Twelfth Edition

Critical Thinking

Brooke Noel Moore
Richard Parker

California State University, Chico

with help in Chapter 12
from Nina Rosenstand and Anita Silvers

Mc
Graw
Hill
Education

CRITICAL THINKING, TWELFTH EDITION

Published by McGraw-Hill Education, 2 Penn Plaza, New York, NY 10121. Copyright © 2017 by McGraw-Hill
Education. All rights reserved. Printed in the United States of America. Previous editions © 2015, 2012, and 2009.
No part of this publication may be reproduced or distributed in any form or by any means, or stored in a database
or retrieval system, without the prior written consent of McGraw-Hill Education, including, but not limited to,
in any network or other electronic storage or transmission, or broadcast for distance learning.

Some ancillaries, including electronic and print components, may not be available to customers outside the
United States.

This book is printed on acid-free paper.

1 2 3 4 5 6 7 8 9 DOW 21 20 19 18 17 16

ISBN 978-1-259-69087-7
MHID 1-259-69087-3

Chief Product Officer, SVP Products & Markets: *G. Scott Virkler*
Vice President, General Manager, Products & Markets: *Michael Ryan*
Managing Director: *David Patterson*
Brand Manager: *Penina Braffman and Jamie Laferrera*
Director, Product Development: *Meghan Campbell*
Product Developer: *Anthony McHugh*
Marketing Manager: *Meredith Leo*
Director, Content Design & Delivery: *Terri Schiesl*
Program Manager: *Jennifer Shekleton*
Content Project Managers: *Jane Mohr, Sandra Schnee, and Samantha Donisi-Hamm*
Buyer: *Laura M. Fuller*
Design: *Studio Montage, St. Louis, MO*
Content Licensing Specialist: *Jacob Sullivan*
Cover Image: © *diephosi/Getty Images RF*
Compositor: *Aptara®, Inc.*
Printer: *R. R. Donnelley*

All credits appearing on page or at the end of the book are considered to be an extension of the copyright page.

Library of Congress Cataloging-in-Publication Data

Names: Moore, Brooke Noel, author. | Parker, Richard (Richard B.), author.
Title: Critical thinking / Brooke Noel Moore, Richard Parker, California
    State University, Chico; with help in chapter 12 from Nina Rosenstand and
    Anita Silvers.
Description: Twelfth Edition. | Dubuque, IA : McGraw-Hill Education, 2016.
Identifiers: LCCN 2016021518 | ISBN 9781259690877 (alk. paper) | ISBN
    1259690873 (alk. paper)
Subjects: LCSH: Critical thinking.
Classification: LCC B105.T54 M66 2016 | DDC 160—dc23 LC record available at https://lccn.loc.gov/2016021518

The Internet addresses listed in the text were accurate at the time of publication. The inclusion of a website does
not indicate an endorsement by the authors or McGraw-Hill Education, and McGraw-Hill Education does not
guarantee the accuracy of the information presented at these sites.

mheducation.com/highered

Brief Contents

Contents

Chapter 3   Clear Thinking, Critical Thinking, and Clear Writing   64

Chapter 6   Relevance (Red Herring) Fallacies   173

Chapter 12   Moral, Legal, and Aesthetic Reasoning   390

©Getty Images/iStockphoto

McGraw-Hill Connect®
Learn Without Limits

Connect is a teaching and learning platform that is proven to deliver better results for students and instructors.

Connect empowers students by continually adapting to deliver precisely what they need, when they need it, and how they need it, so your class time is more engaging and effective.

> 73% of instructors who use **Connect** require it; instructor satisfaction **increases** by 28% when **Connect** is required.

Analytics —————
Connect Insight®

Connect Insight is Connect's new one-of-a-kind visual analytics dashboard—now available for both instructors and students—that provides at-a-glance information regarding student performance, which is immediately actionable. By presenting assignment, assessment, and topical performance results together with a time metric that is easily visible for aggregate or individual results, Connect Insight gives the user the ability to take a just-in-time approach to teaching and learning, which was never before available. Connect Insight presents data that empowers students and helps instructors improve class performance in a way that is efficient and effective.

Mobile —————

Connect's new, intuitive mobile interface gives students and instructors flexible and convenient, anytime–anywhere access to all components of the Connect platform.

Connect's Impact on Retention Rates, Pass Rates, and Average Exam Scores

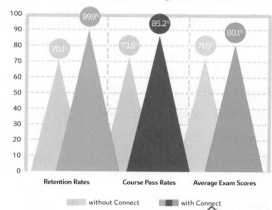

> Using **Connect** improves passing rates by **12.7%** and retention by **19.8%**.

Impact on Final Course Grade Distribution

without Connect		with Connect
22.9%	A	31.0%
27.4%	B	34.3%
22.9%	C	18.7%
11.5%	D	6.1%
15.4%	F	9.9%

> Students can view their results for any **Connect** course.

Adaptive

More students earn **A's** and **B's** when they use McGraw-Hill Education **Adaptive** products.

SmartBook®

Proven to help students improve grades and study more efficiently, SmartBook contains the same content within the print book, but actively tailors that content to the needs of the individual. SmartBook's adaptive technology provides precise, personalized instruction on what the student should do next, guiding the student to master and remember key concepts, targeting gaps in knowledge and offering customized feedback, and driving the student toward comprehension and retention of the subject matter. Available on smartphones and tablets, SmartBook puts learning at the student's fingertips— anywhere, anytime.

Over **5.7 billion questions** have been answered, making McGraw-Hill Education products more intelligent, reliable, and precise.

www.mheducation.com

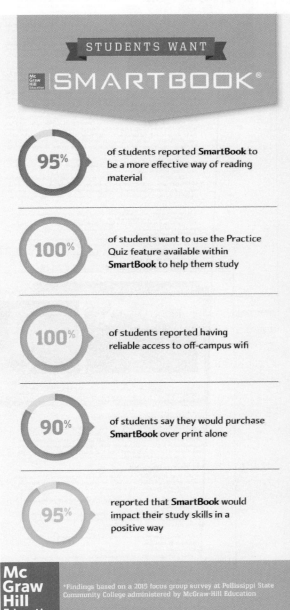

THE **ADAPTIVE READING EXPERIENCE** DESIGNED TO TRANSFORM THE WAY STUDENTS READ

STUDENTS WANT

SMARTBOOK®

95% of students reported **SmartBook** to be a more effective way of reading material

100% of students want to use the Practice Quiz feature available within **SmartBook** to help them study

100% of students reported having reliable access to off-campus wifi

90% of students say they would purchase **SmartBook** over print alone

95% reported that **SmartBook** would impact their study skills in a positive way

Mc Graw Hill Education

*Findings based on a 2015 focus group survey at Pellissippi State Community College administered by McGraw-Hill Education

Critical Thinking . . . Skills for

More Engaging

Moore & Parker are known for fresh and lively writing. They rely on their own classroom experience and on feedback from instructors in getting the correct balance between explication and example.

- Examples and exercises are drawn from today's headlines.
- Students learn to apply critical thinking skills to situations in a wide variety of areas: advertising, politics, the media, popular culture.

I love the sense of humor of the authors, the very clear and elegant way they make critical thinking come alive with visuals, exercises and stories.

—Gary John, *Richland College*

[Before reading this chapter] most students don't realize the extent of product placement and other similar attempts at subtle manipulation.

—Christian Blum, *Bryant & Stratton, Buffalo*

More Relevant

Moore & Parker spark student interest in skills that will serve them throughout their lives, making the study of critical thinking a meaningful endeavor.

- Boxes show students how critical thinking skills are relevant to their day-to-day lives.
- Striking visuals in every chapter show students how images affect our judgment and shape our thinking.

The variety [in the exercises] was outstanding. [They] will provide ample opportunity for the students to put into practice the various logical principles being discussed.

—Ray Darr, *Southern Illinois University*

it is impossible to think that good judgment or rational thought would lead them to such excess.*

Yet another possible source of psychological distortion is the **overconfidence effect,** one of several self-deception biases that may be found in a variety of contexts.** If a person estimates the percentage of his or her correct answers on a subject, the estimate will likely err on the high side—at least if the questions are difficult or the subject matter is unfamiliar.† Perhaps some manifestation of the overconfidence effect explains why, in the early stages of the *American Idol* competition, many contestants appear totally convinced they will be crowned the next American Idol—and are speechless when the judges inform them they cannot so much as carry a tune.††

■ Does Kanye West dress well? The issue is subjective, or, as some people say, "a matter of opinion."

Closely related to the overconfidence effect is the **better-than-average illusion.** The illusion crops up when most of a group rate themselves as better than most of the group relative to some desirable characteristic, such as resourcefulness or driving ability. The classic illustration is the 1976 survey of SAT takers, in which well over 50 percent of the respondents rated themselves as better than 50 percent of other SAT takers with respect to such qualities as leadership ability.‡ The same effect has been observed when people estimate how their intelligence, memory, or job performance stacks up with the intelligence, memory, and job performances of other members of their profession or workplace. In our own informal surveys, more than 80 percent of our students rate themselves in the top 10 percent of their class with respect to their ability to think critically.‡‡

Unfortunately, evidence indicates that even when they are informed about the better-than-average illusion, people may *still* rate themselves as better than most in their ability to not be subject to it.‡‡

That beliefs are generated as much by psychology and impulse as by evidence should come as no surprise. The new car that was well beyond our means yesterday seems entirely affordable today—though our finances haven't changed. If someone invited us to The Olive Garden we'd expect decent fare; but if they suggested we

*Jamey Keaton, Associated Press. Reported in *The Sacramento Bee,* Thursday, March 19, 2010. Did the subjects suspect the shocks weren't real? Their statements afterward don't rule out the possibility but certainly seem to suggest they believed they truly were administering painful electrical shocks to the actor.
**However, a universal tendency among humans to irrationally exaggerate their own competencies hasn't been established. For an online quiz purportedly showing the overconfidence effect, see www.tim-richardson.net/joomla15/finance-articles-problems-7073-over-confidence-test.html.
†See Sarah Lichtenstein and other authors, "Calibration of Probabilities: The State of the Art to 1980," in Daniel Kahneman, Paul Slovic, and Amos Tversky, *Judgment under Uncertainty: Heuristics and Biases* (Cambridge, England: Cambridge University Press, 1982), 306–34.
††This possibility was proposed by Gad Saad, *Psychology Today.* www.psychologytoday.com/blog/homo-consumericus/200901/self-deception-american-idol-is-it-adaptive.
‡See Mark D. Alicke and other authors in "The Better-Than-Average Effect," in Mark D. Alicke and others, *The Self in Social Judgment: Studies in Self and Identity* (New York: Psychology Press, 2005), 85–106. The better-than-average illusion is

---

Appealing to Tradition

According to Representative Steve King of Ohio (pictured here), "Equal protection [under the Constitution] is not equal protection for same sex couples to marry. Equal protection has always been for a man and a woman to be able to get married to each other."

FALLACIES RELATED TO CAUSE AND EFFECT

It can be difficult to prove a cause-and-effect relationship between two variables, which is why mistaken reasoning can occur in this context. In this section we explore two important fallacies that can be made in reasoning about cause and effect. What the two fallacies have in common is this. Both assume that the timing of two variables relative to each other, in and of itself, is sufficient to establish that one is the cause and the other is the effect. This assumption is incorrect.

Post Hoc, Ergo Propter Hoc

Post Hoc, Ergo Propter Hoc means "After this, therefore because of it." A speaker or writer commits this fallacy when he or she assumes that the fact that one event came after another establishes that it was caused by the other. Here is an example:

> After I took Zicam my cold went away fast. Therefore taking Zicam caused my cold to go away fast.

The speaker makes a mistake to assume that Zicam caused the cold to go away fast. The argument is no better than this one:

> After I played poker my cold went away fast. Therefore playing poker caused my cold to go away fast.

Here is a slightly different example, a classic illustration of *post hoc, ergo propter hoc:*

> Every day the sun comes up right after the rooster crows; therefore the rooster causes the sun to come up.

the course. Skills for life.

More Student Success

Moore & Parker provide a path to student success, making students active participants in their own learning while teaching skills they can apply in all their courses.

- Learning objectives link to chapter sections and in turn to print and online activities, so that students can immediately assess their mastery of the learning objective.

- Exercises are dispersed throughout most chapters, so that they link tightly with the concepts as they are presented.

- Students have access to over 2,000 exercises that provide practice in applying their skills.

Hands-on, practical, and one might say, even "patient" with the students' learning as it emphatically repeats concepts and slowly progresses them step by step through the process.

—Patricia Baldwin, *Pitt Community College*

There are a lot of exercises, which provides nice flexibility. The . . . mix of relatively easy and more challenging pieces . . . is useful in providing some flexibility for working in class.

—Dennis Weiss, *York College of Pennsylvania*

Additional Exercises

Exercise 8-4

Here are 106 examples of the fallacies discussed in this chapter. Match each item to one or more of the following categories or otherwise answer as indicated:

a. affirming the consequent
b. denying the antecedent
c. undistributed middle fallacy
d. confusing explanations with excuses
e. equivocation
f. composition
g. division
h. miscalculating probabilities

Note

Your instructor may or may not ask you to further assign miscalculating probabilities into the following subcategories: Incorrectly combining the probabilities of independent events, the gambler's fallacy, overlooking prior probabilities, and faulty inductive conversion.

1. Professor Parker can tell you if you are sick; after all, he is a doctor.
2. If this man is the president, then he believes in immigration reform. If this man is vice president, then he believes in immigration reform. Therefore, if this man is president, then he is vice president.
3. If global warming is for real, then the mean global temperature will have risen over the past ten years. And that is what happened. Therefore, global warming is for real.
4. My chance of being born on December 25 was the same as yours. So the chances we were both born on December 25 have to be twice as good.
5. Sodium is deadly poisonous, and so is chlorine. Salt consists of sodium and chlorine, which must be why we're told not to eat too much of it.
6. The Bible commands you to leave life having made the world a better place. And therefore it commands you to make the world a better place each and every day.
7. A dialogue:
   JILL: Helen has her mother's eyes.
   BILL: Good lord! Can the woman still see?
8. Is an explanation clearly being offered as an excuse/justification? I didn't buy tickets to see Chris Angel's show because I heard that he spends half his act with his shirt off strutting around in front of the ladies in the audience.
9. If Congress changes marijuana from a Class 1 drug to something lesser, next year the penalties for possession will be much less than they are now. But Congress is not going to declassify marijuana anytime soon. So we'll have to live with the drastic penalties for at least another year.
10. If you are rich, then your car is something like a Mercedes or a Bentley. Oh! Is that your Bentley, you rich old thing, you?
11. Man! Three sons in a row? Your next kid is bound to be a girl.

Changes to the 12th Edition

Having arrived at an even dozen editions, we still have our original goal constantly in mind: helping teach students to think and reason critically and make better decisions and making life a bit easier for instructors of critical thinking courses. We invite both students and instructors to get in touch with us with any ideas they have that might help us pursue these goals.

As usual, this edition updates names and events in examples and exercises in the hope that they will be familiar to the current crop of students. As we've mentioned before, what to many of us instructors are recent events are obscure history to many new freshmen. Other changes are as follows.

CHAPTER-SPECIFIC CHANGES

- Chapter 1 begins with a fuller accounting of what we take critical thinking to be. It also goes into a bit more depth regarding cognitive biases that affect our thinking.

- Chapter 2 contains a revised section on inference to the best explanation (IBE).

- Chapter 3 is somewhat leaner, but still makes a wealth of points about the important concepts of vagueness and generality and it contains a revised account of several types of definitions.

- Chapter 4 gets the usual updating here and there plus a new section on credibility in social media.

- Chapter 5 gets updating, new photos, and a subsection on significant mention under the innuendo heading.

- Chapter 6 is left largely unchanged aside from some new examples and photos.

- Chapter 7 is also much the same as the previous version, although "fallacious" appeals have been changed to "mistaken" appeals; why use a word students have trouble spelling when there is one they don't?

- Chapter 8 was new in the previous edition. It gets updated this time around, including a replacement of the section entitled "Overlooking False Positives" with an easier to understand "Faulty Inductive Conversion" section.

- Chapter 9 gets a bit of reformatting to make examples stand out more easily. Also, existential assumption gets its own subsection so it will be more difficult to miss.

Rhetoric, the Art of Persuasion

5

Students will learn to . . .

1. Explain the concepts of rhetorical force and emotive power

2. Identify and critique the use of euphemisms, dysphemisms, weaselers, and downplayers

3. Identify and critique the use of stereotypes, innuendo, and loaded questions

4. Identify and critique the use of ridicule, sarcasm, and hyperbole

5. Identify and critique the use of rhetorical definitions, explanations, analogies, and misleading comparisons

6. Identify and critique the use of proof surrogates and repetition

7. Identify and critique the persuasive aspects of visual images

8. Detect the techniques used in the extreme rhetoric of demagoguery

Rhetoric, the venerable art of persuasive writing and speaking, has been one of the twin anchors of Western education since the days of Aristotle. The other, which also dates from Aristotle, is logic. You use rhetoric to win someone to your point of view; you use logic to demonstrate a claim or support it. These are separate enterprises. You can use logic to persuade people, but all too often they are persuaded by poor logic and unmoved by good logic. This is why education increasingly emphasizes critical thinking, to help people improve their logic and to help them distinguish between proof and persuasion.

In this chapter we do three things. First, we introduce the important concept of rhetorical force. Then we explain several rhetorical devices. Good writers and speakers employ many of these devices to make their cases as persuasive as possible. None of the devices, however, have logical force or probative weight ("probative" means tending to prove). We, as critical thinkers, should be able to recognize them for what they are—devices of persuasion.

Last, after we examine the various devices, we examine four principal techniques of demagoguery. Demagogues use inflammatory rhetoric to win acceptance for false and misleading ideas. They appeal to the fears and prejudices of an audience,

■ Chapter 10 now makes the electrical circuit box a bit less distracting and adds a couple of new exercises to aid in learning to symbolize claims. But the biggest change from the previous edition is the reinsertion of a section that gives a briefer version of truth-functional arguments. This allows an instructor (like Moore) to deal quickly with this subject or (like Parker) to deal with it in much more detail by going on to the longer treatment that completes the chapter.

■ Chapter 11 has the sections on analogies and generalizations fine-tuned, while the section on causal hypotheses remains in its previous pristine form.

■ Chapter 12 has been left alone aside from a bit of updating of examples.

■ Vladimir Putin asks Hillary Clinton if she can get him a copy of Moore/Parker.

Acknowledgments

We, Moore and Parker, feel about this textbook the way people usually feel about their children. It has been a wonderful thing to watch it grow up through these (now) dozen editions, although it has caused us the occasional pain in the backside along the way. Those pains—often in the form of criticism in reviews and correspondence from adopters—have usually been growing pains, however, and they have contributed to the improvement of the book. We are pretty pleased with the book, as proud parents are wont to be, but we realize that there are always things—smaller and smaller things, we hope—that can be changed for the better. We hope this edition incorporates changes of just that sort. Many of them are listed below.

The online accompaniment to the text continues to expand and, we trust, become more and more useful to adopters and their students. The preceding pages briefly describe LearnSmart and Connect, the principal components of the online material. These programs promise help for the student and an easier and more productive time for the instructor. We hope you find they live up to this promise.

Having escaped from the mysterious clutches of Mark Georgiev, former KGB operative and our editor a couple of editions ago, we have been blessed by guidance this time around from the gentle hands of Penina Braffman, Brand Manager; Anthony McHugh, Product Developer; Jane Mohr, Content Project Manager; as well as Erin Guendelsberger, Reshmi Rajeesh, and the **ansr**source team, Development Editors, who encourage us even when we don't quite toe the McGraw-Hill line.

The guidance of the following reviewers of current and previous editions and others who have written to us has been invaluable:

Keith Abney, California Polytechnic State University, San Luis Obispo
James Anderson, San Diego State University
Benjamin Arah, Bowie State University
Sheldon Bachus
Patricia Baldwin, Pitt Community College
Monique Bindra
Tim Black, California State University, Northridge
Charles Blatz, University of Toledo
Christian Blum, Bryant & Stratton, Buffalo
K. D. Borcoman, Coastline College/CSUDH
Keith Brown, California State University, East Bay
Rosalie Brown
Lee Carter, Glendale Community College
Jennifer Caseldine-Bracht, Indiana University-Purdue University, Fort Wayne
Lynne Chandler-Garcia, Pikes Peak Community College
David Connelly
Anne D'Arcy, California State University, Chico
Michelle Darnelle, Fayetteville State University
Ray Darr, Southern Illinois University, Edwardsville
William J. Devlin, Bridgewater State University
Paul Dickey, Metropolitan Community College
Sandra Dwyer, Georgia State University
Jeffrey Easlick, Saginaw Valley State University

Aaron Edlin, University of California, Berkeley
Dorothy Edlin
Noel Edlin
Ellery Eells, University of Wisconsin–Madison
Ben Eggleston, University of Kansas
Geoffrey B. Frasz, Community College of Southern Nevada
Josh Fulcher
Rory Goggins
Geoffrey Gorham, University of Wisconsin–Eau Claire
Joseph Graves, North Carolina A&T University
Dabney Gray, Stillman College
Patricia Hammer, Delta College
Anthony Hanson, De Anza College
Rebecca Hendricks
Judith M. Hill, Saginaw Valley State University
Steven Hoeltzel, James Madison University
Steven R. Huizenga, Central Ohio Technical College
J. F. Humphrey, North Carolina A&T University
Amro Jayousi
Gary John, Richland College
Sunghyun Jung
Allyn Kahn, Champlain College
David Kelsey, Coastline Community College
David Keyt, University of Washington
Paulina Kohan
William Krieger, California State University–Pomona
Michael LaBossiere, Florida A&M University
Sunita Lanka, Hartnell College
Bill Lawson
Marisha Lecea, Western Michigan University
Marion Ledwig, University of Nevada–Las Vegas
Vern Lee, University of Phoenix
Terrance MacMullon, Eastern Washington University
Andrew Magrath, Kent State University
Alistair Moles, Sierra College
Ralph J. Moore, Jr.
Jeffry Norby, Northcentral Technical College
Eric Parkinson, Syracuse University
Steven Patterson, Marygrove College
Carmel Phelan, College of Southern Nevada
Jamie L. Phillips, Clarion University
Domenick Pinto, Sacred Heart University
Ayaz Pirani, Hartnell College
Ed Pluth, California State University, Chico
Scott Rappold, Our Lady of Holy Cross College
N. Mark Rauls, College of Southern Nevada
Victor Reppert, Glendale Community College
Matthew E. Roberts, Patrick Henry College
Greg Sadler, Fayetteville State University
Matt Schulte, Montgomery College
Richard Scott, Glendale Community College

Laurel Severino, Santa Fe Community College
Mehul Shah, Bergen Community College
Robert Shanab, University of Nevada at Las Vegas
Steven Silveria
Robert Skipper, St. Mary's University
Aeon J. Skoble, Bridgewater State University
Taggart Smith, Purdue University–Calumet
Richard Sneed, University of Central Oklahoma
Alan Soble, Drexel University
Chris Soutter
James Stump, Bethel College
Lou Suarez
Susan Vineberg, Wayne State University
Michael Ventimiglia, Sacred Heart University
Helmut Wautischer, Sonoma State University
Dennis Weiss, York College of Pennsylvania
Linda L. Williams, Kent State University
Amy Goodman Wilson, Webster University
Christine Wolf
Wayne Yuen, Ohlone College
Marie G. Zaccaria, Georgia Perimeter College

Over the years, our Chico State colleague Anne Morrissey has given us more usable material than anybody else. She's also given us more unusable material, but never mind. We've also had fine suggestions and examples from Curtis Peldo of Chico State and Butte College; Dan Barnett, also of Butte College, has helped in many ways over the years.

We thank colleagues at Chico State, who are ever ready with a suggestion, idea, or constructive criticism; in particular, Marcel Daguerre, Randy Larsen, Becky White, Wai-hung Wong, Zanja Yudell, and Greg Tropea, whose death in 2010 left us saddened beyond words. Greg was a dear friend whose deep wisdom and quiet insight contributed significantly to our thinking over the course of many years. We are also grateful to Bangs Tapscott, Linda Kaye Bomstad, Ann Bykerk-Kauffman, Sue Patterson, and Jeffrey Ridenour for contributions both archival and recent.

Last, and especially, we give thanks to two people who put up with us with patience, encouragement, and grace, Leah Blum and Marianne Moore.

A Note to Our Colleagues

No surprise, reading a book (or taking a course) in critical thinking won't make anyone a genius. It won't tell you who to vote for or whether to believe in God or whether to contribute to the Humane Society, But it can, we hope, help students tell whether a given reason for doing or not doing one of those things is a good reason. It can help them spot irrelevancies in a discussion, emotional appeals, empty rhetoric, and bogus argument. Other courses can do these things too, of course. But speaking generally, other courses are probably not focused so intensely on those things.

There are differences about how best to go about teaching critical thinking. One of us, Parker likes to emphasize formal logic. Moore, not quite so much. One thing Moore and Parker both agree on, and possibly so do many instructors, is that drill and practice are essential to improving students' critical thinking ability. And one thing we have found is that technology can be helpful in this regard. The personalized digital reading experience of this text (called *SmartBook*) questions students as they read, and the credit they get depends on the proportion of the questions they answer correctly. (We instructors can also see how long they spent on a reading assignment.) Additionally, *Connect,* McGraw-Hill's assignment and assessment platform through which *SmartBook* is accessed, gives us the means to put a whole lot of exercises online. And these two things enable us to do even more drilling in class.

If you don't use *Connect* or *LearnSmart*, this text contains hundreds and hundreds and hundreds of exercises of the sort (we think) that can be applied directly to the world at large. And they are all answered in the *Instructor's Manual*. The explanatory material found in the text is (we hope) both concise and fairly readable for even first-year university students.

If you use this text or the online peripherals, we would appreciate hearing from you. We both can be contacted through McGraw-Hill Education, or via the philosophy department at Chico State.

About the Authors

Brooke Moore and Richard Parker have taught philosophy at California State University, Chico, for almost as long as they can remember. Moore has been that university's Outstanding Professor, and both he and Parker have received top academic honors on their campus. Moore has seen several terms as department chair, and Parker has served as chair of the academic senate and dean of undergraduate education.

Moore has a bachelor's degree in music from Antioch College and a PhD in philosophy from the University of Cincinnati; Parker did his undergraduate degree at the University of Arkansas and his PhD at the University of Washington, both in philosophy.

Moore has finally given up being the world's most serious amateur volleyball player. He and Marianne share their house and life with Sparky, as cute a pup as you'll ever see. He has never sold an automobile.

Parker gets around in a 1962 MG or on a Harley softail. He plays golf for fun, shoots pool for money, and plays guitar for a semiprofessional flamenco troupe. He lives with Djobi, a hundred-pound Doberman.

Moore and Parker have remained steadfast friends through it all. They are never mistaken for one another.

To:

Alexander and Levi
From Richard

Sherry and Bill; and Sydney, Darby,
Peyton Elizabeth, and Griffin
From Brooke

This is not entirely a work of nonfiction.

Don't Believe Everything You Think

A little before noon on December 14, 2015, a man wearing a black stocking cap, black gloves, and a green sweat shirt with a four-leaf clover and the words "Get Lucky" printed on the front entered the Sterling State Bank in Rochester, Minnesota.* He demanded cash and gave the teller a note saying he was armed. Police officers arrived and followed the man's tracks in the snow to the parking lot of a Comfort Inn nearby, but by then the man had driven off in a car.

The next day, a reporter from KIMT-TV had set up in front of the bank to update the story, and right then and there the same man tried to rob the same bank again. When the teller saw the man he yelled out, "That's the robber!" and the reporter called the police. This time when the police followed the suspect's footprints they spotted his vehicle and apprehended him.

Now, educators will disagree about what exactly critical thinking is, but there will be no disputing that, whatever it is, "Get Lucky" wasn't doing it. First of all, robbing banks isn't necessarily the best way to make a living. But if you insist on robbing a bank, then probably you don't want to leave footprints to your car, and probably you don't want to try to rob the bank when a TV crew is filming it. Among other things, critical thinking involves considering the possible outcomes of an action.

*http://www.postbulletin.com/news/crime/robber-hits-rochester-bank-a-second-time-arrested-at-gunpoint/article_c0f55ab9-97b5-5a52-95d7-484ef2b6fcc9.html.

Students will learn to . . .

1. Define critical thinking

2. Explain the role of beliefs and claims in critical thinking

3. Identify issues in real-world situations

4. Recognize an argument

5. Define and identify the common cognitive biases that affect critical thinking

6. Understand the terms "truth" and "knowledge" as used in this book

1

Among what other things? Speaking generally, if we just think or do stuff, that's not thinking critically. Critical thinking kicks in when we *evaluate* beliefs and actions—when we critique them. On the one hand, there is good, old-fashioned thinking. That's what we do when we form opinions, make judgments, arrive at decisions, develop plans, come to conclusions, offer hypotheses, and the like. On the other hand, there is *critical* thinking. That's what we do when we *rationally evaluate* the first kind of thinking. *Critical thinking is thinking that critiques.* It involves critiquing opinions, judgments, decisions, plans, conclusions, and reasoning in general. We engage in it when we consider whether our thinking (or someone else's) abides by the criteria of good sense and logic.

If you are taking other courses, chances are your *instructor* will think critically about the work you turn in. He or she will offer critical commentary on what you submit. If you want to think critically, you have to do this yourself to your own work. Try to leave your instructor with nothing to say except, "Good job!"

It can be the same in the workplace or in the military. You might perhaps be asked to solve a problem or troubleshoot a situation or come up with a recommendation, or any number of other things that involve arriving at conclusions. Your colleagues or friends or supervisors may give you feedback or commentary. They are thinking critically about your reasoning.

Of course, if you are so brilliant that you never err in your thinking, then you may not need feedback from others. Unfortunately, there is evidence that people who think they are experts are more likely to believe they know things they don't really know.* Anyway, almost everyone makes mistakes. We overlook important considerations, ignore viewpoints that conflict with our own, or in other ways don't think as clearly as we might. Most of us benefit from a little critical commentary, and this includes commentary that comes from ourselves. The chances of reaching defensible conclusions improve if we don't simply conclude willy-nilly, but reflect on our reasoning and try to make certain it is sound.

Being able to think critically can be useful in another way. Others try to influence what we think and do. There is much to be said for being able to critically evaluate a sales pitch, whether it comes from a stranger or a friend, or is about kitchen gadgets or for whom to vote for president. Critical thinking helps us recognize a scam when we see it.

Some educators equate critical thinking with problem solving or innovative thinking ("thinking outside the box"). This is fine, though at a certain point proposed solutions and possible innovations have to be tested. That's where critical thinking comes in.

This is a book in *critical* thinking because it offers guidance about *critiquing* thinking. The book and the course you are using it in, if you are, explain the minimum criteria of good reasoning—the requirements a piece of reasoning must meet if it is worth paying attention to, *no matter what the context*. Along the way we will explore the most common and important obstacles to good reasoning, as well as some of the most common mistakes people make when coming to conclusions. Other courses you take offer refinements. In them you will learn what considerations are important from the perspective of individual disciplines. But in no course anywhere, at least in no course that involves arriving at conclusions, will thinking that violates the standards set forth in this book be accepted.

If it does nothing else, what you read here and learn in your critical thinking course should help you avoid at least a few of the more egregious common errors people make when they reason. If you would have otherwise made these mistakes, you will have become smarter. Not smarter in some particular subject, mind you, but

---

**Scientific American Mind*, January/February 2016, p. 13.

smarter in general. The things you learn from this book (and from the course you may be reading it for) apply to nearly any subject people can talk or think or write about.

To a certain extent, questions we should ask when critiquing our own—or someone else's—thinking depend on what is at issue. Deciding whom to vote for, whether to buy a house, whether a mathematical proof is sound, which toothpaste to buy, or what kind of dog to get involve different considerations. In all cases, however, we should want to avoid making or accepting weak and invalid arguments. We should also avoid being distracted by irrelevancies or ruled by emotion, succumbing to fallacies or bias, and being influenced by dubious authority or half-baked speculation. These are not the only criteria by which reasoning might be evaluated, but they are central and important, and they provide the main focus of this book.

Critical Thinking, the Long Version

The Collegiate Learning Assessment (CLA) Project of the Council for Aid to Education has come up with a list of skills that covers almost everything your authors believe is important in critical thinking. If you achieve mastery over all these or even a significant majority of them, you'll be well ahead of most of your peers—and your fellow citizens. In question form, here is what the council came up with:

How well does the student

- determine what information is or is not pertinent;
- distinguish between rational claims and emotional ones;
- separate fact from opinion;
- recognize the ways in which evidence might be limited or compromised;
- spot deception and holes in the arguments of others;
- present his/her own analysis of the data or information;
- recognize logical flaws in arguments;
- draw connections between discrete sources of data and information;
- attend to contradictory, inadequate, or ambiguous information;
- construct cogent arguments rooted in data rather than opinion;
- select the strongest set of supporting data;
- avoid overstated conclusions;
- identify holes in the evidence and suggest additional information to collect;
- recognize that a problem may have no clear answer or single solution;
- propose other options and weigh them in the decision;
- consider all stakeholders or affected parties in suggesting a course of action;
- articulate the argument and the context for that argument;
- correctly and precisely use evidence to defend the argument;
- logically and cohesively organize the argument;
- avoid extraneous elements in an argument's development;
- present evidence in an order that contributes to a persuasive argument?

www.aacu.org/peerreview/pr_sp07_analysis1.cfm.

■ The judges on *The Voice* critique singers, but that doesn't automatically qualify as thinking critically.

BELIEFS AND CLAIMS

Why bother thinking critically? The ultimate objective in thinking critically is to come to conclusions that are correct and to make decisions that are wise. Because our decisions reflect our conclusions, we can simplify things by saying that *the purpose of thinking critically is to come to correct conclusions.* The method used to achieve this objective is to evaluate our thinking by the standards of rationality. Of course, we can also evaluate someone else's thinking, though the objective there might simply be to help the person.

When we come to a conclusion, we have a belief. Concluding involves believing. If you *conclude* the battery is dead, you *believe* the battery is dead. Keeping this in mind, let's define a few key terms.

A belief is, obviously, something you believe. It is important to understand that a belief is *propositional,* which means it can be expressed in a declarative sentence—a sentence that is either true or false. A good bit of muddleheaded thinking can be avoided if you understand that beliefs are propositional entities, but more on this later.

As we use these words, *beliefs* are the same as *judgments* and *opinions.* When we express a belief (or judgment or opinion) in a declarative sentence, the result is a *statement* or *claim* or *assertion,* and for our purposes these are the same thing. Claims can be used for other purposes than to state beliefs, but this is the use we're primarily concerned with.

> Beliefs and claims are *propositional:* they can be expressed in true-or-false declarative sentences.

Objective Claims and Subjective Claims

Before we say something more about conclusions, we should make a distinction between objective and subjective claims. An **objective claim** has this characteristic:

whether it is true or false is independent of whether people think it is true or false. "There is life on Mars" is thus an objective claim, because whether or not life exists there doesn't depend on whether people think it does. If everyone suddenly believed there is life on Mars, that doesn't mean that suddenly there would be life on Mars. Likewise, "God exists" is an objective claim because whether it is true doesn't depend on whether people think it is true.

■ That could be you under the snow if you don't think critically.

Although objective claims are either true or false, we may not know which a given claim is. "Portland, Oregon, is closer to the North Pole than to the equator" is a true objective claim. "Portland, Oregon, is closer to the equator than to the North Pole" is a false objective claim. "More stamp collectors live in Portland, Oregon, than in Portland, Maine" is an objective claim whose truth or falsity is not known, at least not by us.

Not every claim is objective, of course. "Bruno Mars has swag" is not objective, for it lacks the characteristic mentioned previously. That is, whether or not someone has swag *does* depend on whether people think he does. If nobody thinks Bruno Mars has swag, then he doesn't. If Parker thinks he does and Moore doesn't, you will say that Parker and Moore are each entitled to their opinions. Whether someone has swag is in the eyes of the beholder.

Claims of this variety are **subjective.** Whether a subjective claim is true or false is not independent of whether people think it is true or false. Examples of subjective claims would be judgments of taste, such as "Rice vinegar is too sweet." Is rice vinegar too sweet? It depends on what you think. Some kinds of comparisons also are subjective. Is snowboarding more fun than skiing? Again, it depends on what you think, and there is no further "truth" to consider. However, many statements contain both objective and nonobjective elements, as in "Somebody stole our nifty concrete lawn duck." Whether the lawn duck is *concrete* is an objective question; whether it is *our* lawn duck is an objective question; and whether it was *stolen* is an objective question. But whether the stolen concrete lawn duck is *nifty* is a subjective question.

Fact and Opinion

Sometimes people talk about the difference between "fact" and "opinion," having in mind the notion that *all* opinions are subjective. But some opinions are not subjective, because their truth or falsity is independent of what people think. Again, in this book "opinion" is just another word for "belief." If you believe that Portland, Oregon, is closer to the North Pole than to the equator, that opinion happens to be true, and would continue to be true even if you change your mind. You can refer to objective opinions as *factual* opinions or beliefs, if you want—*but that doesn't mean factual opinions are all true.* "Portland, Oregon, is closer to the equator than to the North Pole" is a factual opinion that is false.

Factual opinion/belief/claim = objective opinion/belief/claim = opinion/belief/claim whose truth is independent of whether anyone thinks it is true.

Thinking About Thinking

Remember, an *objective* statement is not made true by someone thinking it is true. "Wait a minute," you might say. "Isn't the statement 'Joanie is thinking about Frank' made true by her thinking that it is true?" The answer is no! It is made true by her *thinking about Frank.*

Relativism

Relativism is the idea that truth is relative to the standards of a given culture. More precisely, relativism holds that if your culture and some other culture have different standards of truth or evidence, there is no independent "God's-eye view" by which one culture's standards can be seen to be more correct than the others'.

Whatever may be said of this as an abstract philosophical doctrine, it cannot possibly mean that an objective statement could be made true by a culture's thinking that it is true. If it is universally believed in some culture that "water" is not H_2O, then either the people in that culture are mistaken or their word "water" does not refer to water.

Moral Subjectivism

Moral subjectivism is the idea that moral opinions, such as "Bullfighting is morally wrong" or "Jason shouldn't lie to his parents," are subjective. It is the idea, in other words, that if you think bullfighting is morally wrong, then it is morally wrong for you and you don't need to consider any further truth. It is the idea expressed by Hamlet in the famous passage, "There is nothing either good or bad, but that thinking makes it so."

You should be wary of Hamlet's dictum. Ask yourself this: If someone actually believed there is nothing wrong with torturing donkeys or stoning women to death for adultery, would you say, well, if that's what he thinks, then it's fine for him to torture donkeys or stone women to death? Of course you wouldn't. Those ideas can't be made true by thinking they are true anymore than drinking battery acid can be made good for you by thinking it is.

ISSUES

An **issue,** as we employ that concept in this book, is simply a question. Is Moore taller than Parker? When we ask that question, we raise the issue as to *whether* Moore is taller than Parker. To put it differently, we are considering whether the claim "Moore is taller than Parker" is true. Let us note in passing that as with claims, some issues are objective. Is Moore taller than Parker? Whether he is or isn't doesn't depend on whether we think he is, so this is an objective issue (question).

Other issues, such as whether P. Diddy dresses well, are subjective, in the sense explained previously.

The first order of business when it comes to thinking critically about an issue is to determine what, exactly, the issue *is.* Unfortunately, in many real-life situations, it is difficult to identify exactly what the issue is—meaning it is difficult to identify exactly what claim is in question. This happens for lots of reasons, from purposeful obfuscation to ambiguous terminology to plain muddleheaded thinking. In his inaugural address President Warren G. Harding said,

> We have mistaken unpreparedness to embrace it to be a challenge of the reality and due concern for making all citizens fit for participation will give added strength of citizenship and magnify our achievement.

This is formidable. Do you understand what issue Harding is addressing? Neither does anyone else, because his statement is perfectly meaningless. (American satirist H. L. Mencken described it as a "sonorous nonsense driven home with gestures."*) Understanding what is meant by a claim has so many aspects that we'll devote a large part of Chapter 3 to the subject.

However, if you have absolutely no clue as to what an issue actually is, there isn't much point in considering it further—you don't know what "it" is. There also isn't much point in considering it further if you have no idea as to what would count toward settling it. For example, suppose someone asks, "Is there an identical you in a different dimension?" What sort of evidence would support saying either there is or isn't? Nobody has any idea. (Almost any question about different "dimensions" or "planes" or "universes" would be apt to suffer from the same problem unless, possibly, it were to be raised from someone well educated in physics who used those concepts in a technical way.) "Is everything really one?" would also qualify as something you couldn't begin to settle, as would wondering if "the entire universe was created instantly five minutes ago with all false memories and fictitious records."**

Obscure issues aren't always as metaphysical as the preceding examples. Listen carefully and you may hear more than one politician say something like, "It is human nature to desire freedom." Oh, really? This sounds good, but if you look at it closely it's hard to know exactly what sort of data would support the remark.

This isn't to imply that only issues that can be settled through scientific test or via the experimental method are worth considering. Moral issues cannot be settled in that way, for example. Mathematical and historical questions are not answered by experiment, and neither are important philosophical questions. Does God exist? Is there free will? What difference does it make if he does or doesn't or there is or isn't? Legal questions, questions of aesthetics—the list of important questions not subject to purely scientific resolution is very long. The point here is merely that if a question is to be taken seriously, or if you want others to take it seriously, or if you want others who can think critically to take it seriously, you must have *some* idea as to what considerations bear on the answer.

ARGUMENTS

In our experience, lots of college students seriously contemplate getting a dog or cat. But they are conflicted. On the one hand, it would be sweet to have a nice pet; but on the other, it would be extra work and cost money, and they aren't sure what to do with the animal if they take a trip.

If you are such a student, you weigh the arguments pro and con. An **argument** presents a consideration for accepting a claim. For example, this is an argument:

> A dog would keep me company; so I should get one.

---

*Reported on NBC News, *Meet the Press,* January 16, 2005.
**This famous example comes from philosopher Bertrand Russell.

Are You Good at Reasoning?

Are you the kind of person who reasons well? Some people are. Unfortunately, maybe people who *aren't* very good at reasoning are the most likely to overestimate their reasoning ability.*

*See Justin Kruger and David Dunning, "Unskilled and Unaware of It: How Difficulties in Recognizing One's Own Incompetence Lead to Inflated Self-Assessments," *Psychology* 1 (2009): 30–46.

And so is this:

> My landlord will raise my rent; so I shouldn't get one.

The first example is an argument for getting a dog. The second is an argument for not getting one.

As you can see from these two examples, an argument consists of two parts. One part gives a reason for accepting the other part. The part that provides the reason is called the **premise** of the argument,* though an argument may have more than one premise. The other part is called the conclusion. The **conclusion** of an argument is what the premise supposedly supports or demonstrates.

You should always think of the conclusion of an argument as stating a position on an issue, and of the premise or premises as giving reasons for taking that position.

Want an example? Look at the two arguments previously shown. They both address the issue of *whether I should get a dog*. The premise of the first example ("A dog would keep me company") gives a reason for saying I *should* get a dog. The premise of the second example ("My landlord will raise my rent") gives a reason for saying I *should not* get a dog.

What does this have to do with critical thinking? Everything. You want to make the best decision on an important issue—in this case, whether to get a dog. You evaluate the arguments pro and con. Being able to do this intelligently may not be the sum total of critical thinking, but it is an essential part of it.

A large part of this book is devoted to understanding how to evaluate arguments, and all this will begin in Chapter 2. However, right now, two minor points about arguments are worth noticing:

1. The two arguments given as examples are not very long or complicated. Some arguments can be very long and complicated. Einstein's revolutionary theory that $E = mc^2$ was based on complex mathematical reasoning, and that reasoning was his argument for saying that $E = mc^2$.
2. Not every issue requires an argument for resolution. Is your throat sore? You can just tell directly, and no argument is necessary.

We will now offer you a few exercises to help you understand these fundamental concepts. In the next section we will look at psychological factors that impede clear thought.

*Unfortunately, sometimes people use the word "argument" to refer only to the premise or premises of an argument.

Answer the questions based on your reading to this point, including the boxes.

▲ —See the answers section at the back of the book.

Exercise 1-1

▲ 1. What is an argument?

2. T or F: A claim is what you use to state an opinion or a belief.

3. T or F: Critical thinking consists in attacking other people's ideas.

▲ 4. T or F: Whether a passage contains an argument depends on how long it is.

5. T or F: When a question has been asked, an issue has been raised.

6. T or F: All arguments have a premise.

▲ 7. T or F: All arguments have a conclusion.

8. T or F: You can reach a conclusion without believing it is true.

9. T or F: Beliefs, judgments, and opinions are the same thing.

▲ 10. T or F: All opinions are subjective.

11. T or F: All factual claims are true.

12. "There is nothing either good or bad but that thinking makes it so" expresses a doctrine known as _____.

▲ 13. The first order of business when it comes to thinking critically about an issue is (a) to determine whether the issue is subjective or objective, (b) to determine whether the issue can be resolved, or (c) to determine what exactly the issue is.

14. T or F: The conclusion of an argument states a position on an issue.

15. T or F: Issues can be resolved only through scientific testing.

▲ 16. T or F: Statements, claims, and assertions are the same thing.

17. T or F: The claim "Death Valley is an eyesore" expresses a subjective opinion.

18. T or F: Every issue requires an argument for a resolution.

▲ 19. T or F: Relativism is the idea that if the standards of evidence or truth are different for two cultures, there is no independent way of saying which standards are the correct ones.

20. T or F: It is not possible to reason correctly if you do not think critically.

On the basis of a distinction covered so far, divide these items into two groups of five items each such that all the items in one group have a feature that none of the items in the second group have. Describe the feature on which you based your classifications. The items that belong in one group are listed at the back of the book.

Exercise 1-2

■ Can bears and other animals think critically? Find out by checking the answers section at the back of the book.

▲ 1. You shouldn't buy that car because it is ugly.

2. That car is ugly, and it costs more than $25,000, too.

3. Rainbows have seven colors, although it's not always easy to see them all.

▲ 4. Walking is the best exercise. It places the least stress on your joints.

5. The ocean on the central coast is the most beautiful shade of sky blue, but it gets greener as you go north.

6. Her favorite color is yellow because it is the color of the sun.

▲ 7. Pooh is my favorite cartoon character because he has lots of personality.

8. You must turn off the lights when you leave the room. They cost a lot of money to run, and you don't need them during the day.

9. Television programs have too much violence and immoral behavior. Hundreds of killings are portrayed every month.

▲ 10. You'll be able to find a calendar on sale after the first of the year, so it is a good idea to wait until then to buy one.

Exercise 1-3

Which of the following claims are objective?

▲ 1. Nicki Minaj can fake a great English accent.

2. On a baseball field, the center of the pitcher's mound is 59 feet from home plate.

3. Staring at the sun will damage your eyes.

▲ 4. Green is the most pleasant color to look at.

5. Yellow is Jennifer's favorite color.

6. With enough experience, a person who doesn't like opera can come to appreciate it.

▲ 7. Opera would be easier to listen to if they'd leave out the singing.

8. Sailing is much more soothing than sputtering about in a motorboat.

9. Driving while drowsy is dangerous.

▲ 10. Pit vipers can strike a warm-blooded animal even when it is pitch dark.

11. P. Diddy is totally bink.

12. P. Diddy is totally bink to me.

Exercise 1-4

Which of the following are subjective?

▲ 1. Fallon tells better jokes than Colbert.

2. In 2013 Miguel Cabrera hit the most home runs on a 3–0 count.

3. Your teacher will complain if you text in class.

▲ 4. Your teacher would be crazy not to complain if you text in class.

5. There is life on Mars.

6. Golf wastes time.

▲ 7. *Warcraft* scared the you-know-what out of my sister.

8. *Warcraft* is lousy. A total letdown.

9. Movies like *Warcraft* lack redeeming social value. [*Hint:* An assertion might have more than one subjective element.]

▲ 10. Donald Trump has unusual hair.

Exercise 1-5

Some of these items are arguments, and some are not. Which are which?

▲ 1. Tipsarevic is unlikely to win the U.S. Open this year. He has a nagging leg injury, plus he doesn't have the drive he once had.

2. Hey there, Marco! Don't go giving that cat top sirloin. What's the matter with you? You got no brains?

3. If you've ever met a pet bird, you know they are busy creatures.

4. Everybody is saying the president earned the Nobel Prize. What a stupid idea! She hasn't earned it at all. There's not a lick of truth in that notion.

5. "Is the author really entitled to assert that there is a degree of unity among these essays which makes this a book rather than a congeries? I am inclined to say that he is justified in this claim, but articulating this justification is a somewhat complex task."

—From a book review by Stanley Bates

6. As a long-time customer, you're already taking advantage of our money management expertise and variety of investment choices. That's a good reason for consolidating your other eligible assets into an IRA with us.

7. PROFESSOR X: Well, I see where the new chancellor wants to increase class sizes.

PROFESSOR Y: Yeah, another of his bright ideas.

PROFESSOR X: Actually, I don't think it hurts to have one or two extra people in class.

PROFESSOR Y: What? Of course it hurts. Whatever are you thinking?

PROFESSOR X: Well, I just think there are good reasons for increasing the class size a bit.

8. Yes, I charge a little more than other dentists. But I feel I give better service. So my billing practices are justified.

9. Since you want to purchase the house, you should exercise your option before June 30, 2018. Otherwise, you will forfeit the option price.

10. John Montgomery has been the Eastern Baseball League's best closer this season. Unfortunately, when a closer gets shelled, as Montgomery did last night, it takes him a while to recover. Nobody will say he is the best closer after that performance.

Determine which of the following passages contain arguments. For any that do, identify the argument's conclusion. There aren't hard-and-fast rules for identifying arguments, so you'll have to read closely and think carefully about some of these.

Exercise 1-6

1. The Directory of Intentional Communities lists more than 200 groups across the country organized around a variety of purposes, including environmentally aware living.

2. Carl would like to help out, but he won't be in town. We'll have to find someone else who owns a truck.

3. Once upon a time Washington, DC, passed an ordinance prohibiting private ownership of firearms. After that, Washington's murder rate shot up 121 percent. Bans on firearms are clearly counterproductive.

4. Computers will never be able to converse intelligently through speech. A simple example proves this. The sentences "How do you recognize speech?" and "How do you wreck a nice beach?" have different meanings, but they sound similar enough that a computer could not distinguish between the two.

■ Think you are welcome? Think again and think critically.

5. *The Carrie Diaries* isn't very good. It's just a repackage of *Sex and the City*.

6. "Like short-term memory, long-term memory retains information that is encoded in terms of sense modality and in terms of links with information that was learned earlier (that is, meaning)."

—*Neil R. Carlson*

7. Fears that chemicals in teething rings and soft plastic toys may cause cancer may be justified. Last week, the Consumer Product Safety Commission issued a report confirming that low amounts of DEHP, known to cause liver cancer in lab animals, may be absorbed from certain infant products.

8. "It may be true that people, not guns, kill people. But people with guns kill more people than people without guns. As long as the number of lethal weapons in the hands of the American people continues to grow, so will the murder rate."

—*Susan Mish'alani*

9. Then: A Miami man gets thirty days in the stockade for wearing a flag patch on the seat of his trousers. Now: Miami department stores sell boxer trunks made up to look like an American flag. Times have changed.

10. Dockers are still in style, but skinny legs are no longer trending.

Exercise 1-7

For each numbered passage, identify which lettered item best states the primary issue discussed in the passage. Be prepared to say why you think your choice is the correct one.

1. Let me tell you why Hank ought not to take that math course. First, it's too hard, and he'll probably flunk it. Second, he's going to spend the whole term in a state of frustration. Third, he'll probably get depressed and do poorly in all the rest of his courses.

   a. whether Hank ought to take the math course
   b. whether Hank would flunk the math course
   c. whether Hank will spend the whole term in a state of frustration
   d. whether Hank will get depressed and do poorly in all the rest of his courses

2. The county has cut the library budget for salaried library workers, and there will not be enough volunteers to make up for the lack of paid workers. Therefore, the library will have to be open fewer hours next year.

   a. whether the library will have to be open fewer hours next year
   b. whether there will be enough volunteers to make up for the lack of paid workers

3. Pollution of the waters of the Everglades and of Florida Bay is due to multiple causes. These include cattle farming, dairy farming, industry, tourism, and urban development. So it is simply not true that the sugar industry is completely responsible for the pollution of these waters.

   a. whether pollution of the waters of the Everglades and Florida Bay is due to multiple causes
   b. whether pollution is caused by cattle farming, dairy farming, industry, tourism, and urban development
   c. whether the sugar industry is partly responsible for the pollution of these waters
   d. whether the sugar industry is completely responsible for the pollution of these waters

▲ 4. It's clear that the mainstream media have lost interest in classical music. For example, the NBC network used to have its own classical orchestra conducted by Arturo Toscanini, but no such orchestra exists now. One newspaper, the no-longer-existent *Washington Star*, used to have thirteen classical music reviewers; that's more than twice as many as *The New York Times* has now. H. L. Mencken and other columnists used to devote considerable space to classical music; nowadays, you almost never see it mentioned in a major column.

   a. whether popular taste has turned away from classical music
   b. whether newspapers are employing fewer writers on classical music
   c. whether the mainstream media have lost interest in classical music

5. This year's National Football League draft lists a large number of quarterbacks among its highest-ranking candidates. Furthermore, quite a number of teams do not have first-class quarterbacks. It's therefore likely that an unusually large number of quarterbacks will be drafted early in this year's draft.

   a. whether teams without first-class quarterbacks will choose quarterbacks in the draft
   b. whether this year's NFL draft includes a large number of quarterbacks
   c. whether an unusually large number of quarterbacks will be drafted early in this year's draft

6. An animal that will walk out into a rainstorm and stare up at the clouds until water runs into its nostrils and it drowns—well, that's what I call the world's dumbest animal. And that's exactly what young domestic turkeys do.

   a. whether young domestic turkeys will drown themselves in the rain
   b. whether any animal is dumb enough to drown itself in the rain
   c. whether young domestic turkeys are the world's dumbest animal

▲ 7. The defeat of the school voucher initiative was a bad thing for the country because now public schools won't have any incentive to clean up their act. Furthermore, the defeat perpetuates the private-school-for-the-rich, public-school-for-the-poor syndrome.

   a. whether public schools now have any incentive to clean up their act
   b. whether the defeat of the school voucher initiative was bad for the country
   c. whether public schools now have any incentive to clean up their act and whether the private-school-for-the-rich, public-school-for-the-poor syndrome will be perpetuated (issues are equally stressed)

8. From an editorial in a newspaper outside Southern California: "The people in Southern California who lost a fortune in the wildfires last year could have

bought insurance that would have covered their houses and practically every-thing in them. And anybody with any foresight would have made sure there were no brush and no trees near the houses so that there would be a buffer zone between the house and any fire, as the Forest Service recommends. Finally, anybody living in a fire danger zone ought to know enough to have a fireproof or fire-resistant roof on the house. So, you see, most of the losses those people suffered were simply their own fault."

a. whether fire victims could have done anything to prevent their losses
b. whether insurance, fire buffer zones, and fire-resistant roofs could have prevented much of the loss
c. whether the losses people suffered in the fires were their own fault

9. "Whatever we believe, we think agreeable to reason, and, on that account, yield our assent to it. Whatever we disbelieve, we think contrary to reason, and, on that account, dissent from it. Reason, therefore, is allowed to be the principle by which our belief and opinions ought to be regulated."

—*Thomas Reid,* Essays on the Active Powers of Man

a. whether reason is the principle by which our beliefs and opinions ought to be regulated
b. whether what we believe is agreeable to reason
c. whether what we disbelieve is contrary to reason
d. both b and c

10. Most people you find on university faculties are people who are interested in ideas. And the most interesting ideas are usually new ideas. So most people you find on university faculties are interested in new ideas. Therefore, you are not going to find many conservatives on university faculties, because conser-vatives are not usually interested in new ideas.

a. whether conservatives are interested in new ideas
b. whether you'll find many conservatives on university faculties
c. whether people on university faculties are interested more in new ideas than in older ideas
d. whether most people are correct

COGNITIVE BIASES

When a poll is really, really out of whack with what I want to happen, I do have a tendency to disregard it.

—Rush Limbaugh, recognizing his own confirmation bias

Unconscious features of psychology can affect human mental processes, sometimes in unexpected ways. Recent research suggests that donning formal business attire or a physician's white lab coat might improve a person's performance on a cognitive test.* Seeing a fast food logo (e.g., McDonald's golden arches) may make some individuals attempt to process information more hastily.** In one experiment, sub-jects being told that the expensive sunglasses they were asked to wear were fake increased their propensity to cheat on tests that involved cash payments for correct answers.† In another experiment, male subjects, if dressed in sweats, made less prof-itable deals in simulated negotiations than did subjects dressed in suits.

---

*Referenced in *Scientific American Mind,* January/February 2016, p. 13.
**Referenced in a posting dated April 13, 2010, by Christopher Peterson in *Psychology Today.* https://www.psychologytoday.com/blog/the-good-life/201004/fast-food-and-impatience.
†This and the experiment cited in the next sentence also are referenced in *Scientific American Mind,* January/February 2016, p. 13.

Were we entirely rational, our conclusions would be grounded in logic and based on evidence objectively weighed. The unconscious features of human psychology affecting belief formation that have been reasonably well established include several that are widely referred to as *cognitive biases*.* They skew our apprehension of reality and interfere with our ability to think clearly, process information accurately, and reason objectively.

For example, we tend to evaluate an argument based on whether we agree with it rather than on the criteria of logic. Is the following specimen good reasoning?

> All pit bulls are dogs.
> Some dogs bite.
> Therefore some pit bulls bite.

It isn't. You might as well conclude some pit bulls are fox terriers. After all, all pit bulls are dogs and some dogs are fox terriers. If it took you a moment to see that the first argument is illogical, it's because its conclusion is something you know is true.

The tendency to evaluate reasoning by the believability of its conclusion is known as **belief bias.** A closely related cognitive bias is **confirmation bias,** which refers to the tendency to attach more weight to evidence that supports our viewpoint. If you are a Democrat, you may view evidence that Fox News is biased as overwhelming; if you are a Republican you may regard the same evidence as weak and unconvincing. In science, good experiments are designed to ensure that experimenters can't "cherry-pick" evidence, that is, search for evidence that supports the hypothesis they think is true while ignoring evidence to the contrary.

There isn't any hard-and-fast difference between confirmation bias and belief bias; they are both unconscious expressions of the human tendency to think our side of an issue must be the correct side. Thinking critically means being especially critical of arguments that support our own points of view.

Some cognitive biases involve **heuristics,** general rules we unconsciously follow in estimating probabilities. An example is the **availability heuristic,** which involves unconsciously assigning a probability to a type of event on the basis of how often one thinks of events of that type. After watching multiple news reports of an earthquake or an airplane crash or a case of child abuse, thoughts of earthquakes and airplane crashes and child abuse will be in the front of one's mind. Accordingly, one may overestimate their probability. True, if the probability of airplane crashes were to increase, then one might well think about airplane crashes more often; but it does not follow that if one thinks about them more often, their probability has increased.

The availability heuristic may explain how easy it is to make the mistake known as generalizing from anecdote, a logical fallacy

> People will generally accept facts as truth only if the facts agree with what they already believe.
>
> —Andy Rooney, nicely explaining belief bias

> ■ Bad-mouthing someone is not the same as thinking critically about what he or she says.

we discuss later in the book. Generalizing from anecdote happens when one accepts a sweeping generalization based on a single vivid report. The availability heuristic is also probably related to the **false consensus effect,** which refers to the inclination we may have to assume that our attitudes and those held by people around us are shared by society at large.*

Another source of skewed belief is the **bandwagon effect,** which refers to an unconscious tendency to align one's thinking with that of other people. The bandwagon effect is potentially a powerful source of cognitive distortion. In famous experiments, psychologist Solomon Asch found that what other people say *they* see may actually alter what we think *we* see.** We—the authors—have students take tests and quizzes using smartphones and clickers, with software that instantly displays the opinion of the class in a bar graph projected on a screen. Not infrequently it happens that, if opinion begins to build for one answer, almost everyone switches to that option—even if it is incorrect or illogical.

If you have wondered why consumer products are routinely advertised as bestsellers, you now know the answer. Marketers understand the bandwagon effect. They know that getting people to believe that a product is popular generates further sales.

Political propagandists also know we have an unconscious need to align our beliefs with the opinions of other people. Thus, they try to increase support for a measure by asserting that everyone likes it, or—and this is even more effective—by asserting that *nobody* likes whatever the opposition has proposed. Given alternative measures X and Y, "Nobody wants X!" is even more likely to generate support for Y than is "Everyone wants Y!" This is because of **negativity bias,** the tendency people have to weight negative information more heavily than positive information when evaluating things. Negativity bias is hard-wired into us: the brain displays more neural activity in response to negative information than to positive information.† A corollary to negativity bias from economics is that people generally are more strongly motivated to avoid a loss than to accrue a gain, a bias known as **loss aversion.**

It also should come as no surprise that we find it easier to form negative opinions of people who don't belong to our club, church, party, nationality, or other group. This is a part of **in-group bias,** another cognitive factor that may color perception and distort judgment. We may well perceive the members of our own group as exhibiting more variety and individuality than the members of this or that out-group, who we may view as indistinguishable from one another and as conforming to stereotypes. We may attribute the achievements of members of our own group to gumption and hard work and our failures to bad luck, whereas we may attribute *their* failures—those of the members of out-groups—to their personal shortcomings, while grudgingly discounting their achievements as mere good luck. The tendency to not appreciate that others' behavior is as much constrained by events and circumstances as our own would be if we were in their position is known as the **fundamental attribution error.**††

Experiments suggest that people find it extraordinarily easy to forge group identities. When assigned to a group on the basis of something as trivial as a coin

*See L. Ross, "The 'False Consensus Effect': An Egocentric Bias in Social Perception and Attribution Processes," *Journal of Experimental Social Psychology* 13, no. 3 (May 1977): 279–301.

**A copy of Asch's own summary of his experiments can be found at www.panarchy.org/asch/social.pressure.1955.html.

†See Tiffany A. Ito, et al., "Negative Information Weighs More Heavily on the Brain," *Journal of Personality and Social Psychology* 75, no. 4 (1998): 887–900.

††E. E. Jones and V. A. Harris, "The Attribution of Attitudes," *Journal of Experimental Social Psychology* 3 (1967): 1–24. For in-group biases, see Henri Tajfel, *Human Groups and Social Categories* (Cambridge, England: Cambridge University Press, 1981).

Rational Choice?

Critical thinking is aimed at coming to correct conclusions and making wise choices or decisions. We know from everyday experience that desires, fears, personal objectives, and various emotions affect choices. As explained in the text, experimental psychologists have discovered other, more unexpected and surprising, influences on our thinking.

■ In a recent experiment, researchers at Yale and Harvard Universities asked subjects to evaluate a job candidate by reading an applicant's résumé, which had been attached to a clipboard. Some of the clipboards weighed ¾ pound; the others weighed 4½ pounds. Subjects holding the heavier clipboard rated the applicant as better overall. Evidently a "rational evaluation" of a person's qualifications may be affected by irrelevant physical cues.*

*Reported by Randolph E. Schmid of the Associated Press, in *The Sacramento Bee,* June 23, 2010.

flip, subjects will immediately begin exhibiting in-group and attribution biases.* In a famous experiment in social psychology, the Robber's Cave Experiment, twenty-two 12-year-old boys who previously hadn't known each other were divided *arbitrarily* into two groups. When the two groups were forced to compete, the members of each group instantly exhibited hostility and other indicators of in-group bias toward the members of the other group.**

People make snap judgments about who is and who is not a member of their group. Students transferring into a new high school are branded swiftly. Once, one of the authors and his wife were walking their dogs, not necessarily the world's best-behaved pooches, along a street in Carmel, an affluent town on California's central coast. When the author fell a few paces behind his wife, a well-dressed woman walked by and glanced disapprovingly at the dogs. "Did you see that woman?" she asked indignantly, unaware that she was referring to the wife of the man she was addressing. "You can tell she isn't from around here," she said. She seems to have assumed that the author was from the Carmel in-group, simply because he wasn't connected to the misbehaving dogs.

In a series of famous experiments in the 1960s regarding **obedience to authority,** psychologist Stanley Milgram discovered that a frightening percentage of ordinary men and women will administer apparently lethal electrical shocks to innocent people, when told to do so by an experimenter in a white coat.† The findings are subject to multiple interpretations and explanations, but the tendency of humans to obey authority simply for the sake of doing so hardly needs experimental confirmation. Not long ago French researchers created a fake TV game show that was much like the Milgram experiment. The host instructed contestants to deliver electrical shocks to an individual who was said to be just another contestant, but who in reality was an actor. The contestants complied—and delivered shocks right up to a level that (if the shock was really being delivered) might execute the man. Whether the subjects were blindly following the instructions of an authority or were responding to some other impulse isn't completely clear, but

*Tajfel, *Human Groups and Social Categories.*
**A report of the Robber's Cave experiment is available online at http://psychclassics.yorku.ca/Sherif/.
†Milgram discusses his experiments in *Obedience to Authority: An Experimental View* (New York: HarperCollins, 1974).

■ Does Kanye West dress well? The issue is *subjective,* or, as some people say, "a matter of opinion."

it is impossible to think that good judgment or rational thought would lead them to such excess.*

Yet another possible source of psychological distortion is the **overconfidence effect,** one of several self-deception biases that may be found in a variety of contexts.** If a person estimates the percentage of his or her correct answers on a subject, the estimate will likely err on the high side—at least if the questions are difficult or the subject matter is unfamiliar.[†] Perhaps some manifestation of the overconfidence effect explains why, in the early stages of the *American Idol* competition, many contestants appear totally convinced they will be crowned the next American Idol—and are speechless when the judges inform them they cannot so much as carry a tune.[††]

Closely related to the overconfidence effect is the **better-than-average illusion.** The illusion crops up when most of a group rate themselves as better than most of the group relative to some desirable characteristic, such as resourcefulness or driving ability. The classic illustration is the 1976 survey of SAT takers, in which well over 50 percent of the respondents rated themselves as better than 50 percent of other SAT takers with respect to such qualities as leadership ability.[‡] The same effect has been observed when people estimate how their intelligence, memory, or job performance stacks up with the intelligence, memory, and job performances of other members of their profession or workplace. In our own informal surveys, more than 80 percent of our students rate themselves in the top 10 percent of their class with respect to their ability to think critically.

Unfortunately, evidence indicates that even when they are informed about the better-than-average illusion, people may *still* rate themselves as better than most in their ability to not be subject to it.[‡‡]

That beliefs are generated as much by psychology and impulse as by evidence should come as no surprise. The new car that was well beyond our means yesterday seems entirely affordable today—though our finances haven't changed. If someone invited us to The Olive Garden we'd expect decent fare; but if they suggested we

---

*Jamey Keaton, Associated Press. Reported in *The Sacramento Bee,* Thursday, March 18, 2010. Did the subjects suspect the shocks weren't real? Their statements afterward don't rule out the possibility but certainly seem to suggest they believed they truly were administering painful electrical shocks to the actor.

**However, a universal tendency among humans to irrationally exaggerate their own competencies hasn't been established. For an online quiz purportedly showing the overconfidence effect, see www.tim-richardson.net/joomla15/finance-articles-profmenu-70/73-over-confidence-test.html.

[†]See Sarah Lichtenstein and other authors, "Calibration of Probabilities: The State of the Art to 1980," in Daniel Kahneman, Paul Slovic, and Amos Tversky, *Judgment under Uncertainty: Heuristics and Biases* (Cambridge, England: Cambridge University Press, 1982), 306–34.

[††]This possibility was proposed by Gad Saad, *Psychology Today,* www.psychologytoday.com/blog/homo-consumericus/200901/self-deception-american-idol-is-it-adaptive.

[‡]See Mark D. Alicke and other authors in "The Better-Than-Average Effect," in Mark D. Alicke and others, *The Self in Social Judgment: Studies in Self and Identity* (New York: Psychology Press, 2005), 85–106. The better-than-average illusion is sometimes called the Lake Wobegon effect, in reference to Garrison Keillor's story about the fictitious Minnesota town "where all the children are above average."

[‡‡]http://weblamp.princeton.edu/~psych/FACULTY/Articles/Pronin/The%20Bias%20Blind.PDF. The better-than-average bias has not been found to hold for all positive traits. In some things, people underestimate their abilities. The moral is that for many abilities, we are probably not the best judges of how we compare to others. And this includes our ability to avoid being subject to biasing influences.

try dining at, say, The Lung Garden, we'd hesitate—even if we were told the food is identical. People will go out of their way to save $10 when buying a $25 pen, but won't do the same to save the same amount buying a $500 suit.* Programmed into our psyches are features that distort our perception, color our judgment, and impair our ability to think objectively.

The best defense? Making it a habit to think critically—and to be especially critical of arguments and evidence that seem to accord with what we already believe.

The following exercises may help you understand the cognitive biases discussed in the previous section.

The following questions are for thought or discussion. Your instructor may ask you to write a brief essay addressing one or more of them. **Exercise 1-8**

▲ 1. Which of the cognitive biases discussed in this section do you think you might be most subject to? Why?

2. Can you think of other psychological tendencies you have that might interfere with the objectivity of your thinking? For example, are you unusually generous or selfish?

3. Think again about a student (or anyone) contemplating getting a pet. Is there a cognitive bias a person in that position might be especially prone to, when weighing the arguments on both sides?

▲ 4. Explain belief bias (or confirmation bias) in your own words, and give an example of a time when you may have been subject to it.

5. What might you do to compensate for a bias factor you listed in questions 1 or 2 in this exercise?

For each of the following attributes, rate yourself in comparison with other students in your class. Are you **Exercise 1-9**

a. in the top 10 percent?
b. in the top 50 to 89 percent?
c. in the lower 25 to 49 percent?
d. below the top 75 percent?

▫ ability to think clearly
▫ ability to think logically
▫ ability to think critically
▫ ability to be objective
▫ ability to think creatively
▫ ability to read with comprehension
▫ ability to spot political bias in the evening news
▫ IQ

If you answered (a) or (b) about one of the preceding abilities, would you change your mind if you learned that most of the class also answered (a) or (b) about that ability? Why or why not?

*Daniel Ariely, *Predictably Irrational* (New York: HarperCollins, 2008), 19–20.

Exercise 1-10

Select one of the following claims you are inclined to strongly agree or disagree with. Then produce the best argument you can think of for the opposing side. When you are finished, ask someone to read your argument and tell you honestly whether he or she thinks you have been fair and objective.

- "There is (is not) a God."
- "Illegal immigrants should (should not) be eligible for health care benefits."
- "Handgun owners should (should not) be required to register each handgun they own."
- "The words 'under God' should (should not) be removed from the Pledge of Allegiance."
- "Sex education should (should not) be taught in public schools."

TRUTH AND KNOWLEDGE

At the end of the day, when we are ready to turn out the lights and go to bed, we want the conclusions we have reached through painstaking critical thinking to be *true*—and we want to *know* they are true. However, what are truth and knowledge? Through the years, many competing theories have been offered to account for their real nature, but fortunately for you, we can tell you what you need to know for this discussion without getting mired in those controversies.

As for truth, the most important thing is to understand that an objective belief or claim is either true or false in the normal, commonsense way. Truth and falsity are properties of propositional entities like beliefs, opinions, judgments, statements, claims, and the like. As mentioned previously, when any of those entities is objective, whether it is true or false does not depend on whether we think it is true or false.

You can assert a claim's truth in a number of ways. In normal conversation, we'd take each of the following as making the same statement:

> A book is on the table.
> It is true a book is on the table.
> It is a fact a book is on the table.
> Yes, a book is on the table.

The concept of knowledge is another that philosophers have contested at a deep, theoretical level despite a general agreement that in everyday life, we understand well enough what we mean when we say we know something.

Ordinarily, you are entitled to say you *know* a book is on the table, provided that (1) you believe a book is on the table, (2) you have justification for this belief in the form of an argument beyond a reasonable doubt that a book is on the table, and (3) you have no reason to suspect you are mistaken, such as that you haven't slept for several nights or have recently taken hallucinogenic drugs. Skeptics may say it is impossible to know anything, though one wonders how they know that. Presumably, they'd have to say they're just guessing.

WHAT CRITICAL THINKING CAN AND CAN'T DO

We think critically when we evaluate the reasoning we and others use in coming to conclusions. Perhaps this remark strikes you as restricted and narrow. A composer, for example, thinks critically when he or she tries to find the right instrumentation to introduce a musical theme. A general thinks critically when he or she defines a military objective and weighs various strategies for achieving it. Dentists think critically when they weigh the likely duration of alternative dental repairs against a patient's life expectancy. Mechanics think critically when they attempt to diagnose mechanical problems by listening to the sound of an engine. People in each walk of life examine considerations that are unique to them.

Yet every discipline, every walk of life, every enterprise without exception involves the two kinds of reasoning we will begin examining in the next chapter. And critical thinking anywhere can be waylaid by emotion, self-interest, wishful thinking, desire to be accepted, confirmation bias, and various other psychological propensities that come with being a human being, and that also will be considered in this book.

Thinking critically won't necessarily tell you whether you should get a dog or whom to vote for or whether there is global warming or why your car won't start. It can, however, help you spot bad reasoning about all these things.

A WORD ABOUT THE EXERCISES

To get good at tennis, golf, playing a musical instrument, or most other skills, you have to practice, practice, and practice more. It's the same way with critical thinking, and that's why we provide so many exercises. For some exercises in this book, there is no such thing as only one correct answer, just as there is no such thing as only one correct way to serve a tennis ball. Some answers, however—just like tennis serves—are better than others, and that is where your instructor comes in. In many exercises, answers you give that are different from your instructor's are not necessarily incorrect. Still, your instructor's answers will be well thought out, reliable, and worth your attention. We recommend taking advantage of his or her experience to improve your ability to think critically.

Answers to questions marked with a triangle are found in the answers section at the back of the book.

We think critically when we evaluate reasoning used in coming to conclusions. Conclusions are beliefs; when they are expressed using true-or-false declarative sentences, they are claims (or statements or assertions). A belief (or opinion or claim or statement, etc.) whose truth is independent of whether people think it is true is objective.

An issue is simply a question. One uses an argument to establish a position on an issue; the position is the conclusion of the argument. Evaluation of arguments can be skewed by emotion, wishful thinking, self-interest, confirmation bias, and other psychological impediments to objectivity.

What follows is a more complete list of ideas explored in this chapter.

Recap

■ **Claim:** When a belief (judgment, opinion) is asserted in a declarative sentence, the result is a claim, statement, or assertion.

■ **Objective claim vs. subjective claim:** An objective claim is true or false regardless of whether people think it is true or false. Claims that lack this property are said to be subjective.

- **"Fact vs. opinion"**: People sometimes refer to true objective claims as "facts," and use the word "opinion" to designate any claim that is subjective.

- **"Factual claim"**: An objective claim. Saying that a claim is "factual" is not the same as saying it is true. A factual claim is simply a claim whose truth does not depend on our thinking it is true.

- **Moral subjectivism:** Moral subjectivism is the idea that moral judgments are subjective. "There is nothing either good or bad but that thinking makes it so."

- **Issue:** A question.

- **Argument:** An argument consists of two parts—one part of which (the premise or premises) is intended to provide a reason for accepting the other part (the conclusion).

- **"Argument":** People sometimes use this word to refer just to an argument's premise.

- **Arguments and issues:** The conclusion of an argument states a position on the issue under consideration.

- **Cognitive bias:** A feature of human psychology that skews belief formation. The ones discussed in this chapter include the following:

  - **Belief bias:** Evaluating reasoning by how believable its conclusion is.

  - **Confirmation bias:** A tendency to attach more weight to considerations that support our views.

  - **Availability heuristic:** Assigning a probability to an event based on how easily or frequently it is thought of.

  - **False consensus effect:** Assuming our opinions and those held by people around us are shared by society at large.

  - **Bandwagon effect:** The tendency to align our beliefs with those of other people.

  - **Negativity bias:** Attaching more weight to negative information than to positive information.

  - **Loss aversion:** Being more strongly motivated to avoid a loss than to accrue a gain.

  - **In-group bias:** A set of cognitive biases that make us view people who belong to our group differently from people who don't.

  - **Fundamental attribution error:** Having one understanding of the behavior of people in the in-group and another for people not in the in-group.

  - **Obedience to authority:** A tendency to comply with instructions from an authority.

  - **Overconfidence effect:** A cognitive bias that leads us to overestimate what percentage of our answers on a subject are correct.

  - **Better-than-average illusion:** A self-deception cognitive bias that leads us to overestimate our own abilities relative to those of others.

- **Truth:** A claim is true if it is free from error.

- **Knowledge:** If you believe something, have an argument beyond a reasonable doubt that it is so, and have no reason to think you are mistaken, you can claim you know it.

Here are more exercises to help you identify objective and subjective claims, recognize arguments, identify issues, and tell when two people are addressing the same issue. In addition, you will find writing exercises as well as an exercise that will give you practice in identifying the purpose of a claim.

Additional Exercises

Exercise 1-11

Identify the conclusion of any arguments contained in the following passages.

1. There is trouble in the Middle East, there is a recession at home, and all economic indicators are trending downward. It seems likely, then, that the only way the stock market can go is down.

2. Lucy is too short to reach the bottom of the sign.

3. "Can it be established that genetic humanity is sufficient for moral humanity? I think there are very good reasons for not defining the moral community in this way."

   —Mary Anne Warren

4. Pornography often depicts women as servants or slaves or as otherwise inferior to men. In light of that, it seems reasonable to expect to find more women than men who are upset by pornography.

5. "My folks, who were Russian immigrants, loved the chance to vote. That's probably why I decided that I was going to vote whenever I got the chance. I'm not sure [whom I'll vote for], but I am going to vote. And I don't understand people who don't."

   —Mike Wallace

6. "Dynamism is a function of change. On some campuses, change is effected through nonviolent or even violent means. Although we too have had our demonstrations, change here is usually a product of discussion in the decision-making process."

   —Hillary Clinton, while a student at Wellesley College in the 1960s

7. What does it take to make a good soap? You need good guys and bad guys, sex, babies, passion, infidelity, jealousy, hatred, and suspense. And it must all be believable. Believability is the key.

8. We need to make clear that sexual preference, whether chosen or genetically determined, is a private matter. It has nothing to do with an individual's ability to make a positive contribution to society.

9. The report card on charter schools is mixed. Some show better results than public schools, others show worse. Charter schools have this advantage when it comes to test scores: the kids attending them are more apt to have involved parents.

10. *American Idol* is history, but when you remember whose careers were launched by *AI,* you know it was the best talent show on TV.

Exercise 1-12

For each numbered passage in this exercise, identify which lettered item best states the primary issue discussed in the passage. Be prepared to say why you think your choice is the correct one.

1. In pre-civil war Spain, the influence of the Catholic Church must have been much stronger on women than on men. You can determine this by looking at the number of religious communities, such as monasteries, nunneries, and so forth. A total of about 5,000 such communities existed in 1931; 4,000 of them were female, whereas only 1,000 of them were male. This proves my point about the Church's influence on the sexes.

   a. whether the Catholic Church's influence was stronger on women than on men in pre-civil war Spain
   b. whether the speaker's statistics really prove his point about the Church's influence
   c. whether the figures about religious communities really have anything to do with the overall influence of the Catholic Church in Spain

2. *Breaking Bad* might have been a good series without all the profanity. But without the profanity, it would not have been believable. Those people just talk that way. If you have them speaking Shakespearean English, nobody will pay attention. Yes, like many programs with offensive features—whether it's bad language, sex, or whatever—it will never appeal to the squeamish.

   a. whether movies with offensive features can appeal to the squeamish
   b. whether *Breaking Bad* would have been entertaining without the bad language
   c. whether *Breaking Bad* would have been believable without the profanity
   d. whether believable programs must always have offensive features

3. Siri is great, but it isn't an encyclopedia. It will tell you where the nearest Round Table is, but right now it won't tell you how late the place is open.

   a. whether Siri is great
   b. whether Siri has encyclopedic knowledge
   c. whether Siri will have encyclopedic knowledge
   d. whether Siri knows a lot about Round Table

4. From the way it tastes, you might think French roast has more caffeine in it than regular coffee, but it has less. The darker the roast, the less caffeine there is in it. I read this in *Consumer Reports*.

   a. whether *Consumer Reports* is a good source of information about coffee
   b. whether French roast has more caffeine than regular coffee
   c. whether most people think French roast has more caffeine than regular coffee

5. In Miami–Dade County, Florida, schools superintendent Rudy Crew was inundated with complaints after a police officer used a stun gun on a six-year-old student. As a result, Crew asked the Miami–Dade police to ban the use of stun guns on elementary school children. Crew did the right thing. More than 100 deaths have been linked to tasers.

   a. whether a police officer used a stun gun on a six-year-old student
   b. whether the superintendent did the right thing by asking the police to ban the use of stun guns on elementary school children

   c.   whether 100 deaths have been linked to tasers

   d.   whether the fact that 100 deaths have been linked to tasers shows that the superintendent did the right thing when he asked the police not to use tasers on children

6. Letting your children surf the net is like dropping them off downtown to spend the day doing whatever they want. They'll get in trouble.

   a.   whether letting your children off downtown to spend the day doing whatever they want will lead them into trouble

   b.   whether letting your children surf the net will lead them into trouble

   c.   whether restrictions should be placed on children's activities

▲ 7. The winner of this year's spelling bee is a straight-A student whose favorite subject is science, which isn't surprising, since students interested in science learn to pay attention to details.

   a.   whether the winner of this year's spelling bee is a straight-A student

   b.   whether science students learn to pay attention to details

   c.   whether learning science will improve a student's ability to spell

   d.   whether learning science teaches a student to pay attention to details

   e.   none of the above

8. Illinois state employees, both uniformed and nonuniformed, have been serving the state without a contract or cost-of-living pay increase for years, despite the fact that legislators and the governor have accepted hefty pay increases. All public employee unions should launch an initiative to amend the Illinois constitution so that it provides compulsory binding arbitration for all uniformed and nonuniformed public employees, under the supervision of the state supreme court.

   a.   whether Illinois state employees have been serving the state without a contract or cost-of-living pay increase for years

   b.   whether public employee unions should launch an initiative to amend the Illinois constitution so that it provides compulsory binding arbitration for all uniformed and nonuniformed public employees, under the supervision of the Illinois Supreme Court

   c.   neither of the above

9. In 2007, the Dominican Republic banned the sale of two brands of Chinese toothpaste because they contained a toxic chemical responsible for dozens of poisoning deaths in Panama. The company that exported the toothpaste, the Danyang Household Chemical Company, defended its product. "Toothpaste is not something you'd swallow, but spit out, and so it's totally different from something you would eat," one company manager said. The company manager was taking a position on which issue?

   a.   whether the Danyang Household Chemical Company included toxic chemicals in its toothpaste

   b.   whether Danyang Household Chemical Company toothpaste prevents cavities

   c.   whether the Danyang Household Chemical Company did anything wrong by exporting its toothpaste

   d.   whether China should have better product safety controls

▲ 10. YOU: So, what do you think of the governor?

   YOUR FRIEND: Not much, actually.

   YOU: What do you mean? Don't you think she's been pretty good?

   YOUR FRIEND: Are you serious?

YOU: Well, yes. I think she's been doing a fine job.

YOUR FRIEND: Oh, come on. Weren't you complaining about her just a few days ago?

a.   whether your friend thinks the governor has been a good governor
b.   whether you think the governor has been a good governor
c.   whether the governor has been a good governor
d.   whether you have a good argument for thinking the governor has been a good governor

Exercise 1-13

On what issue is the speaker taking a position in each of the following?

1. Police brutality does not happen very often. Otherwise, it would not make headlines when it does.

2. We have little choice but to concentrate crime-fighting efforts on enforcement because we don't have any idea what to do about the underlying causes of crime.

3. A lot of people think the gender of a Supreme Court justice doesn't matter. But with three women on the bench, cases dealing with women's issues are handled differently.

4. "The point is that the existence of an independent world explains our experiences better than any known alternative. We thus have good reason to believe that the world—which seems independent of our minds—really is essentially independent of our minds."

   —*Theodore W. Schick Jr. and Lewis Vaughn,* How to Think About Weird Things

5. Sure, some hot-doggers get good grades in Bubacz's class. But my guess is if Algernon takes it, all it'll get him is flunked out.

6. It's so dumb to think sales taxes hit poor people harder than rich people. The more money you have, the more you spend; and the more you spend, the more sales taxes you pay. And rich people spend more than poor people.

7. If you're going to buy a synthesizer, sign up for lessons on how to use the thing. A synthesizer won't work for you if you don't know how to make it work.

8. Intravenous drug use with nonsterile needles is one of the leading causes of the spread of AIDS. Many states passed legislation allowing officials to distribute clean needles in an effort to combat this method of infection. But in eleven states, including some of the most populous, possession of hypodermic syringes without a prescription is illegal. The laws in these foot-dragging states must be changed if we hope to end this epidemic.

9. The best way to avoid error is to suspend judgment about everything except what is certain. Because error leads to trouble, suspending judgment is the right thing to do.

10. "[Readers] may learn something about their own relationship to the earth from a people who were true conservationists. The Indians knew that life was equated with the earth and its resources, that America was a paradise,

and they could not comprehend why the intruders from the East were determined to destroy all that was Indian as well as America itself."

—*Dee Brown*, Bury My Heart at Wounded Knee

Exercise 1-14

Is the second person addressing the issue raised by the first person?

Example

> ELMOP: Toilet paper looks better unwinding from the back of the spool.
>
> MARWOOF: Get real! That is so stupid! It should unwind the other way.

Analysis

> Marwoof addresses the issue raised by Elmop.

1. MR.: Next weekend, we go on standard time again. We have to set the clocks ahead.
   MRS.: It isn't next weekend; it's the weekend after. And you set the clocks back an hour.

2. MOORE: Getting out of Afghanistan is only going to make us vulnerable to terrorism.
   PARKER: Yeah, right. You're just saying that 'cause you don't like Obama.

3. SHE: You don't give me enough help around the house. Why, you hardly ever do anything!
   HE: What??? I mowed the lawn on Saturday, and I washed both of the cars on Sunday. What's more, I clean up after dinner almost every night, and I hauled all that garden stuff to the dump. How can you say I don't do anything?
   SHE: Well, you sure don't want to hear about what I do! I do a lot more than that!

4. HEEDLESS: When people complain about what we did in Afghanistan, they just encourage terrorists to think America won't fight. People who complain like that ought to just shut up.
   CAUTIOUS: I disagree. Those people are reminding everyone it isn't in our interest to get involved in wars abroad.

5. MR. RJ: If you ask me, there are too many casinos around here already. We don't need more.
   MR. JR: Yeah? Well that's a strange idea coming from you; you play the lottery all the time.

6. JOE FITNESS: Whoa, look at that! The chain on my bike is starting to jump around! If I don't fix it, it'll stop working.
   COUCH POTATO: What you need is to stop worrying about it. You get too much exercise as it is.

7. YOUNG GUY: Baseball players are better now than they were forty years ago. They eat better, have better coaching, you name it.
   OLD GUY: They aren't better at all. They just seem better because they get more publicity and play with juiced equipment.

8. STUDENT ONE: Studying is a waste of time. Half the time, I get better grades if I don't study.
    STUDENT TWO: I'd like to hear you say that in front of your parents.

9. PHILATELIST: Did you know that U.S. postage stamps are now being printed in Canada?
    PATRIOT: What an outrage! If there is one thing that ought to be made in the United States, it's U.S. postage stamps!
    PHILATELIST: Oh, c'mon. If American printing companies can't do the work, let the Canadians have it.

10. FIRST NEIGHBOR: See here, you have no right to make so much noise at night. I have to get up early for work.
    SECOND NEIGHBOR: Yeah? Well, if you have the right to let your idiot dog run loose all day long, I have the right to make noise at night.

11. STUDY PARTNER ONE: Let's knock off for a while and go get pizza. We'll function better if we eat something.
    STUDY PARTNER TWO: Not one of those pizzas you like! I can't stand anchovies.

12. FEMALE STUDENT: The Internet is overrated. It takes forever to find something you can actually use in an assignment.
    MALE STUDENT: Listen, it takes a lot longer to drive over to the library and find a place to park.

13. RAMON: Hey, this English course is a complete waste of time. You don't need to know how to write anymore.
    DEVON: That's ridiculous. You're just saying that because you're a PE major.

14. CULTURALLY CHALLENGED PERSON: A concert! You think I'm going to a concert when I can be home watching football?
    CULTURALLY CHALLENGED PERSON'S SPOUSE: Yes, if you want dinner this week.

15. REPUBLICAN: I don't think Obama's budget requests make sense.
    DEMOCRAT: You just can't stand more taxes, can you?

16. MOORE: I've seen the work of both Thomas Brothers and Vernon Construction, and I tell you, Thomas Brothers does a better job.
    PARKER: Listen, Thomas Brothers is the highest-priced company in the whole state. If you hire them, you'll pay double for every part of the job.

17. URBANITE: The new requirements will force people off septic tanks and make them hook up to the city sewer. That's the only way we'll ever get the nitrates and other pollutants out of the groundwater.
    SUBURBANITE: You call it a requirement, but I call it an outrage! They're going to charge us from five to fifteen thousand dollars each to make the hookups! That's more than anybody can afford!

18. CRITIC: I don't think it's proper to sell junk bonds without emphasizing the risk involved, but it's especially bad to sell them to older people who are investing their entire savings.
    ENTREPRENEUR: Oh, come on. There's nothing the matter with making money.

19. ONE HAND: What with the number of handguns and armed robberies these days, it's hard to feel safe in your own home.
    THE OTHER HAND: The reason you don't feel safe is you don't have a handgun yourself. Criminals would rather hit a house where there's no gun than a house where there is one.

20. ONE GUY: Would you look at the price they want for these computer tablets? They're making a fortune on every one of these things!

   ANOTHER: Don't give me that. I know how big a raise you got last year—you can afford a truckload of those things!

21. FED UP: This city is too cold in the winter, too hot in the summer, and too dangerous all the time. I'll be happier if I exercise my early retirement option and move to my place in Arkansas.

   FRIEND: You're nuts. You'll be miserable if you don't work, and if you move, you'll be back in six months.

▲ 22. KATIE: Hey Jennifer, I hate to say this, but you would be better off riding a bike to school.

   JENNIFER: What, this from someone who drives everywhere she goes?

23. DEZRA: What are you thinking, mowing the lawn in your bare feet? That's totally unsafe.

   KEN: Like you never did anything you could get hurt doing?

24. YAO: Nice thing about an iMac. It never gets viruses.

   MAO: Of course you would say that; you own one.

▲ 25. HERR ÜBERALLES: We spend too much on heating. We must show more fortitude.

   FRAU ÜBERALLES: But you know I get cold easily.

Exercise 1-15

Which of the following claims pertain to right/wrong, good/bad, or should/shouldn't?

▲ 1. We did the right thing getting rid of Saddam. He was a sadistic tyrant.

2. That guy is the smartest person I know.

3. Contributing to the Humane Society is good to do.

▲ 4. It's time you start thinking about somebody other than yourself!

5. Your first duty is to your family; after that, to God and country, in that order.

6. You know what? I always tip 15 percent.

▲ 7. The FBI and CIA don't share information all that often, at least that's what I've heard.

8. You might find the parking less expensive on the street.

9. Help him! If the situation were reversed, he would help you.

▲ 10. Hip hop is better than country, any day.

11. Rodin was a master sculptor.

12. Whatever happened to Susan Boyle? You don't hear about her anymore.

▲ 13. If we want to stop the decline in enrollments here at Chaffee, we need to give students skills they can use.

Exercise 1-16

This exercise will give you another opportunity to identify when someone is offering an argument, as distinct from doing something else.

Decide which of the lettered options serves the same kind of purpose as the original remark. Then think critically about your conclusion. Do you have a reason for it? Be ready to state your reasoning in class if called on.

Example

Be careful! This plate is hot.

    a.   Watch out. The roads are icy.
    b.   Say—why don't you get lost?

Conclusion: The purpose of (a) is most like the purpose of the original remark. Reason: Both are arguments.

1. I'd expect that zipper to last about a week; it's made of cheap plastic.

    a.   The wrinkles on that dog make me think of an old man.
    b.   Given Sydney's spending habits, I doubt Adolphus will stick with her for long.

2. If you recharge your battery, sir, it will be almost as good as new.

    a.   Purchasing one CD at the regular price would entitle you to buy an unlimited number of CDs at only $4.99.
    b.   I will now serve dinner, after which you can play if you want.

3. To put out a really creative newsletter, you should get in touch with our technology people.

    a.   Do unto others as you would have them do unto you.
    b.   To put an end to this discussion, I'll concede your point.
    c.   You'd better cut down on your smoking if you want to live longer.

4. GE's profits during the first quarter were short of GE's projections. Therefore, we can expect GE's stock to fall sharply in the next day or so.

    a.   The senator thought what he did in private was nobody's business but his own.
    b.   The dog is very hot. Probably he would appreciate a drink of water.
    c.   The dog's coat is unusually thick. No wonder he is hot.

5. How was my date with your brother? Well . . . he has a great personality.

    a.   How do I like my steak? Not dripping blood like this thing you just served me.
    b.   How do I like your dress? Say, did you know that black is more slimming than white?

6. The wind is coming up. We'd better head for shore.

    a.   They finally arrived. I guess they will order soon.
    b.   We shouldn't leave yet. We just got here.

7. Good ties are made out of silk. That's why they cost so much.

    a.   Belts are like suspenders. They both keep your pants up.
    b.   Rugby has lots of injuries because rugby players don't wear pads.

8. Daphne owns an expensive car. She must be rich.

    a.   This dog has fleas. I'll bet it itches a lot.
    b.   This dog has fleas. That explains why it scratches a lot.

9. Dennis's salary is going up. He just got a promotion.

    a.   Dennis's salary went up after he got a promotion.
    b.   Dennis's salary won't be going up; he didn't get a promotion.

▲　10. Outlawing adult websites may hamper free speech, but pornography must be curbed.

　　　a.　The grass must be mowed even though it is hot.
　　　b.　The grass is getting long; time to mow.

Writing Exercises

1. Do people choose the sex they are attracted to? Write a one-page answer to this question, defending your answer with at least one supporting reason. Take about ten minutes to do this. Do not put your name on your essay. When everyone is finished, your instructor will collect the essays and redistribute them to the class. In groups of four or five, read the essays that have been given to your group. Divide the drafts into two batches, those that contain an argument and those that do not. Your instructor will ask each group to read to the class an essay that contains an argument and an essay that does not contain an argument (assuming that each group has at least one of each). The group should be prepared to explain why they feel each essay contains or fails to contain an argument.

2. Is it ever okay to tell a lie? Take a position on this issue and write a short essay supporting it.

Two Kinds of Reasoning

Students will learn to . . .

1. Recognize general features of arguments

2. Distinguish between deductive and inductive arguments and evaluate them for validity, soundness, strength, and weakness

3. Identify unstated premises

4. Identify a balance of considerations argument and an inference to the best explanation (IBE)

5. Distinguish between ethos, pathos, and logos as means of persuasion

6. Use techniques for understanding and evaluating the structure and content of arguments

Time to look more closely at arguments—the kind that actually show something (unlike the red herrings and emotional appeals and other fallacies we are going to be talking about later).

ARGUMENTS: GENERAL FEATURES

To repeat, an argument consists of two parts. One part, the premise, is intended to provide a reason for accepting the second part, the conclusion. This statement is *not* an argument:

> God exists.

It's just a statement.

Likewise, *this* is not an argument:

> God exists. That's as plain as the nose on your face.

It's just a slightly more emphatic statement.

Nor is this an argument:

> God exists, and if you don't believe it, you will go to hell.

It just tries to scare us into believing God exists.

Also not an argument:

> I think God exists, because I was raised a Baptist.

Yes, it looks a bit like an argument, but it isn't. It merely explains why I believe in God.

On the other hand, this *is* an argument:

> God exists because something had to cause the universe.

The difference between this and the earlier examples? This example has a premise ("something had to cause the universe") and a conclusion ("God exists").

As we explained in Chapter 1 (see page 8), an argument always has two parts: a premise part and a conclusion part. The premise part is intended to give a reason for accepting the conclusion part.

This probably seems fairly straightforward, but one or two complications are worth noting.

Conclusions Used as Premises

The same statement can be the conclusion of one argument and a premise in another argument:

> **Premise:** The brakes aren't working, the engine burns oil, the transmission needs work, and the car is hard to start.
> **Conclusion 1:** The car has outlived its usefulness.
> **Conclusion 2:** We should get a new car.

In this example, the statement "The car has outlived its usefulness" is the conclusion of one argument, and it is also a premise in the argument that we should get a new car.

Clearly, if a premise in an argument is uncertain or controversial or has been challenged, you might want to defend it—that is, argue that it is true. When you do, the premise becomes the conclusion of a new argument. However, every chain of reasoning must begin somewhere. If we ask a speaker to defend each premise with a further argument, and each premise in that argument with a further argument, and so on and so on, we eventually find ourselves being unreasonable, much like four-year-olds who keep asking "Why?" until they become exasperating. If we ask a speaker why he thinks the car has outlived its usefulness, he may mention that the car is hard to start. If we ask him why he thinks the car is hard to start, he probably won't know what to say.

Unstated Premises and Conclusions

Another complication is that arguments can contain unstated premises. For example:

> **Premise:** You can't check out books from the library without an ID.
> **Conclusion:** Bill won't be able to check out any books.

The unstated premise must be that Bill has no ID.

An argument can even have an unstated conclusion. Here is an example:

Conclusion Indicators

When the words in the following list are used in arguments, they usually indicate that a premise has just been offered and that a conclusion is about to be presented. (The three dots represent the claim that is the conclusion.)

Thus . . .   Consequently . . .
Therefore . . .   So . . .
Hence . . .   Accordingly . . .
This shows that . . .   This implies that . . .
This suggests that . . .   This proves that . . .

Example:

Stacy drives a Porsche. This suggests that either she is rich or her parents are.

The conclusion is

Either she is rich or her parents are.

The premise is

Stacy drives a Porsche.

The political party that best reflects mainstream opinion will win the presidency in 2020 and the Republican Party best reflects mainstream opinion.

If a person said this, he or she would be implying that the Republican Party will win the presidency in 2020; that would be the unstated conclusion of the argument.

Unstated premises are common in real life because sometimes they seem too obvious to need mentioning. The argument "the car is beyond fixing, so we should get rid of it" actually has an unstated premise to the effect that we should get rid of any car that is beyond fixing; but this may seem so obvious to us that we don't bother stating it.

Unstated conclusions also are not uncommon, though they are less common than unstated premises.

We'll return to this subject in a moment.

TWO KINDS OF ARGUMENTS

Good arguments come in two varieties: deductive demonstrations and inductive supporting arguments.

Deductive Arguments

The premise (or premises) of a good *deductive* argument, if true, *proves or demonstrates* (these being the same thing for our purposes) its conclusion. However, there is more to this than meets the eye, and we must begin with the fundamental concept

Premise Indicators

When the words in the following list are used in arguments, they generally introduce premises. They often occur just *after* a conclusion has been given. A premise would replace the three dots in an actual argument.

Since . . .
For . . .
In view of . . .
This is implied by . . .

Example:

Either Stacy is rich or her parents are, since she drives a Porsche.

The premise is the claim that Stacy drives a Porsche; the conclusion is the claim that either Stacy is rich or her parents are.

of deductive logic, *validity.* An argument is **valid** *if it isn't possible for the premise (or premises) to be true and the conclusion false.* This may sound complicated, but it really isn't. An example of a valid argument will help:

Premises: Jimmy Carter was president immediately before Bill Clinton, and George W. Bush was president immediately after Bill Clinton.
Conclusion: Jimmy Carter was president before George W. Bush.

As you can see, it's impossible for these premises to be true and this conclusion to be false. So the argument is valid.

However, you may have noticed that the premises contain a mistake. Jimmy Carter was not president immediately before Bill Clinton. George H. W. Bush was president immediately before Bill Clinton. Nevertheless, even though a premise of the preceding argument is not true, the argument is still valid, because it isn't possible for the premises to be true and the conclusion false. Another way to say this: If the premises *were* true, the conclusion *could not* be false—and that's what "valid" means.

Now, when the premises of a valid argument *are* true, there is a word for it. In that case, the argument is said to be **sound.** Here is an example of a sound argument:

Premises: Bill Clinton is taller than George W. Bush, and Jimmy Carter is shorter than George W. Bush.
Conclusion: Therefore, Bill Clinton is taller than Jimmy Carter.

This argument is sound because it is valid and the premises are true. As you can see, if an argument is sound, then its conclusion has been demonstrated.

Inductive Arguments

Again, the premise of a good deductive argument, if true, demonstrates that the conclusion is true. This brings us to the second kind of argument, the *inductive* argument. The premise of a good *inductive* argument doesn't demonstrate its conclusion; it *supports* it. For example:

> After 2 P.M. the traffic slows to a crawl on the Bay Bridge.
> Therefore, it probably does the same thing on the Golden Gate Bridge.

The fact that traffic slows to a crawl after 2 P.M. on the Bay Bridge does not demonstrate or prove that it does that on the Golden Gate Bridge; it *supports* that conclusion. It makes it somewhat more likely that traffic on the Golden Gate Bridge slows to a crawl after 2 P.M.

Here is another example of an inductive argument:

> Nobody has ever run a mile in less than three minutes.
> Therefore, nobody will ever run a mile in less than three minutes.

Like the first argument, the premise supports the conclusion but does not demonstrate or prove it.

If you are thinking that support is a matter of degree and that it can vary from just a little to a whole lot, you are right. Thus, inductive arguments are better or worse on a scale, depending on how much support their premises provide for the conclusion. Logicians have a technical word to describe this situation. The more support the premise of an inductive argument provides for the conclusion, the **stronger** the argument; the less support it provides, the **weaker** the argument. Put another way, one argument for a conclusion is weaker than another if it fails to raise the probability of the conclusion by as much. Thus, the first argument given above is weaker than the following argument:

> After 2 P.M. the traffic slows to a crawl on the Bay Bridge, the San Mateo Bridge, the San Rafael Bridge, and the Dumbarton Bridge.
> Therefore, it probably does the same thing on the Golden Gate Bridge.

This argument is stronger than the first argument because its premise makes the conclusion more likely. The more bridges in a region on which traffic slows at a given time, the more likely it is that that phenomenon is universal on the bridges in the region.

One more example of an inductive argument:

> Alexandra rarely returns texts.
> Therefore, she probably rarely returns emails.

Once again, the premise supports but does not demonstrate or prove the conclusion. The differences between texting and emailing are sufficiently significant that the premise does not offer a great deal of support for the conclusion, but it does offer some. If Alexandra rarely returned telephone calls or letters as well as texts, that would make the argument stronger.

In Chapter 11 we will explain the criteria for evaluating inductive arguments.

BEYOND A REASONABLE DOUBT

In common law, the highest standard of proof is proof "beyond a reasonable doubt." If you are a juror in a criminal trial, evidence will be presented to the court—facts that the interested parties consider relevant to the crime. Additionally, the prosecutor and counsel for the defense will offer arguments connecting the evidence to (or disconnecting it from) the guilt or innocence of the defendant. When the jury is asked to return a verdict, the judge will tell the jury that the defendant must be found not guilty unless the evidence proves guilt *beyond a reasonable doubt.*

Proof beyond a reasonable doubt actually is a lower standard than deductive demonstration. Deductive demonstration corresponds more to what, in ordinary English, might be expressed by the phrase "beyond any *possible* doubt." Recall that in logic, a proposition has been demonstrated when it has been shown to be the conclusion of a sound argument—an argument in which (1) all premises are true and (2) it is impossible for the premises to be true and for the conclusion to be false. In this sense, many propositions people describe as having been demonstrated or proved, such as that smoking causes lung cancer or that the DNA found at a crime scene was the defendant's, have not actually been proved in the logician's sense of the word. So, in real life, when people say something has been demonstrated, they may well be speaking informally. They may not mean that something is the conclusion of a sound deductive argument. However, when we—the authors—say that something has been demonstrated, that is *exactly* what we mean.

TELLING THE DIFFERENCE BETWEEN DEDUCTIVE AND INDUCTIVE ARGUMENTS

A useful strategy for telling the difference between deductive and inductive arguments is to memorize a good example of each kind. Here are good examples of each:

> **Valid Deductive Argument:** Juan lives on the equator. Therefore, Juan lives midway between the North and South poles.

> **Relatively Strong Inductive Argument:** Juan lives on the equator. Therefore, Juan lives in a humid climate.

Study the two examples so that you understand the difference between them. In the left example, if you know the definition of "equator," you already know it is midway between the poles. The right example is radically different. The definition of "equator" does not contain the information that it is humid. So:

> If the conclusion of an argument is true *by definition* given the premise or premises, it is a valid deductive argument.

Often it is said that a valid deductive argument is valid due to its "form." Thus, consider this argument:

> If Juan is a fragglemop, then Juan is a snipette. Juan is not a snipette. Therefore, Juan is not a fragglemop.

What makes this argument valid is its form:

> If P then Q.
> Not-Q.
> Therefore not-P.

You can see, however, that ultimately what makes the argument valid, and makes its form a valid form, is the way the words "If . . . then" and "not" work. If you know the way those words work, then you already know that the conclusion must be true given the two premises.

Another way of telling the difference between a deductive argument and an inductive argument is this: You generally would not say of a deductive argument that it supports or provides evidence for its conclusion. It would be odd to say that Juan's living on the equator is *evidence* that he lives midway between the poles, or that it *supports* that claim. Thus:

> If it sounds odd to speak of the argument as providing evidence or support for a contention, that's an indication it is a deductive argument.

It would sound very odd to say, "The fact that Fido is a dog is evidence Fido is a mammal." Fido's being a dog isn't *evidence* Fido is a mammal: it's *proof*. "Fido is a dog; therefore Fido is a mammal" is a valid deductive argument.

DEDUCTION, INDUCTION, AND UNSTATED PREMISES

Somebody announces, "Rain is on its way." Somebody else asks how he knows. He says, "There's a south wind." Is the speaker trying to *demonstrate* rain is coming? Probably not. His thinking, spelled out, is probably something like this:

> **Stated premise:** The wind is from the south.
> **Unstated premise:** Around here, south winds are usually followed by rain.
> **Conclusion:** There will be rain.

In other words, the speaker was merely trying to show that rain was a good possibility.

Notice, though, that the unstated premise in the argument could have been a universal statement to the effect that a south wind *always* is followed by rain at this particular location, in which case the argument would be deductive:

> **Stated premise:** The wind is from the south.
> **Unstated premise:** Around here, a south wind is always followed by rain.
> **Conclusion:** There will be rain.

Spelled out this way, the speaker's thinking is deductive: It isn't possible for the premises to be true and the conclusion to be false. So one might wonder abstractly what the speaker intended—an inductive argument that supports the belief that rain is coming, or a deductive demonstration.

There is, perhaps, no way to be certain short of asking the speaker something like, "Are you 100 percent positive?" But experience ("background knowledge") tells us that wind from a particular direction is not a surefire indicator of rain. So probably the speaker did have in mind merely the first argument. He wasn't trying to present a 100 percent certain, knock-down demonstration that it would rain; he was merely trying to establish there was a good chance of rain.

You can always turn an inductive argument with an unstated premise into a deductively valid argument by supplying the right universal premise—a statement that something holds without exception or is true everywhere or in all cases. Is that what the speaker really has in mind, though? You have to use background knowledge and common sense to answer the question.

For example, you overhear someone saying,

> Stacy and Justin are on the brink of divorce. They're always fighting.

One could turn this into a valid deductive argument by adding to it the universal statement "Every couple fighting is on the brink of divorce." But such an unqualified universal statement seems unlikely. Probably the speaker wasn't trying to demonstrate that Stacy and Justin are on the brink of divorce. He or she was merely trying to raise its likelihood. He or she was presenting evidence that Stacy and Justin are on the brink of divorce.

Often it is clear that the speaker does have a *deductive* argument in mind and has left some appropriate premise unstated. You overhear Professor Greene saying to Professor Brown,

> "Flunk her! This is the second time you've caught her cheating."

It would be strange to think that Professor Greene is merely trying to make it more likely that Professor Brown should flunk the student. Indeed, it is hard even to make sense of that suggestion. Professor Greene's argument, spelled out, must be this:

> **Stated premise:** This is the second time you've caught her cheating.
> **Unstated premise:** Anyone who has been caught cheating two times should be flunked.
> **Conclusion:** She should be flunked.

So context and content often make it clear what unstated premise a speaker has in mind and whether the argument is deductive or inductive.

Unfortunately, though, this isn't always the case. We might hear someone say,

> The bars are closed; therefore it is later than 2 A.M.

If the unstated premise in the speaker's mind is something like "In this city, the bars all close at 2 A.M.," then presumably he or she is thinking deductively and is evidently proffering proof that it's after 2. But if the speaker's unstated premise is something like "Most bars in this city close at 2 A.M." or "Bars in this city usually close at 2 A.M.," then we have an inductive argument that merely supports the conclusion. So which is the unstated premise? We really can't say without knowing more about the situation or the speaker.

Is an Ad Photo an Argument?

The short answer: No. The longer version: Still no. An advertising photograph can "give you a reason" for buying something only in the sense that it can *cause* you to think of a reason. A photo is not an argument.

The bottom line is this. Real-life arguments often leave a premise unstated. One such unstated premise might make the argument inductive; another might make it deductive. Usually, context or content make reasonably clear what is intended; other times they may not. When they don't, the best practice is to attribute to a speaker an unstated premise that at least is believable, everything considered. We'll talk about believability in Chapter 4.

BALANCE OF CONSIDERATIONS

Should I get a dog? Miss class to attend my cousin's wedding? Get chemo? Much everyday reasoning requires weighing considerations for and against thinking or doing something. Such reasoning, called **balance of considerations reasoning,** often contains both deductive and inductive elements. Here is an example:

> Should assault weapons be banned? On the one hand, doing that would violate the Second Amendment to the U.S. Constitution. But on the other hand, when guns were outlawed in Australia the number of accidental gun deaths fell dramatically; that would probably happen here, too. It is a tough call.

The first consideration mentioned in this passage—that banning assault weapons would violate the Second Amendment and therefore should not be done—is a deductive argument. The second consideration mentioned—that banning assault weapons would reduce the number of accidental gun deaths—is an inductive argument.

Inductive arguments can be compared as to strength and weakness; deductive arguments can be compared as to validity and soundness. Assigning weight to considerations can be difficult, of course, but it is not hopelessly arbitrary. In Chapter 12 of this book, we discuss the perspectives within which moral evaluations are made; you will see there that weighing considerations of the sort presented in the example above depend to a certain extent on the moral perspective one adheres to.

INFERENCE TO THE BEST EXPLANATION (IBE)

An **Inference to the Best Explanation (IBE)** concludes that something exists or holds true or is a fact because that supposition best explains something we have observed or otherwise know. An example:

> Neither the dog nor my husband is home, and the dog's leash is gone. The best explanation of this is that my husband is out walking the dog. Therefore, my husband is out walking the dog.

Here is another example:

> Sometimes my back really aches. Let's see. Could it be due to gardening? Or lifting weights perhaps? No—it hurts all the time. Plus it seems to hurt more in the morning. And it started right after I bought that expensive mattress. Therefore, it's the mattress that is hurting my back.

The conclusion of the argument is that the mattress is hurting my back; that supposition best explains the fact that my back hurts. Notice that the argument explicitly compares alternative explanations. It thus qualifies as a balance of considerations argument as well as an IBE, the "considerations" in this instance being alternative explanations.

Two more examples:

> Sarah and another candidate were finalists for the teaching position. Sarah had better qualifications, but she had tattoos. The candidate who got the position didn't have tattoos. Therefore, the fact she had tattoos caused Sarah to lose out on the position.

> There is water on the floor. Neither the bathtub nor the sink has been used and the ceiling isn't leaking. The only source of water in the room is the toilet. Therefore, the toilet is leaking.

In the first example, the best explanation of Sarah's not getting the position is thought to be the fact that she has tattoos. Since no other explanation was considered, you might say the tattoo explanation wins by default. In the second example, the leaking-toilet explanation was explicitly compared to other possible explanations and declared the winner.

Sometimes IBE is referred to as "abduction." We treat it as a type of inductive reasoning, reasoning used to support rather than demonstrate a conclusion. In Chapter 11, we explore factors in terms of which one type of explanation might be said to be better than another.

WHAT ARE NOT PREMISES, CONCLUSIONS, OR ARGUMENTS

We hope you've noticed, when we use the word "argument," we are not talking about two people having a feud or fuss about something. That use of the word has nothing much to do with critical thinking, though many a heated exchange could use some critical thinking. Arguments in our sense do not even need two people; we make arguments for our own use all the time. And when we evaluate them, we think critically.

Speaking of what arguments are not, it's important to realize that not everything that might look like an argument, or like a premise or a conclusion, is one.

Pictures

Pictures are not premises, conclusions, or arguments. Neither are movies. Your iPhone can do lots of things, but it isn't an argument. Sorry. Arguments have two parts, a premise part and a conclusion part, and both parts are propositional entities, which means (to repeat) that both parts must be expressible in declarative, true-or-false sentences. Movies and pictures can be moving, compelling, beautiful, complex, realistic, and so forth—but they cannot be either true or false. You can ask if what is depicted in a movie actually happened, or if the story upon which it is based is a true story, but you can't really ask if a movie itself is true or false—or valid or invalid or relatively strong or weak. Such questions don't make literal sense. If it doesn't make sense to think of a thing as true or false, it cannot be a premise or a conclusion. If it doesn't make sense to think of it as valid or invalid, or as being relatively strong or weak, it cannot be an argument.

The list of things that aren't premises or conclusions or arguments therefore also includes emotions, feelings, landscapes, faces, gestures, grunts, groans, bribes, threats, amusement parks, and hip-hop. Since they may *cause* you to have an opinion or to form a judgment about something or produce an argument, you might be tempted to think of them as premises, but causes are not premises. A cause isn't a propositional entity: it is neither true nor false. So it cannot be a premise.

If . . . then . . . Sentences

Sometimes sentences like the following are taken to state arguments:

> If you wash your car now, then it will get spots.

This statement might be the premise of an argument whose conclusion is "Therefore you shouldn't wash your car now." It might also be the conclusion of an argument whose premise is "It is raining." But though it *could* be a premise or a conclusion, it is not *itself* an argument. An argument has a premise and a conclusion, and, though the preceding statement has two parts, neither part by itself is either a premise or a conclusion. "If you wash your car now" is not a statement, and neither is "Then it will get spots." Neither of these phrases qualifies as either a premise or a conclusion. Bottom line: "If . . . then . . ." sentences are not arguments.

Lists of Facts

Though the following might look like an argument, it is nothing more than a list of facts:

> Identity theft is up at least tenfold over last year. More people have learned how easy it is to get hold of another's Social Security number, bank account numbers, and such. The local police department reminds everyone to keep close watch on who has access to such information.

Although they are related by being about the same subject, none of these claims is offered as a reason for believing another, and thus there is no argument here. But the following passage is different. See if you can spot why it makes an argument:

> The number of people who have learned how to steal identities has doubled in the past year. So you are now more likely to become a victim of identity theft than you were a year ago.

Here, the first claim offers a reason for accepting the second claim; we now have an argument.

"A because B"

Sometimes the word "because" refers to the cause of something. But other times it refers to a premise of an argument. Mike walks into the motel lobby, wearing a swimsuit and dripping wet. Consider these two statements:

> "Mike is in his swimsuit because he was swimming."

> "Mike was swimming because he's in his swimsuit."

These two sentences have the same form, "X because Y." But the sentence on the left *explains why* Mike is wearing a swimsuit. The sentence on the right offers an argument *that* Mike was swimming. Only the sentence on the right is an argument. Put it this way: What follows "because" in the sentence on the left is the *cause.* What follows "because" in the right-hand sentence is *evidence.*

Be sure you understand the difference between these two sentences. Arguments and cause-and-effect statements can both employ the phrase *"X because Y."* But there the similarity ends. When what follows "because" is a *reason* for accepting a contention, or evidence for it, we have an argument; when what follows "because" states the *cause* of something, we have a cause-and-effect explanation. These are entirely different enterprises. Arguing *that* a dog has fleas is different from explaining what *gave* it fleas. Arguing *that* violent crime has increased is different from explaining what *caused* it to increase.

ETHOS, PATHOS, AND LOGOS

When he was a young man, Alexander the Great conquered the world. Alexander was enormously proud of his accomplishment, and named several cities after himself. Alexander's teacher, the Greek philosopher Aristotle, had no cities named after him (there is no indication that this disappointed Aristotle). Nevertheless, Aristotle's imprint on civilization turned out to be even more profound than Alexander's.

■ First known pic of Aristotle taking a selfie.

Aristotle, who now is regarded as the father of logic, biology, and psychology, made enduring contributions to virtually every subject. These include (in addition to those just mentioned) physics, astronomy, meteorology, zoology, metaphysics, political science, economics, ethics, and rhetoric.

Among Aristotle's contributions in the last field (rhetoric) was a theory of persuasion, which famously contained the idea that there are three modes by which a speaker may persuade an audience. Paraphrasing very loosely, Aristotle's idea was that we can be persuaded, first of all, by a speaker's personal attributes, including such things as his or her background, reputation, accomplishments, expertise, and similar things. Aristotle referred to this mode of persuasion as *ethos*. Second, a speaker can persuade us by connecting with us on a personal level, and by arousing and appealing to our emotions by a skillful use of rhetoric. This mode of persuasion Aristotle termed *pathos*. And third, the speaker may persuade us by using information and arguments—what he called *logos*.

Unfortunately, logos—rational argumentation—is one of the least effective ways of winning someone to your point of view. That's why advertisers rarely bother with it. When the sellers of the first home automatic breadmaker found that its new kitchen device didn't interest people, they advertised the availability of a second model of the same machine, which was only slightly larger but much more expensive. When consumers saw that the first model was a great buy, they suddenly discovered they wanted one, and began snapping it up. Why try to persuade people by rational argument that they need a breadmaker when you can get them to think they do simply by making them believe they have sniffed out a bargain?*

Still, despite the general inefficacy of logos as a tool of persuasion, people do frequently use arguments when they try to persuade others. This might lead you to *define* an argument as an attempt to persuade. But that won't do. Remember, there are two kinds of argument. Deductive arguments are either sound or unsound, and whether a deductive argument is one or the other doesn't depend in the least on whether anyone is persuaded by it. Likewise, inductive arguments are in varying degrees strong or weak; their strength depends on the degree to which their premises elevate the probability of the conclusion, and that, too, is independent of whether anyone finds them persuasive. The very same argument might be persuasive to Parker but not to Moore, which shows that the persuasiveness of an argument is a subjective question of psychology, not of logic. Indeed, the individual who does *not* think critically is precisely the person who is persuaded by specious reasoning. People notoriously are unfazed by good arguments while finding even the worst arguments compelling. If you want to persuade people of something, try propaganda. Flattery has been known to work, too.

We will be looking at alternative modes of persuasion—what Aristotle called ethos and pathos—in considerable detail in Chapters 4, 5, 6, 7, and 8. However, we do this not so you can persuade people, but so you can be alert to the influence of ethos and pathos on your own thinking.

Now, we aren't suggesting it is a bad thing to be a persuasive writer or speaker. Obviously it isn't; that's what rhetoric courses are for—to teach you to write persuasively. Let's just put it this way: Whenever you find yourself being persuaded by what someone says, find the "logos" in the "pathos," and be persuaded by it alone.

---

*Dan Ariely, *Irrational Predictability* (New York: HarperCollins, 2008), 14, 15.

The following exercises will give you practice (1) identifying premises and conclusions as well as words that indicate premises and conclusions, (2) telling the difference between deductive demonstrations and inductive supporting arguments, and (3) identifying balance of considerations arguments and inferences to the best explanation.

▲—See the answers section at the back of the book.

Exercise 2-1

Indicate which blanks would ordinarily contain premises and which would ordinarily contain conclusions.

▲ 1. ___a___, and ___b___. Therefore, ___c___.
▲ 2. ___a___. So, since ___b___, ___c___.
▲ 3. ___a___, clearly. After all, ___b___.
▲ 4. Since ___a___ and ___b___, ___c___.
▲ 5. ___a___. Consequently, ___b___, since ___c___ and ___d___.

Identify the premise(s) and conclusion in each of the following arguments.

Exercise 2-2

▲ 1. Since all Communists are Marxists, all Marxists are Communists.
2. The Lakers almost didn't beat the Kings. They'll never get past Dallas.
3. If the butler had done it, he could not have locked the screen door. Therefore, since the door was locked, we know the butler is in the clear.
▲ 4. That cat loves dogs. Probably she won't be upset if you bring home a new dog for a pet.
5. Hey, he can't be older than his mother's daughter's brother. His mother's daughter has only one brother.
6. Mr. Hoover will never make it into the state police. They have a weight limit, and he's over it.
▲ 7. Presbyterians are not fundamentalists, but all born-again Christians are. So, no born-again Christians are Presbyterians.
8. I guess Thork doesn't have a thing to do. Why else would he waste his time watching daytime TV?
9. "There are more injuries in professional football today than there were twenty years ago," he reasoned. "And if there are more injuries, then today's players suffer higher risks. And if they suffer higher risks, then they should be paid more. Consequently, I think today's players should be paid more," he concluded.
▲ 10. Let's see . . . since the clunk comes only when I pedal, the problem must be in the chain, the crank, or the pedals.

Identify the premises and the conclusions in the following arguments.

Exercise 2-3

▲ 1. The darned engine pings every time we use the regular unleaded gasoline, but it doesn't do it with super. I'd bet that there is a difference in the octane ratings between the two in spite of what my mechanic says.
2. Chances are I'll be carded at JJ's, since Kera, Sherry, and Bobby were all carded there, and they all look as though they're about thirty.

3. Seventy percent of first-year students at Cal Poly San Luis Obispo come from wealthy families; therefore, probably about the same percentage of all Cal Poly San Luis Obispo students come from wealthy families.

▲ 4. When blue jays are breeding, they become aggressive. Consequently, scrub jays, which are very similar to blue jays, can also be expected to be aggressive when they're breeding.

5. I am sure Marietta comes from a wealthy family. She told me her parents benefited from the cut in the capital gains tax.

6. According to *Nature*, today's thoroughbred racehorses do not run any faster than their grandparents did. But human Olympic runners are at least 20 percent faster than their counterparts of fifty years ago. Most likely, racehorses have reached their physical limits but humans have not.

▲ 7. Dogs are smarter than cats, since it is easier to train them.

8. "Let me demonstrate the principle by means of logic," the teacher said, holding up a bucket. "If this bucket has a hole in it, then it will leak. But it doesn't leak. Therefore, obviously, it doesn't have a hole in it."

9. We shouldn't take a chance on this new candidate. She's from Alamo Polytech, and the last person we hired from there was incompetent.

▲ 10. If she was still interested in me, she would have called, but she didn't.

Exercise 2-4

Five of these items are best viewed as deductive arguments and five as inductive arguments. Which are which?

▲ 1. No mayten tree is deciduous, and all nondeciduous trees are evergreens. It follows that all mayten trees are evergreens.

2. Mike must belong to the Bartenders and Beverage Union Local 165, since almost every Las Vegas bartender does.

3. Either Colonel Mustard or Reverend Green killed Professor Plum. But whoever ran off with Mrs. White did not kill the professor. Since Reverend Green ran off with Mrs. White, Colonel Mustard killed Professor Plum.

▲ 4. I've never met a golden retriever with a nasty disposition. I bet there aren't any.

5. Since some grapes are purple, and all grapes are fruit, some fruit is purple.

6. Why is Shrilla so mean to Timeeda? The only thing I can think of is that she's jealous. Jealousy is what's making her mean.

▲ 7. Biden would have made a fine president. After all, he made a fine vice president.

8. The figure he drew has only three sides, so it isn't a square.

9. It was the pizza that made my stomach churn. What else could it be? I was fine until I ate it.

▲ 10. It's wrong to hurt someone's feelings, and that is exactly what you are doing when you speak to me like that.

Exercise 2-5

Which of the following items are intended to be deductive arguments?

▲ 1. Miss Scarlet's fingerprints were on the knife used to kill Colonel Mustard. Furthermore, he was killed in the pantry, and she was the only person who had a key to the pantry. Clearly she killed the colonel.

2. Outlawing guns would be a violation of the U.S. Constitution. Therefore, they should not be outlawed.

3. There are sunfish in the water behind this dam, but none in the water released from it. Ordinarily this kind of thing happens only when the released water comes from the bottom of the dam, because then the released water is too cold for sunfish. Therefore the water released from this dam comes from the bottom.

▲ 4. Sparky is scratching again. He must either have a skin infection or flea bites.

5. Outlawing guns reduced gun deaths in Australia; therefore it would do the same here.

6. I'm sleepy again. I guess I didn't get enough sleep last night.

▲ 7. I didn't get enough sleep last night; therefore I should get to bed earlier tonight.

8. The victims' blood was on a glove found behind Simpson's house. This shows that Simpson committed the murders, because he alone had access to that area.

9. The indentation on the west coast of Africa is about the same size as the bulge on the east coast of South America, indicating that the two continents were once connected.

▲ 10. I can hear you lots better now! You must be holding the phone in a different position.

Identify each of the following as either

   a. IBE
   b. balance of considerations reasoning
   c. neither of the above

Exercise 2-6

▲ 1. Let's go now. I know you wanted to work in the yard, but if we wait longer, we won't make the movie. Plus, it's gonna get cold if we don't make tracks.

2. He said he was for the bill when it was proposed, and now he vetoes it? The only thing I can see is, he must be trying to get the teachers' vote.

3. Yes, a card laid is a card played, but I kept my hand on it, so I didn't actually lay it.

▲ 4. All things considered, we'd be better off taking the Suburban. Plus, let's get AAA to help us make reservations.

5. Jackson will get an A in the course, since he aced the final.

6. "A gentleman goes forth on a showery and miry day. He returns immaculate in the evening with the gloss still on his hat and his boots. He has been a fixture therefore all day. He is not a man with intimate friends. Where, then, could he have been? Is it not obvious?"

         —*Arthur Conan Doyle,* The Hound of the Baskervilles, Chapter 3

▲ 7. It's longer taking the 405, but you can drive faster—though who knows what the traffic's like at this hour. I would say if you want to play it safe, stay on the 5.

8. He made threats, plus he had the motive. Not only that, but who else had access to a gun? If Mitchell didn't do it, I don't know who did.

9. The question is, are you running a temperature? Because if you are, it can't be a cold. The runny nose and the sore throat could be a cold, but not the temperature. Only the flu would give you a temperature.

▲ 10. Sherry seems right for the job to me. She speaks French, knows biology, has people skills, and makes a great impression. The only down side is, she can't start until October. That pretty much eliminates her, unfortunately.

Exercise 2-7   Identify each of the following as either

      a. IBE
      b. balance of considerations reasoning
      c. neither of the above

    ▲   1. These tomatoes got plenty of sunlight and water. The only thing that could account for their being rotten is the soil.

        2. Should we outlaw assault weapons? No. That would be a violation of the Second Amendment.

        3. Should we outlaw assault weapons? Well, that depends. The Second Amendment gives us the right to bear arms, but outlawing them might make the country a safer place.

    ▲   4. Priglet messed on the carpet again! Is he sick do you suppose? Or is he trying to tell us something? It seems like he does that only when we leave him alone for a long time. I bet he just has a weak bladder.

        5. Either God exists or He does not. By believing that He exists, you lose nothing if you are wrong; but if you are right, He will reward you with happiness and eternal life. By believing He does not exist, you lose nothing if you are right; but if you are wrong, you may suffer eternal damnation. It is therefore prudent to believe that He exists.

                                            —*A paraphrase of Blaise Pascal (1623–1662)*

        6. Professor Stooler has been teaching here thirty years and he still hasn't unpacked his boxes from graduate school. It seems likely he won't ever unpack them.

    ▲   7. "The man I found in the room was definitely a fighter and a smart one too. He hid his gun, chest rack, and hand grenades just out of reach and well enough for us not to see them on our initial entry into the room."

                                            —*Mark Owen*, No Easy Way

        8. I don't like Mr. Biden's personality, but I think he may be better than Mrs. Clinton at working with people. Plus he has been around longer than she. That's why I support him.

        9. Susan doesn't laugh at my jokes anymore. Maybe I'm not as funny as I think I am.

    ▲   10. I am reading this sentence; therefore I am alive.

TECHNIQUES FOR UNDERSTANDING ARGUMENTS

If an argument has been offered to us, before we can evaluate it we must understand it. Many arguments are difficult to understand because they are spoken and go by so quickly we cannot be sure of the conclusion or the premises. Others are difficult to understand because they have a complicated structure. Still others are difficult to understand because they are embedded in nonargumentative material consisting of background information, prejudicial coloring, illustrations, parenthetical remarks, digressions, subsidiary points, and other window dressing. And some arguments are difficult to understand because they are confused or because the reasons they contain are so poor that we are not sure whether to regard them as reasons.

In understanding an argument that has been given to us, the first task is to find the conclusion—the main point or thesis of the passage. The next step is to locate the reasons that have been offered for accepting the conclusion—that is, to find the premises. Next, we look for the reasons, if any, offered for accepting these premises. To proceed through these steps, you have to learn both to spot premises and conclusions when they occur in spoken and written passages and to understand the interrelationships among these claims—that is, the structure of the argument.

Clarifying an Argument's Structure

Let's begin with how to understand the relationships among the argumentative claims, because this problem is sometimes easiest to solve. If you are dealing with written material that you can mark up, one useful technique is to number the premises and conclusions and then use the numbers to lay bare the structure of the argument. Let's start with this argument as an example:

> I don't think we should get Carlos his own car. He is not responsible in view of the fact that he doesn't care for his things. And anyway, we don't have enough money for a car for him, since we even have trouble making our own car payments. Last week you yourself complained about our financial situation, and you never complain without really good reason.

We want to display the structure of this argument clearly. First, circle all premise and conclusion indicators, and then bracket each premise and conclusion, numbering them consecutively, like this:

> ① [I don't think we should get Carlos his own car.] ② [He is not responsible] in view of the fact that ③ [he doesn't care for his things.] And anyway, ④ [we don't have enough money for a car for him], since ⑤ [we even have trouble making our own car payments.] ⑥ [Last week you yourself complained about our financial situation], and ⑦ [you never complain without really good reason.]

Then we diagram the argument. Using an arrow to mean therefore, we diagram the first three claims in the argument as follows:

Now, ⑥ and ⑦ together support ④; that is, they are part of the same argument for ④. To show that ⑥ and ⑦ go together, we simply draw a line under them, put a plus sign between them, and draw the "therefore" arrow from the line to ④, like this:

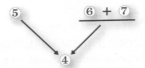

Because ⑤ and ⑥ + ⑦ are separate arguments for ④, we can represent the relationship between them and ④ as follows:

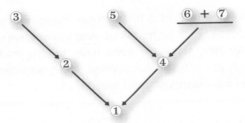

Finally, because ④ and ② are separate arguments for ①, the diagram of the entire passage is this:

So the conventions governing this approach to revealing argument structure are very simple: First, circle all premise- and conclusion-indicating words. Then, assuming you can identify the claims that function in the argument (a big assumption, as you will see before long), number them consecutively. Then display the structure of the argument, using arrows for "therefore" and plus signs over a line to connect two or more premises that depend on one another.

Some claims, incidentally, may constitute reasons for more than one conclusion. For example:

① [Carlos continues to be irresponsible.] ② [He certainly should not have his own car], and, as far as I am concerned, ③ [he can forget about that trip to Hawaii this winter, too.]

Structure:

Frequently, too, a passage may entertain counterarguments to its ultimate conclusion. For example, this passage contains a counterargument:

① We really should have more African Americans on the faculty. ② That is why the new diversity program ought to be approved. True, ③ it may involve an element of unfairness to whites, but ④ the benefits to society of having more black faculty outweigh the disadvantages.

As you can see, claim ③ introduces a consideration that runs counter to the conclusion of the passage, which is stated in ②. We can indicate counterclaims by crossing the "therefore" arrow with lines, thus:

This diagram indicates that item ③ has been introduced by the writer as a consideration that runs counter to ②.

Of course, one might adopt other conventions for clarifying argument structure—for example, circling the main conclusion and drawing solid lines under supporting premises and wavy lines under the premises of subarguments. The technique we have described is simply one way of doing it; any of several others might work as well for you. However, *no* technique for revealing argument structure will work if you cannot spot the argumentative claims in the midst of a lot of background material.

Distinguishing Arguments from Window Dressing

It is not always easy to isolate the argument in a speech or a written piece. Often, speakers and writers think that because their main points are more or less clear to them, they will be equally apparent to listeners and readers. But it doesn't always work that way.

If you have trouble identifying a conclusion in what you hear or read, it *could* be the passage is not an argument at all. Make sure the passage in question is not a report, a description, an explanation, or something else altogether, rather than an argument. The key here is determining whether the speaker or writer is offering reasons intended to support or demonstrate one or more claims.

The problem could also be that the conclusion is left unstated. Sometimes it helps simply to put the argument aside and ask yourself, "What is this person trying to prove?" In any case, the first and essential step in understanding an argument is to spot the conclusion.

If you are having difficulty identifying the *premises,* consider the possibility that you have before you a case of rhetoric (see Chapter 5). (You can't find premises in a piece of pure rhetoric because there *are* no premises.) You will have an advantage over many students in having learned about rhetorical devices in Chapters 5, 6, 7, and 8. By that time, you should be getting pretty good at recognizing them.

As you apply what you learn in this book to arguments you encounter in real life, you are apt to encounter arguments and argumentative essays whose organization is difficult to comprehend. When you do, you may find diagramming a useful technique. Also, as is obvious, what we have said in this section applies to arguments that others give us or that we otherwise encounter. You don't diagram what's in your head, though you need to be clear on your own conclusions, tentative or otherwise, and the reasons you have for accepting them. However, the diagramming technique does apply to material you write for others. If you find you have difficulty diagramming your arguments, you should reorganize your essay and make the structure of your reasoning clearer.

EVALUATING ARGUMENTS

Thinking critically requires us to evaluate arguments, and evaluating arguments has two parts. First, there is the *logic* part: Does the argument either demonstrate or support its conclusion? Is this argument either deductively valid or inductively relatively strong? You know now what these questions mean theoretically; over the course of this book, you will see what they involve in fact.

The other part, of course, is the *truth* part. Are the premises actually true? As we explain in Chapter 4, it is best to be suspicious of a premise that conflicts with our background information or other credible claims, as well as a premise that comes from a source that lacks credibility. And, as we develop at length in Chapters 5, 6, and 7, we want to avoid being tricked into accepting a claim by rhetoric or other psychological gimmickry. It also almost goes without saying that premises that are unclear require clarification before one accepts them—as we explain in Chapter 3. In general, determining the truth of premises requires knowledge, experience, a level head, and the inclination to look into things.

Recap

The main ideas of the chapter are these:

- Arguments always have two parts, a premise (or premises) and a conclusion.
- The same statement can be a premise in one argument and a conclusion in a second argument.
- The two fundamental types of reasoning are deductive demonstration and inductive support.
- A deductive argument is used to demonstrate or prove a conclusion, which it does if it is sound.
- An argument is sound if it is valid and its premise (or premises) is true.
- An argument is valid if it isn't possible for its premise or premises to be true and its conclusion to be false.
- An inductive argument is used to support rather than to demonstrate a conclusion.
- An argument supports a conclusion if it increases the likelihood that the conclusion is true.
- Support is a matter of degrees: An argument supports a conclusion to the extent its premise (or premises) makes the conclusion likely.
- An argument that offers more support for a conclusion is said to be stronger than one that offers less support; the latter is said to be weaker than the former.

▪ Some instructors use the word "strong" in an absolute sense to denote inductive arguments whose premise (or premises) makes the conclusion more likely than not.

▪ If it doesn't make sense to think of an argument as providing evidence or support for a contention, it is probably because it is a deductive argument.

▪ Inductive arguments and deductive arguments can have unstated premises.

▪ Whether an argument is deductive or inductive may depend on what the unstated premise is said to be.

▪ If an argument is written, diagramming it may help you understand it.

▪ Balance of considerations reasoning often involves deductive and inductive elements.

▪ Inference to best explanation is a common type of inductive reasoning in which a supposition is said to be true because it states the best explanation of something we have observed or otherwise know.

These exercises will test your comprehension of the chapter. They will also give you additional practice (1) distinguishing between deductive demonstrations and inductive supporting arguments, (2) recognizing when a passage contains more than a single argument, (3) recognizing the difference between arguments and explanations, (4) identifying unstated assumptions, and (5) diagramming arguments.

Additional Exercises

Exercise 2-8

Fill in the blanks where called for, and answer true or false where appropriate.

▲ 1. Arguments that are relatively strong or weak are called _____ arguments.

2. All valid arguments are sound arguments.

3. All sound arguments are valid arguments.

▲ 4. If a valid argument has a false conclusion, then not all its premises can be true.

5. A sound argument cannot have a false conclusion.

6. "Strong" and "weak" are absolute terms.

▲ 7. If you try to demonstrate a conclusion, you are using _____ reasoning.

8. When a conclusion has been proved beyond a reasonable doubt, it has always been demonstrated.

9. An argument can never have an unstated conclusion.

▲ 10. When you try to support a conclusion, you are using _____ reasoning.

11. The most effective way to convince someone is through argument.

12. "If . . . then . . ." sentences may be arguments.

▲ 13. "If . . . then . . ." sentences may be premises.

14. Logic should be defined as the art of persuasion.

15. "A because B" is always an argument.

16. "A because B" is never an argument.

17. "IBE" refers to a type of deductive argument.

18. Inductive and deductive arguments both may occur in balance of considerations reasoning.

Exercise 2-9

Some of these passages are best viewed as attempted deductive demonstrations, and others are best viewed as offering inductive support. Which are which?

1. All mammals are warm-blooded creatures, and all whales are mammals. Therefore, all whales are warm-blooded creatures.

2. The brains of rats raised in enriched environments with a variety of toys and puzzles weigh more than the brains of rats raised in more barren environments. Therefore, the brains of humans will weigh more if humans are placed in intellectually stimulating environments.

3. Jones won't plead guilty to a misdemeanor, and if he won't plead guilty, then he will be tried on a felony charge. Therefore, he will be tried on a felony charge.

4. We've interviewed 200 professional football players, and 60 percent of them favor expanding the season to twenty games. Therefore, 60 percent of all professional football players favor expanding the season to twenty games.

5. Jose is taller than Bill, and Bill is taller than Margaret. Therefore, Jose is taller than Margaret.

6. Exercise may help chronic male smokers kick the habit, says a study published today. The researchers, based at McDuff University, put thirty young male smokers on a three-month program of vigorous exercise. One year later, only 14 percent of them still smoked, according to the report. An equivalent number of young male smokers who did not go through the exercise program were also checked after a year, and it was found that 60 percent still smoked.

7. Believe in God? Yes, of course I do. The universe couldn't have arisen by chance, could it? Besides, I read the other day that more and more physicists believe in God, based on what they're finding out about the big bang and all that stuff.

8. From an office memo: "I've got a good person for your opening in Accounting. Jesse Brown is his name, and he's as sharp as they come. Jesse has a solid background in bookkeeping, and he's good with computers. He's also reliable, and he'll project the right image. He will do a fine job for you."

Exercise 2-10

Diagram the arguments contained in the following passages.

1. North Korea is a great threat to its neighbors. It has a million-person army ready to be unleashed at a moment's notice, and it also has nuclear weapons.

2. Shaun is going to the party with Mary, so she won't be going alone.

3. Michael should just go ahead and get a new car. The one he's driving is junk; also, he has a new job and can afford a new car.

4. If Karper goes to Las Vegas, he'll wind up in a casino; and if he winds up in a casino, it's a sure thing he'll spend half the night at a craps table. So you can be sure: If Karper goes to Las Vegas, he'll spend half the night at a craps table.

5. It's going to be rainy tomorrow, and Serj doesn't like to play golf in the rain. It's going to be cold as well, and he *really* doesn't like to play when it's cold. So you can be sure Serj will be someplace other than the golf course tomorrow.

▲ 6. Hey, you're overwatering your lawn. See? There are mushrooms growing around the base of that tree—a sure sign of overwatering. Also, look at all the worms on the ground. They come up when the earth is oversaturated.

7. "Will you drive me to the airport?" she asked. "Why should I do that?" he wanted to know. "Because I'll pay you twice what it takes for gas. Besides, didn't you say you were my friend?"

8. If you drive too fast, you're more likely to get a ticket, and the more likely you are to get a ticket, the more likely you are to have your insurance premiums raised. So, if you drive too fast, you are more likely to have your insurance premiums raised.

▲ 9. If you drive too fast, you're more likely to get a ticket. You're also more likely to get into an accident. So you shouldn't drive too fast.

▲ 10. There are several reasons why you should consider installing a solarium. First, you can still get a tax credit. Second, you can reduce your heating bill. Third, if you build it right, you can actually cool your house with it in the summer.

11. From a letter to the editor: "By trying to eliminate Charles Darwin from the curriculum, creationists are doing themselves a great disservice. When read carefully, Darwin's discoveries only support the thesis that species change, not that they evolve into new species. This is a thesis that most creationists can live with. When read carefully, Darwin actually supports the creationist point of view."

12. Editorial comment: "The Supreme Court's ruling, that schools may have a moment of silence but not if it's designated for prayer, is sound. Nothing stops someone from saying a silent prayer at school or anywhere else. Also, even though a moment of silence will encourage prayer, it will not favor any particular religion over any other. The ruling makes sense."

▲ 13. We must paint the house now! Here are three good reasons: (a) If we don't, then we'll have to paint it next summer; (b) if we have to paint it next summer, we'll have to cancel our trip; and (c) it's too late to cancel the trip.

Exercise 2-11 ⎯⎯⎯⎯⎯⎯⎯⎯⎯⎯⎯⎯⎯⎯⎯⎯⎯⎯⎯

Which of the following instances of "because" are followed by a cause, and which are followed by a premise?

▲ 1. We've had so much hot weather recently because the jet stream is unusually far north.

2. Ms. Mossbarger looks so tired because she hasn't been able to sleep for three nights.

3. It's a bad idea to mow the lawn in your bare feet because you could be seriously injured.

▲ 4. Ken mows the lawn in his bare feet because he doesn't realize how dangerous it is.

5. Ryan will marry Beth because he told me he would.

6. I'd change before going into town because your clothes look like you slept in them.

▲ 7. You have high blood pressure because you overeat.

8. You'd better cut back on the salt because you could become hypertensive.

▲ 9. It's a good bet Iran wants to build nuclear weapons because the UN inspectors found devices for the enrichment of plutonium.

10. Iran wants to build nuclear weapons because it wants to gain control over neighboring Middle Eastern countries.

Exercise 2-12

Which of the following statements could not possibly be false?

▲ 1. Squares have four sides.

2. You will not live to be 130 years old.

3. A cow cannot yodel.

▲ 4. A six-foot person is taller than a five-foot person.

5. If the sign on the parking meter says "Out of Order" the meter won't work.

6. Nobody can be her own mother.

▲ 7. God exists or does not exist.

8. They will never get rid of all disease.

9. The ice caps couldn't melt entirely.

▲ 10. The day two days after the day before yesterday is today.

Exercise 2-13

For each of the following, supply a universal principle (a statement that says that something holds without exception) that turns it into a valid deductive argument.

Example

Tay is opinionated. She should be more open-minded.

One universal principle that makes it valid

Opinionated people should all be more open-minded. (*Note:* There are alternative ways of phrasing this.)

▲ 1. Jamal keeps his word, so he is a man of good character.

2. Betty got an A in the course, so she must have received an A on the final.

3. Iraq posed a threat to us, so we had a right to invade it.

▲ 4. Colonel Mustard could not have murdered Professor Plum, because the two men were in separate rooms when the professor was killed.

5. Avril is no liberal, since she voted against gun control.

6. Jimmi has a gentle soul; if there is a heaven, he should go there when he dies.

▲ 7. Of course that guy should be executed; he committed murder, didn't he?

8. I don't think you could call the party a success; only eight people showed up.

9. Mzbrynski proved Goldbach's conjecture; that makes him the greatest mathematician ever.

▲ 10. The fan needs oil; after all, it's squeaking.

Exercise 2-14

For each of the following arguments, supply a principle that makes it inductive rather than deductive.

Example

Ryder is sharp, so he will get a good grade in this course.

One claim that makes it inductive

Most sharp people get good grades in this course.

▲ 1. There are puddles everywhere; it must have rained recently.

2. The lights are dim; therefore, the battery is weak.

3. Simpson's blood matched the blood on the glove found at the victim's condo: He killed her.

▲ 4. Of course it will be cold tomorrow! It's been cold all week, hasn't it?

5. Ambramoff isn't very good with animals. I doubt he'd make a great parent.

6. The dog has either fleas or dry skin; it's scratching a lot.

▲ 7. Why do I say their party wasn't a success? Remember all the leftovers?

8. Cheston owns a rifle; he's sure to belong to the NRA.

9. The dessert contained caffeine, so you might have trouble sleeping tonight.

▲ 10. I took Zicam, and my cold disappeared like magic. Obviously, it works.

Exercise 2-15

Diagram the following "arguments."

▲ 1. ①, in light of the fact that ② and ③. [Assume ② and ③ are part of the same argument for ①.]

2. ① and ②; therefore ③. [Assume ① and ② are separate arguments for ③.]

3. Since ①, ②; and since ③, ④. And since ② and ④, ⑤. [Assume ② and ④ are separate arguments for ⑤.]

▲ 4. ①; therefore ② and ③. And in light of the fact that ② and ③, ④. Consequently, ⑤. Therefore, ⑥. [Assume ② and ③ are separate arguments for ④.]

5. ①, ②, ③; therefore ④. ⑤, in view of ①. And ⑥, since ②. Therefore ⑦. [Assume ①, ②, and ③ are part of the same argument for ④.]

Exercise 2-16

What does each diagram display—a or b?

▲   1.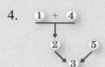

   a. 1 supports 3, as does 2.
   b. 1 in combination with 2 demonstrates 3.

   2.   ① + ②
        │
        ③

   a. 1 demonstrates 3, as does 2,
   b. 1 in combination with 2 demonstrates 3.

   3.   ①
        │
        ③
       ╱ ╲
      ②   ④

   a. 3, which is supported by 1, supports two things, 2 and 4.
   b. 3, which is supported by 1, supports 2, which in turn supports 4.

▲   4.   ① + ④
         │
       ②   ⑤
        ╲ ╱
         ③

   a. In view of 5, 3 must be true, and it must also be true because of 2, which
      follows from 1 combined with 4.
   b. 2 must be true because of 1 in combination with 4; and 2 and 5 combined
      demonstrate 3.

   5.   ① + ②
       ③ │ ④
         ⑤
          ╲
           ⑥

   a. 1 in combination with 2 support 5. In addition, 3 supports 5, as does 4. So
      despite the fact that 6 indicates that 5 is false, 5.
   b. 6 follows from 3, and it follows from 4 as well. It is also supported by 5,
      which follows from 1 in combination with 2.

Exercise 2-17

Diagram the arguments contained in the following passages.

▲   1. Dear Jim,

   Your distributor is the problem. Here's why. There's no current at the spark
   plugs. And if there's no current at the plugs, then either your alternator is shot
   or your distributor is defective. But if the problem were in the alternator, then

your dash warning light would be on. So, since the light isn't on, the problem must be in the distributor. Hope this helps.

> Yours,
> Benita Autocraft

2. The slide in the dollar must be stopped. It contributes to inflation and increases the cost of imports. True, it helps exports, but on balance it is bad for the economy.

3. It's high time professional boxing was outlawed. Boxing almost always leads to brain damage, and anything that does that ought to be done away with. Besides, it supports organized crime.

4. They really ought to build a new airport. It would attract more business to the area, not to mention the fact that the old airport is overcrowded and dangerous.

5. Vote for Cuomo? No way. He's too radical, and he's too inexperienced, and those two things make him dangerous. I do like his stand on trade, but I still don't think you should vote for him.

Exercise 2-18

Diagram the arguments contained in the following passages.

1. Cottage cheese will help you be slender, youthful, and more beautiful. Enjoy it often.

2. If you want to listen to loud music, do it when we are not at home. It bothers us, and we're your parents.

3. If you want to see the best version of *The Three Musketeers*, try the 1948 version. Lana Turner is luscious; Vincent Price is dastardly; Angela Lansbury is exquisitely regal; and nobody ever has or ever will portray D'Artagnan with the grace, athleticism, or skill of Gene Kelly. Download it. It's a must.

4. From a letter to the editor: "The idea of a free press in America today is a joke. A small group of people, the nation's advertisers, control the media more effectively than if they owned it outright. Through fear of an advertising boycott, they can dictate everything from programming to news report content. Politicians as well as editors shiver in their boots at the thought of such a boycott. This situation is intolerable and ought to be changed. I suggest we all listen to National Public Radio and public television."

5. Too many older Americans, veterans with disabilities, and families with children are paying far too much of their incomes for housing. Proposition 168 will help clear the way for affordable housing construction for these groups. Proposition 168 reforms the outdated requirement for an election before affordable housing can even be approved. Requiring elections for every publicly assisted housing venture, even when there is no local opposition, is a waste of taxpayers' money. No other state constitution puts such a roadblock in front of efforts to house senior citizens and others in need. Please support Proposition 168.

6. Decades after President John F. Kennedy's assassination, it's no easier to accept the idea that a loser like Lee Harvey Oswald committed the crime of the century all by himself with a $12.78 mail-order rifle and a $7.17 scope.

Yet even though 2,000+ books and films about the episode have been made, there is no credible evidence to contradict the Warren Commission finding that "the shots which killed President Kennedy and wounded Governor Connally were fired by Lee Harvey Oswald" and that "Oswald acted alone."

After all these years, it's time to accept the conclusion. The nation pays a heavy price for chronic doubts and mistrust. Confidence in the government has declined. Participation in the voting process has steadily slid downward. The national appetite for wild theories encourages peddlers to persist. Evil is never easy to accept. In the case of JFK, the sooner we let it go, the better.

7. Most schools should offer single-sex classes. Single-sex classes promote learning. Girls do better in math and science courses when they are alone with other girls. Gender offers distractions that interfere with learning. Research also shows that in mixed classrooms most instructors will spend more time answering questions from boys. Schools that offer single-sex classes always report learning gains for students of both sexes.

8. "And we thought we'd heard it all. Now the National Rifle Association wants the U.S. Supreme Court to throw out the ban on private ownership of fully automatic machine guns.

"As the nation's cities reel under staggering murder totals, as kids use guns simply to get even after feuds, as children are gunned down by random bullets, the NRA thinks it is everybody's constitutional right to have their own personal machine gun.

"This is not exactly the weapon of choice for deer hunting or for a homeowner seeking protection. It is an ideal weapon for street gangs and drug thugs in their wars with each other and the police.

"To legalize fully automatic machine guns is to increase the mayhem that is turning this nation—particularly its large cities—into a continual war zone. Doesn't the NRA have something better to do?"

—Capital Times, *Madison, Wisconsin*

9. From a letter to the editor: "Recently the California Highway Patrol stopped me at a drunk-drive checkpoint. Now, I don't like drunk drivers any more than anyone else. I certainly see why the police find the checkpoint system effective. But I think our right to move about freely is much more important. If the checkpoint system continues, then next there will be checkpoints for drugs, seat belts, infant car seats, drivers' licenses. We will regret it later if we allow the system to continue."

10. "Well located, sound real estate is the safest investment in the world. It is not going to disappear, as can the value of dollars put into savings accounts. Neither will real estate values be lost because of inflation. In fact, property values tend to increase at a pace at least equal to the rate of inflation. Most homes have appreciated at a rate greater than the inflation rate (due mainly to strong buyer demand and insufficient supply of newly constructed homes)."

—*Robert Bruss,* The Smart Investor's Guide to Real Estate

11. "The constitutional guarantee of a speedy trial protects citizens from arbitrary government abuse, but it has at least one other benefit, too. It prevents crime.

"A recent Justice Department study found that more than a third of those with serious criminal records—meaning three or more felony convictions—are arrested for new offenses while free on bond awaiting federal court trial. You don't have to be a social scientist to suspect that the longer the delay, the greater the likelihood of further violations. In short, overburdened courts mean much more than justice delayed; they quite literally amount to the infliction of further injustice."

—Scripps Howard News Service

12. As we enter a new decade, about 200 million Americans are producing data on the Internet as rapidly as they consume it. Each of these users is tracked by technologies ever more able to collate essential facts about them—age, address, credit rating, marital status, etc.—in electronic form for use in commerce. One website, for example, promises, for the meager sum of seven dollars, to scan "over two billion records to create a single comprehensive report on an individual." It is not unreasonable, then, to believe that the combination of capitalism and technology poses a looming threat to what remains of our privacy.

—Loosely adapted from Harper's

13. Having your car washed at the car wash may be the best way to go, but there are some possible drawbacks. The International Carwashing Association (ICA) has fought back against charges that automatic car washes, in recycling wash water, actually dump the salt and dirt from one car onto the next. And that brushes and drag cloths hurt the finish. Perhaps there is some truth to these charges.

The ICA sponsored tests that supposedly demonstrated that the average home car wash is harder on a car than an automatic wash. Maybe. But what's "the average" home car wash? And you can bet that the automatic car washes in the test were in perfect working order.

There is no way you or I can tell for certain if the filtration system and washing equipment at the automatic car wash are properly maintained. And even if they are, what happens if you follow some mud-caked pickup through the wash? Road dirt might still be caught in the bristles of the brushes or strips of fabric that are dragged over your car.

Here's my recommendation: Wash your own car.

14.   **Argument in Favor of Measure A**

"Measure A is consistent with the City's General Plan and City policies directing growth to the City's non-agricultural lands. A 'yes' vote on Measure A will affirm the wisdom of well-planned, orderly growth in the City of Chico by approving an amendment to the 1982 Rancho Arroyo Specific Plan. Measure A substantially reduces the amount of housing previously approved for Rancho Arroyo, increases the number of parks and amount of open space, and significantly enlarges and enhances Bidwell Park.

"A 'yes' vote will accomplish the following: • Require the development to dedicate 130.8 acres of land to Bidwell Park • Require the developer to dedi-cate seven park sites • Create 53 acres of landscaped corridors and greenways • Preserve existing arroyos and protect sensitive plant habitats and other envi-ronmental features • Create junior high school and church sites • Plan a series of villages within which, eventually, a total of 2,927 residential dwelling units will be developed • Plan area which will provide onsite job opportunities and retail services."

—County of Butte sample ballot

15.   **Rebuttal to Argument in Favor of Measure A**

"Villages? Can a project with 3,000 houses and 7,000 new residents really be regarded as a 'village'? The Sacramento developers pushing the Rancho Arroyo project certainly have a way with words. We urge citizens of Chico to ignore their flowery language and vote no on Measure A.

"These out-of-town developers will have you believe that their project protects agricultural land. Hogwash! Chico's Greenline protects valuable farmland. With the Greenline, there is enough land in the Chico area available for development to build 62,000 new homes. . . .

"They claim that their park dedications will reduce use of our overcrowded Bidwell Park. Don't you believe it! They want to attract 7,000 new residents to Chico by using Rancho Arroyo's proximity to Bidwell Park to outsell other local housing projects.

"The developers imply that the Rancho Arroyo project will provide a much needed school site. In fact, the developers intend to sell the site to the school district, which will pay for the site with taxpayers' money.

"Chico doesn't need the Rancho Arroyo project. Vote no on Measure A."

—County of Butte sample ballot

16. Letter to the editor: "I recently read about a man who killed another man several years ago, then he made a plea-bargain with the District Attorney's office and thus got a reduced charge and a shorter sentence. He didn't even serve all of that sentence, because he got some time off for good behavior. After being out of prison for only a few months, he killed somebody else!

"I cannot understand how our so-called system of 'justice' allows this sort of thing to happen. According to FBI statistics, not a half-hour goes by without there being a murder somewhere in this country. How many of these murders are committed by people who have been released from prison? I can answer that: too many!

"The main reason there are so many people released from prisons is that there are not enough prisons to hold them all. If, on average, there is a murder every half hour, then, on average, there should be an execution every half hour. That would open up some more room in prisons and allow the authorities to keep both killers and non-killers off the streets. We'd all be safer as a result.

"It isn't like the people I'm saying should be executed don't deserve to die. They gave up their right to live the minute they pulled the trigger or wielded the knife or whatever means they used in their crime. We have to get tough about this or none of us will be safe."

—Corning News & Review

▲ 17. Letter to the editor: "In regard to your editorial, 'Crime bill wastes billions,' let me set you straight. Your paper opposes mandatory life sentences for criminals convicted of three violent crimes, and you whine about how criminals' rights might be violated. Yet you also want to infringe on a citizen's right to keep and bear arms. You say you oppose life sentences for three-time losers because judges couldn't show any leniency toward the criminals no matter how trivial the crime. What is your definition of trivial, busting an innocent child's skull with a hammer?"

—North State Record

▲ 18. Freedom means choice. This is a truth antiporn activists always forget when they argue for censorship. In their fervor to impose their morality, groups like

Enough Is Enough cite extreme examples of pornography, such as child porn, suggesting that they are easily available in video stores.

This is not the way it is. Most of this material portrays not actions such as this but consensual sex between adults.

The logic used by Enough Is Enough is that, if something can somehow hurt someone, it must be banned. They don't apply this logic to more harmful substances, such as alcohol or tobacco. Women and children are more adversely affected by drunken driving and secondhand smoke than by pornography. Few Americans would want to ban alcohol or tobacco, even though these substances kill hundreds of thousands of people each year.

Writing Exercises

1. Write a one-page essay in which you determine whether and why it is better (you get to define "better") to look younger than your age, older than your age, or just your age. Then number the premises and conclusions in your essay and diagram it.

2. Should there be a death penalty for first-degree murder? On the top half of a sheet of paper, list considerations supporting the death penalty, and on the bottom half, list considerations opposing it. Take about ten minutes to compile your two lists.

   After everyone is finished, your instructor will call on people to read their lists. He or she will then give everyone about twenty minutes to write a draft of an essay that addresses the issue "Should there be a death penalty for first-degree murder?" Put your name on the back of your essay. After everyone is finished, your instructor will collect the essays and redistribute them to the class. In groups of four or five, read the essays that have been given to your group. Do not look at the names of the authors. Select the best essay in each group. Your instructor will ask each group to read the essay it has selected as best.

   As an alternative, your instructor may have each group rank-order their essays and ask a neighboring group which of their top-ranked essays is best. The instructor will read the top-ranking essays to the class, for discussion.

3. Is it possible to tell just by looking at someone whether he or she is telling the truth? Do a little Internet research and then take a position on the issue and defend it in a two-page essay. This assignment will help prepare you for Chapter 4.

Clear Thinking, Critical Thinking, and Clear Writing

3

Students will learn to . . .

1. Determine acceptable and unacceptable degrees of vagueness

2. Understand and identify types of ambiguity

3. Identify the problems generality causes in language

4. Understand the uses and types of definitions

5. Acquire skills for writing an effective argumentative essay

This appeared as part of an agreement one of your authors was required to sign for a credit card:

> All transactions effected pursuant to this instrument shall be effected for the account and risk and in the name of the undersigned; and the undersigned hereby agrees to indemnify and hold harmless from, and to pay promptly on demand, any and all losses arising therefrom or any debit balance due thereon.

This turns out to mean simply that the cardholder is responsible for anything owed on the account. It is an example of gobbledygook, which is pretentious or unintelligible jargon designed as much to bewilder as to inform.*

This chapter is about dealing with this and other obstacles to clear thinking, speaking, and especially writing. Here's another example of bewildering prose, from former Canadian

---

*The word "gobbledygook" was first used by Texas representative Maury Maverick in 1944 to apply to language often used by government officials.

Let Obscurity Bloom

Allan Bloom, the famous American educator who authored *The Closing of the American Mind*, which was read (or at least purchased) by millions, wrote in that book:

> If openness means to "go with the flow," it is necessarily an accommodation to the present. That present is so closed to doubt about so many things impeding the progress of its principles that unqualified openness to it would mean forgetting the despised alternative to it, knowledge of which makes us aware of what is doubtful in it.

> Is this true? Well, that's hard to say. The problem is that we don't know exactly what Professor Bloom is asserting. It may look profound, but it may be that it simply makes no sense. Whatever he has in mind, he has asked us to work too hard to understand it.

prime minister Jean Chrétien, when asked in Parliament about old versus new money in the health care program:

> They say that the money we had promised three years ago to be new money this year is not new money. We have not paid it yet and it is old money versus new money. For me new money is new money if paying in $5 or $10, it's the same money.*

We have no clue what he had in mind.

One of the authors noticed this tease on the front page of a newspaper: "49ers upset." This probably means that somebody who was not supposed to beat the San Francisco football team managed to beat them. On the other hand, it *could* mean that the team is dismayed about something.

Although obscurity can issue from various causes, four are paramount: excessive vagueness, ambiguity, excessive generality, and undefined terms. In this chapter, we will consider vagueness, ambiguity, and generality in some detail and then talk about definitions. We will also provide pointers about writing an argumentative essay, an essay in which one takes a position, supports it, and rebuts contrary positions.

VAGUENESS

A word or phrase is **vague** if we cannot say with certainty what it includes and excludes. Consider the word "bald." It's clear that Kim Kardashian is *not* bald. It's equally clear that Pitbull *is* bald. (See box on next page.) But there are lots of people in between (including both your authors). Many are borderline cases: It is not clear whether the word "bald" should apply to them—it's the sort of thing about which reasonable people could disagree. Baldness is a vague concept.

Those who survived the San Francisco earthquake said, "Thank God, I'm still alive." But, of course, those who died—their lives will never be the same again.

—U.S. Senator Barbara Boxer (D), California

■ That we might find Einstein's essay "Foundation of General Relativity" difficult to understand does not mean it is obscure to a trained physicist.

*Reported in the *Globe and Mail*, February 7, 2003.

Vagueness at the Border

Vagueness results when the scope of a concept is not clear—that is, when there are borderline cases. "Bald" is a typical example. Kim Kardashian is clearly *not* bald and Pitbull clearly *is* bald. But whether Bruce Willis is bald or not is a good question. He has hair—although it seems to be on the wane—but much of the time he keeps his head shaved and thus appears bald. How much hair would he have to lose to be bald whether or not he shaved his head? There is no correct answer. Vague words like "bald," "blond," and "wealthy" clearly apply in some cases, but they all have borderline cases to which it isn't clear whether they apply.

■ Kim Kardashian

■ Willis, with . . .

■ . . . and without

■ Pitbull

Vagueness plays an important role in much that we do. In the law, for example, how we deal with vagueness is crucial. Whether the word "torture" applies to various types of interrogation techniques, especially including "waterboarding," for example, has been a serious issue for several years. Whether your driving is "reckless" or not may determine whether you pay a small fine or a large one—or even go to jail. Because "driving too fast for the conditions" is vague, speed limits are clearly spelled out.

Sometimes vagueness is annoying. Suppose it's late and you're looking for someone's house and you're instructed, "go down this street a ways until you get to the first major intersection, make a sharp right, then, when the street starts to curve to the left, you'll be there." The vagueness in these directions is more likely to get your blood pressure up than to help you find your destination. How do you decide that a particular intersection is "major," for example?

Vagueness is often intentionally used to avoid giving a clear, precise answer. Politicians often resort to vague statements if they don't want their audience to know exactly where they stand. A vague answer to the question "Do you love me?" may mean there's trouble ahead in the relationship.

Vagueness occurs in varying degrees, and it is impossible to get rid of it entirely. Fortunately, there is no need to do this. We live comfortably with vagueness in much of what we say. "Butte City is a small town" presents no problems under ordinary circumstances, despite the vagueness of "small town." "Darren has no school loans because his parents are rich" doesn't tell us how much money his parents have, but it tells us enough to be useful. "Rich" and "small," like "bald," are vague words; there is no accepted clear line between the things to which they apply and those to which they don't. Nonetheless, they have their uses. Problems arise with vagueness when there is too much of it, as in our previous direction-giving example.

So, when is a level of vagueness acceptable and when is it not? It's difficult to give a general rule, aside from urging due care and common sense, but we might say this:

> When a claim is too vague to convey appropriately useful information, its level of vagueness is not acceptable.

For example, if you tell your mechanic you have an engine problem, he or she will ask you to be more specific. If we tell you that missing too many classes will have consequences, you will ask us for more details. If the rental car agent tells you there will be refueling charges if you return the car with less than a full tank, you would do well to ask if these include costs other than for gasoline.

AMBIGUITY

A word, phrase, or sentence is said to be **ambiguous** when it has more than one meaning. Does "Paul cashed a check" mean that Paul gave somebody cash, or that somebody gave cash to him? It could mean either. "Jessica is renting her house" could mean that she's renting it *to* someone or *from* someone. Jennifer gets up from her desk on Friday afternoon and says, "My work here is finished." She might mean that she has finished the account she was working on, or that her whole week's work is done and she's leaving for the weekend, or that she's fed up with her job and is leaving the company. If you look online, you can find several collections of amusing headlines that are funny because of their ambiguity: "Kids make nutritious snacks," for example, or "Miners refuse to work after death."

Most of the time the interpretation that a speaker or writer intends for a claim is obvious, as in the case of these headlines. But ambiguity can have consequences beyond making us smile.

In discussions of gay rights, we've seen an ambiguity in the term "rights" that often stymies rational debate. The issue is whether laws should be passed to prevent discrimination against gays in housing, in the workplace, and so forth. One side claims that such laws would themselves be discriminatory because they would specifically grant to gay people rights that are not specifically guaranteed to others—they would be "special" rights. The other side claims that the laws are only to guarantee for gays the right to be treated the same as others under the law. When the two sides fail to sort out just what

Ask a man which way he is going to vote, and he will probably tell you. Ask him, however, why, and vagueness is all.

—BARNARD LEVIN

Asked why the desertion rate in the army had risen so much, director of plans and resources for Army personnel Roy Wallace replied, "We're asking a lot of soldiers these days."

You might at first want to know what they're asking the soldiers, until you see the ambiguity in Wallace's remark.

■ Marco Rubio is not pleased with this book. Of course, he is not displeased, either, since it's almost certain he's never heard of it. Note the ambiguity in the original statement.

they mean by their key terms, the result is at best a great waste of breath and at worst angry misunderstanding.

Semantic Ambiguity

What day is the day after three days before the day after tomorrow?

Complicated, but neither vague nor ambiguous.

A claim can be ambiguous in more than one way. The most obvious way is by containing an ambiguous word or phrase, which produces a case of **semantic ambiguity.** See if you can explain the ambiguity in each of the following claims:

> Collins, the running back, always lines up on the right side.
> Jessica is cold.
> Aunt Delia never used glasses.

In the first case, it may be that it's the right and not the left side where Collins lines up, *or* it may be that he always lines up on the correct side. The second example may be saying something about Jessica's temperature or something about her personality. In the third case, it may be that Aunt Delia always had good eyes, but it also might mean that she drank her beer directly from the bottle (which was true of one of your authors' Aunt Delia). Semantically ambiguous claims can be made unambiguous ("disambiguated") by substituting a word or phrase that is not ambiguous for the one making the trouble. "Correct" for "right," for example, in #1; "eyeglasses" for "glasses" in #3.

Grouping Ambiguity

The story goes that a burglar and his 16-year-old accomplice tripped a silent alarm while breaking into a building. The accomplice was carrying a pistol, and when police arrived and tried to talk him out of the weapon, the older burglar said, "Give it to him!" whereupon the youngster shot the policeman.

—Courtesy of COLLEN JOHNSON, currently of the California State Prison, Tehachapi

Ambiguity can be dangerous!

There is a special kind of semantic ambiguity, called **grouping ambiguity,** that results when it is not clear whether a word is being used to refer to a group collectively or to members of the group individually. Consider:

> Secretaries make more money than physicians do.

The example is true if the speaker refers to secretaries and physicians collectively, since there are many more secretaries than there are physicians. But it is obviously false if the two words refer to individual secretaries and physicians.

"Lawn mowers create more air pollution than dirt bikes do" is something a dirt biker might say in defense of his hobby. And, because it is ambiguous, there is an interpretation under which his claim is probably true as well as one under which it is probably false. Taken collectively, lawn mowers doubtlessly create more pollution because there are many more of them. Individually, we'd bet it's the dirt bike that does more damage.

Like other types of ambiguity, grouping ambiguity can be used intentionally to interfere with clear thinking. When taxes are increased, opponents can smear it as "the biggest tax increase in history" if the total revenue brought in by the increase is very large, even if individual taxes have not gone up much.

Syntactic Ambiguity

Syntactic ambiguity occurs when a claim is open to two or more interpretations because of its *structure*—that is, its syntax. Not long ago, one of us received information from the American Automobile Association prior to driving to British

Columbia. "To travel in Canada," the brochure stated, "you will need a birth certificate or a driver's license and other photo ID." What does this mean? There are two possibilities:

> [You will need a birth certificate or a driver's license] *and* [other photo ID].
> [You will need a birth certificate] *or* [a driver's license and other photo ID].

Depending on the intended interpretation, the original should have been written as either:

> You will need either a birth certificate or a driver's license *and you will also need* an additional photo ID.
> Or
> You will need either a birth certificate or *both* a driver's license and an additional photo ID.

Neither of these is ambiguous.

Here are some other examples of syntactic ambiguity, along with various possible interpretations, to help you get the idea.

> Players with beginners' skills only may use Court 1.

In this case, we don't know what the word "only" applies to. This word, as we'll see in later chapters, is both useful and easy to use incorrectly. Here, it might mean that beginners may use *only Court 1*. Or it might mean that players with *only beginners' skills* may use Court 1. Finally, it might mean that *only players with beginners' skills* may use Court 1. Obviously, whoever puts up such a sign needs to be more careful. (And so does the person who put up a sign in our university's student union that said, "Cash only this line." Do you see the ambiguity?)

> Susan saw the farmer with binoculars.

This ambiguity results from a modifying phrase ("with binoculars") that is not clear in its application. Who had the binoculars in this case? Presumably Susan, but it looks as though it was the farmer. "Looking through her binoculars, Susan saw the farmer" clears it up.

> People who protest often get arrested.

This is similar to the previous example: Does "often" apply to protesting or to getting arrested?

> There's somebody in the bed next to me.

Does "next to me" apply to a person or to a bed? One might rewrite this either as "There's somebody next to me in the bed" or as "There's somebody in the bed next to mine."

Ambiguous pronoun references occur when it is not clear to what or whom a pronoun is supposed to refer. "The boys chased the girls and they giggled a lot"

Making Ambiguity Work for You

Have you ever been asked to write a letter of recommendation for a friend who was, well, incompetent? To avoid either hurting your friend's feelings or lying, Robert Thornton of Lehigh University has some ambiguous statements you can use. Here are some examples:

I most enthusiastically recommend this candidate with no qualifications whatsoever.

I am pleased to say that this candidate is a former colleague of mine.

I can assure you that no person would be better for the job.

I would urge you to waste no time in making this candidate an offer of employment.

All in all, I cannot say enough good things about this candidate or recommend the candidate too highly.

In my opinion, you will be very fortunate to get this person to work for you.

does not make clear who did the giggling. "They" could be either the boys or the girls. A similar example: "After their father removed the trash from the pool, the kids played in it." A less amusing and possibly more trouble-making example: "Paul agreed that, once Gary removed the motor from the car, he could have it." What does Gary have permission to take, the motor or the car? We'd predict a lawsuit.

Sometimes examples of ambiguity are difficult to classify. Imagine telling a server, "You can bring the sauce separately, and I'll put it on myself." The ambiguity, obviously, is in *how* the speaker will put the sauce on versus *where* he or she will put it. This could be called either semantic ambiguity or syntactic ambiguity. However, it's more important to see *that* a claim is ambiguous than to be able to classify the type of ambiguity.

GENERALITY

We turn now to the notion of generality, which is closely related to both vagueness and ambiguity and which can cause trouble in the same way they do.

From what we learned of vagueness, we realize that the word "child" is vague, since it is not clear where the line is drawn between being a child and no longer being a child. It can also be ambiguous, because it can refer not only to a person of immature years but also to a person's offspring. As if this weren't enough, it is also general because it applies to both boys and girls. **Generality** is lack of specificity. A term that refers to all the members of a group is more general than a term that refers to fewer than all members of that group. "Dog" is more general than "otterhound." "Otterhound" is more general than "blue-eyed otterhound." "Clarence was arrested" is more general than "Clarence was arrested for trespassing."

If you learn that Clarence was arrested, it may well lower your estimate of him and may prevent you from hiring him to do work around your house, for example. But if some more detail were supplied—for instance, that he had been arrested during a protest against a company that was polluting the local river—it might well make a difference in your opinion of him. The difference between a very general description and one with more specificity can be crucial to nearly any decision.

Widely discussed these days is whether the War on Terror should really be called a "war" at all. The phrase has continued to be used because "war" is both

The traveler must, of course, always be cautious of the overly broad generalization. But I am an American, and a paucity of data does not stop me from making sweeping, vague, conceptual statements, and, if necessary, following these statements up with troops.

—GEORGE SAUNDERS, *The Guardian*, July 22, 2006

vague and general. Some believe that the word as traditionally used requires an enemy that is organized and identifiable, such as a country or province, and those are difficult to identify in the War on Terror. Still less clearly a war is the so-called War on Drugs. This seems to be a purely metaphorical use of the word "war," meant to show only that somebody is serious about the issue and to justify the expense of prosecuting drug cases.

We don't mean to confuse you with these closely related and overlapping pitfalls—vagueness, ambiguity, and generality. In practical fact, it is less important that you classify the problem that infects a claim or idea than that you see what's going on and can explain it. For example, "Just what do you mean by 'war'?" is a good response to someone who is using the word too loosely. In some of the exercises that follow, we'll ask you to identify problems in different passages in order to help you become familiar with the ideas. In others, we'll simply ask you to explain what is needed for clarification.

Anyhow, with all these potential pitfalls to clear thinking and clear communication, what is a critically thinking person to do? To start, we can do the best we can to be clear in what our words mean. So after the following exercises we will turn our attention to the definition of terms.

Here are several exercises to give you practice identifying precision (or lack thereof) in sentences.

The lettered words and phrases that follow each of the following fragments vary in their precision. In each instance, determine which is the most precise and which is the least precise; then rank the remainder in order of precision, to the extent possible. If these exercises are discussed in class, you'll discover that many leave room for disagreement. Discussion with input from your instructor will help you and your classmates reach closer agreement about items that prove especially difficult to rank.

Exercise 3-1

▲ —See the answers section at the back of the book.

Example

Over the past ten years, the median income of wage earners in St. Paul

a. nearly doubled
b. increased substantially
c. increased by 85.5 percent
d. increased by more than 85 percent

Answer

Choice (b) is the least precise because it provides the least information; (c) is the most precise because it provides the most detailed figure. In between, (d) is the second most precise, followed by (a).

 1. Eli and Sarah

a. decided to sell their house and move
b. made plans for the future
c. considered moving
d. talked
e. discussed their future
f. discussed selling their house

2. Manuel

   a. worked in the yard all afternoon
   b. spent the afternoon planting flowers in the yard
   c. was outside all afternoon
   d. spent the afternoon planting salvia alongside his front sidewalk
   e. spent the afternoon in the yard

3. The American Civil War

   a. was the bloodiest in American history
   b. resulted in the highest percentage of deaths of U.S. males of any war
   c. saw 10 percent of young Northern males and 30 percent of young Southern males lose their lives
   d. resulted in the deaths of approximately 750,000 soldiers, North and South

▲ 4. The recent changes in the tax code

   a. will substantially increase taxes paid by those making more than $200,000 per year
   b. will increase by 4 percent the tax rate for those making more than $200,000 per year; will leave unchanged the tax rate for people making between $40,000 and $200,000; and will decrease by 2 percent the tax rate for those making less than $40,000
   c. will make some important changes in who pays what in taxes
   d. are tougher on the rich than the provisions in the previous tax law
   e. raise rates for the wealthy and reduce them for those in the lowest brackets

5. Smedley is absent because

   a. he's not feeling well
   b. he's under the weather
   c. he has an upset stomach and a fever
   d. he's nauseated and has a fever of more than 103°
   e. he has flulike symptoms

6. Candice

   a. had a nice trip to her home town
   b. took a vacation
   c. visited her mother back in Wichita Falls
   d. was out of town for a while
   e. visited her mother

▲ 7. Hurricane Sandy

   a. was the second most costly storm to hit the United States
   b. took over 200 lives in seven countries along its path
   c. killed people in several countries
   d. killed 253 people from Jamaica to Canada and did $65 million worth of damage
   e. was the most lethal storm to hit the United States since Katrina

8. The Miami Heat

   a. beat the Atlanta Hawks last night
   b. 104, the Atlanta Hawks 101
   c. squeaked by the Atlanta Hawks last night
   d. beat the Atlanta Hawks by three points in a playoff game last night
   e. won last night

9. Roy and Jaydee are

    a. driving less because they want to reduce auto emissions

    b. trying to reduce their carbon footprint

    c. concerned about the effects of carbon emissions on the world's climate

    d. carpooling with neighbors to keep down the amount of carbon they cause to be emitted

    e. worried about global climate change

10. The Tea Party

    a. was unsuccessful in at least one Senate race

    b. has supported candidates who failed to win in the general election

    c. has caused a shift in the policies adopted by the Republican Party

    d. supported a candidate for the Senate in Missouri who lost the election

Exercise 3-2

You do not always have to classify problematic sentences as too vague, ambiguous, or too general, but practice in doing so can help you learn to spot problems quicker.

For each of the following, determine if it is too vague or too ambiguous, or simply not useful because of either of these faults. Explain your answer.

Example

Full implementation of the Affordable Care Act ("Obamacare") will cause a serious increase in health care costs.

Answer

This claim is too vague to be very useful. The problem is the phrase "serious increase," which could mean anything within a wide range of cost increases. What is a serious increase to one person may not be serious at all to another.

 1. Full implementation of the Affordable Care Act ("Obamacare") will cause a noticeable decrease in health care costs.

2. I would not advise going to Raymond's party; he invites all kinds of people to those things.

3. Sign in store window: Help Wanted.

 4. He chased the girl in his car.

5. Remember, you have an appointment tomorrow afternoon.

6. The new tax plan will only affect rich people.

 7. He gave her cat food.

8. Professional football needs new rules about excessive violence in the game.

9. She had her daughter's family over and served them a very nice meal.

10. Headline: Killer sentenced to die for the second time in ten years.

 11. You only need modest exercise to stay healthy.

12. Yes, I saw the robber; he looked perfectly ordinary.

13. Prostitutes appeal to the mayor.

14. Athletes have to stay in training year round.

15. They're looking for teachers of Spanish, French, and German.

Source: Hi and Lois: © 1986 King Features Syndicate, Inc., World Rights Reserved.

Exercise 3-3

Which of each set of claims suffers least from excessive vagueness, ambiguity, or excessive generality?

Example

   a. The trees served to make shade for the patio.
   b. He served his country proudly.

Answer

   The use of "served" in (b) is more vague than that in (a). We know exactly what the trees did; we don't know what he did.

1. a. Rooney served the church his entire life.
   b. Rooney's tennis serve is impossible to return.

2. a. The window served its purpose.
   b. The window served as an escape hatch.

3. a. Throughout their marriage, Alfredo served her dinner.
   b. Throughout their marriage, Alfredo served her well.

4. a. Minta turned her ankle.
   b. Minta turned to religion.

5. a. These scales will turn on the weight of a hair.
   b. This car will turn on a dime.

6. a. Fenner's boss turned vicious.
   b. Fenner's boss turned out to be forty-seven.

7. a. Time to turn the garden.
   b. Time to turn off the sprinkler.

8. a. The wine turned to vinegar.
   b. The wine turned out to be vinegar.

9. a. Harper flew around the world.
   b. Harper departed around 3:00 A.M.

10. a. Clifton turned out the light.
   b. Clifton turned out the vote.

11. a. The glass is full to the brim.
   b. Mrs. Couch has a rather full figure.

12. a. Kathy gave him a full report.
    b. "Oh, no, thank you! I am full."

13. a. Oswald was dealt a full house.
    b. Oswald is not playing with a full deck.

14. a. Money is not the key to happiness.
    b. This is not the key to the garage.

▲ 15. a. Porker set a good example.
    b. Porker set the world record for the 100-meter dash.

DEFINING TERMS

When today's typical student hears the word "definition," we wouldn't be surprised if the first thing to come to mind is television. "Ultra-high definition" is now the standard of clarity in what we see on the home screen. This is directly analogous to the clarity and distinctness we're looking for as critical thinkers, and the careful definition of terms is one of our most useful tools in pursuing this goal. While the business of definitions may seem straightforward ("'carrot' refers to a tapering, orange-colored root eaten as a vegetable"), you'll soon see that there's more to it than you might have thought. For example, a multitude of attempts have been made to construct a definition of "person" (or, if you like, "human being"). Everything from "rational animal" to "featherless biped" has been suggested. But such important issues as whether abortion is morally permissible, whether fetuses have rights, whether a fetus is correctly referred to as an "unborn child," and doubtless many others—all turn on how we define "person" and some of these other basic concepts. Indeed, if we define "abortion" as "the murder of an unborn child," the debate on abortion is over before it begins.

> A definition is the start of an argument, not the end of one.
>
> —NEIL POSTMAN, author of *Amusing Ourselves to Death: Public Discourse in the Age of Show Business*

Some arguments against the acceptance of rights for gay men and lesbians depend on the claim that their orientation is "unnatural."* But to arrive at a definition of "natural" (or "unnatural") is no easy task. If you spend a few minutes thinking about this difficulty—even better, if you discuss it with others—we think you'll see what we mean. What is "natural," depending on who is defining the term, can mean anything from "occurs in nature" to "correct in the eyes of God."

As you will see in Chapter 12, the definition of the word "use" by the U.S. Supreme Court made a difference of thirty years in the sentence of John Angus Smith in a recent criminal case.** Definitions matter. Now, let's have a look at how to deal with them.

Purposes of Definitions

Definitions can serve several purposes, but we want to call your attention to three:

1. **Lexical definitions** are definitions like those we find in dictionaries; they tell us what a word ordinarily means. (An example from the dictionary: "*Tamarin. noun:* a small, forest-dwelling south American monkey of the marmoset family,

---

*Here is an example: "[W]e're talking about a particular behavior that most American's [*sic*] consider strange and unnatural, and many Americans consider deeply immoral." "Equal Rights for Homosexuals," by Gregory Kouki, www.str.org/site/News2?page=NewsArticle&id=5226.

**See Exercise 12–13, p. 89, for details.

typically brightly colored and with tufts and crests of hair around the face and neck.") You might ask, Isn't this what all definitions do? A good question, and the answer is *no*. Check the following.

2. **Precising or stipulative definitions** are designed to make a term more precise (i.e. less vague or general) or to stipulate a new or different meaning from the ordinary one. For example, the word "dollars" is too general to be used in its normal sense in an international sales contract, because it could apply to U.S. dollars, Canadian dollars, Australian dollars, etc. So we make the meaning precise by *stipulating* that, *In this contract, the term 'dollars' will refer exclusively to Canadian dollars.*

We can also stipulate that a word will have a new meaning in a given context. For example, *In this environment, 'desktop' means the basic opening screen of the operating system—the one with the trash can.*

3. **Persuasive** or **rhetorical definitions** are used *to persuade or slant* someone's attitude or point of view toward whatever the "defined" term refers to. This kind of definition can be troublesome, because it often distorts the real meaning of a term in order to cause the listener or reader to favor or disfavor a person, policy, object, or event.

If a liberal friend tries to "define" a conservative as *a hidebound, narrow-minded hypocrite who thinks the point to life is making money and ripping off poor people,* you know the point here is not the clarification of the meaning of the word "conservative." It is a way of trashing conservatives. Such rhetorical uses of definitions frequently make use of the *emotive meaning* or the *rhetorical force* of words. By this we mean the positive or negative associations of a word. Consider the difference between *government guaranteed health care* and *a government takeover of health care.* These terms might reasonably be used to refer to the same thing, but they clearly have different emotional associations—one positive and one negative. The word "connotation" is the traditional term for these associations.* Our definition of "abortion" as "the murder of an unborn child" at the beginning of this section is another much-quoted example of this use of definition.

Kinds of Definitions

The purpose of a definition and the kind of definition it is are different things. (Compare: The *purpose* of food is to nourish our bodies and please our palettes, whereas *kinds* of food are vegetables, meat, Pringles, etc.) Regardless of what purpose is served by defining a term, most definitions are of one of the three following kinds:

1. **Definition by example** (also called **ostensive definition**): Pointing to, naming, or otherwise identifying one or more examples of the sort of thing to which the term applies: *"By 'scripture,' I mean writings like the Bible and the Koran." "A mouse is this thing here, the one with the buttons."*

2. **Definition by synonym:** Giving another word or phrase that means the same as the term being defined. *"'Fastidious' means the same as 'fussy.'" "'Pulsatile' means 'throbbing.'" "To be 'lubricious' is the same as to be 'slippery.'"*

> It's bad poetry executed by people who can't sing. That's my definition of Rap.
>
> —PETER STEELE
>
> **We're guessing he doesn't like it.**

---

*Much more will be said about rhetorical force (emotive meaning, connotation) in Chapter 5.

3. **Analytical definition:** Specifying the features a thing must possess in order for the term being defined to apply to it. These definitions often take the form of a genus-and-species classification. For example, *"A samovar is an urn that has a spigot and is used especially in Russia to boil water for tea." "A mongoose is a ferret-sized mammal native to India that eats snakes and is related to civets."*

Almost all dictionary definitions, often said to be **lexical definitions,** are of the analytical variety.

Tips on Definitions

So far, we've seen that definitions serve a variety of purposes and take several forms. Combinations can be of many sorts: a definition by synonym that is precising *("minor" means under eighteen)*; an analytical definition designed just to persuade *(a liberal is somebody who wants the able and willing to take care of both the unable and the unwilling)*. But what makes a definition a good one?

First, definitions should not prejudice the case against one side of a debate or the other. This is one form of *begging the question,* which will be discussed in detail in Chapter 6. For now, just recall that one cannot usually win a debate simply by insisting on one's own favored definition of key terms, since those who disagree with your position will also disagree with your definitions. Definitions are instances in which people have to try to achieve a kind of neutral ground.

Second, definitions should be clear. They are designed to clear the air, not muddy the water. This means they should be expressed in language that is as clear and simple as the subject will allow. If we define a word in language that is more obscure than the original word, we accomplish nothing. This includes avoiding emotionally charged language.

Third, realize that sometimes you must get along with incomplete definitions. In real life, we sometimes have to deal with claims that include such big-league abstractions as friendship, loyalty, fair play, freedom, rights, and so forth. If you have to give a *complete* definition of "freedom" or "fair play," you'd best not plan on getting home early. Such concepts have subtle and complex parameters that

Arguments and Tainted Definitions

Definitions, or the lack of them, can cause great confusion in argumentation. Consider the following "argument"

> *Whenever you can, you act so as to satisfy your desires.*
>
> *Acting to satisfy your desires is acting selfishly.*
>
> *Therefore, whenever you can, you act selfishly.*

We hope you're not persuaded by this. If you look carefully at this argument you should notice that hidden in it is an odd "definition" of acting selfishly—acting so as to satisfy your desires. Indeed, given this definition, you act selfishly whenever you can. But the ordinary understanding of acting selfishly is putting your own interests above those of others. Given the ordinary definition of the phrase, you do not necessarily always act selfishly.

If an argument leads to a surprising result, the first thing to do is check definitions!

might take a lifetime to pin down. (Plato, generally recognized as a smart cookie, wrote an entire book in an attempt to define "justice.") For practical purposes, what is usually needed for words like these is not a complete definition but a precise definition that focuses on one aspect of the concept and provides sufficient guidance for the purposes at hand something like, *"To me, the word 'justice' does not include referring to a person's private life when evaluating his or her work performance."*

The following exercise will give you practice with definitions:

Exercise 3-4

In groups (or individually if your instructor prefers), determine what term in each of the following is being defined and whether the definition is by example or by synonym or an analytical definition. If it is difficult to tell which kind of definition is present, describe the difficulty.

1. A piano is a stringed instrument in which felt hammers are made to strike the strings by an arrangement of keys and levers.

2. "Decaffeinated" means without caffeine.

3. Carly Fiorina is my idea of a successful philosophy major.

4. The red planet is Mars.

5. "UV" refers to ultraviolet light.

6. The Cheyenne perfectly illustrate the sort of Native Americans who were Plains Indians.

7. Data, in our case, is raw information collected from survey forms, which is then put in tabular form and analyzed.

8. "Chiaroscuro" is just a fancy word for shading.

9. Bifocals are glasses with two different prescriptions ground into each lens, making it possible to focus at two different distances from the wearer.

10. Red is the color that we perceive when our eyes are struck by light waves of approximately seven angstroms.

11. A significant other can be taken to be a person's spouse, lover, long-term companion, or just girlfriend or boyfriend.

12. "Assessment" means evaluation.

13. A blackout is "a period of total memory loss, as one induced by an accident or prolonged alcoholic drinking." When your buddies tell you they loved your rendition of the Lambada on Madison's pool table the other night and you don't even remember being at Madison's, that is a blackout.

   —*Adapted from the CalPoly, San Luis Obispo,* Mustang Daily

14. A pearl, which is the only animal-produced gem, begins as an irritant inside an oyster. The oyster then secretes a coating of nacre around the irritating object. The result is a pearl, the size of which is determined by the number of layers with which the oyster coats the object.

15. According to my cousin, who lives in Tulsa, the phrase "bored person" refers to anybody who is between the ages of sixteen and twenty-five and lives in Eastern Oklahoma.

WRITING ARGUMENTATIVE ESSAYS

In an argumentative essay you state an issue, take a position on it, support or defend it, and rebut contrary arguments. This isn't a book on writing, but writing an argumentative essay is so closely related to thinking critically that we would like to take the opportunity to offer our recommendations. We know professors who have retired because they could not bear to read another student essay. As a result, we offer our two bits' worth here in hopes of continuing to see familiar faces.

As we just said, an argumentative essay generally has four components:

> **A statement of the issue**
> **A statement of one's position on that issue**
> **Arguments that support one's position**
> **Rebuttals of arguments** that **support contrary positions**

Ideally, your essay should begin with an introduction to the issue that demonstrates that the issue is important or interesting. This is not always easy, but even when you are not excited about the subject yourself, it is still good practice to try to make your reader interested. Your statement of the issue should be fair; that is, don't try to state the issue in such a way that your position on it is obviously the only correct one. This can make your reader suspicious; the burden of convincing him or her will come later, when you give your arguments.

Your position on the issue should be clear. Try to be brief. If you have stated the issue clearly, it should be a simple matter to identify your position.

Your arguments in support of your position also should be as succinct as you can make them, but it is much more important to be clear than to be brief. After all, this is the heart of your essay. The reasons you cite should be clearly relevant, and they should be either clearly reliable or backed up by further arguments. Much of the rest of this book is devoted to how this is done; hang in there.

If there are well-known arguments for the other side of the issue, you should acknowledge them and offer some reason to believe that they are unconvincing. You can do this either by attacking the premises that are commonly given or by trying to show that those premises do not actually support the opposing conclusion. More on these topics later too.

Following are some more detailed hints that might be helpful in planning and writing an argumentative essay:

1. *Focus.* Make clear at the outset what issue you intend to address and what your position on the issue will be. However, nothing is quite so boring as starting off with the words "In this essay, I will argue that X, Y, and Z," and then going on to itemize everything you are about to say, and at the end concluding with the words "In this essay, I argued that X, Y, and Z." As a matter of style, you should let the reader know what to expect without using trite phrases and without going on at length. However, you should try to find an engaging way to state your position. For example, instead of "In this essay, I will discuss the rights of animals to inherit property from their masters," you might begin, "Could your inheritance wind up belonging to your mother's cat?"

2. *Stick to the issue.* All points you make in an essay should be connected to the issue under discussion and should always either (a) support, illustrate, explain, clarify, elaborate on, or emphasize your position on the issue or (b) serve as responses to anticipated objections. Rid the essay of irrelevancies and dangling thoughts.

3. *Arrange the components of the essay in a logical sequence.* This is just common sense. Make a point before you clarify it, for example, not the other way around.

When supporting your points, bring in examples, clarification, and the like in such a way that a reader knows what in the world you are doing. A reader should be able to discern the relationship between any given sentence and your ultimate objective, and he or she should be able to move from sentence to sentence and from paragraph to paragraph without getting lost or confused. If a reader cannot outline your essay with ease, you have not properly sequenced your material. Your essay might be as fine as a piece of French philosophy, but it would not pass as an argumentative essay.

4. *Be complete.* Accomplish what you set out to accomplish, support your position adequately, and anticipate and respond to possible objections. Keep in mind that many issues are too large to be treated exhaustively in a single essay. The key to being complete is to define the issue sharply enough that you can be complete. Thus, the more limited your topic, the easier it is to be complete in covering it.

Also, be sure there is closure at every level. Sentences should be complete, paragraphs should be unified as wholes (and usually each should stick to a single point), and the essay should reach a conclusion. Incidentally, reaching a conclusion and summarizing are not the same thing. Short essays do not require summaries.

Good Writing Practices

Understanding the four principles just mentioned is one thing, but actually employing them may be more difficult. Fortunately, there are five practices that a writer can follow to improve the organization of an essay and to help avoid other problems. We offer the following merely as a set of recommendations within the broader scope of thinking critically in writing.

I'm for abolishing and doing away with redundancy.

—J. Curtis McKay, of the Wisconsin State Elections Board (reported by Ross and Petras)

We ourselves are also for that too.

1. At some stage *after* the first draft, outline what you have written. Then, make certain the outline is logical and that every sentence in the essay fits into the outline as it should. Some writers create an informal outline before they begin, but many do not. Our advice: Just identify the issue and your position on it, and start writing by stating them both.

   Incidentally, for most people, the hardest sentence to write is the first one. H. L. Mencken once said, "Writing is easy. All you do is stare at a blank piece of paper until drops of blood form on your forehead." We have better advice: Just begin using your keyboard. Say anything. You can always throw away what you write at first, but just the act of writing will help you get started. Eventually, you'll say something relevant to your topic and then you're off and running.

2. Revise your work. Revising is the secret to good writing. Even major-league writers revise what they write, and they revise continuously. Unless you are more gifted than the very best professional writers, revise, revise, revise. Don't think in terms of two or three drafts. Think in terms of *innumerable* drafts.

3. Have someone else read your essay and offer criticisms of it. Revise as required.

4. If you have trouble with grammar or punctuation, reading your essay out loud may help you detect problems your eyes have missed.

5. After you are completely satisfied with the essay, put it aside. Then, come back to it later for still further revisions.

Essay Types to Avoid

Seasoned instructors know that the first batch of essays they get from a class will include samples of each of the following types. We recommend avoiding these mistakes:

- **The Windy Preamble.** Writers of this type of essay avoid getting to the issue and instead go on at length with introductory remarks, often about how important the issue is, how it has troubled thinkers for centuries, how opinions on the issue are many and various, and so on, and so on. Anything you write that smacks of "When in the course of human events . . . " should go into the trash can immediately.

- **The Stream-of-Consciousness Ramble.** This type of essay results when writers make no attempt to organize their thoughts and simply spew them out in the order in which they come to mind.

- **The Knee-Jerk Reaction.** In this type of essay, writers record their first reaction to an issue without considering the issue in any depth or detail. It always shows.

- **The Glancing Blow.** In this type of essay, writers address an issue obliquely. If they are supposed to evaluate the health benefits of bicycling, they will bury the topic in an essay on the history of cycling; if they are supposed to address the history of cycling, they will talk about the benefits of riding bicycles throughout history.

- **Let the Reader Do the Work.** Writers of this type of essay expect the reader to follow them through *non sequiturs,* abrupt shifts in direction, and irrelevant sidetracks.

And While We're on the Subject of Writing

Don't forget these rules of good style:

1. Avoid clichés like the plague.
2. Be more or less specific.
3. NEVER generalize.
4. The passive voice is to be ignored.
5. Never, ever be redundant.
6. Exaggeration is a billion times worse than understatement.
7. Make sure verbs agree with their subjects.
8. Why use rhetorical questions?
9. Parenthetical remarks (however relevant) are (usually) unnecessary.
10. Proofread carefully to see if you any words out.
11. And it's usually a bad idea to start a sentence with a conjunction.

This list has been making the rounds on the Internet.

Persuasive Writing

The primary aim of argumentation and the argumentative essay is to support or demonstrate a position on an issue. Good writers, however, write for an audience and hope their audience will find what they write persuasive. If you are writing for an audience of people who think critically, it is helpful to adhere to these principles:

Confine your discussion of an opponent's point of view to issues rather than personal considerations.

When rebutting an opposing viewpoint, avoid being strident or insulting. Don't call opposing arguments absurd or ridiculous.

If an opponent's argument is good, concede that it is good.

If space or time is limited, be sure to concentrate on the most important considerations. Don't become obsessive about refuting every last criticism of your position.

Present your strongest arguments first.

There is nothing wrong with trying to make a persuasive case for your position. However, in this book we place more emphasis on making and recognizing good arguments than on simply devising effective techniques of persuasion. Some people can be persuaded by poor arguments and doubtful claims, and an argumentative essay can be effective as a piece of propaganda even when it is a rational and critical failure. One of the most difficult things you are called upon to do as a critical thinker is to construct and evaluate claims and arguments independently of their power to win a following. The remainder of this book—after a section on writing and diversity—is devoted to this task.

Writing in a Diverse Society

In closing, it seems appropriate to mention how important it is to avoid writing in a manner that reinforces questionable assumptions and attitudes about people's gender, ethnic background, religion, sexual orientation, physical ability or disability, or other characteristics. This isn't just a matter of ethics; it is a matter of clarity and good sense. Careless word choices relative to such characteristics not only are imprecise and inaccurate but also may be viewed as biased even if they were not intended to be, and thus they may diminish the writer's credibility. Worse, using sexist or racist language may distort the writer's own perspective and keep him or her from viewing social issues clearly and objectively.

But language isn't entirely *not* a matter of ethics, either. We are a society that aspires to be just, a society that strives not to withhold its benefits from individuals on the basis of their ethnic or racial background, skin color, religion, gender, or disability. As a people, we try to end practices and change or remove institutions that are unjustly discriminatory. Some of these unfair practices and institutions are, unfortunately, embedded in our language.

Some common ways of speaking and writing, for example, assume that "normal" people are all white males. It is still not uncommon, for instance, to mention a person's race, gender, or ethnic background if the person is *not* a white male, and *not* to do so if the person *is*. Of course, it may be relevant to whatever you are writing about to state that this particular individual is a male of Irish descent, or whatever; if so, there is absolutely nothing wrong with saying so.

"Always" and "never" are two words you should always remember never to use.

—WENDELL JOHNSON

Another tip on writing.

Some language practices are particularly unfair to women. Imagine a conversation among three people, you being one of them. Imagine that the other two talk only to each other. When you speak, they listen politely; but when you are finished, they continue as though you had never spoken. Even though what you say is true and relevant to the discussion, the other two proceed as though you were invisible. Because you are not being taken seriously, you are at a considerable disadvantage. You have reason to be unhappy.

In an analogous way, women have been far less visible in language than men and have thus been at a disadvantage. Another word for the human race is not "woman," but "man" or "mankind." The generic human has often been referred to as "he." How do you run a project? You *man* it. Who supervises the department or runs the meeting? The chair*man*. Who heads the crew? The fore*man*. Picture a research scientist to yourself. Got the picture? Is it a picture of a *woman?* No? That's because the standard picture, or stereotype, of a research scientist is a picture of a man. Or, read this sentence: "Research scientists often put their work before their personal lives and neglect their husbands." Were you surprised by the last word? Again, the stereotypical picture of a research scientist is a picture of a man.

A careful and precise writer finds little need to converse in the lazy language of stereotypes, especially those that perpetuate prejudice. As long as the idea prevails that the "normal" research scientist is a man, women who are or who wish to become research scientists will tend to be thought of as out of place. So they must carry an *extra* burden, the burden of showing that they are *not* out of place. That's unfair. If you unthinkingly always write, "The research scientist . . . he," you are perpetuating an image that places women at a disadvantage. Some research scientists are men, and some are women. If you wish to make a claim about male research scientists, do so. But if you wish to make a claim about research scientists in general, don't write as though they were all males.

The rule to follow in all cases is this: Keep your writing free of *irrelevant implied evaluation* of gender, race, ethnic background, religion, or any other human attribute.

Recap

This list summarizes the topics covered in this chapter:

- Clarity of language is extremely important to the ability to think critically.
- Clarity of language can often be lost as a result of multiple causes, including, importantly, vagueness, ambiguity, and generality.
- Vagueness is a matter of degree; what matters is not being too vague for the purposes at hand.
- A statement is ambiguous when it is subject to more than one interpretation and it isn't clear which interpretation is the correct one.
- Some main types of ambiguity are semantic ambiguity, syntactic ambiguity, grouping ambiguity, and ambiguous pronoun reference.
- A claim is overly general when it lacks sufficient detail to restrict its application to the immediate subject.
- To reduce vagueness or eliminate ambiguity, or when new or unfamiliar words are brought into play, or familiar words are used in an unusual way, definitions are our best tool.

■ The most common types of definitions are definition by synonym, definition by example, and analytical definition.

■ Some "definitions" are used not to clarify meaning but to express or influence attitude. This is known as the rhetorical use of definition.

■ The rhetorical use of definitions accomplishes its ends by means of the rhetorical force (emotive meaning) of terms.

■ Critical thinking done on paper is known as an argumentative essay, a type of writing worth mastering, perhaps by following our suggestions.

Additional Exercises

Exercise 3-5

Are the italicized words or phrases in each of the following too imprecise given the implied context? Explain.

▲ 1. Please cook this steak *longer*. It's too rare.

2. If you get ready for bed quickly, Mommy has a *surprise* for you.

3. This program contains language that some viewers may find offensive. It is recommended for *mature* audiences only.

▲ 4. *Turn down the damned noise!* Some people around here want to sleep!

5. Based on our analysis of your eating habits, we recommend that you *lower* your consumption of sugar and refined carbohydrates.

6. NOTICE: Hazard Zone. *Small* children not permitted beyond this sign.

▲ 7. SOFAS CLEANED: $150 & *up*. MUST SEE TO GIVE *EXACT* PRICES.

8. And remember, all our mufflers come with a *lifetime guarantee.*

9. CAUTION: *To avoid* unsafe levels of carbon monoxide, do not set the wick on your kerosene stove *too high*.

▲ 10. Uncooked Frosting: Combine 1 unbeaten egg white, ½ cup corn syrup, ½ teaspoon vanilla, and dash salt. Beat with electric mixer until of fluffy spreading consistency. Frost cake. Serve *within a few hours* or refrigerate.

Exercise 3-6

Read the following passage, paying particular attention to the italicized words and phrases. Determine whether any of these expressions are too vague in the context in which you find them here.

Term paper assignment: Your paper *should be* typed, *between eight and twelve pages in length,* and double-spaced. You should *make use of* at least three *sources.* Grading will be based on *organization, use of sources, clarity of expression, quality of reasoning,* and *grammar.*

A *rough draft* is due *before Thanksgiving.* The final version is due *at the end of the semester.*

Exercise 3-7

▲ Read the following passage, paying particular attention to the italicized words and phrases. All of these expressions would be too imprecise for use in *some* contexts; determine which are and which are not too imprecise in *this* context.

> In view of what can happen in twelve months to the fertilizer you apply at any one time, you can see why just one annual application may not be adequate. Here is a guide to timing the *feeding* of some of the more common types of garden flowers.
>
> Feed begonias and fuchsias *frequently* with label-recommended amounts or less frequently with *no more than half* the recommended amount. Feed roses with *label-recommended amounts* as a *new year's growth begins* and as *each bloom period ends*. Feed azaleas, camellias, rhododendrons, and *similar* plants *immediately after bloom* and again *when the nights begin cooling off*. Following these simple instructions can help your flower garden be as attractive as it can be.

Exercise 3-8

Rewrite the following claims to remedy problems of ambiguity. Do *not* assume that common sense by itself solves the problem. If the ambiguity is intentional, note this fact, and do not rewrite.

Example

> Former professional football player Jim Brown was accused of assaulting a thirty-three-year-old woman with a female accomplice.

Answer

> This claim is syntactically ambiguous because grammatically it isn't clear what the phrase "with a female accomplice" modifies—Brown, the woman who was attacked, or, however bizarre it might be, the attack itself (he might have thrown the accomplice at the woman). To make it clear that Brown had the accomplice, the phrase "with a female accomplice" should have come right after the word "Brown" in the original claim.

▲ 1. The Raider tackle threw a block at the Giants linebacker.

2. Please close the door behind you.

3. We heard that he informed you of what he said in his letter.

▲ 4. "How Therapy Can Help Torture Victims"

—Headline in newspaper

5. Charles drew his gun.

6. They were both exposed to someone who was ill a week ago.

▲ 7. Chelsea has Hillary's nose.

8. I flush the cooling system regularly and just put in new thermostats.

9. "Tuxedos Cut Ridiculously!"

—An ad for formal wear, quoted by Herb Caen

▲ 10. "Police Kill 6 Coyotes After Mauling of Girl."

—Headline in newspaper

11. "We promise nothing."

—*Aquafina advertisement*

12. A former governor of California, Pat Brown, viewing an area struck by a flood, is said to have remarked, "This is the greatest disaster since I was elected governor."

—*Quoted by Lou Cannon in the* Washington Post

13. "Besides Lyme disease, two other tick-borne diseases, babesiosis and HGE, are infecting Americans in 30 states, according to recent studies. A single tick can infect people with more than one disease."

—Self *magazine*

14. "Don't freeze your can at the game."

—*Commercial for Miller beer*

15. Volunteer help requested: Come prepared to lift heavy equipment with construction helmet and work overalls.

16. "GE: We bring good things to life."

—*Television commercial*

17. "Tropicana 100% Pure Florida Squeezed Orange Juice. You can't pick a better juice."

—*Magazine advertisement*

18. "It's biodegradable! So remember, Arm and Hammer laundry detergent gets your wash as clean as can be [pause] without polluting our waters."

—*Television commercial*

19. If you crave the taste of a real German beer, nothing is better than Dunkelbrau.

20. Independent laboratory tests prove that Houndstooth cleanser gets your bathroom cleaner than any other product.

21. We're going to look at lots this afternoon.

22. Jordan could write more profound essays.

23. "Two million times a day Americans love to eat, Rice-a-Roni—the San Francisco treat."

—*Advertisement*

24. "New York's first commercial human sperm-bank opened Friday with semen samples from 18 men frozen in a stainless steel tank."

—*Strunk and White,* The Elements of Style

25. She was disturbed when she lay down to nap by a noisy cow.

26. "More than half of expectant mothers suffer heartburn. To minimize symptoms, suggests Donald O. Castell, M.D., of the Graduate Hospital in Philadelphia, avoid big, high-fat meals and don't lie down for three hours after eating."

—Self *magazine*

27. "Abraham Lincoln wrote the Gettysburg address while traveling from Washington to Gettysburg on the back of an envelope."

—Richard Lederer

▲ 28. "When Queen Elizabeth exposed herself before her troops, they all shouted 'harrah.'"

—Richard Lederer

29. "In one of Shakespeare's famous plays, Hamlet relieves himself in a long soliloquy."

—Richard Lederer

30. The two suspects fled the area before the officers' arrival in a white Ford Mustang, being driven by a third male.

▲ 31. "AT&T, for the life of your business."

▲ 32. The teacher of this class might have been a member of the opposite sex.

▲ 33. "Woman gets 9 years for killing 11th husband."

—Supposedly, a Headline in newspaper

34. "Average hospital costs are now an unprecedented $3,146 per day in California. Many primary plans don't pay 20% of that amount."

—AARP Group Health Insurance Program advertisement

35. "I am a huge Mustang fan."

—Ford Mustang advertisement

36. "Visitors are expected to complain at the office between the hours of 9:00 and 11:00 A.M. daily."

—Supposedly, a sign in an Athens, Greece, hotel

37. "Order your summers suit. Because is big rush we will execute customers in strict rotation."

—Supposedly, a sign in a Rhodes tailor shop

38. "Please do not feed the animals. If you have any suitable food, give it to the guard on duty."

—Supposedly, a sign at a Budapest zoo

39. "Our wines leave you with nothing to hope for."

—Supposedly, from a Swiss menu

40. "Our Promise—Good for life."

—Cheerios

41. Thinking clearly involves hard work.

42. "Cadillac—Break Through"

Exercise 3-9

Determine which of the italicized expressions are ambiguous, which are more likely to refer to the members of the class taken as a group, and which are more likely to refer to the members of the class taken individually.

Example

Narcotics are habit forming.

Answer

In this claim, *narcotics* refers to individual members of the class because it is specific narcotics that are habit forming. (One does not ordinarily become addicted to the entire class of narcotics.)

▲ 1. *Swedes* eat millions of quarts of yogurt every day.

2. *Professors at the university* make millions of dollars a year.

3. *Our amplifiers* can be heard all across the country.

▲ 4. *Students at Pleasant Valley High School* enroll in hundreds of courses each year.

5. *Cowboys* die with their boots on.

6. The *angles of a triangle* add up to 180 degrees.

▲ 7. *The New York Giants* played mediocre football last year.

8. On our airline, *passengers* have their choice of three different meals.

9. On our airline, *passengers* flew fourteen million miles last month without incident.

▲ 10. *Hundreds of people* have ridden in that taxi.

11. *All our cars* are on sale for two hundred dollars over factory invoice.

▲ 12. *Chicagoans* drink more beer than *New Yorkers*.

13. *Power lawn mowers* produce more pollution than *motorcycles*.

14. *The Baltimore Orioles* may make it to the World Series in another six or seven years.

▲ 15. *People* are getting older.

Exercise 3-10

Determine which of the following definitions are more likely designed to persuade and which are not.

1. "Punk is musical freedom. It's saying, doing and playing what you want. In Webster's terms, 'nirvana' means freedom from pain, suffering and the external world, and that's pretty close to my definition of Punk Rock."

—Kurt Cobain

2. "Congress's definition of torture . . . [is] the infliction of severe mental or physical pain."

—John Yoo

3. "Democrats' definition of 'rich'—always seems to be set just above whatever the salary happens to be for a member of Congress. Perhaps that says it all."

—Steve Steckler

4. "That is the definition of faith—acceptance of that which we imagine to be true, that which we cannot prove."

—Dan Brown

5. "Sin: That's anything that's so much fun it's difficult not to do it."

—*Dave Kilbourne*

Exercise 3-11

Make up six definitions, two of which are designed to make the thing defined look good, two of which are designed to make it look bad, and two of which are neutral.

Exercise 3-12

The sentences in this Associated Press health report have been scrambled. Rearrange them so that the report makes sense.

1. The men, usually strong with no known vices or ailments, die suddenly, uttering an agonizing groan, writhing and gasping before succumbing to the mysterious affliction.

2. Scores of cases have been reported in the United States during the past decade.

3. In the United States, health authorities call it "Sudden Unexplained Death Syndrome," or "SUDS."

4. Hundreds of similar deaths have been noted worldwide.

5. The phenomenon is known as "lai tai," or "nightmare death," in Thailand.

6. In the Philippines, it is called "bangungut," meaning "to rise and moan in sleep."

7. Health officials are baffled by a syndrome that typically strikes Asian men in their thirties while they sleep.

8. Researchers cannot say what is killing SUDS victims.

Exercise 3-13

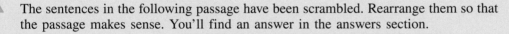

The sentences in the following passage have been scrambled. Rearrange them so that the passage makes sense. You'll find an answer in the answers section.

1. Weintraub's findings were based on a computer test of 1,101 doctors twenty-eight to ninety-two years old.

2. She and her colleagues found that the top ten scorers aged seventy-five to ninety-two did as well as the average of men under thirty-five.

3. "The test measures memory, attention, visual perception, calculation, and reasoning," she said.

4. "The studies also provide intriguing clues to how that happens," said Sandra Weintraub, a neuropsychologist at Harvard Medical School in Boston.

5. "The ability of some men to retain mental function might be related to their ability to produce a certain type of brain cell not present at birth," she said.

6. The studies show that some men manage to escape the trend of declining mental ability with age.

7. Many elderly men are at least as mentally able as the average young adult, according to recent studies.

Exercise 3-14

This billboard, one of many put up across the country in recent times, was sponsored by the local (Butte County, California) Coalition of Reason and the national United Coalition of Reason. The billboards created controversy in many towns, and as happened in many other parts of the country, at least one local billboard was vandalized. (The word "Don't" was painted over.)

In a brief essay of no more than two pages, present a case on one side or the other of this issue: Should an organization be allowed to put up billboards that many members of a community will find offensive?

Exercise 3-15

Rewrite each of the following claims in gender-neutral language.

Example

We have insufficient manpower to complete the task.

Answer

We have insufficient personnel to complete the task.

1. A student should choose his major with considerable care.
2. When a student chooses his major, he must do so carefully.
3. The true citizen understands his debt to his country.
4. If a nurse can find nothing wrong with you in her preliminary examination, she will recommend a physician to you. However, in this city the physician will wish to protect himself by having you sign a waiver.
5. You should expect to be interviewed by a personnel director. You should be cautious when talking to him.
6. The entrant must indicate that he has read the rules, that he understands them, and that he is willing to abide by them. If he has questions, then he should bring them to the attention of an official, and he will answer them.
7. A soldier should be prepared to sacrifice his life for his comrades.
8. If anyone wants a refund, he should apply at the main office and have his identification with him.

9. The person who has tried our tea knows that it will neither keep him awake nor make him jittery.

▲ 10. If any petitioner is over sixty, he (she) should have completed form E-7.

11. Not everyone has the same beliefs. One person may not wish to put himself on the line, whereas another may welcome the chance to make his view known to his friends.

12. God created man in his own image.

▲ 13. Language is nature's greatest gift to mankind.

14. Of all the animals, the most intelligent is man.

15. The common man prefers peace to war.

▲ 16. The proof must be acceptable to the rational man.

▲ 17. The Founding Fathers believed that all men are created equal.

18. Man's pursuit of happiness has led him to prefer leisure to work.

19. When the individual reaches manhood, he is able to make such decisions for himself.

▲ 20. If an athlete wants to play for the National Football League, he should have a good work ethic.

21. The new city bus service has hired several women drivers.

22. The city is also hiring firemen, policemen, and mailmen; and the city council is planning to elect a new chairman.

23. Harold Vasquez worked for City Hospital as a male nurse.

▲ 24. Most U.S. senators are men.

25. Mr. and Mrs. Macleod joined a club for men and their wives.

26. Mr. Macleod lets his wife work for the city.

▲ 27. Macleod doesn't know it, but Mrs. Macleod is a women's libber.

28. Several coeds have signed up for the seminar.

29. A judge must be sensitive to the atmosphere in his courtroom.

▲ 30. To be a good politician, you have to be a good salesman.

Classroom/Writing Exercise

This exercise is designed for use in the classroom, although your instructor may make a different kind of assignment. Consider the claim, "genetically modified food is unnatural." Many people agree or disagree with this statement even though they have only the most rudimentary idea of what it might mean. Discuss what you think might be meant by the claim, taking note of any vagueness or ambiguity that might be involved.

More Writing Exercises

Everyone, no matter how well he or she writes, can improve. And the best way to improve is to practice. Since finding a topic to write about is often the hardest part of a writing assignment, we're supplying three subjects for you to write about. For each—or whichever your instructor might assign—write a one- to two-page essay in which you clearly identify the issue (or issues), state your position on the issue (a hypothetical position if you don't have one), and give at least one good reason in support of your position. Try also to give at least one reason why the opposing position is wrong.

1. The exchange of dirty hypodermic needles for clean ones, or the sale of clean ones, is legal in many states. In such states, the transmission of HIV and hepatitis from dirty needles is down dramatically. But bills [in the California legislature] to legalize clean-needle exchanges have been stymied by the last two governors, who earnestly but incorrectly believed that the availability of clean needles would increase drug abuse. Our state, like every other state that has not yet done it, should immediately approve legislation to make clean needles available.

—Adapted from an editorial by Marsha N. Cohen,
professor of law at Hastings College of Law

2. On February 11, 2003, the Eighth Circuit Court of Appeals ruled that the state of Arkansas could force death-row prisoner Charles Laverne Singleton to take antipsychotic drugs to make him sane enough to execute. Singleton was to be executed for felony capital murder but became insane while in prison. "Medicine is supposed to heal people, not prepare them for execution. A law that asks doctors to make people well so that the government can kill them is an absurd law," said David Kaczynski, the executive director of New Yorkers Against the Death Penalty.

3. Some politicians make a lot of noise about how Canadians and others pay much less for prescription drugs than Americans do. Those who are constantly pointing to the prices and the practices of other nations when it comes to pharmaceutical drugs ignore the fact that those other nations lag far behind the United States when it comes to creating new medicines. Canada, Germany, and other countries get the benefits of American research but contribute much less than the United States does to the creation of drugs. On the surface, these countries have a good deal, but in reality everyone is worse off, because the development of new medicines is slower than it would be if worldwide prices were high enough to cover research costs.

—Adapted from an editorial by Thomas Sowell,
senior fellow at the Hoover Institution

4. If a law is unjust, but the lawmaking process can't overturn the law in a timely way, then justice demands that the law be broken.

—Paraphrase of Henry David Thoreau

4 Credibility

Raymond James Merrill was in a funk. He had broken up with his girlfriend, and he did not want to be alone. Then a website that featured "Latin singles" led him to Regina Rachid, an attractive woman with a seductive smile who lived in southern Brazil, and suddenly Merrill was in love. Desperately so, it seems. He believed everything Rachid told him and was credulous enough to make three trips to Brazil to be with her, to give her thousands of dollars in cash, and to buy her a $20,000 automobile. He even refused to blame her when thousands of dollars in unexplained charges turned up on his credit card account. Sadly, Rachid was more interested in Merrill's money than in his affection, and when he went to Brazil the third time, to get married and begin a new life, he disappeared. The story ended tragically: Merrill's strangled and burned body was found in an isolated spot several miles out of town. Rachid and two accomplices were put in jail for the crime.* The moral of the story: It can be a horrible mistake to let our needs and desires overwhelm our critical abilities when we are not sure with whom or with what we're dealing. Our focus in this chapter is on how to determine when a claim or a source of a claim is credible enough to warrant belief.

A second story, less dramatic but much more common, is about a friend of ours named Dave, who not long ago received

Students will learn to . . .

1. **Evaluate the sources of claims**

2. **Evaluate the content of claims**

3. **Evaluate the credibility of sources**

4. **Understand the influences and biases behind media messages**

5. **Understand the impact of advertising on consumer behavior**

*The whole story can be found at www.justice4raymond.org.

an email from Citibank. It notified him that there might be a problem with his credit card account and asked him to visit the bank's website to straighten things out. A link was provided to the website. When he visited the site, he was asked to confirm details of his personal information, including account numbers, Social Security number, and his mother's maiden name. The website looked exactly like the Citibank website he had visited before, with the bank's logo and other authentic-appearing details. But very shortly after this episode, he discovered that his card had paid for a new smart phone, a home theater set, and a couple of expensive car stereos, none of which he had ordered or received.

Dave was a victim of "phishing," a ploy to identify victims for identity theft and credit card fraud. The number of phishing scams continues to rise, with millions of people receiving phony emails alleging to be from eBay, PayPal, and other Internet companies as well as an assortment of banks and credit card companies. Some of these phishing expeditions threaten to suspend or close the individual's account if no response is made. Needless to say, a person should give *no credibility* to an email that purports to be from a bank or other company and asks for personal identifying information via email or a website.

There are two grounds for suspicion in cases where credibility is the issue. The first ground is the claim itself. Dave should have asked himself just how likely it is that Citibank would notify him of a problem with his account by email and would ask him for his personal identifying information. (Once again, *no* bank will approach its customers for such information by email or telephone.) The second ground for suspicion is the source of the claim. In this case, Dave believed the source was legitimate. But here's the point, one that critical thinkers are well aware of these days: *On the Internet, whether by website or email, the average person has no idea where the stuff on the computer screen comes from.* Computer experts have methods that can sometimes identify the source of an email, but most of us are very easy to mislead.

The Nigerian Advance Fee 4-1-9 Fraud: The Internet's Longest-Running Scam Is Still Running Strong

If you have an email account, chances are you've received an offer from someone in Nigeria, probably claiming to be a Nigerian civil servant, who is looking for someone just like you who has a bank account to which several millions of dollars can be sent—money that results from "overinvoicing" or "double invoicing" oil purchases or otherwise needs laundering outside the country. You will receive a generous percentage of the money for your assistance, but you will have to help a bit at the outset by sending some amount of money to facilitate the transactions, or to show *your* good faith!

This scam, sometimes called "4-1-9 Fraud," after the relevant section of Nigeria's criminal code, is now celebrating more than forty years of existence. (It operated by letter, telephone and fax before the web was up and running.) Its variations are creative and numerous. Critical thinkers immediately recognize the failure of credibility such offers have, but thousands of people have not, and from a lack of critical thinking skills or from simple greed, hundreds of millions of dollars have been lost to the perpetrators of this fraud.

To read more about this scam, google "419 scam."

Dave is no dummy; being fooled by such scams is not a sign of a lack of intelligence. His concern that his account might be suspended caused him to overlook the ominous possibility that the original request might be a fake. In other cases, such as the one described in the "4-1-9 Fraud" box, it may be wishful thinking or a touch of simple greed that causes a person to lower his or her credibility guard.

Every time we revise and update this book, we feel obliged to make our warnings about Internet fraud more severe.* And every time we seem to be borne out by events. The level of theft, fraud, duplicity, and plain old vandalism seems to rise like a constant tide. We'll have some suggestions for keeping yourself, your records, and your money safe later in the chapter. For now, just remember that you need your critical thinking lights on whenever you open your browser.

THE CLAIM AND ITS SOURCE

As indicated in the phishing story, there are two arenas in which we assess credibility: the first is that of *claims* themselves; the second is the claims' *sources*. If we're told that ducks can communicate by quacking in Morse code, we dismiss the claim immediately. Such claims lack credibility no matter where they come from. (They have no initial plausibility, a notion that will be explained later.) But the claim that ducks mate for life is not at all outrageous; it might be true: it's a credible claim.** Whether we should believe it depends on its source; if we read it in a bird book or hear it from a bird expert, we are much more likely to believe it than if we hear it from our editor, for example.

There are degrees of credibility and incredibility; they are not all-or-nothing kinds of things, whether we're talking about claims or sources. Consider the claim that a month from now everyone in the world will die in an epidemic caused by a mysterious form of bacteria. This is highly unlikely, of course, but it is not as unlikely as the claim that everyone in the world will die a month from now due to an invasion of aliens from outer space. Sources (i.e., people) vary in their credibility just as do the claims they offer. If the next-door neighbor you've always liked is arrested for bank robbery, his denials will probably seem credible to you. But he loses credibility if it turns out he owns a silencer and a .45 automatic with the serial numbers removed. Similarly, a knowledgeable friend who tells us about an investment opportunity has a bit more credibility if we learn he has invested his own money in the idea. (At least we could be assured he believed the information himself.) On the other hand, he has less credibility if we learn he will make a substantial commission from our investment in it.

So, there are always two questions to be asked about a claim with which we're presented. First, when does a *claim itself* lack credibility—that is, when does its *content* present a credibility problem? Second, when does the *source* of a claim lack credibility?

We'll turn next to the first of these questions, which deals with what a claim actually says. The general answer is

> A claim lacks inherent credibility to the extent that it conflicts with what we have observed or what we think we know—our background information—or with other credible claims.

---

*Recently, one of the authors had his bank account raided and four phony payments totaling almost $2,000 were made to his utility company. The money actually went to some private source. Both the author and his credit union were reimbursed for the loss. Moral: check accounts frequently!

**Bank vultures, swans, albatrosses, and several other species reportedly mate for life.

Just what this answer means will be explained in the section that follows. After that, we'll turn our attention to the second question we asked earlier, about the credibility of sources.

ASSESSING THE CONTENT OF THE CLAIM

So, some claims stand up on their own; they tend to be acceptable regardless of from whom we hear them. But when they fail on their own, as we've said, it's because they come into conflict either with our own observations or with what we call our "background knowledge." We'll discuss each of these in turn.

Does the Claim Conflict with Our Personal Observations?

Our own observations provide our most reliable source of information about the world. It is therefore only reasonable to be suspicious of any claim that comes into conflict with what we've observed. Imagine that Moore has just come from the home of Mr. Marquis, a mutual friend of his and Parker's, and has seen his new red Mini Cooper automobile. He meets Parker, who tells him, "I heard that Marquis has

---

Incredible Claims!

Lunatic headlines from the supermarket tabloids (as well as from "straight" newspapers) provide more fun than information. Most of the following are from the *Weekly World News.*

Statistics show that teen pregnancy drops off significantly after age 25.
[Amazing what you can prove with statistics.]

Homicide victims rarely talk to police.
[Or to anybody else.]

Starvation can lead to health hazards.
[Dr. Donohue's health column breaking new dietary ground.]

End of World Confirmed (December 20, 2012)
[Mayan archaeologists met in Guatemala and confirmed the end date of December 20, 2012.]

End of the World Postponed (December 21, 2012)
[Make up your mind.]

China Buys Grand Canyon
[They're trying to figure out how to move it nearer to Beijing.]

Aliens Abduct Cheerleaders
[They say they want to learn how to make those pyramids.]

When Personal Observation Fails . . .

According to the Innocence Project, a group in New York that investigates wrongful convictions, eyewitness misidentification is the single greatest cause of conviction of innocent persons. Of all the convictions overturned by DNA analysis, witness misidentification played a role in over 75 percent. Of the first 239 DNA exonerations, 62 percent of the defendants were misidentified by one witness; in 25 percent of the cases, the defendant was misidentified by two witnesses; and *in 13 percent of the cases the same innocent defendant was misidentified by three or more separate eyewitnesses.* Even though eyewitness testimony can be persuasive before a judge and jury, it may be *much* more unreliable than we generally give it credit for being.

From http://www.innocenceproject.org/causes-wrongful-conviction/the-science-behind-eyewitness-identification-reform.

bought a new Mini Cooper, a bright blue one." Moore does not need critical thinking training to reject Parker's claim about the color of the car, because of the obvious conflict with his earlier observation.

But observations and short-term memory are far from infallible. Stories abound of recalled observations that turned out to be mistaken, from cases of surgeons operating on the wrong limb of a patient to, most notoriously, cases in which witnesses misidentified the perpetrators of a crime. The box above, "When Personal Observation Fails . . ." gives startling statistics about innocent persons being wrongly convicted as a result of faulty eyewitness identifications.

Our observations and our recollections of them can go wrong for all manner of reasons. An observer might be tired, distracted, worried about an unrelated matter, emotionally upset, feeling ill, and so on. (A crime victim would be an extreme example of such a person!) Further, such physical conditions as bad lighting, noise, and speed of events can affect our observations.

It's also important to remember that people are not all created equal when it comes to making observations. We hate to say it, dear reader, but there are lots of people who see better, hear better, and remember better than you. Of course, that goes for us as well.

Our beliefs, hopes, fears, and expectations affect our observations. Tell us that a house is infested with fleas, we are apt to see every little black bug as a flea. Inform someone who believes in ghosts that a house is haunted, and she may well believe she sees evidence of ghosts.* At séances staged by the Society for Psychical Research to test the observational powers of people under séance conditions, some observers insist that they see numerous phenomena that simply do not exist.** Teachers who are told that the students in a particular class are brighter than usual may be apt to believe that the work those students produce is better than average, even when it is not.

In Chapter 6, we discuss a very common error called *wishful thinking,* which occurs when we allow hopes and desires to influence our judgment and color our beliefs. Most of the people who fall for the 4-1-9 Fraud Internet scam (see the box on page 94) are almost surely victims of wishful thinking. It is unlikely that somebody, somewhere, wants to send you millions of dollars just because you have a bank account and that the money the person asks for really is just to facilitate the transaction. The most gullible victim, with no stake in the matter, would probably realize this. But the idea of getting one's hands on a great pile of money can blind a person to even the most obvious facts.

Our personal interests and biases affect our perceptions and the judgments we base on them. We overlook many of the mean and selfish actions of the people we like or love—and when we are infatuated with someone, everything that person does seems wonderful. By contrast, people we detest can hardly do anything that we don't perceive

Incredible but True

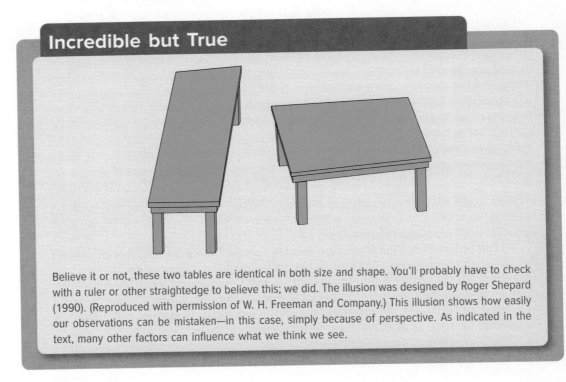

Believe it or not, these two tables are identical in both size and shape. You'll probably have to check with a ruler or other straightedge to believe this; we did. The illusion was designed by Roger Shepard (1990). (Reproduced with permission of W. H. Freeman and Company.) This illusion shows how easily our observations can be mistaken—in this case, simply because of perspective. As indicated in the text, many other factors can influence what we think we see.

---

*C. E. M. Hansel, *Parapsychology, A Scientific Evaluation.*
**Ibid.

as mean and selfish. If we desperately wish for the success of a project, we are likely to see more evidence for that success than is actually present. On the other hand, if we wish for a project to fail, we may exaggerate flaws that we see in it or imagine flaws that are not there at all. If a job, chore, or decision is one that we wish to avoid, we tend to draw worst-case implications from it and thus come up with reasons for not doing it. However, if we are predisposed to want to do the job or make the decision, we are more likely to focus on whatever positive consequences it might have.

Finally, as we hinted earlier, above, the reliability of our observations is no better than the reliability of our memories, except in those cases where we have the means at our disposal to record our observations. And memory, as most of us know, can be deceptive. Critical thinkers are always alert to the possibility that what they remember having observed may not be what they did observe.

But even though firsthand observations are not infallible, they are still the best source of information we have. Any report that conflicts with our own direct observations is subject to serious doubt.

Does the Claim Conflict with Our Background Information?

Reports must always be evaluated against our **background information**—that immense body of justified beliefs that consists of facts we learn from our own direct observations and facts we learn from others. Such information is "background" because we may not be able to specify where we learned it, unlike something we know because we witnessed it this morning. Much of our background information is well confirmed by a variety of sources. Reports that conflict with this store of information are usually quite properly dismissed, even if we cannot disprove them through direct observation. We immediately reject the claim "Palm trees grow in abundance near the North Pole," even though we are not in a position to confirm or disprove the statement by direct observation.

Indeed, this is an example of how we usually treat claims when we first encounter them: We begin by assigning them a certain **initial plausibility,** a rough assessment of how credible a claim seems to us. This assessment depends on how consistent the claim is with our background information—how well it "fits" with that information. If it fits very well, we give the claim some reasonable degree of initial plausibility— there is a reasonable expectation of its being true. If, however, the claim conflicts with our background information, we give it low initial plausibility and lean toward rejecting it unless very strong evidence can be produced on its behalf. The claim "More guitars were sold in the United States last year than saxophones" fits very well with the background information most of us share, and we would hardly require detailed evidence before accepting it. However, the claim "Charlie's eighty-seven-year-old grandmother swam across Lake Michigan in the middle of winter" cannot command much initial plausibility because of the obvious way it conflicts with our background information about eighty-seven-year-old people, about Lake Michigan, about swimming in cold water, and so on. In fact, short of observing the swim ourselves, it isn't clear just what *could* persuade us to accept such a claim. And even then, we should consider the likelihood that we're being tricked or fooled by an illusion.

Obviously, not every oddball claim is as outrageous as the one about Charlie's grandmother. Several years ago, we read a report about a house being stolen in Lindale, Texas—a brick house. This certainly is implausible—how could anyone steal a home? Yet there is credible documentation that it happened,* and even stranger things

There are three types of men in the world. One type learns from books. One type learns from observation. And one type just has to urinate on the electric fence.

—DR. LAURA SCHLESSINGER
(reported by Larry Englemann)

The authority of experience.

---
*Associated Press report, March 25, 2005.

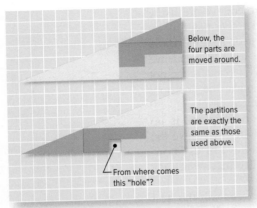

Below, the four parts are moved around.

The partitions are exactly the same as those used above.

From where comes this "hole"?

■ This optical illusion has made the rounds on the web. It takes a very close look to identify how the illusion works, although it's *certain* that *something* sneaky is going on here. The problem is solved in the answers section at the back of the book.

occasionally turn out to be true. That, of course, means that it can be worthwhile to check out implausible claims if their being true might be of consequence to you.

Unfortunately, there are no neat formulas that can resolve conflicts between what you already believe and new information. Your job as a critical thinker is to trust your background information when considering claims that conflict with that information—that is, claims with low initial plausibility—but at the same time to keep an open mind and realize that further information may cause you to give up a claim you had thought was true. It's a difficult balance, but it's worth getting right. For example, let's say you've been suffering from headaches and have tried all the usual methods of relief: aspirin, antihistamines, whatever your physician has recommended, and so on. Finally, a friend tells you that she had headaches that were very similar to yours, and nothing worked for her, either, until she had an aromatherapy treatment. Then, just a few minutes into her aromatherapy session, her headaches went away. Now, we (Moore and Parker) are not much inclined to believe that smelling oils will make your headache disappear, but we think there is little to lose and at least a small possibility of something substantial to be gained by giving the treatment a try. It may be, for example, that the treatment relaxes a person and relieves tension, which can cause headaches. We wouldn't go into it with great expectations, however.

The point is that there is a scale of initial plausibility ranging from quite plausible to only slightly so. Our aromatherapy example would fall somewhere between the plausible (and in fact true) claim that Parker went to high school with Bill Clinton and the rather implausible claim that Kim Kardashian has a PhD in physics.

As mentioned, background information is essential to adequately assess a claim. It is difficult to evaluate a report if you lack background information relating

Fib Wizards

In *The Sleeping Doll,* novelist Jeffery Deaver invents a character who is incredibly adept at reading what people are thinking from watching and listening to them. This is fiction, but there seems to be at least a bit of substance to the claim that such talents exist.

After testing 13,000 people for their ability to detect deception, Professor Maureen O'Sullivan of the University of San Francisco identified 31 who have an unusual ability to tell when someone is lying to them. These "wizards," as she calls them, are especially sensitive to body language, facial expressions, hesitations in speech, slips of the tongue, and similar clues that a person may not be telling the truth. The wizards are much better than the average person at noticing these clues and inferring the presence of a fib from them.

Professor O'Sullivan presented her findings to the American Medical Association's 23rd Annual Science Reporters Conference.

Maybe a few people can reliably tell when someone is lying. But we'd bet there are many more who merely *think* they can do this. We want to play poker with them.

From an Associated Press report.

to the topic. This means the broader your background information, the more likely you are to be able to evaluate any given report effectively. You'd have to know a little economics to evaluate assertions about the dangers of a large federal deficit, and knowing how Social Security works can help you know what's misleading about calling it a savings account. Read widely, converse freely, and develop an inquiring attitude; there's no substitute for broad, general knowledge.

▲   —See the answers section at the back of the book.

Exercise 4-1

1. The text points out that physical conditions around us can affect our observations. List at least four such conditions.

2. Our own mental state can affect our observations as well. Describe at least three of the ways this can happen, as mentioned in the text.

3. According to the text, there are two ways credibility should enter into our evaluation of a claim. What are they?

4. A claim lacks inherent credibility, according to the text, when it conflicts with what?

5. Our most reliable source of information about the world is _____.

6. The reliability of our observations is not better than the reliability of _____.

7. True/False: Initial plausibility is an all-or-nothing characteristic; that is, a claim either has it or it doesn't.

▲   In your judgment, are any of these claims less credible than others? Discuss your opinions with others in the class to see if any interesting differences in background information emerge.

Exercise 4-2

1. They've taught crows how to play poker.

2. The center of Earth consists of water.

3. Stevie Wonder is just faking his blindness.

4. The car manufacturers already can build cars that get more than 100 miles per gallon; they just won't do it because they're in cahoots with the oil industry.

5. If you force yourself to go for five days and nights without any sleep, you'll be able to get by on less than five hours of sleep a night for the rest of your life.

6. It is possible to read other people's minds through mental telepathy.

7. A diet of mushrooms and pecans supplies all necessary nutrients and will help you lose weight. Scientists don't understand why.

8. Somewhere on the planet is a person who looks exactly like you.

9. The combined wealth of the world's 225 richest people equals the total annual income of the poorest 2.5 billion people, which is nearly half the world's total population.

10. The *Kansas City Star* has reported that the Kansas Anti-Zombie Militia is preparing for a zombie apocalypse. A spokesperson said, "If you're ready for zombies, you're ready for anything."

11. Daddy longlegs are the world's most poisonous spider, but their mouths are too small to bite.

12. Static electricity from your body can cause your gas tank to explode if you slide across your seat while fueling and then touch the gas nozzle.

13. Japanese scientists have created a device that measures the tone of a dog's bark to determine what the dog's mood is.

14. Barack Obama (a) is a socialist, (b) is a Muslim, (c) was not born in the United States.

15. Hugh Hefner, founder of *Playboy* magazine, was eighty-seven years old when he married Crystal Harris, who was twenty-seven at the time.

THE CREDIBILITY OF SOURCES

We turn now from the credibility of claims themselves to the credibility of the sources from which we get them. We are automatically suspicious of certain sources of information. (If you were getting a divorce, you wouldn't ordinarily turn to your spouse's attorney for advice.) We'll look at several factors that should influence how much credence we give to a source.

Interested Parties

Gold and silver are money,
Everything else is credit.

—J. P. MORGAN

We'll begin with a very important general rule for deciding whom to trust. Our rule makes use of two correlative concepts, interested parties and disinterested parties:

> A person who stands to gain from our belief in a claim is known as an **interested party,** and interested parties must be viewed with much more suspicion than **disinterested parties,** who have no stake in our belief one way or another.

Not All That Glitters

When the U.S. dollar began to decline seriously in about 2004, quite a few financial "experts" claimed that gold is one of the few ways to protect one's wealth and provide a hedge against inflation. Some of their arguments make some good sense, but it's worth pointing out that many of the people advocating the purchase of gold turn out to be brokers of precious metals themselves, or are hired by such brokers to sell their product. As we emphasize in the text: Always beware of interested parties!

It would be hard to overestimate the importance of this rule—in fact, if you were to learn only one thing from this book, this would be a good candidate. Of course, not all interested parties are out to hoodwink us, and certainly not all disinterested parties have good information. But, all things considered, the rule of trusting the latter before the former is a crucially important weapon in the critical thinking armory.

We'll return to this topic later, both in the text and in some exercises.

Physical and Other Characteristics

The feature of being an interested or disinterested party is highly relevant to whether he, she, it, or they should be trusted. Unfortunately, we often base our judgments on irrelevant considerations. Physical characteristics, for example, tell us little about a person's credibility or its lack. Does a person look you in the eye? Does he perspire a lot? Does he have a nervous laugh? Despite being generally worthless in this regard, such characteristics are widely used in sizing up a person's credibility. Simply being taller, louder, and more assertive can enhance a person's credibility, according to a Stanford study.* A practiced con artist can imitate a confident teller of the truth, just as an experienced hacker can cobble up a genuine-appearing website. ("Con," after all, is short for "confidence.")

Other irrelevant features we sometimes use to judge a person's credibility include gender, age, ethnicity, accent, and mannerisms. People also make credibility judgments

Does Your Face Give You Away?

Some researchers, like Alan Stevens in Australia, believe that conclusions about your character and health can be drawn from your facial structures. Here are some examples:

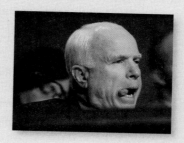

Face width: A man with a wide face (they say) generally has higher levels of testosterone and is more likely to be aggressive than one with a narrower face.

Cheek size: Fuller cheeks (they say) may indicate a person's greater likelihood of catching illnesses and infections. According to Benedict Jones at Glasgow University, larger-cheeked people are more likely to be depressed or anxious.

Nose size and shape: A large nose supposedly indicates a person is ambitious, confident, and self-reliant, a born leader. People who have neutral nose tips—neither round nor sharp—are said to be sweet, mild-tempered, and have endearing personalities.

We have our doubts. There may be weak associations between genetically determined facial structures and not-entirely-genetically-determined character traits, but we don't need to look at Santa's nose to know he is sweet.

From http://www.bustle.com/articles/110866-what-your-facial-features-say-about-you-according-to-science.
Also see *In Your Face: What Facial Features Reveal About People You Know and Love,* by Bill Cordingley.

*The study, conducted by Professor Lara Tiedens of the Stanford University Graduate School of Business, was reported in *USA Today,* July 18, 2007.

on the basis of the clothes a person wears. A friend told one of us that one's sunglasses "make a statement"; maybe so, but that statement doesn't say much about credibility. A person's occupation certainly bears a relationship to his or her knowledge or abilities, but as a guide to moral character or truthfulness, it is hardly reliable.

Which considerations are relevant to judging someone's credibility? We will get to these in a moment, but appearance isn't one of them. You may have the idea that you can size up a person just by looking into his or her eyes. This is a mistake. Just by looking at someone, we cannot ascertain that person's truthfulness, knowledge, or character. (Although this is generally true, there may be rare exceptions. See the "Fib Wizards" box on page 100.)

Of course, we sometimes get in trouble even when we accept credible claims from credible sources. Many rely, for example, on credible advice from qualified and honest professionals in preparing our tax returns. But qualified and honest professionals can make honest mistakes, and we can suffer the consequences. In general, however, trouble is much more likely if we accept either doubtful claims from credible sources or credible claims from doubtful sources (not to mention doubtful claims from doubtful sources). If a mechanic says we need a new transmission, the claim itself may not be suspicious—maybe the car we drive has many miles on it; maybe we neglected routine maintenance; maybe it isn't shifting smoothly. But remember that the mechanic is an interested party; if there's any reason to suspect he or she would exaggerate the problem to get work, we'd get a second opinion.

One of your authors has an automobile which the dealership said had an oil leak it would cost almost a thousand dollars to fix. Because he'd not seen oil on his garage floor, your cautious author decided to wait to see how serious the problem was. Well, a year after the "problem" was diagnosed, there was still no oil on the garage floor, and the car had used less than half a quart of oil, about what one would have expected over the course of a year. What to conclude? The dealership is an interested party. If its service rep convinces your author that the oil leak is serious, the dealership makes almost a thousand dollars. This makes it worth a second opinion, or, in this case, the author's own investigation. He now believes his car will never need this thousand-dollar repair.

> Remember: Interested parties are less credible than other sources of claims.

I looked the man in the eye. I found him to be very straightforward and trustworthy. We had a very good dialogue. I was able to sense his soul.

—GEORGE W. BUSH, commenting on his first meeting with Russian president Vladimir Putin

Bush later changed his mind about Putin, seeing him as a threat to democracy. So much for the "blink" method of judging credibility.

War-Making Policies and Interested Parties

In the 1960s, the secretary of defense supplied carefully selected information to President Lyndon Johnson and to Congress. Would Congress have passed the Gulf of Tonkin Resolution, which authorized the beginning of the Vietnam War, if its members had known that the secretary of defense was determined to begin hostilities there? We don't know, but certainly they and the president should have been more suspicious if they had known this fact. Would President Bush and his administration have been so anxious to make war on Iraq if they had known that Ahmad Chalabi, one of their main sources of information about that country and its ruler, Saddam Hussein, was a very interested party? (He hoped to be the next ruler of Iraq if Hussein were overthrown, and much of his information turned out to be false or exaggerated.) We don't know that either, of course. But it's possible that more suspicion of interested parties may have slowed our commitment to two costly wars.

Expertise

Much of our information comes from people about whom we have no reason to suspect prejudice, bias, or any of the other features that make interested parties bad sources. However, we might still doubt a source's actual knowledge of an issue in question. A source's knowledge depends on a number of factors, especially expertise and experience. Just as you generally cannot tell merely by looking at a source whether he or she is speaking truthfully, objectively, and accurately, you can't judge his or her knowledge or expertise by looking at surface features. A British-sounding scientist may appear more knowledgeable than a scientist who speaks, say, with a Texas drawl, but accent, height, gender, ethnicity, and clothing don't bear on a person's knowledge. In the municipal park in our town, it can be difficult to distinguish people who teach at the university from people who live in the park, based on physical appearance.

So, then, how do you judge a person's **expertise?** Education and experience are often the most important factors, followed by accomplishments, reputation, and position, in no particular order. It is not always easy to evaluate the credentials of a source, and credentials vary considerably from one field to another. Still, there are useful guidelines worth mentioning.

Education includes, but is not strictly limited to, formal education—the possession of degrees from established institutions of learning. (Some "doctors" of this and that received their diplomas from mail-order houses that advertise on matchbook covers. The title "doctor" is not automatically a qualification.)

Experience—both the kind and the amount—is an important factor in expertise. Experience is important if it is relevant to the issue at hand, but the mere fact that someone has been on the job for a long time does not automatically make him or her good at it.

Accomplishments are an important indicator of someone's expertise but, once again, only when those accomplishments are directly related to the question at hand. A Nobel Prize winner in physics is not necessarily qualified to speak publicly about toy safety, public school education (even in science), or nuclear proliferation. The last issue may involve physics, it's true, but the political issues are the crucial ones, and they are not taught in physics labs.

A person's reputation is obviously very important as a criterion of his or her expertise. But reputations must be seen in a context; how much importance we should attach to somebody's reputation depends on the people among whom the person has that reputation. You may have a strong reputation as a pool player among the denizens of your local pool hall, but that doesn't necessarily put you in the same league with Allison Fisher. Among a group of people who know nothing about investments, someone who knows the difference between a 401(k) plan and a Roth IRA may seem like quite an expert. But you certainly wouldn't want to take investment advice from somebody simply on that basis.

Most of us have met people who were recommended as experts in some field but who turned out to know little more about that field than we ourselves knew. (Presumably, in such cases those doing the recommending knew even less about the subject, or they would not have been so quickly impressed.) By and large, the kind of reputation that counts most is the one a person has among other experts in his or her field of endeavor.

The positions people hold provide an indication of how well *somebody* thinks of them. The director of an important scientific laboratory, the head of an academic department at Harvard, the author of a work consulted by other experts—in each case the position itself is substantial evidence that the individual's opinion on a relevant subject warrants serious attention.

But expertise can be bought. Our earlier discussion of interested parties applies to people who possess real expertise on a topic as well as to the rest of us. Sometimes a person's position is an indication of what his or her opinion, expert or not, is likely to be. The opinion of a lawyer retained by the National Rifle Association, offered at a hearing on firearms and urban violence, should be scrutinized much more carefully (or at least viewed with more skepticism) than that of a witness from an independent firm or agency that has no stake in the outcome of the hearings. The former can be assumed to be an interested party, the latter not. It is too easy to lose objectivity where one's interests and concerns are at stake, even if one is *trying* to be objective.

Here's a more complicated story: In the 1960s and 1970s, a national concern arose about the relationship between the consumption of sugar and several serious conditions, including diabetes and heart disease. An artificial sweetener, cyclamate, was introduced to replace sugar in sodas and other products. The sugar industry, afraid of lost sales, countered with an assault on cyclamates, and Dr. John Hickson led the charge. Later, when Hickson was research director of the Cigar Research Council, he was described in a confidential memo as "a supreme scientific politician who had been successful in condemning cyclamates, on behalf of the Sugar Research Council, on somewhat shaky evidence."* The substance was banned by the FDA in 1969. A quick web search on "cyclamate ban" will reveal the story: By 1989, FDA officials were admitting they had made a mistake in issuing the ban, which was done under pressure from the U.S. Congress, which in turn was pressured by the sugar industry.

The moral of this story is that politics, and interested parties with deep pockets, can and do influence findings that are supposed to be entirely scientific.

Experts sometimes disagree, especially when the issue is complicated and many different interests are at stake. In these cases, a critical thinker is obliged to suspend judgment about which expert to endorse, unless one expert clearly represents a majority viewpoint among experts in the field or *unless one expert can be established as more authoritative or less biased than the others.*

Of course, majority opinions sometimes turn out to be incorrect, and even the most authoritative experts occasionally make mistakes. For example, various economics experts predicted good times ahead just before the Great Depression. The same was true for many advisers right up until the 2008 financial meltdown. Jim Denny, the manager of the Grand Ole Opry, fired Elvis Presley after one performance, stating that Presley wasn't going anywhere and ought to go back to driving a truck. A claim you accept because it represents the majority viewpoint or comes from the most authoritative expert may turn out to be thoroughly wrong. Nevertheless, take heart: At the time, you were rationally justified in accepting the majority viewpoint as the most authoritative claim. The reasonable position is the one that agrees with the most authoritative opinion but allows for enough open-mindedness to change if the evidence changes.

Finally, we sometimes make the mistake of thinking that whatever qualifies someone as an expert in one field automatically qualifies that person in other areas.

---

*http://legacy.library.ucsf.edu/tid/bon57a99.

Not Paying Attention to Experts Can Be Deadly

David Pawlik called the fire department in Cleburne, Texas, in July to ask if the "blue flames" he and his wife were seeing every time she lit a cigarette were dangerous, and an inspector said he would be right over and for Mrs. Pawlik not to light another cigarette. However, anxious about the imminent inspection, she lit up and was killed in the subsequent explosion. (The home was all electric, but there had been a natural gas leak underneath the yard.)

—*Fort Worth Star Telegram,* July 11, 2007

Sometimes it is *crucial* that you take the word of an expert.

Being a top-notch programmer, for example, might not be an indication of top-notch management skills. Indeed, many programmers get good at what they do by shying away from dealing with other people—or so the stereotype runs. Being a good campaigner may not always translate into being a good office-holder. Even if the intelligence and skill required to become an expert in one field could enable someone to become an expert in any field—which is doubtful—having the ability to become an expert is not the same as actually being an expert. Claims put forth by experts about subjects outside their fields are not automatically more acceptable than claims put forth by nonexperts.

Exercise 4-3

A. List as many factors as you can think of that are unreliable indicators of a source's truthfulness (e.g., the firmness of a handshake).
B. List as many factors as you can that *are* reliable.

Exercise 4-4

A. List as many factors as you can think of that often are mistakenly taken as reliable signs of expertise on the part of a source (e.g., appearing self-confident).
B. List as many factors as you can that are reliable indicators of a source's expertise.

Exercise 4-5

Expertise doesn't transfer automatically from one field to another: Being an expert in one area does not automatically qualify a person as an expert (or even as competent) in other areas. Is it the same with dishonesty? Many people think dishonesty does transfer, that being dishonest in one area automatically discredits that person in all areas. For example, when Bill Clinton lied about having sexual encounters with his intern, some said he couldn't be trusted about anything.

If someone is known to have been dishonest about one thing, should we automatically be suspicious of his or her honesty regarding other things? In a short paper of no more than two pages, defend your answer to this question.

Exercise 4-6

1. In a sentence, describe the crucial difference between an interested party and a disinterested party.
2. Which of the two parties mentioned in item 1 should generally be considered more trustworthy? Why?
3. Invent an issue, and then identify someone who would likely be an interested party regarding that issue; then identify someone who is likely *not* to be an interested party. Explain why in each case.

Exercise 4-7 ▲

Suppose you're in the market for a new television, and you're looking for advice as to what to buy. Identify which of the following persons or subjects is likely to be an interested party and which is not.

1. a flyer from a local store that sells televisions
2. the *Consumer Reports* website
3. a salesperson at a local electronics store
4. the Sony website
5. an article in a major newspaper about television, including some rankings of brands

Now let's say you've narrowed your search to two brands: LG and Panasonic. Which of the following are more likely interested parties?

6. a friend who owns an LG
7. a friend who used to own a Panasonic and now owns an LG
8. a salesperson at a store that sells both Panasonic and LG

CREDIBILITY AND THE NEWS MEDIA

The First Amendment to the U.S. Constitution was designed to encourage a free press—freedom for journalists and publications to print (and, now, to broadcast on the airwaves or the Internet) whatever they found that would enhance public opinion. The importance of such a free press was emphasized in a famous quotation from President Thomas Jefferson: "The only security of all is in a free press. The force of public opinion cannot be resisted when permitted freely to be expressed. The agitation it produces must be submitted to. It is necessary, to keep the waters pure."*

But the waters have become less pure over the last few decades, and the press has fallen on hard times. The newspaper industry shrank to less than half of what it was at the turn of this century—and this in less than fifteen years! Consumption of news on the web and on cells seemingly increases by the hour. But it is possible people no longer believe as much of what they read or see—unless they're getting news from a source that caters to their own personal beliefs. Among other things, we'll look next at reasons why confidence in the mainstream media seems to be eroding.

Consolidation of Media Ownership

Although it is not well known to most citizens, the media have become controlled by fewer and fewer corporations, the result of many mergers and buyouts over the past three or so decades. Since 2001, when the Federal Communications Commission loosened the regulations regarding ownership of newspapers, radio stations, and television stations, the concentration of media in fewer and fewer hands has been accelerating. From thousands of independent media outlets in the mid-twentieth century, media ownership dropped to only fifty companies by 1983. As we write this, approximately 90 percent of all media companies in the United States were controlled by just five companies: Time Warner (Warner Bros., Time, Inc., HBO, CNN, etc.), Disney (ABC, ESPN, Miramax Films, etc.), News Corp. (Fox Television, Wall Street Journal, New York Post, etc.), Comcast (NBC, Universal Studios, E! Entertainment Television, etc.), and Viacom/CBS (Paramount Pictures, MTV, Comedy Central, etc.). The subsidiaries listed in parentheses are only a tiny portion of these companies' holdings.** No matter what you see on television, the great likelihood is that one or more of these companies had a hand in producing it or getting it onto your screen. The fewer hands that control the media, the easier it is for the news we get to be "managed"—either by the owners themselves or by their commercial advertisers or even, as we'll next see, by the government.

Government Management of the News

For a while there, our only known source of *fake* news was *The Daily Show*. But the federal government got into the fake news business as well. In recent years, a number of fake news reports, paid for by the government, have appeared on television touting the virtues of government schemes from the prescription drug program to airport safety to education programs. No criticism of the programs was included, and no mention was made that these were not legitimate independent news reports but rather were produced by the very same governmental departments that implemented the policies in question.

---

*See, among other places, http://famguardian.org/Subjects/Politics/thomasjefferson/jeff1600.htm.

**For a more thorough treatment, see www.freepress.net/ownership chart.

"The online version just doesn't offer as much coverage as printed media."

These practices provide material for stations that cannot afford to produce a full plate of news themselves, which includes many, many stations across the country. Unfortunately, many viewers accept as news what is essentially official propaganda.

Leaving aside news reporting, problems also crop up on the op-ed page. Opinion and editorial pages and television commentaries are usually presumed to present the opinions of the writers or speakers who write or speak in them. But, as it turned out, some of those are bought and paid for as well. Our favorite example turned up in 2005: Syndicated columnist Michael McManus was paid $10,000 by the Department of Health and Human Services for writing positively about one of its programs. Ironically enough, his column is titled "Ethics and Religion."

The military has had its own methods for managing the media, from not allowing photographs to be taken of the coffins of slain American soldiers when they were being brought home from Iraq to more elaborately produced examples, such as the highly staged rescue of Private Jessica Lynch from an Iraqi hospital in 2003. Sometimes management takes the form of simple suppression of news, as when it took a whistle-blower to finally make public the video of a 2007 helicopter attack that killed a news photographer, his driver, and several others in Iraq.

It's Up to Me and Fox News

In early 2013, as a bipartisan group of senators announced a plan for immigration reform, radio host Rush Limbaugh took to the air to denounce their proposal. "I don't know that there's any stopping this," he said. "It's up to me and Fox News."

Wait. Isn't Fox News supposed to be "fair and balanced"?

Bias Within the Media

It is commonly said that the media are biased politically. Conservatives are convinced that they have a liberal bias and liberals are convinced the bias favors conservatives.

The usual basis for the conservative assessment is that, generally speaking, reporters and editors are more liberal than the general population. Indeed, several polls have indicated that this is the case. On the other hand, the publishers and owners of media outlets tend to be conservative—not surprisingly, since they have an orientation that places a higher value on the bottom line: They are in business to make a profit. A book by Eric Alterman* argues that the "liberal media" has always been a myth and that, at least in private, well-known conservatives like Patrick Buchanan and William Kristol are willing to admit it. On the other hand, Bernard Goldberg, formerly of CBS, argues that the liberal bias of the press is a fact.**

Making an assessment on this score is several miles beyond our scope here. But it is important to be aware that a reporter or a columnist or a broadcaster who draws conclusions without presenting sufficient evidence is no more to be believed than some guy from down the street, even if the conclusions happen to correspond nicely to your own bias—indeed, *especially* if they correspond to your own bias!

What is important to remember is that there are many forces at work in the preparation of news besides a desire to publish or broadcast the whole truth. That said, our view is that the major network news organizations are generally credible, exceptions like those noted notwithstanding. We especially prefer the Public Broadcasting System and National Public Radio; others have different preferences. Also in our view, the printed media, the *New York Times*, the *Washington Post*,

Bias in the universities? According to Lou Dobbs, former CNN news anchor (now with Fox Business News), citing a *Washington Post* survey, 72 percent of collegiate faculty across the country say they are liberal; 15 percent say they are conservative. At "elite" universities, 87 percent say they are liberal, and 3 percent say they are conservative.

*What Liberal Bias? (New York: Basic Books, 2003).
**Bias (Washington, DC: Regnery Publishing, 2001).

Media Bias?

Mainstream media, or "lame stream" as Sarah Palin prefers it, came under increased attack during the [2012] presidential campaign, mostly among conservatives who railed against a perceived liberal tilt.

"It goes without saying that there is definitely media bias," said Paul Ryan on the stump, claiming that most people in media "want a left-of-center president." Fox News commentator Bill O'Reilly surmised that liberal bias in media gave President Obama a 3 or 4 percentage point boost, enough to have determined the outcome.

But what are today's mainstream media? The most popular news channel is Fox News; the most powerful radio talk hosts are Rush Limbaugh and Sean Hannity; and among the Internet's loudest information voices is The Drudge Report—all severely conservative. In terms of audience and influence, these outlets are about as mainstream as it gets.

Newspapers are certainly in the mainstream, but they've always been divided politically, starting with two of the nation's biggest dailies, the conservative *Wall Street Journal* and the liberal *New York Times*. In the [2012] election, the nation's 100 largest papers split almost evenly in endorsements for Obama and Romney. Romney even won more swing state newspaper endorsements, 24 to 15, according to analysis by the Poynter organization.

It seems reasonable to assume that any paper that endorsed Romney was not likely to be simultaneously biased in favor of Obama. Yet, that is what some conservatives seem to be suggesting.

Then there are legacy broadcast networks—specifically the news departments of CBS, NBC and ABC, and their principal TV news anchors. Diane Sawyer of ABC once worked for Richard Nixon; neither Brian Williams of NBC nor Scott Pelley of CBS has ever dabbled in government or politics. In my view, having worked for two of these companies, network news personnel actually bend over backwards—at times too far—trying to avoid even a hint of bias. And having written for the nation's three largest papers, I conclude that most bias is confined to the opinion pages, where it belongs.

However, the media landscape is changing in ways that do, indeed, involve bias. It's the overt posturing of Fox News Channel on the right, MSNBC on the left, and dozens of opinion-based Internet sites serving both sides. What these outlets share is an obsessive desire to protest each other's slanted reporting.

Republicans tend to distrust media more than Democrats. According to Pew polling, Republican respondents gave only two news sources high credibility ratings: Fox News and local TV news. Democrats gave high marks to a much longer list of broadcasters and newspapers.

. . .

When it comes to actual bias, there's significantly more of it in new media than in legacy media. Meanwhile, the mainstream is gradually becoming a collection of smaller streams—the most influential of which are divided politically, and even lean toward the conservative side. It's ironic that protesting by conservatives over media bias is growing in direct proportion to the emerging power of those on the right to shape media content.

. . .

Funt, Peter, "Examining Media 'Bias,'" Monterey County Herald, December 7, 2012.

the *Los Angeles Times,* and other major newspapers are generally credible, even though mistakes are sometimes made here as well. News magazines fall in the same category: usually credible but with occasional flaws.

For several years, cable news had a great influence on what became news. CNN (which stands, unsurprisingly, for "Cable News Network") began in 1980 as the first twenty-four-hours-a-day news broadcaster. Fox News and MSNBC now also compete for viewers' attention both day and night. While spreading across the hours of the day, these networks have also spread across the political spectrum. You can now find "news" that satisfies nearly any political bias. What's more, with the need to fill screens for so many hours, the notion of what actually counts as news has had to be expanded. The result has affected not just the cable networks but traditional news programs as well: "Feature stories" from prison life to restaurant kitchen tours take up more and more space that used to be devoted to so-called hard news. One of our northern California newspapers, the *Sacramento Bee,* did a story on how "silly news" was taking up more and more space in local news programs. Ben Bagdikian, author and former dean of the Graduate School of Journalism at the University of California, Berkeley, has pointed out that a commercial for Pepsi-Cola seems to connect better after a fluff piece or a sitcom than after a serious piece on, say, massacres in Rwanda or an ambush in the Middle East.*

It would be difficult to boil down our advice regarding accepting claims from the news media, but it would certainly include keeping the following points in mind:

> Like the rest of us, people in the news media sometimes make mistakes; they sometimes accept claims with insufficient evidence or without confirming the credibility of a source.
>
> The media are subject to pressure and sometimes to manipulation from government and other news sources.
>
> The media, with few exceptions, are driven in part by the necessity to make a profit, and this can bring pressure from advertisers, owners, and managers.

Finally, we might remember that the news media are to a great extent a reflection of the society at large. If we the public are willing to get by with superficial, sensationalist, or manipulated news, then we can rest assured that, eventually, that's all the news we'll get.

Talk Radio

On the surface, talk radio seems to offer a wealth of information not available in news reports from conventional sources. And at least some talk radio hosts employ people to scour traditional legitimate news sources for information relevant to their political agenda, and to the extent that they document the source, which they often do, they provide listeners with many interesting and important facts. But radio hosts from all sides are given to distortion, misplaced emphasis, and bias with regard to selection of which facts to report. And, really, the shouting gives us a headache.

Advocacy Television

We mentioned earlier that some cable networks have moved left while others have moved right on the political spectrum, so the news you can expect from them comes

---

*Interview on *Frontline,* http://www.pbs.org/wgbh/pages/frontline/smoke/interviews/bagdikian.html.

with a predictable slant. This is good insofar as it exposes people to opinions different from their own; it is not so good insofar as it simply reinforces what the viewer already believes, especially if there is no evidence offered in support of the opinions.

MSNBC offers *All In with Chris Hayes, The Last Word with Lawrence O'Donnell,* and *The Rachel Maddow Show,* all of which offer a liberal perspective on the news of the day, and all of which editorialize from that perspective.

Fox News features Bill O'Reilly, Sean Hannity, and Megyn Kelly, who represent various conservative constituencies and do something similar from the other side.

We could write an entire chapter on this subject, and maybe, given the influence the media have on American public opinion these days, we should. We could discuss other channels and other organizations (e.g., Accuracy in Media on the right and MoveOn.org on the left, to name just two of a thousand), but we think you get the idea: We remind you to always listen with a skeptical ear to political news and commentary. We know it's difficult, but it's important to be especially careful about accepting claims (without good evidence), and in particular, those with which you sympathize.

The Internet, Generally

It is difficult to overestimate the importance of the Internet—that amalgamation of electronic lines and connections that allows nearly anyone with a computer or a smart phone to link up with nearly any other similarly equipped person on the planet. Although the Internet offers great benefits, the information it provides must be evaluated with even *more* caution than information from the print media, radio, or television. We presented two stories at the beginning of the chapter that show just how wrong things can go.

There are basically two kinds of information sources on the Internet. The first consists of commercial and institutional sources; the second, of individual and group sites on the World Wide Web. In the first category, we include sources like the LexisNexis facility, as well as the online services provided by newsmagazines, large electronic news organizations, and government institutions. The second category includes everything else you'll find on the web—an amazing assortment of good information, entertainment of widely varying quality, hot tips, advertisements, come-ons, fraudulent offers, and outright lies. Just as the fact that a claim appears in print or on television doesn't make it true, so it is for claims you run across online. Keep in mind that the information you get from a source is only as good as that source.

Wikipedia

Possibly the fastest-growing source of information in terms of both its size and its influence is the online encyclopedia Wikipedia. "Wiki" refers to a collaborative voluntary association (although the word seems to have been coined by a programmer named Ward Cunningham from the Hawaiian term "wiki-wiki"—"quick-quick"). Begun in 2001 by Larry Sanger and Jimmy Wales, the encyclopedia's content and structure are determined by its users. This accounts for its major strengths as well as its major weaknesses. Because there are many thousands of contributors, the coverage is immense. There are well over four million articles in English alone, and more than two hundred other languages and dialects are also employed. Because access is available to virtually everybody who has a computer or smartphone, coverage is often very fast; articles often appear within hours of breaking events.

Evaluating Website Credibility: A Tip from the Professionals

In a study done a few years ago,* it was determined that when it comes to evaluating the credibility of a website, experts in a field go about it much differently than do ordinary consumers. Since, as we've indicated, credibility varies hugely on the web, we must do the best job we can in assessing this feature of any website we consider important. Unfortunately, as was shown in the study just mentioned, most ordinary visitors do a much less effective job of evaluating credibility than do people knowledgeable about the field. In particular, while professionals attend most carefully to the information given at a website, most of the rest of us pay more attention to its visual appeal. Layout, typography, color schemes, and animation affect the general public's estimate of a site's credibility— 54 percent of comments are about these features—whereas the professionals' interest is more in the quality of the site's references, the credentials of individuals mentioned, and so on. Only 16 percent of professional evaluators' comments had to do with a website's visual design.

What should we take from this? A general rule: Don't be taken in by how visually attractive a website might be. A flashy design with attractive colors and design features is no substitute for information that is backed up by references and put forward by people with appropriate credentials.

*Experts vs. Online Consumers, a Consumer Reports WebWatch research report, October 2009 (www.consumerwebwatch.org).

But also because of this wide access, the quality of the articles varies tremendously. You should be especially wary of recent articles; they are more likely to contain uncorrected errors that will eventually disappear as knowledgeable people visit the page and put right whatever mistakes are present. Not just factual errors, but bias and omission can affect the quality of material found on Wikipedia's pages. Occasionally, a writer will do a thorough job of reporting the side of an issue that he or she favors (or knows more about, or both), and the other side may go underreported or even unmentioned. Over time, these types of errors tend to get corrected after visits by individuals who favor the other side of the issue. But at any given moment, in any given Wikipedia entry, there is the possibility of mistakes, omissions, citation errors, and plain old vandalism.

Our advice: We think Wikipedia is an excellent starting point in a search for knowledge about a topic. We use it frequently. But you should always check the sources provided in what you find there; it should never be your sole source of information if the topic is important to you or is to become part of an assignment to be turned in for a class. That said, we add that articles dealing with technical or scientific subjects tend to be more reliable (although errors are often more difficult to spot), with an error rate (according to one study) about the same as that found in the *Encyclopedia Britannica.** (Britannica announced in March 2012 that it would no longer publish a paper version; it now exists only online.) Such articles and, as mentioned, articles that have been around for a while can be extremely helpful in whatever project you are engaged in.

*"Internet Encyclopedias Go Head to Head," by Jim Giles, *Nature,* December 12, 2005.

Webcheckers

Along with other sites we've already mentioned, here are some other places where you can go to get to the bottom of an issue you've seen brought up on the web. We believe these to be among the most reliable sources currently available; we use them all ourselves.

Snopes.com. The original site for checking out rumors, stories, urban legends, and any other type of strange claim that turns up on the web. Run by Daniel and Barbara Mikkelson since 1996, it classifies as true or false a host of claims that circulate on the Internet. Analysis of the history and nature of the claims under investigation is usually provided.

TruthorFiction.com. A general fact-finding, debunking site. Generally up-to-date findings by owner Rich Buhler. Analyses tend to be less thorough than those found on Snopes, but a generally trustworthy site.

Factcheck.org. Run by Brooks Jackson, a former CNN and *Wall Street Journal* reporter out of the University of Pennsylvania's Annenberg Public Policy Center. Neutral politically, the site attacks anybody who stretches the truth concerning any topic in politics.

PolitiFact.com. Operated by the *St. Petersburg* (Florida) *Times* newspaper. Reporters and editors fact-check claims made by politicians, lobbyists, and interest groups. The website won a Pulitzer Prize in 2009 for its work during the presidential election of 2008.

ConsumerReports.org. Evaluates consumer issues (including health care and financial planning) and products. Not to be confused with other organizations with similar names, this site, like the magazine of the same name that sponsors it, accepts no advertising and bends over backward to avoid bias. Careful evaluation and analysis can be expected. The organization buys products to be evaluated from stores, just like we do, rather than being given them by manufacturers. Unbiased help in shopping for electronics can also be found at Decide.com, a recent addition to the consumer's arsenal.

For the general evaluation of websites, several checklists are available. You will find Cornell University's and the University of Maryland's checklists at www.library.cornell.edu/olinuris/ref/research/skill26.htm and www.lib.umd.edu/guides/evaluate.html.

News from Social Media: The Echo Chamber

Until lately, the social media on the web (Facebook, Twitter, YouTube, Google Plus, and maybe a dozen more by the time you read this) have not been much thought of as sources of news. But times have changed. In 2015 alone, some of the most viewed news pieces resulted from amateur- or police-recorded video that made it onto the web and went viral.

Facebook is the number one social media source of news for the greatest number of people, with about 30 percent of U.S. adults getting news there.* YouTube and Twitter come in at 10 and 8 percent, respectively. While entertainment news is the category that garners the most interest (and that by itself is worrisome to some of us), social media has been instrumental in many breaking news events. Individual users have posted photos and videos that have sometimes made the difference in how the country understands a news event.

---

*See http://www.pewresearch.org/fact-tank/2014/09/24/how-social-media-is-reshaping-news/, on which this and much of the current section relies.

While we welcome the first-hand video of breaking events, whether recorded by private individuals or by police cameras, we have to remember that nearly every photo or video is open to interpretation in varying degrees. Furthermore, much viral video that is passed around on web is accompanied by one hysterical voice or another. We urge caution when looking at accounts—written or video—of news events, especially when presented by people who have a stake in the subject. They are, remember, the very sort of interested parties we spoke of earlier in the chapter.

A second, and maybe more serious problem, is the false impression that can be created by repeated viewings of an event or type of event. Remember from Chapter 1 how the availability heuristic affects us: The more frequently we think of an event or type of event, the greater the probability we assign to its occurrence. And seeing something happen frequently on television, on the computer, or on the smart phone is certain to cause us to think more frequently about it.

Finally, remember that social media may know more about us than we might be inclined to think. The things sent to us are frequently tailored to our interests by our website-viewing history, thus echoing and reinforcing our interests, preferences, and biases.

To sum up: More sources of news, everything being equal, are a good thing. But everything is not always equal, and we must proceed with caution and with our critical thinking faculties turned on when digesting news from any source, whether the *New York Times* or your cousin's videos.

Blogs

Now we come to blogs. Blogs are simply journals, the vast majority of them put up by individuals, that are left open to the public on an Internet site. Originally more like public diaries dealing with personal matters, they now encompass specialties of almost every imaginable sort. Up to three million blogs were believed to be up and running by the end of 2004; by July 2011, there were an estimated 164 million.* We are afraid to guess how many there are now.

You can find blogs that specialize in satire, parody, and outright fabrication. They represent all sides of the political spectrum, including some sides that we wouldn't have thought existed at all. The Drudge Report is a standard on the right; the Huffington Post is equally well known on the left. On a blog site, like any other website that isn't run by a responsible organization such as most of those previously indicated, you can find *anything that a person wants to put there,* including all kinds of bad information. You can take advantage of these sources, but you should always exercise caution, and if you're looking for information, always consult another source, but be especially careful about any that are linked to your first source!

Before we leave the topic of web worthiness, we want to pass along a warning that comes from Barbara Mikkelson, co-founder of Snopes.com. (See the box, "Web-checkers," on the previous page.) She reminds us that rumors often give people a great sense of comfort; people are quick to reject nuance and facts that are contrary to their own point of view, but quickly accept them when they are agreeable to the hearer. (This is called "confirmation bias." See Chapter 1.) "When you're looking at truth versus gossip," Mikkelson says, "truth doesn't stand a chance." We hope she's being unduly pessimistic.

---

*Rightmixmarketing.com; blogging statistics.

So remember, when you take keyboard and mouse in hand, be on guard. You have about as much reason to believe the claims you find on most sites as you would if they came from any other stranger, except you can't look this one in the eye.

Exercise 4-8

See who in the class can find the strangest news report from a credible source. Send it to us at McGraw-Hill. If your entry is selected for printing in our next edition, Moore might send you $100. (In the next chapter you'll see why we call the word "might" a weaseler in this context.)

Exercise 4-9

Identify at least three factors that can cause inaccuracies or a distortion of reports in the news media.

ADVERTISING

> Advertising [is] the science of arresting the human intelligence long enough to get money from it.
>
> —*Stephen Leacock*

It is estimated that about a half-trillion dollars are spent each year trying to get people to buy or do something. Six billion dollars were spent during the 2012 elections, most of it on advertising.

People watching a sexual program are thinking about sex, not soda pop. Violence and sex elicit very strong emotions and can interfere with memory for other things.

—BRAD BUSHMAN of Iowa State University, whose research indicated that people tend to forget the names of sponsors of violent or sexual TV shows (reported by Ellen Goodman)

"Doctor recommended."

This ambiguous ad slogan creates an illusion that many doctors, or doctors in general, recommend the product. However, a recommendation from a single doctor is all it takes to make the statement true.

If there is anything in modern society besides politics that truly puts our sense of what is credible to the test, it's advertising. As we hope you'll agree after reading this section, skepticism is a good policy when considering advertisements and promotions.

Ads are used to sell many products other than toasters, televisions, and toilet tissue. They can encourage us to vote for a candidate, agree with a political proposal, take a tour, give up a bad habit, or join the Tea Party or the army. They can also be used to make announcements (for instance, about job openings, lectures, concerts, or the recall of defective automobiles) or to create favorable or unfavorable climates of opinion (e.g., toward labor unions or offshore oil drilling). A "public service announcement" may even be used surreptitiously to create a climate of opinion about something or someone. To simplify this discussion, let's just refer to all these things as products.

Three Kinds of Ads

The three modes of persuasion first written about by Aristotle and discussed in Chapter 2 of this book present a useful way of classifying ads.

1. *Logos ads:* These ads emphasize information about a product—information advertisers hope favorably influence our decision about buying their products. (Remember that "product" includes everything from balsamic vinegar to ballot initiatives.) Unfortunately, to make an informed decision on a purchase, you may need to know more than the advertiser is willing to claim, particularly because advertisers won't tell you what's wrong with their products or what's right with their competitors'. After all, they are *interested parties*. Ads are written to *sell something;* they are not designed to be informative except to help with the sales job.

   Sometimes, of course, a *logos* advertisement can provide you with information that can clinch your decision to make a purchase. Sometimes the mere existence, availability, or affordability of a product—all information an ad can convey—is all you need to make a reason-based decision to buy.

2. *Ethos ads:* These ads display a product as being used or endorsed by people we admire or identify with or feel we can trust. Potential buyers of a product are probably aware that individuals who star in advocacy ads (as they are sometimes called) are paid to be in them and are therefore interested parties. But the strategy behind such ads primarily is to create favorable associations with the product and to give the product prominent shelf space in our mind, i.e., to make us remember it when we go shopping. Obviously, neither the fact that we remember a product nor the fact that someone we like has been paid to promote it is a reason to buy it.

3. *Pathos ads:* These ads are primarily intended to arouse emotions in us. Pleasurable emotions stimulate positive memories of a product and help it stand out in a positive way when we are shopping. Negative emotions—the staple of negative political advertising—are intended to help make us think poorly of something or someone.

A common *pathos* ad technique is the narrative ad, which situates a product in an emotionally charged story. Many car ads use this technique: a good example is the 2014 ad for a Chevy Silverado which features a man, his truck, a broken fence, and a lost calf—which the man finds while driving his truck through freezing rain. Such ads often use stereotypes, in this case the positive stereotype of the tough-yet-caring cowboy, a central and iconic figure in American mythology. The ad may not make you want to rush out and buy a Silverado, but the story is compelling and may stick in your thoughts. The local Chevy dealership may be happy that, if you contemplate getting a truck, the lost-calf story comes to mind more readily than frequency of repair data you read about in *Consumer Reports*.

Of course, memories created by an advertising narrative, whether favorable or unfavorable, are not reasons to buy or avoid a product.

For people on whom good fortune has smiled, those who don't care what kind of *whatsit* they buy, or those to whom mistaken purchases simply don't matter, all that is important is knowing that a product is available. Most of us, however, need more information than ads provide to make reasoned purchasing decisions. Of course,

"Chevy runs deep."

Meaningless but catchy slogan for Chevy trucks. Being catchy is no substitute for being relevant or being true.

we all occasionally make purchases solely on the basis of advertisements, and sometimes we don't come to regret them. In such cases, though, the happy result is due as much to good luck as to the ad.

A final suggestion on this subject. We know of only one source that maintains a fierce independence and still does a good job of testing and reporting on products in general. That's Consumers Union, the publishers of *Consumer Reports,* a magazine (mentioned in the box on page 121) that accepts no advertising and that buys all

When Is an Ad Not an Ad? When It's a Product Placement!

When Katharine Hepburn threw Humphrey Bogart's Gordon's gin overboard in *The African Queen,* it was an early example of product placement, since the makers of Gordon's paid to have their product tossed in the drink, as it were. More recent examples of placement ads include Dodge vehicles in the Fast and Furious movies and Apple laptops just about everywhere.

These days, the paid placement of products in both movies and television (and possibly even in novels) is a serious alternative to traditional commercials, and it has the advantage of overcoming the Tivo/DVR effect: the viewer records programs and skips over the commercials when watching them.

■ We suspect the Coke can is there because Pepsi wouldn't pay enough.

WAY Too Good to Be True!

After the country fell into a serious recession in 2008, many people found themselves unable to meet their mortgage payments, and many found themselves saddled with more credit card debt than they could manage. Easy debt-relief schemers to the rescue! Some cable TV and radio ads promised to help get your mortgage paid off, make your credit card debt shrink or disappear altogether, or make you rich by teaching you to make quick killings in real estate.

According to a *Consumer Reports Money Adviser* article (April 2010), these schemes, which are still around, tend more toward guaranteeing fees for the operators than for debt relief or riches, quick or otherwise, for the client. Many clients wind up worse off than they started after signing up for these plans. Advertising is designed to help the folks who pay for the ads. If it looks too good to be true, you can bet it *is*.

the objects it tests and reports on (rather than accepting them for free from the manufacturers, as do several other "consumer" magazines). For reliable information and fair-mindedness, we recommend them. They're also on the web at www.consumersunion.org. Also on the web, decide.com does the same for electronic gear. They're mentioned in the same box, above.

This list summarizes the topics covered in this chapter.

Recap

- Claims lack credibility to the extent they conflict with our observations, experience, or background information, or come from sources that lack credibility.
- The less initial plausibility a claim has, the more extraordinary it seems, and the less it fits with our background information, the more suspicious we should be.
- Interested parties should be viewed with more suspicion than disinterested parties.
- Doubts about sources generally fall into two categories: doubts about the source's knowledge or expertise and doubts about the source's veracity, objectivity, and accuracy.
- We can form reasonably reliable judgments about a source's knowledge by considering his or her education, experience, accomplishments, reputation, and position.
- Claims made by experts, those with special knowledge in a subject, are the most reliable, but the claims must pertain to the area of expertise and must not conflict with claims made by other experts in the same area.
- Major metropolitan newspapers, national newsmagazines, and network news shows are generally credible sources of news, but it is necessary to keep an open mind about what we learn from them.
- Governments have been known to influence and even to manipulate the news.
- Sources like Wikipedia, institutional websites, and news organizations can be helpful, but skepticism is the order of the day when we obtain information from unknown Internet sources or advocacy TV.

■ What goes for advocacy television also goes for talk radio.

■ Advertising assaults us at every turn, attempting to sell us goods, services, beliefs, and attitudes. Because substantial talent and resources are employed in this effort, we need to ask ourselves constantly whether the products in question will really make the differences in our lives that their advertising claims or hints they will make. Advertisers are more concerned with selling something than with improving your life. They are concerned with improving their own lives.

Additional Exercises

Exercise 4-10

In groups, decide which is the best answer to each question. Compare your answers with those of other groups and your instructor.

1. "SPACE ALIEN GRAVEYARD FOUND! Scientists who found an extraterrestrial cemetery in central Africa say the graveyard is at least 500 years old! 'There must be 200 bodies buried there and not a single one of them is human,' Dr. Hugo Schild, the Swiss anthropologist, told reporters." What is the appropriate reaction to this report in the *Weekly World News?*

   a. It's probably true.
   b. It almost certainly is true.
   c. We really need more information to form any judgment at all.
   d. None of the above.

2. Is Elvis really dead? Howie thinks not. Reason: He knows three people who claim to have seen Elvis recently. They are certain that it is not a mere Elvis look-alike they have seen. Howie reasons that, since he has absolutely no reason to think the three would lie to him, they must be telling the truth. Elvis must really be alive, he concludes!

   Is Howie's reasoning sound? Explain.

3. VOICE ON TELEPHONE: Hello, Mr. Roberts, this is HSBC calling. Have you recently made a credit card purchase of $347 at Macy's in New York City?

   MR. ROBERTS: Why, no, I haven't . . .

   VOICE: We thought not, Mr. Roberts. I'm sorry to report that it is very likely that your credit card has been compromised and is being used by another party. However, we are prepared to block that card and send you another immediately, at no expense to you.

   MR. ROBERTS: Well, that's fine, I suppose.

   VOICE: Let me emphasize, you will experience very little inconvenience and no expense at all. Now, for authorization, just to make sure that we are calling the correct person, Mr. Roberts, please state the number on your credit card and the expiration date.

   Question: What should Mr. Roberts, as a critical thinker, do?

4. One Thanksgiving Day, an image said by some to resemble the Virgin Mary was observed on a wall of St. Dominic's Church in Colfax, California. A physicist asked to investigate said the image was caused by sunlight shining through a stained glass window and reflecting from a newly installed hanging

light fixture. Others said the image was a miracle. Whose explanation is more likely true?

a. the physicist's
b. the others'
c. more information is needed before we can decide which explanation is more likely

5. It is late at night around the campfire when the campers hear awful grunting noises in the woods around them. They run for their lives! Two campers, after returning the next day, tell others they found huge footprints around the campfire. They are convinced they were attacked by Bigfoot. Which explanation is more likely true?

a. The campers heard Bigfoot.
b. The campers heard some animal and are pushing the Bigfoot explanation to avoid being called chickens, or are just making the story up for unknown reasons.
c. Given this information, we can't tell which explanation is more likely.

6. Megan's aunt says she saw a flying saucer. "I don't tell people about this," Auntie says, "because they'll think I'm making it up. But this really happened. I saw this strange light, and this, well, it wasn't a saucer, exactly, but it was round and big, and it came down and hovered just over my back fence, and my two dogs began whimpering. And then it just, whoosh! It just vanished."
   Megan knows her aunt, and Megan knows she doesn't make up stories.

a. She should believe her aunt saw a flying saucer.
b. She should believe her aunt was making up the story.
c. She should believe that her aunt may well have had some unusual experience, but it was probably not a visitation by extraterrestrial beings.

7. According to Dr. Edith Fiore, author of *The Unquiet Dead,* many of your personal problems are really the miseries of a dead soul who has possessed you sometime during your life. "Many people are possessed by earthbound spirits. These are people who have lived and died, but did not go into the afterworld at death. Instead they stayed on Earth and remained just like they were before death, with the fears, pains, weaknesses and other problems that they had when they were alive." She estimates that about 80 percent of her more than 1,000 patients are suffering from the problems brought on by being possessed by spirits of the dead. To tell if you are among the possessed, she advises that you look for such telltale symptoms as low energy levels, character shifts or mood swings, memory problems, poor concentration, weight gain with no obvious cause, and bouts of depression (especially after hospitalization). Which of these reactions is best?

a. Wow! I'll bet I'm possessed!
b. If these are signs of being possessed, how come she thinks that only 80 percent of her patients are?
c. Too bad there isn't more information available, so we could form a reasonable judgment.
d. Dr. Fiore doesn't know what she's talking about.

8.   **EOC—Engine Overhaul in a Can**

Developed by skilled automotive scientists after years of research and laboratory and road tests! Simply pour one can of EOC into the oil in your crankcase. EOC contains long-chain molecules and special thermo-active metallic

alloys that bond with worn engine parts. NO tools needed! NO need to disassemble engine.

Question: Reading this ad, what should you believe?

9. ANCHORAGE, Alaska (AP)—Roped to her twin sons for safety, Joni Phelps inched her way to the top of Mount McKinley. The National Park Service says Phelps, 54, apparently is the first blind woman to scale the 20,300-foot peak.

This report is

a. probably true
b. probably false
c. too sketchy; more information is needed before we can judge

10. You read rave reviews of *The Life Plan,* a book that promises to slow aging, promote strength, enhance one's sex life, and so on through diet, exercise, and hormone therapy. Should a reader of the book expect to achieve the results described? Are there cautions you should heed before beginning such a program?

Exercise 4-11

Within each group of observers, are some especially credible or especially not so?

1. Judging the relative performances of the fighters in a heavyweight boxing match
   a. the father of one of the fighters
   b. a sportswriter for *Sports Illustrated* magazine
   c. the coach of the American Olympic boxing team
   d. the referee of the fight
   e. a professor of physical education

2. You (or your family or your class) are trying to decide whether you should buy a Mac computer or a Windows PC. You might consult
   a. a friend who owns either a Mac or a Windows machine
   b. a friend who now owns one of the machines but used to own the other
   c. a dealer for either Mac or Windows computers
   d. a computer column in a big-city newspaper
   e. reviews in computer magazines

3. The Surgical Practices Committee of Grantville Hospital has documented an unusually high number of problems in connection with tonsillectomies performed by a Dr. Choker. The committee is reviewing her surgical practices. Those present during a tonsillectomy are
   a. Dr. Choker
   b. the surgical proctor from the Surgical Practices Committee
   c. an anesthesiologist
   d. a nurse
   e. a technician

4. The mechanical condition of the used car you are thinking of buying
   a. the used-car salesperson
   b. the former owner (who we assume is different from the salesperson)
   c. the former owner's mechanic
   d. you
   e. a mechanic from an independent garage

5. A demonstration of psychokinesis (the ability to move objects at a distance by nonphysical means)

    a. a newspaper reporter
    b. a psychologist
    c. a police detective
    d. another psychic
    e. a physicist
    f. a customs agent
    g. a magician

Exercise 4-12

For each of the following items, discuss the credibility and authority of each source relative to the issue in question. Whom would you trust as most reliable on the subject?

1. Issue: Is Crixivan an effective HIV/AIDS medication?

    a. *Consumer Reports*
    b. Stadtlander Drug Company (the company that makes Crixivan)
    c. the owner of your local health food store
    d. the U.S. Food and Drug Administration
    e. your local pharmacist

2. Issue: Should possession of handguns be outlawed?

    a. a police chief
    b. a representative of the National Rifle Association
    c. a U.S. senator
    d. the father of a murder victim

3. Issue: What was the original intent of the Second Amendment to the U.S. Constitution, and does it include permission for every citizen to possess handguns?

    a. a representative of the National Rifle Association
    b. a justice of the U.S. Supreme Court
    c. a constitutional historian
    d. a U.S. senator
    e. the president of the United States

4. Issue: Is decreasing your intake of dietary fat and cholesterol likely to reduce the level of cholesterol in your blood?

    a. *Time* magazine
    b. *Runner's World* magazine
    c. your physician
    d. the National Institutes of Health
    e. the *New England Journal of Medicine*

5. Issue: When does a human life begin?

    a. a lawyer
    b. a physician
    c. a philosopher
    d. a minister
    e. you

Exercise 4-13

Each of these items consists of a brief biography of a real or imagined person, followed by a list of topics. On the basis of the information in the biography, discuss the credibility and authority of the person described on each of the topics listed.

1. Anne St. Germain teaches sociology at the University of Illinois and is the director of its Population Studies Center. She is a graduate of Harvard College, where she received a BA in 1985, and of Harvard University, which granted her a PhD in economics in 1988. She taught courses in demography as an assistant professor at UCLA until 1992; then she moved to the sociology department of the University of Nebraska, where she was associate professor and then professor. From 1997 through 1999, she served as acting chief of the Population Trends and Structure Section of the United Nations Population Division. She joined the faculty at the University of Illinois in 1999. She has written books on patterns of world urbanization, the effects of cigarette smoking on international mortality, and demographic trends in India. She is president of the Population Association of America.

Topics

   a. The effects of acid rain on humans
   b. The possible beneficial effects of requiring sociology courses for all students at the University of Illinois
   c. The possible effects of nuclear war on global climate patterns
   d. The incidence of poverty among various ethnic groups in the United States
   e. The effects of the melting of glaciers on global sea levels
   f. The change in death rate for various age groups in all Third World countries between 1980 and 2000
   g. The feasibility of a laser-based nuclear defense system
   h. Voter participation among religious sects in India
   i. Whether the winters are worse in Illinois than in Nebraska

2. Tom Pierce graduated cum laude from Cornell University with a BS in biology in 1980. After two years in the Peace Corps, during which he worked on public health projects in Venezuela, he joined Jeffrey Ridenour, a mechanical engineer, and the pair developed a water pump and purification system that is now used in many parts of the world for both regular water supplies and emergency use in disaster-struck areas. Pierce and Ridenour formed a company to manufacture the water systems, and it prospered as they developed smaller versions of the system for private use on boats and motor homes. In 1988, Pierce bought out his partner and expanded research and development in hydraulic systems for forcing oil out of old wells. Under contract with the federal government and several oil firms, Pierce's company was a principal designer and contractor for the Alaskan oil pipeline. He is now a consultant in numerous developing countries as well as chief executive officer and chair of the board of his own company, and he sits on the boards of directors of several other companies.

Topics

   a. The image of the United States in Latin America
   b. The long-range effects of the leftward turn in Venezuela on South America
   c. Fixing a leaky faucet

d. Technology in Third World countries
e. The ecological effects of the Alaskan pipeline
f. Negotiating a contract with the federal government
g. Careers in biology

Exercise 4-14

According to certain pollsters, quite a number of people vote for candidates for president not because they especially like those candidates' policies and programs or their idea of where the country should be going, but because they like (or dislike) the candidates personally. Discuss what features a candidate from the recent past may have that might cause such people to vote for (or against) him or her. Which of these features, if any, might be relevant to how good a job the candidate would do as president?

Exercise 4-15

From what you know about the nature of each of the following claims and its source, and given your general knowledge, assess whether the claim is one you should accept, reject, or suspend judgment on due to ambiguity, insufficient documentation, vagueness, or subjectivity (e.g., "Sam Claflin is cute"). Compare your judgment with that of your instructor.

1. "Campbell Soup is hot—and some are getting burned. Just one day after the behemoth of broth reported record profits, Campbell said it would lay off 650 U.S. workers, including 175—or 11% of the workforce—at its headquarters in Camden, New Jersey."

   —Time

2. [The claim to evaluate is the first one in this passage.] Jackie Haskew taught paganism and devil worship in her fourth-grade classroom in Grand Saline, Texas, at least until she was pressured into resigning by parents of her students. (According to syndicated columnist Nat Hentoff, "At the town meeting on her case, a parent said firmly that she did not want her daughter to read anything that dealt with 'death, abuse, divorce, religion, or any other issue.'")

3. "By 1893 there were only between 300 and 1,000 buffaloes remaining in the entire country. A few years later, President Theodore Roosevelt persuaded Congress to establish a number of wildlife preserves in which the remaining buffaloes could live without danger. The numbers have increased since, nearly doubling over the past 10 years to 130,000."

   —*Clifford May, in the* New York Times Magazine

4. Lee Harvey Oswald, acting alone, was responsible for the death of President John F. Kennedy.

   —*Conclusion of the Warren Commission on the assassination of President Kennedy*

5. "[N]ewly released documents, including the transcripts of telephone conversations recorded by President Lyndon B. Johnson in November and December 1963, provide for the first time a detailed . . . look at why and how the seven-member Warren [Commission] was put together. Those documents, along with

a review of previously released material . . . describe a process designed more to control information than to elicit and expose it."

—*"The Truth Was Secondary,"* Washington Post National Weekly Edition

6. "Short-sighted developers are determined to transform Choco [a large region of northwestern Colombia] from an undisturbed natural treasure to a polluted, industrialized growth center."

—*Solicitation letter from the World Wildlife Fund*

7. "Frantic parents tell shocked TV audience: space aliens stole our son."

—Weekly World News

8. "The manufacturer of Sudafed 12-hour capsules issued a nationwide recall of the product Sunday after two people in the state of Washington who had taken the medication died of cyanide poisoning and a third became seriously ill."

—Los Angeles Times

9. "In Canada, smoking in public places, trains, planes or even automobiles is now prohibited by law or by convention. The federal government has banned smoking in all its buildings."

—*Reuters*

10. "In October 2012, People for the Ethical Treatment of Animals petitioned Irvine, California, to create a roadside memorial for the truckload of live fish that perished in a recent traffic accident."

—Orange County Register

11. "Maps, files and compasses were hidden in Monopoly sets and smuggled into World War II German prison camps by MI-5, Britain's counter-intelligence agency, to help British prisoners escape, according to the British manufacturer of the game."

—*Associated Press*

12. "Cats that live indoors and use a litter box can live four to five years longer."

—*From an advertisement for Jonny Cat litter*

13. "The collapse of WTC Building 7 represents one of the worst structural failures in modern history. The official story contends that fires weakened the structures, resulting in a gravitational collapse. The evidence, obvious to so many researchers but omitted from NIST's Final Report, supports a very different conclusion—one that points squarely to explosive controlled demolition. If WTC 7 was intentionally brought down, then clearly it becomes a 'smoking gun' that must be investigated."

—*http://www.ae911truth.org/news/41-articles/344-building-7-implosion-the-smoking-gun-of-911.html*

14. "Because of cartilage that begins to accumulate after age thirty, by the time . . . [a] man is seventy his nose has grown a half inch wider and another half inch longer, his earlobes have fattened, and his ears themselves have grown a quarter inch longer. Overall, his head's circumference increases a quarter inch every decade, and not because of his brain, which is shrinking. His head is fatter apparently because, unlike most other bones in the body, the skull seems to thicken with age."

—*John Tierney (a staff writer for* Esquire)

15. "Gardenias . . . need ample warmth, ample water, and steady feeding. Though hardy to 20°F or even lower, plants fail to grow and bloom well without summer heat."

—The Sunset New Western Garden Book *(a best-selling gardening reference in the West)*

16. "It's stunningly beautiful. The weather is near perfect. The community of locals and expats is welcoming and friendly. The road here is good and you don't want for any modern conveniences or amenities. But hardly anyone knows about it—and real estate is still affordable.

"Once the word gets out about this place, the real estate market is set to explode. But right now . . . you can get lake view lots perched above the boat dock, with a down payment of $1,900 and monthly payment of just $143."

—International Living *(an online advertiser for foreign real estate), about Costa Rica*

17. "On Tuesday, Dec. 4, DJs Mel Greig and Michael Christian phoned the King Edward VII hospital pretending to be Prince Charles and Queen Elizabeth in order to get information about the Duchess of Cambridge. Saldanha, [a nurse] who had been tending to Middleton during her stay, fell victim to the prank and passed the callers on to another employee, who then proceeded to give confidential details about the pregnant royal's condition.

Three days later, Saldanha, known to friends and colleagues as 'Jess,' was found dead of an apparent suicide."

—US Weekly

18. "In our new print issue, which begins hitting newsstands today, the superstar's [John Travolta's] former gay lover breaks his long silence to reveal the shocking details of an intimate six-year sexual relationship. In a bombshell world exclusive ENQUIRER interview, former pilot DOUG GOTTERBA discloses that Travolta's Hollywood image as a big-screen heartthrob throughout the '80s was a total sham."

—National Enquirer, *online*

19. "The Encinitas (California) Union School District is facing the threat of a lawsuit as it launches what is believed to be the country's most comprehensive yoga program for a public school system. Parents opposed to the program say the classes will indoctrinate their children in Eastern religion and are not just for exercise."

—*Associated Press*

▲ 20. "Taliban terrorists have a secret weapon to destroy the infidel American enemy—monkey marksmen. According to the *People's Daily* in China, the Taliban in Afghanistan is 'training monkeys to use weapons to attack American troops.' . . . Islamic insurgents have drafted macaques and baboons to be all that they can be, arming them with AK-4 rifles, machine guns and trench mortars in the Waziristan tribal region near the border between Pakistan and Afghanistan. The monkeys, being rewarded with bananas and peanuts, are being turned into snipers at a secret Taliban training base."

—New York Post, *July 13, 2010*

Exercise 4-16

The following appeared in a local newspaper, criticizing the position on global warming taken by local television weather forecaster and political activist Anthony Watts.

Read it carefully and decide whether anything the newspaper alleges should affect the credibility of Watts or the project he endorsed. Compare your judgment with those of your classmates.

"[Anthony] Watts endorsed the 'Petition Project,' which refutes man-made global warming. Besides many fictitious names submitted, only about one percent of the petition signers had done any climate research.

"The petition was prepared by Frederick Seitz, a scientist who, from 1975 to 1989, was paid \$585,000 by the tobacco industry to direct a \$45 million scientific effort to hide the health impact of smoking. Does Watts agree that cigarettes are not harmful, as Seitz's studies showed?"

—Chico News & Review

Exercise 4-17

Find five *ethos* or *pathos* advertisements. Explain how each ad attempts to make the product seem attractive.

Exercise 4-18

Watch Fox News, MSNBC, and CNN news programs on the same day. Compare the three on the basis of (1) the news stories covered, (2) the amount of air time given to two or three of the major stories, and (3) any difference in the slant of the presentations of a controversial story. Make notes. Be prepared to discuss in class the differences in coverage on the basis of the three criteria just mentioned.

Writing Exercises

1. Although millions of people have seen professional magicians like David Copperfield and Siegfried and Roy perform in person or on television, it's probably a safe assumption that almost nobody believes they accomplish their feats by means of real magical or supernatural powers—that is, that they somehow "defy" the laws of nature. But even though they've never had a personal demonstration, a significant portion of the population is said to believe that certain psychics are able to accomplish apparent miracles by exactly such means. How might you explain this difference in belief?

2. In the text, you were asked to consider the claim "Charlie's eighty-seven-year-old grandmother swam across Lake Michigan in the middle of winter." Because of the implausibility of such a claim—that is, because it conflicts with our background information—it is reasonable to reject it. Suppose, however, that instead of just telling us about his grandmother, Charlie brings us a photocopy of a page of the *Chicago Tribune* with a photograph of a person in a wet suit walking up onto a beach. The caption underneath reads, "Eighty-Seven-Year-Old Grandmother Swims Lake Michigan in January!" Based on this piece of evidence, should a critical thinker decide that the original claim is significantly more likely to be true than if it were backed up only by Charlie's word? Defend your answer.

3. Are our schools doing a bad job educating our kids? Do research in the library or on the Internet to answer this question. Make a list (no more than one page long) of facts that support the claim that our schools are not doing as good a job as they should. Then list facts that support the opposite view

(or that rebut the claims of those who say our schools aren't doing a good job). Again, limit yourself to one page. Cite your sources.

Now, think critically about your sources. Are any stronger or weaker than the others? Explain why on a single sheet of paper. Come prepared to read your explanation, along with your list of facts and sources, to the class.

4. Jackson says you should be skeptical of the opinion of someone who stands to profit from your accepting that opinion. Smith disagrees, pointing out that salespeople are apt to know a lot more about products of the type they sell than do most people.

"Most salespeople are honest, and you can trust them," Smith argues. "Those who aren't don't stay in business long."

Take about fifteen minutes to defend either Smith or Jackson in a short essay. When everyone is finished, your instructor will collect the essays and read three or more to the class to stimulate a brief discussion. After discussion, can the class come to any agreement about who is correct, Jackson or Smith?

5. Search the Internet for answers to one or more of the following questions. Write an essay in which you take a position on the question and defend your position with an argument, and explain which Internet source you came across is most credible and why.

a. Can smoking stunt bone growth?
b. Is it safe to smoke tobacco using a hookah?
c. Should toasters be unplugged when not in use?
d. Will regular, vigorous exercise make you live longer?
e. Are sea levels rising?
f. How harmful is it to get too little sleep?
g. Is it better to feed dogs raw meat than dog food?
h. Are psychics really able to solve crimes?
i. Why do hands and feet get wrinkled if you are in a bath for a long time?
j. Do smoking laws improve public health?

6. Raise a question you are interested in, research it on the Internet, take a position on it and support it with an argument, and explain which Internet source you came across is most credible and why.

Rhetoric, the Art of Persuasion

Students will learn to . . .

1. Explain the concepts of rhetorical force and emotive power

2. Identify and critique the use of euphemisms, dysphemisms, weaselers, and downplayers

3. Identify and critique the use of stereotypes, innuendo, and loaded questions

4. Identify and critique the use of ridicule, sarcasm, and hyperbole

5. Identify and critique the use of rhetorical definitions, explanations, analogies, and misleading comparisons

6. Identify and critique the use of proof surrogates and repetition

7. Identify and critique the persuasive aspects of visual images

8. Detect the techniques used in the extreme rhetoric of demagoguery

Rhetoric, the venerable art of persuasive writing and speaking, has been one of the twin anchors of Western education since the days of Aristotle. The other, which also dates from Aristotle, is logic. You use rhetoric to win someone to your point of view; you use logic to demonstrate a claim or support it. These are separate enterprises. You can use logic to persuade people, but all too often they are persuaded by poor logic and unmoved by good logic. This is why education increasingly emphasizes critical thinking, to help people improve their logic and to help them distinguish between proof and persuasion.

In this chapter we do three things. First, we introduce the important concept of rhetorical force. Then we explain several rhetorical devices. Good writers and speakers employ many of these devices to make their cases as persuasive as possible. None of the devices, however, have logical force or probative weight ("probative" means tending to prove). We, as critical thinkers, should be able to recognize them for what they are—devices of persuasion.

Last, after we examine the various devices, we examine four principal techniques of demagoguery. Demagogues use inflammatory rhetoric to win acceptance for false and misleading ideas. They appeal to the fears and prejudices of an audience, and depend on its inability to see through their tricks. Famous demagogues include Adolf Hitler, Joseph McCarthy, and others, including the occasional candidate for the U.S. presidency. Spotting demagoguery and resisting it is perhaps the most important skill a critical thinker can have.

RHETORICAL FORCE

Words and expressions have more than a literal or "dictionary" meaning. They also have what is known as **emotive meaning** or **rhetorical force** (these being the same thing). This is their power to express and elicit various psychological and emotional responses. For example, "elderly gentleman" and "old codger" evoke different emotions, the first pleasing and the second less so. To say that someone's opinion is "mistaken" is one thing; to refer to it as "bull" is quite another. The two expressions have the same literal meaning, but the second has a negative emotive meaning. Read this statement from a famous speech by Barack Obama, in which he conceded a primary election to Hillary Clinton. Then compare it with the paraphrase that immediately follows:

> And so tomorrow, as we take this campaign South and West; as we learn that the struggles of the textile worker in Spartanburg are not so different than the plight of the dishwasher in Las Vegas; that the hopes of the little girl who goes to a crumbling school in Dillon are the same as the dreams of the boy who learns on the streets of LA; we will remember that there is something happening in America; that we are not as divided as our politics suggests; that we are one people; we are one nation; and together, we will begin the next great chapter in America's story with three words that will ring from coast to coast; from sea to shining sea—Yes. We. Can.
>
> —*Barack Obama speech, January 8, 2008*

Paraphrase:

> Let us continue campaigning.

The message conveyed by the two passages is essentially the same. The difference between them is due entirely to the powerful rhetorical force of the first passage, which is inspirational and uplifting, and exhorts listeners toward a common shining goal. The passage illustrates the point made above about rhetoric: It may be psychologically compelling, but by itself it establishes nothing. It has no probative weight. If we allow our attitudes and beliefs to be formed solely by the rhetorical force of words, we fall short as critical thinkers.

Now, before we get in trouble with your English professor, let's make it clear once again that there is nothing wrong with someone's trying to make his or her case as persuasive as possible. Good writers use well-chosen, rhetorically effective words and phrases. But we, as critical thinkers, must be able to distinguish the argument (if any) contained in a passage from the rhetoric; we must distinguish between the logical force of a set of remarks and its psychological force. You won't find much rhetoric of the sort we discuss here in science journals because it carries no probative weight. Scientists may hope readers accept their findings, but it's risky for them to try to sell their findings by couching them in the language of persuasion. It's not that rhetoric weakens an argument; it just doesn't strengthen it.*

Political language is designed to make lies sound truthful . . . and to give the appearance of solidity to pure wind.

—George Orwell

---

*A body of scholarly work known as the "Rhetoric of Science," views science *as* a species of rhetoric. However, if you are looking for examples of the kind of rhetorical devices and techniques explored in this chapter, you won't find many in (for instance) the *Journal of Cell Biology* or the *Journal of the Royal Statistical Society*.

RHETORICAL DEVICES I

The first group of **rhetorical devices** are usually single words or short phrases designed to give a statement a positive or negative slant. For this reason, they are sometimes called **slanters.**

Euphemisms and Dysphemisms

Euphemisms are unpleasant truths wearing diplomatic cologne.

—QUENTIN CRISP, *Manners from Heaven*

A **euphemism** is a neutral or positive expression used in place of one that carries negative associations. "Detainee" means what most of us call "prisoner," but it seems more benign. At first glance, "waterboarding" sounds like something you'd expect to see young people doing on a California beach, not a torture technique. "Collateral damage" is a sanitized way of saying "civilian casualties."

Euphemisms obviously can be used to whitewash wrongdoing; but they have positive uses as well. It would be insensitive to tell friends you were sorry they killed their dog. Instead, you say you were sorry they had to put their dog to sleep.

A **dysphemism** is used to produce a negative effect on someone's attitude about something, or to tone down the positive associations it may have. It sounds worse to be obscenely rich than to be very wealthy. Eating animal flesh sounds worse than eating meat. The tax imposed on an inheritance is sometimes called a death tax, which leaves a bad taste because it suggests the deceased rather than the inheritors is being taxed. Dismissing a legislative proposal as a "scheme" also qualifies as a dysphemism. We would be hard pressed to explain the difference between "conservative" and "far-right" or between "liberal" and "ultra-liberal," but the second of each of these pairs sounds worse than the first, and they both qualify as dysphemisms. "Wing nut" qualifies as a dysphemism for either end of the political spectrum.

You naturally expect to find a generous sprinkling of dysphemisms when a speaker or writer tries to get us to dislike someone or something. (During political campaigns, they crop up everywhere.) Of course, what counts as a euphemism or a dysphemism is, to some extent, in the eyes of the beholder. One person's junkyard is another person's automotive recycling business; one person's sanitary land fill is another person's garbage dump.

Finally, there is this: Some facts are just plain repellent, and for that reason, even neutral reports of them sound appalling. "Lizzie killed her father with an ax" is not a dysphemism; it simply reports a horrible fact about Lizzie.

Weaselers

Great Western pays up to 12 percent *more interest on checking accounts.*

—Radio advertisement

Even aside from the "up to" weaseler, this ad can be deceptive about what interest rate it's promising. Unless you listen carefully, you might think Great Western is paying 12 percent on checking accounts. The presence of the word "more" changes all that, of course. If you're getting 3 percent now, and Great Western gives you "up to 12 percent more" than that, they'll be giving you about 3½ percent—hardly the fortune the ad seems to promise.

When inserted into a claim, **weaselers** help protect it from criticism by watering it down somewhat, weakening it, and giving the claim's author a way out in case the claim is challenged.

Without doubt you've heard the words "up to" used as a weaseler a thousand times, especially in advertising. "Up to five more miles per gallon." "Up to twenty more yards off the tee." "Lose up to ten pounds a week." None of these guarantee anything. Sure, you might lose ten pounds, but you might lose nothing. The statement still stands, thanks to "up to."

Let's make up a statistic. Let's say that 98 percent of American doctors believe that aspirin is a contributing cause of Reye's syndrome in children, and that the other 2 percent are unconvinced. If we then claim that "some doctors are unconvinced that aspirin is related to Reye's syndrome," we cannot be held accountable for having said something false, even though our claim might be misleading to someone who did not know the complete story. The word "some" has allowed us to weasel the point. Remember: A claim does not have to be false in order to be misleading.

Words that sometimes weasel—such as "perhaps," "possibly," "maybe," and "may be," among others—can be used to produce innuendo (to be explained below), to plant a suggestion without actually making a claim that a person can be held to. We can suggest that Berriault is a liar without actually saying so (and thus without saying something that might be hard to defend) by saying that Berriault *may be* a liar. Or we can say it is *possible* that Berriault is a liar (which is true of all of us, after all). "*Perhaps* Berriault is a liar" works nicely, too. All of these are examples of weaselers used to create innuendo.

Not every use of words and phrases like these is a weaseling one, of course. Words that can weasel can also bring very important qualifications to bear on a claim. The very same word that weasels in one context may not weasel at all in another. For example, a detective who is considering all the possible angles on a crime and who has just heard Smith's account of events may say to an associate, "Of course, it is *possible* that Smith is lying." This need not be a case of weaseling. The detective may simply be exercising due care. Other words and phrases that are sometimes used to weasel can also be used legitimately. Qualifying phrases such as "it is arguable that," "it may well be that," and so on have at least as many appropriate uses as weaseling ones. Others, such as "some would say that," are likely to be weaseling more often than not, but even they can serve an honest purpose in the right context. Our warning, then, is to be watchful when qualifying phrases turn up. Is the speaker or writer adding a reasonable qualification, insinuating a bit of innuendo, or preparing a way out? We can only warn; you need to assess the speaker, the context, and the subject to establish the grounds for the right judgment.

Downplayers

Downplayers attempt to make someone or something look less important or less significant. Stereotypes, rhetorical comparisons, rhetorical explanations, and innuendo (all discussed later) can all be used to downplay something. The remark "Don't mind what Mr. Pierce says; he thinks he is an educator" downplays Mr. Pierce and his statements. (What educator doesn't think he or she is one?) We can also downplay by careful insertion of certain words or other devices. Let's amend the preceding example like this: "Don't mind what Mr. Pierce says; he's just another educator." Notice how the phrase "just another" downplays Mr. Pierce's status still further.

Perhaps the words most often used as downplayers are "mere" and "merely." If Kim tells you her sister has a mere green belt in Pujo (a Tibetan martial art), she is downplaying her sister's accomplishment.

The term "so-called" is another standard downplayer. We might say, for example, that the woman who made the diagnosis is a "so-called medical professional," which downplays her credentials. Quotation marks can be used to accomplish the same thing:

> She got her "degree" from a correspondence school.

Use of quotation marks as a downplayer is somewhat different from their use to indicate irony, as in this remark:

> John "borrowed" Hank's umbrella, and Hank hasn't seen it since.

The idea in the latter example isn't to downplay John's borrowing the umbrella; it's to indicate that it wasn't really a case of borrowing at all.

"Fifteen minutes could save you fifteen percent or more on car insurance."

—GEICO car insurance advertisements

Then again, it might not.

Many conjunctions—such as "nevertheless," "however," "still," and "but"—can be used to downplay claims that precede them. Others, like "although" and "even though," can downplay claims that follow them. Such uses are more subtle than the first group of downplayers. Compare the following two versions of what is essentially the same pair of claims:

> (1) The leak at the plant was terrible, but the plant provided good jobs to thousands of people.
>
> (2) Although the plant provided good jobs to thousands of people, the leak there was terrible.

The first statement downplays the leak; the second statement downplays the good the plant produces.

The context of a claim can determine whether it downplays or not. Consider the remark "Chavez won by only six votes." The word "only" may or may not downplay Chavez's victory, depending on how thin a six-vote margin is. If ten thousand people voted and Chavez won by six, then the word "only" seems perfectly appropriate: Chavez won by just the skin of his teeth. But if the vote was in a committee of, say, twenty, then six is quite a substantial margin (it would be thirteen votes to seven, if everybody voted—almost two to one), and applying the word "only" to the result is clearly a slanting device designed to give Chavez's margin of victory less importance than it deserves.

Downplayers really can't—and shouldn't—be avoided altogether. They can give our writing flair and interest. What *can* be avoided is being unduly swayed by them. Learning to appreciate the psychological and emotional nuances of language decreases your chances of being taken in by the manipulations of a writer or speaker.

Exercise 5-1

Identify rhetorical devices you find in the following from the previous section of the text (euphemisms, dysphemisms, weaselers, downplayers). *Not every example may contain such a device.*

▲ —See the answers section at the back of the book.

▲   1. There, there; it could be worse.

2. You should install solar panels. They could save you a lot of money.

3. Smithers might have visited a gentleman's club once or twice, but that hardly could disqualify him from the race.

▲   4. This president wakes up every morning and pretends to speak for the people.

5. Whistle-blower? Dude's a snitch.

6. These self-appointed experts have nothing better to do with their time than tell us what we should do with ours.

▲   7. Excuse me, Dear. I must powder my nose.

8. I suppose we could go listen to her speech. No doubt some people think she is an expert.

9. We have to take poor Fido to the animal shelter.

▲   10. "It doesn't say anywhere in the Constitution this idea of the separation of church and state."

—*Sean Hannity*

11. You say you are in love with Oscar, but are you sure he's right for you? Isn't he a little too . . . uh, mature for you?

12. He was at the bar for two hours, officer, but I know he had only four drinks during that time.

▲ 13. "The key principle is 'responsible energy exploration.' And remember, it's NOT drilling for oil. It's responsible energy exploration."

—Republican pollster Frank Luntz

14. Of course, it may be that Aaron Hernandez didn't even commit the assaults he was accused of.

15. Try the Neutron Diet for just four weeks, and you can lose as many as twenty pounds!

▲ 16. Republicans stand on principle against the schemes of the environmental extremists.

17. Despite the downplaying by bought-off scientists, climate change is very real.

18. Obama and his Democrat–Communist party bloated the already bloated federal bureaucracy by 25 percent in ONE YEAR.

▲ 19. Charles, be sure to tinkle before we leave!

20. Him? Oh, that's just my brother.

RHETORICAL DEVICES II

These next three slanting devices rely, in one way or another, on unwarranted assumptions. We have to depend on unstated assumptions all the time, but as you'll see, we can get into trouble when those assumptions are not trustworthy.

Stereotypes

A **stereotype** is a cultural belief or idea about a social group's attributes, usually simplified or exaggerated. It can be positive or negative. Americans are sometimes stereotyped as friendly and generous, other times as boorish and insensitive. Southern Caucasian males are sometimes stereotyped as genteel or mannerly; other times as bigoted rednecks. Of course, a moment's thought tells us that none of these characteristics could reasonably apply to all the members of these groups. Stereotypes are unreliable characterizations of people; and when speakers or writers use them to try to win us to their point of view, we must be on guard. For example, if someone used the idea of a "welfare queen" (a pejorative stereotype of a lazy mother who prefers collecting welfare checks to finding a job) to persuade us that taxpayers are spending too much money on welfare, we should be aware that the speaker is trying to persuade us with an image rather than with data.*

But stereotyping can work in the other direction as well. If we hear that so-and-so "tells it like it is," we have been given a positive stereotype, that of the outspoken truthteller. Linking people with a stereotype we like can create a favorable impression of them.

Stereotypes come from multiple sources, many from popular literature or the entertainment or recording industries, and are often supported by a variety of prejudices and group interests. Native American tribes of the Great Plains were portrayed

Mention the *strict regulations*—not protocols or rules—governing nuclear power plants.

—Republican pollster FRANK LUNTZ, in "An Energy Policy for the 21st Century," advising Republicans how to sell nuclear energy

---

*In 2012, welfare accounted for less than one-half of 1 percent of the federal budget.

Do Blondes Make Us Dumber? Cognitive Functioning in the Presence of Stereotypes

According to research reported by Shelley Emling of the Cox News Service, when subjects (both men and women) were shown photos of women with blonde hair, their ability to answer Trivial Pursuit game questions declined. This did not happen when they saw women with other hair colors. The authors of the study said that it confirmed other findings that people's cognitive functioning is affected by exposure to stereotypes. "The mere knowledge of a stereotype can influence our behavior," one researcher said. One example given for this was that, when people are exposed to elderly people, they tend to walk and talk more slowly.

■ Maybe seeing a picture of German Chancellor Angela Merkel, a very bright blonde woman, who has a PhD in quantum chemistry, would improve subjects' abilities on Trivial Pursuit.

—*Shelley Emling, Cox News Service,* http://thesituationist.wordpress.com/2008/01/22/.

---

favorably in the popular literature of white Americans until just before the mid-nineteenth century. But as the westward expansion of the United States continued, and conflicts with white settlers escalated, depictions became increasingly pejorative.

Bottom line: Undeniably, some stereotypes carry much rhetorical force, but they have no evidentiary or probative (tendency to prove) force. Rhetoric that contains them may be persuasive psychologically, but it is neither strengthened nor weakened logically.

Incidentally, does the fact that members of a group utter negative stereotypes about themselves make it okay for others to use those stereotypes? We are not aware of an argument to that effect that can withstand scrutiny. "They say bad things about themselves; therefore those things are true" is illogical; and so is "since they say bad things about themselves, it is okay for us to do so too."

Innuendo

Innuendo uses the power of suggestion to disparage (say something bad about) someone or something. Unlike dysphemisms—expressions having obvious negative rhetorical force—innuendo relies on neutral (or even positive) phrasing to insinuate something derogatory. Consider for example this statement:

> Ladies and gentlemen, I am proof that at least one candidate in this race doesn't make stuff up.

The city voluntarily assumed the costs of cleaning up the landfill to make it safe for developers.

—Opponents of a local housing development

Oops, the opponents didn't mention that the law required the city to assume the costs. The omission of course suggests that the city was in cahoots with the developers. Leaving out important information in order to convey a negative message about someone or something is another form of innuendo.

Innuendo with Statistics

> Taxpayers with incomes over $200,000 could expect on average to pay about $99,000 in taxes under [the proposed] plan.
>
> —*Wall Street Journal*

This statement plants the suggestion that the tax proposal will soak anyone who makes over $200,000. But, in the words of the *New Republic* (February 3, 2003), "The *Journal's* statistic is about as meaningful as asserting that males over the age of six have had an average of three sexual partners." Bill Gates and many billionaires like him are among those who make over $200,000.

As you can see, the statement does not say that the speaker's opponent makes stuff up. But it conveys that message nevertheless. Another example:

> Jim: Is Ralph is telling the truth?
> Joe: Yes, this time.

Joe is insinuating that Ralph doesn't usually tell the truth. Yet another example, maybe our all-time favorite, is this remark from W. C. Fields.

> I didn't say the meat was tough. I said I didn't see the horse that is usually outside.

Another example would be:

> She's just the aerobics instructor, at least that's what he tells his wife.

Saying, "He may think he made a good speech" would also count as innuendo, because it insinuates that his speech wasn't very good. So would, "I bet he actually thinks he made a good speech." What we bet is that most people who make good speeches actually think they made good speeches.

Some examples of innuendo are known as **significant mention.** This occurs when someone states a claim that ordinarily would not need making. Here's an example:

> I noticed that Sueanne's latest rent check didn't bounce.

It's clear that the speaker mentions this fact because there was some expectation that the check *would* bounce. Thus the idea that she bounces checks regularly is clearly insinuated.

The key to recognizing innuendo is that it relies entirely on suggestion and implication, rather than on wording that has overtly negative associations. "His speech was vaporous and stupid" is not innuendo.

Loaded Questions

A **loaded question,** like innuendo, implies something without coming out and saying it. For example, the question "Why does the president hate rich people?" implies without quite saying it that the president hates rich people. "Have you always loved being in debt?" implies without quite saying it that you love being in debt.

■ Photographs, like rhetoric, have suggestive power. For example, what does this picture of Russian President Vladimir Putin suggest about him? Is it favorable or unfavorable, or does it depend entirely on your point of view?

Here is how this works. Every question rests on assumptions. Even an innocent question like "What time is it?" depends on the assumptions that the hearer speaks English and probably has means of finding out the time. A loaded question, however, rests on one or more *unwarranted* (unjustified) assumptions. The world's oldest example, "Have you stopped beating your wife?" rests on the assumption that the person asked has beaten his wife in the past. If there is no reason to think that this assumption is true, then the question is loaded.

Loaded questions thus count as a form of innuendo if they imply something negative about someone. However, they can be used to carry a positive message as well, as in the example: "How did Melanie acquire such a wonderful voice?"

Exercise 5-2	1. Watch an episode of *Big Bang Theory, Two and a Half Men,* or *Shades of Blue* and see how many stereotyped characters you can identify.
	2. Watch an episode of *Good Morning America* or one of the network or cable news programs and see how many stereotyped characters you can spot in the commercials.
Exercise 5-3	Identify any stereotypes, innuendo, or loaded questions you find in the following text.

    ▲   1. Devon is a total jock. Don't go making him your study partner.

        2. Went to my philosophy class today. The professor showed up sober.

        3. At least his wife isn't rude.

    ▲   4. Don't you have anything better to wear than that?

        5. Give the work to Brockston. He's a real man. He'll get it done.

        6. You're going to go see what? That's such a chick flick!

    ▲   7. Who do like better, me or Sydney?

        8. For some reason, President Obama has never shown his birth certificate.

        9. An attorney questioning a witness: "So, if you were awake when you crossed the bridge, just when did you go to sleep at the wheel?"

    ▲ 10. No, I'm sure you'll enjoy playing tennis with Jerome. He gets around pretty well for a guy his age.

      11. Frankly, I believe that flash memory will make any kind of moving-part memory, such as hard drives, completely obsolete.

12. Larry Kudlow, on CNBC (in an *American Spectator* interview): "[Former Treasury secretary] Bob Rubin's a smart guy, a nice man, but he hates tax cuts. To listen to Rubin on domestic issues, you could just die. He's a free-spending left-winger."

13. Has Harry been a faithful husband? Well, he's not been through a Tiger Woods phase.

14. Why is it, do you suppose, that pit bulls are all mean and vicious?

15. I wouldn't worry about the train being late. This is Germany, you know.

16. Keep your kid away from that dog! Didn't you know that's a pit bull?

17. It goes without saying that his kid will do well in school. His kind always do.

18. There is no proof the president deals drugs. On the other hand, there's no proof he doesn't, either.

19. Does Sydney still drink like a fish?

20. Of course Christie had nothing to do with shutting down the lanes on the George Washington Bridge. He's only the governor of New Jersey, after all.

RHETORICAL DEVICES III

Humor and a bit of exaggeration are part of our everyday speech. But they can also be used to sway opinions if the listener is not being careful.

Ridicule/Sarcasm

Also known as the **horse laugh,** this device includes ridicule and vicious humor of all kinds. Ridicule is a powerful rhetorical tool—most of us hate being laughed at. So it's important to remember that somebody who simply gets a laugh at the expense of another person's position has not raised any objection to that position.

One may simply laugh outright at a claim ("Send aid to Egypt? Har, har, har!"), tell an unrelated joke, use sarcastic language, or simply laugh at the person who is trying to make the point.

The next time you watch a debate, remember that the person who has the funniest lines and who gets the most laughs may be the person who *seems* to win the debate, but critical thinkers should be able to see the difference between argumentation on one hand and entertainment on the other.

Notice that we are not saying there's anything *wrong* with entertainment, nor with making a valid point in a humorous way.

Hyperbole

Hyperbole is extravagant overstatement, or exaggeration. "The Democrats want everyone to be on welfare" is hyperbole. So is "Nobody in the Tea Party likes African Americans." Describing your

■ Stephen Colbert's stock in trade is making fun of celebrities and politicians.

A feminazi is a woman to whom the most important thing in life is seeing to it that as many abortions as possible are performed.

—RUSH LIMBAUGH

A rhetorical definition with hyperbole. (A straw man, too, but that's for a later chapter.)

parents as "fascists" because they don't want you to major in art also counts. People exaggerate—we all exaggerate—not only to express how strongly we feel about something but also, sometimes, to persuade our listeners of a lesser claim. For example, to persuade your son not to text while driving, you might tell him he's likely to kill half the population of Los Angeles. To convince his girlfriend he really loves her, a young man may state that he loves her more than anyone has ever loved anyone. And so on.

Therefore, the thing to remember when you encounter hyperbole is that, even if you reject it as exaggeration, you might be moved in the direction of a lesser claim even in the absence of argument. If a server tells you that the salmon is the best you will ever eat, you may end up ordering it. If somebody tells you that Clara thinks of nobody but herself, you might be tempted to think that Clara is a little self-centered. If you hear somebody you respect confidently predict "*nobody* will vote for Jackson," you might find yourself surprised when Jackson actually is elected.

It may almost go without saying that other rhetorical devices often involve hyperbole. For example, when we describe a member of the opposing political party as traitorous, we are using a dysphemism that involves hyperbole. And negative stereotyping always involves exaggerating how often some undesirable characteristic is found in the targeted social group.

Exercises for these last two rhetorical devices can be found in Exercise 5-8.

RHETORICAL DEVICES IV

Definitions, explanations, analogies, and comparisons are all used in straightforward ways most of the time. But, as we'll see, they can also be used in rhetorical fashion to slant a point one way or another.

Rhetorical Definitions and Rhetorical Explanations

As explained in Chapter 3, **rhetorical definitions** employ rhetorically charged language to express or elicit an attitude about something. Defining abortion as "the murder of an unborn child" does this—and stacks the deck against those who think abortion is morally defensible. Restricting the meaning of "human being" to an organism to which a human has given birth stacks the deck the other way.

In Chapter 3, we explained that when we define a concept by providing an example of it, we are "defining by example." It's worth noting here that even definitions by example can slant a discussion if the examples are prejudicially chosen. Defining "conservative" by pointing to a white supremacist would be a case in point. If one wants to see all sides of an issue, one must avoid definitions and examples that slant a discussion.

Rhetorical explanations use the language of standard explanations to disguise their real purpose, which is to express or elicit an attitude.

For example, consider this "explanation" we found in a letter to an editor:

> I am a traditional liberal who keeps asking himself, why has there been such a seismic shift in affirmative action? It used to be affirmative action stood for equal opportunity; now it means preferences and quotas. Why the change? It's because the people behind affirmative action aren't for equal rights anymore; they're for handouts.

This isn't a dispassionate scholarly explanation of causation, but a way of expressing an opinion about, and trying to evoke anger at, affirmative action policies.

Legislative Misnomers

Several polls have reported that voters sometimes indicate approval of a measure when they hear its title but indicate disapproval after they've heard an explanation of what the measure actually proposes. This isn't surprising, given the misleading proposal titles assigned by members of Congress and state legislatures, and by authors of ballot measures. Here are a few examples of recent laws, initiatives, and so on, the names of which don't exactly tell the whole story:

Healthy Forests Initiative (federal)—Reduces public involvement in decision making regarding logging, reduces environmental protection requirements, and provides timber companies greater access to national forests

Clear Skies Act (federal)—Loosens regulation of mercury, nitrous oxide, and sulphur dioxide, and puts off required reductions of these substances for several years beyond the limits of the current Clean Air Act; allows companies to trade off "pollution credits" so that some communities would get cleaner air and others dirtier air

Defense of Marriage Act (federal)—Does nothing to preserve traditional marriages, but does outlaw same-sex marriages; many parts have been declared invalid

Limitations on Enforcement of Unfair Business Competition Laws (California)—Makes it impossible for consumer groups of all types to sue corporations and businesses to prevent fraud, false advertising, and other deceptions before they take place

Right to Work (many states)—Prevents unions from collecting fees from nonmembers of bargaining units

Prohibition of Discrimination and Preferential Treatment (California)—Weakens or eliminates affirmative action programs

Rhetorical Analogies and Misleading Comparisons

A **rhetorical analogy** likens two or more things to make one of them appear better or worse than another. This may lead us to change our opinions about something even though we have not been given an argument. For example, hearing Social Security likened to a Ponzi scheme (a Ponzi scheme is a pyramid scheme designed to bilk people who fall for it) might make us suspicious of Social Security. Constant likening of Saddam Hussein to Adolf Hitler may have influenced some people's attitudes about the Iraq invasion. In late 2015 and 2016, we heard Donald Trump compared to Benito Mussolini, the facist dictator of Italy in the early 1940s, in an attempt to paint Trump as a facist.

Of course, people use analogies for straightforward explanatory purposes. If a friend knows nothing about rugby, you might promote his understanding by noting its similarity to football. But when Joseph Goebbels likened intellectuals to "bubbles of fat that float on the surface without affecting the liquid below" (see page 144), it is clear that his intent was to denigrate intellectuals—and lead his listeners to do so as well. On the other hand, when humorist Dave Barry likens having kids to having a bowling alley in your brain, he is simply trying to entertain us.

Rhetorical analogies also include comparisons, like "You have a better chance of being struck by lightning than of winning the lottery." But some comparisons can lead us into error if we are not careful. A female smoker has a much better chance of surviving lung cancer than does a male, but that would not be a good reason for

Doonesbury   BY GARRY TRUDEAU

a female smoker not to quit. Advertising sometimes offers vague comparisons, such as "Now 25 percent larger," "New and improved," and "Quietest by far." Unless both sides of a comparison are made clear, the comparison isn't worth much.

Here are a few questions that you could keep in mind when considering comparisons. They include reference to omissions and distortions, which can be among the more subtle forms of rhetorical devices.

1. *Is the comparison vague?* What do you mean, James is a *better swimmer* than Ray? In what way is Sarah *happier* than Santana? What specifically do you have in mind, when you assert that women are *better equipped to deal with grief?* The appropriate question for comparisons like these is not," What makes you think that is true," but rather, "What do you mean?"

2. *Is important information missing?* It is nice to hear that the unemployment rate has gone down, but not if you learn the reason is that a larger percent of the workforce has given up looking for work. Or, suppose someone says that 90 percent of heroin addicts once smoked marijuana. Without other information, the comparison is meaningless, since 90 percent of heroin addicts no doubt ate carrots, too.

3. *Is the same standard of comparison used?* Are the same reporting and recording practices being used? A change in the jobless rate doesn't mean much if the government changes the way it calculates joblessness, as sometimes happens. In 1993, the number of people in the United States with AIDS suddenly increased dramatically. Had a new form of the AIDS virus appeared? No; the federal government had expanded the definition of AIDS to include several new indicator conditions. As a result, overnight 50,000 people were considered to have AIDS who had not been so considered the day before.

4. *Are the items comparable?* It is hard to compare professional golfers Jack Nicklaus and Tiger Woods, since they played against different competitors and had different types of equipment. It's hard to derive a conclusion from the fact that this April's retail business activity is way down as compared with last April's, if Easter came early this year and the weather was especially cold. That more male than female drivers are involved in traffic fatalities doesn't mean much by itself, since male drivers collectively drive more miles than do female drivers. Comparing share values of two mutual funds over the past ten years won't be useful to an investor if the comparison doesn't take into account a difference in fees.

5. *Is the comparison expressed as an average?* The average rainfall in Seattle is about the same as that in Kansas City. But you'll spend more time in the rain in Seattle because it rains there twice as often as in Kansas City. If Central Valley Components, Inc. (CVC), reports that average salaries of a majority of

Misleading Graphic Comparisons

Comparisons displayed on graphs should be viewed with caution, as this graph illustrates.

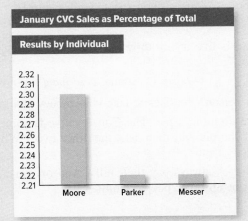

January CVC Sales as Percentage of Total

Results by Individual

If you just glance at the bars, you might think Moore's sales at CVC (a fictitious company) are many times greater than Parker's or Messer's. That's because Moore's bar is much taller than Parker's or Messer's. But if you look closely at the scale on the vertical axis, you can see that, in fact, the sales of all three salespeople are only about eight one-hundredths of a percent different.

its employees have more than doubled over the past ten years, it sounds good, but CVC still may not be a great place to work. Perhaps the increases were due to converting the majority of employees, who worked half-time, to full-time and firing the rest. Comparisons that involve averages omit details that can be important, simply because they involve averages.

Averages are measures of central tendency, and there are different kinds of measures or averages. Consider, for instance, the average cost of a new house in your area, which may be $210,000. If that is the *mean,* it is the total of the sales prices divided by the number of houses sold, and it may be quite different from the *median,* which is an average that is the halfway figure (half the houses cost more and half cost less). The *mode,* the most common sales price, may be different yet. If there are likely to be large or dramatic variations in what is measured, one must be cautious of figures that represent an unspecific "average."

Never try to wade a river just because it has an average depth of four feet.

—MILTON FRIEDMAN

The wrong average can put you under.

Cause for Alarm?

According to the National Household Survey on Drug Abuse, cocaine use among Americans twelve to seventeen years of age increased by a whopping 166 percent between 1992 and 1995. Wow, right?

Except that the increase *in absolute terms* was a little less spectacular: In 1992, 0.3 percent of Americans aged twelve to seventeen had used cocaine; in 1995, the percentage was 0.8 percent of that population.

Be wary of comparisons expressed as percentage changes.

Exercise 5-4   Identify each of the following as either a rhetorical explanation, rhetorical analogy, or rhetorical definition.

▲   1. "The *New York Times* editorial page is like a Ouija board that has only three answers, no matter what the question. The answers are: higher taxes, more restrictions on political speech and stricter gun control."

—*Ann Coulter*

2. "Listening to him is like trying to read *Playboy* magazine with your wife turning the pages."

—*Barry Goldwater, describing fast-talking Hubert Humphrey*

3. A Democrat is a person who likes to take your money and give it to lazy people.

▲   4. Three people are dividing a pie. The Conservative is someone who takes all but one piece of the pie and then asks the other two, "Why is that guy trying to take your piece of pie?"

5. "Good Conservatives always pay their bills. And on time. Not like the Socialists, who run up other people's bills."

—*Margaret Thatcher*

6. "Yeah, I'm obnoxious, yeah, I cut people off, yeah, I'm rude. You know why? Because you're busy."

—*Bill O'Reilly*

▲   7. "Republicans believe every day is the 4th of July, but Democrats believe every day is April 15."

—*Ronald Reagan*

8. "Liberals would rather see a child aborted than a tree chopped down."

—*Ann Coulter*

9. Philosophers love to argue because they don't have anything better to do with their time.

▲   10. "Liberal soccer moms are precisely as likely to receive anthrax in the mail as to develop a capacity for linear thinking."

—*Ann Coulter*

11. "A liberal interprets the Constitution. A conservative quotes it."

—*Rush Limbaugh*

12. "New Rule: Gay marriage won't lead to dog marriage. It is not a slippery slope to rampant inter-species coupling. When women got the right to vote, it didn't lead to hamsters voting. No court has extended the Equal Protection Clause to salmon."

—*Bill Maher*

Exercise 5-5   Explain how rhetorical definitions, rhetorical comparisons, and rhetorical explanations differ. Find an example of each in a newspaper, magazine, or other source.

Exercise 5-6   Critique these comparisons, using the questions about comparisons discussed in the text as guides.

Example

You get much better service on Air Atlantic.

Answer

Better than on what? (One term of the comparison is not clear.)

In what way better? (The claim is much too vague to be of much use.)

▲ 1. New improved Morning Muffins! Now with 20 percent more real dairy butter!

2. The average concert musician makes less than a plumber.

3. Major league ballplayers are much better than they were thirty years ago.

▲ 4. What an arid place to live. Why, they had less rain here than in the desert.

5. On the whole, the mood of the country is more conservative than it was in the last decade.

6. Which is better for a person, coffee or tea?

▲ 7. The average GPA of graduating seniors at Georgia State is 3.25, as compared with 2.75 twenty years ago.

8. Women can tolerate more pain than men.

9. Try Duraglow with new sunscreening polymers. Reduces the harmful effect of sun on your car's finish by up to 50 percent.

▲ 10. What a brilliant season! Attendance was up 25 percent over last year.

PROOF SURROGATES AND REPETITION

These last two devices don't fit comfortably into any of the other groups, so we've made a group of just the two of them.

Proof Surrogates

A **proof surrogate** suggests there is evidence or authority for a claim without actually citing such evidence or authority. When someone can't prove or support something, he or she may hint that proof or support is available without being specific as to what it is. Using "informed sources say" is a favorite way of making a claim seem more authoritative. "It's obvious that" sometimes precedes a claim that isn't obvious at all. "It's clear to anyone who has thought the matter through carefully that blahblahblah" is another example, one that by its sheer length might silence push-back.

A more general strategy speakers and writers use to win acceptance for a claim without providing actual proof or evidence is to insinuate themselves into our confidence. If a salesperson can establish common personal ground with a potential buyer, he or she may be more likely to make a sale. The same strategy may be followed by someone trying to sell us an idea—we may be more inclined to accept claims made by people we feel bonded with. As discussed in Chapter 1, it is a part of in-group bias to be more favorably disposed to a spokesperson who belongs to our own tribe; we naturally are inclined to assign him or her high marks for credibility. And it might be hard to question someone who says "As we all know" because it might sound disrespectful, and nobody wants to show disrespect to a fellow member of the club.

Other proof surrogates are less subtle: "Studies show" crops up a lot in advertising. Note that this phrase tells us nothing about how many studies are involved,

In 2003, the administration proposed a tax cut that, it was said, would give the average taxpayer $1,083.

The "average" here is the mean average. However, most taxpayers, according to the Urban Institute–Brookings Institution Tax Policy Center, would have received less than $100 under the administration's proposal.

There is no other country in the Middle East except Israel that can be considered to have a stable government. . . . Is Saudi Arabia more stable? Egypt? Jordan? Kuwait? Judge for yourself!

—"Facts and Logic About the Middle East"

Proof surrogates often take the form of questions. This strategy can also be analyzed as switching the burden of proof (see Chapter 6).

how good they are, who did them, or any other important information. Here's another example, from *The Wall Street Journal:*

> We hope politicians on this side of the border are paying close attention to Canada's referendum on Quebec. . . .
>
> Canadians turned out en masse to reject the referendum. There's every reason to believe that voters in the United States are just as fed up with the social engineering that lumps people together as groups rather than treating them as individuals.

There may be "every reason to believe" that U.S. voters are fed up, but nobody has yet told us what any of them are.

Bottom line: Proof surrogates are just that—surrogates. They are not proof or evidence. Such proof or evidence may exist, but until it has been presented, the claim at issue remains unsupported.

Repetition

> The most brilliant propagandist technique will yield no success unless one fundamental principle is borne in mind constantly—it must confine itself to a few points and repeat them over and over.
>
> —Joseph Goebbels
>
> A lie told often enough becomes the truth.
>
> —Vladimir Lenin

The technique of **repetition,** simply making the same point over and over at every opportunity, is a widely used rhetorical device, and not just in the propaganda of people like Joseph Goebbels and Vladimir Lenin. It may be found in advertising and

The Great Depression of the 1930s was needlessly prolonged by government policies now recognized in retrospect as foolish and irresponsible.

—Syndicated columnist Thomas Sowell

The phrase "now recognized in retrospect" is a proof surrogate, which hides the fact that the writer has done nothing more than offer his personal opinion.

■ Putting campaign signs up everywhere is a form of repetition. Everything else being equal, we'd bet the winning candidate is the one who puts up the most visible signs. (Of course, usually everything else isn't equal.)

in everyday politics. The constant repetition of a theme seems eventually to have a dulling effect on our critical faculties, and we can become lulled into believing something simply because we've become used to hearing it. This is attributable to the availability heuristic, discussed in Chapter 1. A critical thinker needs to remember: it takes evidence and argument to provide believability; if a claim is not likely to be true on the first hearing, simple repetition does not make it more likely on the hundredth.

List as many proof surrogates (e.g., "It is very clear that . . . ") as you can.

Exercise 5-7

Identify these passages as ridicule/sarcasm, hyperbole, or proof surrogates.

Exercise 5-8

▲ 1. "Everything about the Left is perception, manipulation, and lies. Everything. Everything is 'Wag the Dog.' Everything is a structured deception."

—*Rush Limbaugh*

2. "Mr. Obama has an ingenious approach to job losses: He describes them as job gains."

—*Karl Rove*

3. "How come liberals never admit that they're liberal? They've now come up with a new word called 'progressive,' which I thought was an insurance company but apparently it's a label."

—*Marco Rubio*

▲ 4. "Obviously there is global warming; no responsible climate scientist disputes that."

—*Al Gore*

5. "I might be in favor of national healthcare if it required all Democrats to get their heads examined."

—*Ann Coulter*

6. "We had a national tragedy this week, and the President of the United States and Sarah Palin both made speeches on the same day. Obama came out against lunatics with guns, she gave the rebuttal."

—*Bill Maher*

▲ 7. "Rick Santorum doesn't like sex. He doesn't like the pill. He really doesn't like condoms. He said if men are going to pull something on to prevent procreation, nothing works better that a sweater vest."

—*Bill Maher (Rick Santorum, a GOP presidential contender in 2008, 2012, and 2016, was frequently seen wearing a sweater vest)*

8. "The idea that being black and being gay is the same is simply not true. There are all sorts of studies out there that suggest just the contrary and there are people who were gay and lived the gay life style who aren't any more."

—*Rick Santorum, addressing the question whether being gay is a matter of heredity like being black*

9. "So the majority of Americans are conservatives. They believe in things like the Constitution. I know that's weird to some people, but they believe in it."

—*Marco Rubio*

▲ 10. "You want to have two guys making out in front of your 4-year-old? It's OK with them. A guy smoking a joint, blowing the smoke into your little kid's face? OK with them. And I'm not exaggerating here. This is exactly what the secular movement stands for."

—*Bill O'Reilly*

Exercise 5-9

Identify these passages as ridicule/sarcasm, hyperbole, or proof surrogates.

▲ 1. Medical school, huh? Right. You and your fancy 2.9 grade point are going to get into a fine medical school all right.

2. Laboratory tests have shown that Cloyon produces a sweeter taste than any other artificial sweetener.

3. My wife is nuts. When we go shopping she buys out the entire store.

▲ 4. Anybody who drinks can tell you that three drinks are enough to make that guy seriously impaired.

5. *Rachet & Clank* is the best video game ever made. Try it. You can't stop playing.

6. The only thing you hear on Fox News is right-wing rants, and the only thing you hear on MSNBC are left-wing rants.

▲ 7. That the president is a Marxist simply cannot be denied by any serious observer of contemporary politics.

8. In the 1988 U.S. presidential election, campaigners for Democrat Michael Dukakis took a photograph of Dukakis in an M1 Abrams Tank. The photo was supposed to make Dukakis look strong on defense. Unfortunately, Dukakis had a silly grin and was wearing a helmet too large for his head, and the effect of the photograph was to make him appear diminutive and goofy. The photo was widely shown in the months preceding the election—but not by the Dukakis people. Instead, it was picked up and shown by his opponent, George H. W. Bush. After looking at the photo at the following link, state which technique was being used by the Bush campaign: http://en.wikipedia.org/wiki/File:Michael_Dukakis_in_tank.jpg.

9. If you want to work your way up from being a host to being a server at The Cheesecake Factory, it'll take forever.

▲ 10. The proposal isn't bad when you consider it comes from a group of knuckle-dragging morons.

PERSUASION THROUGH VISUAL IMAGERY

Images affect emotions profoundly. Pictures of lakes and meadows make us feel good. Videos of chuckling babies cause us to laugh. Pictures of kind faces soothe us. Photos of suffering people or animals lead us to make donations.

Imagery affects emotions, and emotions are the wellsprings of actions. Advertisers and political campaigners know this. They use focus groups and other empirical methods to find out which pictures and videos sell the most beer or cars, or generate the most enthusiastic response among potential voters. When it comes to selling a product, political candidate, or even an idea, imagery seems to work better than reasoned argument. At least it is more common.

Apparently, which images work best to motivate behavior is not fully understood and may actually be surprising. Are people more apt to buy a product when they see a beautiful person using it or when they see someone they can relate to using it? Many Superbowl ads are funny visually, but it's not clear that humor works well if you want to sell a laxative.

Adding the right music or other sounds to a video only enhances its power to persuade. Watch an ad produced by a presidential campaign while muting the soundtrack. It will not seem as compelling.

What, then, is the defense when imagery—with or without sound—is enlisted to persuade us to buy a product or vote for a candidate or enlist in the military? After all, nobody wants to be led blindly by emotions; we all want to make intelligent decisions about political candidates, ballot initiatives, and even household products.

One solution might be simply not to watch. The TV remote has made this easier than it used to be, except that online advertising is now pervasive and hard to click your way out of.

Our recommendation is pretty elementary, though not as foolproof as we would like. It begins with remembering that an image is *not* an argument (see Chapter 2). It is not a premise, and it is not a conclusion. A picture is *nonpropositional:* it's neither true nor false. Of course, a picture can be the basis of an argument. A surveillance camera can provide unimpeachable photographic evidence that a car went through a red light. Pictures of mistreated chickens might give officials an excellent reason for shutting down a poultry farm. News photos keep us informed and help us make better decisions. Looked at in this light, a photograph can be informational. And if it is, it is the *information* documented in it that carries weight, not the emotions it generates. Emotions may be the springs of actions, but information alone can be the basis of a reasoned argument. The best defense against being swayed by "photographic rhetoric," if we may call it that, is to focus on the informational content of the photograph or video—assuming the photograph isn't fraudulent. These days sophisticated photo-editing software makes it easy to alter photos to achieve almost any effect. But this is no different from written records and other forms of information, because they can be faked and altered, too.

Don't Get Carried Away!

Once you're familiar with the ways rhetorical devices are used to try to influence us, you may be tempted to dismiss a claim or argument *just because it contains strongly rhetorical language*. But true claims as well as false ones, good reasoning as well as bad, can be couched in such language. Remember that rhetoric *itself* gives us no reason to accept a position on an issue; that doesn't mean that there *are* no such reasons.

These days there are more ways than ever before to deceive us with images. It is often hard to determine whether an image is Photoshopped, which this one, from a Ted Cruz campaign ad, was.

Of course, reasonable people can disagree about what information actually is provided by a visual. In 2005, a Florida woman named Terri Schiavo, became the center of a nationwide controversy regarding whether she was in a "persistent vegetative state" and could ever be expected to regain consciousness. A videotape made by family members appeared to show her responding to the presence of her mother. Some doctors saw the tape and said that Schiavo seemed to be responding to visual stimuli; other doctors said that her facial expressions were not signs of awareness. The first group of doctors thought life support should not be withdrawn; the second group felt that it should. But there is nothing unique about photographic evidence in this regard; other forms of evidence too mean different things to different people. Thus, when you see compelling imagery—meaning imagery that has been used to promote an idea—focus on the information that may or may not be contained within the images, and evaluate it relative to the issue at hand.

THE EXTREME RHETORIC OF DEMAGOGUERY

No account of rhetoric in a book on critical thinking could be complete without a discussion of the rhetoric of demagoguery. Demagogues fan the flames of fanaticism, and use extreme rhetoric to propagate false ideas and preposterous theories—even among people who might otherwise be generous, kind, and honorable. In this section, we highlight four broad rhetorical techniques that demagogues persistently employ.

Otherizing, which is pervasive in demagoguery, divides people into two groups—*us* and *them*—and portrays *them* as suspicious, dangerous, or repulsive. *Them* includes ideological opponents and other social groups who can be blamed for *our* problems. Minorities with their "unreasonable demands" make easy targets. The following passage will illustrate the technique. It is from a speech by Joseph Goebbels, the head of the Nazi Ministry of Information. Goebbels, who had a PhD in literature, once boasted that you can convince people that 2 + 2 is 5 if you know how to do it. In this passage, Goebbels otherizes intellectuals and critics of the Nazi regime:

One cannot make history with such quivering people [intellectuals and dissenters]. They are only chaff in God's breath. Thankfully, they are only a thin intellectual or social upper class, particularly in the case of Germany. They are not an upper class in the sense that they govern the nation, but rather more a fact of nature like the bubbles of fat that always float on the surface of things.

The people want nothing to do with them. These Philistines are the 8/10 of one percent of the German people who have always said "no," who always say "no" now, and who will always say "no" in the future. We cannot win them over, and do not even want to . . . . One does not need to take them all that seriously. They do not like us, but they do not like themselves any better. Why should we waste words on them?

If you think about it, this is pretty obvious. Reading this, whose side would you want to be on, the side of "the people," or on the side of "them," who are so contemptible "we" should not even "waste words on them"? The *fundamental attribution error* and *in-group bias,* which you read about in Chapter 1, have obvious connections with otherizing.

The second pervasive rhetorical technique used by demagogues is *demonizing*—trying to induce loathing of someone or something by portraying the person or thing as evil. Demonizing is often used with otherizing, and the two are frequently blended together so completely that they are impossible to separate out. In 1962, many white Alabamians thought that George Wallace was insufficiently opposed to racial integration to warrant their vote for governor of Alabama. To shore up his credentials as a hardline segregationist, Wallace hired the head of the Ku Klux Klan to write his speeches—and won election. In the following excerpt from his 1963 inaugural address, referred to as his "Segregation Now, Segregation Forever" speech, Wallace demonized the U.S. Supreme Court and the U.S. president, Dwight D. Eisenhower:

It is this theory that led the Supreme Court for the first time in American history to issue an edict, based not on legal precedent, but upon a volume, the editor of which said our Constitution is outdated and must be changed, and the writers of which admitted belonging to as many as half a hundred communist-front organizations. It is this theory that led the same group of men to briefly bare the ungodly core of that philosophy, in forbidding little school children to say a prayer. And we find evidence of that ungodliness even in the removal of the words "In God we trust" from some of our dollars. . . . It is the spirit of power thirst that caused a president in Washington [Eisenhower] to take up Caesar's pen and with one stroke of it make a law . . . that tells us that we can or cannot buy or sell our very homes except by HIS conditions and except at HIS discretion. It is the spirit of power thirst that led the same president to launch a full offensive of twenty-five thousand troops against a university of all places in his own country and against his own people.

George Wallace attempts to block the integration of the University of Alabama in 1963.

As Wallace portrayed them, the members of the Supreme Court were atheistic communists who removed God from our currency and even forbade little school children from praying; and Eisenhower, according to Wallace, was a dictator who told people when they could buy or sell their own homes. He (Eisenhower) even launched an assault against one of our own universities. Notice that Wallace demonized his targets without resorting to many dysphemisms. And without looking too hard, you can find demonizing statements like these on political blogs today.

Fostering xenophobia is the third pervasive rhetorical strategy employed by demagogues, and it goes hand-in-hand with otherizing and demonizing. Xenophobia is the fear or dislike of what is foreign or strange. When we are suspicious of people simply because they dress or talk differently from "us," are from a foreign country, or simply are not "from around here," we are being xenophobic. Demagogues use xenophobia to elicit the worst in human nature. Excerpts from people like Joseph Goebbels and Adolf Hitler are so repugnant that we decline to provide examples.

Fourth, demagogues invariably try to stimulate an audience's fear, resentment, and hatred. *Fear and hate mongering* are used in conjunction with otherizing, demonization, and xenophobia, and you can see how they all work together. Here is

The innocent-looking Joseph Goebbels, PhD, shown here accepting an award from a youngster, used stock propaganda techniques to sell the vile and malignant concepts of the Third Reich.

a passage from another Goebbels' speech, which uses fear and hate mongering to support the other demagogic techniques discussed.

> When Mr. Bramsig or Mrs. Knöterich [names of everyday Germans] feel pity for an old woman wearing the Jewish star, they should also remember that a distant nephew of this old woman by the name of Nathan Kaufmann sits in New York and has prepared a plan by which all Germans under the age of 60 will be sterilized. They should recall that a son of her distant uncle is a warmonger named Baruch or Morgenthau or Untermayer who stands behind Mr. Roosevelt, driving him to war, and that if they succeed, a fine but ignorant U.S. soldier may one day shoot dead the only son of Mr. Bramsig or Mrs. Knöterich. It will all be for the benefit of Jewry, to which this old woman also belongs, no matter how fragile and pitiable she may seem.

Goebbels used fear and hate to prime his audience, something like loading a gun for further use, so that at the right time they would be willing or able to harm the "other," even if the "other" was a helpless old woman.

The four techniques we have just discussed—otherizing, demonization, fostering xenophobia, and fear and hate mongering—are persistently used by demagogues to manipulate the opinion of an audience. Here's the lesson: When you feel yourself enthralled by a speaker, with your blood pumping and your pulse rising—and, in particular, if you are being turned against some person or group of people this is when you most need to think critically. Step back and analyze what is being said. Set aside the temptation to strike out at someone or something. Dial down the anger. Look hard for arguments. You might find there aren't any. This is the only way, short of censorship, to make sure there is never another Joseph Goebbels.

Recap

Things to remember from this chapter:

- ▪ Persuasion attempts to win someone to one's own point of view.
- ▪ Rhetoric seeks to persuade through the rhetorical force of language and other devices.
- ▪ Although it can exert a profound psychological influence, rhetoric has no logical force or probative value.
- ▪ There are a multitude of rhetorical devices in common use; they include:
  - **Euphemisms:** seek to mute the disagreeable aspects of something or to emphasize its agreeable aspects
  - **Dysphemisms:** seek to emphasize the disagreeable aspects of something
  - **Weaselers:** seek to protect a claim by weakening it
  - **Downplayers:** seek to tone down the importance of something
  - **Stereotypes:** a cultural belief about a social group's attributes, usually simplified or exaggerated
  - **Innuendo:** using the power of suggestion to disparage someone or something

— **Loaded questions:** questions that depend on unwarranted assumptions

— **Ridicule and sarcasm:** widely used to put something in a bad light

— **Hyperbole:** overdone exaggeration

— **Rhetorical definitions and explanations:** definitions and explanations used to express or influence attitudes or affect behavior by invoking images with emotional associations

— **Rhetorical analogies:** analogies used to express or influence attitudes or affect behavior by invoking images with emotional associations

— **Proof surrogates** suggest there is evidence or authority for a claim without actually saying what the evidence or authority is

— **Repetition:** hearing or reading a claim over and over can sometimes mistakenly encourage the belief that it is true

■ These devices can affect our thinking in subtle ways, even when we believe we are being objective.

■ Although photographs and other images are not claims or arguments, they can enter into critical thinking by offering information bearing on an issue. They can also affect us psychologically in the same way that emotional language affects us, and often even more powerfully.

■ Demagogues use extreme rhetoric to spread false ideas and to gain power over people. Four rhetorical techniques persistently used by demagogues are otherizing, demonizing, fostering xenophobia, and fear and hate mongering. One of the most important tasks of critical thinking is to recognize these techniques for what they are.

Additional Exercises

Exercise 5-10

Identify each of the following passages as otherizing, demonizing, fear or hate mongering, or fostering xenophia. Some passages may fit more than one category. One passage does not fit any of these categories.

▲ 1. "They aren't from around here. You know that just by looking at them."

—*Overheard conversation*

2. "Whether they are defending the Soviet Union or bleating for Saddam Hussein, liberals are always against America. They are either traitors or idiots, and on the matter of America's self-preservation, the difference is irrelevant."

—*Ann Coulter*

3. "It [Poland] was a State built on force and governed by the truncheons of the police and the military. The fate of Germans in this State was horrible. There is a difference between people of low culture being governed by a culturally significant people and people of high cultural significance having forced upon them the tragic fate of being oppressed by an inferior."

—*Adolf Hitler*

▲ 4. "Barack *Hussein* Obama."

—*Emphasis on middle name, used by some Obama opponents to refer to him*

5. The fact is that public schools in this country have become nothing better than government indoctrination centers. Teachers look constantly for ways to brainwash our students and make them incapable of independent thought or critical judgment. Our children spend their lives in government prison camps where their heads are filled with propaganda. They are told what to think, not how to think. No wonder high school students seem so dumb. Why would anyone want to subject their children to this?

> —Adapted from *The American Dream* http://endoftheamericandream.com/
> archives/category/commentary

6. "These people don't care about our country."

> —*Charles Rangel, referring to Republicans*

▲ 7. "Our intellectual, cultural, and political elites are today engaged in one of the most audacious and ambitious experiments in history. They are trying to transform a Western Christian republic into an egalitarian democracy made up of all the tribes, races, creeds, and cultures of planet Earth. They have dethroned our God, purged our faith from public life, and repudiated the Judeo-Christian moral code by which previous generations sought to live."

> —*Patrick Buchanan*

8. Ew. Don't play with *her*.

9. "Once the Republicans get rolling, they assume they're going to win everything. They are zealots, and zealots assume the last five percent of whatever their plan is will be taken care of by their own greatness or momentum or divinity."

> —*Keith Olbermann*

▲ 10. "Let us therefore brace ourselves to our duties, and so bear ourselves that, if the British Empire and its Commonwealth last for a thousand years, men will still say, 'This was their finest hour!'"

> —*Winston Churchill*

11. "What's really funny is seeing these [gay] activists supporting Muslim governments. They don't want us to bomb them. . . . Do they know what would happen to them outside of the United States? Do they know what would happen to them if Islamists took over this country? They are lucky that they live in a privileged country . . . a country which gives them every right to do whatever they want no matter how much they happen to hate it. It's all very ironic."

> —*Sarah Palin*

12. "As a mom, I was vigilant about food safety. Right, moms? I mean, if you could depend on the government for one thing, it was you had to be able to trust the water that our kids drank and the food that they ate. But this [the Republican Party] is the *E. coli* club. They do not want to spend money to do that."

> —*Nancy Pelosi*

▲ 13. "They keep coming."

> —*1996 reelection campaign ad for California governor Pete Wilson, in reference to
> undocumented immigrants*

14. "Mitt Romney. He's not one of us."

—*2012 Obama Ohio campaign ad*

15. "When Mexico sends its people, they're not sending their best. They're sending people who have lots of problems, and they're bringing those problems to us. They're bringing drugs. They're bringing crime. They're rapists. And some, I assume, are good people."

—*Donald Trump*

Exercise 5-11

In the first ten examples, identify which, if any, of the listed rhetorical strategies are being employed. In the second ten, identify which, if any, of the listed slanting devices are being employed.

1. "Yes, a lot of innocent civilians are being killed by the bombing in both North and South Vietnam, but do remember that Asians do not believe in the importance of individual lives like we do. Life just doesn't mean as much to them."

—*Overheard conversation during the Vietnam War*

   a. demonizing
   b. fostering xenophobia
   c. otherizing
   d. fear or hate mongering
   e. no rhetorical import

2. No, we should not raise the minimum wage for agricultural workers. Many of those people are illegal, and besides, they're happy to work for low wages or they would not have come to this country to begin with.

   a. demonizing
   b. fostering xenophobia
   c. otherizing
   d. fear or hate mongering
   e. no rhetorical import

3. Immigrants, legal and illegal, are coming over here by the thousands and taking jobs away from us—and jobs are already hard enough for us to find.

   a. demonizing
   b. fostering xenophobia
   c. otherizing
   d. fear or hate mongering
   e. no rhetorical import

4. About 47 percent of the American public receive benefits from the government and about the same percentage pay no income tax. They are takers, not like you and me.

   a. demonizing
   b. fostering xenophobia
   c. otherizing
   d. fear or hate mongering
   e. no rhetorical import

5. The motorcycle gangs that come through here regularly are like nothing you've ever seen. They are filthy, they dress like wild people, they are foul-mouthed, and their motorcycles make such a racket it drives you crazy. Decent folk can hardly go out in the street while they're here. We have got to get the city council to do something to stop this terrible invasion of our town.

   a. demonizing
   b. fostering xenophobia
   c. otherizing
   d. fear or hate mongering
   e. no rhetorical import

6. It is indeed an unintended consequence of the new voting laws here in our state that a few people who do not have government-issued photo identification will have trouble voting. The purpose of the laws was to help discourage voter fraud, although nobody is certain whether that has been a problem in our state.

   a. demonizing
   b. fostering xenophobia
   c. otherizing
   d. fear or hate mongering
   e. no rhetorical import

7. Planned Parenthood is badly named. "Planned Population Control" is more like it. The head of that outfit said she's for killing any infant that survived an abortion. That's murder! These are fiends! They give hundreds of presentations a year in Los Angeles schools. They are insinuating their foul views of humanity into our own children!

   a. demonizing
   b. fostering xenophobia
   c. otherizing
   d. fear or hate mongering
   e. no rhetorical import

8. An upper-class British woman around the turn of the last century: "Working people are supposed to work; what could they possibly want with a day off?"

   —*Paraphrase of Bertrand Russell, from* In Praise of Idleness

   a. demonizing
   b. fostering xenophobia
   c. otherizing
   d. fear or hate mongering
   e. no rhetorical import

9. It isn't just the *numbers* of illegals that are streaming across our borders. It's the fact that they are universally poor, mainly illiterate, and without real means of self-support. That means our welfare system, the one you and I pay dearly to support, will be clogged with these invaders.

   a. demonizing
   b. fostering xenophobia
   c. otherizing
   d. fear or hate mongering
   e. no rhetorical import

▲ 10. Crime is going to get nothing but worse with the growth in population, and neither your family nor your property is safe anymore. There have been break-ins, home invasions, and muggings right here in our town. Get an alarm system. Better yet, get a gun.

   a. demonizing
   b. fostering xenophobia
   c. otherizing
   d. fear or hate mongering
   e. no rhetorical import

11. "Making a former corporate CEO the head of the Securities and Exchange Commission is like putting a fox in charge of the henhouse." This is best seen as an example of

   a. rhetorical analogy
   b. rhetorical explanation
   c. innuendo
   d. dysphemism
   e. not a slanter

12. "Right. George Bush 'won' the election in 2000, didn't he?" The use of quotation marks around "won" has the effect of

   a. a weaseler
   b. a dysphemism
   c. a downplayer
   d. a rhetorical explanation
   e. not a slanter

▲ 13. "The obvious truth is that bilingual education has been a failure." In this statement, "the obvious truth" might best be viewed as

   a. a proof surrogate
   b. a weaseler
   c. innuendo
   d. a dysphemism
   e. not a slanter

14. After George W. Bush announced he wanted to turn a substantial portion of the federal government operation over to private companies, Bobby L. Harnage Sr., president of the American Federation of Government Employees, said Bush had "declared all-out war on federal employees." Would you say that the quoted passage is

   a. a rhetorical explanation
   b. a euphemism
   c. a weaseler
   d. hyperbole/a rhetorical analogy
   e. not a slanter

15. "Harry and his daughter had a little discussion about her outfit . . . one that left her in tears." This statement contains

   a. a loaded question
   b. a euphemism
   c. both a and b
   d. neither a nor b

▲ 16. "Before any more of my tax dollars go to the military, I'd like answers to some questions, such as why are we spending billions of dollars on weapons programs that don't work." This statement contains

   a. a downplayer
   b. a dysphemism
   c. a proof surrogate
   d. a loaded question
   e. hyperbole and a loaded question

17. "Can Governor Evans be believed when he says he will fight for the death penalty? You be the judge." This statement contains

   a. a dysphemism
   b. a proof surrogate
   c. innuendo
   d. hyperbole
   e. no slanters

18. President Obama promised change, but he continued to turn government operations over to private companies, especially in Iraq and Afghanistan, just like his predecessor did.

   a. hyperbole
   b. a dysphemism
   c. a loaded question
   d. a proof surrogate
   e. a downplayer

▲ 19. "Studies confirm what everyone knows: smaller classes make kids better learners."

   —*Bill Clinton*

   This statement is

   a. a proof surrogate
   b. a weaseler
   c. hyperbole
   d. an innuendo
   e. no slanter

20. MAN SELLING HIS CAR: "True, it has a few dents, but that's just normal wear and tear." This statement contains

   a. a loaded question
   b. innuendo
   c. a dysphemism
   d. a euphemism

Exercise 5-12

▲ Determine which of the numbered, italicized words and phrases are used as rhetorical devices in the following passage. If the item fits one of the text's categories of rhetorical devices, identify it as such.

   The National Rifle Association's campaign to *arm every man, woman, and child in America*[1] received a setback when the president came out for gun control. But *the gun-pushers*[2] know this is only *a small skirmish in a big war*[3] over guns in America. They can give up some of their more *fanatical*[4] positions on such things as protecting the *"right"*[5] to possess *cop-killer bullets*[6] and still win on the one that counts: regulation of manufacture and sale of handguns.

Exercise 5-13

Follow the directions for Exercise 5-12.

The *big money guys*[1] who have *smuggled*[2] the Rancho Vecino development onto the November ballot *will stop at nothing to have this town run just exactly as they want.*[3] *It is possible*[4] that Rancho Vecino will cause traffic congestion on the east side of town, and *it's perfectly clear that*[5] the number of houses that will be built will overload the sewer system. *But*[6] a small number of individuals have taken up the fight. *Can the developers be stopped in their desire to wreck our town?*[7]

Exercise 5-14

Follow the directions for Exercise 5-12.

The U.S. Congress has cut off funds for the superconducting super-collider that the *scientific establishment*[1] wanted to build in Texas. The *alleged*[2] virtues of the supercollider proved no match for the *huge*[3] *cost overruns*[4] that had piled up *like a mountain alongside a sea of red ink.*[5] Despite original estimates of five to six billion dollars, the latest figure was over eleven billion and *growing faster than weeds.*[6]

Exercise 5-15

Read the passage below, then answer the questions that follow it. Your instructor may have further directions.

"There is something called 'carried-interest' that occupies a peculiar spot in the U.S. tax code; it represents one of the most glaring injustices in a tax law that is chock full of injustice. While most of the people who make a substantial income—and I include here surgeons, stockbrokers, baseball players, and corporate lawyers—will have to pay the new higher marginal rate of 39.6% on the top part of their earnings, there are a few who are exempted from the higher rate.

"The beneficiaries of this tax giveaway are private equity and hedge fund managers, venture capitalists, and partners in real estate investment trusts. Their income, which comes from managing other people's money—they do not have to invest a dime of their own money, mind you, to get this benefit—is taxed as 'carried-interest' at a rate of only 20%. So, a tiny group of individuals who are already stupendously wealthy, manage to get away with a tax burden 19.6% lower than others who earn their money in some other way. For a million-a-year single filer, that could make a difference in taxes of almost a quarter of a million dollars, and all because one made his money by managing other people's money.

"The unfairness of this loophole, which was crafted in large part by Senator Charles Schumer (Democrat of New York), should be obvious to anyone. The New York Times referred to it as 'crony capitalism,' since it favors certain kinds of work over others. Myself, I call it cheating."

—*From a speech by Joel Trajan, at the Northstate Economic Forum, March 2013*

1. What issue is the author addressing?
2. What is the author's position on that issue?
3. Does the author support that position with an argument (or arguments)? If you think so, state that argument (or one of those arguments) in your own words.
4. Are there rhetorical devises or strategies employed in the passage? If so, identify any that fall into the categories described in this chapter.

Exercise 5-16

Follow the directions for Exercise 5-15, using the same list of questions.

Schools are not a microcosm of society, any more than an eye is a microcosm of the body. The eye is a specialized organ which does something that no other part of the body does. That is its whole significance. You don't use your eyes to lift packages or steer automobiles. Specialized organs have important things to do in their own specialties. So schools, which need to stick to their special work as well, should not become social or political gadflies.

—*Thomas Sowell*

Exercise 5-17

Follow the directions for Exercise 5-15, using the same list of questions.

The core of the Judeo-Christian tradition says that we are utterly and distinctly apart from other species. We have dominion over the plants and the animals on Earth. God gave it to us, it's ours—as stated succinctly in the book of Genesis. Liberals would sooner trust the stewardship of the Earth to Shetland ponies and dung beetles. All their pseudoscience supports an alternative religion that says we are an insignificant part of nature. Environmentalists want mass infanticide, zero population growth, reduced standards of living, and vegetarianism. The core of environmentalism is that they hate mankind.

—*Ann Coulter*, Godless: The Church of Liberalism

Exercise 5-18

Follow the directions for Exercise 5-15, using the same list of questions.

Asked whether he would be resigning, [U.N. Secretary General Kofi] Annan replied, "Hell, no. I've got lots of work to do, and I'm going to go ahead and do it." That's doubtful. His term is up at the end of 2006, and few—after the mess he's caused—take him seriously. He may have a lot of "work" he'd like to do, but he won't be permitted to do it. All around Annan is the wreckage of the U.N.'s spirit of high-level cronyism.

—*Editorial in the* National Review Online, *April 1, 2005*

Exercise 5-19

Follow the directions for Exercise 5-15, using the same list of questions.

"It is not the job of the state, and it is certainly not the job of the school, to tell parents when to put their children to bed," declared David Hart of the National Association of Head Teachers, responding to David Blunkett's idea that parents and teachers should draw up "contracts" (which you could be fined for breaching) about their children's behavior, time-keeping, homework and bedtime. Teachers are apparently concerned that their five-to-eight-year-old charges are staying up too late and becoming listless truants the next day.

While I sympathize with Mr. Hart's concern about this neo-Stalinist nannying, I wonder whether it goes far enough. Is it not high time that such concepts as Bathtime, Storytime and Drinks of Water were subject to regulation as well? I for one would value some governmental guidance as to the number of humorous swimming toys (especially Hungry Hippo) allowable per gallon of water. Adopting silly voices while reading *Spot's Birthday* or *Little Rabbit Foo-Foo* aloud is something crying out for regulatory guidelines, while the right of children to demand and receive wholly unnecessary glasses of liquid after lights-out needs a Statutory Minimum Allowance.

—*Walsh, John,* "I say there, are you absolved?" The Independent, August 30, 1998. Copyright © 1998 by The Independent. All rights reserved. Used with permission.

Exercise 5-20

Choose which answer is best from among the alternatives provided.

▲   1. "The Clintons have indeed employed elite accountants to help limit their own family's tax liability. Because they're so very concerned about the wealth gap, you see."

—*Guy Benson, Town Hall.com, January 5, 2016*

This contains
a. a downplayer
b. sarcasm, ridicule
c. hyperbole

2. "Liberals need to understand the global health argument for abortion is deeply offensive. It is like fighting disease by killing everyone who has a disease."
This contains
a. a euphemism
b. a dysphemism
c. a rhetorical definition
d. none of the above

3. "Why does Senator Schmidt collect child pornography? Only the Senator can answer that." This contains

   a. a loaded question
   b. a euphemism
   c. a dysphemism
   d. none of the above

▲ 4. "Does Senator Schmidt collect child pornography? Only the Senator can answer that." This contains

   a. innuendo
   b. a downplayer
   c. a euphemism
   d. a stereotype

5. "Better lock up your whisky before Patrick gets here. Didn't you know he is Irish?" This contains

   a. a loaded question
   b. a rhetorical definition
   c. a stereotype
   d. a euphemism.
   e. none of the above

6. "Ecology? I will tell you what ecology is. Ecology is the Marxist 'science' that tries to shove bogus facts about global warming down everyone's throat." This contains

   a. a rhetorical definition
   b. a rhetorical explanation
   c. a rhetorical analogy

▲ 7. "Ecology? I will tell you what ecology is. Ecology is the Marxist 'science' that tries to shove bogus facts about global warming down everyone's throat." The quotation marks around "science" are

   a. hyperbole
   b. a proof surrogate
   c. a downplayer
   d. a stereotype

8. "Ecology? I will tell you what ecology is. Ecology is the Marxist 'science' that tries to shove bogus facts about global warming down everyone's throat." "Marxist" and "bogus" are

   a. proof surrogates
   b. dysphemisms
   c. hyperbole
   d. rhetorical comparisons
   e. none of the above

9. "The reason Republicans oppose health care is that they don't care about anyone except their friends in the insurance industry." This sentence contains

   a. a rhetorical definition
   b. a rhetorical explanation
   c. a rhetorical analogy
   d. none of these

▲ 10. "Rush Limbaugh doesn't make things up? C'mon, it's been shown over and over that he makes things up." This contains

    a. a stereotype
    b. hyperbole
    c. ridicule
    d. a proof surrogate

Exercise 5-21

Identify any rhetorical devices you find in the following selections, and classify those that fit the categories described in the text. For each, explain its function in the passage.

▲ 1. I trust you have seen Janet's file and have noticed the "university" she graduated from.

2. The original goal of the Milosevic government in Belgrade was ethnic cleansing in Kosovo.

3. Obamacare: The compassion of the IRS and the efficiency of the post office, all at Pentagon prices.

▲ 4. Although it has always had a bad name in the United States, socialism is nothing more or less than democracy in the realm of economics.

5. We'll have to work harder to get Representative Burger reelected because of his little run-in with the law.

6. It's fair to say that, compared with most people his age, Mr. Beechler is pretty much bald.

▲ 7. During World War II, the U.S. government resettled many people of Japanese ancestry in internment camps.

8. "Overall, I think the gaming industry would be a good thing for our state."

—From a letter to the editor, Plains Weekly Record

9. Capitalism, after all, is nothing more or less than freedom in the realm of economics.

▲ 10. I'll tell you what capitalism is: Capitalism is Charlie Manson sitting in Folsom Prison for all those murders and still making a bunch of bucks off T-shirts.

11. Clearly, Antonin Scalia was the most corrupt Supreme Court justice in the history of the country.

12. If MaxiMotors gave you a good price on that car, you can bet there's only one reason they did it: It's a piece of serious junk.

▲ 13. It may well be that many faculty members deserve some sort of pay increase. Nevertheless, it is clearly true that others are already amply compensated.

14. "The only people without [cable or satellite TV] are Luddites and people too old to appreciate it."

—Todd Mitchell, industry analyst

15. I love some of the bulleting and indenting features of Microsoft Word. I think it would have been a nice feature, however, if they had made it easy to turn some of them off when you don't need them.

Exercise 5-22

Identify any rhetorical devices you find in the following passages, and explain their purposes. *Note:* Some items may contain *no* rhetorical devices.

1. "The Obama administration is shamelessly rolling Homeland Security Secretary Janet Napolitano out this week to make sure Americans everywhere know that terrorists will be crawling through their children's bedroom windows as early as next week if the Republicans don't back down on this budget thing."

   —*Matt Taibbi,* Rolling Stone Magazine

2. "If the United States is to meet the technological challenge posed by Japan, Inc., we must rethink the way we do everything from design to manufacture to education to employee relations."

   —Harper's

3. According to UNICEF reports, several thousand Iraqi children died each month because of the UN sanctions.

4. I did see someone sleeping through her lecture, but of course that could have been just a coincidence.

5. I can't find it in myself to sympathize with people with drug problems. I mean, I didn't have anything to do with causing their "problem"; I don't see why I should have anything to do with getting them over it. Let the do-gooders help these druggies. These addicts are like pets—they accept care from others but they can't do anything for themselves.

6. Maybe Professor Stooler's research hasn't appeared in the first-class journals as recently as that of some of the other professors in his department; that doesn't necessarily mean his work is going downhill. He's still a terrific teacher, if the students I've talked to are to be believed.

7. Let's put it this way: People who make contributions to my campaign fund get access. But there's nothing wrong with constituents having access to their representatives, is there?

   —*Loosely paraphrased from an interview with a California state senator*

8. In the 2000 presidential debates, Al Gore consistently referred to his own tax proposal as a "tax plan" and to George W. Bush's tax proposal as a "tax scheme."

9. George Bush got us into two wars, and Jeb is his brother after all. . . .

10. "They'll have to pry my gun out of my cold, dead hands."

    —*Charlton Heston*

11. Wayne Lapierre? Hah! He's worse than Charlton Heston. He's at the point now where he believes that the only—the *only*—solution to the country's problems is more guns! That the solution to *all* the country's problems is more guns!

12. I pulled my child out of school because I learned that his teacher is an atheist. I was amazed that they'd hire an atheist to teach small children. Those people are not satisfied to condemn themselves in the eyes of God; they want to bring our children along with them with their Godless teachings. These are really the most dangerous people in the world, when you think about it. Let's get them out of the schools!

13. All I know is that they started reporting small amounts of money missing not too long after she started working in their house.

14. [*Note:* Dr. Jack Kevorkian was instrumental in assisting a number of terminally ill people in committing suicide during the 1990s.] "We're opening the door to Pandora's Box if we claim that doctors can decide if it's proper for someone to die. We can't have Kevorkians running wild, dealing death to people."

    —*Larry Bunting, assistant prosecutor, Oakland County, Michigan*

15. "LOS ANGELES—Marriott Corp. struck out with patriotic food workers at Dodger Stadium when the concession-holder ordered them to keep working instead of standing respectfully during the National Anthem. . . . Concession stand manager Nick Kavadas . . . immediately objected to a Marriott representative.

    "Marriott subsequently issued a second memo on the policy. It read: 'Stop all activities while the National Anthem is being played.'"

    "Mel Clemens, Marriott's general manager at the stadium, said the second memo clarified the first memo."

    —*Associated Press*

16. These so-called forfeiture laws are a serious abridgment of a person's constitutional rights. In some states, district attorneys' offices have only to claim that a person has committed a drug-related crime to seize the person's assets. So fat-cat DAs can get rich without ever getting around to proving that anybody is guilty of a crime.

17. "A few years ago, the deficit got so horrendous that even Congress was embarrassed. Faced with this problem, the lawmakers did what they do best. They passed another law."

    —*Abe Mellinkoff, in the* San Francisco Chronicle

18. "[U]mpires are baseball's designated grown-ups and, like air-traffic controllers, are paid to handle pressure."

    —*George Will*

19. "Last season should have made it clear to the moguls of baseball that something still isn't right with the game—something that transcends residual fan anger from the players' strike. Abundant evidence suggests that baseball still has a long way to go."

    —*Stedman Graham,* Inside Sports

20. "As you know, resolutions [in the California State Assembly] are about as meaningful as getting a Publishers' Clearinghouse letter saying you're a winner."

    —*Greg Lucas, in the* San Francisco Chronicle

21. The entire gain in the stock market in the first four months of the year was due to a mere fifty stocks.

22. "The climate has changed considerably over the last few decades, with the last two years being the hottest on record in several places around the globe and we've seen the hottest overall global temperatures recently as well. There is every reason to believe that this trend is going to continue, with the result that the planet will gradually become more and more unlivable."

    —*Jim Holt,* Slate *online magazine*

23. "[Supreme Court Justice Antonin] Scalia's ideology is a bald and naked concept called 'Majoritarianism.' Only the rights of the majority are protected."

—*Letter to the editor of the* San Luis Obispo Telegram-Tribune

24. When the government has finished taking over health care—and believe me, the so-called "Affordable Care Act" is just the first step—government bureaucrats will be deciding who gets treated for what. You'll wait while you're dying while some clerk with a rubber stamp figures out whether you get treated or not. Oh yes, and if treatment and death are the alternatives, there will be death squads to make that decision for you. A bunch of government goons will be deciding whether you're worth saving or not. It's going to be wonderful, just like these "progressives" say. You betcha.

▲ 25. "We are about to witness an orgy of self-congratulation as the self-appointed environmental experts come out of their yurts, teepees, and grant-maintained academic groves to lecture us over the impending doom of the planet and agree with each other about how it is evil humanity and greedy 'big business' that is responsible for it all."

—*Tim Worstall, in* New Times

26. "In the 1980s, Central America was awash in violence. Tens of thousands of people fled El Salvador and Guatemala as authoritarian governments seeking to stamp out leftist rebels turned to widespread arrests and death squads."

—USA Today

Exercise 5-23

Discuss the following stereotypes in class. Do they invoke the same kind of images for everyone? Which are negative and which are positive? How do you think they came to be stereotypes? Is there any "truth" behind them?

1. soccer mom
2. Religious Right
3. dumb blonde
4. tax-and-spend liberal
5. homosexual agenda
6. redneck
7. radical feminist
8. contented housewife
9. computer nerd
10. Tea Partier
11. interior decorator
12. Washington insider
13. old hippie
14. frat rat
15. Barbie doll
16. trailer trash

Exercise 5-24

Your instructor will give you three minutes to write down as many positive and negative stereotypes as you can. Are there more positive stereotypes on your list or more negative ones? Why do you suppose that is?

Exercise 5-25

Write two brief paragraphs describing the same person, event, or situation—that is, both paragraphs should have the same informative content. The first paragraph should be written in a *purely* informative way, using language that is as neutral as possible; the second paragraph should be slanted as much as possible either positively or negatively (your choice).

Exercise 5-26

Explain the difference between a weaseler and a downplayer. Find a clear example of each in a newspaper, magazine, or other source. Next find an example of a phrase that is sometimes used as a weaseler or downplayer but that is used appropriately or neutrally in the context of your example.

Exercise 5-27

Critique these comparisons, using the questions discussed in the text as guides.

▲ 1. You've got to be kidding. Paltrow is much superior to Blanchett as an actor.

2. Blondes have more fun.

3. The average chimp is smarter than the average monkey.

▲ 4. The average grade given by Professor Smith is a C. So is the average grade given by Professor Algers.

5. Crime is on the increase. It's up by 160 percent over last year.

6. Classical musicians, on the average, are far more talented than rock musicians.

▲ 7. Long-distance swimming requires much more endurance than long-distance running.

8. "During the monitoring period, the amount of profanity on the networks increased by 45–47 percent over a comparable period from the preceding year. A clear trend toward hard profanity is evident."

—*Don Wildmon, founder of the National Federation for Decency*

9. As a company, Google is a greater benefit to the country than Amazon.

▲ 10. Which is more popular, the movie *Gone With the Wind* or Bing Crosby's version of the song "White Christmas"?

Exercise 5-28

In groups, or individually if your instructor prefers, critique these comparisons, using the questions discussed in the text as guides.

▲ 1. A course in critical thinking will make you smarter.

2. Students are much less motivated than they were when I first began teaching at this university.

3. Offhand, I would say the country is considerably more religious than it was twenty years ago.

4. In addition, for the first time since 1960, a majority of Americans now attend church regularly.

5. Science is not appreciated in this country like it was 50 years ago.

6. Hire Ricardo. He's more knowledgeable than Annette.

7. Why did I give you a lower grade than your roommate? Her paper contained more insights than yours, that's why.

8. Golf is a considerably more demanding sport than tennis.

9. Yes, our prices are higher than they were last year, but you get more value for your dollar.

10. So, tell me, which do you like more, fried chicken or Volkswagens?

Writing Exercises

1. The illustration below is for an article on banks and bankers in *Rolling Stone Magazine* online. After seeing the illustration but before reading the article, how sympathetic to bankers would you expect it to be? Try to come up with a couple of sentences that you think the image illustrates—you'll probably need some forceful language.

Juhasz, Victor, Cartoon from The Rolling Stone, April 15, 2010. Copyright © 2010 by Victor Juhasz. All rights reserved. Used with permission.

2. Over the past decade, reportedly more than 2,000 illegal immigrants have died trying to cross the border into the Southwestern United States. Many deaths have resulted from dehydration in the desert heat and from freezing to death

on cold winter nights. A San Diego–based nonprofit humanitarian organization now leaves blankets, clothes, and water at stations throughout the desert and mountain regions for the immigrants. Should the organization do this? Its members say they are providing simple humanitarian aid, but critics accuse them of encouraging illegal activity. Take a stand on the issue and defend your position in writing. Then identify each rhetorical device you used.

3. Until recently, tiny Stratton, Ohio, had an ordinance requiring all door-to-door "canvassers" to obtain a permit from the mayor. Presumably, the ordinance was intended to protect the many senior citizens of the town from harm by criminals who might try to gain entry by claiming to be conducting a survey. The ordinance was attacked by the Jehovah's Witnesses, who thought it violated their First Amendment right to free speech. The Supreme Court agreed and struck down the law in 2002. Should it have? Defend your position in a brief essay without using rhetoric. Alternatively, defend your position and use rhetorical devices, but identify each device you use.

6 Relevance (Red Herring) Fallacies

T ime now to talk about fallacies.

A **fallacy** is a mistake in reasoning, an argument that doesn't really support or prove the contention it is supposed to support or prove. Here is an example of a fallacy:

> You tell me it's dangerous to text when I'm driving, but I have seen you doing it.

The speaker is dismissing someone's claim that it's dangerous to drive and text. However, the fact that the other person texts while he or she drives has no bearing on whether texting while driving is dangerous. This argument is a fallacy—a mistake in reasoning. It is also an example of a **relevance fallacy** because its premise (I have seen you doing it) is not relevant to the issue in question (whether texting while driving is dangerous).

The fallacies we discuss in this chapter are all relevance fallacies. A relevance fallacy's premise may seem relevant and may resonate psychologically, but it isn't relevant.

Relevance fallacies are also called **red herrings.** A herring is a smelly fish that, if dragged across the trail a hound is

Students will learn to . . .

1. Define and recognize *argumentum ad hominem* fallacies

2. Define and recognize straw man fallacies

3. Define and recognize false dilemma fallacies

4. Define and recognize fallacies involved in misplacing the burden of proof

5. Define and recognize fallacies involved in begging the question

6. Define and recognize fallacies classified as appeals to emotion

7. Define and recognize other fallacies involved in arriving at irrelevant conclusions

tracking, might lead the hound on a wild goose chase; the fish is merely a distracting irrelevancy.

In this chapter, we will look at the most common red herrings (relevance fallacies).

ARGUMENTUM AD HOMINEM

The example just given about texting is a relevance fallacy (or red herring) known as an ***Argumentum Ad Hominem*** (pronounced the way it is spelled). This type of argument is the most common fallacy on planet Earth. The name translates as "argument to the person." You commit this fallacy if you think you dismiss someone's *position* (idea, proposal, claim, argument, etc.) by dismissing *him* or *her.* Take the example about texting and driving. Recall what was going on: the issue was whether it is dangerous to text and drive. But instead of discussing the other person's position on the issue, the speaker (the person committing the fallacy) started talking about *the other person.* The speaker's argument was directed at *the person (ad hominem),* not at what the other person said.

Let's modify that example slightly:

> Not only have I seen you drive and text, but just last week you were saying it isn't dangerous to do that.

This too is an *argumentum ad hominem.* Instead of addressing whether it is dangerous to text, the speaker (the person committing the fallacy) is still talking about the other person, apparently thinking that the fact the individual has changed positions on the issue somehow nullifies what he or she said. You might wonder how anyone could reason this way, but you hear this type of argument all the time. Accusations of doing a "flip-flop" are standard in political campaigns, despite the fact that a person's being inconsistent or changing his or her mind has no bearing on the wisdom of his or her position either now or at any other time.

Here is a different kind of example of *argumentum ad hominem:*

> What do I think about the president's proposal for immigration reform? It's ridiculous. He just wants Latino votes.

The speaker is just bad-mouthing the president, which doesn't tell us anything at all about the strengths or weaknesses of the president's proposal. If the speaker wants to show that the president's proposal is ridiculous, the speaker had better talk about the proposal.

Another slightly different example:

> You can forget what Father Hennessey said about the dangers of abortion, because Father Hennessey is a priest and priests are required to hold such views.

The speaker in this example isn't exactly bad-mouthing Father Hennessey, but he or she still isn't talking about what Father Hennessey said. Instead, he or she is talking about Hennessey's circumstances (being a priest). If someone gave you this argument, you wouldn't have the faintest idea what Father Hennessey actually thinks the dangers of abortion are, let alone what is wrong with his thinking.

To repeat, the *argumentum ad hominem* fallacy occurs when someone attempts to dismiss another person's position on an issue by discussing the person, and not by discussing the issue or that person's position on it. The person committing the fallacy might discuss the other individual's circumstances, character, motivation, lack of consistency, or any number of other attributes, but he or she hasn't really commented on the strengths or weaknesses of the other individual's *position.*

Poisoning the Well

Speakers and writers sometimes try to get us to dismiss what someone is *going* to say by talking about the person's consistency or character or circumstances. This is known as **Poisoning the Well.** An example:

> You can forget what Father Hennessey will say this evening about abortion, because Father Hennessey is a priest and priests are required to think that abortion is a mortal sin.

As you can see, this is like the previous example about Father Hennessey, except in this example Father Hennessey hasn't said anything yet. The person who made the previous statement is poisoning the well, hoping we are not thinking critically and will dismiss whatever Father Hennessey says when he does speak.

Guilt by Association

Outside the logic classroom, the phrase "guilt by association" refers to the concept that a person is judged by the company he or she keeps. For example, if you hang out with unsavory people, then others may think that you too have unsavory qualities. We, however, mean something different by the phrase "guilt by association." We use the phrase to denote a very common version of the *argumentum ad hominem.* The fallacy **Guilt by Association** occurs when a speaker or writer tries to persuade us to dismiss a belief by telling us that someone we don't like has that belief. For example:

> You think waterboarding is torture? That sounds like something these left-wing college professors would say.

The speaker wants listeners to dismiss the idea that waterboarding is torture. So he or she tries to taint that idea by associating it with "left-wing college professors," people he or she thinks listeners don't like or trust. The argument isn't a straightforward *argumentum ad hominem,* because the speaker doesn't imply that "left-wing college professors" came up with the idea that waterboarding is torture. He or she is just saying that they likely have that idea. The fact that the idea is *associated* with such people is offered as a reason for dismissing it. The belief is "guilty" by virtue of its alleged association with supposedly left-wing college professors.

Genetic Fallacy

One other version of the *argumentum ad hominem* deserves your attention. It's known as the **Genetic Fallacy.** A speaker or writer commits this fallacy when he or

---

We've arrived at a point where the President of the United States is going to lead a war on traditional marriage.

—RUSH LIMBAUGH, on President Obama's endorsement of gay marriage (Limbaugh's first, second, third, and fourth wives could not be reached for comment.)

The comment about the wives is a humorous *argumentum ad hominem* dismissal by About.com of something Rush Limbaugh said. See the Political Humor section of About.com.

Could somebody please show me one hospital built by a dolphin? Could somebody show me one highway built by a dolphin? Could someone show me one automobile invented by a dolphin?

—RUSH LIMBAUGH, responding to *The New York Times* claim that dolphins' behavior and large brains suggest they are as intelligent as human beings.

Good point. Anyone know of a hospital or highway built by Rush Limbaugh or an automobile invented by him?

(The "good point" comment is an *argumentum ad hominem* on our part. We couldn't resist.)

she argues that the origin of a contention in and of itself automatically renders it false. Here are two examples:

> That idea is absurd. It's just something the Tea Party put out there.

> Where on earth did you hear that? On talk radio?

As you can see, both examples imply that a view should be rejected simply because of its origin (genesis).

Here's another example of the genetic fallacy:

> God is just an idea people came up with way back before they had science.

The speaker is dismissing the idea of God because of its origin.

STRAW MAN

The **Straw Man** fallacy occurs when a speaker or writer attempts to dismiss a contention by distorting or misrepresenting it. Here's an example of the straw man fallacy:

> What do I think about outlawing large ammunition clips? I think the idea of disarming everyone is ridiculous and dangerous.

As you can see, the speaker has turned the proposal to outlaw large ammunition clips into something far different, a proposal to disarm everyone. He has set up a straw man (one that is easy to knock over).

The straw man fallacy is almost as common as the *argumentum ad hominem*. Here is another example of the straw man fallacy:

> YOU: I think we should legalize medical marijuana.
> YOUR FRIEND: Maybe you think everyone should go around stoned, but I think that's absurd.

Your Friend has transformed your position into one that nobody would accept. Another example:

> CONSERVATIVE: It would be bad for the economy to tighten emission standards for sulfur dioxide.
> PROGRESSIVE: How can you say that? Having more sulfur dioxide in the atmosphere is the last thing we need!

Conservative never said she wanted *more* sulfur dioxide in the atmosphere; Progressive is putting words into her mouth. He has misstated her position.

Whereas an *argumentum ad hominem* attempts to dismiss a claim on the basis of irrelevant considerations about the person making it, the straw man fallacy attempts to dismiss a claim by misrepresenting it.

FALSE DILEMMA (IGNORING OTHER ALTERNATIVES)

The **False Dilemma** fallacy happens when someone tries to establish a conclusion by offering it as the only alternative to something we will find unacceptable, unattainable, or implausible.

> We either eliminate Social Security or the country will go bankrupt. Therefore, we must eliminate Social Security.

This is a fallacy. The speaker doesn't present all the options. He ignores, for example, the alternative of cutting something other than Social Security, or raising the age of eligibility, or having better off earners pay more into the system.

Here is another example:

> Either we allow the oil companies to drill for oil in the Gulf or we will be at the mercy of OPEC. Therefore, we shouldn't prevent the oil companies from drilling for oil in the Gulf.

This is a false dilemma. The speaker thinks oil companies should be free to drill in the Gulf, and tries to support his position by pretending that it's either that or be at the mercy of OPEC, an alternative he assumes we will find unacceptable. The speaker ignores other options. Saving fuel might be one. Getting oil from shale is another. Going solar is possibly a third. Maybe you can think of others.

Here is another example. A man says to his spouse:

> "Look, either we clean out the garage, or this junk will run us out of house and home."

The man is pretending the only alternative to cleaning out the garage is being run out of house and home, an unacceptable alternative. He has ignored other options, such as not acquiring more junk.

Which Do You Want in Your Backyard?

 This?   ■ Or this!

We've seen flyers advocating a position on a zoning-law proposal that imply we must choose between settings like these. Vote one way, you get a lush creek in your backyard; vote the other, you get a pig farm. We're pretty sure there are other alternatives.

The false dilemma fallacy is often referred to as the black/white fallacy, the either/or fallacy, the false choice fallacy, and the false alternative fallacy. Perhaps the best name would be "ignoring other options," but unfortunately that name hasn't caught on.

The Perfectionist Fallacy

Two false dilemma arguments are so common that they have their own names. One is called the **Perfectionist Fallacy.** The fallacy is committed when a speaker or writer ignores options between "perfection" and "nothing." Here's an example:

> A single English course won't make anyone a great writer, so I don't see why we have to take one.

The speaker has presented us with a perfectionist fallacy. He has restricted our options. He is arguing that unless a single English course can make us great writers ("perfection"), we shouldn't have to take one at all. He has ignored the possibility that a single English course might make us *better* writers.

Here is another example of the perfectionist fallacy:

> Drilling for oil in the Gulf won't give us independence from OPEC; therefore, we shouldn't drill.

Unlike the speaker in the previous oil drilling example, this speaker tries to establish that we should *not* drill in the Gulf. She gives us a perfectionist fallacy, because she ignores the less-than-perfect possibility that drilling for oil in the Gulf could make us *less* dependent on OPEC.

The Line-Drawing Fallacy

The other version of the false dilemma fallacy is the **Line-Drawing Fallacy.** This fallacy occurs when a speaker or writer assumes that either a crystal-clear line can be drawn between two things, or else there is no difference between them. Here is an example:

> It doesn't make sense to say that someone is rich. After all, nobody can say just how much money a person has to have in order to be "rich."

The speaker has assumed that, if we cannot say *exactly* how many dollars a person must have in order to be rich, then we can never say that person is rich. But he ignores the fact that there are obvious cases of rich people as well as people who are not rich. An imprecise line between the two is still useful.

Here is another example of the line-drawing version of the false dilemma fallacy—a person trying to argue that video games are not excessively violent:

> You can't say exactly when a videogame is too violent; therefore, no videogame is too violent.

The speaker has restricted our options to either being able to draw a *clear* line between violent and nonviolent videos (which is implausible to think could be done), or not making a distinction between them. He has ignored the possibility that an imprecise line can be drawn and that it might have some value in assessing level of violence.

Antonin Scalia Uses the Line-Drawing Fallacy

Antonin Scalia was a justice on the United States Supreme Court until his death in early 2016. Attorney Theodore B. Olson represented those who sought to have the Supreme Court rule that California's Proposition 8, which banned gay marriage, is unconstitutional. The following is from the oral arguments made before the U. S. Supreme Court on Proposition 8.

SCALIA: When did it become constitutional [When did gays have a constitutional right to marry?]?

OLSON: When we as a culture determined that sexual orientation is a characteristic that individuals cannot control.

SCALIA: I see. When did that happen? When did that happen?

OLSON: There is no specific date in time.

SCALIA: How am I supposed to know how to decide the case then?

MISPLACING THE BURDEN OF PROOF

If your doctor says you are infected with West Nile virus, you will say, "Doctor, what makes you think that?" If she says, "What makes you think you aren't?" you will get a new doctor. Her remark is absurd because it is *her* job to tell you why she thinks you are infected with West Nile, not *your* job to tell her why you think you aren't.

As in this case, sometimes the burden of proof clearly falls more heavily on one side than another. When people try to support or prove their position by misplacing the burden of proof, they commit the fallacy called **Misplacing the Burden of Proof.** Here is a less far-fetched example:

I believe our former president's birth certificate was a forgery. Can you prove it isn't?

The burden of proof is on the speaker to give us a reason for thinking the birth certificate was forged, and he or she has tried to transfer the burden to the listener. Why is the burden of proof on the speaker? Because forging a birth certificate is the exception rather than the rule. If everyone normally forged his or her birth certificate, then it would be common to want proof that one *wasn't* forged. But in the real world, forging a birth certificate is rare, so the person who makes the accusation has the burden of proof.

Another example:

> Guns should be outlawed. I'll bet you can't think of a single good reason they shouldn't.

The speaker has incorrectly shifted the burden of proof to the listener. In the United States, the Constitution is interpreted as giving people the right to own a gun, so the burden of proof is on the speaker to explain why the right should be removed.

Sometimes you have to be on your toes to spot the fallacy. Here is an example:

> JILL: We should invest more money in expanding the interstate highway system.
> ALICE: That would be a mistake.
> JILL: How could anyone object to more highways?

With her last remark, Jill has tried to put the burden of proof on Alice. This tactic can put Alice in a defensive position, if she takes the bait. Alice may think she must show why we should not spend more on highways, when in fact it is Jill who has the burden of proof. We don't even know whether Alice is against more highways; she might think we shouldn't be spending any money because of budget problems.

Which side has the burden of proof often depends on context, but speaking generally, if the issue is a factual one, the side making the more outlandish claim (the claim having the lowest initial credibility) has the burden of proof. Also, other things being equal, the burden of proof falls on the person who wants to change something, rather than on the person who wants to leave things alone. That was the case in the last two examples. Of course, in a criminal court, the burden of proof always falls on the prosecution. The defense is not required to prove innocence: it must only try to keep the prosecution from succeeding in its attempt to prove guilt. This is what is meant by the phrase "Innocent until proved guilty."

When someone asserts that we should believe a claim because nobody has proved it false, the fallacy is a version of misplacing the burden of proof known as **Appeal to Ignorance.** Here is an example:

> Nobody has proved ghosts don't exist; therefore they do.

This is a fallacy because proof requires more than an absence of disproof.

Here is our recommendation: Be suspicious when somebody regards your inability to disprove his or her position as evidence for it. Take note of where the burden of proof falls in such situations; your speaker may be trying erroneously to place that burden on you.

Shifty Sales Strategies

BEGGING THE QUESTION (ASSUMING WHAT YOU ARE TRYING TO PROVE)

In everyday language, to *beg* the question has lately come to mean simply to *raise* the question. Traditionally, and in logic, **Begging the Question** means something else. A speaker or writer is guilty of begging the question logically when he or she tries to "support" a contention by offering as "evidence" what amounts to a repackaging of the very contention in question.

Here is an example:

> Obviously the governor told the truth about the budget. He wouldn't lie to us about it.

In essence, the reason given here for believing the governor is that he wouldn't lie. This isn't *exactly* the same thing, but it is so close that it could not really be counted as evidence. If we aren't sure the governor told the truth, we can't be sure he wouldn't lie.

If an argument is of such a nature that a person who disputes its conclusion logically must also dispute its premise, then it begs the question. The classic example of begging the question is this:

> That God exists is proved by scripture, because scripture is the word of God and thus cannot be false.

If someone disputes that God exists, then he or she must also dispute that anything is the word of God.

Here is another example:

> Women should not be allowed in combat, because it is prohibited by the Defense Department.

This is merely saying that something shouldn't be allowed because it isn't, which does not explain why it shouldn't.

Often loaded questions (discussed as rhetorical devices in Chapter 5) beg the question. This dialogue will serve as an example:

> BILL: Do Republicans hate women because they are angry white males? Yes or no.
>
> JILL: Uhhhhhh...
>
> BILL: Well?

Bill hasn't given a legitimate argument for his belief that Republicans hate women. He has simply asked a question which assumes that very point. He is just smuggling his belief into his question—which amounts to trying to establish something simply by assuming it.

APPEAL TO EMOTION

When a speaker or writer "supports" a contention by playing on our emotions rather than by producing a real argument, the result is the fallacy called an **Appeal to Emotion.** This can happen in various ways depending on the specific emotion involved. We will explain the most common varieties of this fallacy.

The idea behind [talk radio] is to keep the base riled.

—Republican political adviser BRENT LAUDER, explaining what talk radio is for

Argument from Outrage

The **Argument from Outrage** attempts to convince us by making us angry rather than by giving us a relevant argument. Here is an example:

> Do you think Apple doesn't know it hires 12-year-old children to make its electronics? You think it isn't aware it pays them slave wages and has them work in buildings without heat or air conditioning? It knows. Apple products can't be any good.

The passage doesn't support the contention that Apple products aren't any good. Rather, it tries to *induce* us to have that belief by making us angry.

Here is another example:

> You expect me to believe BP cleaned up its mess in the Gulf? Just look at those ads it runs, trying to make it sound like everything is beautiful and even better than before. Does the company take us for fools?

This argument has no probative weight. It tries to persuade us that BP hasn't cleaned up its mess, by making us indignant, rather than by proving or supporting.

The argument from outrage occurs frequently in political contexts, where the conclusion is often just implied that we should vote against someone or something.

Scare Tactics

The **Scare Tactics** fallacy occurs when a speaker or writer tries to scare us into accepting an irrelevant conclusion.

Debate Evaluations

Here is an example:

> You really should get a Prudential life insurance policy. What would happen to your spouse and children if you die? Remember, you are their main source of income. Would they be forced to move?

This argument tries to scare you into buying a Prudential life insurance policy. But even if it is true that your spouse and children will be forced to move if you die, that is no reason to favor insurance from this particular company.

Threats too, if they substitute for argument, are regarded as scare tactics. Here is an example:

> Gavin Newsom would make a terrible governor. Do you seriously think I could be interested in being your girlfriend if you vote for him?

The speaker hasn't said a thing to support the idea that Gavin Newsom would make a terrible governor. She is just threatening the other person. Obviously, if a speaker issues a credible threat, it would not be a fallacy to protect yourself. "If you vote for Newsom, I will shoot your dog" would be a compelling reason for not voting for Newsom, if the speaker actually would carry out the threat. But no threat to you is related to whether Newsom would make a terrible governor.

One final example of a scare tactic:

> Obviously the federal government must cut spending. You agree with the rest of us on that, I assume.

The speaker hasn't given the listener a reason for cutting government spending. He or she is simply trying to make the listener fear being made an outcast. This is sometimes called the **Peer Pressure Fallacy.**

Scare Tactics versus Fear Mongering

Speakers and writers often make inflammatory or scary statements just to rile people up or frighten them, without pretending that the statements support a specific conclusion. When that happens, it's just fear or hate mongering, as discussed in Chapter 5. Here, for example, is a famous fear-mongering statement from Joseph McCarthy, the U.S. senator from Wisconsin in the 1950s who furthered his own political objectives by alarming people with false accusations of treason and communism.

> I have here in my hand a list of two hundred and five people that were known to the Secretary of State as being members of the Communist Party and who nevertheless are still working and shaping the policy of the State Department.

The statement wasn't offered with any specific "conclusion." So you can't really call it an argument or a fallacy. It's just scary rhetoric about Communists infiltrating the government. Obviously there is a fine line between the scare tactic fallacy and fear mongering, and between the argument from outrage and hate mongering. If there is no specific conclusion stated or implied, then you can call it fear or hate mongering.

Appeal to Pity

The **Appeal to Pity** fallacy occurs when a speaker or writer tries to convince us of something by arousing our pity rather than by giving a relevant argument. Here is an example:

> Jane is the best qualified candidate: after all, she is out of work and desperately needs a job.

The speaker has not given a reason for thinking that Jane is the best qualified candidate; he or she is just tugging on our heartstrings.

Other Appeals to Emotion

Emotions other than fear, anger, and pity are used to manipulate an audience into believing or doing something. Instead of providing actual support for a claim, a speaker or writer may issue remarks designed to make us feel envious or jealous, proud, guilty, or anything else, in the hope that we will then accept the claim. These other "arguments" have names—playing on our pride is called **Apple Polishing,**

■ Guns aren't arguments, but that hardly means you should ignore what an armed man tells you to do.

trying to make us feel guilty is referred to as **Guilt Tripping,** arousing envy is called **Appeal to Envy,** and playing on someone's jealousy is called **Appeal to Jealousy.** What these and the other appeals to emotion all have in common is that they actually are pieces of *persuasion* masquerading as arguments.

This brings up the final and very important point about appeals to emotion. Considerations that *truly support* a contention often arouse our emotions. So you cannot conclude, just because someone appears to be trying to scare you or make you angry, or feel some other way, that he or she has committed a fallacy. If he or she offers evidence having probative value, then it is a mistake to consider the argument a fallacy. Here is an example of a legitimate (no fallacy) argument that might arouse a listener's pity.

> You should let that dog out of your car, because it is suffering from heat and thirst and will die very soon if you don't.

This is *not* the appeal to pity fallacy or any other kind of fallacy. The speaker has given us an excellent reason for letting the dog out of our car.

And here is an example of a legitimate (no fallacy) argument that might arouse a listener's fear:

> You should not drive on the 50 tonight. It is icy and dangerous and you could get killed.

This is *not* scare tactics or any other kind of fallacy. Dangerous conditions on a road are relevant to whether we should drive on it. Look very carefully at what speakers and writers say before concluding that a fallacy has been committed. Seeing "fallacies" where none are present is also a breakdown in critical thinking.

■ Scare tactics? Not really. The ad is actually aimed at reducing one's fear.

IRRELEVANT CONCLUSION

Relevance fallacies that do not fit comfortably into the above categories may be said to commit the fallacy of **Irrelevant Conclusion.** Here is an example from a student talking to a professor:

> I don't think I missed too many classes to pass. My attendance has been much better lately.

An improvement in attendance doesn't show you didn't miss too many classes to pass.

Here is a car salesperson:

> This new Honda gets better mileage than any other car in its class. After all, Honda has completely redesigned the engine.

Hooray; good for Honda. Now let's hear figures on mileage.

A similar example is as follows:

> Fracking* won't hurt the water around here. Don't you know that we have invested millions in safety controls?

Perhaps the speaker's company deserves kudos for its safety controls, but we haven't been given evidence that the controls work at all, let alone perfectly.

---

*Hydraulic fracturing, or fracking, is the process of drilling and injecting fluid into the ground at a high pressure in order to fracture shale rocks to release natural gas or oil inside.

This is a different sort of example:

> Why should I tell them they undercharged me? You think they would say something if they overcharged me?

The speaker is trying to justify not doing anything about having been undercharged. However, the fact that they (whoever they are) wouldn't inform him of an overcharge (assuming it is even true that they wouldn't) only supports a negative appraisal of *their* ethics, not a positive appraisal of *his*. This is an example of the fallacy **Two Wrongs Make a Right.**

Two other common irrelevant conclusion fallacies are **Wishful Thinking** and **Denial.** Wishful thinking happens when we forget that wanting something to be true is irrelevant to whether it is true. Denial happens when we forget that wanting something to be false is irrelevant to whether it is false. The two fallacies are flip sides of the same thing, of course.

Here is an example of wishful thinking:

> I really really hope I will be the next American Idol. Therefore, I'm sure I will be.

Did *American Idol* contestants really think this? Some at any rate seemed stunned when they were eliminated.

Here is an example of denial:

> I'm *positive* I didn't miss class as many times as the professor says and the records show! I just know it!!!

Being "in denial" about the likely consequences of harmful behavior—smoking, eating poorly, drinking excessively, and so forth—does not seem uncommon.

Ducking with Irrelevancies

David Muir (*of ABC News***):** Does Carfax report the entire history of the car?

Larry Gamache (Carfax communications director): Yes, we give people the entire Carfax history.

David Muir: Is that the entire history of the car?

Larry Gamache: You can't give the entire history of anything.

■ David Muir, of ABC News

Sometimes irrelevancies are introduced into a discussion when someone attacks a counterargument *to* his or her position rather than offering an argument *for* that position. Here is an example:

> Republicans hated Obama due to their racist attitudes. If the polls didn't show it, it's because people lie.

The speaker here hasn't supported the assertion that Republicans hated Obama because they are racist. Rather than produce evidence to support this assertion, he or she claims that people lied to pollsters. This is logically irrelevant at this point in the discussion.

Recap

The fallacies in this chapter are relevance fallacies—arguments that may seem relevant to their conclusion but logically are not. We specifically examined the following:

- ■ *Argumentum ad hominem*—attempting to dismiss a source's position by discussing the source rather than the position
- ■ Straw man—attempting to dismiss a source's position by misrepresenting it
- ■ False dilemma—attempting to establish a point by pretending it is the only alternative to something we will find unacceptable, unattainable, or implausible
- ■ Misplacing the burden of proof—attempting to place the burden of proof on the wrong side of an issue
- ■ Begging the question—attempting to "support" a contention by offering as "evidence" what amounts to a repackaging of the very contention in question
- ■ Appeal to emotion—attempting to "support" a contention by playing on our emotions rather than by producing a real argument
- ■ Irrelevant conclusion—relevance fallacies that do not fit into the previous categories

EXERCISES

Here are 100 examples of the fallacies discussed in this chapter.* Match each item to one or more of the following categories:

    a. *argumentum ad hominem*
    b. straw man
    c. false dilemma
    d. misplacing the burden of proof
    e. begging the question
    f. appeal to emotion
    g. irrelevant conclusion

*Exercises from previous editions may be found in the appendix at the end of the book.

Notes

- Some items arguably fall into more than one category; this is true in real life as well. But no item in this list could plausibly be said to fall into every category. Your instructor will tell you if your categorization is too much of a stretch.

- Your instructor may or may not ask you to further match instances of *argumentum ad hominem* to one or another of these categories:

    a. Arguments that dismiss a source's position because of the source's alleged hypocrisy or inconsistency (inconsistency *ad hominem*)

    b. Arguments that dismiss a source's position because of other alleged deficiencies on the part of the source (personal attack or abusive *ad hominem*)

    c. Arguments that dismiss a source's position because of the source's circumstances (circumstantial *ad hominem*)

    d. Arguments that dismiss a source's position before the source has presented it (poisoning the well)

    e. Arguments that dismiss a claim by associating it with someone we are assumed to despise (guilt by association)

    f. Arguing that the source of a contention in and of itself renders it false (genetic fallacy)

- Your instructor may also ask you to identify any examples of perfectionist or line-drawing versions of the false dilemma fallacy.

- Finally, your instructor may ask you to identify specific emotional appeals, including argument from outrage, appeal to pity, and scare tactics.

1. Save your money. Nothing will make your teeth perfectly white.

2. Jane complains because she doesn't like the way I clean. Of course, she wants to be able to eat off the floor.

3. Don't read *The New York Times*. It's filled with liberal propaganda.

4. Limbaugh! That pompous windbag. You can't believe what he says about climate science.

5. If you don't support same-sex marriage, then you are a homophobe who hates gays.

6. It isn't *guns* that need controlling. It's *people* who need controlling! *Guns* don't kill people; *people* kill people! I get furious when I hear people miss this point!

7. SKEPTIC: Why is Genesis the only acceptable account of how the world came to be?
   BELIEVER: Show me an explanation that makes more sense.

8. The prices at Starbucks? A rip-off. I get better coffee at McDonald's.

9. I'm telling you, something was holding me in bed in the middle of the night. I didn't see or hear anything, but there were hands—or something—on my chest and stomach pushing me into the bed. You can't convince me it wasn't something supernatural doing it.

10. Acid indigestion, if untreated, might burn a hole in your stomach lining. Get Pepcid AC.

11. Not picking up after your dog is unsanitary, since it is so unhygienic.

12. Baking powder is toxic. How could you doubt that?

13. We have every right to be late on the rent! Management won't fix anything. The toilet is leaking and the doorbell doesn't work. They won't even let us paint or keep a pet!

14. Don't you get sick and tired of hearing her brag? I'll bet she expects us to believe her, too.

15. BILL: Students these days are lazy and shiftless. They don't care about learning.
    JILL: Are you just saying that, or do you have evidence?
    BILL: Well, remember how hard we worked when we were students?

16. Portman says we ought to allow gays to marry, but he wouldn't say that if his son weren't gay.

17. Obama did an excellent job, when you consider how the Republicans tried to destroy him with endless attacks and *ad hominem* arguments.

18. Their proposal is 90 percent predictable, and 90 percent bad for the country. But what would you expect, coming from Republicans.

19. BILL: Space aliens are real.
    JILL: Oh, Bill, how can you say such a thing?
    BILL: Because only space aliens would have the power to erase all evidence of their existence.

20. Sure, it sounds good in theory, but curbing violence in movies doesn't make sense. It's crazy to think they should only make movies for kids.

21. If you don't align yourself a little better with conservatism you might find yourself facing a challenge come next primary. Just saying.

22. He wants to lower the drinking age? Forget about that. He owns a liquor store.

23. ANTI-GUN PERSON: Most homicides are committed with guns that were originally purchased legally.
    GUN PERSON: Where did you hear that?
    ANTI-GUN PERSON: Where did you hear they weren't?

24. How could God have created the world if God didn't exist?

25. Sure, a cruise would be nice, but we can't spend every last cent on vacations.

26. Honey, you are so understanding. Would you do the dishes this once?

27. The Democrats say they want the government to help all Americans. Translation: They want the government to run everything.

28. High-speed rail travel between here and St. Louis is something we should support, unless you can explain to me why we shouldn't.

29. Vote for the new parking garage! If we don't build it, people will have no place to park.

30. "You can't believe in all three religions, because that is the same as not believing in any of them."

    —The Life of Pi

31. Don't bother listening. He's just going to give us a bunch of emotional garbage.

32. Look out there. See those people bent over those vegetables? Know how hot it is out there? Know how many hours they put in? And are you aware that they have a special minimum wage, lower than anyone else's? Are you still going to say they take jobs away from citizens?

33. He wants to lower the drinking age? Since he is eighteen, I'm not surprised.

34. You see what the vandals did to Sharp's store over across the street? You need protection from that. You need to buy a little "security insurance" from us, you know what I'm saying?

▲ 35. Public schools are unfixable. Prove me wrong.

36. You can't possibly think pot is good for you, in view of how harmful it is.

37. The city council says the city needs a sales tax, but I don't buy it. Look at all the stuff they force down our throat—like, no plastic bags. Why, we can't even cut down the trees in our own backyards. They are after our hard-earned money and want to spend it on art projects and other so-called civic enhancements.

38. Your mom doesn't even own a cell, and you listen to her when she tells you not to text and drive?

39. We have been very frugal of late, so it is time to get a new car.

▲ 40. Staring at the sun will hurt your eyes. If it weren't for that, you could try it yourself and find out.

41. That's ridiculous. Sounds like something Nancy Pelosi would say.

42. "Wholistic" or "holistic," it doesn't matter. The guy talking tonight probably believes in crystals and pyramids. Totally New Age. I wouldn't even go, let alone listen.

43. FIRST GUY: I'm going to buy a new Mazda.
SECOND GUY: Hey, I think a Honda is a better deal.
FIRST GUY: What makes you think so?
SECOND GUY: What makes you think the Mazda is better?

44. The CEO of BlackBerry says iPhones are passé. That's clearly false. He wouldn't say that if he worked for Apple.

▲ 45. The Republican budget can't be all bad, when you consider the Democrats haven't proposed a budget in years.

46. JILL: I think we need a little more accountability in public schools. There should be sanctions for incompetent teachers.
BILL: Oh I see. Eliminate tenure, huh?

47. Ashley makes me so mad! Who does she think she is, trying to tell me what I can do. If I want to play music loud, that's my right!

48. Honey, I invested our savings in equities. I didn't want to lose it all to inflation.

49. We don't need to drill in the Santa Barbara Channel. It won't solve our fuel problems, and the ugly rigs will ruin the beauty of our pristine coast.

▲ 50. This pamphlet is put out by the people who have been trying to suppress minority voters. You won't find a word of truth in it.

51. You can't believe that! That's the kind of stuff you hear on Fox.

52. JILL: I see that the editor of the newspaper is going to retire, which is a good thing, because he has caused a lot of trouble for the Downtown Business Association.

BILL: I don't know about that. The paper has made a lot of money under his editorship.

53. We must honor the agreement, because it binds us.

54. Are you saying Candace's voice is better than Amber's? I disagree. You have to factor in how Amber went through so many hardships—illness, abandoned as a child. . . . Candace didn't face anything like that.

▲ 55. What, more shoes? C'mon, nobody needs a thousand pairs of shoes!

56. Bombing the despot's airports won't bring his reign to an end, so why do it?

57. Tell me this. If you aren't losing your hearing, then how come you can't hear so well?

58. Do I agree with Rand's brand of conservatism? Not entirely. He isn't doing himself any favors by pushing those ideas.

59. He wants to raise the drinking age? Are you going to accept that coming from him? Isn't he the very same person who thinks we should legalize pot?

▲ 60. You know, when you say things like that, I think you've been hanging out with the Sierra Club or something.

61. Class, when you fill out these student evaluations, I hope you remember how hard I have tried.

62. I used to think Mike Savage made a lot of sense. Then I found out he lied about his background.

63. SENATOR TED CRUZ: The question that I would pose to the senior senator from California is: Would she deem it consistent with the Bill of Rights for Congress to engage in the same endeavor that we are contemplating doing with the Second Amendment in the context of the First or Fourth Amendment? Namely, would she consider it constitutional for Congress to specify that the First Amendment shall apply only to the following books and shall not apply to the books that Congress has deemed outside the protection of the Bill of Rights? SENATOR DIANE FEINSTEIN: I'm not a sixth grader. Senator, I've been on this committee for 20 years. I was a mayor for nine years. I walked in and I saw people shot. I've looked at bodies that have been shot with these weapons. After 20 years, I've been up close and personal to the Constitution. It's fine if you want to lecture me on the Constitution. I appreciate it. Just know I've been here for a long time. I passed on [sic] a number of bills. I study the Constitution myself. I am reasonably well educated, and I thank you for the lecture. Incidentally, this does not prohibit—you used the word "prohibit." It exempts 2,271 weapons. Isn't that enough for the people in the United States?

64. Estelle claims we should have the kids vaccinated, but that doesn't persuade me, since she works for Amgen or one of those other drug companies.

▲ 65. Is the EPA trying to ruin the oil industry, or is it just plain incompetent?

66. You want to keep defense spending at current levels? What, you don't think we should be able to defend ourselves even from a place like Iceland?

67. I deserved to pass. I couldn't have missed every question!

68. Either we increase troop strength, or the Taliban will overrun the country. I know which I would choose.

69. Drink less? And why should I believe that coming from a chain smoker like you?

▲ 70. Hey, Professor, do you give extra credit? I missed a few classes, but I want to major in English. I love your class!

71. Pryor's diatribe against gun control is flat-out nonsense. He probably doesn't believe that stuff himself.

72. "Mark Pryor's liberal record is out of touch with Arkansans, and it's time to hold him accountable. Mark Pryor stood with Obama on Obamacare, the failed stimulus, and bailing out the Wall Street banks. While Arkansans have had to balance their checkbooks, Mark Pryor has joined with the liberals in Washington to recklessly spend our tax dollars on the Obama agenda."

    —*Club for Growth President Chris Chocola*

73. "Only $100? Isn't it worth more than that? We really need the money for our daughter's tuition."

    —*A couple trying to sell a stove on* Hardcore Pawn

74. Ladies and gentlemen of the jury, you can't trust this witness. Counsel for the defense has not produced a shred of evidence that he is trustworthy.

▲ 75. Drinking wine is good for you? Where did that idea come from, Gallo?

76. Buy now while supplies last!

77. Forget those polls. They come from CBS.

78. The War on Drugs has been a disaster. It has cost us billions and hasn't reduced drug use at all. Obviously the sane thing is to legalize drugs.

79. That's nuts. That's just something someone like Ayn Rand would think.

▲ 80. Armed guards in public schools? You think that's a solution to gun violence? That's just something the NRA put out there.

81. Heidegger was a mean, thoughtless, self-serving man—an ex-Nazi. He couldn't have been a great philosopher.

82. I don't like the idea of getting a second pet. We aren't running a zoo.

83. Mold is the leading cause of illness in the home. Schedule an appointment with our technicians now, for peace of mind.

84. Accept Jesus or rot in hell.

▲ 85. Aryan superiority is demonstrated, if a demonstration is even needed, by the manifest inferiority of the other races.

86. He thinks we should outlaw large ammunition clips. I don't buy it at all, coming from him. He also thinks we don't need the police.

87. You can hardly eliminate all carbs from your diet, so there is no point going on a low-carb diet.

88. All right. We have to decide who will be the final boss in this outfit. Clearly, the person who invested the most money ought to have the final say, and I invested the most. Therefore, I should have the final say. And since I have the final say, that's that.

89. The president lied through his teeth all through the debate, and now he expects us to agree with his ideas?

▲ 90. Cutting back on salt doesn't sound like a good idea. A person has to eat some salt, you know.

91. Not many people could appreciate the distinction, but I know it wasn't lost on you.

92. Terry will win the raffle. That girl has worked her fingers off putting this event together! She and her three sick babies deserve it.

93. All this negative publicity has hurt the Boy Scouts. They deserve our support.

94. Jackson is at least a hundred pounds overweight. He has a simple choice: Lose it, or die.

▲ 95. The idea will never work. Of course, the mainstream media like it, but they are known for their liberal bias.

96. Why raise taxes on the richest 3 percent? It would bring in only a fraction of the revenue needed to balance the budget.

97. Professor Stooler assigned two extra paragraphs to read. Dude thinks we don't have anything better to do.

98. The tax bill would derail the economic recovery. If you vote for it, many of your supporters might have difficulty contributing to your campaign.

99. He is so full of himself, it's disgusting. Don't expect me to agree with him.

▲ 100. She is trustworthy; after all, she swears she is, and you can't doubt that.

7 Induction Fallacies

In this chapter we examine common **Fallacies of Induction**—arguments that are supposed to raise the probability of their conclusions, but are so weak as to fail almost entirely to do so. In Chapter 11 we will discuss the basic principles of inductive reasoning. However, you do not need to read Chapter 11 to understand the fallacies discussed here.

GENERALIZATIONS

A little background here: General claims (claims that lack specificity) are made by people every second of every day.

> Pit bulls bite.
> This town is dead.
> The food in L.A. is lousy.
> My aunt is so mean.
> This country is going down the tubes.
> Most people believe in God.

However, general statements are often supported by feeble, inadequate reasoning. In this section we look at two important ways this can happen. We also consider the reverse mistake, one that can be involved when we reason from a general statement to a specific case.

Students will learn to . . .

1. **Define and recognize fallacies involved in generalizing**

2. **Define and recognize fallacies involved in arguments based on weak analogies**

3. **Define and recognize fallacies involved in citing authorities**

4. **Define and recognize fallacies involved in citing popular beliefs or customs**

5. **Define and recognize fallacies involved in cause-and-effect claims**

6. **Define and recognize fallacies involved in slippery slope arguments**

7. **Define and recognize fallacies involved in arguments based on untestable explanations**

Every Kroger apple I've have had has tasted great. Therefore, all great tasting apples come from Kroger.

Everyday backwards generalizing

Generalizing from Too Few Cases (Hasty Generalization)

Arriving at a general statement or rule by citing too few supporting cases is the fallacy known as **Generalizing from Too Few Cases,** or more commonly, **Hasty Generalization.** Here is an example:

> The food in L.A. is lousy, judging from this meal.

Assuming the speaker is dining at a restaurant, he or she has made a sweeping generalization about food sold at restaurants in a very large city, based on his or her experience at one restaurant. This "support" is so weak as to count as nonexistent. The speaker has offered us what might be called a lonely fact; indeed a very appropriate alternative name for the fallacy of hasty generalization is the **Fallacy of the Lonely Fact.**

Here is another example of hasty generalization:

> The police stopped me for driving five miles over the speed limit. Around here they will stop you for everything.

That you were cited for driving five miles over the speed limit in and of itself is a "lonely fact," insufficient for thinking the police will stop everyone for every infraction.

One version of hasty generalization is known as the **Argument by Anecdote.** An anecdote is a story. When a speaker or writer tries to support a general claim by offering a story, he commits this fallacy. A story is just a single incident. It may carry psychological weight, but it has little logical force. Here is an example of an argument by anecdote:

> Did you read where John Travolta flew his plane into LAX and parked it on the tarmac—right out there in everyone's way? That's the trouble with these Hollywood actors. They don't care about anyone but themselves.

A story about John Travolta is just that—a story about John Travolta. Generalizing from that story to all Hollywood actors is a fallacy.

Here is another example of argument by anecdote:

> They say the unemployment rate is around 8 percent but I don't buy that at all. Anybody who wants a job can get one. You just have to be willing to settle for something less than ideal. When my husband was laid off he didn't sit around crying about it. He got a job with a yard service. It didn't pay much, but you know what? He learned the ropes and now he owns his own yard service and hires several employees.

Often an argument by anecdote is used in the vain hope that it *disproves* a general claim. That is what has happened here. You can't disprove a statement about the unemployment rate by telling a story, no matter how interesting the story is.

Here is another example of an argument by anecdote used to try to disprove a general claim:

> They say the health care is excellent in Canada? Well, it isn't. My new neighbor just moved here from Toronto, and she says the health care up there is terrible. She says everyone in Canada comes to the United States for any serious medical condition.

The speaker tells us a little story, a factoid. In itself it proves or disproves nothing about overall health care in Canada. (It sounds as if the new neighbor is guilty of her own hasty generalization, too.)

The fallacy of hasty generalization frequently occurs when someone tries to derive a statement about all or most members of a **population** from a statement about a tiny sample of the population. This is sometimes called the **Fallacy of Small Sample.** Here is an example:

> People who live in Cincinnati have no idea where Akron is. I didn't, when I lived in Cincinnati.

The speaker provides a solitary piece of evidence for the knowledge level of everyone in Cincinnati. He thinks he has supported a conclusion about a large population by considering a sample consisting of a single person.

Good Reasoning Can Be Based on Small Samples

Generalizations based on small samples are not necessarily fallacies, if the sampled population is known to be homogeneous. For example, if every member of a small random sample of ball bearings had the same defect, and it was known that the ball bearings were all manufactured by the same process, it would not be a fallacy to expect the next ball bearing to have the same defect.

Also, a generalization based on a small random sample from even a nonhomogeneous population is not mistaken if an appropriate error margin or confidence level is built into it. This is discussed in Chapter 11.

Here is one final example of the small sample version of hasty generalization:

> Things cost less at Costco. I bought lawn fertilizer there for a ridiculously low price.

You can view the items Costco sells as a "population"; lawn fertilizer would then be a "sample" of that population. This argument does offer some support for the general conclusion it reaches, but the support is very weak. Lawn fertilizer might be an isolated case.

Generalizing from Exceptional Cases

Arriving at a general statement or rule by citing an atypical supporting case is the fallacy known as **Generalizing from Exceptional Cases.** Here is an example:

> The police aren't required to get a search warrant if they arrest a suspect while a robbery is in progress and search him for a weapon. Therefore, they shouldn't be required to get a search warrant for any kind of search.

The speaker is generalizing about all police searches, from a premise about searches in exceptional circumstances.

Here is another example of generalizing from exceptional cases:

> Animals will live longer if they are on a calorie-restricted diet. This has been shown in experiments with rats.

Rats may have unusual responses to calorie-restricted diets. Yes, what holds for rats *might* hold for other animals; the argument offers some support for its conclusion. But the conclusion overstates things. That animals will live longer on calorie-restricted diets has not been "shown" by the experiments. Further testing is called for.

One very important variety of generalizing from exceptional cases is known as the **Fallacy of Biased Sample.** It occurs when a speaker or writer incautiously bases a generalization about a large population on an atypical or skewed sample. For example:

> Almost everyone in a large survey of Tea Party members thinks the president should be impeached. Therefore, most Americans think the president should be impeached.

The problem here isn't that the survey is small, because it might be large. Rather, the problem is that Tea Party members might have atypical opinions.

When logicians call a sample "biased," they don't mean that it is a sample of people who have unfounded opinions about something. They mean that the sample is potentially atypical or skewed. Here is another example of the fallacy of biased sample:

> Judging from what car dealers say, most businesspeople now think the economy is improving.

It is unsafe to generalize about what most businesspeople think from what car dealers think, because car dealers see the economy from their own perspective. This is a biased sample, meaning not that car dealers' opinions are unfounded, but that they do not reflect every perspective.

Whom Do You Trust?

- When it comes to deciding which kind of car to buy, which do you trust more—the reports of a few friends or the results of a survey based on a large sample?

- When it comes to deciding whether an over-the-counter cold remedy (e.g., vitamin C) works, which do you trust more—a large clinical study or the reports of a few friends?

Some people trust the reports of friends over more reliable statistical information. We hope you aren't among 'em. (According to R. E. Nisbett and L. Ross, *Human Inference: Strategies and Shortcomings of Human Social Judgment* [Englewood Cliffs, N.J.: Prentice Hall, 1980], people may be quite insensitive to sample size when evaluating some products, being swayed more by the judgments of a few friends than by the results of a survey based on a large sample.)

Another version of generalizing from an exceptional case is known as the **Self-Selection Fallacy.** This fallacy happens when someone generalizes incautiously from a self-selected sample. A self-selected sample is one whose members are included by their own decision. Here is an example of the self-selection fallacy:

> Most Americans have a favorable view of the president as a person, judging from an online survey conducted by CNN.

The opinions of respondents to an online survey constitute a skewed sample, because the respondents select themselves into the sample by their own decision. Such samples underrepresent people who don't have the inclination or time or means to respond.

Accident

The fallacy of **Accident** occurs when a speaker or writer assumes that a general statement automatically applies to a specific case that is (or could well be) exceptional. This is an example:

> It is illegal to use a cell phone while driving; therefore, that police officer committed a crime when she used her cell while driving.

The general statement that it is illegal to use a cell phone while driving does not automatically apply to the special circumstance mentioned. It is easy to imagine situations when police business might best be conducted on a cell. In addition, police presumably have intensive training handling a car in challenging conditions.

The fallacy of accident has various unnamed varieties so we will provide various examples. Here is one:

> Everyone should have access to a college education. Therefore, anyone who applies should be admitted to Cal Poly.

A general rule is being applied here to an exceptional case in which it does not automatically hold. Among other things, students who attend Cal Poly may need special skills or training that Cal Poly cannot itself provide.

Here is another example:

> In this country we have a right to free speech. Therefore, if I want to threaten the mayor, that is my right.

The right to free speech does not include the right to issue threats. Even so-called absolute rights are subject to limitations where there is a compelling social interest.

Here is a slightly different type of example. It will sound familiar.

> Costco sells for less. Therefore, lawn fertilizer will cost less at Costco.

At first glance this might seem to be a good argument. However, remember what we said earlier. If you found that lawn fertilizer costs less at Costco than at other stores, you would not conclude from *that information alone* that Costco *in general* sells for less. That would be a case of hasty generalization. The reverse argument also is a fallacy, the fallacy of accident. The fact that Costco *in general* sells for less raises the probability only slightly that it will sell *this specific item* for less.

One final example:

> This city has a very high crime rate; therefore, it will be dangerous to shop in this neighborhood.

This is similar to the Costco example. It would be hasty generalization to draw a conclusion about a city's overall crime rate from what you observed in one particular location, at least if the city is large. Likewise, it is the fallacy of accident to infer from the city's overall high crime rate, considered in and of itself without regard to anything else, that a particular location in the city has a high crime rate.

WEAK ANALOGY

The fallacy known as **Weak Analogy** (sometimes called **False Analogy**) is a weak argument based on debatable or unimportant similarities between two or more things.

> My mom is just like Adolf Hitler. I doubt she will let me go out with you guys.

The speaker offers an analogy between her mom and Adolf Hitler, presumably to support the contention that she is a ruthless dictator who won't allow her daughter to do something with us. The similarities between Adolf Hitler and her mother, if there are any, are almost certainly superficial. For one thing, Adolf Hitler was a sociopath. We hope few other human beings are like him.

Here is another example:

> The federal government is just like a private household. If it doesn't balance its budget, it will go bankrupt.

This argument likens the federal government to a household like yours or mine, to support the idea that the federal government will go bankrupt if it doesn't balance its budget. But the analogy is weak because the federal government has ways of avoiding bankruptcy indefinitely that are not available to a private household. These include being able to raise taxes, print more money, and stimulate economic growth and foreign investment.

This is another example:

> If you knife someone to death, you will be charged with murder. Therefore, if a surgeon kills someone, she should be charged with murder.

A difference is that a surgeon's error is accidental. If it isn't, he or she should be brought up on charges.

Another example:

> In the wild, wolves eat nothing but raw meat. Therefore, we should feed our dog nothing but raw meat.

The conclusion may be true, but this argument is weak support. Canine digestive systems may have evolved differently from wolves'.*

One more example:

> In the 1960s scientists were worried about global cooling, and their worries turned out to be unjustified. Therefore, their present concern with global warming will also turn out to be unjustified.

A difference is that the present concern is based on fifty years of additional and improved data, including many more monitoring stations, satellite measurements of glaciers and artic sea ice, and so forth.

Most assuredly, not every argument based on an analogy is a fallacy. To take an obvious example, a court ruling based on a legal precedent draws an analogy between the present case and a past ruling. Such arguments are the basis of legal reasoning. But jurists always look for relevant differences between an alleged legal precedent and the case currently before them. We should be similarly cautious when we are offered arguments based on analogies.

---

*www.nature.com/news/dog-s-dinner-was-key-to-domestication-1.12280.

MISTAKEN APPEAL TO AUTHORITY

A speaker or writer commits the **Mistaken Appeal to Authority** when he or she tries to support a contention by offering as evidence the opinion of a nonauthoritative source. Here is an example:

> My father thinks the president lied. Therefore, the president lied.

The fact that it is one's father who thinks the president lied does not affect the probability that he did—unless, of course, the subject is something the father would have special knowledge about. There is no reason to suppose that is the case here.

Here is another example of a mistaken appeal to authority:

> My doctor thinks my car has leaking valves. Therefore, my car has leaking valves.

Everything else being equal, that your doctor thinks you have leaking heart valves raises the probability that you do. But everything else being equal, that your doctor thinks your car has leaking engine valves does not raise the probability that it does.

Of course special circumstances can diminish a physician's authoritativeness in regard to medical conditions, too—just as special circumstances can diminish any expert's authoritativeness within his or her sphere of expertise. One of the most common occurrences of mistaken appeal to authority occurs when an authority in one field, domain, or discipline is assumed without further ado to be an authority in an unrelated field, domain, or discipline. We have discussed credibility and authoritativeness at length in Chapter 4 and refer you to that material now.

MISTAKEN APPEAL TO POPULARITY (MISTAKEN APPEAL TO COMMON BELIEF)

The fallacy known as **Mistaken Appeal to Popularity** (sometimes called **Mistaken Appeal to Common Belief**) happens when a speaker or writer treats an issue that cannot be settled by public opinion as if it can. Here is an example:

> The Iranians have nuclear weapons. Everyone knows that.

Even if you had a way of telling what "everyone" thinks on this subject, and even if everyone believed the claim in question, the argument does not provide much support for it. To find out if Iran has nuclear weapons, the International Atomic Energy Agency has technical means of investigation that do not include consulting popular opinion polls.

Here is another example:

> Almost everyone knows that plastic is contaminating the oceans. Therefore, plastic is contaminating the oceans.

Whether plastic is contaminating the oceans cannot be determined by consulting popular sentiment.

Another example:

> Hondas get great gas mileage. Everyone knows that.

To find out whether a car gets good gas mileage you have to run tests, not ask people what they think.

However, not every argument of the form *"X is true because most people think X is true"* is a fallacy. If most people around a stream say you need a fishing license to fish those waters, that would be a good reason for thinking you do. But notice that whether or not you need a fishing license is something people from around there might well know. You would not find out *definitively* if you need a fishing license by asking people—they might be wrong—but this is the sort of circumstance in which popular belief counts as evidence for the truth of a claim.

The ANECDOTAL EVIDENCE *Detective*

PROOF! CLIMATE CHANGE IS A HOAX.

PROOF! MORE GUNS MAKE US SAFER. STORY OF GUN OWNER WHO SHOT CRIMINAL.

PROOF! ALL MUSLIMS ARE TERRORISTS. ISIS INSPIRED ATTACK

Let's leave matters this way: Ask yourself, Would a scientist writing in a scientific journal offer popular opinion as evidence of something's truth or falsity? If not, then you would commit the mistaken appeal to popularity if you did. This rule of thumb won't help in every case, but it will help to weed out egregious instances of the fallacy.

Mistaken Appeal to Common Practice

Sometimes speakers and writers try to justify a *practice* on the grounds that is traditional or is commonly practiced. The **Mistaken Appeal to Common Practice** (sometimes called **Mistaken Appeal to Tradition**) is a variant of the mistaken appeal to popularity. Here is an example:

> This is the right way; it's the way it has always been done.

If tradition by itself truly justified a practice, then human slavery, burning people at the stake, and any other extreme and deplorable behavior would have been justified if it happened to have been "traditional."

Bandwagon Fallacy

Sometimes by mentioning the popularity of a proposition, a speaker or writer may not be trying to offer "evidence" of its truth. Instead, he or she may be dangling a psychological inducement to believe it. He or she may be playing on the natural human tendency to want to be a part of things, to be one of the group. When a speaker or writer uses "everyone thinks" (and other such phrases) as a psychological ploy, he or she commits the **Bandwagon Fallacy.** Here is an example:

> Hillary Clinton has earned your support. Everyone is endorsing her.

An Example of Appeal to Common Practice

"Shell [Oil Company] was charged with misleading advertising in its Platformate advertisements. A Shell spokesman said: 'The same comment could be made about most good advertising of most products.'"

—SAMM S. BAKER, *The Permissible Lie*

A perfect example of a mistaken appeal to common practice.

The speaker wants us to jump on the bandwagon. He or she has not shown that Hillary Clinton has earned our support.

Here is one more example:

> Let's get a spa. They are very popular these days.

The speaker hasn't really shown that we *need* a spa. He wants us to get on the bandwagon.

A final example:

> You shouldn't shop at Walmart. None of us does that.

If you overheard someone say this, you would have no idea what is supposed to be wrong with Walmart. You would know, however, that the speaker was employing the bandwagon fallacy.

The bandwagon fallacy also can be classified as an appeal to emotion, but its similarity to the mistaken appeal to popularity justifies its inclusion here.

Appealing to Tradition

According to Representative Steve King of Ohio (pictured here), "Equal protection [under the Constitution] is not equal protection for same sex couples to marry. Equal protection has always been for a man and a woman to be able to get married to each other."

FALLACIES RELATED TO CAUSE AND EFFECT

It can be difficult to prove a cause-and-effect relationship between two variables, which is why mistaken reasoning can occur in this context. In this section we explore two important fallacies that can be made in reasoning about cause and effect. What the two fallacies have in common is this. Both assume that the timing of two variables relative to each other, in and of itself, is sufficient to establish that one is the cause and the other is the effect. This assumption is incorrect.

Post Hoc, Ergo Propter Hoc

Post Hoc, Ergo Propter Hoc means "After this, therefore because of it." A speaker or writer commits this fallacy when he or she assumes that the fact that one event came after another establishes that it was caused by the other. Here is an example:

> After I took Zicam my cold went away fast. Therefore taking Zicam caused my cold to go away fast.

The speaker makes a mistake to assume that Zicam caused the cold to go away fast. The argument is no better than this one:

> After I played poker my cold went away fast. Therefore playing poker caused my cold to go away fast.

Here is a slightly different example, a classic illustration of *post hoc, ergo propter hoc:*

> Every day the sun comes up right after the rooster crows; therefore the rooster causes the sun to come up.

The Easy Way to Make a Killing in the Stock Market!

Sophisticated mathematical schemes for predicting the behavior of the stock market abound, but you may think you don't need any of them. You may think all you need to do is watch the Super Bowl every winter. In 80 percent of the years since the first Super Bowl in 1967, a win by a National Conference team has been followed by a good year in the market, and a win by an American Conference team has been followed by a bad year. So getting into the market after an NFC win and out of it after an AFC win should produce good results 80 percent of the time, right?

Not a sports fan? Another indicator of how the market will perform is known as the "hemline indicator," first presented in 1926 by economist George Taylor. The idea is that when the hemlines of ladies' skirts go up, it signals good economic times; and when they go down, bad times are ahead. The hemline-market correlation has held more frequently than chance would dictate.

Are you intrigued by either of these correlations? This doesn't have anything to do with the stock market, but in 17 out of the last 18 presidential elections, when the Washington Redskins football team won its last home game, the nation's presidential election went to the party of the incumbent president. Good enough odds for a big bet on the next election, no?

Well, no. The fact is, if you look at enough *possible* correlations, you will certainly find some that look like sure things. Of the many, many things that go up and down in some sort of cycle, *some* of them are coincidentally going to match the movement of the market; and of the many, many things that either happen or don't, some of them are going to match the outcome of presidential elections.

Correlation does not equal causation! If no causal link exists between two things, then the correlation is mere coincidence, and you're best off treating it as a joke rather than the basis for making decisions. In Chapter 11, we discuss ways of eliminating the possibility that a correlation between two things is coincidental.

http://online.wsj.com/article/SB10001424127887324105204578384832555959160.html.

As you can see from this example, the fact that one event *invariably* follows another event *still* doesn't establish that the first event caused the second event. This fact is often expressed by saying *"Correlation does not prove causation,"* a phrase worth remembering.

Post hoc ergo propter hoc often is referred to simply as *post hoc*. Here is another example of the *post hoc* fallacy:

> After you drove my car it was hard to start. Therefore, it was something you did that made my car hard to start.

You may think this is a reasonable argument. Indeed, when an unusual event is followed by another unusual event and we can see how the first might cause the second, it is not a fallacy to think that it *might* have done that. A fallacy occurs only when we assume that the sequential timing of events, in and of itself, *establishes* cause and effect between them, as in the example just given.

Overlooking the Possibility of Coincidence

A special case of the *post hoc* fallacy is known as **Overlooking the Possibility of Coincidence.** Here is an example:

> After Susan threw out the chain letter, she was in an automobile accident. Therefore throwing out the chain letter caused her to get in an automobile accident.

The speaker has overlooked the possibility that the sequential events were coincidental.

Overlooking a Possible Common Cause

Another instance of the *post hoc* fallacy is known as **Overlooking a Possible Common Cause.** Here is an example:

> I left the lights on when I went to bed. Next morning I woke up with a headache. Therefore leaving the lights on caused the headache.

The speaker has overlooked the possibility that leaving the lights on and waking up with a headache may each be the effects of a common cause, such as having gone to bed unusually tired or intoxicated.

Overlooking the Possibility of Random Variation

Yet another instance of *post hoc* reasoning occurs when we ignore the fact that values of variables fluctuate randomly. For example, the average distance that one randomly selected group of men can throw a football will vary randomly from the average distance another randomly selected group of men can throw a football. Likewise, the average distance a randomly selected group of men can throw a football will vary randomly from the average distance the *same* group of men can throw a football on a second try. If you assume that this random fluctuation is due to causation, you make the mistake known as **Overlooking the Possibility of Random Variation.** Here is an example:

> In our tests, we asked randomly selected men to drive a golf ball as far as they could. We then had them wear our magnetic bracelet and try again. On the second occasion, the men hit the ball an average of ten feet further. Our bracelet can lengthen your drive as well.

The speaker is implying that the magnetic bracelet caused the improvement in the average drive lengths. However, the improvement might simply have been due to random variation. Until he has eliminated that possibility, the speaker has committed a fallacy. (In Chapter 11 we explain what is required to reduce the likelihood that such changes are due to randomness.) If we performed the test again, the average drive length might decrease. In any case the average drive length is almost certain to change randomly from one trial to the next. So we should not by a change, or assume it must be due to something other than random fluctuation.

Overlooking the Possibility of Regression

A directly related fallacy is known as **Overlooking the Possibility of Regression.** This mistake is committed when we overlook this fact: *If the average value of a variable is atypical on one measurement, it is likely to be less atypical on a subsequent measurement.* This may sound complicated, but it isn't. If the average distance the randomly selected men drove a golf ball is relatively distant from the "true average" for all men, then on the second try, the average is apt to be closer to the true average. This phenomenon is known as *regression to the statistical mean.* The more atypical the value of a variable is on one measurement, the more likely it is that it will be less atypical on the next measurement. If we overlook this fact, we commit the fallacy of overlooking the possibility of regression. Here is an example:

> We measured the IQs of a group of students and found the average to be relatively low. Then we had them take a course in critical thinking, after which we measured their IQs again. Their IQs were higher. Therefore the course in critical thinking raised their IQs.

As you now know, their average IQs were apt to be higher on the second measurement (closer to the "true average") anyway. The speaker has overlooked that fact and attributed the change in IQ scores to the critical thinking course, which is a fallacy.

Here is another example—one high school basketball coach talking to another coach:

> The girls shot well below their average on Monday, so I made them do fifty sets of pushups. Guess what? Their average was much better on Tuesday. Pushups did the trick.

The coach has overlooked the fact that the girls' shooting was apt to improve even if she had served them cookies rather than having them do pushups.

For obvious reasons, researchers conducting clinical trials are careful not to overlook the possibility of regression before they conclude that a drug works. If, for example, the members of a group of people have atypically high average blood pressure on one measurement, their average blood pressure is apt to be closer to the human norm on a second measurement—even if they have had nothing fancier than a glass of water. We go into the matter in more detail in Chapter 11.

For equally obvious reasons, unscrupulous makers of magnetic bracelets might simply run "trials" in which men hit golf balls, until a trial happened in which the average drive was fairly short. At that point, the manufacturer of the bracelet could ask the men to put on bracelets, knowing that on the next trial their average drive is likely to improve and could be attributed, mistakenly, to the bracelet. Such misuses of data are not limited to magnetic bracelet manufacturers, of course. Any device that might be alleged to improve a measurement people are interested in could be shown to "work" by this simple technique.

Cum Hoc, Ergo Propter Hoc

Cum Hoc, Ergo Propter Hoc means "With this, therefore because of it." A speaker or writer commits this fallacy when he or she assumes that the fact that two events happen at about the same time establishes that one caused the other. This fallacy is so similar to *post hoc, ergo propter hoc* that not all logicians list the two as separate fallacies. However, we have found that confusion can crop up if the two are not listed separately. Here, then, is an example of *cum hoc, ergo propter hoc:*

> John had a heart attack while he was saying a prayer. Therefore the prayer caused the heart attack.

Now, the fact that two unusual events happen at the same time can be a reason for thinking that one *might* have caused the other; but it is never sufficient to *establish* that this happened, as the speaker in the previous example implies.

Here is another example of *cum hoc:*

> Children with long hair are better spellers than children with short hair. Therefore having long hair makes a child a better speller.

This premise is perhaps absurd (though perhaps not!), but the conclusion does not follow in any case. The example is another illustration that correlation does not prove causation.

Overlooking the Possibility of Coincidence

Overlooking the Possibility of Coincidence can occur as a special case of *cum hoc* mistaken reasoning as well as a special case of *post hoc* mistaken reasoning. For example, the speaker in the hair/spelling example just given overlooks the possibility that the correlation between having longer hair and being better spellers is coincidental.

Here is another example of *cum hoc* in which a speaker overlooks the possibility of coincidence:

> I got cancer when I lived under a high-voltage power line. Therefore the high-voltage power line caused my cancer.

The speaker is overlooking the possibility that the two events are coincidental. Again, when two unusual events happen at the same time it is not necessarily a fallacy to think that one *might* be causative. It is a fallacy, however, to think that the juxtaposition in and of itself *establishes* that one is causative.

Overlooking a Possible Common Cause

It was said previously that **Overlooking a Possible Common Cause** is a special case of the *post hoc* fallacy. It can also be a special case of the *cum hoc* fallacy. Here is an example:

> Chimney fires and long underwear purchases increase in frequency at the very same time. Therefore chimney fires cause people to buy long underwear.

The speaker in this example has ignored the possibility that the events in question are both the effects of a common cause, the weather turning colder.

Overlooking the Possibility of Reversed Causation

Sometimes a speaker or writer who commits the *cum hoc* fallacy is guilty of **Overlooking the Possibility of Reversed Causation.** Here is an example:

> People who walk long distances enjoy good health. Therefore, walking long distances will make you healthy.

This speaker has assumed that the walking accounts for the good health. Maybe he or she has it backward. Maybe being healthy accounts for the walking.

Here is another example of overlooking the possibility of reversed causation:

> Successful businesspeople often drive expensive cars. Therefore, driving an expensive car will help make you a successful businessperson.

This speaker has overlooked the possibility that driving an expensive car is the *result* of being successful, not a *cause* of it.

Argument by Anecdote (Causal Variety)

Finally, before we leave *post hoc* and *cum hoc* mistaken reasoning, we should note this: Just as it is a fallacy to try to support (or disprove) a *general* claim by telling a story, it is a fallacy to try to support (or disprove) a cause-and-effect claim by telling a story. Attempting to do the latter is also known as the fallacy of **Argument by Anecdote.** Here is an example:

> I've heard doctors say eating red meat daily increases your risk of heart disease, but I don't believe it. My uncle was a rancher and he lived to be 100. His entire life he ate red meat three times a day. He didn't die of a heart attack, either. He died when he fell down a well.

A single story like this does not establish the presence or absence of causation. The matter is treated extensively in Chapter 11.

SLIPPERY SLOPE

The **Slippery Slope** fallacy is an argument that rests on an unsupported warning that is controversial and tendentious, to the effect that something will progress by degrees to an undesirable outcome. (A tendentious assertion is one that is slanted toward a particular point of view.) Here is an example:

> We should not require gun owners to carry liability insurance, because if we do that, before long they will repeal the Second Amendment.

The speaker has made a surprising and controversial statement. This is not like saying that if you run your AC twenty-four hours a day, your utility bill will go up. The speaker should support his theory. Until he does, his argument is a slippery slope fallacy.

Here is another example:

> No, I don't think we should tip servers 20 percent. The next thing you know we will be tipping them 25 percent, then 30 percent, then who knows what. We will be giving out our entire paycheck every time we eat out.

What we should say to this speaker is "Why couldn't we stop at 20 percent?" We could also just say, "Give me a break."

Another example:

> Raising the Pentagon's budget by 5 percent this year will just lead to a continuous 5 percent increase. In twenty years, the *whole budget* will go to the military!

There has to be support for the claim that the increases will continue. Otherwise this is a slippery slope fallacy.

For obvious reasons, some logicians treat the slippery slope fallacy as a version of scare tactics. You would not be wrong to regard any of these three examples in that light. Incidentally, a slight change in wording can convert many slippery slope fallacies into false dilemma fallacies (discussed in Chapter 6) and *vice versa*. For instance, the last example can be made into a false dilemma by wording it this way:

> Either we deny the Pentagon a 5 percent increase this year, or in twenty years it will get the entire budget.

Both versions have the same objective: to get a listener to oppose the 5 percent increase for the Pentagon.

UNTESTABLE EXPLANATION

When someone offers an explanation that could not be tested even in principle, he or she is said to commit the fallacy of **Untestable Explanation.** Here is an example:

> He has heart issues because of sins done in a previous life.

This explanation is untestable. There is no way to tell if someone is a previous-life sinner. In fact we cannot even identify people who have had previous lives. Plus, who is to say that someone's past life was in a human form? Perhaps some of us had previous lives as bugs and such. We do not know if bugs are capable of sin, but we do know that we cannot distinguish a bug that has sinned from one that has not.

Some explanations are untestable because they are circular. They merely repackage themselves in alternative language. Here is a stock example:

> Hooray! The Kings are winning again. That's because they are gaining momentum.

This explanation is not quite as circular as saying that the Kings are winning because they are ahead. Still, it does basically just repeat itself using different words. One could not test it. The only way to identify a gain in momentum is to look at the scoreboard.

Finally, some explanations are untestable because they are too vague. Here is an example:

> The crime rate has gone up because of general moral decay.

This argument isn't circular; moral decay, whatever it is, is not identical to a rising crime rate. Rather, the problem here is vagueness. We do not know what moral decay is exactly, and so we do not know how to test the assertion.

LINE-DRAWING AGAIN

When exactly does an analogy become weak? Precisely where do you draw the line between a credible authority and one who lacks credibility? When exactly does a report cease to be a report and become an anecdote? When exactly does a slippery slope become tendentious or controversial? You can't say in any of these cases. However, don't forget the line-drawing fallacy discussed in Chapter 6. That you cannot draw a precise demarcation between a weak analogy and one that is not weak, does not mean that every analogy is weak or that none are, or that there is no such thing as the fallacy of weak analogy. Similar remarks hold for the other distinctions just mentioned.

The fallacies in this chapter are inductive fallacies—arguments that offer at best only weak support for their conclusions. We specifically examined the following:

Recap

- Hasty generalization—generalizing from too few cases or from samples that are too small
- Generalizing from exceptional cases—generalizing from cases that are exceptional or from samples that are biased (skewed)
- Accident—applying a general statement to a possibly exceptional case
- Weak analogy—offering an argument based on debatable similarities between two or more things
- Mistaken appeal to authority—attempting to support a claim by citing a source that is not really an authority
- Mistaken appeal to popularity—treating an issue that cannot be settled by public opinion as if it could
- *Post hoc, ergo propter hoc*—thinking that a temporal succession between two variables, in and of itself, establishes a cause-and-effect connection between them
- *Cum hoc, ergo propter hoc*—thinking that simultaneity between two variables, in and of itself, establishes a cause-and-effect connection between them
- Slippery slope—offering an argument resting on an unsupported warning that something will progress by degrees to an undesirable outcome
- Untestable explanation—an argument based on an untestable explanation

EXERCISES

Here are 125 examples of the fallacies discussed in this chapter.* Match each item to one or more of the following categories:

- a. hasty generalization/generalizing from exceptional cases
- b. accident
- c. weak analogy
- d. mistaken appeal to authority
- e. mistaken appeal to popularity
- f. *post hoc, ergo propter hoc/cum hoc, ergo propter hoc*
- g. overlooking the possibility of random variation or regression
- h. slippery slope
- i. untestable explanation

Notes

- Some items arguably fall into more than one category; this is true in real life as well. But no item in this exercise could plausibly be said to fall into every category. Your instructor will tell you if your categorization is too much of a stretch.

*Exercises from previous editions may be found in the appendix at the end of the book.

- It may be especially difficult to distinguish hasty generalization from generalizing from an exceptional case; and to distinguish *post hoc, ergo propter hoc* from *cum hoc, ergo propter hoc.* Your instructor may or may not ask you to do so.

- Your instructor may or may not ask you to further assign examples into one or more of the following subcategories: argument by anecdote, fallacy of small sample, fallacy of biased sample, overlooking the possibility of coincidence, overlooking the possibility of a common cause, and overlooking the possibility of reversed causation.

1. I'd better not eat this lemony dessert thing. If I do, there will be no end. Hamburgers, chips, ice cream, chocolates—you name it and I will eat all of it. I will explode.

2. Stress bad for you? That's a myth. I know all sorts of Type A people who are in excellent health.

3. These university kids drink like crazy on Halloween and St. Patrick's Day. They probably drink like crazy on Christmas, too.

4. I had a great time at the party last night; I'll bet all university parties are great.

5. The prayer leader cured her rheumatism. She said he did, and who would know better than she?

6. Salmon is very bad for dogs. You shouldn't let your cat eat it either, I'd guess.

7. You have to stand up for what you believe. Ignore it if your wife complains about how fast you are driving.

8. Most Americans watch *American Idol.* That's clear since over one million people cast votes on the season finale.

9. ONE GUY: The guy Paulson shot had climbed through a window and was coming down the darkened hallway.

   ANOTHER GUY: Doesn't matter; he still should have been charged with murder because the guy he shot was unarmed.

10. I tried to buy a portable heater from the Saber Company last winter, and it was back-ordered. After a month, I just canceled and decided not to do any more business with them.

11. "In a message about discrimination in private clubs, he [Morley Safer] wrote that all clubs, by definition, discriminate through admissions policies and hefty annual dues. 'What will be next?' he asked. 'Disassociation with clubs that do not cater to vegans on their menus? Kosher dining rooms? Special facilities for nudists and transsexuals?'"

   —New York Times

12. The heart attack rate spikes the day clocks are set ahead for daylight saving time, demonstrating how time change can affect our health.

13. The professor is a fantastic teacher. He should run for Congress.

14. These days young people don't like expensive cars. You hardly ever see a teenager driving a Maserati.

15. Prostate cancer is almost unheard of in countries where they don't eat meat, proof positive that meat in your diet will lead to prostate cancer.

16. When the government bailed out General Motors it set a bad precedent. Now it'll be bailing out banks and the automobile industry and any company that isn't competent enough to stay in business on its own.

17. The new law says everybody who takes a firearms course can carry a concealed weapon, so I don't see why I can't take my gun to school.

18. My son thinks Galaxies are better than iPhones, and he should know since he is a teenager.

19. I'm putting my money in a Vanguard account. My history teacher thinks the firm has the best mutual funds, and he is a smart man.

▲ 20. Be prepared. We are traveling to a Third World country; there won't be good hotels.

21. You would not go into the woods if you knew there were bears there, and the same thing therefore holds for getting into a bear market. Hang on to your money until the market changes.

22. Given the right circumstances, humans will always revert to savages. Look at the Nazis.

23. We live in a democracy. That's why children should be allowed to vote.

24. My student evaluations were better this year. I'll bet it's because I had to cancel class two times.

▲ 25. Statistics show that smokers disproportionately come from low-income areas. We are trying to figure out what it is about poverty that makes people smoke.

26. Global warming is not caused by human activity—and the latest polls show the majority of Americans agree.

27. Jean plays the flute beautifully. I'll bet she could learn the guitar in no time.

28. Just after I started doing yoga in the mornings, my golf swing improved. Yoga lowered my score!

29. Hank has sold Subarus for years, and he knows them as well as anybody. So when he says they make a better car than Toyota, I believe it.

▲ 30. Eating fish three times a week is supposed to be good for you, but I tried it for several months and never noticed an improvement.

31. Women are still paid less than men. Look at Walmart. The company is always getting sued for discrimination.

32. I assume my doctor watched the Super Bowl, since it is the most popular TV program in existence.

33. If I can make time for a movie, you can make time for a movie.

34. The chancellor now requires us to post syllabi online. Before long there won't be such a thing as face-to-face teaching.

▲ 35. In Stephen Hunter's new novel he showed how a conspiracy was involved in the murder of John F. Kennedy. After reading the book, I've decided the Warren Commission was mistaken and that Lee Harvey Oswald did not act alone.

36. Over the long haul, Obamacare will cut medical expenses. Informed people all say that.

37. My blasted pen leaked and ruined my shirt. I'll never buy another Bic.

38. Don't be alarmed if the pilot seems a little tipsy. After all, flying is safer than driving.

39. The country was safer after Obama was elected. That's why the economy improved.

▲ 40. The air in American cities is pretty bad. I was in Houston the other day and the air was foul.

41. If the delays in this flight are any indication, this is not an airline I want to fly again.

42. I don't think the president's trip to the Middle East is a good idea. It will lead to our sending "advisers" there, and the next thing you know we'll have troops there and be involved in another war we can't get out of.

43. TV is fabulous these days. Just look at *Downton Abbey.* Refined, cultured, superb.

44. We don't have freedom of religion in this country. Public schools can't even lead kids in prayer. Atheism is being crammed down our throats.

▲ 45. Gay parents cannot raise children correctly. Reverend Jacobs says that, and as a man of God, he should know.

46. Judging from the way she carries herself, I'd say she is very self-centered.

47. My kindergarten class seemed unusually antsy today. I wonder if they were all on a sugar high.

48. No, I don't want to join a hiking club. That would just be the start, and then we'd be doing mountaineering and rock climbing and who knows what. I've got too much to do to spend all that time in the great outdoors.

49. Last year student test scores at our school were lower than usual. We responded by having teachers emphasize spelling. This year the scores were higher, showing how spelling helps kids learn.

▲ 50. It's well and good that Apple hired you, but don't expect to be paid much. In this country women still get shafted when it comes to pay.

51. They say stretching before exercising reduces your chances of a sprain. I'm skeptical. I don't stretch before I run and I'm perfectly healthy.

52. Boiled eggs are great. I'll bet boiled salmon would be great, too.

53. Tom Wolfe characterized Freud's theory of sexual repression as similar to the way a boiler works. A boiler builds up pressure over time, and if the steam isn't let off somehow, an explosion will result. Similarly, therefore, if sexual "pressure" isn't released, the result will be an emotional explosion.

54. "More and more, women are determining what everybody watches on TV. Just look at that show on HBO, starring Lena Dunham, *Girls,* it's called. Everybody's watching that show. Everybody."

—Rush Limbaugh

▲ 55. Being overweight can't be all that bad for you. Eighty percent of the population over twenty-five is overweight.

56. I didn't pray hard enough. That's why my prayers weren't answered.

57. Yawns are contagious. Ask anyone.

58. Well I'll be! Look at the great gas mileage we got on this trip! Not a whole lot better than usual, but still nothing to sneeze at. Shows what a tune-up will do.

59. Hey, it works! After I sprinkled Arm & Hammer around the sink, the ants disappeared.

▲ 60. Attendance is up today. They must think there is a test.

61. Sex before marriage is the road to perdition. You will end up in hell.

62. I find it very hard to lie; therefore I bet Casanova here isn't lying when he says he wants to marry me.

63. The average temperature in Arizona is much hotter than what you're used to. So I wouldn't plan on taking my vacation at the Grand Canyon. If I were you.

64. Secondhand smoke isn't harmful. My parents both smoked and I am perfectly healthy.

▲ 65. Amber isn't very good. After all, she was voted off *The X Factor.*

66. They make us come home by ten! Our parents don't let us do anything!

67. God displays his love by making Earth a paradise.

68. The park seems almost deserted today. Must be something going on downtown.

69. Siri, are there snakes around here?

▲ 70. After my granddad had his heart attack, his hair turned completely white. I didn't know a heart attack could cause that.

71. Low-fat milk has a lot of sugar in it. You want to stay away from those low-fat frozen dinners unless you want extra sugar in your diet.

72. It's not dangerous to tube here. Look at all the people doing it.

73. Most people here in Stockton think the recession will last several more years, judging from the call-in survey on Channel 5.

74. My father died at a young age. God's will.

▲ 75. I took Psych 100 last semester and it was terrible. The instructor went on and on about stuff that never turned up on any of the quizzes or exams. I'm glad I never have to take another psychology class.

76. Watts has been doing the weather on the local channel for over ten years. I put more stock in what he says about global warming than on somebody I never heard of.

77. Look at Bill Gates. He didn't go to college, and he's a millionaire. College is such a waste of time.

78. Some skin products must help a person's skin look and feel better. After all, *Vogue* did a poll of its readers and found that most American women use them.

79. Don't start messing around with Facebook. Once you get involved with one of those social media traps you'll wind up living your whole life online.

▲ 80. There's no freedom of speech in this country. Look at how country radio wouldn't play the Dixie Chicks after they criticized George W. Bush.

81. My son loves the Boy Scouts; your son will too.

82. Facebook has to be a positive force in the world. Billions of people are signed up for it.

83. My students' scores have improved dramatically since I started giving tests online, which indicates that students learn more on online courses.

84. A person should defend his principles. Farley did the right thing slugging Wonderson during the debate last night.

85. The first time I played that golf course, I shot an 82. It must have affected my mental state, because I didn't score that well again for almost a year.

86. Since the SEC is the strongest conference in the country, Vanderbilt, long an SEC member, will doubtless beat whomever it plays in a bowl game.

87. We did a poll in my math class and found that most people believe there is sufficient tutoring help for students. So I don't think there's that much demand for more tutoring services.

88. Shoot, millions of people sunbathe. It can't hurt you.

89. Whenever I go to Kroger I'm hungry; do you suppose going to Kroger makes me hungry?

90. Obesity is more prevalent among people who live below the poverty line. It is paradoxical that a low-income level can make you fat, but it's the truth.

91. This student isn't good at math. Therefore she won't be good at writing, either.

92. What's all this fuss about airport delays? I arrived at the airport this morning, and fifteen minutes later I had checked my bag, passed through security, and was at my gate, where I had to wait another hour to board my flight. It was dumb to have to arrive so early.

93. How can you deny global warming? This was the hottest summer on record.

94. A lot more people are near-sighted these days. Check out those kids over there on their computers. They all wear glasses.

95. It took years for Jennifer to get pregnant the first time, but it took only eighteen months after the first child for her to get pregnant again. Clearly, having one child raises the odds of having another.

96. Fatal accidents have decreased in recent years despite the fact speed limits are gradually being raised. The only conclusion you can draw from this is that driving fast makes people more careful.

97. I had severe arthritis until—thank goodness—I started taking glucosamine.

98. According to studies, people who live in poverty are much more likely to take drugs, showing how taking drugs can have economic consequences.

99. There's no unemployment in this country. I had no problem finding a job.

100. I have every right to burn tires in my backyard. It's a free country.

101. We wouldn't let the government force people to eat broccoli; therefore we should not let the government make people carry medical insurance.

102. I failed the final. But then I didn't get much sleep the night before. That explains it.

103. The police report said there were four arrests involving alcohol over the weekend near the university. Student drinking is now an epidemic.

104. Liquid egg whites are good for your health. It says so right here on the web page of this outfit that sells liquid egg whites.

105. Bad luck brought the airplane down.

106. People don't like Southwest Air. Check it out on Yelp. You will find several negative reviews.

107. Retailers have declared a war on Christmas. Walmart has replaced the traditional "Merry Christmas" greeting with "Happy Holidays."

108. Once *American Idol* started to lose its popularity, nothing could reverse the trend. Therefore if our restaurant starts to lose its popularity, we will have a hard time stopping the trend.

109. It isn't legal to text when you drive. I'll bet it's not legal to text when you ride a bike.

110. They want to make it illegal for a running back to hit someone with his helmet? Next thing you know they won't even allow tackling.

111. You can't walk fifty feet down the Las Vegas Strip without somebody handing you a card advertising call girls. The economy of this town must be built on prostitution.

112. I've always known that wine was good for your health. Do you think 40 million French people can be wrong?

113. You know about the *SI* jinx, don't you? Players who appear on the cover of *Sports Illustrated* almost always have a poorer showing shortly afterward. Probably the extra attention affects their game.

114. In the nineties, the United States helped out in Bosnia. We should use the same strategy in Syria.

115. When I retake this stupid physiology course, I'll get an athlete to tutor me. He's bound to know the subject.

116. People have no right to keep vicious animals. Therefore my neighbors have no right to keep a dog that snarls at me through the fence.

117. Protein power builds muscle mass, according to my weight trainer. Obviously she would be someone who knows.

118. You shouldn't break your word. Therefore you shouldn't break your word to save someone's life.

119. I signed up for one of those car giveaways at a casino, and bam! My inbox started to fill up with spam within a week. Don't sign up for one of those things, ever.

120. Alicia doesn't think it would be illegal, and she played an attorney in the senior play. That's good enough for me.

121. TV is garbage these days. Just look at *2 Broke Girls*. Pornographic garbage.

122. Everyone should have access to a college education. Therefore there should be no entrance requirements here at Cal Poly.

123. There they go again, the Democrats smearing us conservatives with a single brush. They all do that. Just look at this left-wing editorial in the *Washington Post*, pretending the congressperson from Missouri speaks for us all.

124. I just read about a study of obese people who went on a low-carb diet? After a year, almost none had achieved a normal weight. Shows me that this low-carb business doesn't really do the job for most folks.

125. There are about three million Muslims in England today, and it has been the fastest-growing religion in the country so far this century. If something isn't done soon, the English are all going to be facing Mecca and praying five times a day.

Formal Fallacies and Fallacies of Language

Students will learn to . . .

1. Define and recognize the three formal fallacies of affirming the consequent, denying the antecedent, and the undistributed middle

2. Define and recognize the fallacies of equivocation and amphiboly

3. Define and recognize the fallacies of composition and division

4. Define and recognize the fallacies of confusing explanations with excuses

5. Define and recognize the fallacies of confusing contraries with contradictories

6. Define and recognize fallacies related to consistency and inconsistency

7. Define and recognize four fallacies involved in calculating probabilities

I n this chapter we'll turn our attention to fallacies that result either from a failure of form—which refers to the way the argument is set up—or from certain misuses of language.

THREE FORMAL FALLACIES: AFFIRMING THE CONSEQUENT, DENYING THE ANTECEDENT, AND UNDISTRIBUTED MIDDLE

We'll take these three in order.

Affirming the Consequent

Let's start with an example:

> (1) If Jane is a member of a sorority, then Jane is female.
> (2) Jane is female.
> Therefore (3), Jane is a member of a sorority.

The structure, or "form," of this argument is what makes it invalid rather than its content.

Here is the form of the argument presented previously:

If P then Q.
Q.
Therefore, P.

"P" and "Q" stand for independent clauses—parts of claims that are true or false. (The part of the first premise after the "if" is the **antecedent** of the claim; the part after the "then" is the **consequent.**) Whatever clauses the two letters might stand for, if they are arranged according to the previous form, the result is an invalid argument.* Any argument of this form commits the fallacy of **Affirming the Consequent.** Do you see why the following is also an example of this form?

If this dog is pregnant, then it is a female.
This dog is female.
Therefore, this dog is pregnant.

This form is so called because one premise affirms the consequent of the other premise. Remember, the consequent of an "if . . . then . . ." sentence like our first premise (*If this dog is pregnant, then it is a female*) is the part after the word "then." And that's all the second premise affirms.

Here is another example:

If the theory is correct, then the specimen is acidic.
The specimen is acidic.
Therefore, the theory is correct.

However valid this argument might look, it isn't—the second premise merely affirms the consequent of the first premise. The argument's form is exactly that of the previous example. One more:

If Sandy passed the final, then she passed the course.
She did pass the course.
Therefore, she passed the final.

Again, the argument is invalid. There may have been more than one way for Sandy to pass the course, for example, either by passing the final or by doing extra work. If she passed by doing extra work, the premises are both true and the conclusion is false.

Denying the Antecedent

Just as we get an invalid argument when one premise affirms the consequent of the other, the same thing happens when one premise denies the antecedent of the other.

---

*An exception occurs if the conclusion is a necessary truth or the premises are inconsistent. This is a technical matter and occurs only in very rare circumstances.

For example:

> If Sandy passed the final, then she passed the course.
> Sandy did not pass the final.
> Therefore, Sandy did not pass the course.

Here, the second premise is **Denying the Antecedent** of the first premise (the antecedent is the part after the "if"). The form of the argument is:

> If P then Q.
> Not-P.
> Therefore, not-Q.

The circumstances that showed the previous example invalid do the same for this one: It may be that Sandy could *either* have passed the final *or* done extra work in order to pass the course, and she did the extra work and passed. In that case, the premises are true and the conclusion is false.

The Undistributed Middle

The fallacy of **Undistributed Middle*** happens when a speaker or writer (or you!) assumes that two things related to a third thing, the "middle," are otherwise related to each other. The fallacy appears in a variety of guises. Here is one example:

> All cats are mammals.
> All dogs are mammals.
> Therefore, all cats are dogs.

The fact that cats and dogs are both mammals does not mean they are otherwise related.

Here is another example, one you might fall for if you aren't careful:

> All German Shepherds are dogs.
> Some dogs bite.
> Therefore, some German Shepherds bite.

Surprise! This conclusion does *not* follow. Both premises could be true and the conclusion false, as would be the case if, for example, all the biting German Shepherds (but not other types of biting dogs) suddenly died. If this happened, the remaining German Shepherds would all still be dogs, and it would still be true that some dogs bite, but it would not be true that some German Shepherds bite.

So that you can see that this really is a fallacy, here is an identical argument that you would never fall for:

> All German Shepherds are animals.
> Some animals are cats.
> Therefore, some German Shepherds are cats.

---

*The precise meaning of "undistributed middle" is explained in Chapter 9.

Here is slightly different example of the undistributed middle fallacy:

> The sniper had to be a great shot, have access to the roof, have a high-powered rifle and scope, and be able to get through the crowd in the ballroom without being noticed.
>
> Aaron is a great shot, had access to the roof, had a high-powered rifle and scope, and was wearing a tux so he would not have been noticed going through the crowd in the ballroom.
>
> Therefore, Aaron was the sniper.

The fact that Aaron and the sniper are both great shots, had access, have the right kind of rifle, and could go through the crowd in the ballroom without being noticed doesn't *prove* that Aaron is the sniper. These facts make Aaron look suspicious, but they don't deductively demonstrate that Aaron and the sniper are one and the same.

The scheme of the sniper argument was this:

> X has features a, b, c, etc.
> Y has features a, b, c, etc.
> Therefore, X is Y.

Here is another schema:

> All Xs are Ys.
> *a* (some individual) is a Y.
> Therefore, a is an X.

Another schema:

> If something is an X then it is a Y.
> *a* (some individual) is a Y.
> Therefore, *a* is an X.

Still another schema:

> X is a Z.
> Y is a Z.
> Therefore, X is a Y.

And there is one more way to do it:

> If P is true, then Q is true.
> If R is true then Q is true.
> Therefore, if P is true, then R is true.

---

*This looks very much like affirming the consequent. However, for technical reasons, logicians do not think of this as AC, but rather as a shorthand version of this argument:

  All Xs are Ys.

  All things identical to this particular individual, *a*, are Ys.

  Therefore, all things identical to this particular individual, *a*, are Xs.

This will be covered in the next chapter.

An example of the last version: If Bill wins the lottery, then he'll be happy. If Bill buys a new car, then he'll be happy. Therefore, if Bill wins the lottery, then he'll buy a new car.

As you can see, these are all basically the same kind of fallacy, just packaged differently.

The three fallacies just discussed (affirming the consequent, denying the antecedent, and undistributed middle) are not to be confused with three valid argument structures that resemble them. In the box below, the three invalid structures are displayed side by side with the three valid structures. For more information on these structures, please see Chapters 9 and 10.

Common Valid and Invalid Argument Structures

	Valid		Invalid
Modus ponens	If in a sorority then female In a sorority Therefore, female	Affirming the consequent	If in a sorority then female Female Therefore, in a sorority
Modus tollens	If in a sorority then female Not female Therefore, not in sorority	Denying the antecedent	If in a sorority then female Not in a sorority Therefore, not female
Chain argument	If in a sorority then female If female then have longer life expectancy Therefore, if in a sorority then have longer life expectancy	Undistributed middle	If in a sorority then female If pregnant then female Therefore, if in a sorority then pregnant

[Note: There are other forms of "undistributed middle" arguments. See text, pages 272–274]

THE FALLACIES OF EQUIVOCATION AND AMPHIBOLY

Ambiguous claims can produce a fallacy. Here is a simple example:

> All banks are alongside rivers, and the place where I keep my money is a bank. Therefore, the place where I keep my money is alongside a river.

The fallacy in this example is called **Equivocation.** It is related to semantic ambiguity, which was discussed in Chapter 3, and occurs when a sentence contains a word or phrase that is open to more than one interpretation. Clearly, the word "bank" is used in two different senses in the premises of the argument, and this makes the argument invalid. Here's a somewhat more sophisticated example:

> The *Washington Times* engaged in censorship by refusing to publish controversial authors.
> Censorship is a violation of the First Amendment.
> Therefore, the *Washington Times* violated the First Amendment.

The word "censorship" is used equivocally in the premises. For the second premise to be true, the word must mean that some governmental agency has prevented publication by threats of punishment. But that is not the meaning of the term required to make the first premise true. In that case, all it means is that the *Times* decided not to publish something that it could have published.

The fallacy of equivocation does not crop up too often, but when it does it can be slippery. In Chapter 3, we noted that clear definitions are crucial to argumentation, and one way they can fail is to be equivocal. For example, we saw that if one defines a selfish action as any action performed because we desire to perform it, we could conclude that all our actions are selfish. But if we then conclude that all our actions are selfish *in the ordinary sense,* we commit the fallacy of equivocation.

Just as equivocation makes use of semantic ambiguity, the fallacy known as **Amphiboly** makes use of syntactic ambiguity. In these cases, it is the structure of the sentence that causes the ambiguity rather than a single word or phrase. Recall examples like these from Chapter 3:

> If you want to take the motor out of the car, I'll sell it to you cheap.

The sentence's structure does not make it clear enough whether "it" refers to the motor or the car. If someone used a sentence like this to try to mislead us about what was for sale cheap, he or she would be guilty of amphiboly.

And here is another example of amphiboly.

> AGENT: You must show a birth certificate and a driver's license or a passport in order to apply to the program.
> APPLICANT: Okay. I have my passport.
> AGENT: And a birth certificate?
> APPLICANT: You said *or* a passport, and that's what I have here.

The agent meant that a birth certificate was required, *plus* either a license or a passport; the applicant understood that either a birth certificate and license were required *or* a passport. This kind of problem crops up now and then when people are not careful enough about punctuation in their directions.

THE FALLACIES OF COMPOSITION AND DIVISION

The fallacy known as **Composition** occurs when a feature of the parts of something is erroneously attributed to the whole. Here is a simple example:

> This building is built from rectangular bricks; therefore, it must be rectangular.

The fallacy is also related to the grouping ambiguity covered in Chapter 3: It is fallacious to reason from a claim about members of a group taken individually to a conclusion about the group taken collectively. For example:

> The public thinks highly of individual members of Congress.
> Therefore, the public thinks highly of Congress as a whole.

This is fallacious reasoning, because what is true of individual members of Congress may not be true of the whole collective.

■ Do you need curved bricks to build a curved wall?

The fallacy known as **Division** is the same as composition but going the other direction. An example:

> During the recent recovery my financial portfolio gained considerably in value. Therefore, Microsoft stock, which is in my portfolio, gained considerably in value.

The fact that the speaker's portfolio as a whole increased in value during the recovery does not show that any particular investment within it increased in value during the recovery.

Like the fallacy of composition, division also can hinge on the grouping ambiguity. Here's an example.

> Letter carriers in this town walk hundreds of miles each day. Cheryl, who delivers letters to my block and doesn't look very athletic, must be exhausted every day after walking that far.

Obviously, in the first sentence it was letter carriers taken collectively, not individually, who are said to walk hundreds of miles. So one cannot conclude from that premise that any single carrier walks so far.

Another example of division:

> The Miami Dolphins are the only team that ever went an entire NFL season, all the way through the Super Bowl, without suffering a tie or defeat. Clearly, they were the best team in the league that year. Therefore, that year the team's quarterback, Bob Griese, was the best in the league at his position, and running back Larry Csonka and wide receiver Mercury Morris likewise were the best at their positions.

No, what was just said of the individuals on the team does not follow. What is true of the whole may not be true of the individual parts. To turn our earlier example around: The fact that a building is round does not mean it must be made of round bricks.

Confusing Fallacies I: Composition versus Hasty Generalization

The fallacy of composition is easily confused with hasty generalization (covered in Chapter 7). When we jump from a fact about the individual members of a collection (*The senators are all large*) to a conclusion about the members taken collectively (*Therefore, the senate is large*), we have a case of composition. But when we jump from a fact about an individual member of a collection (*Senator Brown is overweight*) to a conclusion about all the members of the collection taken individually (*Therefore, all the senators are overweight*), it's hasty generalization.

Confusing Fallacies II: Division versus Accident

The fallacy of division is also easily confused with the fallacy of accident. If we jump from a fact about the members of a collection taken collectively (*It is a large senate*) to a conclusion about the members taken individually (*Therefore, the senators are large*), that's division. Accident occurs when we jump from a generalization about the individual members of a collection (*Senators are wealthy*) to a conclusion about this or that member of the collection (*Therefore, Senator Brown is wealthy*).

CONFUSING EXPLANATIONS WITH EXCUSES

Back in Chapters 1 and 2 we made a careful distinction between arguments and explanations. We reason fallaciously when we take the one to be the other, as in this case:

> SPEAKER: The young man who killed all those people at Sandy Hook Elementary School was suffering from a half dozen mental disorders.
>
> HECKLER: Oh, so now you're going to tell us he had an excuse for the horrible things he did!

Not necessarily. The speaker may simply be trying to explain why things happened as they did, which is not the same thing as *excusing,* never mind *justifying* those actions.

After the September 11, 2001, suicide attacks on the World Trade Center, a speaker at our university attempted to explain possible causes of the attacks. Some assumed him to be excusing or justifying the attacks; Rush Limbaugh invited him to move to Afghanistan.

It is one thing to *explain* why or how something may have happened, and it is another thing entirely to *justify* or *excuse* the event. To mistake the first for the others is to commit a fallacy we'll call **Confusing Explanations with Excuses.** An attempt to *excuse* or *justify* a thing or event requires an argument the conclusion of which

Several excuses are always less convincing than one.

—Aldous Huxley

is that the thing or event is justifiable or excusable.* But an attempt to *explain* the thing or event requires a story—an account of a causal chain—showing how the thing or event may have come to be.

Here is another example:

> I heard on the History Channel about how the weak German economy after World War I contributed to the rise of Adolf Hitler. What's that about? Why would the History Channel try to excuse the Germans?

It is one thing to seek to understand how Hitler came to power in Germany, but it is quite another thing to excuse or justify its happening. To assume without further reason that a person (or a television show) that explains an event is thereby trying to excuse or justify it is to commit this fallacy. One *can* propose an explanation for something *and then go on* to use this explanation as part of an excuse or justification, but that is going beyond the explanation itself.

> He that is good for making excuses is seldom good for anything else.
>
> —Benjamin Franklin

Money to Burn

Inflation in Germany was so severe in the 1920s that what could be purchased for four marks very quickly required 8000 marks. Marks were soon worth so little people used them for fuel in their stoves. Such facts are usually cited as part of the explanation for German discontent and belligerence after World War I. But it would be a mistake to assume that someone who cites them is trying to excuse or justify German belligerence.

---

*Technically speaking, justifications and excuses are not exactly the same. To justify an action is to show that it was reasonable under the circumstances; to excuse it is to relieve the actor of blame or criticism. One discourages the latter actions, but not the former. The point is, to assume that an explanation automatically is either an attempted justification or attempted excuse is to commit the fallacy that, for brevity, we call "confusing explanations with excuses."

CONFUSING CONTRARIES AND CONTRADICTORIES

Here is how contraries and contradictories can be confused:

> VISITOR: I understand that all the fish in this pond are carp.
>
> CURATOR: No, quite the opposite, in fact.
>
> VISITOR: What? No carp?

The visitor's conclusion does not follow. "None are carp" is not the opposite of "All are carp." A pair of claims that are exact opposites of each other are **contradictories,** meaning they *never* have the same truth value. But two claims that cannot both be true but can both be *false* are not exact opposites: they are **contraries.** "None are carp" and "All are carp" are contraries, not contradictories.

Two terms—"alive" and "dead," for example—may seem to be the exact opposite of each other. If that frog isn't alive, then it must be dead. But that doesn't follow about just any old object, as can be seen from this example:

> The instructions for the scavenger hunt said to bring back something dead. So I brought this rock. Now you're telling me it doesn't count? Do you think maybe it's alive?

The speaker here does not understand how "alive" and "dead" relate to one another. Being dead implies that the thing in question was once alive. Thus, it is not correct to say that rocks are dead. The point is that "X is alive" and "X is dead" can both be false (as in the case of the rocks). They are contraries. Now consider the two sentences "X is alive" and "It is not true that X is alive." These sentences really *are* exact opposites in that they cannot both be true (of the same X) *and* they cannot both

■ Confusion at the putter factory? If we take these markings to mean "This is a heavy putter" and "This is a mid-weight putter," then clearly something is wrong. Are these two claims contradictories or contraries?

be false. Such sentences are contradictories. To treat contraries as if they were contradictories is fallacious reasoning.

Exercise 8-1

For each of the following pairs of sentences, determine whether they are contraries, contradictories, or neither.

▲—See the answers section at the back of the book.

▲ 1. a. Some of the exercises are difficult.
       b. None of the exercises are difficult.

    2. a. All kangaroos are marsupials.
       b. No kangaroos are marsupials.

    3. a. There is only a little gas in the tank.
       b. There is a lot of gas in the tank.

▲ 4. a. John comes here every Tuesday.
       b. John comes here every day.

    5. a. Today is Friday.
       b. Today is not Friday.

    6. a. Many over-the-counter medicines are expensive.
       b. Many over-the-counter medicines are not expensive.

▲ 7. a. Hillary ran a better campaign than Marco.
       b. Marco ran a better campaign than Hillary.

    8. a. The Bible is divinely inspired writing.
       b. The Koran is divinely inspired writing.

    9. a. The Bible is the only divinely inspired writing.
       b. The Koran is the only divinely inspired writing.

▲ 10. a. All Dobermans are aggressive.
       b. My dog is a Doberman and he is not aggressive.

CONSISTENCY AND INCONSISTENCY

How many times have you heard a politician accused of doing a "flip-flop"? The term is used to describe politicians who have changed their position on something. But what is so bad about flip-flopping? Aren't you ever supposed to

change your mind? We'll look at that question in a moment, but first let's get a couple of simple concepts clear. A group of beliefs is *consistent* if, and only if, it is possible that each and every one of them is true at the same time. A group of beliefs is *inconsistent* if and only if it *isn't* possible for all of them to be true at the same time.

An individual claim is also consistent or inconsistent. It is consistent if it is at least *possible* for it to be true, and it is inconsistent if it simply cannot be true—in which case it is *self-contradictory*. "It is raining on my window as I write this" is a consistent statement. It is false, but it at least could be true. But "it is raining on my window as I write this and it is not raining on my window as I write this" is self-contradictory.

Now, let's remind ourselves that knowing that a *person* has been inconsistent does not tell us a thing about his or her *position*. To think that it does is to commit an *argumentum ad hominem*, as explained on pages 174–176. Flip-flopping is *never* a reason for thinking that the person's *position* is defective. An inconsistent position is unacceptable, but the position of an inconsistent person might not be.

In early 2013, Senator Rand Paul was questioning Kathleen Hogan in a Senate Energy and Natural Resources hearing. Among his remarks was a charge of inconsistency: "You favor choice in the matter of a woman's right to an abortion, but you don't favor a woman's or a man's right to choose what kind of light bulb, what kind of dishwasher or washing machine [they will buy]." Evaluate whether the inconsistency charge is reasonable.

Exercise 8-2

MISCALCULATING PROBABILITIES

In this section, we examine four mistakes people sometimes make when they calculate probabilities.

Incorrectly Combining the Probability of Independent Events

Sometimes people make a mistake when they combine the probability of unrelated events. For example:

> Bill's chances of becoming a professional football player are about 1 in 1,000, and Hal's chances of becoming a professional hockey player are about 1 in 5,000. So the chance of both of them becoming professionals in their respective sports is about 1 in 6,000.

The conclusion is incorrect. The two events—Bill's becoming a professional football player and Hal's becoming a professional hockey player—are independent events. One *independent event* cannot affect the outcome of another; whether one happens does not change the probability of the other. When we gauge the probability of two independent events, we multiply their two individual probabilities. So, to find the probability of Bill and Hal both becoming professionals, we multiply 1/1,000 times 1/5,000. The probability of both making pro teams is thus 1 in 5,000,000. We hope they have backup plans.

Gun Owners and the Second Amendment

Possibly 100% of gun owners support the right to bear arms. What is the probability that someone who supports the right to bear arms owns a gun? You would need to know what percent of people who don't own guns support the right to bear arms as well as the base rate or "prior probability" of gun ownership. This is explained in the text.

Another example of the same mistake:

> Since there are six sides on a die, the chances of rolling a 1 (a "snake eye") are 1 in 6. Therefore, the chances of rolling two of them in a row are 2 in 12.

Nope. These events are independent, so we multiply $\frac{1}{6}$ times $\frac{1}{6}$ and we get $\frac{1}{36}$. The chances of two consecutive snake eyes are 1 in 36, or a little less than 3 percent.

The principles behind combining probabilities will be further explained in Chapter 11.

Gambler's Fallacy

The *Gambler's Fallacy* is a common and seductive mistake that happens when we don't realize that independent events *really are independent*. Like this speaker:

> The last three coin flips have all been heads, so the next flip is more likely to come up tails.

It's true that four heads in a row is fairly unlikely ($\frac{1}{2} \times \frac{1}{2} \times \frac{1}{2} \times \frac{1}{2} = \frac{1}{16}$ or 6.25 percent), but once the first three heads have come up, the odds of the fourth flip coming up heads is still 1 in 2, that is, 50 percent. Remember when dealing with independent events: past history has no effect.

Overlooking Prior Probabilities

The **prior probability** of something is its probability everything else being equal. (What that last phrase means should be clear in a moment.) The prior probability of a coin flip coming up heads is 1 in 2, or .5. The prior probability of a given newborn baby's being male is also .5, since about 50 percent of newborns are male. If 20 percent of the students at your college are business majors, then the prior probability of any given student at your college being a business major is .2, or 2 in 10.

The fallacy of **Overlooking Prior Probabilities** occurs when someone fails to take these underlying probabilities into account. Here's an example:

> Bill is the best football player in our high school, and Hal is the best hockey player in our high school. So it appears that Bill's chances of becoming a professional football player and Hal's chances of becoming a professional football player are equally good.

What is overlooked here is that the prior probability of someone's becoming a professional football player is greater than the prior probability of someone's becoming a professional hockey player. Now you can see what we meant earlier by "everything else being equal." Bill has a 1/1,000 chance to play pro ball, let's say, presuming he has the same chance as any other player at his level. If Bill were a high school All-American, that would improve his chances, but then "everything else" would not be equal—he would have an odds advantage over other players. Similarly, if the dice we are rolling are loaded, the prior probabilities of a given number coming up will change, since not all the numbers will have an equal chance of coming up.

Faulty Inductive Conversion

Information about the percentage of As that are Bs does not in itself tell you anything about the percentage of Bs that are As. Those who think it does are guilty of a **Faulty Inductive Conversion,** the fourth mistake people sometimes make when they calculate probabilities.

Here is an example:

> Most professional football players are men.
> Therefore, most men are professional football players.

Here is another example:

> Almost everyone who has Alzheimer's disease once ate carrots.
> Therefore, eating carrots makes it more likely that you will get Alzheimer's disease.

These examples are so obviously mistaken nobody would be fooled by them. Here, however, is a less obvious example:

Ten percent of the students living in the dorm came down with a stomach ailment, and most of them ate at the student union. It seems wise to steer clear of student union food.

Our speaker fears the food at the student union, because most of the dorm students who fell ill ate it. He or she thinks eating the food at the student union is apt to cause illness.

But what if most of the students in the dorm who *didn't* fall ill also ate at the student union?

Let's presume the following numbers: The dorm (let us say) has 100 students. Thus ten became ill and ninety didn't. Let's say that seven of the ten dorm residents who became ill ate at the student union. But let's also suppose that 70 percent of the ninety dorm residents who *didn't* fall ill also ate at the student union. That's an additional sixty-three students who ate student union food. So a total of seventy students ate student union food, and only six of them fell ill. That means that only 8.5 percent of the people who ate student union food fell ill. Nothing in these facts should make our speaker leery of dining at the student union.

One more example:

Sam's parents have learned that, at Blue Mountain State, 60 percent of students on academic probation (AP) party every week. Sam, who attends Blue Mountain, has confided that her sorority hosts a party every Friday. Her parents worry that this makes it more likely she will end up on AP.

Sam's parents are guilty of a faulty inductive conversion, jumping from the fact that most AP students party to the conclusion that partying increases a student's chances of ending up on AP. Sam's parents need more information. Specifically, they need to know what percentage of Blue Mountain students who are *not* on AP party every week, and what percentage of Blue Mountain students are on AP in the first place. For all they know, Sam's parents should be encouraging her to party.

Don't believe it? Let's say only 10 percent of Blue Mountain students are on AP. That means that, out of every 100 students at Blue Mountain, ninety are *not* on AP. Suppose now that of these ninety students who are *not* on AP, 60 percent—fifty-four students—party every week. Now we have the situation that fifty-four students who are *not* on AP party every week and six students who *are* on AP party every week. Do the math. At Blue Mountain, a student who parties every week is more apt to *not* be on AP.

So, to repeat, information about the percentage of As that are Bs doesn't by itself tell you anything about the percentage of Bs that are As. You need to know as well the percentage of *not-As* that are Bs, and how many of them there are to begin with. More details coming up in Chapter 11.

Exercise 8-3	Show that the reasoning in the next paragraph is unsound based on what you've read in this section.

The test said I was allergic to cats. It says "yes" 90 percent of the time when people really do have the allergy and it says "yes" 10 percent of the time when people really do not have it. So more than likely I have the allergy, which is unlucky since only 1 percent of the population has this affliction.

In this chapter, we examined fallacies and mistakes in reasoning that generally are based on a faulty argument structure or a careless use of language. Specifically, we discussed the following:

Recap

- Affirming the consequent—affirming the consequent of an "if . . . then . . ." claim and attempting to infer its antecedent

- Denying the antecedent—denying the antecedent of an "if . . . then . . ." claim and attempting to infer the denial of its consequent

- Undistributed middle—assuming that two things that are related to a third thing must be related to each other

- Equivocation—the use of claims as premises and/or conclusions that contain words or phrases that are interpreted in more than one way

- Amphiboly—the use of claims as premises and/or conclusions that contain ambiguity because of their grammatical structure

- Composition—assuming that what is true of a group of things taken individually must also be true of those same things taken collectively; or assuming that what is true of the parts of a thing must be true of the thing itself

- Division—assuming that what is true of a group of things taken collectively must also be true of those same things taken individually; or assuming that what is true of a whole is also true of its parts

- Confusing explanations and excuses—presuming that, because someone is explaining how or why some event came to pass, he or she is attempting to excuse or justify that event

- Confusing contraries and contradictories—to fail to notice that two conflicting claims can be either contraries (cannot both be true but can both be false) or contradictories (cannot both be true and cannot both be false)

- Consistency and inconsistency—consistency in one's beliefs is a requirement of rationality, but the inconsistency of a person (in changing from one belief to another inconsistent with the first) does not impugn either the previously held belief or the current one

- Incorrectly combining the probabilities of independent events—failing to realize that the probability of several independent events is determined by multiplying the probabilities of the various events

- Gambler's fallacy—believing that the past performance of independent events will have an effect on a further independent event

- Overlooking prior probabilities—failing to take into consideration the likelihood of an event all other things being equal; that is, its likelihood apart from any outside influences

- Faulty inductive conversion—mistakenly thinking that, from information about the percentage of As that are Bs, you can derive a conclusion about the percentage of Bs that are As

29. A couple dozen great singers came to the audition. Just think of what a great chorus they would make.

30. Mercedes-Benz is the most expensive car line in the world, on average. Therefore, its top-of-the-line model will be more expensive than the top-of-the-line Bentley.

31. Sucrose is a necessary nutrient. Without it the body cannot generate energy. So, since sucrose is sugar, it is important to have a sufficient amount of sugar in your diet.

32. Is an explanation clearly being offered as an excuse/justification? Billy behaves poorly in restaurants because he's a little kid. What would you expect?

33. Dooley wants to conserve clean air and water. If that doesn't make him a conservative, I don't know what does.

34. All German shepherds are dogs, and some dogs are trained to attack people. Therefore, some German shepherds are trained to attack people.

35. If the government response to Hurricane Sandy is large enough and fast enough, then New Jersey and the surrounding area will avoid years of economic hard times. But there is no chance its response will be both big enough and fast enough. Therefore, there will be years of hard times in that part of the country.

36. Is this an explanation or an excuse/justification? You shouldn't condemn bull-fighting on account of the bulls' well-being. After all, the bulls that enter the ring have had lives that are many times better than the cattle that are raised to be killed in slaughterhouses.

37. With college board scores like these, Charles can probably get into Princeton as easily as State.

38. Is an explanation clearly being offered as an excuse/justification? Tiger Woods isn't winning tournaments like he once was because he has messed with his golf swing too many times.

39. Small pieces of litter are barely visible; therefore, as long as you throw out only small pieces of litter, there shouldn't be a problem.

40. Rare diseases are very common and hemophagocytic lymphohistiocytosis is a rare disease. Therefore, you should be on the lookout for it.

41. The paint store is the best place to work on your diet. You can get thinner there.

42. Is an explanation clearly being offered as an excuse/justification? When former candidate for vice president John Edwards was asked why he did not favor gay marriage, he replied, "I don't know. It was just the way I was raised, I guess."

43. All feral cats are wild creatures, and many wild creatures cannot be successfully socialized. Therefore, many feral cats cannot be successfully socialized.

44. If she hates her parents as much as she says, she has her own apartment. She doesn't hate her parents as much as she says. Therefore, she does not have her own apartment.

45. Everybody who can legally drink in this state is twenty-one or older. Sally is twenty-one or older. Therefore, she can legally drink.

46. Most Parkinson's disease victims were once wine drinkers; therefore, drinking wine raises your chances of having Parkinson's disease.

47. Lightning struck that barn a year ago, and everybody knows lightening never strikes twice in the same spot. So the barn is safe.

48. Each individual has the right to be heard. Therefore, our group has the right to be heard.

49. Sandra has had some bad arthritis in her left hand. But, on the other hand, she's just fine.

▲ 50. Is an explanation clearly being offered as an excuse/justification? It's true, Geoffrey said some very unpleasant things to some of the people at the table last night. But that's because he's had a lot to drink and he really doesn't hold his liquor all that well. He's a completely different person when he's sober.

51. Is an explanation clearly being offered as an excuse/justification? Well, yes, I read Christine's diary—but that's because, good grief, she read mine!

52. All members of the club have strong views, and all the men in this community have strong views. So all the men in this community are members of the club.

53. If you are not twenty-one or older, then it is not legal for you to drink. You are twenty-one. Therefore, it is legal for you to drink.

54. If Sally is over twenty-one, then she can legally drink. Sally can legally drink. Therefore, she is over twenty-one.

▲ 55. If it is legal for Sally to drink, then she is twenty-one or older. It is not legal for Sally to drink. Therefore, she is not twenty-one or older.

56. If Sally is over twenty-one, then it is legal for her to drink. Sally is not over twenty-one. Therefore, it is not legal for her to drink.

57. Posey hit two home runs in the last game, so you know he's on track to hit at least one today.

58. Is the speaker viewing an explanation as an excuse/justification? Her car broke down is why she says she isn't here? Why does she try to duck her responsibilities all the time?

59. Virtually every heroin addict once smoked marijuana. Therefore, your chances of becoming a heroin addict are increased if you smoke marijuana.

▲ 60. Water is liquid. Water consists of hydrogen and oxygen molecules. Therefore, hydrogen and oxygen molecules are liquid.

61. Somebody drilled a hole in the nudist camp wall. The police are looking into it.

62. Is an explanation clearly being offered as an excuse/justification? Monica was unable to take the test today because she was very ill with the flu and a high fever.

63. Jackson believes in democracy—you know, let the voters decide. And as a Democrat he will support whomever the party decides to nominate.

64. If she passed the course, she is very bright. If she did well on the final, she is very bright. Therefore, if she did well on the final, she passed the course.

▲ 65. If a person dropped out of college, that person will not make much money. Chris doesn't make much money. Therefore, he dropped out of college.

66. Is an explanation clearly being offered as an excuse/justification? Dinner is late because I had to work late is why, so don't get on my case.

67. Don't worry about your recital tonight. Every note sounds great on a Steinway.

68. Laura's physics class came out with an A-minus average on the exam. She has to be a smart cookie to do so well in such a difficult class.

69. The sign at the drug rehabilitation center said "Keep off the grass." They're even doing propaganda out in the yard!

▲ 70. In my child's class there are thirty students, and ten of them got flu shots this year. Five of the kids who got shots wound up getting the flu. The shots were a bad idea: kids were just as likely to get the flu as not, even after their shots!

71. You say he's had his fill of flies? Gross. Does he eat rats, too?

72. She wouldn't have said it if she didn't believe it. And she didn't do it if she didn't believe it. Therefore, she wouldn't have said it if she didn't do it.

73. This zinfandel would have a smooth finish if it came from very old vines. In fact, it does have a smooth finish, so it came from very old vines.

74. Nearly all advanced prostate cancer victims have elevated PSA levels. Therefore, if you have an elevated PSA level, you probably have advanced prostate cancer.

▲ 75. Is SUE clearly offering an explanation as an excuse/justification?
SUE: I'm sorry, Mom. I really didn't know I was supposed to be home by ten.
SUE'S MOM: Stop making excuses, Sue!

76. I read somewhere that Ford owners buy lots more gas than Chrysler and Jeep owners put together. So Chryslers and Jeeps must get better mileage.

77. "The sign said 'Fine for parking here' so I parked there. And damned if I didn't get a ticket. Don't they follow their own rules?"

—Steven's Guide

78. The menu said, "Soup or salad and dessert." So I asked for salad and desert.

79. If you like Ayn Rand, you are a libertarian. And, of course, if you're an anarchist, you're a libertarian. Therefore, if you like Ayn Rand, you are an anarchist.

▲ 80. It's true, if Ms. Presson is accepted into law school, then you know she had to have very good grades. And I'm telling you, you should see her transcript; she's made straight As for the past two years. So I wouldn't worry about her being accepted into law school; she'll be accepted without a doubt.

81. Most straight-A students own cell phones. Obviously owning a cell enhances learning.

82. They told me their computers were down, but I am sick and tired of people blaming everything on computer issues.

83. If you aren't wealthy, adding a single dollar to your bank account won't change things. Therefore, single dollars cannot make you wealthy.

84. Councilman Smith says he thinks we should make liberal payouts to local organizations. I knew he was a liberal in conservative's clothing!

▲ 85. Of course he couldn't see your point. Dude's blind.

86. Everybody who took the exam passed the course, and everybody who did an outside project passed the course too. So everybody who did an outside project took the exam.

87. If global warming is for real, then the mean global temperature would have risen over the past ten years. Global warming is not for real. Therefore, the mean global temperature didn't rise over the past ten years.

88. Don't play that number. It won the lottery last week!

89. He can lift every weight in that stack; therefore, he can lift the entire stack.

▲ 90. The chance of rain in Washington, D.C., tomorrow is 50% and it's 50% in London too. So we're pretty much 100% sure to get rain in one capital or the other.

91. Well, as you know, if you had taken aspirin daily, your blood would have become thinner. According to your latest blood test, you have no problem in that department, so I conclude that you've been taking aspirin.

92. MARINA: Given how harsh he was, it was wrong for us to support the Shah.

OLIVIA: Well, he was harsh because strong measures were needed to improve his country's economy. Given his motives, he did not act immorally.

Is OLIVIA's explanation being offered to justify the Shah's harsh measures?

93. I've always wondered how they could breathe, there on the Underground Railway.

94. All mammals bear their young live. Guppies also bear their young live. So, surprisingly, guppies must be mammals.

▲ 95. When James gets the paper on the porch every day, Mr. Fields gives him a small tip at the end of the month. I noticed he gave him a tip yesterday, so James was doing a good job of getting the paper on the porch.

96. The chances of my bus to the airport being late is about 50 percent, but the chance of my flight taking off late is also about 50 percent. So together the chance of them happening is 100 percent.

97. The San Francisco Giants won the World Series. No way the San Francisco 49ers won the Super Bowl the same year!

98. Smoke from a single fireplace can hardly pollute the air; therefore, people should be able to use their fireplaces anytime they want.

99. That field of flowers is really colorful. Some of the plants in there are hostas; they must be quite colorful.

▲ 100. I'll tell you right now, Horace. No daughter of mine is going to work in a strip mall.

101. Is an explanation clearly being offered as an excuse/justification? No surprise that pit bulls are involved in more attacks on people than most other breeds. I mean, after all, those dogs are bred to be aggressive and to fight. That was the whole point of the breed.

102. If it weren't for a gerrymandered district, our local congressperson would never be reelected. Therefore, since the district is gerrymandered, our person will be elected again.

103. If you had cooked this meat for at least three hours, it would be tender enough to go in the stew. But you cooked it for only two hours, so it won't be tender enough.

104. Given the number of tickets I bought, I have a 33 percent chance of winning a raffle prize, and Bill also has a 33 percent chance, and Juanita has a 33 percent chance too. So one of us is bound to win something!

▲ 105. I read that tiger mosquitos are spreading across the country more rapidly than any other type. I'm thinking they must be able to fly faster than other mosquitos.

106. A dialogue:

JILL: Professor Heinz is delivering a paper to a scientific meeting.
BILL: The *Post* or the *Times?*

Deductive Arguments I

Categorical Logic

Students will learn to . . .

1. **Recognize the four types of categorical claims and the Venn diagrams that represent them**

2. **Translate claims into standard form**

3. **Use the square of opposition to identify logical relationships between corresponding categorical claims**

4. **Use conversion, obversion, and contraposition with standard form to make valid arguments**

5. **Recognize and evaluate the validity of categorical syllogisms**

The Science of Deduction and Analysis is one which can only be acquired by long and patient study, nor is life long enough to allow any mortal to attain the highest possible perfection in it.

> —*From an article by Sherlock Holmes,*
> *in* A Study in Scarlet *by Sir Arthur Conan Doyle*

Fortunately, the greatest detective was exaggerating in this quotation. While it may be that few of us mortals will attain "the highest possible perfection" in "the Science of Deduction," most of us can learn quite a bit in a short time if we put our minds to it. In fact, you already have an understanding of the basics from Chapter 2.* In this chapter and the next, you'll learn two kinds of techniques for making and evaluating deductive inferences—in other words, arguments.

If you flip through the pages of this chapter, you'll see diagrams with circles and Xs, and in the next chapter you will see weird symbols that remind some people of mathematics. These pages may look intimidating, but there's nothing complicated about them if you keep in mind that each paragraph builds on those that

---

*An understanding that's somewhat better than Sherlock's, as a matter of fact. As mentioned in Chapter 2, many instances of what Holmes calls deduction actually turn out to be induction. We mean no disrespect to Sherlock.

came before. If you try to skip ahead, you may have trouble. We recommend reading slowly, carefully, and thoughtfully, and even taking a break now and then.

You may remember from Chapter 2 that deductive arguments depend on the meanings of the words that occur in their premises for their validity. In particular, it is words like "all," "and," "or," "if . . . then . . ." that carry this burden. We'll see how this works as we go along. Recall also that valid deductive arguments actually *prove* or *demonstrate* their conclusion—that is, if the premises of such an argument are true, the conclusion cannot fail to be true as well. That said, we'll move on to our treatment of the first general type of deductive argument.

The first topic we'll take up is **categorical logic.** Categorical logic is logic based on the relations of inclusion and exclusion among classes (or "categories") as stated in categorical claims. Its methods date back to the time of Aristotle, and it was the principal form that logic took among most knowledgeable people for more than 2,000 years. During that time, all kinds of bells and whistles were added to the basic theory, especially by monks and other scholars during the medieval period. So as not to weigh you down with unnecessary baggage, we'll just set forth the basics of the subject in what follows.

Like propositional logic, the subject of the next chapter, categorical logic is useful in clarifying and analyzing deductive arguments. But there is another reason for studying the subject: *There is no better way to understand the underlying logical structure of our everyday language than to learn how to put it into the kinds of formal terms we'll introduce in these chapters.*

To test your analytical ability, take a look at these claims. Just exactly what is the difference between them?

(1) Everybody who is ineligible for Physics 1A must take Physical Science 1.

(2) No students who are required to take Physical Science 1 are eligible for Physics 1A.

■ For over a hundred years, the symbol of "the Science of Deduction." The smaller photo has Holmes and Watson portrayed by Basil Rathbone and Nigel Bruce, the classic cast in over a dozen films. Benedict Cumberbatch and Martin Freeman have starred in some excellent recent films about the famous detective.

Here's another pair of claims:

> (3) Harold won't attend the meeting unless Vanessa decides to go.
> (4) If Vanessa decides to go, then Harold will attend the meeting.

You might be surprised at how many college students have a hard time trying to determine whether the claims in each pair mean the same thing or something different. In this chapter and the next, you'll learn a foolproof method for determining how to unravel the logical implications of such claims and for seeing how any two such claims relate to each other. (Incidentally, claims 1 and 2 do not mean the same thing at all, and neither do 3 and 4.) If you're signing a lease or entering into a contract of any kind, it pays to be able to figure out just what is said in it and what is not; those who have trouble with claims like the ones above risk being left in the dark.

Studying categorical and truth-functional logic can teach us to become more careful and precise in our own thinking. Getting comfortable with this type of thinking can be helpful in general, but for those who will someday apply to law school, medical school, or graduate school, it has the added advantage that many admission exams for such programs deal with the kinds of reasoning discussed in these chapters.

Let's start by looking at the four basic kinds of claims on which categorical logic is based.

CATEGORICAL CLAIMS

In logic, a *category* is a group or a class or a population; any bunch of things can serve as a category for our purposes. *Terms* are noun phrases, like "dogs," "cats," "Christians," "Arabs," "people who read logic books," and so on. These terms are labels for categories (or classes or populations, all of which for our purposes are the same thing). There are all kinds of ways to express claims about categories, but we are interested in four standard-form types of sentences—the names of which are simple: A, E, I, and O—sentences that result from putting terms in the blanks of the following:

> A: All _____ are _____.
> (Example: All pianists are musicians.)
> E: No _____ are _____.
> (Example: No otterhounds are pianists.)
> I: Some _____ are _____.
> (Example: Some musicians are prodigies.)
> O: Some _____ are not _____.
> (Example: Some politicians are not criminals.*)

The phrases that go in the blanks are **terms;** the one that goes into the first blank is the **subject term** of the claim, and the one that goes into the second blank is the **predicate term.** Thus, "musicians" is the predicate term of the first example and the subject term of the third example. In many of the examples and explanations that follow, we'll use the letters S and P (for "subject" and "predicate") to stand for terms in categorical claims. And we'll talk about the subject and predicate *classes,* which are just the classes (or populations) the terms refer to.

*We actually believe this.

But first, a caution: Only nouns and noun phrases will work as terms. An adjective alone, such as "red," won't do. "All fire engines are red" is *not* a standard-form categorical claim, because "red" by itself does not name a class of things.

Looking back at the standard-form structures just given, notice that each one has a letter to its left. These are the traditional names of the four types of standard-form categorical claims. The claim "All pianists are musicians" is an A-claim, and so are "All idolaters are heathens," "All people born after the year 2000 are millennials," and any other claim of the form "All S are P." The same is true for the other three letters, E, I, and O, and the other three kinds of claims.

Venn Diagrams

Each of the standard forms has its own visual illustration in a **Venn diagram,** as shown in Figures 1 through 4. Named after British logician John Venn, these diagrams graphically represent the four standard-form categorical claim types.

The following are conventions that govern the diagrams:

1. Circles represent classes ("categories").
2. A shaded area indicates that nothing is in it. It means that this part of a class (or classes, if the area is where two or more circles overlap) is "empty."
3. An X in an area indicates that at least one thing is in that part of a class or classes.
4. An area that is blank does NOT mean that it is empty. It means we have no information about that part of the category or class.

Now let's understand the diagrams:

Figure 1 is the diagram for A-claims. It shows that All S are P. It shows this by shading out all the S area that is *outside* the P area, thus showing that if anything is an A it must be in the P area.

Figure 2 is the diagram for E-claims. It shows that No S are P, by showing that the category "SP" is empty.

Figure 3 is the diagram for I-claims. It shows that Some S are P, by placing an X in the "SP" area. For our purposes, *the word "some" means "at least one."*

Figure 4 is the diagram for O-claims. It shows that there is at least one thing that is an S but which is outside the P area.

Finally, notice that the A- and I-claims are **affirmative,** and the E- and O-claims are **negative.**

Although there are only four standard-form claim types, it's remarkable how versatile they are. A large portion of what we want to say can be rewritten, or "translated,"

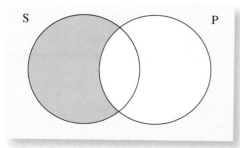

FIGURE 1   **A-claim:** All S are P.

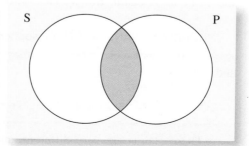

FIGURE 2   **E-claim:** No S are P.

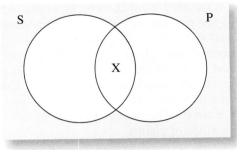

FIGURE 3   **I-claim:** Some S are P.

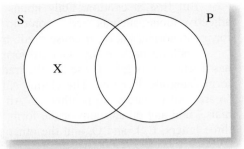

FIGURE 4   **O-claim:** Some S are not P.

into one or another of them. Because this task is sometimes easier said than done, we'd best spend a little while making sure we understand how to do it. And we warn you: A lot of standard-form translations are not pretty—but it's accuracy we seek, not style.

TRANSLATION INTO STANDARD FORM (INTRODUCTION)

The idea here is to turn an ordinary claim into a standard-form categorical claim that is equivalent. We'll say that two claims are **equivalent claims** if, and only if, they would be true in exactly the same circumstances—that is, under no circumstances could one of them be true and the other false. (You can think of such claims as "saying the same thing.")

Lots of ordinary claims in English are easy to translate into standard form. A claim of the sort "Every X is a Y," for example, turns into the standard-form A-claim "All Xs are Ys." And "Minors are not eligible" turns into the E-claim "No minors are eligible people."

All standard-form claims are in the present tense, but even so, we can use them to talk about the past. For example, we can translate "There were creatures weighing more than four tons that lived in North America" as "Some creatures that lived in North America are creatures that weighed more than four tons."

Translating Claims in Which the Word "Only" or the Phrase "The Only" Occurs

The word "only" is not only versatile (see the box on the next page), it can cause confusion when it occurs in a claim you need to translate into standard form. An example:

> ORIGINAL: Only sophomores are eligible candidates.

A careful reading and a moment's thought will probably indicate that this should be an A-claim. But we have to decide between

> INCORRECT TRANSLATION: All sophomores are eligible candidates.

and

> CORRECT TRANSLATION: All eligible candidates are sophomores.

These claims are very different, and only one of them say the same thing as our original statement. Notice that the original says something about *every* eligible candidate; we're saying something about *all* eligible candidates. So eligible candidates form the *subject* class of the A-claim. The correct translation is the claim at the bottom of the preceding page. Notice that the word "only" introduced the class of sophomores in the original sentence. That provides us with a general rule:

The word "only," used by itself, introduces the *predicate* term of an A-claim.

Now look at this example:

> ORIGINAL: The only people admitted are people over twenty-one.

Here, the class being restricted is the class of people admitted, right? *Every one of them* has to be over twenty-one. So we're talking about *all* people admitted:

> TRANSLATION: All people admitted are people over twenty-one.

And this is always the case when a term in an A-claim is introduced by the phrase "the only"; it works in the opposite way from how the word "only" works by itself:

The phrase "the only" introduces the *subject* term of an A-claim.

Note that, in accordance with these rules, we would translate both of these claims:

> ORIGINAL: Only matinees are half-price shows.

and

> ORIGINAL: Matinees are the only half-price shows.

as

> TRANSLATION: All half-price shows are matinees.

Translating Claims About Times and Places

Sometimes statements that look to be about one thing need to be interpreted to be about something else in order to make them work as standard form categorical claims. For example:

> ORIGINAL: I always get nervous when I take logic exams.

This looks like a claim about the speaker, but it is best seen as a claim about *times* or *occasions*. The speaker is saying, "Every time I take a logic exam is a time I get nervous," which of course translates into standard form:

> TRANSLATION: All times I take logic exams are times I get nervous.

The Most Versatile Word in English

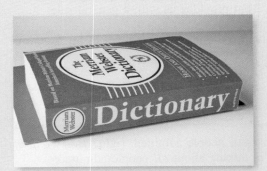

Only one word can be placed anywhere in the following sentence (at the beginning, at the end, or between any other two words) and still make sense:

> I gave my son the money he needed yesterday.

That word is "only," the most versatile word in the English language. Each placement, with a hint as to the different meanings produced, is given below:

1. Only I gave my son the money he needed yesterday.
   (Nobody else gave him any.)
2. I only gave my son the money he needed yesterday.
   (He wanted the car, too, but I would not give it to him.)
3. I gave only my son the money he needed yesterday.
   (His friend wanted money too, but I refused.)
4. I gave my only son the money he needed yesterday.
   (I have a daughter, but only the one son.)
5. I gave my son only the money he needed yesterday.
   (He'll need more for tomorrow.)
6. I gave my son the only money he needed yesterday.
   (He didn't need much. . . .)
7. I gave my son the money only he needed yesterday.
   (Everybody else must have had their money.)
8. I gave my son the money he only needed yesterday.
   (He won't need any money the rest of the week.)
9. I gave my son the money he needed only yesterday.
   (And already he's needing more?)
10. I gave my son the money he needed yesterday only.
   (And I told him that was the first and last time.)

—Based on an idea from Marilyn Vos Savant, author of the "Ask Marilyn" column in Parade Magazine

The word "whenever" can be a good clue that you have such a claim on your hands. For example:

> Whenever Peg shows up, Dick gets anxious.

The word "whenever" tells us two things: that we probably have a claim about times or occasions, and that the term it introduces will be the subject term. There can be exceptions to this, depending on how "whenever" is used, but this rule of thumb is always worth keeping in mind.

Places are handled much like times in categorical claims. Consider this:

> ORIGINAL: It's snowing everywhere in Massachusetts.

This is about snow, and it's about today, but we're best seeing it as about places: places where it's snowing and places in Massachusetts. Once you see it that way, it's easily translated into standard form:

> TRANSLATION: All places in Massachusetts are places it's snowing.

The word "wherever" is an indicator for places in the way that "whenever" is for times. When you see it, it is likely that it introduces the subject term of an A-claim. For example:

> The lamb goes wherever Bo Peep goes.

This clearly should translate as "All places Bo Peep goes are places the lamb goes."

So, to recap the two rules of thumb for this section:

"Whenever" usually introduces the subject term of an A-claim about times; "wherever" usually introduces the subject term of an A-claim about places.

Translating Claims About Specific Individuals

The next claims that can confuse efforts at translation are claims about one individual person, thing, event, and so on. Consider the example, Aristotle is a logician.

It's clear that this claim specifies a class, "logicians," and places Aristotle as a member of that class. The problem is that categorical claims are always about *two* classes, and Aristotle isn't a class. (We certainly don't talk about *some* of Aristotle being a logician.) What we want to do is treat such claims as if they were about classes with exactly one member—in this case, Aristotle. One way to do this is to use the term "people who are identical with Aristotle," which of course has only Aristotle as a member. The important thing to remember about such claims can be summarized in the following rule:

Claims about single individuals should be treated as A-claims or E-claims.

So our example

> ORIGINAL: Aristotle is a logician.

can be translated as:

> TRANSLATION: All people identical with Aristotle are logicians.

Which is an A-claim. Similarly, "Aristotle is not left-handed" becomes the E-claim "No people identical with Aristotle are left-handed people." (Your instructor may prefer to leave the claim in its original form and simply *treat* it as an A-claim or an E-claim. This avoids the awkward "people identical with Aristotle" wording and is certainly okay with us.)

It isn't just people that crop up in individual claims. For example, the preferred translation of

> ORIGINAL: St. Louis is on the Mississippi.

is

> TRANSLATION: All cities identical with St. Louis are cities on the Mississippi.

We warned you that some of these translations would not be pretty.

Translating Claims that Use Mass Nouns

Other claims that cause translation difficulty contain what are called *mass nouns*. Example:

> ORIGINAL: Boiled okra is too ugly to eat.

This claim is about a *kind of stuff.* The best way to deal with it is to treat it as a claim about *examples* of this kind of stuff. The present example translates into an A-claim about *all* examples of the stuff in question:

> TRANSLATION: All examples of boiled okra are things that are too ugly to eat.

An example such as

> ORIGINAL: Most boiled okra is too ugly to eat.

translates into the I-claim,

> TRANSLATION: Some examples of boiled okra are things that are too ugly to eat.

As we noted, it's not possible to give rules or hints about every kind of problem you might run into when translating claims into standard-form categorical versions. Only practice and discussion can bring you to the point where you can handle this part of the material with confidence. The best thing to do now is to turn to some exercises.

Translate each of the following into a standard-form claim. Make sure that each answer follows the exact form of an A-, E-, I-, or O-claim and that each term you use is a noun or noun phrase that refers to a class of things.

Exercise 9-1

1. Every one of the senators is a politician.
2. Not all senators are politicians.
3. If somebody is a senator, then that person must be a politician.
4. You can be a senator only if you're a politician.
5. The only politicians I know are senators.
6. Being a senator is all it takes to be a politician.
7. Being a politician is not enough to make you a senator.
8. You can be a senator only if you're a politician.
9. Nobody who is a politician is also a senator.
10. A few senators are not politicians.
11. There are scholars who are philosophers.
12. There are no philosophers who are not scholars.
13. Philosophers are not the only scholars.
14. Philosophers are the only scholars.
15. Not every scholar is a philosopher.

Follow the directions for the previous exercise. Remember that you're trying to produce a claim that's equivalent to the one given; it doesn't matter whether the given claim is actually true.

Exercise 9-2

1. Every salamander is a lizard.
2. Not every lizard is a salamander.
3. Only reptiles can be lizards.
4. Snakes are the only members of the suborder Ophidia.
5. The only members of the suborder Ophidia are snakes.
6. None of the burrowing snakes are poisonous.
7. Anything that's an alligator is a reptile.
8. Anything that qualifies as a frog qualifies as an amphibian.
9. There are frogs wherever there are snakes.
10. Wherever there are snakes, there are frogs.
11. Whenever the frog population decreases, the snake population decreases.
12. Nobody arrived except the cheerleaders.
13. Except for vice presidents, nobody got raises.
14. Unless people arrived early, they couldn't get seats.
15. Most home movies are as boring as dirt.
16. Socrates is a Greek.
17. The bank robber is not Jane's fiancé.

18. If an automobile was built before 1950, it's an antique.
▲ 19. Salt is a meat preservative.
20. Most corn does not make good popcorn.

Exercise 9-3   Follow the directions for the previous exercises.

▲ 1. Students who wrote poor exams didn't get admitted to the program.
2. None of my students are failing.
3. If you live in the dorms, you can't own a car.
▲ 4. There are a few right-handed first basemen.
5. People make faces every time Joan sings.
6. The only tests George fails are the ones he takes.
▲ 7. Nobody passed who didn't make at least 50 percent.
8. You can't be a member unless you're over fifty.
9. Nobody catches on without studying.
▲ 10. I've had days like this before.
11. Roofers aren't millionaires.
12. Not one part of Joan Rivers' face is original equipment.
▲ 13. A few holidays fall on Saturday.
14. Only outlaws own guns.
15. You have nothing to lose but your chains.
▲ 16. Unless you pass this test you won't pass the course.
17. If you cheat, your prof will make you sorry.
18. If you cheat, your friends couldn't care less.
▲ 19. Only when you've paid the fee will they let you enroll.
20. Nobody plays who isn't in full uniform.

THE SQUARE OF OPPOSITION

We can now exhibit the logical relationships between A, E, I, and O claims that have the same subject and predicate terms and have them in the same order. The **square of opposition,** in Figure 5, does this very concisely. The A- and E-claims, across the top of the square from each other, are **contrary claims**—they can both be false, but they cannot both be true. The I- and O-claims, across the bottom of the square from each other, are **subcontrary claims**—they can both be true, but they cannot both be false. The A- and O-claims and the E- and I-claims, which are at opposite diagonal corners from each other, respectively, are **contradictory claims**—they never have the same truth values.

Existential Assumption and the Square of Opposition

Throughout this chapter, we are assuming that we are talking about classes that are not empty—that is, that our standard form claims have subject and predicate classes that have at least one member each. This is known as an **existential assumption.** The relationships between contraries and between subcontraries depend on this assumption. Here's how to see why: First let's diagram an A-claim. We color in the left portion of the subject class circle (see Figure 6). Now diagram an E-claim on the same diagram. To do this we color in the right-side portion of the subject class circle. But look what we've done: We've made both A- and E-claims true on the diagram, but we've eliminated the entire subject class!

So, if every class *does* have a member, both of those areas of the circle cannot be empty, in which case either the A- or the E-claim must be false. That is why both contraries cannot be true.* A similar explanation will show why both the I- and O-claims cannot be false under our assumption.

Inferences Across the Square

Sometimes, if we know the truth value (T or F) of a standard form claim, we can deduce the value of all three of the corresponding standard form claims. This happens when we begin with a true claim from the top of the square (A or E) or a false one from the bottom of the square (I or O). For example, if we know that an A-claim is true, we can infer that the E is false, that the O is also false, and that the I is true. A close look at the square will show why this is so. Similarly, begin with a false I- or O-claim and see if you can deduce the truth values of the other three claims.

On a first reading, the preceding may sound like a lot of complicated stuff. But believe us, it's not as difficult as it sounds. Take it slowly, and you'll find it isn't all that difficult.

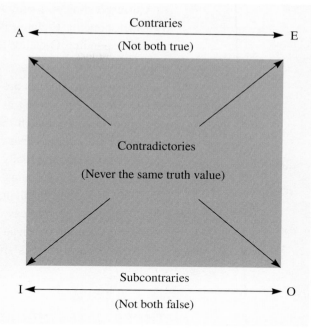

FIGURE 5 The square of opposition.

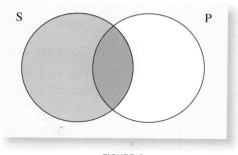

FIGURE 6

*Many contemporary logicians do not make existential assumptions, allowing both A- and E-claims to be true and both I- and O-claims to be false, thus reducing the square of opposition to contradiction alone. We are making the assumption, however; at the level at which we're operating, it seems much more natural to see "All Cs are Ds" as conflicting with "No Cs are Ds."

Translate the following into standard-form claims, and determine the three corresponding standard-form claims. Then, assuming the truth value in parentheses for the given claim, determine the truth values of as many of the other three as you can.

Exercise 9-4

Example

Most snakes are harmless. (True)

Translation (I-claim): Some snakes are harmless creatures. (True)

Corresponding A-claim: All snakes are harmless creatures. (Undetermined)

Corresponding E-claim: No snakes are harmless creatures. (False)

Corresponding O-claim: Some snakes are not harmless creatures. (Undetermined)

1. Not all anniversaries are happy occasions. (True)
2. There's no such thing as a completely harmless drug. (True)
3. There have been such things as just wars. (True)
4. There are allergies that can kill you. (True)
5. Woodpeckers sing really well. (False)
6. Mockingbirds can't sing. (False)
7. Some herbs are medicinal. (False)
8. Logic exercises are easy. (False)
9. Some Central American countries have no standing army. (True)
10. Not all colorful frogs are poisonous. (True)

THREE CATEGORICAL RELATIONS

The square of opposition allows us to make inferences from one claim to another, as you were doing in the last exercise. We'll turn next to three operations that can be performed on standard-form categorical claims. They, too, will allow us to make simple valid inferences and, in combination with the square, some not-quite-so-simple valid inferences.

Conversion

You find the **converse** of a standard-form claim by switching the positions of the subject and predicate terms. The E- and I-claims, but not the A- and O-claims, contain just the same information as their converses; that is,

All E- and I-claims, but not A- and O-claims, are equivalent to their converses.

Each member of the following pairs is the converse of the other:

> E: No Norwegians are Slavs.
> No Slavs are Norwegians.
> I: Some state capitals are large cities.
> Some large cities are state capitals.

Notice that the claims that are equivalent to their converses are those with symmetrical Venn diagrams.

Obversion

The next categorical relation is between a claim and its obverse. In order to arrive at a claim's obverse, we first need to introduce a couple of auxiliary notions. First, there's the notion of a *universe of discourse*. With rare exceptions, we make claims within contexts that limit the scope of the terms we use. For example, if your instructor walks into class and says, "Everybody passed the last exam," the word "everybody" does not include everybody in the world. Your instructor is not claiming, for example, that your mother and the Queen of England passed the exam. There is an unstated but obvious restriction to a smaller universe of people—in this case, the people in your class who *took* the exam. Now, for every class within a universe of discourse, there is a *complementary class* that contains everything in the universe of discourse that is *not* in the first class. Terms that name complementary classes are complementary terms. So "students" and "nonstudents" are **complementary terms.** Indeed, putting the prefix "non" in front of a term is often the easiest way to produce its complement. Some terms require different treatment, though. The complement of "people who took the exam" is probably best stated as "people who did not take the exam" because the universe is pretty clearly restricted to people in such a case. (We wouldn't expect, for example, the complement of "people who took the exam" to include *everything* that didn't take the exam, including your Uncle Bob's hairpiece.)

Now, we can get on with it: To find the **obverse** of a claim, (a) change it from affirmative to negative, or vice versa (i.e., go horizontally across the square—an A-claim becomes an E-claim and an O-claim becomes an I-claim then (b) replace the predicate term with its complementary term.

> All categorical claims of all four types, A, E, I, and O, are equivalent to their obverses.

Here are some examples; each claim is the obverse of the other member of the pair:

> A: All Presbyterians are Christians.
>   No Presbyterians are non-Christians.
> E: No fish are mammals.
>   All fish are nonmammals.
> I: Some citizens are voters.
>   Some citizens are not nonvoters.
> O: Some contestants are not winners.
>   Some contestants are nonwinners.

Contraposition

You find the **contrapositive** of a categorical claim by (a) switching the places of the subject and predicate terms, just as in conversion and (b) replacing both terms with complementary terms. Each of the following is the contrapositive of the other member of the pair:

> A: All Mongolians are Muslims.
>   All non-Muslims are non-Mongolians.
> O: Some citizens are not voters.
>   Some nonvoters are not noncitizens.

All A- and O-claims, but not E- and I-claims, are equivalent to their contrapositives.

The operations of conversion, obversion, and contraposition are important to much of what comes later, so make sure you can do them correctly and that you know which claims are equivalent to the results.

Immediate Inferences on Venn Diagrams

Here are Venn diagrams for the four standard-form categorical statements, A, E, I, and O. You will see how each statement relates to its converse, obverse, and contrapositive.

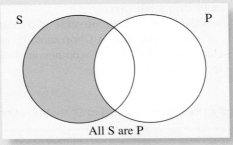

All S are P

If you study the diagram for "All S are P," you will see that the diagram also shows the following:

- No S are nonP (the obverse).
- All nonP are nonS (the contrapositive).

However, it does *not* show the following:

- All P are S (the converse).

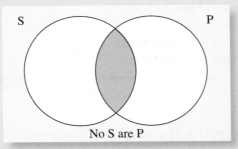

No S are P

The above, the diagram for "No S are P," also shows the following:

- No P are S (the converse).
- All S are nonP (the obverse).

It does *not* show the following:

- No nonP are nonS (the contrapositive).

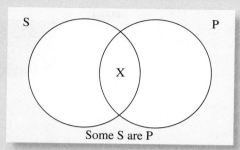

Some S are P

This diagram, the diagram for "Some S are P," also shows the following:

- Some P are S (the converse).
- Some S are not nonP (the obverse).

It does *not* show the following:

- Some nonP are nonS (the contrapositive).

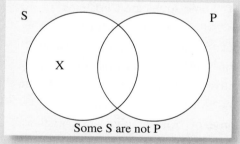

Some S are not P

This diagram (for "Some S are not P") also shows the following:

- Some S are not nonP (the obverse).
- Some nonP are not nonS (the contrapositive).

It does *not* show the following:

- Some P are not S (the converse).

As you can see,

- Logically, the diagram of *every* categorical statement is also a diagram of its obverse.
- Logically, the diagram of an A or O statement is also a diagram of its contrapositive.
- Logically, the diagram of an E or I statement is also a diagram of its converse.

Some Do, So Some Don't?

Some mosquitoes carry West Nile virus. So it must be that there are some that don't. The conclusion of this type of argument ("Some don't"), while it may be *true*, does *not* follow from the premise, because it could just as easily be false.

You sometimes hear arguments like this worked in reverse: "Some mosquitoes don't carry West Nile; therefore, some do." Equally invalid. The only way to get an I-claim from an O-claim is by obverting the O-claim.

Exercise 9-5

Find the claim described, and determine whether it is equivalent to the claim you began with.

▲ 1. Find the contrapositive of "No Sunnis are Christians."
    2. Find the obverse of "Some Arabs are Christians."
    3. Find the obverse of "All Sunnis are Muslims."
▲ 4. Find the converse of "Some Kurds are not Christians."
    5. Find the converse of "No Hindus are Muslims."
    6. Find the contrapositive of "Some Indians are not Hindus."
▲ 7. Find the converse of "All Shiites are Muslims."
    8. Find the contrapositive of "All Catholics are Christians."
    9. Find the converse of "All Protestants are Christians."
▲ 10. Find the obverse of "No Muslims are Christians."

Exercise 9-6

Follow the directions given in the preceding exercise.

▲ 1. Find the obverse of "Some students who scored well on the exam are students who wrote poor essays."
    2. Find the obverse of "No students who wrote poor essays are students who were admitted to the program."
    3. Find the contrapositive of "Some students who were admitted to the program are not students who scored well on the exam."
▲ 4. Find the contrapositive of "No students who did not score well on the exam are students who were admitted to the program."
    5. Find the contrapositive of "All students who were admitted to the program are students who wrote good essays."
    6. Find the obverse of "No students of mine are unregistered students."
▲ 7. Find the contrapositive of "All people who live in the dorms are people whose automobile ownership is restricted."

8. Find the contrapositive of "All commuters are people whose automobile ownership is unrestricted."

9. Find the contrapositive of "Some students with short-term memory problems are students who do poorly in history classes."

 10. Find the obverse of "No first basemen are right-handed people."

Exercise 9-7

For each of the following, find the claim that is described.

Example

Find the contrary of the contrapositive of "All Greeks are Europeans." First, find the contrapositive of the original claim. It is "All non-Europeans are non-Greeks." Now, find the contrary of that. Going across the top of the square (from an A-claim to an E-claim), you get "No non-Europeans are non-Greeks."

1. Find the contradictory of the converse of "No clarinets are percussion instruments."

 2. Find the contradictory of the obverse of "Some encyclopedias are definitive works."

3. Find the contrapositive of the subcontrary of "Some English people are Celts."

4. Find the contrary of the contradictory of "Some sailboats are not sloops."

5. Find the obverse of the converse of "No sharks are freshwater fish."

Exercise 9-8

For each of the numbered claims below, determine which of the lettered claims that follow is equivalent. You may use letters more than once if necessary. (*Hint:* This is a lot easier to do after all the claims are translated, a fact that indicates at least one advantage of putting claims into standard form.)

1. Some people who have not been tested can give blood.

2. People who have not been tested cannot give blood.

3. Nobody who has been tested can give blood.

4. Nobody can give blood except those who have been tested.

    a. Some people who have been tested cannot give blood.
    b. Not everybody who can give blood has been tested.
    c. Only people who have been tested can give blood.
    d. Some people who cannot give blood are people who have been tested.
    e. If a person has been tested, then he or she cannot give blood.

Exercise 9-9

Follow the directions given in the preceding exercise. (Presume that the universe of discourse consists of people who signed either before or after the first of the year.)

1. None of the people who signed before the first of the year are bound by the terms of the lease.

2. Some of the people who are bound by the terms of the lease are not people who signed before the first of the year.

3. Everybody who signed after the first of the year is bound by the terms of the lease.

4. You are not bound by the terms of the lease unless you signed before the first of the year.

   a. Some people who are not bound by the terms of the lease are not people who signed after the first of the year.
   b. The only people who are bound by the terms of the lease are those who signed after the first of the year.
   c. None of the people who are not bound by the terms of the lease are people who signed after the first of the year.
   d. If you did not sign before the first of the year, you are not bound by the terms of the lease.

Exercise 9-10

Try to make the claims in the following pairs correspond to each other—that is, arrange them so that they have the same subject and the same predicate terms. Use only those operations that produce equivalent claims; for example, don't convert A- or O-claims in the process of trying to make the claims correspond. You can work on either member of the pair or both. (The main reason for practicing on these is to make the problems in the next two exercises easier to do.)

Example

   a. Some students are not unemployed people.
   b. All employed people are students.

These two claims can be made to correspond by obverting claim (a) and then converting the result (which is legitimate because the claim has been turned into an I-claim before conversion). We wind up with "Some employed people are students," which corresponds to (b).

1. a. Some Slavs are non-Europeans.
   b. No Slavs are Europeans.

2. a. All Europeans are Westerners.
   b. Some non-Westerners are non-Europeans.

3. a. All Greeks are Europeans.
   b. Some non-Europeans are Greeks.

4. a. No members of the club are people who took the exam.
   b. Some people who did not take the exam are members of the club.

5. a. All people who are not members of the club are people who took the exam.
   b. Some people who did not take the exam are members of the club.

6. a. Some cheeses are not products high in cholesterol.
   b. No cheeses are products that are not high in cholesterol.

7. a. All people who arrived late are people who will be allowed to perform.
   b. Some of the people who did not arrive late will not be allowed to perform.

8. a. No nonparticipants are people with name tags.
   b. Some of the people with name tags are participants.

9. a. Some perennials are plants that grow from tubers.
   b. Some plants that do not grow from tubers are perennials.

10. a. Some flash drives that can be reformatted are not capable of defragmentation.
    b. All devices capable of defragmentation are drives that cannot be reformatted.

Which of the following arguments is valid? (Remember, an argument is valid when the truth of its premises guarantees the truth of its conclusion.)

Exercise 9-11

1. Whenever the battery is dead, the screen goes blank; that means, of course, that whenever the screen goes blank, the battery is dead.

2. For a while there, some students were desperate for good grades, which meant some weren't, right?

3. Some players in the last election weren't members of the Reform Party. Obviously, therefore, some members of the Reform Party weren't players in the last election.

4. Since some of the students who failed the exam were students who didn't attend the review session, it must be that some students who weren't at the session failed the exam.

5. None of the people who arrived late were people who got good seats, so none of the good seats were occupied by latecomers.

6. Everybody who arrived on time was given a box lunch, so the people who did not get a box lunch were those who didn't get there on time.

7. None of the people who gave blood are people who were tested, so everybody who gave blood must have been untested.

8. Some of the people who were not tested are people who were allowed to give blood, from which it follows that some of the people who were *not* allowed to give blood must have been people who were tested.

9. Everybody who was in uniform was able to play, so nobody who was out of uniform must have been able to play.

10. Not everybody in uniform was allowed to play, so some people who were not allowed to play must not have been people in uniform.

For each pair of claims, assume that the first has the truth value given in parentheses. Using the operations of conversion, obversion, and contraposition along with the square of opposition, decide whether the second claim is true, is false, or remains undetermined.

Exercise 9-12

Example

    a. No aardvarks are nonmammals. (True)
    b. Some aardvarks are not mammals.

Claim (a) can be obverted to "All aardvarks are mammals." Because all categorical claims are equivalent to their obverses, the truth of this claim follows from that of (a). Because this claim is the contradictory of claim (b), it follows that claim (b) must be false.

Note: If we had been unable to make the two claims correspond without performing an illegitimate operation (such as converting an A-claim), then the answer is automatically *undetermined*.

1. a. No mosquitoes are poisonous creatures. (True)
    b. Some poisonous creatures are mosquitoes.

2. a. Some students are not ineligible candidates. (True)
   b. No eligible candidates are students.

3. a. Some sound arguments are not invalid arguments. (True)
   b. All valid arguments are unsound arguments.

▲ 4. a. Some residents are nonvoters. (False)
   b. No voters are residents.

5. a. Some automobile plants are not productive factories. (True)
   b. All unproductive factories are automobile plants.

Many of the following will have to be rewritten as standard-form categorical claims before they can be answered.

6. a. Most opera singers take voice lessons their whole lives. (True)
   b. Some opera singers do not take voice lessons their whole lives.

▲ 7. a. The hero gets killed in some of Gary Brodnax's novels. (False)
   b. The hero does not get killed in some of Gary Brodnax's novels.

8. a. None of the boxes in the last shipment are unopened. (True)
   b. Some of the opened boxes are not boxes in the last shipment.

9. a. Not everybody who is enrolled in the class will get a grade. (True)
   b. Some people who will not get a grade are enrolled in the class.

▲ 10. a. Persimmons are always astringent when they have not been left to ripen. (True)
   b. Some persimmons that have been left to ripen are not astringent.

CATEGORICAL SYLLOGISMS

A **syllogism** is a two-premise deductive argument. A **categorical syllogism** (in standard form) is a syllogism whose every claim is a standard-form categorical claim and in which three terms each occur exactly twice and in exactly two of the claims. Study the following example:

All Americans are consumers.
Some consumers are not Democrats.
Therefore, some Americans are not Democrats.

Notice how each of the three terms "Americans," "consumers," and "Democrats" occurs exactly twice in exactly two different claims. The *terms of a syllogism* are sometimes given the following labels:

Major term: the term that occurs as the predicate term of the syllogism's conclusion

Minor term: the term that occurs as the subject term of the syllogism's conclusion

Middle term: the term that occurs in both of the premises but not at all in the conclusion

The most frequently used symbols for these three terms are *P* for major term, *S* for minor term, and *M* for middle term. We use these symbols throughout to simplify the discussion.

In a categorical syllogism, each of the premises states a relationship between the middle term and one of the other terms. If both premises do their jobs correctly—that is, if the proper connections between S and P are established via the middle term, M—then the relationship between S and P stated by the conclusion will have to follow—that is, the argument is valid.

Let's begin by looking at three candidates for syllogisms. In fact, only one of the following qualifies as a categorical syllogism. Can you identify which one? What is wrong with the other two?

> 1. All cats are mammals.
>   Not all cats are domestic.
>   Therefore, not all mammals are domestic.
> 2. All valid arguments are good arguments.
>   Some valid arguments are boring arguments.
>   Therefore, some good arguments are boring arguments.
> 3. Some people on the committee are not students.
>   All people on the committee are local people.
>   Therefore, some local people are nonstudents.

We hope it was fairly obvious that the second argument is the only proper syllogism. The first example has a couple of things wrong with it: Neither the second premise nor the conclusion is in standard form—no standard-form categorical claim begins with the word "not"—and the predicate term must be a noun or noun phrase. The

Abe Knew His Logic

Validity and Soundness in the Lincoln–Douglas Debates

Here's Abraham Lincoln speaking in the fifth Lincoln–Douglas debate:

> Nothing in the Constitution . . . can destroy a right distinctly and expressly affirmed in the Constitution.
>
> The right of property in a slave is distinctly and expressly affirmed in the Constitution.
>
> Therefore, nothing in the Constitution can destroy the right of property in a slave.

Lincoln goes on to say:

> There is a fault [in the argument], but the fault is not in the reasoning; but the falsehood in fact is a fault of the premises. I believe that the right of property in a slave is *not* distinctly and expressly affirmed in the Constitution.

second premise can be translated into "Some cats are not domestic creatures" and the conclusion into "Some mammals are not domestic creatures," and the result is a syllogism. The third argument is okay up to the conclusion, which contains a term that does not occur anywhere in the premises: "nonstudents." However, this argument can be turned into a proper syllogism by obverting the conclusion, producing "Some local people are not students."

Once you're able to recognize syllogisms, it's time to learn how to determine their validity. We'll turn now to our first method, the Venn diagram test.

The Venn Diagram Method of Testing for Validity

Diagramming a syllogism requires three overlapping circles, one representing each class named by a term in the argument. We will diagram the following syllogism step by step:

> No Republicans are collectivists.
> All socialists are collectivists.
> Therefore, no socialists are Republicans.

Here's how we diagram this argument: Figure 7 shows the three circles, labeled appropriately.

First, we diagram the first premise (Figure 8). Then we diagram the second premise (Figure 9). Then we look at our diagram (Figure 9) and consider whether it shows that the conclusion is true. It does! It shows that no socialists are Republicans. The argument therefore is valid. In general, a syllogism is valid if and only if diagramming the premises automatically produces a correct diagram of the conclusion.* (The one exception is discussed later.)

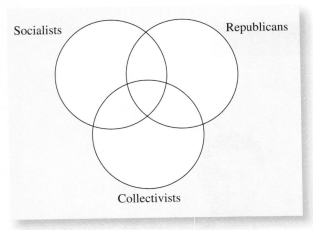

FIGURE 7   Before either premise has been diagrammed.

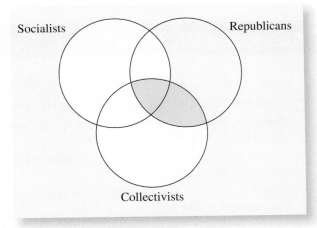

FIGURE 8   One premise diagrammed.

*It might be helpful for some students to produce two diagrams, one for the premises of the argument and one for the conclusion. The two can then be compared: Any area of the conclusion diagram that is colored must also be colored in the premises diagram, and any area of the conclusion diagram that has an X must also have one in the premises diagram. If both of these conditions are met, the argument is valid. (Thanks to Professor Ellery Eells of the University of Wisconsin, Madison, for the suggestion.)

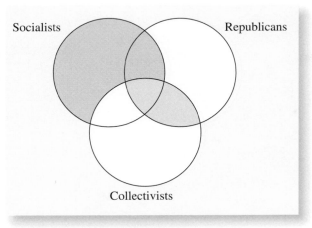

FIGURE 9 Both premises diagrammed.

When one of the premises of a syllogism is an I- or O-premise, there can be a problem about where to put the required X. The following example presents such a problem (see Figure 11 for the diagram). Note in Figure 10 that we have numbered the different areas in order to refer to them easily.

Some S are not M.
All P are M.
Some S are not P.

(The horizontal line separates the premises from the conclusion.)

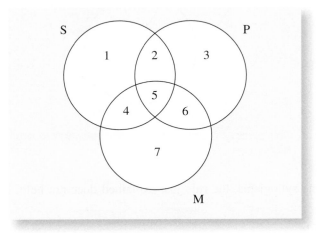

FIGURE 10

An X in either area 1 or area 2 of Figure 10 makes the claim "Some S are not M" true, because an inhabitant of either area is an S but not an M. How do we determine which area should get the X? In some cases, the decision can be made for us: *When one premise is an A- or E-premise and the other is an I- or O-premise,*

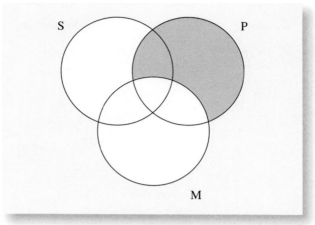

FIGURE 11

diagram the A- or E-premise first. (Always color areas in before putting in Xs.) Refer to Figure 12 to see what happens with the current example when we follow this rule.

Once the A-claim has been diagrammed, there is no longer a choice about where to put the X—it has to go in area 1. Hence, the completed diagram for this argument looks like Figure 11. And from this diagram, we can read the conclusion "Some S are not P," which tells us that the argument is valid.

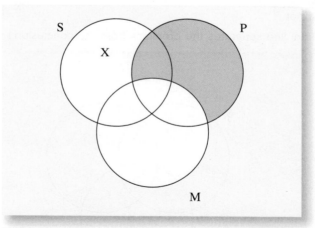

FIGURE 12

In some syllogisms, the rule just explained does not help. For example:

All P are M.
Some S are M.
Some S are P.

A syllogism like this one still leaves us in doubt about where to put the X, even after we have diagrammed the A-premise (Figure 13): Should the X go in area 4 or 5?

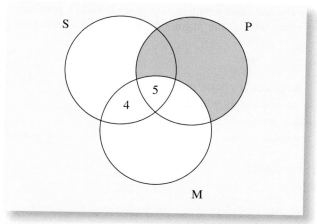

FIGURE 13

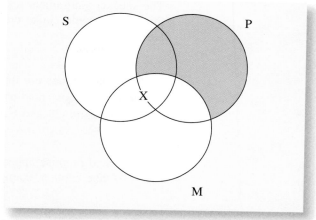

FIGURE 14

When such a question remains unresolved, here is the rule to follow: *An X that can go in either of two areas goes on the line separating the areas,* as in Figure 14.

In essence, an X on a line indicates that the X belongs in one or the other of the two areas, maybe both, but we don't know which. When the time comes to see whether the diagram yields the conclusion, we look to see whether there is an X *entirely* within the appropriate area. In the current example, we would need an X entirely within the area where S and P overlap; because there is no such X, the argument is invalid. An X *partly* within the appropriate area fails to establish the conclusion.

Existential Assumption in Categorical Syllogisms

Please notice this about Venn diagrams: When both premises of a syllogism are A- or E-claims and the conclusion is an I- or O-claim, diagramming the premises cannot possibly yield a diagram of the conclusion (because A- and E-claims produce only coloring of areas, and I- and O-claims require an X to be read from the diagram). In such a case, remember our assumption that every class we are dealing with has at least one member. This assumption justifies our looking at the diagram and determining whether any circle has all but one of its areas colored. *If any circle has only one area remaining uncolored, an X should be put in that area.* This is the case because any member of that class has to be in that remaining area. Sometimes placing the X in this way will enable us to read the conclusion, in which case the argument is valid (on the assumption that the relevant class is not empty); sometimes placing the X will not enable us to read the conclusion, in which case the argument is invalid, with or without any assumptions about the existence of a member within the class.

Categorical Syllogisms with Unstated Premises

Many "real-life" categorical syllogisms have unstated premises. For example, suppose somebody says,

You shouldn't give chicken bones to dogs. They could choke on them.

The speaker's argument rests on the unstated premise that you shouldn't give dogs things they could choke on. In other words, the argument, when fully spelled out, is this:

> All chicken bones are things dogs could choke on.
> [No things dogs could choke on are things you should give dogs.]
> Therefore, no chicken bones are things you should give dogs.

The unstated premise appears in brackets.

To take another example:

> Driving around in an old car is dumb, since it might break down in a dangerous place.

Here, the speaker's argument rests on the unstated premise that it's dumb to risk a dangerous breakdown. In other words, when fully spelled out, the argument is this:

> All examples of driving around in an old car are examples of risking dangerous breakdown.
> [All examples of risking dangerous breakdown are examples of being dumb.]
> Therefore, all examples of driving around in an old car are examples of being dumb.

When you hear (or give) an argument that looks like a categorical syllogism that has only one stated premise, usually a second premise has been assumed and not stated. Ordinarily, this unstated premise remains unstated because the speaker thinks it is too obvious to bother stating. The unstated premises in the arguments above are good examples: "You shouldn't give dogs things they could choke on," and "It is dumb to risk a dangerous breakdown."

When you encounter (or give) what looks like a categorical syllogism that is missing a premise, ask: Is there a reasonable assumption I could make that would make this argument valid? We covered this question of unstated premises in more detail in Chapter 2, and you might want to look there for more information on the subject.

At the end of this chapter, we have included a few exercises that involve missing premises.

Real-Life Syllogisms

We'll end this section with a word of advice. Before you use a Venn diagram (or the rules method described on pages 272–274) to determine the validity of real-life arguments, it helps to use a letter to abbreviate each category mentioned in the argument. This is mainly just a matter of convenience: It is easier to write down letters than to write down long phrases.

The World's Two Most Common Syllogisms

We're pretty sure the syllogism you'll run across most frequently is of this form:

All As are Bs.
All Bs are Cs.
All As are Cs.

Some real-life versions are easier to spot than others. Here's an example: "The chords in that song are all minor chords because every one of them has a flatted third, and that automatically makes them minor chords." Here's another: "Jim will be on a diet every day next week, so you can expect him to be grumpy the whole time. He's *always* grumpy when he's on a diet."

If a real, live syllogism turns out not to have the form just described, there's a very good chance it has this form:

All As are Bs.
No Bs are Cs.
No As are Cs.

Here's an example: "Eggs and milk are obviously animal products, and since real vegans don't eat any kind of animal product at all, they surely don't eat eggs or milk."

Take the first categorical syllogisms given on page 268:

You shouldn't give chicken bones to dogs because they could choke on them.

The argument spelled out, once again, is this:

All chicken bones are things dogs could choke on.
[No things dogs could choke on are things you should give dogs.]
Therefore, no chicken bones are things you should give dogs.

Abbreviating each of the three categories with a letter, we get

C = chicken bones; D = things dogs could choke on; and S = things you should give dogs.

Then, the argument is

All C are D
[No D are S]
Therefore, no C are S.

Likewise, the second argument was this:

> Driving around in an old car is dumb, since it might break down in a dangerous place.

When fully spelled out, the argument is

> All examples of driving around in an old car are examples of risking dangerous breakdown.
> [All examples of risking dangerous breakdown are examples of being dumb.]
> Therefore, all examples of driving around in an old car are examples of being dumb.

Abbreviating each of the three categories, we get the following abbreviation key:

> D = examples of driving around in an old car; R = examples of risking dangerous breakdown; S = examples of being dumb.

Then, the argument is

> All D are R
> [All R are S]
> Therefore, all D are S.

A final tip: Take the time to write down your abbreviation key clearly.

■ We're not certain exactly what the AT&T people had in mind here, but it *looks* like a syllogism with the conclusion unstated. With the conclusion "Your world is AT&T," is the argument valid? In fact, you can't get any conclusion at all about AT&T and "your world" from this billboard, as much as it might appear otherwise.

Use the diagram method to determine which of the following syllogisms are valid and which are invalid.

Exercise 9-13

1. All paperbacks are books that use glue in their spines.
   No books that use glue in their spines are books that are sewn in signatures.
   No books that are sewn in signatures are paperbacks.

2. All sound arguments are valid arguments.
   Some valid arguments are not interesting arguments.
   Some sound arguments are not interesting arguments.

3. All topologists are mathematicians.
   Some topologists are not statisticians.
   Some mathematicians are not statisticians.

4. Every time Louis is tired, he's edgy. He's edgy today, so he must be tired today.

5. Every voter is a citizen, but some citizens are not residents. Therefore, some voters are not residents.

6. All the dominant seventh chords are in the mixolydian mode, and no mixolydian chords use the major scale. So no chords that use the major scale are dominant sevenths.

7. All halyards are lines that attach to sails. Painters do not attach to sails, so they must not be halyards.

8. Only systems with no moving parts can give you instant access. Standard hard drives have moving parts, so they can't give you instant access.

9. All citizens are residents. So, since no noncitizens are voters, all voters must be residents.

10. No citizens are nonresidents, and all voters are citizens. So, all residents must be nonvoters.

Put the following arguments in standard form (you may have to use the obversion, conversion, or contraposition operations to accomplish this); then determine whether the arguments are valid by means of diagrams.

Exercise 9-14

1. No blank drives contain any data, although some blank drives are formatted. Therefore, some formatted drives do not contain any data.

2. All ears of corn with white tassels are unripe, but some ears are ripe even though their kernels are not full-sized. Therefore, some ears with full-sized kernels are not ears with white tassels.

3. Prescription drugs should never be taken without a doctor's order. So no over-the-counter drugs are prescription drugs, because all over-the-counter drugs can be taken without a doctor's order.

4. All tobacco products are damaging to people's health, but some of them are addictive substances. Some addictive substances, therefore, are damaging to people's health.

5. A few digital players use 3.0 transfer rates, so some of them must cost at least twenty dollars because you can't buy any player with a 3.0 rate for less than twenty dollars.

6. Everything that Pete won at the carnival must be junk. I know that Pete won everything that Bob won, and all the stuff that Bob won is junk.

▲   7. Only people who hold stock in the company may vote, so Mr. Hansen must not hold any stock in the company, because I know he was not allowed to vote.

8. No off-road vehicles are allowed in the unimproved portion of the park, but some off-road vehicles are not four-wheel-drive. So some four-wheel-drive vehicles are allowed in the unimproved part of the park.

9. Some of the people affected by the new drainage tax are residents of the county, and many residents of the county are already paying the sewer tax. So, it must be that some people paying the sewer tax are affected by the new drainage tax, too.

▲   10. No argument with false premises is sound, but some of them are valid. So, some unsound arguments must be valid.

The Rules Method of Testing for Validity

The diagram method of testing syllogisms for validity is intuitive, but there is a faster method that makes use of three simple rules. These rules are based on two ideas, the first of which has been mentioned already: affirmative and negative categorical claims. (Remember, the A- and I-claims are affirmative; the E- and O-claims are negative.) The other idea is that of *distribution*.

Distribution

A-claim:	All ⓈＳ are P.
E-claim:	No Ⓢ are Ⓟ.
I-claim:	Some S are P.
O-claim:	Some S are not Ⓟ.

FIGURE 15   Distributed terms.

Terms that occur in categorical claims are either distributed or undistributed: Either the claim says something about every member of the class the term names, or it does not.* Three of the standard-form claims distribute one or more of their terms. In Figure 15, the circled letters stand for distributed terms, and the uncircled ones stand for undistributed terms. As the figure shows, the A-claim distributes its subject term, the O-claim distributes its predicate term, the E-claim distributes both, and the I-claim distributes neither.

The Three Rules

We can now state the three *rules of the syllogism*. A syllogism is valid if, and only if, all of these conditions are met:

1. **The number of negative claims in the premises must be the same as the number of negative claims in the conclusion.** (Because the conclusion is always one claim, this implies that no valid syllogism has two negative premises.)

2. **At least one premise must distribute the middle term.**

3. **Any term that is distributed in the conclusion of the syllogism must be distributed in its premises.**

These rules are easy to remember, and with a bit of practice, you can use them to determine quickly whether a syllogism is valid.

---

*This is a rough-and-ready definition of distribution. If you'd like a more technical version, here's one: A term is *distributed* in a claim if, and only if, on the assumption that the claim is true, the class named by the term can be replaced by *any* subset of that class without producing a false claim. Example: In the claim "All senators are politicians," the term "senators" is distributed because, assuming the claim is true, you can substitute *any* subset of senators (Democratic ones, Republican ones, tall ones, short ones) and the result must also be true. "Politicians" is not distributed: The original claim could be true while "All senators are honest politicians" was false.

Which of the rules is broken in this example?

> All pianists are keyboard players.
> Some keyboard players are not percussionists.
> Some pianists are not percussionists.

The term "keyboard players" is the middle term, and it is undistributed in both premises. The first premise, an A-claim, does not distribute its predicate term; the second premise, an O-claim, does not distribute its subject term. So this syllogism breaks rule 2.

Another example:

> No dogs up for adoption at the animal shelter are pedigreed dogs.
> Some pedigreed dogs are expensive dogs.
> Some dogs up for adoption at the animal shelter are expensive dogs.

This syllogism breaks rule 1 because it has a negative premise but no negative conclusion.

A last example:

> No mercantilists are large landowners.
> All mercantilists are creditors.
> No creditors are large landowners.

A Guide to Dweebs, Dorks, Geeks, and Nerds

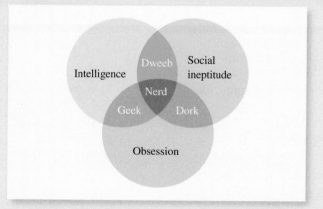

We found this Venn diagram floating around on the web. It gives us a tongue-in-cheek (we think) sorting of various categories of people based on three characteristics: intelligence, social ineptitude, and obsession. You can interpret this in the same way we interpreted such diagrams in this chapter (e.g., a dweeb is a member of the class of intelligent people and of the class of the socially inept, but not a member of the class of the obsessed).

The minor term "creditors" is distributed in the conclusion (because it's the subject term of an E-claim) but not in the premises (where it's the predicate term of an A-claim). So this syllogism breaks rule 3.

Recap

The following list of topics covers the basics of categorical logic as discussed in this chapter:

- ■ The four types of categorical claims include A, E, I, and O.
- ■ There are Venn diagrams for the four types of claims.
- ■ Ordinary English claims can be translated into standard-form categorical claims. Some rules of thumb for such translations are as follows:
  — "only" introduces predicate term of A-claim
  — "the only" introduces subject term of A-claim
  — "whenever" means times or occasions
  — "wherever" means places or locations
  — claims about individuals are treated as A- or E-claims
- ■ The square of opposition displays contradiction, contrariety, and subcontrariety among corresponding standard-form claims.
- ■ Conversion, obversion, and contraposition are three relations that result from operations performed on standard-form claims; some are equivalent to the original, and some are not.
- ■ Categorical syllogisms are standardized deductive arguments; we can test them for validity by the Venn diagram method or by the rules method—the latter relies on the notions of distribution and the affirmative and negative qualities of the claims involved.

Additional Exercises

Exercise 9-15

In each of the following items, identify whether A, B, or C is the middle term.

1. All A are B.
   All A are C.
   _____
   All B are C.

2. All B are C.
   No C are D.
   _____
   No B are D.

3. Some C are not D.
   All C are A.
   _____
   Some D are not A.

4. Some A are not B.
   Some B are C.
   _____
   Some C are not A.

5. No C are A.
   Some B are A.
   _____
   Some C are not B.

Exercise 9-16

Which terms are distributed in each of the following?

▲ 1. All A are B.
   a. A only
   b. B only
   c. both A and B
   d. neither A nor B

2. No A are B.
   a. A only
   b. B only
   c. both A and B
   d. neither A nor B

3. Some A are B.
   a. A only
   b. B only
   c. both A and B
   d. neither A nor B

▲ 4. Some A are not B.
   a. A only
   b. B only
   c. both A and B
   d. neither A nor B

Exercise 9-17

How many negative claims appear in the premises of each of the following arguments? (In other words, how many of the premises are negative?) Your options are 0, 1, or 2.

▲ 1. All A are B.
   All A are C.
   Therefore, all B are C.

2. All B are C.
   No C are D.
   Therefore, no B are D.

3. Some C are not D.
   All C are A.
   Therefore, some D are not A.

▲ 4. Some A are not B.
   Some B are C.
   Therefore, some C are not A.

5. No A are B.
   Some B are not C.
   Some A are C.

Exercise 9-18

Which rules (if any) are broken in each of the following? Select from these options:

    a. breaks rule 1 only
    b. breaks rule 2 only
    c. breaks rule 3 only
    d. breaks more than one rule
    e. breaks no rule

▲   1. All A are B.
       All A are C.
       Therefore, all B are C.

     2. All B are C.
       No C are D.
       Therefore, no B are D.

     3. Some C are not D.
       All C are A.
       Therefore, some D are A.

▲   4. Some A are not B.
       Some B are C.
       Therefore, some C are not A.

     5. Some A are C.
       Some C are B.
       Therefore, some A are B.

     6. Some carbostats are framistans.
       No framistans are arbuckles.
       Some arbuckles are not carbostats.

▲   7. All framistans are veeblefetzers.
       Some veeblefetzers are carbostats.
       Some framistans are carbostats.

     8. No arbuckles are framistans.
       All arbuckles are carbostats.
       No framistans are carbostats.

     9. All members of the class are registered students.
       Some registered students are not people taking fifteen units.
       Some members of the class are not people taking fifteen units.

▲   10. All qualified mechanics are people familiar with hydraulics.
       No unschooled people are people familiar with hydraulics.
       No qualified mechanics are unschooled people.

Exercise 9-19

Which rules (if any) are broken in each of the following?

    Note: If an argument breaks a rule, *which* rule is broken depends on how you translate the claims in the argument. For example, the claim "Dogs shouldn't be given chicken bones" could be translated as an *E-claim:* "No dogs are animals that should be given chicken bones." But it also could be translated as an *A-claim:* "All dogs are animals that shouldn't be given chicken bones." If the original claim appeared in an invalid argument, one rule would be broken if you translated it as the E-claim. A different rule would be broken if you translated it as the A-claim.

1. All tigers are ferocious creatures. Some ferocious creatures are zoo animals. Therefore, some zoo animals are tigers. (For this and the following items, it will help if you abbreviate each category with a letter. For example, let T = tigers, F = ferocious creatures, and Z = zoo animals.)

2. Some pedestrians are not jaywalkers. Therefore, some jaywalkers are not gardeners, since no gardeners are pedestrians.

3. Because all shrubs are ornamental plants, it follows that no ornamental plants are cacti, since no cacti qualify as shrubs.

4. Weightlifters aren't really athletes. Athletics requires the use of motor skills; and few, if any, weightlifters use motor skills.

5. The trick to finding syllogisms is to think categorically, as well as to focus on the key argument in a passage. For example, some passages contain a good bit of rhetoric, and some passages that do this make it hard to spot syllogisms, with the result that it is hard to spot syllogisms in some passages.

6. Every broadcast network has seen its share of the television audience decline during the past six years. But not every broadcast network that has a decline in television audience share has lost money. So, not every broadcast network has lost money.

7. Many students lift papers off the Internet, and this fact is discouraging to teachers. However, it must be noted that students who do this are only cheating themselves, and anyone who cheats himself or herself loses in the long run. Therefore, lifting papers off the Internet is a losing proposition in the long run.

8. When he was Speaker of the House, Newt Gingrich could be counted on to advance Republican causes. At the time, nobody who would do that could be accused of being soft on crime, which explains why, at the time, Gingrich could hardly be accused of being soft on crime.

9. It would be in everyone's interest to amend the Constitution to permit school prayer. And it is obviously in everyone's interest to promote religious freedom. It should be no surprise, then, that amending the Constitution to permit school prayer will promote religious freedom.

10. If you want to stay out all night dancing, it is fine with me. Just don't cry about it if you don't get good grades. Dancing isn't a total waste of time, but dancing the whole night certainly is. There are only so many hours in a day, and wasting time is bound to affect your grades negatively. So, fine, stay out dancing all night. It's your choice. But you have to expect your grades to suffer.

Exercise 9-20

Refer back to Exercises 9-13 and 9-14 (pages 271–272), and check the arguments for validity using the rules. We recommend abbreviating each category with a letter.

Once again, remember: If an argument breaks a rule, *which* rule is broken depends on how you translate the claims in the argument. For example, the claim "Dogs shouldn't be given chicken bones" could be translated as an E-claim: "No dogs are animals that should be given chicken bones." But it could also be translated as an A-claim (the obverse of the other version): "All dogs are animals that shouldn't be given chicken bones." If the original claim appeared in an invalid argument, one rule would be broken if you translated it as an E-claim. A different rule would be broken if you translated it as an A-claim.

Answers to 2, 5, 7, and 8 of both exercises are given in the answers section.

Exercise 9-21

For each of the following items: Abbreviate each category with a letter, then translate the argument into standard form using the abbreviations. Then test the argument for validity using either the diagram method or the rules method.

Note: For many of these items, it can be difficult to translate the arguments into standard form.

1. Some athletes are not baseball players, and some baseball players are not basketball players. Therefore, some athletes are not basketball players.

2. Rats are disease-carrying pests and, as such, should be eradicated because such pests should all be eradicated.

3. All creationists are religious, and all fundamentalists are religious, so all creationists are fundamentalists.

4. Every sportscaster is an athlete, and no athlete is a college professor. Therefore, no sportscasters are college professors.

5. Anyone who voted for the Democrats favors expansion of medical services for the needy. So, the people who voted for the Democrats all favor higher taxes, since anyone who wants to expand medical services must favor higher taxes.

6. All cave dwellers lived before the invention of the radio, and no one alive today is a cave dweller. Thus, no person who lived before the invention of the radio is alive today.

7. Conservationists don't vote for Republicans, and all environmentalists are conservationists. Thus, environmentalists don't vote for Republicans.

8. Since all philosophers are skeptics, it follows that no theologian is a skeptic, since no philosophers are theologians.

9. Each philosopher is a skeptic, and no philosopher is a theologian. Therefore, no skeptic is a theologian.

10. Peddlers are salespeople, and confidence men are, too. So, peddlers are confidence men.

11. Drug addicts are a burden on society. So are criminals of all sorts. That's why I say all addicts are criminals.

12. Critical thinkers recognize invalid syllogisms; therefore, critical thinkers are logicians, since logicians can spot invalid syllogisms, too.

13. The Mohawk Indians are Algonquin, and so are the Cheyenne. So, the Mohawks are really just Cheyenne.

14. Idiots would support the measure, but no one else would. Whatever else you may think of the school board, you can't say they are idiots. [Therefore . . .]

15. This is not the best of all possible worlds, because the best of all possible worlds would not contain mosquitoes, and *this* world contains plenty of mosquitoes!

16. From time to time, the police have to break up parties here on campus, since some campus parties get out of control, and when a party gets out of control, well, you know what the police have to do.

17. I know that all fundamentalist Christians are evangelicals, and I'm pretty sure that all revivalists are also evangelicals. So, if I'm right, at least some fundamentalist Christians must be revivalists.

▲ 18. "Their new lawn furniture certainly looks cheap to me," she said. "It's made of plastic, and plastic furniture just looks cheap."

19. None of our intramural sports are sports played in the Olympics, and some of the intercollegiate sports are not Olympic sports, either. So, some of the intercollegiate sports are also intramural sports.

20. The moas were all Dinornithidae, and no moas exist anymore. So, there aren't any more Dinornithidae.

▲ 21. Everybody on the district tax roll is a citizen, and all eligible voters are also citizens. So, everybody on the district tax roll is an eligible voter.

22. Any piece of software that is in the public domain may be copied without permission or fee. But that cannot be done in the case of software under copyright. So, software under copyright must not be in the public domain.

23. None of the countries that have been living under dictatorships for these past few decades are familiar with the social requirements of a strong democracy—things like widespread education and a willingness to abide by majority vote. Consequently, none of these countries will make a successful quick transition to democracy, since countries where the aforementioned requirements are unfamiliar simply can't make such a transition.

▲ 24. Trust Senator Cobweb to vote with the governor on the new tax legislation. Cobweb is a liberal, and liberals just cannot pass up an opportunity to raise taxes.

25. Investor-held utilities should not be allowed to raise rates, since all public utilities should be allowed to raise rates, and public utilities are not investor held.

26. Masterpieces are no longer produced on cassettes. This is because masterpieces belong to the classical repertoire, and classical music is no longer produced on cassettes.

27. It isn't important to learn chemistry, since it isn't very useful, and there isn't much point in learning something that isn't useful.

28. Stockholders' information about a company's worth must come from the managers of that company, but in a buy-out, the managers of the company are the very ones who are trying to buy the stock from the stockholders. So, ironically, in a buyout situation, stockholders must get their information about how much a company is worth from the very people who are trying to buy their stock.

▲ 29. All the networks devoted considerable attention to reporting poll results during the last election, but many of those poll results were not especially newsworthy. So, the networks have to admit that some unnewsworthy items received quite a bit of their attention.

▲ 30. If a person doesn't understand that the earth goes around the sun once a year, then that person can't understand what causes winter and summer. Strange as it may seem, then, there are many American adults who don't know what causes winter and summer, because a survey a year or so ago showed that many such adults don't know that the earth goes around the sun.

31. Congress seems ready to impose trade sanctions on China, and perhaps it should. China's leaders cruelly cling to power. They flout American interests in their actions in Tibet, in their human-rights violations, in their weapons sales, and in their questionable trade practices. Any country with a record like this deserves sanctions.

▲ 32. Since 1973, when the U.S. Supreme Court decided *Miller v. California,* no work can be banned as obscene unless it contains sexual depictions that are "patently offensive" to "contemporary community standards" and unless the work as a whole possesses no "serious literary, artistic, political, or scientific value." As loose as this standard may seem when compared with earlier tests of obscenity, the pornographic novels of "Madame Toulouse" (a pseudonym, of course) can still be banned. They would offend the contemporary standards of *any* community, and to claim any literary, artistic, political, or scientific value for them would be a real joke.

Exercise 9-22

This exercise is a little different, and you may need to work one or more such items in class in order to get the hang of them. Your job is to try to prove each of the following claims about syllogisms true or false. You may need to produce a general argument—that is, show that *every* syllogism that does *this* must also do *that*—or you may need to produce a counterexample, that is, an example that proves the claim in question false. The definition of categorical syllogism and the rules of the syllogism are of crucial importance in working these examples.

▲ 1. Every valid syllogism must have at least one A- or E-claim for a premise.

2. Every valid syllogism with an E-claim for a premise must have an E-claim for a conclusion.

3. Every valid syllogism with an E-claim for a conclusion must have an E-claim for a premise.

▲ 4. It's possible for a syllogism to break two of the rules of the syllogism.

5. No syllogism can break all three of the rules of the syllogism.

Exercise 9-23

For each of these, identify a premise (or conclusion) that makes the item a valid, standard-form categorical syllogism. If this cannot be done, say so.

▲ 1. All A are B.
   ???
   Therefore, all A are C.

2. All B are C.
   ???
   Therefore, no B are D.

3. Some C are D.
   ???
   Therefore, some D are not A.

▲ 4. All A are B.
   Some B are not C.
   Therefore, ???

5. Some A are B.
   Some B are C.
   Therefore, ???

6. Some A are not C.
   Some A are not D.
   Therefore, ???

▲ 7. All A are B.
   No A are C.
   Therefore, ???

8. No A are B.
   ???
   Therefore, some B are not C.

9. No B are A.
   ???
   Therefore, no B are C.

▲ 10. Some A are B.
   Some B are not C.
   Therefore, ???

Exercise 9-24

Follow the instructions for each item.

▲ 1. "All business executives have accounting experience, and some business executives are not economists."
   Which of the following statements follows validly from these premises?

   a. Some economists do not have accounting experience.
   b. Some people with accounting experience are not economists.
   c. All people with accounting experience are business executives.
   d. More than one of the above.
   e. None of the above.

2. "Coffee is a stimulant, since coffee contains caffeine."
   What statement must be added to this syllogism to make it valid?

   a. All substances that contain caffeine are stimulants.
   b. All stimulants are substances that contain caffeine.
   c. Neither of the above makes it valid.
   d. Both of the above make it valid.

3. "All musicians can read music; plus, all Washington University music majors can read music."
   Which of the following statements follows validly from these premises?

   a. Anyone who can read music is a musician.
   b. All Washington University music majors are musicians.
   c. Neither of the above.
   d. Both of the above.

▲ 4. "All CEOs are college grads. Therefore, some college grads are not economists."
   What statement must be added to this syllogism to make it valid?

   a. Some CEOs are not economists.
   b. Some economists are not CEOs.
   c. Neither of the above makes it valid.
   d. Both of the above make it valid.

5. "Some economists are historians; therefore, some radicals are not historians." What statement must be added to this syllogism to make it valid?

    a. No economists are radicals.

    b. Some economists are not radicals.

    c. Some radicals are not economists.

    d. None of the above make it valid.

6. "All online businesses are modern businesses, from which an obvious conclusion follows, since modern businesses don't include any brick-and-mortar businesses." What conclusion, if any, makes this a valid categorical syllogism?

▲ 7. "Political radicals never become Navy SEALS, from which it follows that some patriots are not Navy SEALS." What premise must be added to make this a valid categorical syllogism?

8. "All NASCAR drivers are NASCAR fans, but no Minnesotans are NASCAR fans." What conclusion, if any, makes this a valid categorical syllogism?

9. "All physicians own mutual funds, from which it follows that no professors are physicians." What premise must be added to make this a valid categorical syllogism?

▲ 10. "Some private investigators carry sidearms, and some people who carry side-arms are not licensed to do so." What conclusion, if any, makes this a valid categorical syllogism?

Exercise 9-25

The following is an anonymous statement of opinion that appeared in a newspaper call-in column.

> This is in response to the person who called in that we should provide a shelter for the homeless, because I think that is wrong. These people make the downtown area unsafe because they have nothing to lose by robbing, mugging, and so on. The young boy killed by the horseshoe pits was attacked by some of these bums, assuming that witnesses really saw people who were homeless, which no doubt they did, since the so-called homeless all wear that old worn-out hippie gear, just like the people they saw. They also lower property values. And don't tell me they are down and out because they can't find work. The work is there if they look for it. They choose for themselves how to live, since if they didn't choose, who did?

A lot of things might be said in criticism of this tirade, but what we want you to notice is the breakdown of logic. The piece contains, in fact, a gross logic error, which we ask you to make the focus of a critical essay. Your audience is the other members of your class; that is, you are writing for an audience of critical thinkers.

Exercise 9-26

> Pornography violates women's rights. It carries a demeaning message about a woman's worth and purpose and promotes genuine violence. This is indeed a violation of women's civil rights and justifies the Minneapolis City Council in attempting to ban pornography.

This letter to the editor is, in effect, two syllogisms. The conclusion of the first is that pornography violates women's rights. This conclusion also functions as a premise in the second syllogism, which has as its own conclusion the claim that the Minneapolis City Council is justified in attempting to ban pornography. Both syllogisms have unstated premises. Translate the entire argument into standard-form syllogisms, supplying missing premises, and determine whether the reasoning is valid.

Exercise 9-27

Each of the following arguments contains an unstated premise, which, together with the stated premise, makes the argument in question valid. Your job is to identify this unstated premise, abbreviate each category with a letter, and put the argument in standard form.

▲
1. Ladybugs eat aphids; therefore, they are good to have in your garden.
2. CEOs have lots of responsibility; therefore, they should be paid a lot.
3. Anyone who understands how a computer program works knows how important logic is. Therefore, anyone who understands how a computer program works understands how important unambiguous writing is.

▲
4. Self-tapping screws are a boon to the construction industry. They make it possible to screw things together without drilling pilot holes.
5. No baseball player smokes anymore. Baseball players all know that smoking hampers athletic performance.
6. You really ought to give up jogging. It is harmful to your health.
7. Camping isn't much fun. It requires sleeping on the hard ground and getting lots of bug bites.
8. Drinking too much coffee makes you sleep poorly. That's why you shouldn't do it.
9. Do you have writer's block? No problem. You can always hire a secretary.
10. You think those marks were left by a—snake? That's totally crazy. Snakes don't leave footprints.

Exercise 9-28

Diagram the argument found in the passage in Exercise 9-26 using the methods described in Chapter 2.

Writing Exercises

1. Should dogs be used in medical experiments, given that they seem to have the capacity to experience fear and feel pain? Write a short paper defending a negative answer to this question, taking about five minutes to do so. When you have finished, exchange arguments with a friend and rewrite each other's argument as a categorical syllogism or a combination of categorical syllogisms. Remember that people often leave premises unstated.
2. Follow the instructions for Writing Exercise 1, but this time defend the position that it is not wrong to use dogs in medical experiments.

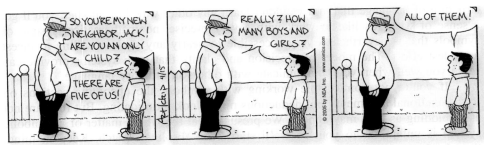

■ The word "and," when used in questions, can produce some interesting and amusing results. In this case, Brutus means to ask, "How many of them are boys, and how many of them are girls?" But Jack thinks he asks, "How many of them are girls or boys?" Our way of treating "and" in this chapter will not allow for any such ambiguities.
Source: THE BORN LOSER © 2005 Art and Chip Sansom. Reprinted by permission of Universal Uclick for UFS. All rights reserved.

the truth value from T to F or from F to T, depending on P's values." Because it's handy to have a name for negations that you can say aloud, we read ~P as "not-P." So, if P were "Parker is at home," then ~P would be "It is not the case that Parker is at home," or, more simply, "Parker is not at home." In a moment we'll define other symbols by means of truth tables, so make sure you understand how this one works.

Because any given claim is either true or false, two claims, P and Q, must both be true, both be false, or have opposite truth values, for a total of four possible combinations. Here are the possibilities in truth-table form:

P	Q
T	T
T	F
F	T
F	F

A **conjunction** is a compound claim made from two simpler claims, called *conjuncts. A conjunction is true if and only if both of the simpler claims that make it up (its conjuncts) are true.* An example of a conjunction is the claim "Parker is at home and Moore is at work." We'll express the conjunction of P and Q by connecting them with an ampersand (&). The truth table for conjunctions looks like this:

P	Q	P & Q
T	T	T
T	F	F
F	T	F
F	F	F

P & Q is true in the first row only, where both P and Q are true. Notice that the "truth conditions" in this row match those required in the italicized statement above the truth table.*

---

*Some of the words that have truth-functional meaning have other kinds of meanings as well. For example, "and" can signify not only that two things happened but that one happened earlier than the other. An example: "Melinda got on the train and bought her ticket" is quite different from "Melinda bought her ticket and got on the train." In this case, "and" operates as if it were "and then."

Here's another way to remember how conjunctions work: If either part of a conjunction is false, the conjunction itself is false. Notice finally that, although the word "and" is the closest representative in English to our ampersand symbol, there are other words that are correctly symbolized by the ampersand: "but" and "while," for instance, as well as such phrases as "even though." So, if we let P stand for "Parsons is in class" and let Q stand for "Quincy is absent," then we should represent "Parsons is in class even though Quincy is absent" by P & Q. The reason is that the compound claim is true only in one case: where both parts are true. And that's all it takes to require an ampersand to represent the connecting word or phrase.

A **disjunction** is another compound claim made up of two simpler claims, called *disjuncts. A disjunction is false if and only if both of its disjuncts are false.* Here's an example of a disjunction: "Either Parker is at home, or Moore is at work." We'll use the symbol ∨ ("wedge") to represent disjunction when we symbolize claims—as indicated in the example, the closest word in English to this symbol is "or." The truth table for disjunctions is this:

P	Q	P ∨ Q
T	T	T
T	F	T
F	T	T
F	F	F

Notice here that a disjunction is false only in the last row, where both of its disjuncts are false. In all other cases, a disjunction is true.

The third kind of compound claim made from two simpler claims is the **conditional claim.** In ordinary English, the most common way of stating conditionals is by means of the words "if . . . then . . . ," as in the example "If Parker is at home, then Moore is at work."

We'll use an arrow to symbolize conditionals: P → Q. The first claim in a conditional, the P in the symbolization, is the **antecedent,** and the second—Q in this case—is the **consequent.** *A conditional claim is false if and only if its antecedent is true and its consequent is false.* The truth table for conditionals looks like this:

P	Q	P → Q
T	T	T
T	F	F
F	T	T
F	F	T

Only in the second row, where the antecedent P is true and the consequent Q is false, does the conditional turn out to be false. In all other cases, it is true.*

---

*Like the conjunction, conditionals in ordinary language can have more than the meaning we assign to the arrow. The arrow represents what is often called the "material conditional," conditionals that are true except when the antecedent is true and the consequent false.

Differences between material conditionals and the conditionals used in ordinary language have held the attention of logicians and philosophers for a long time and are still controversial. See, for example, Richard Bradley, "A Defence of the Ramsey Test," in the philosophical journal *Mind* 116, no. 461 (January 2007): 1–21.

The systematic way to construct such a table is to alternate Ts and Fs in the right-hand column, then alternate *pairs* of Ts and *pairs* of Fs in the next column to the left, then sets of *four* Ts and sets of *four* Fs in the next, and so forth. The leftmost column will always wind up being half Ts and half Fs.

The second thing we have to know is that the truth value of a compound claim in any particular case (i.e., any row of its truth table) depends entirely upon the truth values of its parts; and if these parts are themselves compound, their truth values depend upon those of their parts; and so on, until we get down to letters standing alone. The columns under the letters, which you have just learned to construct, will then tell us what we need to know. Let's build a truth table for P → (Q & R) and see how this works.

P	Q	R	Q & R	P → (Q & R)
T	T	T	T	T
T	T	F	F	F
T	F	T	F	F
T	F	F	F	F
F	T	T	T	T
F	T	F	F	T
F	F	T	F	T
F	F	F	F	T

The three columns at the left, under P, Q, and R, are our *reference columns,* set up just as we discussed previously. They determine what goes on in the rest of the table. From the second and third columns, under the Q and the R, we can fill in the column under Q & R. Notice that this column contains a T only in the first and fifth rows, where both Q and R are true. Next, from the column under the P and the one under Q & R, we can fill in the last column, which is the one for the entire symbolized claim. It contains Fs only in rows two, three, and four, which are the only ones where its antecedent is true and its consequent is false.

Test Yourself

e   d   6   3

These cards are from a deck that has letters on one side and numbers on the other. They are supposed to obey the following rule: "If there is a vowel on one side, then the card has an even number on the other side."

Question: To see that the rule has been kept, which card(s) must be turned over and checked? (Many university students flunk this simple test of critical thinking.)

Truth-Functional Trickery

Using what you know about truth-functional logic, can you identify how the sender of this encouraging-looking notice can defend the claim (because it *is* true), even though the receiver is not really going to win one nickel?

You Have Absolutely Won
$1,000,000.00

If you follow the instructions inside
and return the winning number!

Answer: Because there is not going to be any winning number inside (there are usually several *losing* numbers, in case that makes you feel better), the conjunction "you follow the instructions inside and [you] return the winning number" is going to be false, even if you do follow the instructions inside. Therefore, because this conjunction is the antecedent of the whole conditional claim, the conditional claim turns out to be true.

Of course, uncritical readers will take the antecedent to be saying something like "If you follow the instructions inside *by returning the winning number inside*" (as if there were a winning number inside). These are the people who may wind up sending their own money to the mailer.

What our table gives us is a *truth-functional analysis* of our original claim. Such an analysis displays the compound claim's truth value, based on the truth values of its simpler parts. Remember, "truth-functional" is just a fancy term for saying that the truth of the compound claim results entirely from the truth values of the smaller parts.

If you've followed everything so far without problems, that's great. If you've not yet understood the basic truth-table idea, however, as well as the truth tables for the logical symbols, then by all means stop now and go back over this material. You should also understand how to build a truth table for symbolizations consisting of three or more letters. What comes later builds on this foundation, and as with any construction project, without a strong foundation the whole thing collapses.

A final note before we move on: Two claims are **truth-functionally equivalent** if they have exactly the same truth table—that is, if the Ts and Fs in the column under one claim are in the same arrangement as those in the column under the other. Generally speaking, when two claims are equivalent, one can be used in place of another—truth-functionally, they each imply the other.

Okay. It's time now to consider some tips for symbolizing propositional claims.

SYMBOLIZING COMPOUND CLAIMS

Most of the things we can do with symbolized claims are pretty straightforward; that is, if you learn the techniques, you can apply them in a relatively clear-cut way. What's less clear-cut is how to symbolize a claim in the first place. We'll cover tips for symbolization in this section and then give you a chance to practice with exercises.

Remember, when you symbolize a claim, you're displaying its truth-functional structure. The idea is to produce a version that will be truth-functionally equivalent to the original informal claim—that is, one that will be true under all the same circumstances as the original and false under all the same circumstances. Let's go through some examples that illustrate a few of the most frequently encountered symbolization problems.

"If" and "Only If"

In symbolizing truth-functional claims, as in translating categorical claims in Chapter 9, nothing can take the place of a careful reading of what the claim in question says. It always comes down to a matter of exercising careful judgment.

Of all the basic truth-functional types of claim, the conditional is probably the most difficult for students to symbolize correctly. There are so many ways to make these claims in ordinary English that it's not easy to keep track. Fortunately, the phrases "if" and "only if" account for a large number of conditionals, so you'll have a head start if you understand their uses. Here are some general rules to remember:

The word "if," used alone, introduces the antecedent of a conditional. The phrase "only if" introduces the consequent of a conditional.

To put it another way: It's not the location of the part in a conditional that tells us whether it is the antecedent or the consequent; it's the logical words that identify it. Consider this example:

> Moore will get wet *if* Parker capsizes the boat.

The "Parker" part of the claim is the antecedent, even though it comes *after* the "Moore" part. It's as though the claim had said,

> If Parker capsizes the boat, Moore will get wet.

We would symbolize this claim as P → M. Once again, it's the word "if" that tells us what the antecedent is.

> Parker will pay up *only if* Moore sinks the nine ball.

This claim is different. In this case, the "Parker" part is the antecedent because "only if" introduces the consequent of a conditional. This is truth-functionally the same as

> If Parker pays up (P), then Moore sunk (or must have sunk) the nine ball (M).

Using the letters indicated in parentheses, we'd symbolize this as

> P → M

Damned If You Do, But If You Don't . . .

The fearful, and unbelieving, and the abominable, and murderers, and whoremongers, and sorcerers, and idolators, and all liars, shall have their part in the lake which burneth with fire and brimstone.

—Revelation 21:8

This came to us in a brochure from a religious sect offering salvation for the believer. Notice, though, that the passage from the Bible doesn't say that, if you believe, you *won't* go to hell. It says, if you don't believe, you *will* go to hell.

Don't worry about the grammatical tenses; we'll adjust those so that the claims make sense. We can use "if" in front of a conditional's antecedent, or we can use "only if" in front of its consequent; we produce exactly equivalent claims in the two cases. As is the case with "if," it doesn't matter where the "only if" part of the claim occurs. The part of this claim that's about Moore is the consequent, even though it occurs at the beginning of this version:

Only if Moore sinks the nine ball will Parker pay up.

Once again: P → M.

Symbolize the following using the claim variables P and Q. (You can ignore differences in past, present, and future tense.)

Exercise 10-1

▲ 1. If Quincy learns to symbolize, Paula will be amazed.
▲ 2. Paula will teach him if Quincy pays her a big fee.
▲ 3. Paula will teach him only if Quincy pays her a big fee.
▲ 4. Only if Paula helps him will Quincy pass the course.
▲ 5. Quincy will pass if and only if Paula helps him.

Claim 5 in the preceding exercise introduces a new wrinkle, the phrase "if and only if." Remembering our general rules about how "if" and "only if" operate separately, it shouldn't surprise us that "if and only if" makes both antecedent and consequent out of the claim it introduces. We can make P both antecedent and consequent this way:*

$$(P \rightarrow Q) \ \& \ (Q \rightarrow P)$$

---

*Many texts introduce a new symbol ("P ↔ Q") to represent "P if and only if Q." It works exactly like our version; that is, it has the same truth table as "(P → Q) & (Q → P)." Under some circumstances, the extra symbol provides some efficiencies, but for us it is unnecessary and would be merely something else to learn and remember.

There are other ways to produce conditionals, of course. In one of its senses, the word "provided" (and the phrase "provided that") works like the word "if" in introducing the antecedent of a conditional. "Moore will buy the car, provided the seller throws in a ton of spare parts" is equivalent to the same expression with the word "if" in place of "provided."

Necessary and Sufficient Conditions

Conditional claims are sometimes spelled out in terms of necessary and sufficient conditions. Consider this example:

> The presence of oxygen is a necessary condition for combustion.

This tells us that we can't have combustion without oxygen, or "If we have combustion (C), then we must have oxygen (O)." Notice that *the necessary condition becomes the consequent of a conditional:* $C \rightarrow O$.

A sufficient condition *guarantees* whatever it is a sufficient condition for. Being born in the United States is a sufficient condition for U.S. citizenship—that's *all* one needs to be a U.S. citizen. *Sufficient conditions are expressed as the antecedents of conditional claims,* so we would say, "If Juan was born in the United States (B), then Juan is a U.S. citizen (C)": $B \rightarrow C$.

You should also notice the connection between "if" and "only if" on the one hand and necessary and sufficient conditions on the other. The word "if," by itself, introduces a sufficient condition; the phrase "only if" introduces a necessary condition. So the claim "X is a necessary condition for Y" would be symbolized as "$Y \rightarrow X$."

From time to time, one thing will be both a necessary and a sufficient condition for something else. For example, if Jean's payment of her dues to the National Truth-Functional Logic Society (NTFLS) guaranteed her continued membership (making such payment a sufficient condition) and there were no way for her to continue membership *without* paying her dues (making payment a necessary condition as well), then we could express such a situation as "Jean will remain a member of the NTFLS (M) if and only if she pays her dues (D)": $(M \rightarrow D) \ \& \ (D \rightarrow M)$.

■ This student shouldn't automatically assume that "only if" means "if and only if."

"What do you mean I flunked??? You told me I would pass the course only if I passed the final, and I passed the final!"

Another "If" and "Only If" Confusion

Do you want to install and run Flasher 3.0 distributed by SE Digital Arts? Caution: SE Digital Arts claims that this content is safe. You should install or view this content if you trust SE Digital Arts to make that assertion.

—A typical download caution

Presumably, they mean not "if" but "only if." Do you see why?

We often play fast and loose with how we state necessary and sufficient conditions. A parent tells his daughter, "You can watch television only if you clean your room." Now, the youngster would ordinarily take cleaning her room as both a necessary and a sufficient condition for being allowed to watch television, and probably that's what a parent would intend by those words. But notice that the parent actually stated only a necessary condition; technically, he would not be going back on what he said if room cleaning turned out not to be sufficient for television privileges. Of course, he'd better be prepared for more than a logic lesson from his daughter in such a case, and most of us would be on her side in the dispute. But, literally, it's the necessary condition that the phrase "only if" introduces, not the sufficient condition.

"Unless"

Consider the claim "Paula will foreclose unless Quincy pays up." Asked to symbolize this, we might come up with ~Q → P because the original claim is equivalent to "If Quincy doesn't pay up, then Paula will foreclose."* But there's an even simpler way to do it. Ask yourself, What is the truth table for ~Q → P? If you've gained familiarity with the basic truth tables by this time, you realize that it's the same as the table for P ∨ Q. And, as a matter of fact, you can treat the word "unless" exactly like the word "or" and symbolize it with a "∨".

"Either . . . Or"

Sometimes we need to know exactly where a disjunction begins; it's the job of the word "either" to show us. Compare the claims

Either P and Q or R

and

P and either Q or R.

These two claims say different things and have different truth tables, but the only difference between them is the location of the word "either"; without that word, the claim would be completely ambiguous. "Either" tells us that the disjunction begins

---

*Just as "if" sometimes is used to state both necessary and sufficient conditions, "unless" can be used the same way. Thus, "P unless Q" can be taken to mean "If ~Q then P and if Q then ~P." So the text's example could be used to mean that if Quincy doesn't pay up, Paula will foreclose, and if he does pay up, Paula will not foreclose." Remember, only the first of these is literally stated; the second may be taken as implied.

with P in the first claim and Q in the second claim. So, we would symbolize the first (P & Q) ∨ R and the second P & (Q ∨ R). Notice that P is not part of a disjunction at all in the second symbolization.

The word "if" does much the same job for conditionals that "either" does for disjunctions. Notice the difference between

P and if Q then R

and

If P and Q then R.

"If" tells us that the antecedent begins with Q in the first example and with P in the second. Hence, the second must have P & Q for the antecedent of its symbolization.

In general, the trick to symbolizing a claim correctly is to pay careful attention to exactly what the claim says—and this often means asking yourself just exactly what would make this claim false (or true). Then, try to come up with a symbolization that says the same thing—that is false (or true) in exactly the same circumstances. There's no substitute for practice, so here's an exercise to work on.

Exercise 10-2

Determine whether each of the following symbolizations is a negation, a conjunction, a disjunction, or a conditional.

1. ~P → Q
2. ~(P → Q)
3. (P → Q) ∨ (R → Q)
4. R → (P ∨ Q)
5. (P ∨ Q) & (R → S)
6. R → (P & Q)
7. (R → P) & Q
8. P → (Q → R)
9. ~(P ∨ (Q & R))
10. ~(P ∨ Q) & R

Exercise 10-3

Determine whether each of the following is a negation, a conjunction, a disjunction, or a conditional.

1. I will either go to the movies this evening or I'll come over to your house.
2. If I don't go to the movies this evening, I'll come over to your house.
3. It is not true that I'll go to the movies *and* come over to your house.
4. I'll come over to your house if I don't go to the movies this evening.
5. I'll come over to your house unless I go to the movies this evening.
6. My car is really dirty and it isn't running well either.
7. It is not true that, if you advance the timing, the car will start more easily.

8. I'll sell Meredith the car provided she brings the cash with her.

9. Either the team will win on Saturday or, if they lose again on Sunday, they'll be out of the tournament.

10. The team will neither win the tournament nor get to go on to the post season.

When we symbolize a claim, we're displaying its truth-functional structure. Show that you can figure out the structures of the following claims by symbolizing them. Use these letters for the first ten items:

Exercise 10-4

P = Parsons signs the papers.

Q = Quincy goes (or will go) to jail.

R = Rachel files (or will file) an appeal.

Use the symbols ~, &, ∨, and →. We suggest that, at least at first, you make symbolization a two-stage process: First, replace simple parts of claims with letters; then, replace logical words with logical symbols, and add parentheses as required. We'll do an example in two stages to show you what we mean.

Example

If Parsons signs the papers, then Quincy will go to jail but Rachel will not file an appeal.

Stage 1: If P, then Q but ~R

Stage 2: P → (Q & ~R)

1. If Parsons signs the papers then Quincy will go to jail, and Rachel will file an appeal.

2. If Parsons signs the papers, then Quincy will go to jail and Rachel will file an appeal.

3. If Parsons signs the papers and Quincy goes to jail then Rachel will file an appeal.

4. Parsons signs the papers and if Quincy goes to jail Rachel will file an appeal.

5. If Parsons signs the papers then if Quincy goes to jail Rachel will file an appeal.

6. If Parsons signs the papers Quincy goes to jail, and if Rachel files an appeal Quincy goes to jail.

7. Quincy goes to jail if either Parsons signs papers or Rachel files an appeal.

8. Either Parsons signs the papers or, if Quincy goes to jail, then Rachel will file an appeal.

9. If either Parsons signs the papers or Quincy goes to jail then Rachel will file an appeal.

10. If Parsons signs the papers then either Quincy will go to jail or Rachel will file an appeal.

For the next ten items, use the following letters:

C = My car runs well.

S = I will sell my car.

F = I will have my car fixed.

▲   11. If my car doesn't run well, then I will sell it.

▲   12. It's not true that, if my car runs well, then I will sell it.

13. I will sell my car only if it doesn't run well.

14. I won't sell my car unless it doesn't run well.

15. I will have my car fixed unless it runs well.

▲   16. I will sell my car but only if it doesn't run well.

17. Provided my car runs well, I won't sell it.

18. My car's running well is a sufficient condition for my not having it fixed.

19. My car's not running well is a necessary condition for my having it fixed.

▲   20. I will neither have my car fixed nor sell it.

Exercise 10-5   ▲   Construct truth tables for the symbolizations you produced for Exercise 10-4. Determine whether any of them are truth-functionally equivalent to any others. (Answers to the items with triangles are provided in the answers section at the back of the book.)

TRUTH-FUNCTIONAL ARGUMENT PATTERNS (BRIEF VERSION)

This section is an alternative to the two sections that follow ("Truth-Functional Arguments" and "Deductions"). Those instructors who want to go into the subject of truth-functional logic in some depth should skip this section and cover the next two instead; they constitute a fairly thorough treatment and a concise introduction to symbolic logic. For those who want briefer and more practical coverage of the subject, this section should suffice.

Three Common Valid Argument Patterns

Three forms of truth-functional argument are almost ubiquitous; they appear so frequently, and we are so accustomed to them, that we often make use of them almost without thinking. But it is important to understand and be able to recognize them because there are imposters that, because of superficial similarities, may look like valid argument patterns but are not.

First, we should recall what it means for an argument to be valid. To be valid, the truth of the argument's premises must guarantee the truth of its conclusion. Another way to say this is that it is impossible for the premises to be true while the conclusion is false. If it is even possible for the premises to be true without the conclusion being true, the argument is invalid.

Modus Ponens

Modus ponens ("in the affirmative mode," more or less) is a two-premise valid argument form, one premise of which is a conditional and the other of which is the antecedent of that conditional. The conclusion of the argument is the consequent of the conditional. (See pages 287-8 if you need refreshing on the meanings of these terms.) So all cases of modus ponens fit this pattern:

> If P then Q.
> P.
> Therefore Q.

You can see that one premise is the conditional: "If P then Q," and the other premise is the antecedent of that conditional: "P." The conclusion, "Q," is the consequent of the conditional. Every argument that has this form is valid. For example,

Example 1

> If the referee scored the fight in favor of Madderly, then Madderly wins the decision.
> The referee did score the fight in favor of Madderly.
> Therefore, Madderly wins the decision.

Remember from the previous section that there are other ways of stating conditional claims besides using "if . . . then. . . ." For example, this is another way to state the foregoing argument:

Example 2

> Madderly wins the decision provided the referee scored the fight in his favor.
> The referee did score the fight in favor of Madderly.
> Therefore, Madderly wins the decision.

Here are some other examples of arguments that fit the modus ponens form, accompanied by some remarks about why they do. Make sure you understand each one. (We'll continue to separate premises from the conclusion with the horizontal line; it works the same as "therefore" in introducing the conclusion.)

Example 3

> The generator works.
> The generator works only if the polarity of the circuit has been reversed.
> The polarity of the circuit has been reversed.

The second premise is the required conditional, with "only if" introducing the consequent (see page 292). It does not matter which of the two premises is stated first. The full conditional is stated second in this example.

Example 4

> Failure to melt at 2,600 degrees is sufficient for determining that this item is not made of steel.
> The item failed to melt at 2,600 degrees.
> The item is not made of steel.

The first premise is a conditional stated in terms of a sufficient condition (see page 294).

Modus Tollens

Modus tollens ("in the denial mode," approximately) is also a two-premise argument with one of the premises a conditional and the other premise the negation of that conditional's consequent. The conclusion is the negation of the antecedent. It looks like this:

> If P then Q.
> Not-Q.
> Not-P.

It is crucially important to notice that the nonconditional premise is the negation of the consequent of the other premise, not its antecedent. It isn't valid the other way, as you'll see in the following examples. Every argument that fits the form above, however, is valid. You'll sometimes hear someone use modus tollens in this way: "Hey, if X had happened, then Y would have had to happen, but it (Y) didn't happen. So X must not have happened." Here are some examples of modus tollens. Make sure you understand why they fit the modus tollens form.

Example 1

> If the new generator will work, then the polarity of the circuit has been reversed.
> But the polarity of the circuit has not been reversed.
> The new generator will not work.

Example 2

> If the song is in A-minor, there are no black keys in its scale.
> However, there are black keys in its scale.
> The song is not in A-minor.

Example 3

> If he got his forms in on time, he's automatically accepted. But he wasn't automatically accepted; consequently, he must not have gotten his forms in on time.

Example 4

> Bill was not with AT&T; but he'd have to have been with AT&T if he'd had an early iPhone. So he clearly did not have an early iPhone.

A last point about modus tollens: This argument form is the logical structure underlying the technique known as "*reductio ad absurdum*"—literally, to reduce to an absurdity. This technique, widely used in science and mathematics (where it's sometimes known as "indirect proof"), attempts to show that a given claim clearly leads to (implies) a second claim, and that the second claim cannot be true. Thus, by modus tollens, the first claim cannot be true either.

Chain Argument

A **chain argument** comprises two conditionals for premises and another for the conclusion. Here's the form:

> If P then Q.
> If Q then R.
> If P then R.

The important thing is the arrangement of the simple sentences, P, Q, and R. It's crucial that the consequent of one premise be the same as the antecedent of the other premise. The remaining antecedent and consequent get hooked up in the conclusion. This way of laying it out may help:

> If P . . . then Q.
> If Q . . . then R.
> If P . . . then R.

Here, Q is the consequent of the first premise and the antecedent of the second. This makes possible the conclusion with P as antecedent and R as consequent. Here are further examples of the chain argument:

Example 1

> If Simone goes, then Chris will go.
> If Casey goes to the meeting, then Chris will go.

Example 2

> If the stock is lightweight, then it's aluminum; but if it's aluminum, then it will be hard to weld. So, if the stock is lightweight, it will be hard to weld.

Example 3

> If the picture is a daguerreotype, then it has to have been made after 1837; and the man in the picture can't be Hegel if it was made after 1837. So it isn't Hegel in the picture if it's a daguerreotype.

Example 4

> If the oil gusher in the gulf of Mexico continues until August, it will be ten times bigger than the Exxon Valdez spill. And if it's that much bigger than the Exxon Valdez, it'll be the biggest man-made environmental disaster ever. You draw the conclusion.

■ This piece of rationalization is just two chain arguments linked together. See page 301.

Three Mistakes: Invalid Argument Forms

Each of the three foregoing argument forms has an invalid imposter that resembles it fairly closely. We'll have a brief look at each and see why they fail the test of validity.

Affirming the Consequent

This fallacy masquerades as modus ponens, because one of its premises is a conditional and the other premise is a part of that conditional, while the conclusion is the other part of the conditional. But modus ponens, you'll recall, has the antecedent of the conditional as its other premise and its consequent as conclusion. The fallacious version has the consequent as the other premise and the antecedent of the conditional as conclusion. Thus the title, since the second premise "affirms" or states the consequent of the conditional rather than its antecedent. This is easy to see when we lay it out like this:

> If P then Q.
> Q.
> Therefore, P.

You might take a moment to compare this argument form to the one for modus ponens on pages 289-9. In this case, it is entirely possible for both premises to be true and the conclusion false. If Q is true and P is false, then both premises are true* and the conclusion false—exactly the thing that cannot happen with a valid argument. So remember, a conditional with its antecedent as the other premise can validly give the consequent as a conclusion. However, a conditional with its consequent as the other premise cannot validly produce the antecedent as conclusion.

---

*Since a conditional with false antecedent and true consequent is true, remember the truth table for the conditional on page 287.

Example 1

> If Shelley has read the Republic, then she's bound to know who Thrasymachus is. And, since she clearly does know who Thrasymachus is, we can conclude that she must have read the Republic.

Example 2

> This zinfandel would have a smooth finish if it came from very old vines. In fact, it does have a smooth finish, so it must have come from very old vines.

Denying the Antecedent

Here, the fallacy impersonates modus tollens. In modus tollens, a conditional and the negation of its consequent validly give us the negation of its antecedent. But the fallacious version has us trying to draw a conclusion from a conditional and the negation of its antecedent, and this does not produce a valid argument.

Here's the way it looks:

> If P then Q.
> Not-P.
> Therefore, not-Q.

Now, if P is false and Q is true, the premises of the argument are true and the conclusion is false; thus the argument is invalid. A couple of examples:

Example 1

> If Jared studies really hard for the final, he will pass the course.
> [Later:] Well, Jared didn't study for the final, so it's a sure thing that he won't pass.

Example 2

> Joel will automatically be accepted provided he got his forms in on time. Unfortunately, he did not get his forms in on time; so he won't be automatically accepted.

Undistributed Middle (Truth-Functional Version)

Our final invalid form mimics the chain argument. It differs from that argument, though, by having the same consequent for each of its conditional premises:

> If P then Q.
> If R then Q.
> Therefore, if P then R.

If we allow P and Q to be true and R to be false, we'll see that both premises turn out to be true and the conclusion false. So this is clearly not a valid form of argument. Here's what it can look like:

Example 1

> If Robinson had had some great success in business, he'd be well known. Furthermore, if he were extremely rich, he'd be well known. So, of course, if Robinson had had some great success in business, he'd be extremely rich.

Example 2

> If you eat fish, you're a carnivore; and if you're an omnivore, you must be a carnivore. So, if you eat fish, that would make you an omnivore.

Exercise 10-6

Go through the eighteen examples in this section and symbolize each. Alternatively, use "if . . . then . . ." and "not- . . ." in place of the special symbols.

Exercise 10-7

For each of the last six examples (of the invalid forms), explain why each is invalid. For each, try to imagine and describe circumstances in which the premises are true and the conclusion is false.

Exercise 10-8

Determine which of the argument forms mentioned in this section is found in each of the following passages. Which contain valid arguments and which do not?

1. There are Taliban in North Waziristan; and if there are Taliban there, you can be sure they're in South Waziristan, too. So we have to believe there are Taliban in South Waziristan.

2. If the Saints win the Super Bowl, it will be poetic justice for New Orleans, the country's most bad-luck city in recent years. Unfortunately, the Saints have no chance to win, so there'll be no poetic justice this year for "N'awlins."

3. If you read Ayn Rand, you'll be a libertarian. And, of course, if you're an anarchist, you're already a libertarian. Hmm. It looks like if you read Ayn Rand, you'll be an anarchist!

4. If Sheila were ever to become a successful trader, she would have to develop a ruthless personality. But you know her: she could never be ruthless, even for a minute. So it's not going to be in her future to be a successful trader.

5. It's true, Ms. Zerkle will be accepted into law school only if she has excellent grades. But I'm telling you, you should see her transcript; she's made straight A's for the past two years. So don't worry about her getting into law school. She'll be accepted without a doubt.

6. If the Lambda X's continue to throw those open parties, they're going to get cited by the police. So if they continue the parties, they'll get decertified by the university because the university will certainly decertify them if they're cited by the police.

7. Jamal is a devout Muslim only if he follows the Sharia law, and I know for a fact that he follows it to the letter. So he is a devout Muslim.

8. If the carburetor is clogged, the engine will run lean, and running lean will lead to overheating. So overheating can result if the carburetor is clogged up.

TRUTH-FUNCTIONAL ARGUMENTS (FULL VERSION)

A truth-functional argument is an argument whose validity and invalidity can be determined by using a truth table. While categorical syllogisms, discussed in Chapter 9, have a total of 256 forms, a truth-functional argument, by contrast, can take any of an infinite number of forms. Nevertheless, we have methods for testing for validity that are flexible enough to encompass every truth-functional argument. In the remainder of this chapter, we'll look at three of them: the truth-table method, the short truth-table method, and the method of deduction.

Before doing anything else, though, let's quickly review the concept of validity. An argument is *valid,* you'll recall, if and only if the truth of the premises guarantees the truth of the conclusion—that is, if the premises were true, the conclusion could not then be false. (Where validity is concerned, remember, it doesn't matter whether the premises are *actually* true.)

The Truth-Table Method

The *truth-table test for validity* requires familiarity with the truth tables for the four logical symbols (~, &, ∨, →), so go back and check yourself on those if you think you may not understand them clearly. Here's how the method works: We present all of the possible circumstances for an argument by building a truth table for it; then we simply look to see if there are any rows in which the premises are all true and the conclusion false. If there are such rows—one row of the truth table is all that's required—then the argument is invalid.

Let's look at a simple example. Let P and Q represent any two claims. Now, look at the following symbolized argument:

P → Q

~P

Therefore, ~Q

We can construct a truth table for this argument by including a column for each premise and one for the conclusion:

1	2	3	4	5
P	Q	~P	P → Q	~Q
T	T	F	T	F
T	F	F	F	T
F	T	T	T	F
F	F	T	T	T

The first two columns are reference columns; they list truth values for the letters that appear in the argument. The reference columns should be constructed in accordance with the method described on pages 289-90. The third and fourth columns appear under the two premises of the argument, and the fifth column is for the conclusion. The truth values in these columns are determined by those in the appropriate rows of the reference columns. Note that in row 3 of the table, both premises (columns 4 and 5) are true and the conclusion is false. This tells us that it is possible for the premises of this argument to be true while the conclusion is false; thus, the argument is invalid. Because it doesn't matter what claims P and Q might stand for, the same is true for *every* argument of this pattern. Here's an example of such an argument:

> If the Saints beat the 49ers, then the Giants will make the playoffs. But the Saints won't beat the 49ers. So the Giants won't make the playoffs.

Using S for "The Saints beat (or will beat) the 49ers" and G for "The Giants make (or will make) the playoffs," we can symbolize the argument like this:

$$\begin{array}{c} S \rightarrow G \\ \underline{\sim S} \\ \sim G \end{array}$$

The first premise is a conditional, and the other premise is the negation of the antecedent of that conditional. The conclusion is the negation of the conditional's consequent. It has exactly the same structure as the argument for which we just did the truth table; accordingly, it, too, is invalid.

Let's do another simple one:

> We're going to have large masses of arctic air (A) flowing into the Midwest unless the jet stream (J) moves south. Unfortunately, there's no chance of the jet stream moving south. So you can bet there'll be arctic air flowing into the Midwest.

Symbolization gives us

> $$\begin{array}{c} A \vee J \\ \underline{\sim J} \\ A \end{array}$$

Here's a truth table for the argument:

1	2	3	4
A	J	A ∨ J	~J
T	T	T	F
T	F	T	T
F	T	T	F
F	F	F	T

Note that the first premise is represented in column 3 of the table, the second premise in column 4, and the conclusion in one of the reference columns, column 1. Now, let's recall what we're up to. We want to know whether this argument is valid—that is to say, is it possible for the premises to be true and the conclusion false? If there is such a possibility, it will turn up in the truth table because, remember, the truth table represents every possible truth-value combination for the claims A and J. Looking at the truth table, we find that the premises are both true in only one row, row 2, and when we check the conclusion, A, we find it is true in that row. Thus, there is *no* row in which the premises are true and the conclusion false. So, the argument is valid.

Here's an example of a rather more complicated argument:

> If Scarlet is guilty of the crime, then Ms. White must have left the back door unlocked and the colonel must have retired before ten o'clock. However, either Ms. White did not leave the back door unlocked, or the colonel did not retire before ten. Therefore, Scarlet is not guilty of the crime.

Let's assign some letters to the simple claims so that we can show this argument's pattern.

$$S \ = \text{Scarlet is guilty of the crime.}$$
$$W = \text{Ms. White left the back door unlocked.}$$
$$C \ = \text{The colonel retired before ten o'clock.}$$

Now we symbolize the argument to display this pattern:

$$S \rightarrow (W \ \& \ C)$$
$$\underline{{\sim}W \lor {\sim}C}$$
$${\sim}S$$

Let's think this argument through. As you read, refer back to the symbolized version shown previously. Notice that the first premise is a conditional, with S as antecedent and the conjunction W & C as consequent. In order for W & C to be true, both W and C have to be true, as you'll recall from the truth table for conjunctions. Now look at the second premise. It is a disjunction that tells us *either* Ms. White did not leave the back door unlocked *or* the colonel did not retire before ten. But if either or both of those disjuncts are true, at least one of the claims in our earlier conjunction is false. So it cannot be that *both* parts of the conjunction are true. This means the conjunction symbolized by W & C must be false. And so the consequent of the first premise is false. How can the entire premise be true, in that case? The only way is for the antecedent to be false as well. And that means that the conclusion, "Scarlet is not guilty of the crime," must be true.

All of this reasoning (and considerably more that we don't require) is implicit in the following truth table for the argument:

1	2	3	4	5	6	7	8	9
S	W	C	~W	~C	W & C	S → (W & C)	~W ∨ ~C	~S
T	T	T	F	F	T	T	F	F
T	T	F	F	T	F	F	T	F
T	F	T	T	F	F	F	T	F
T	F	F	T	T	F	F	T	F
F	T	T	F	F	T	T	F	T
F	T	F	F	T	F	T	T	T
F	F	T	T	F	F	T	T	T
F	F	F	T	T	F	T	T	T

The first three columns are our reference columns, columns 7 and 8 are for the premises of the argument, and column 9 is for the argument's conclusion. The remainder—4, 5, and 6—are for parts of some of the other symbolized claims; they could be left out if we desired, but they make filling in columns 7 and 8 a bit easier.

Once the table is filled in, evaluating the argument is easy. Just look to see whether there is any row in which the premises are true and the conclusion is false. One such row is enough to demonstrate the invalidity of the argument.

In the present case, we find that both premises are true only in the last three rows of the table. And in those rows, the conclusion is also true. So there is no set of circumstances—no row of the table—in which both premises are true and the conclusion is false. Therefore, the argument is valid.

The Short Truth-Table Method

Although filling out a complete truth table always produces the correct answer regarding a truth-functional argument's validity, it can be tedious—in fact, life is too short to spend it filling in truth tables. Fortunately, there are easier ways to check an argument's validity. The easiest is the *short truth-table method.* Here's the idea: *If an argument is invalid, there is at least one row in the argument's truth table where the premises are true and the conclusion is false.* With the short truth-table method, we simply focus on finding such a row. Consider this symbolized argument:

> $P \rightarrow Q$
> $\sim Q \rightarrow R$
> ———————
> $\sim P \rightarrow R$

We begin by looking at the conclusion. Because it's a conditional, it can be made false only one way, by making its antecedent true and its consequent false. So, we do that by making P false and R false.

Can we now make both premises true? Yes, as it turns out, by making Q true. This case

P	Q	R
F	T	F

makes both premises true and the conclusion false and thus proves the argument invalid. What we've done is produce the relevant row of the truth table without bothering to produce all the rest. Had the argument been valid, we would not have been able to produce such a row.

Here's how the method works with a valid argument. Consider this example:

> $(P \lor Q) \rightarrow R$
> $S \rightarrow Q$
> ———————
> $S \rightarrow R$

The only way to make the conclusion false is to make S true and R false:

P	Q	R	S
		F	T

Now, with S true, the only way we can make the second premise true is by making Q true:

P	Q	R	S
	T	F	T

But now, there is no way at all to make the first premise true, because P ∨ Q is going to be true (because Q is true), and R is already false. Because there is no other way to make the conclusion false and the second premise true, and because this way fails to make the first premise true, we can conclude that the argument is *valid*.

In many cases, there will be more than one way to make the conclusion false. Here's a symbolized example:

P & (Q ∨ R)
R → S   } trying to make these true
P → T
——————
S & T   } trying to make this false

Because the conclusion is a conjunction, it is false if either or both of its conjuncts are false, which means we could begin by making S true and T false, S false and T true, or both S and T false. This is trouble we'd like to avoid if possible, so let's see if there's someplace else we can begin making our assignment. (Remember: The idea is to try to assign true and false to the letters so as

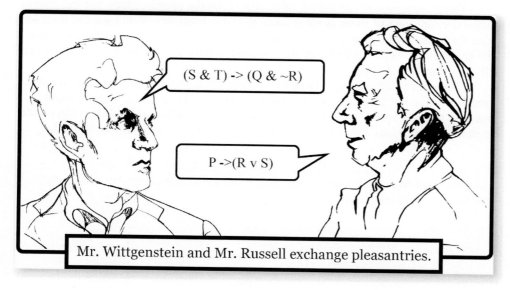

Mr. Wittgenstein and Mr. Russell exchange pleasantries.

(S & T) -> (Q & ~R)

P ->(R v S)

■ Bertrand Russell was among the earliest developers of the system of logic we explore in this chapter. Ludwig Wittgenstein was his student; the two are thought to be among the most important of all twentieth-century philosophers.

to make the premises true and the conclusion false. If we can do it, the argument is invalid.)

In this example, to make the first premise true, we *must* assign true to the letter P. Why? Because the premise is a conjunction, and both of its parts must be true for the whole thing to be true. That's what we're looking for: places where we are *forced* to make an assignment of true or false to one or more letters. Then we make those assignments and see where they lead us. In this case, once we've made P true, we see that, to make the third premise true, we are forced to make T true (because a true antecedent and a false consequent would make the premise false, and we're trying to make our premises true).

After making T true, we see that, to make the conclusion false, S must be false. So we make that assignment. At this point we're nearly done, needing only assignments for Q and R.

P	Q	R	S	T
T			F	T

Are there any other assignments that we're forced to make? Yes: We must make R false to make the second premise true. Once we've done that, we see that Q must be true to preserve the truth of the first premise. And that completes the assignment:

P	Q	R	S	T
T	T	F	F	T

This is one row in the truth table for this argument—the only row, as it turned out—in which all the premises are true and the conclusion is false; thus, it is the row that proves the argument invalid.

In the preceding example, there was a premise that forced us to begin with a particular assignment to a letter. Sometimes, neither the conclusion nor any of the premises forces an assignment on us. In that case, we must use trial and error: Begin with one assignment that makes the conclusion false (or some premise true) and see if it will work. If not, try another assignment. If all fail, then the argument is valid.

Often, several rows of a truth table will make the premises true and the conclusion false; any one of them is all it takes to prove invalidity. Don't get the mistaken idea that, just because the premises are all true in one row and so is the conclusion, the argument is valid. To be valid, the conclusion must be true in *every* row in which all the premises are true.

To review: Try to assign Ts and Fs to the letters in the symbolization so that all premises come out true and the conclusion comes out false. There may be more than one way to do it; any of them will do to prove the argument invalid. If it is impossible to make the premises and conclusion come out this way, the argument is valid.

Exercise 10-9

Construct full truth tables or use the short truth-table method to determine which of the following arguments are valid.

   ▲   1. P ∨ ~Q
         ~Q
         ———
         ~P

2. P → Q

~Q

───────

~P

3. ~(P ∨ Q)

R → P

───────

~R

▲ 4. P → (Q → R)

~(P → Q)

───────

R

5. P ∨ (Q → R)

Q & ~R

───────

~P

6. (P → Q) ∨ (R → Q)

P & (~P → ~R)

───────

Q

▲ 7. (P & R) → Q

~Q

───────

~P

8. P & (~Q → ~P)

R → ~Q

───────

~R

9. L ∨ ~J

R → J

───────

L → ~R

▲ 10. ~F ∨ (G & H)

P → F

───────

~H → ~P

These are simple arguments for you to symbolize; then determine whether they are valid.   Exercise 10-10

▲ 1. If Bobo is smart, then he can do tricks. However, Bobo is not smart. So he cannot do tricks.

2. If God is always on America's side, then America wouldn't have lost any wars. America has lost wars. Therefore, God is not always on America's side.

3. If your theory is correct, then light passing Jupiter will be bent. Light passing Jupiter is bent. Therefore, your theory is correct.

▲ 4. Moore eats carrots and broccoli for lunch, and if he does that, he probably is very hungry by dinnertime. Conclusion: Moore is very hungry by dinnertime.

5. If you value your feet, you won't mow the lawn in your bare feet. Therefore, since you do mow the lawn in your bare feet, we can conclude that you don't value your feet.

6. If Bobo is smart, then he can do tricks; and he can do tricks. Therefore, he is smart.

▲ 7. If Charles had walked through the rose garden, then he would have mud on his shoes. We can deduce, therefore, that he did walk through the rose garden, because he has mud on his shoes.

8. If it rained earlier, then the sidewalks will still be wet. We can deduce, therefore, that it did rain earlier, because the sidewalks are still wet.

9. If you are pregnant, then you are a woman. We can deduce, therefore, that you are pregnant, because you are a woman.

▲ 10. If this stuff is on the final, I will get an A in the class because I really understand it! Further, the teacher told me that this stuff will be on the final, so I know it will be there. Therefore, I know I will get an A in the class.

11. If side A has an even number, then side B has an odd number, but side A does not have an even number. Therefore, side B does not have an odd number.

12. If side A has an even number, then side B has an odd number, and side B does have an odd number. Therefore, side A has an even number.

▲ 13. If the theory is correct, then we will have observed squigglyitis in the specimen. However, we know the theory is not correct. Therefore, we could not have observed squigglyitis in the specimen.

14. If the theory is correct, then we will have observed dilation in the specimen. Therefore, since we did not observe dilation in the specimen, we know the theory is not correct.

15. If we observe dilation in the specimen, then we know the theory is correct. We observed dilation—so the theory is correct.

Exercise 10-11

Use either the long or short truth-table method to determine which of the following arguments are valid.

▲ 1. K → (L & G)
M → (J & K)
B & M
‾‾‾‾‾‾‾
B & G

▲ 2. L ∨ (W → S)
P ∨ ~S
~L → W
‾‾‾‾‾‾‾
P

▲ 3. M & P
R → ~P
F ∨ R
G → M
‾‾‾‾‾‾‾
G & F

4. (D & G) → H
   M & (H → P)
   M → G
   —————
   D & P

5. R → S
   (S & B) → T
   T → E
   —————
   (R ∨ B) → E

6. (D & P) → R
   ~R
   S → R
   —————
   ~D & ~P

7. P → (D & J)
   ~M → ~L
   L ∨ (M → P)
   —————
   J & D

8. M ∨ J
   ~J → R
   —————
   (~R ∨ ~M) → J

9. D → ~M
   (K ∨ L) → (M ∨ R)
   —————————
   (D → ~R) → (D → ~L)

10. (P & R) → (E ∨ ~ S)
    (S → O)
    (N ∨ R) & (S → P)
    ~N
    —————
    S → (O & E)

DEDUCTIONS

The next method we'll look at is less useful for proving an argument *invalid* than the truth-table methods, but it has some advantages in proving that an argument is valid. The method is that of **deduction.**

When we use this method, we actually deduce (or "derive") the conclusion from the premises by means of a series of basic, truth-functionally valid argument patterns. This is a lot like "thinking through" the argument, taking one step at a time to see how, once we've assumed the truth of the premises, we eventually arrive at the conclusion. (We do this for an example on page 307.) We'll consider some extended examples showing how the method works as we explain the first few basic argument patterns. We'll refer to these patterns as truth-functional rules because they govern what steps we're allowed to take in getting from the premises to the conclusion. (Your instructor may ask that you learn some or all of the basic valid argument patterns. It's a good idea to be able to identify these patterns whether you go on to construct deductions from them or not.)

Group I Rules: Elementary Valid Argument Patterns

This first group of rules should be learned before you go on to the Group II rules. Study them until you can work Exercise 10-12 with confidence.

Any argument of the pattern

$$P \to Q$$
$$\underline{P}$$
$$Q$$

Rule 1: Modus ponens (MP), also known as *affirming the antecedent*

is valid. If you have a conditional among the premises, and if the antecedent of that conditional occurs as another premise, then by **modus ponens** the consequent of the conditional follows from those two premises. The claims involved do not have to be simple letters standing alone—it would have made no difference if, in place of P, we had had something more complicated, such as (P ∨ R), as long as that compound claim appeared everywhere that P appears in the previous pattern. For example:

1. (P ∨ R) → Q   Premise
2. <u>P ∨ R</u>   Premise
3. Q   From the premises, by modus ponens

The idea, once again, is that if you have *any conditional whatsoever* on a line of your deduction, and if you have the antecedent of that conditional on some other line, you can write down the consequent of the conditional on your new line.

If the consequent of the conditional is the conclusion of the argument, then the deduction is finished—the conclusion has been established. If it is not the conclusion of the argument you're working on, the consequent of the conditional can be listed just as if it were another premise to use in deducing the conclusion you're after. An example:

1. P → R
2. R → S
3. P   Therefore, S

We've numbered the three premises of the argument and set its conclusion off to the side. (Hereafter we'll use a slash and three dots [/∴] in place of "therefore" to indicate the conclusion.) Now, notice that line 1 is a conditional, and line 3 is its antecedent. Modus ponens allows us to write down the consequent of line 1 as a new line in our deduction:

4. R   1, 3, MP

At the right, we've noted the abbreviation for the rule we used and the lines the rule required. These notes are called the *annotation* for the deduction. We can now make use of this new line in the deduction to get the conclusion we were originally after, namely, S.

> 5. S   2, 4, MP

Again, we used modus ponens, this time on lines 2 and 4. The same explanation as that for deriving line 4 from lines 1 and 3 applies here.

   Notice that the modus ponens rule and all other Group I rules can be used only on whole lines. This means that you can't find the items you need for MP as *parts* of a line, as in the following:

> $(P \rightarrow Q) \vee R$
> P
> _____
> $Q \vee R$ (erroneous!)

This is *not* a legitimate use of MP. We do have a conditional as *part* of the first line, and the second line is indeed the antecedent of that conditional. But the rule cannot be applied to parts of lines. The conditional required by rule MP must take up the entire line, as in the following:

> $P \rightarrow (Q \vee R)$
> P
> _____
> $Q \vee R$

The **modus tollens** pattern is this:

$$P \rightarrow Q$$
$$\frac{\sim Q}{\sim P}$$

Rule 2: Modus tollens (MT), also known as *denying the consequent*

If you have a conditional claim as one premise and if one of your other premises is the negation of the consequent of that conditional, you can write down the negation of the conditional's antecedent as a new line in your deduction. Here's a deduction that uses both of the first two rules:

> 1. $(P \& Q) \rightarrow R$
> 2. S
> 3. $S \rightarrow \sim R$ $/\therefore \sim(P \& Q)$
> 4. $\sim R$ 2, 3, MP
> 5. $\sim(P \& Q)$ 1, 4, MT

In this deduction, we derived line 4 from lines 2 and 3 by modus ponens, and then 4 and 1 gave us line 5, which is what we were after, by modus tollens. The fact that the antecedent of line 1 is itself a compound claim, (P & Q), is not important; our line 5 is the antecedent of the conditional with a negation sign in front of it, and that's all that counts.

$$P \rightarrow Q$$
$$\frac{Q \rightarrow R}{P \rightarrow R}$$

Rule 3: Chain argument (CA)

The **chain argument** rule allows you to derive a conditional from two you already have, provided the antecedent of one of your conditionals is the same as the consequent of the other.

If the Dollar Falls . . . A Chain Argument with 5 Links

The valid argument patterns are in fact fairly common. Here's one from an article in *Time* as to why a weakening dollar is a threat to the stock market:

> Why should we care? . . . If the dollar continues to drop, investors may be tempted to move their cash to currencies on the upswing. That would drive the U.S. market lower. . . . Because foreigners hold almost 40% of U.S. Treasury securities, any pullout would risk a spike in interest rates that would ultimately slaughter the . . . market.

The series of chain arguments here is reasonably obvious. In effect: If the dollar falls, then investors move their cash to currencies on the upswing. If investors move their cash to currencies on the upswing, then the U.S. market goes lower. If the U.S. market goes lower, then interest rates on U.S. Treasury securities rise. If interest rates on U.S. Treasury securities rise, then the . . . market dies. [Therefore, if the dollar falls, then the . . . market dies.]

Zagorin, Adam, "Worried About the Dollar", Time, October 3, 1999.

Rule 4: Disjunctive argument (DA)

$$\frac{P \lor Q}{\sim P} \qquad \frac{P \lor Q}{\sim Q}$$
$$\overline{Q} \qquad \overline{P}$$

From a disjunction and the negation of one disjunct, the other disjunct may be derived.

This one is obvious, but we need it for obvious reasons:

Rule 5: Simplification (SIM)

$$\frac{P \& Q}{P} \qquad \frac{P \& Q}{Q}$$

If the conjunction is true, then of course the conjuncts must all be true. You can pull out one conjunct from any conjunction and make it the new line in your deduction.

Rule 6: Conjunction (CONJ)

$$\frac{P}{Q}$$
$$\overline{P \& Q}$$

This rule allows you to put any two lines of a deduction together in the form of a conjunction.

Rule 7: Addition (ADD)

$$\frac{P}{P \lor Q} \qquad \frac{Q}{P \lor Q}$$

Clearly, no matter what claims P and Q might be, if P is true then *either* P or Q must be true. The truth of one disjunct is all it takes to make the whole disjunction true.

Rule 8: Constructive dilemma (CD)

$$\frac{\begin{array}{c} P \to Q \\ R \to S \\ P \lor R \end{array}}{Q \lor S}$$

Logician at Work

No, really. Problem solving in matters like auto mechanics involves a great deal of deductive reasoning. For example, "The problem had to be either a clogged fuel filter or a defective fuel pump. But we've replaced the fuel filter, and it wasn't that, so it has to be a bad fuel pump." This is an example of one of our Group I rules.

The disjunction of the antecedents of any two conditionals allows the derivation of the disjunction of their consequents.

$$P \rightarrow Q$$
$$R \rightarrow S$$
$$\underline{\sim Q \lor \sim S}$$
$$\sim P \lor \sim R$$

Rule 9: Destructive dilemma (DD)

The disjunction of the negations of the consequents of two conditionals allows the derivation of the disjunction of the negations of their antecedents. (Refer to the previous pattern as you read this, and it will make a lot more sense.)

For each of the following groups of symbolized claims, identify which Group I rule was used to derive the last line.

Exercise 10-12

1. $P \rightarrow (Q \& R)$
    $(Q \& R) \rightarrow (S \lor T)$
    $P \rightarrow (S \lor T)$

▲   2.   (P & S) ∨ (T → R)

        ~(P & S)

        T → R

▲   3.   P ∨ (Q & R)

        (Q & R) → S

        P → T

        S ∨ T

▲   4.   (P ∨ R) → Q

        ~Q

        ~(P ∨ R)

▲   5.   (Q → T) → S

        ~S ∨ ~P

        R → P

        ~(Q → T) ∨ ~R

Exercise 10-13

Go back to Exercise 10-12 and determine which items are instances of modus ponens and which are instances of modus tollens.

Exercise 10-14

Construct deductions for each of the following, using the Group I rules. Each can be done in just a step or two (except number 10, which takes more). Remember, the slash and three dots operate like "therefore" to introduce the conclusion.

▲   1.   1. R → P

        2. Q → R   /∴Q → P

    2.   1. P → S

        2. P ∨ Q

        3. Q → R   /∴S ∨ R

    3.   1. R & S

        2. S → P   /∴P

▲   4.   1. P → Q

        2. ~P → S

        3. ~ Q   /∴S

    5.   1. (P ∨ Q) → R

        2. Q   /∴R

    6.   1. ~P

        2. ~ (R & S) ∨ Q

        3. ~P → ~ Q   /∴ ~ (R & S)

▲ 7. 1. ~ S
   2. (P & Q) → R
   3. R → S   /∴ ~ (P & Q)

8. 1. P → ~ (Q & T)
   2. S → (Q & T)
   3. P   /∴ ~ S

9. 1. (P ∨ T) → S
   2. R → P
   3. R ∨ Q
   4. Q → T   /∴.S

▲ 10. 1. (T ∨ M) → ~ Q
    2. (P → Q) & (R → S)
    3. T   /∴ ~P

Group II Rules: Truth-Functional Equivalences

These rules are different from our Group I rules in important ways. First, they are expressed as truth-functional equivalences. This means that they each take the form of two types of symbolizations that have exactly the same truth table. We'll use a double-headed arrow, ↔, to indicate that we can move from either side to the other. (Remember that Group I rules allow us to go only one direction, from premises to conclusion.) A second major difference is that these rules can be used on *parts* of lines. So, if we have a conjunction in a deduction, and we have a Group II rule that says one of the conjuncts is equivalent to something else, we can substitute that something else for the equivalent conjunct. You'll see how this works after an example or two.

Here is the overall principle that governs how Group II rules work: *A claim or part of a claim may be replaced by a claim to which it is equivalent by one of the following Group II rules.* Once again, how this works should become clear in a moment. As in the case of the first group, the Ps and Qs and so forth in the statement of the rules can stand for any symbolized claim whatever, as long as each letter stands for the same claim throughout.

P ↔ ~~P

Rule 10: Double negation (DN)

This rule allows you to add or remove two negation signs in front of any claim, whether simple or compound. For example, this rule allows the derivation of either of the following from the other,

P → (Q ∨ R)   P → ~~(Q ∨ R)

because the rule guarantees that (Q ∨ R) and its double negation, ~~ (Q ∨ R), are equivalent. This in turn guarantees that P → (Q ∨ R) and P → ~~ (Q ∨ R) are equivalent, and hence that each implies the other.

Here's an example of DN at work:

1. P ∨ ~(Q → R)		
2. (Q → R)	/∴P	
3. ~~(Q → R)	2, DN	
4. P	1, 3, DA	

We use DN on line 2 to get line 3. Now, our new line is the negation of "~(Q → R)," the consequent of line 1. So disjunctive argument allows us to get "P" on the new line.

Rule 11:
Commutation (COM)

$$(P \& Q) \leftrightarrow (Q \& P)$$
$$(P \lor Q) \leftrightarrow (Q \lor P)$$

This rule allows any conjunction or disjunction to be "turned around" so that the conjuncts or disjuncts occur in reverse order. Here's an example:

P → (Q ∨ R)   P → (R ∨ Q)

Either of these symbolized claims can be deduced from the other. Notice that commutation is used on *part* of the claim—just the consequent.

The following rule allows us to change a conditional into a disjunction and *vice versa*.

Rule 12:
Implication (IMPL)

$$(P \to Q) \leftrightarrow (\sim P \lor Q)$$

Notice that the antecedent always becomes the negated disjunct or *vice versa*, depending on which way you're going. Another example:

(P ∨ Q) → R   ~(P ∨ Q) ∨ R

The following rule may remind you of the categorical operation of contraposition (see Chapter 9)—this rule is its truth-functional version.

Rule 13:
Contraposition (CONTR)

$$(P \to Q) \leftrightarrow (\sim Q \to \sim P)$$

This rule allows us to exchange the places of a conditional's antecedent and consequent but only by putting on or taking off a negation sign in front of each. Here's another example:

(P & Q) → (P ∨ Q)   ~(P ∨ Q) → ~(P & Q)

Sometimes you want to perform contraposition on a symbolization that doesn't fit either side of the equivalence because it has a negation sign in front of either the antecedent or the consequent but not both. You can do what you want in such cases, but it takes two steps, one applying double negation and one applying contraposition. Here's an example:

(P ∨ Q) → ~R	
~~(P ∨ Q) → ~R	Double negation
R → ~(P ∨ Q)	Contraposition

Your instructor may allow you to combine these steps (and refer to both DN and CONTR in your annotation).

$$\sim(P \mathbin{\&} Q) \leftrightarrow (\sim P \lor \sim Q)$$
$$\sim(P \lor Q) \leftrightarrow (\sim P \mathbin{\&} \sim Q)$$

Notice that, when the negation sign is "moved inside" the parentheses, the "&" changes into a "∨," or *vice versa*. It's important not to confuse the use of the negation sign in DeMorgan's laws with that of the minus sign in algebra. Notice that when you take ~(P ∨ Q) and "move the negation sign in," you do *not* get (~P ∨ ~Q). The wedge must be changed to an ampersand or *vice versa* whenever DEM is used. You can think of ~(P ∨ Q) and (~P & ~Q) as saying "neither P nor Q," and you can think of ~(P & Q) and (~P ∨ ~Q) as saying "not both P and Q."

$$[P \rightarrow (Q \rightarrow R)] \leftrightarrow [(P \mathbin{\&} Q) \rightarrow R]$$

Square brackets are used exactly as parentheses are. In English, the exportation rule says that "If P, then if Q, then R" is equivalent to "If both P and Q, then R." (The commas are optional in both claims.) If you look back to Exercise 10-4, items 3 and 5 (page 297), you'll notice that, according to the exportation rule, each of these can replace the other.

$$[P \mathbin{\&} (Q \mathbin{\&} R)] \leftrightarrow [(P \mathbin{\&} Q) \mathbin{\&} R]$$
$$[P \lor (Q \lor R)] \leftrightarrow [(P \lor Q) \lor R]$$

Association simply tells us that, when we have three items joined together with wedges or with ampersands, it doesn't matter which ones we group together. If we have a long disjunction with more than two disjuncts, it still requires only one of them to be true for the entire disjunction to be true; if it's a conjunction, then all the conjuncts have to be true, no matter how many of them there are, in order for the entire conjunction to be true. Your instructor may allow you to drop parentheses in such symbolizations, but if you're developing these rules as a formal system, he or she may not.

$$[P \mathbin{\&} (Q \lor R)] \leftrightarrow [(P \mathbin{\&} Q) \lor (P \mathbin{\&} R)]$$
$$[P \lor (Q \mathbin{\&} R)] \leftrightarrow [(P \lor Q) \mathbin{\&} (P \lor R)]$$

This rule allows us to "spread a conjunct across a disjunction" or to "spread a disjunct across a conjunction." In the first example that follows, look at the left-hand side of the equivalence. The P, which is conjoined with a disjunction, is picked up and dropped (distributed) across the disjunction by being conjoined with each part. (This is easier to understand if you see it done on the board than by trying to figure it out from the page in front of you.) The two versions of the rule, like those of DEM, allow us to do exactly with the wedge what we're allowed to do with the ampersand.

$$(P \lor P) \leftrightarrow P$$
$$(P \mathbin{\&} P) \leftrightarrow P$$

This rule allows a few obvious steps; they are sometimes necessary to "clean up" a deduction.

The twelve-step and seven-step examples that follow show some deductions that use rules from both Group I and Group II. Look at them carefully, covering up the lines with a piece of paper and uncovering them one at a time as you progress. This gives you a chance to figure out what you might do before you see the answer. In any case, make sure you understand how each line was achieved before going on. If necessary, look up the rule used to make sure you understand it.

The first example is long but fairly simple. Length is not always proportional to difficulty.

1. P → (Q → R)		
2. (T → P) & (S → Q)		
3. T & S	/∴ R	
4. T → P	2, SIM	
5. S → Q	2, SIM	
6. T	3, SIM	
7. S	3, SIM	
8. P	4, 6, MP	
9. Q	5, 7, MP	
10. P & Q	8, 9, CONJ	
11. (P & Q) → R	1, EXP	
12. R	10, 11, MP	

It's often difficult to tell how to proceed when you first look at a deduction problem. One strategy is to work backward. Look at what you want to get, look at what you have, and see what you would need in order to get what you want. Then determine where you would get *that,* and so on. We'll explain in terms of the following problem.

1. P → (Q & R)		
2. S → ~Q		
3. S	/∴ ~P	
4. ~ Q	2, 3, MP	
5. ~Q ∨ ~ R	4, ADD	
6. ~(Q & R)	5, DEM	
7. ~P	1, 6, MT	

We began by wanting ~P as our conclusion. If we're familiar with modus tollens, it's clear from line 1 that we can get ~P if we can get the negation of line 1's consequent, which would be ~(Q & R). That in turn is the same as ~Q ∨ ~R, by one of DeMorgan's laws, which we can get if we can get either ~Q or ~R. So now we're looking for some place in the first three premises where we can get ~Q. That's easy: from lines 2 and 3, by modus ponens. A little practice and you'll be surprised how easy these strategies are to use, at least *most* of the time!

The table in Figure 2 sums up all the rules introduced so far. Refer back to it as you work through deductions in the remainder of the chapter.

Group I

1. Modus ponens (MP) P → Q P ——— Q	2. Modus tollens (MT) P → Q ~Q ——— ~P	3. Chain argument (CA) P → Q Q → R ——— P → R
4. Disjunctive argument (DA) P v Q P v Q ~P ~Q ——— ——— Q P	5. Simplification (SIM) P & Q P & Q ——— ——— P Q	6. Conjunction (CONJ) P Q ——— P & Q
7. Addition (ADD) P Q ——— ——— P v Q P v Q	8. Constructive dilemma (CD) P → Q R → S P v R ——— Q v S	9. Destructive dilemma (DD) P → Q R → S ~Q v ~S ——— ~P v ~R

Group II

10. Double negation (DN) P ↔ ~~P	11. Commutation (COM) (P & Q) ↔ (Q & P) (P v Q) ↔ (Q v P)	12. Implication (IMPL) (P → Q) ↔ (~P v Q)
13. Contraposition (CONTR) (P → Q) ↔ (~Q → ~P)	14. DeMorgan's Laws (DEM) ~(P & Q) ↔ (~P v ~Q) ~(P v Q) ↔ (~P & ~Q)	15. Exportation (EXP) [P → (Q → R)] ↔ [(P & Q) → R]
16. Association (ASSOC) [P & (Q & R)] ↔ [(P & Q) & R] [P v (Q v R)] ↔ [(P v Q) v R]	17. Distribution (DIST) [P & (Q v R)] ↔ [(P & Q) v (P & R)] [P v (Q & R)] ↔ [(P v Q) & (P v R)]	18. Tautology (TAUT) (P v P) ↔ P (P & P) ↔ P

FIGURE 2   Truth-functional rules for deductions.

The annotations that explain how each line was derived have been left off the following deductions. For each line, supply the rule used and the numbers of any earlier lines the rule requires.

Exercise 10-15

▲ 1.   1. P → Q   (Premise)
      2. R → S   (Premise)
      3. Q → ~S   (Premise) /∴ P → ~ R
      4. P → ~S
      5. ~ S → ~R
      6. P → ~R

2. 1. ~P   (Premise)
    2. (Q → R) & (R → Q)   (Premise)
    3. R ∨ P   (Premise) / ∴ Q
    4. R
    5. R → Q
    6. Q

3. 1. P → Q   (Premise)
    2. R → (~S ∨ T)   (Premise)
    3. ~P → R   (Premise) / ∴ (~ Q & S) → T
    4. ~ Q → ~P
    5. ~ Q → R
    6. ~ Q → (~ S ∨ T)
    7. ~Q → (S → T)
    8. (~Q & S) → T

▲ 4. 1. (P & Q) → T   (Premise)
    2. P   (Premise)
    3. ~Q → ~P   (Premise) / ∴ T
    4. P → Q
    5. Q
    6. P & Q
    7. T

5. 1. ~(S ∨ R)   (Premise)
    2. P → S   (Premise)
    3. T → (P ∨ R)   (Premise) / ∴ ~T
    4. ~S & ~R
    5. ~S
    6. ~P
    7. ~R
    8. ~P & ~R
    9. ~(P ∨ R)
    10. ~T

6. 1. (P ∨ (Q & R)   (Premise)
    2. R → D   (Premise)
    3. M & ~ D   (Premise) / ∴ P
    4. (P ∨ Q) & (P ∨ R)
    5. P ∨ R
    6. ~D
    7. ~R
    8. P

▲ 7. 1. (Q ∨ R) & P   (Premise)
       2. ~M → ~ Q   (Premise)
       3. ~L → ~ R   (Premise) /∴ (P & M) ∨ (P & L)
       4. Q ∨ R
       5. Q → M
       6. R → L
       7. M ∨ L
       8. P
       9. P & (M ∨ L)
      10. (P & M) ∨ (P & L)

    8. 1. (~L ∨ ~ E) & (A → H)   (Premise)
        2. (B & L) ∨ U   (Premise)
        3. M → ~U   (Premise)
        4. ~ A → E   (Premise) /∴ M → H
        5. U ∨ (B & L)
        6. ~ U → (B & L)
        7. M → (B & L)
        8. ~ M ∨ (B & L)
        9. (~ M ∨ B) & (~ M ∨ L)
       10. ~ M ∨ L
       11. M → L
       12. ~ L ∨ ~ E
       13. L → ~ E
       14. M → ~ E
       15. ~ E → A
       16. A → H
       17. M → A
       18. M → H

Derive the indicated conclusions from the premises supplied.   Exercise 10-16

▲ 1. 1. P & Q
       2. P → R   / ∴ R

▲ 2. 1. R → S
       2. ~P ∨ R   /∴ P → S

    3. 1. P ∨ Q
        2. R & ~Q   /∴ P

▲ 4. 1. ~P ∨ (~Q ∨ R)
        2. P   / ∴ Q → R

    5. 1. T ∨ P
        2. P → S   /∴ ~ T → S

6. 1. Q ∨ ~S
    2. Q → P   /∴ S → P

7. 1. ~S ∨ ~R
    2. P → (S & R)   /∴ ~P

  8. 1. ~Q & (~S & ~T)
    2. P → (Q ∨ S)   /∴ ~P

9. 1. P ∨ (S & R)
    2. T → (~P & ~R)   /∴ ~T

10. 1. (S & P) → R
    2. S   /P → R

Exercise 10-17

Derive the indicated conclusions from the premises supplied.

  1. 1. P → R
    2. R → Q   / ∴ ~P ∨ Q

2. 1. ~P ∨ S
    2. ~T → ~S   / ∴ P → T

3. 1. F → R
    2. L → S
    3. ~C
    4. (R & S) → C   / ∴ ~F ∨ ~L

  4. 1. P ∨ (Q & R)
    2. (P ∨ Q) → S   / ∴ S

5. 1. (S & R) → P
    2. (R → P) → W
    3. S   / ∴ W

6. 1. ~L → (~P → M)
    2. ~(P ∨ L)   / ∴ M

  7. 1. (M ∨ R) & P
    2. ~S → ~P
    3. S → ~M   / ∴ R

8. 1. Q → L
    2. P → M
    3. R ∨ P
    4. R → (Q & S)   / ∴ ~M → L

9. 1. Q → S
   2. P → (S & L)
   3. ~P → Q
   4. S → R   / ∴ R & S

▲ 10. 1. P ∨ (R & Q)
   2. R → ~P
   3. Q → T   / ∴ R → T

Conditional Proof

Conditional proof (CP) is both a rule and a strategy for constructing a deduction. It is based on the following idea: Let's say we want to produce a deduction for a conditional claim, P → Q. If we produce such a deduction, what have we proved? We've proved the equivalent of "If P were true, then Q would be true." One way to do this is simply to *assume* that P is true (i.e., to add it as an additional premise) and then to prove that, on that assumption, Q has to be true. If we can do that—prove Q after assuming P—then we'll have proved that, if P then Q, or P → Q. Let's look at an example of how to do this; then we'll explain it again.

Here is the way we'll use CP as a new rule: Simply write down the antecedent of whatever conditional we want to prove, drawing a circle around the number of that step in the deduction; in the annotation, write "CP Premise" for that step. Here's what it looks like:

```
1. P ∨ (Q → R)     Premise
2. Q               Premise   / ∴ ~P → R
③ ~P              CP Premise
```

Then, after we've proved what we want—the consequent of the conditional—in the next step, we write down the full conditional. Then we draw a line in the margin to the left of the deduction from the premise with the circled number to the number of the line we deduced from it. (See the following for an example.) In the annotation for the last line in the process, list *all the steps from the circled number to the one with the conditional's consequent,* and give CP as the rule. Drawing the line that connects our earlier CP premise with the step we derived from it indicates we've stopped making the assumption that the premise, which is now the antecedent of our conditional in our last step, is true. This is known as *discharging the premise.* Here's how the whole thing looks:

```
1. P ∨ (Q → R)       Premise
2. Q                 Premise   / ∴ ~P → R
③ ~P                CP Premise
4. Q → R             1, 3, DA
5. R                 2, 4, MP
6. ~P → R            3–5, CP
```

Here's the promised second explanation. Look at the example. Think of the conclusion as saying that, given the two original premises, *if* we had ~P, we could get R. One way to find out if this is so is to *give ourselves* ~P and then see if we can get R. In step 3, we do exactly that: We give ourselves ~P. Now, by circling the number, we indicate that *this is a premise we've given ourselves* (our "CP premise") and therefore that it's one we'll have to get rid of before we're done. (We can't be allowed to invent, use, and keep just any old premises we like—we could prove *anything* if we could do that.) But once we've given ourselves ~P, getting R turns out to be easy! Steps 4 and 5 are pretty obvious, aren't they? (If not, you need more practice with the other rules.) In steps 3 through 5, what we've actually proved is that *if* we had ~P, then we could get R. So we're justified in writing down step 6 because that's exactly what step 6 says: If ~P, then R.

Once we've got our conditional, ~P → R, we're no longer dependent on the CP premise, so we draw our line in the left margin from the last step that depended on the CP premise back to the premise itself. We *discharge* the premise.

Here are some very important restrictions on the CP rule:

1. CP can be used only to produce a conditional claim: After we discharge a CP premise, the very next step must be a conditional with the preceding step as consequent and the CP premise as antecedent. [Remember that lots of claims are equivalent to conditional claims. For example, to get (~P ∨ Q), just prove (P → Q), and then use IMPL.]

2. If more than one use is made of CP at a time—that is, if more than one CP premise is brought in—they must be discharged in exactly the reverse order from that in which they were assumed. This means that the lines that run from different CP premises must not cross each other. See the following examples.

3. Once a CP premise has been discharged, no steps derived from it—those steps encompassed by the line drawn in the left margin—may be used in the deduction. (They depend on the CP premise, you see, and it's been discharged.)

4. All CP premises must be discharged.

This sounds a lot more complicated than it actually is. Refer back to these restrictions on CP as you go through the examples, and they will make a good deal more sense.

Here's an example of CP in which two additional premises are assumed and discharged in reverse order.

```
    1. P → [Q ∨ (R & S)]         Premise
    2. (~Q → S) → T              Premise        / ∴ P → T
 ┌─(3.) P                        CP Premise
 │  4. Q ∨ (R & S)               1, 3, MP
 │┌(5.) ~Q                       CP Premise
 ││ 6. R & S                     4, 5, DA
 │└ 7. S                         6, SIM
 │  8. ~Q → S                    5–7, CP
 └─ 9. T                         2, 8, MP
   10. P → T                     3–9, CP
```

Notice that the additional premise added at step 5 is discharged when step 8 is completed, and the premise at step 3 is discharged when step 10 is completed. Once again: Whenever you discharge a premise, you must make that premise the antecedent of the next step in your deduction. (You might try the preceding deduction without using CP; doing so will help you appreciate having the rule, however hard to learn it may seem at the moment. Using CP makes many deductions shorter, easier, or both.)

Here are three more examples of the correct use of CP:

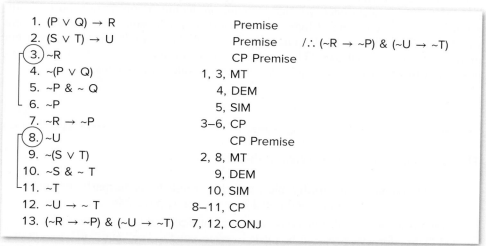

```
1. (R → ~P) → S              Premise
2. S → (T ∨ Q)              Premise   / ∴ ~ (R & P) → (T → Q)
3. ~ (R & P)                CP Premise
4. ~ R ∨ → ~P              3, DEM
5. R → ~P                  4, IMPL
6. S                       1, 5, MP
7. (T ∨ Q)                 2, 6, MP
8. ~ (R & P) → (T ∨ Q)     3–7, CP
```

In this case, one use of CP follows another:

```
1. (P ∨ Q) → R                      Premise
2. (S ∨ T) → U                      Premise    / ∴ (~R → ~P) & (~U → ~T)
3. ~R                               CP Premise
4. ~(P ∨ Q)                         1, 3, MT
5. ~P & ~ Q                         4, DEM
6. ~P                               5, SIM
7. ~R → ~P                          3–6, CP
8. ~U                               CP Premise
9. ~(S ∨ T)                         2, 8, MT
10. ~S & ~ T                        9, DEM
11. ~T                              10, SIM
12. ~U → ~ T                        8–11, CP
13. (~R → ~P) & (~U → ~T)           7, 12, CONJ
```

In this case, one use of CP occurs "inside" another:

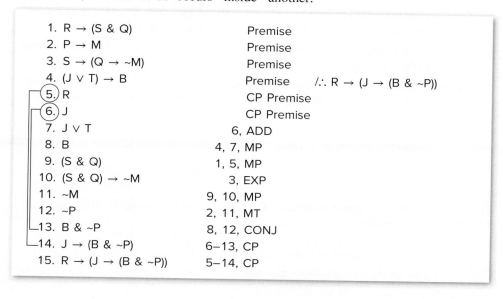

```
1. R → (S & Q)                      Premise
2. P → M                            Premise
3. S → (Q → ~M)                     Premise
4. (J ∨ T) → B                      Premise    / ∴ R → (J → (B & ~P))
5. R                                CP Premise
6. J                                CP Premise
7. J ∨ T                            6, ADD
8. B                                4, 7, MP
9. (S & Q)                          1, 5, MP
10. (S & Q) → ~M                    3, EXP
11. ~M                              9, 10, MP
12. ~P                              2, 11, MT
13. B & ~P                          8, 12, CONJ
14. J → (B & ~P)                    6–13, CP
15. R → (J → (B & ~P))             5–14, CP
```

Before ending this section on deductions, we should point out that our system of truth-functional logic has a couple of properties that are of great theoretical interest: It is both sound and complete. To say that a logic system is sound (in the sense most important to us here) is to say that *every deduction that can be constructed using the rules of the system constitutes a valid argument.* Another way to say this is that no deduction or string of deductions allows us to begin with true sentences and wind up with false ones.

To say that our system is complete is to say that *for every truth-functionally valid argument that there is (or even could be), there is a deduction in our system of rules that allows us to deduce the conclusion of that argument from its premises.* That is, if conclusion C really does follow validly from premises P and Q, then we know for certain that it is possible to construct a deduction beginning with just P and Q and ending with C.

We could have produced a system that is both sound and complete and that had many fewer rules than our system has. However, in such systems, deductions tend to be very difficult to construct. Although our system is burdened with a fairly large number of rules, once you learn them, producing proofs is not too difficult. So, in a way, every system of logic is a trade-off of a sort. You can make the system small and elegant but difficult to use, or you can make it larger and less elegant but more efficient in actual use. (The smaller systems are more efficient for some purposes, but those purposes are quite different from ours in this book.)

Recap

The following topics were covered in this chapter:

- Logical symbols, their truth tables, and their English counterparts: negation, conjunction, disjunction, conditional (see Figure 1, page 288, for a summary).
- Symbolizations of truth functions can represent electrical circuits because "true" and "false" for sentences can be made to correspond to "on" and "off" for circuits. (See the large box at the end of the chapter.)
- Sentences in normal English can be symbolized by claim letters and our four logical symbols; care is required to make sure the result is equivalent.
- The truth-table method and the short truth-table method both allow us to determine whether an argument is truth-functionally valid.
- Deductions can be used to prove the validity of propositional arguments; they make use of the rules on the Figure 2, page 323, and the rule of conditional proof, pages 327-9.

Additional Exercises

Exercise 10-18

Display the truth-functional structure of the following claims by symbolizing them. Use the letters indicated.

D = We do something to reduce the deficit.
B = The balance of payments gets worse.
C = There is (or will be) a financial crisis.

▲ 1. The balance of payments will not get worse if we do something to reduce the deficit.

2. There will be no financial crisis unless the balance of payments gets worse.

3. Either the balance of payments will get worse, or, if no action is taken on the deficit, there will be a financial crisis.

▲ 4. The balance of payments will get worse only if we don't do something to reduce the deficit.

5. Action cannot be taken on the deficit if there's a financial crisis.

6. I can tell you about whether we'll do something to reduce the deficit and whether our balance of payments will get worse: Neither one will happen.

▲ 7. In order for there to be a financial crisis, the balance of payments will have to get worse and there will have to be no action taken to reduce the deficit.

8. We can avoid a financial crisis only by taking action on the deficit and keeping the balance of payments from getting worse.

9. The *only* thing that can prevent a financial crisis is our doing something to reduce the deficit.

Exercise 10-19

For each of the numbered claims below, there is exactly one lettered claim that is equivalent. Identify the equivalent claim for each item.

▲ 1. Oil prices will drop if Venezuela increases its production.

2. Oil prices will drop only if Venezuela increases its production.

3. Neither will oil prices drop, nor will Venezuela increase its production.

▲ 4. Oil prices cannot drop unless Venezuela increases its production.

5. The only thing that can prevent oil prices from dropping is Venezuela increasing its production.

6. A drop in oil prices is necessary for Venezuela to increase its production.

▲ 7. All it takes for Venezuela to increase its production is a drop in oil prices.

8. Venezuela will not increase its production while oil prices drop; each possibility excludes the other.

   a. It's not the case that oil prices will drop, and it's not the case that Venezuela will increase its production.

   b. If Venezuela increases its production, then oil prices will drop.

   c. Only if Venezuela increases its production will oil prices drop.

   d. Either Venezuela will not increase its production, or oil prices will not drop.

   e. If Venezuela does not increase production, then oil prices will drop.

Exercise 10-20

Construct deductions for each of the following. (Try these first without using conditional proof.)

▲ 1. 1. P
   2. Q & R
   3. (Q & P) → S   / ∴ S

2. 1. (P ∨ Q) & R
    2. (R & P) → S
    3. (Q & R) → S   / ∴ S

3. 1. P → (Q → ~R)
    2. (~R → S) ∨ T
    3. ~T & P   / ∴ Q → S

▲   4. 1. P ∨ Q
    2. (Q ∨ U) → (P → T)
    3. ~P
    4. (~P ∨ R) → (Q → S)   / ∴ T ∨ S

5. 1. (P → Q) & R
    2. ~S
    3. S ∨ (Q → S)   / ∴ P → T

6. 1. P → (Q & R)
    2. R → (Q → S)   / ∴ P → S

▲   7. 1. P → Q   / ∴ P → (Q ∨ R)

8. 1. ~P ∨ ~Q
    2. (Q → S) → R   / ∴ P → R

9. 1. S
    2. P → (Q & R)
    3. Q → ~S   / ∴ ~P

▲   10. 1. (S → Q) → ~R
     2. (P → Q) → R   / ∴ ~Q

Exercise 10-21

Use the rule of conditional proof to construct deductions for each of the following.

▲   1. 1. P → Q
    2. P → R   / ∴ P → (Q & R)

2. 1. P → Q
    2. R → Q   / ∴ (P ∨ R) → Q

3. 1. P → (Q → R)   / ∴ (P → Q) → (P → R)

▲ 4. 1. P → (Q ∨ R)
    2. T → (S & ~R)   /∴ (P & T) → Q

  5. 1. ~P → (~Q → ~R)
    2. ~(R & ~P) → ~ S   /∴ S → Q

  6. 1. P → (Q → R)
    2. (T → S) & (R → T)   /∴ P → (Q → S)

▲ 7. 1. P ∨ (Q & R)
    2. T → ~(P ∨ U)
    3. S → (Q → ~R)   /∴ ~ S ∨ ~ T

  8. 1. (P ∨ Q) → R
    2. (P → S) → T   /∴ R ∨ T

  9. 1. P → ~Q
    2. ~R → (S & Q)   /∴ P → R

▲ 10. 1. (P & Q) ∨ R
     2. ~R ∨ Q   /∴ P → Q

Exercise 10-22

Display the truth-functional form of the following arguments by symbolizing them; then use the truth-table method, the short truth-table method, or the method of deduction to prove them valid or invalid. Use the letters provided. (We've used underscores in the example and in the first two problems to help you connect the letters with the proper claims.)

Example

If _M_aria does not go to the movies, then she will _h_elp Bob with his logic homework. Bob will _f_ail the course unless Maria _h_elps him with his logic homework. Therefore, if _M_aria goes to the movies, Bob will _f_ail the course. (M, H, F)

Symbolization

1. ~M → H   (Premise)
2. ~H → F   (Premise)   / ∴ M → F

Truth Table

M	H	F	~M	~H	~M → H	~H → F	M → F
T	T	T	F	F	T	T	T
T	T	F	F	F	T	T	F

We need to go only as far as the second row of the table, since both premises come out true and the conclusion comes out false in that row.

1. If it's cold, Dale's motorcycle won't start. If Dale is not late for work, then his motorcycle must have started. Therefore, if it's cold, Dale is late for work. (C, S, L)

2. If profits depend on unsound environmental practices, then either the quality of the environment will deteriorate, or profits will drop. Jobs will be plentiful only if profits do not drop. So, either jobs will not be plentiful, or the quality of the environment will deteriorate. (U, Q, D, J)

3. The new road will not be built unless the planning commission approves the funds. But the planning commission's approval of the funds will come only if the environmental impact report is positive, and it can't be positive if the road will ruin Mill Creek. So, unless they find a way for the road not to ruin Mill Creek, it won't be built. (R, A, E, M)

4. The message will not be understood unless the code is broken. The killer will not be caught if the message is not understood. Either the code will be broken, or Holmes's plan will fail. But Holmes's plan will not fail if he is given enough time. Therefore, if Holmes is given enough time, the killer will be caught. (M, C, K, H, T)

5. If the senator votes against this bill, then he is opposed to penalties against tax evaders. Also, if the senator is a tax evader himself, then he is opposed to penalties against tax evaders. Therefore, if the senator votes against this bill, he is a tax evader himself. (V, O, T)

6. If you had gone to class, taken good notes, and studied the text, you'd have done well on the exam. And if you'd done well on the exam, you'd have passed the course. Since you did not pass the course and you did go to class, you must not have taken good notes and not studied the text.

7. Either John will go to class, or he'll miss the review session. If John misses the review session, he'll foul up the exam. If he goes to class, however, he'll miss his ride home for the weekend. So John's either going to miss his ride home or foul up the exam.

8. If the government's position on fighting crime is correct, then if more people are locked up, then the crime rate should drop. But the crime rate has not dropped, despite the fact that we've been locking up record numbers of people. It follows that the government's position on fighting crime is not correct.

9. The creation story in the book of Genesis is compatible with the theory of evolution, but only if the creation story is not taken literally. If, as most scientists think, there is plenty of evidence for the theory of evolution, the Genesis story cannot be true if it is not compatible with evolution theory. Therefore, if the Genesis story is taken literally, it cannot be true.

10. The creation story in the book of Genesis is compatible with the theory of evolution, but only if the creation story is not taken literally. If there is plenty of evidence for the theory of evolution, which there is, the Genesis story cannot be true if it is not compatible with evolution theory. Therefore, if the Genesis story is taken literally, it cannot be true.

11. If there was no murder committed, then the victim must have been killed by the horse. But the victim could have been killed by the horse only if he, the victim, was trying to injure the horse before the race; and, in that case, there certainly was a crime committed. So, if there was no murder, there was still a crime committed.

12. Holmes cannot catch the train unless he gets to Charing Cross Station by noon; and if he misses the train, Watson will be in danger. Because Moriarty has thugs watching the station, Holmes can get there by noon only if he goes in disguise. So, unless Holmes goes in disguise, Watson will be in danger.

▲ 13. It's not fair to smoke around nonsmokers if secondhand cigarette smoke really is harmful. If secondhand smoke were not harmful, the American Lung Association would not be telling us that it is. But it is telling us that it's harmful. That's enough to conclude that it's not fair to smoke around nonsmokers.

14. If Jane does any of the following, she's got an eating disorder: If she goes on eating binges for no apparent reason, if she looks forward to times when she can eat alone, or if she eats sensibly in front of others and makes up for it when she's alone. Jane does in fact go on eating binges for no apparent reason. So it's clear that she has an eating disorder.

15. The number of business majors increased markedly during the past decade; and if you see that happening, you know that younger people have developed a greater interest in money. Such an interest, unfortunately, means that greed has become a significant motivating force in our society; and if greed has become such a force, charity will have become insignificant. We can predict that charity will not be seen as a significant feature of this past decade.

Exercise 10-23

Using the method described in Chapter 2, diagram five of the items in the previous exercise.

Writing Exercises

1. a. In a one-page essay evaluate the soundness of the following argument. Write your name on the back of your paper.

    If health care continues to get more expensive, and wages don't go up, then more and more people are going to be suffering from debilitating disease. Furthermore, in this economy, wages are not going up. So, unless something happens to keep health care from getting more expensive, more people are going to suffer from debilitating disease.

   b. When everyone is finished, your instructor will collect the papers and redistribute them to the class. In groups of four or five, read the papers that have been given to your group and select the best one. The instructor will select one group's top-rated paper to read to the class for discussion.

2. Take about fifteen minutes to write an essay responding to the paper the instructor has read to the class in Writing Exercise 1. When everyone is finished, the members of each group will read each other's responses and select the best one to share with the class.

Truth-Functional Logic and Electrical Circuits

We mentioned at the beginning of the chapter that truth-functional logic is the basis of digital computing. This is because, translated into hardware systems, "true" and "false" become "on" and "off." Although there's a lot more to it than this, we can illustrate in a crude way a little of how this works.

Let's construct a simple electrical circuit from an electrical source to a ground and put a lightbulb in it somewhere, like this:

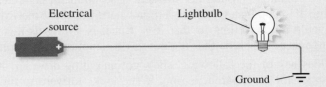

In this situation, the light burns all the time. Now, let's add a switch and give it a name, "P," like so:

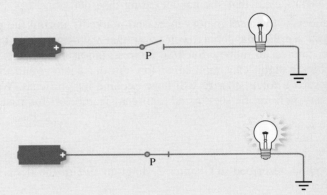

(Switch P represents a sentence that can be true or false, just as the switch can be open or closed.) When the switch is open (corresponding to false), in the second drawing, the light doesn't come on, but when it's closed (corresponding to true) in the third drawing the light comes on. Now, let's add another switch in the same line and call it "Q":

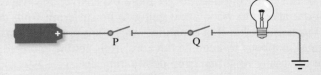

This simple circuit is analogous to a simple conjunction, "P & Q," because *both* switches must be closed for the bulb to come on, just as both conjuncts have to be true in order for the conjunction to be true. So, although there are four possible combinations for the switches (open + open, open + closed, closed + open, closed + closed), only one of them causes the bulb to burn, just as there is only one T in the truth table for conjunction.

We can represent disjunction with a different circuit, one with the switches wired in parallel rather than in series:

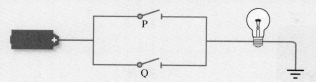

In this case, if *either* the P switch or the Q switch is on, the bulb will light up. So, it lights up in three of the four possible combinations of open/closed for the two switches, just as the disjunction "P ∨ Q" is true in three of the rows in its truth table.

We complicate our circuit-making chores somewhat when we bring in negation. If we have a switch labeled "~P," for example, we just treat it the same as if it were "P": It's either open or closed. But if our circuit contains a switch, P, and another switch, ~P, then we have to connect them (we'll do it with a dotted line), indicating that these switches are always opposite; when one closes, the other automatically opens. Now we get two interesting results: When two switches that are "negations" of each other are wired in series like this

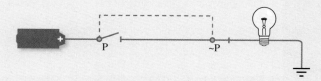

we have a dysfunctional circuit: The light can never come on! But we get the opposite result when we wire the two negation switches in parallel:

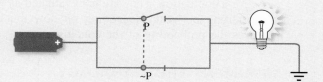

Here, the light can never go off! (This circuit is the exact equivalent of our original one, in which there were no switches at all.) In truth-functional logic, what is being represented here, of course, is that a contradiction is never true (bulb never comes on), and a tautology is never false (bulb never goes off). ("Tautology" is a traditional and somewhat fancy word for a sentence with nothing but "T"s in its truth table.)

This gives you nothing more than a peek at the subject (among other things, truth-functional logic can help us design circuits that are the simplest possible for doing a certain job—i.e., for being on and off under exactly the right circumstances); unfortunately, we don't have room to go further into the subject here. An Introduction to Computer Science class would be the best next step.

Inductive Reasoning

Students will learn to . . .

1. Identify and evaluate arguments from analogy

2. Evaluate generalizations from samples

3. Evaluate scientific generalizations from samples and explain how they differ from everyday generalizations from samples

4. Evaluate the strength of statistical syllogisms and distinguish them from generalizations from samples

5. Identify causal statements, three principles used in forming causal hypotheses, and three types of reasoning used to help confirm causal hypotheses

6. Calculate statistical probabilities

7. Explain how the concept of cause applies to the law

In this chapter we explain how to think critically about inductive reasoning, meaning reasoning used to *support* rather than to demonstrate a conclusion. Inductive arguments offer *evidence* for a contention. They are not evaluated as valid or invalid, but as strong or weak, depending on how much the evidence increases the probability of the conclusion.

ARGUMENT FROM ANALOGY

An **Argument from Analogy** is an argument that something has an attribute because a similar thing has that attribute. Here is an example:

> Bill is a Democrat.
> Therefore, his brother Sam is a Democrat.

The **analogues** in this argument are Bill and Sam. The **conclusion-analogue** (Sam) is argued to have the **attribute of interest** (being a Democrat) because the **premise-analogue** (Bill) is said to have it.

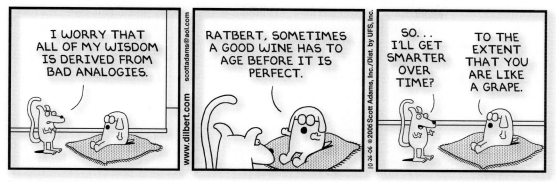

Here is another example:

> Wolves thrive on raw meat.
> Therefore, dogs will thrive on raw meat.

The *analogues* in this argument are wolves and dogs. It is argued that the *conclusion-analogue* (dogs) will have the *attribute of interest* (thriving on raw meat) because the *premise-analogue* (wolves) are said to have it.

One more example:

> Darby is an excellent dog-sitter.
> Therefore, she would be an excellent babysitter.

The analogues in this argument are Darby's performance as a dog-sitter and Darby's performance as a babysitter. The conclusion-analogue (her performance as a babysitter) is argued to have the attribute of interest (being excellent) because the premise-analogue (her performance as a dog-sitter) is said to have it.

The conclusion-analogue is sometimes called the *target analogue,* and the premise-analogue is sometimes called (somewhat misleadingly) the *sample analogue.* Your instructor may find that terminology helpful.

Evaluation of Arguments from Analogy

Evaluating arguments from analogy is basically just a matter of comparing and contrasting the analogues, the same thing you practiced in high school English. It is far from an exact science and requires us mainly to rely on our experience about how similar two or more things are.

Let's bring back the original argument and fiddle with it a bit:

> 1. Bill is a Democrat.
>   Therefore, his brother Sam is a Democrat.

Compare that argument with this one:

> 2. Both Bill and his brother Sam are attorneys and went to the same university.
>   Bill is a Democrat.
>   Therefore Sam is a Democrat, too.

Argument 2 is stronger than Argument 1, because it introduces two additional relevant similarities between the premise analogue (Bill) and the conclusion analogue (Sam). Now look at Argument 3:

> 3. Bill is an attorney. His brother Sam is not. Bill went to Ohio State. Sam did not attend college. Bill is a Democrat.
>   Therefore Sam is too.

Argument 3 is weaker than Arguments 1 and 2, because it introduces relevant differences between the premise and conclusion analogues. Now look at Argument 4:

> 4. Bill has four brothers, including Sam. Bill and three of the brothers are Democrats.
>   Therefore Sam is a Democrat, too.

Argument 4 is just like Argument 1, but stronger, since it increases the number of brothers who are Democrats. Next, look at Argument 5:

> 5. Bill has four brothers, including Sam. All the brothers including Sam are attorneys. Bill and three of the brothers are Democrats.
>   Therefore Sam is a Democrat, too.

Argument 5 is even stronger than Argument 4. It references another attribute (being an attorney) shared by all the brothers.

Here is Argument 6:

> 6. Bill, an attorney, has four brothers, including Sam. One of the other three sells real estate. Another is an unemployed artist. The third owns a restaurant. These three and Bill are all Democrats.
>   Therefore Sam is a Democrat, too.

Actually Argument 6 is as strong as Argument 5, but for a different reason. We still have four premise-analogues (Bill and the three brothers that don't include Sam). Now it is true that, except for Bill, Sam's brothers aren't attorneys. But in Argument 6 we don't know what profession Sam is. The fact that Bill and the other brothers are all Democrats despite exhibiting a diverse array of professions, makes it more likely that, when it comes to this family, it doesn't make any difference what Sam does professionally—he is still apt to be a Democrat.

Guidelines for Thinking Critically About an Argument from Analogy

With these examples in mind, you can see that an argument from analogy can be evaluated using the following guidelines:

- The more similarities between the premise-analogue and the conclusion-analogue the stronger the argument, and the fewer the similarities (or the more the dissimilarities) the weaker the argument.

- Increasing the number of premise-analogues helps strengthen the argument, provided the additional analogues are genuinely similar to the conclusion-analogue.

■ Analogues that lack the attribute of interest are **contrary analogues,** and the fewer of them among the premise-analogues the stronger the argument.

■ If it isn't known whether the conclusion-analogue has a specific attribute, then diversification among the premise-analogues with respect to that attribute strengthens the argument. For example, if Sam's profession is unknown, then if his brothers' professions are diversified, that makes it more likely that Sam is a Democrat if his brothers are Democrats (see Argument 6).

As stated, appraisal of arguments from analogy is not an exact science. Analyzing them blindly according to some formula isn't the best idea. However, we as critical thinkers want to pay special attention to the ways the premise-analogue or analogues and the conclusion-analogue *differ.* **Attacking the analogy** is the time-honored strategy for rebutting an argument from analogy—showing that the premise-analogue or analogues are not as similar to the conclusion-analogue as stated or implied. This could mean showing there are fewer similarities between premise- and conclusion-analogues, or more dissimilarities, or both. Often it means calling attention to a single, glaring dissimilarity between the analogues that undermines the argument.

The fallacy known as **weak analogy** (sometimes called **false analogy**) is a weak argument based on debatable or unimportant similarities between two or more things. It was discussed in Chapter 7.

Three Arguments from Analogy

Here are three examples of analysis of arguments from analogy:

1. Cheryl and Denise are teenage sisters. They attend the same school, watch the same TV shows, like the same music and You Tube videos, and have many friends in common. Cheryl likes *Superman* movies. Therefore, Denise will like *Superman* movies.

The premise-analogue is Cheryl; the conclusion-analogue is Denise, and the attribute of interest is liking *Superman* movies. No differences between the sisters are mentioned. The similarities between the two sisters include attending the same school, watching the same TV shows, liking the same music and You Tube videos, and having many friends in common. This is a relatively diverse list of relevant similarities. This is a relatively strong argument.

2. In an experiment done at the Wisconsin National Primate Research Center in Madison, rhesus monkeys placed on a calorie-restricted diet lived significantly longer than a control group not subject to caloric restriction. Therefore, I will live longer if I place myself on a calorie-restricted diet.

The premise-analogue are the rhesus monkeys placed on a restricted diet; the conclusion-analogue is the writer; and the attribute of interest is longer life. Similarities and differences between rhesus monkeys and humans, generally, are not mentioned. To evaluate this analogy, we would seek authoritative information on possible relevant differences between humans and rhesus monkeys, generally, as well as, of course, authoritative information on the experiment itself. For example, if the diet of the monkeys in the experiment was unhealthy to begin with, then perhaps the better longevity on the part of the calorie-restricted monkeys was due not to consuming fewer calories but to consuming less unhealthy food. Also, how much were the monkeys who weren't placed on reduced calories allowed to eat? Were they allowed to stuff themselves to an unhealthy degree? Without this sort of information, one can only say that the argument is stronger than an identical one based on an analogy with a species less similar to humans, such as rats, and is considerably stronger than one based on an analogy with a species radically different from humans, such as worms.

> 3. Rollerblading is very much like skiing. I am good at rollerblading. Therefore, I will be good at skiing.

The premise-analogue is rollerblading; the conclusion-analogue is skiing, and the attribute of interest is being good at the activity in question. People who know something about the analogues in an analogical argument are in the best place to evaluate the argument; that holds for this example as well as the previous examples. We, not even being novices at skiing or rollerblading, would think the most important similarities between the activities are that both involve standing on an apparatus that is going fast. Both require balance, coordination, and a degree of indifference to bone breakage. Both activities involve equipment without brakes. It might be more difficult to turn on skis than on rollerblades. The problem with rollerblades might be making them not turn.

This is a weaker argument than would be a similar argument based on an analogy between rollerblading and ice skating. But it is stronger than a similar argument based on an analogy between skiing and curling.

Other Uses of Analogy

Analogies are used for nonargumentative purposes. Among the more important of these are to explain how things work and what they are like. Here is an example:

> Electricity going through a wire is like water going through a hose. The wire is the hose; amps are the water; volts create the pressure that pushes the amps through the wire; and ohms measure resistance to the flow.

This is not an argument; it is an analogy used to explain what electricity is like and how it works.

Analogies are also used for persuasion, as explained in Chapter 5. Here is an example:

> Bears are dangerous. If you get too close, you can lose it all. The same holds true of bear markets. In the presence of a bear market, the thing to do is the same as when in the presence of a real bear. Run!

This is not an argument. It offers no reason for thinking that a bear market is dangerous or that a person should avoid one. This is a rhetorical analogy, a concept discussed in Chapter 5.

Guidelines for Thinking Critically About Arguments from Analogy

- The more similarities between the premise-analogue and the conclusion-analogue the stronger the argument, and the fewer the similarities (or the more the dissimilarities) the weaker the argument.

- Increasing the number of premise-analogues helps strength the argument, provided the additional analogues are genuinely similar to the conclusion-analogue.

- Analogues that lack the attribute of interest are contrary analogues, and the fewer of them among the premise analogues the stronger the argument.

- If it isn't known whether the conclusion-analogue has a specific attribute, then diversification among the premise-analogues with respect to that attribute strengthens the argument.

   Note that only similarities and dissimilarities that are related to the attribute of interest should be considered when you evaluate an argument from analogy.

   On the other hand, analogies figure into moral and legal arguments in an important way. A basic moral principle is that we should treat like cases alike. If two people are performing analogous actions in analogous circumstances, it would be wrong to praise one and blame the other. More details about this use of analogies are provided in Chapter 12.

   Similarly, the legal principle of *stare decisis* (stand by things already decided) is the idea that a case currently before the court should be decided by legal precedent—that is, decided in accordance with analogous legal rulings from the past. Again, more details are provided in Chapter 12.

- The legal principle of *stare decisis* (stand by things already decided) is the idea that a case currently before a court should be decided by legal precedent—that is, decided in accordance with analogous legal rulings from the past.

Finally, we should mention that logical analogies are used to rebut or refute arguments. Here is an example:

> BILL: Since all Marxists are progressives, all progressives are Marxists.
>
> JILL: Bill, that is a poor argument. That is like arguing that, since all dogs are animals, all animals are dogs.

The following exercises should help you understand arguing from analogy.

Exercise 11-1

Identify whether each of these is

    A = argument from analogy

    B = an analogy that isn't an argument

1. These shrubs have shiny green leaves, and so does privet. I bet these shrubs keep their leaves in the winter, too.
2. Working in this office is like driving around Florida without AC.
3. Between you and me, Huck has less personality than a pincushion.
4. You don't like picnicking? Well, you won't like camping, either. You can't do either without getting eaten by mosquitoes.
5. As soon as I saw all these formulas and stuff, I knew I'd like symbolic logic. It's just like math, which I love.
6. I love washing dishes like I love cleaning the bathroom.
7. Driving fast is playing with fire.
8. Too much sun will make your face leathery. I suppose it will have that effect on your hands, too.
9. Here, use that screwdriver like a chisel. Just give it a good whack with the hammer.
10. She's no good at tennis. No way she's good at racquetball.
11. "Religion . . . is the opium of the people. To abolish religion as the illusory happiness of the people is to demand their real happiness."

    —*Karl Marx*

12. "Publishing is to thinking as the maternity ward is to the first kiss."

    —*Friedrich von Schlegel*

13. "A book is like a mirror. If an ape looks in, a saint won't look out."

    —*Ludwig Wittgenstein*

14. Historically, the market goes up when the employment situation worsens and goes down when it gets better. Right now, there is bad news on employment, and the latest statistics show unemployment is getting worse. This could be a good time to buy stocks.
15. Yamaha makes great motorcycles. I'll bet their pianos are pretty good, too.
16. "Life is a roll of toilet paper. The closer you get to the end, the faster it goes."

    —*Anonymous*

In each item, identify the premise-analogue, the conclusion-analogue, and the attribute of interest.

Exercise 11-2

▲ 1. Saccharin causes cancer in rats, and rats are like humans, biologically speaking. So saccharin will cause cancer in humans, too.

2. Doug Gray is a successful businessman; he'd make a fine mayor.

3. Haley is very popular in South Carolina. She'd be just as popular in Alabama, since most voters in both states are southern conservatives.

▲ 4. Tell you what, this ant poison looks like Windex. I bet we can clean the windows with it.

5. You need strong, quick fingers if you're going to play a violin or a viola. Angus is great on the violin; he'd probably be great on the viola, too.

6. I liked Will Smith's last movie, so I'll probably like this one too, especially since they have the same story line.

▲ 7. January's heating bill will be high, given that December's was outrageous and January is supposed to be even colder.

8. Expect Hawes to speak his mind at the meeting. He always speaks up in class.

9. Appeasement didn't work with Hitler; why should it work with Kim Jong-IL?

▲ 10. Abortion means killing a live person. If abortion is wrong, then so is capital punishment, since it also involves killing a live person.

In each item, identify the premise-analogue, the conclusion-analogue, and the attribute of interest.

Exercise 11-3

▲ 1. It's easy to use an iPod; it's got to be easy to use an iPad. Apple makes them both.

2. Almonds upset my stomach; I'd bet hazel nuts do, too.

3. The bagels at Safeway are great, so the sourdough's probably fine.

▲ 4. Odwalla carrot juice tastes moldy; I'd bet their orange juice tastes that way as well.

5. My PC slowed way down after a couple of years; it'll happen to yours, too.

6. L.L. Bean makes great sheets; I bet they make great bedspreads.

▲ 7. It's a good thing auto insurance is mandatory; why is it any different with health insurance?

8. The Greek economy collapsed because of all the government pensions. If it happened there, it can happen here.

9. I can't play a baritone; I doubt I could play a Sousaphone.

▲ 10. You don't like *Dancing with the Stars?* Then don't bother watching *So You Think You Can Dance.*

11. Let's get a Whirlpool washing machine. Their dishwashers are great!

Exercise 11-4   ▲   Rank these analogues from most similar to most dissimilar.

    a. football and bowling
    b. football and rugby
    c. football and golf
    d. football and basketball
    e. football and chess
    f. football and tennis

Exercise 11-5   Rank these analogues from most similar to most dissimilar.

    a. going to a rock concert and going to a bluegrass concert
    b. watching Lady Gaga on YouTube and seeing her in concert
    c. going to a ballet and going to a classical concert
    d. going to a ballet and watching Lady Gaga on YouTube
    e. listening to classical music and reading poetry
    f. seeing Lady Gaga in concert or going to a Fourth of July fireworks show

Exercise 11-6   Evaluate the following arguments as relatively strong or weak. To a certain extent this will be a judgment call, but the class as a whole should reach approximate consensus on many items.

▲   1. Earth is like Mars. Since Earth can support life, so can Mars.

    2. Tucker wasn't any good when he managed Big Five Sports; I doubt he'd be good at managing an auto parts store.

    3. Hey, work for Harris if you can. She leaves big tips; she probably pays her employees well, too.

▲   4. Saddam was another Hitler. Obviously we had to take him out.

    5. Julia is good at bowling; I bet she'd be great at poker.

    6. Julia is good at croquet; I bet she'd be great at bowling.

▲   7. Ann takes care of her dog; she'd make a great babysitter.

    8. Hey, Carl? When you don't return something you borrowed, that's like stealing. Give Tony back his wheelbarrow.

    9. Warren shows up to work on time; I bet he pays his rent on time.

▲   10. Norway is like Sweden. There's not much crime in Norway, so there won't be much in Sweden, either.

Exercise 11-7   What kind of argument is this?

> "The proponents of [school] vouchers say, in essence, that if competition produces excellences in other fields—consumer products, athletics, and higher education, to name but three—it would be healthy for the schools as well. Their logic is difficult to refute."
>
> —*Dan Walters, political columnist*

Exercise 11-8   During three earlier years, Kirk has tried to grow artichokes in his backyard garden, and each time, his crop has been ruined by mildew. Billie prods him to try one more time, and he agrees to do so, though he secretly thinks, "This is probably a waste of time. Mildew is likely to ruin this crop, too." How should each of the following suppositions affect his confidence that mildew will ruin this crop, too?

▲   1. Suppose this year Kirk plants the artichokes in a new location.

2. Suppose on the past three occasions Kirk planted his artichokes at different times of the growing season.

3. Suppose this year Billie plants marigolds near the artichokes.

▲   4. Suppose the past three years were unusually cool.

5. Suppose only two of the three earlier crops were ruined by mildew.

6. Suppose one of the earlier crops grew during a dry year, one during a wet year, and one during an average year.

▲   7. Suppose this year, unlike the preceding three, there is a solar eclipse.

8. Suppose this year Kirk fertilizes with lawn clippings for the first time.

9. Suppose this year Billie and Kirk acquire a large dog.

▲ 10. Suppose this year Kirk installs a drip irrigation system.

GENERALIZING FROM A SAMPLE

You **generalize from a sample** when you reason that all, most, or some percentage of the members of a population have an attribute because all, most, or some percentage of a sample of the population have that attribute. A "population" is any identifiable group of things. An example:

> So far, I've liked every one of Professor Stooler's lectures.
> Therefore, I will like all of his lectures.

In this example, the *population* consists of Stooler lectures I will hear. All members of this population are argued to have the *attribute of interest* (being liked by me) because all members of the *sample* of them (the lectures I've heard so far) have that attribute.

Another example:

> Most pit bulls I've met are sweet.
> Therefore, most pit bulls are sweet.

In this example, the *population* is pit bulls. Most members of this population are argued to have the *attribute of interest* (being sweet) because most members of a *sample* of them (the pit bulls I have met) have that attribute.

Another example:

> This sip of coffee is too strong.
> Therefore, all the coffee in this pot is too strong.

It takes getting used to, to think of a pot of coffee as a population, but you can view it as a population of sips.

Studies indicate that more brunettes than blondes or redheads have high-paying corporate jobs.

—From a letter in the *San Francisco Chronicle*

Is this evidence of discrimination against blondes and redheads, as the writer of the letter thought?

Nope; there are more brunettes to begin with. We'd be suspicious if *fewer* brunettes had high-paying corporate jobs.

Another example:

> Whenever I come to this theater it is freezing.
> Therefore, it is always freezing.

The *population* here is occasions within the theater. The *sample* is occasions during which the speaker has been in this theater. The *attribute of interest* is the attribute of being freezing.

One more example:

> Every other peach I have gotten at Kroger was mushy.
> Therefore, about 50 percent of all Kroger peaches are mushy.

In this example, the *population* is Kroger peaches. About 50 percent of this population is said to have the *attribute of interest* (being mushy) because 50 percent of the peaches in a *sample* of Kroger peaches (the Kroger peaches I've had to date) have that attribute.

Evaluation of Arguments That Generalize from a Sample

The most important principles for evaluating generalizations from samples are these three:

■ For the purposes of inductive generalizing, the diversification of a population should be replicated in the sample.

■ **The more atypical the sample, the weaker the generalization.** An **atypical ("biased") sample** is one that doesn't *mirror* or *represent* the overall population. It is one *in which an important variable is disproportionately present or absent.* For example, if the Kroger peaches I'm selecting from have been out on the shelves for several days, my sample will contain a disproportionate number of peaches that other customers have already picked over. It thus may not accurately mirror the entire population of Kroger peaches. It may include more mushy peaches than you would find in the overall Kroger peach population. Any conclusion we might come to about the proportion of mushy peaches in the overall Kroger peach population might be inaccurate if it were based on that sample.

Of course, one does not always know when a sample is atypical (unrepresentative) in an important way. That's because one does not know what variables are related to the attribute we are interested in. Are Georgia peaches prone to being (or not being) mushy? We, at least, don't know. The safest bet therefore is to be cautious about generalizing from a sample that even *could* be atypical (unrepresentative).

Science uses methods (which we discuss later) to help ensure that a sample of a population is not atypical (not unrepresentative). Our best bet in everyday generalizing is to try to make the sample from which we generalize as **diversified** as possible.

- **The less diversified the sample, the weaker the generalization.** Of course, if a sample is too small, it cannot be sufficiently diversified. Thus we go to the next point.
- **Generalizations based on samples too small to accurately mirror the overall population are relatively weak.** If, however, a population is likely to be homogeneous, such as the population of "tastes" in a pot of soup, or a population of ball bearings produced by the same machine, then even a small, undiversified sample is likely to be typical.

Three Arguments That Generalize from a Sample

Here are three arguments together with a brief analysis:

1. There aren't any silverfish in this motel room; therefore, there aren't any silverfish anywhere in Lodi.

The sample (the motel room) is only a single place and probably is atypical: A motel room is more likely than most places to have been treated for pests.

2. I don't like Jane; others probably feel the same.

The speaker is generalizing from himself or herself, to the "population" of people who have feelings about Jane. The sample is too small and undiversified to offer much support for the generalization.

3. OMG! Look at this rash! I'll steer clear of this kind of plant next time.

The population here is all plants of the type in question. Although the "sample" (this specific skin-reaction to this type of plant) is small and undiversified, that doesn't matter much because the "population" (all my skin-reactions to this type of plant) is apt to be relatively homogeneous. A person's physiological responses to the same type of stimulus are apt to be fairly consistent. Number 3 is the strongest of these arguments.

Guidelines for Thinking Critically About Generalizations from a Sample

- The more atypical the sample, the weaker the generalization.
- The less diversified the sample, the weaker the generalization.
- Generalizations based on samples too small to accurately mirror the overall population are relatively weak.

SCIENTIFIC GENERALIZING FROM A SAMPLE

Scientific generalizing from a sample differs from the everyday variety of generalizing in these particulars:

- Scientific populations of interest and attributes of interest are precisely defined by means of a **sampling frame**, a set of criteria that make it clear for any specific thing whether or not it is a member of the population and whether or not it has the attribute of interest.

- Samples are scientifically selected to avoid bias or skew (which refer to the same thing). A **biased (skewed) sample** is what in ordinary English is called an atypical sample, one in which variables that may be linked to the attribute of interest are not present in the same proportion as in the population of interest. (Please notice that "biased sample" does *not* denote a sample of people with strong or unfounded opinions.)

- Random sampling is the most common method used to ensure that a sample is not biased. A **random sample** is one selected by a procedure that gives every member of a population an equal chance of being included.

- No matter how carefully a sample is randomly selected, we cannot always—or even usually—expect it to contain *exactly* the same proportion of items with the attribute of interest as the general population. For example, if the **true proportion** of registered Democrats at a large state university is 30 percent, a given random sample is likely to be *somewhat close* to 30 percent. How likely and how close can both be calculated from the size of the sample. Just how close to that 30 percent mark we can expect our samples to fall is known as the **error margin**. It is reported as a plus-or-minus figure. From a random sample of 250 students at the above-mentioned university, we can say with confidence that the proportion of Democrats in the sample is within six points of the true proportion in the population. That six point leeway is the error margin. With how much confidence can we say the sample is this close? This can be calculated too: With a sample of 250, we are 95 percent confident that it is.

You should now look at Table 11-1, which applies to very large populations. You will see that the confidence level of the table is 95 percent, which is the level scientific polling organizations have settled on. (In a reputable scientific poll, if the confidence level is not mentioned, assume it is 95 percent.) Although we are illustrating things by talking about populations of people, what we say applies to generalizing from a sample of any kind of identifiable entity.

As you look at the table, notice three things:

First, small random samples have huge error margins.

Second, as the random sample size increases, the error margin decreases.

Third, notice that error margins narrow quite a bit as the size of the random sample increases from 10 to 50, but then the narrowing effect slows. By the time we get to a random sample size of 500, which has an error margin of plus or minus 4 percentage points, you would have to increase the sample size by another 500 to narrow the error margin by only a single percentage point. Now that you see this, you won't be surprised to learn that, no matter what a reputable public opinion survey is about, it usually involves between 1,000 and 1,500 in the sample. Trying to reduce the error margin further generally isn't worth the extra expense.

You should take with you from this discussion of scientific generalizing the following three lessons:

Table 11-1

Approximate Error Margins for Various Random Samples from Large Populations

Confidence level of 95 percent in all cases.

Sample Size	Error Margin (%)	Corresponding Range (Percentage Points)
10	± 30	60
25	± 22	44
50	± 14	28
100	± 10	20
250	± 6	12
500	± 4	8
1,000	± 3	6
1,500	± 2	4

The error margin decreases rapidly as the sample size begins to increase, but this decrease slows markedly as the sample gets larger. It is usually pointless to increase the sample beyond 1,500 unless there are special requirements of precision or confidence level.

(We assume, both here and in the text, that the population is large—that is, 10,000 or larger. When the population is small, a correction factor can be applied to determine the appropriate error margin. But most reported polls have large enough populations that we need not concern ourselves here with the calculation methods for correcting the error margin.)

First, at the heart of scientific generalizing are procedures that help minimize bias in samples—in other words, that help ensure that samples are not atypical or skewed. Unfortunately, samples used in everyday generalizing are not selected scientifically, with the result that everyday generalizing is frequently based on atypical samples (the exception is when the samples are from homogeneous populations, like the "population" of tastes of coffee in a pot of coffee). For that reason, the fallacy known as generalizing from exceptional cases, explained in Chapter 7, is common.

Second, also at the heart of scientific generalizing is statistical mathematics, which enables various important probabilities to be precisely calculated, as explained earlier. Everyday generalizing involves at best only approximate or "ball park" estimates of the probability that the members of a large and nonhomogeneous population will have or lack a certain attribute.

Third, as noted, small random samples have huge error margins. Everyday generalizing usually involves small samples that rarely qualify as random. For that reason, examples of the fallacy known as hasty generalization, explained in Chapter 7, are easy to find.

THE STATISTICAL SYLLOGISM

A **statistical syllogism** applies a general statement to a specific case. Here is an example:

Most teachers are Democrats.
York is a teacher.
Therefore, York is a Democrat.

The strength of this argument depends on the general statement "Most teachers are Democrats." The higher the proportion of teachers who are Democrats, the stronger the argument.

Obviously, other considerations bear on the *overall* probability that York is a Democrat. Estimating the probability that he is a Democrat, *everything considered,* involves what logicians refer to as the **Principle of Total Evidence**—the idea that in estimating probabilities of something, you must take into account all available relevant information. But we are not concerned here with the probability, everything considered, that York is a Democrat. We are concerned only with the strength of this argument.

Schematically the argument has this form:

> Such-and-such proportion of Xs are Ys.
> This is an X.
> Therefore, this is a Y.

The strength of such arguments depend on the proportion of Xs that are Ys. The greater the proportion, the stronger the argument. When evaluating the strength of such arguments, don't confuse the strength with the overall probability that the conclusion is true.

Here is another example of a statistical syllogism. This type of argument is encountered ever so frequently; and now you know what kind of argument it is:

> This walks like a duck, talks like a duck, and looks like a duck. Therefore, it is a duck.

Basically, the argument assumes that a high proportion of things that walk, talk, and look like a duck are ducks; therefore, since this thing walks, talks, and looks like a duck, it is a duck.

Among other things, the following exercises will help you explore the difference between statistical syllogisms and generalizing from samples.

Exercise 11-9

Which of the following refer to members of a population in a nonspecific (general) way?

1. Danielle is older than Christina.
2. Annual ryegrass dies out in the summer.
3. Feral donkeys cause considerable damage to the ecology of Death Valley.
4. A significant proportion of small-business owners oppose raising the minimum wage.
5. The president of the senior class didn't wear a tux to the prom, if you can believe it.

6. It costs $55 a year to subscribe to *Consumer Reports*.

7. Glasses purchased online may not be satisfactory for your purposes.

8. Tony the Shark works for No Doz Escobar.

9. The most common seeing-eye dog is the German shepherd.

10. The Toledo museum isn't open this evening.

Which five of the following are generalizations from samples, and which five are statistical syllogisms?

Exercise 11-10

1. Rainbird sprinklers don't last long, judging from my experience.

2. That sprinkler won't last long: it's a Rainbird.

3. Don't worry about your tree losing its leaves; it's a camphor tree.

4. I don't think camphor trees are deciduous; at any rate ours isn't.

5. Blu-ray disks aren't any better than regular old DVDs; so don't expect this disk to be better than what you are used to.

6. Target gives refunds no questions asked. I found that out when I returned a shirt without a receipt.

7. It's difficult to find a grocery store in Fresno; the time I was there I looked all over and only found car parts places and liquor stores.

8. Marsha will be on time; she usually is.

9. Jorge and Susan are both really bright; apparently most music majors are.

10. Jorge and Susan are both really bright; after all, they are music majors.

For each of the following, mark:

   A = statistical syllogism

   B = generalization from a sample

   C = neither

Exercise 11-11

1. Here, try this one. It'll stop your cough. It's a Breezer.

2. Costco charges less than Walmart for comparable items. I've shopped at both for years.

3. Alvid likes the president; after all, he's a Democrat.

4. The local Kia dealership is thriving, which suggests that Kia is doing well nationally.

5. Professor Stooler is a tough grader; he teaches physics.

6. Almost every Shih Tzu I've run into is smart; there probably aren't any anywhere that aren't.

7. A majority of Republicans favor immigration reform, and Horace is a Republican. Connect the dots.

8. Sally is apt to be cranky; she usually is when she skips breakfast.

9. Comcast service has improved a lot over the past year judging from what has happened around here.

10. It will still be cool there in June; the elevation at Denver is over 5,000 feet.

Exercise 11-12   Complete each of these statistical syllogisms by supplying an appropriate premise or conclusion.

Example

> Marilyn is a florist; I bet she's a nice person.
>
> Premise: Most florists are nice people.

▲   1. Don't waste your time trying to teach that dog to fetch. Otterhounds don't do that.

2. I don't see how you could have high blood pressure; you jog, what, ten miles a day?

3. Most people who drive that kind of car have money to burn, so I imagine he has money to burn.

▲   4. Dr. Walker belongs to the ACLU; and most people who belong to the ACLU are liberals.

5. Sharon shops online; I bet she doesn't pay sales tax.

6. York belongs to the NRA; he's probably a Republican.

▲   7. Most members of the NRA are Republicans; therefore, probably York is a Republican.

8. Most smokers drink; I imagine, therefore, that Sally drinks.

9. Melody will be upset; who wouldn't if her husband did that?

▲   10. Verizon provides service to most small towns; so you'll probably get service in Chabot Gap.

Exercise 11-13   Complete each of these statistical syllogisms by supplying an appropriate premise or conclusion.

▲   1. Christine's probably pretty athletic; she's a professional dancer.

2. I doubt Lays have preservatives; most chips these days don't.

3. Aubrey is fibbing; nine times out of ten, when somebody says she doesn't care what people think, she's fibbing.

▲   4. Kids around here generally don't drop out of school, so Jim won't drop out.

5. I don't think their band will be popular; they play jazz.

6. Deanna isn't likely to help; she's too concerned about herself.

▲   7. I expect it's going to rain; it usually does when it's hot.

8. Probably they have a key; most members do.

9. We might have trouble parking; it's New Year's Eve, don't forget.

▲   10. Most governors haven't been good presidents, and Christie is a governor.

Exercise 11-14   Identify the sample, the population, and the attribute of interest in each of the following.

▲   1. I've seen at least ten Disney movies and not one of them has been violent. Apparently Disney doesn't make violent movies.

2. Most of my professors wear glasses; it's a good bet most professors everywhere wear glasses.

3. Conservatives I know don't like Huckabee. Based on that, I'd say most conservatives don't like him.

▲ 4. Judging from what I saw, Columbus State is a fun place to be.

5. Seven of the last ten El Niños were associated with below-average rainfall across southern Canada. Therefore, 70 percent of all El Niños will be associated with below-average rainfall across southern Canada.

6. MRS. BRUDER: Bruder! Bruder! Can you believe it? The Music Department is selling two grand pianos!

   MR. BRUDER: Well, let's check it out. But remember, the last pianos they sold were overpriced. Probably all their pianos are overpriced.

▲ 7. Costco's store-brand coffee tastes as good as any name brand; I'll bet any store brand product from Costco is as good as the name brand.

8. A 55 percent approval rating? Them polls is all rigged! Most people I know think he's a Marxist.

9. The young people around here sure are crazy! Did you see those two dudes drag racing?

▲ 10. The fries at McDonald's are too salty, judging from these.

Identify the sample, the population, and the attribute of interest in each of the following: Exercise 11-15

▲ 1. Whoa, is this joint overpriced or what! Look at what they want for quart of milk!

2. The Hamptons? People there are snobs, judging from what I've seen.

3. PCs are way faster than Macs! Just compare these two puppies!

▲ 4. Life insurance salespeople are always trying to sell you stuff you don't need; anyway, the ones I know do.

5. Did you see that? The drivers in this town are crazy!

6. I get lots of dropped calls with AT&T where I live; it's probably the same everywhere.

▲ 7. After the first test, I knew I'd do well in this class.

8. The doorbell doesn't ring and the hot water heater is busted. Doesn't anything work in this house?

9. I never saw a frost after March. I don't think it can happen this close to the coast.

▲ 10. English classes are boring, judging from the one I took.

▲ Using your background knowledge, rank the following populations from least diversified to most diversified.   Exercise 11-16

1. Television sitcoms

2. Movies

3. Episodes of Survivor

4. Movies rated PG

5. Movies starring Meryl Streep

Exercise 11-17 ▲ Using your background knowledge, rank the following populations from least diversified to most diversified.

1. Professional athletes
2. National Football League referees
3. Physically fit people
4. Major League baseball players
5. Olympic shot-putters

Exercise 11-18 ▲ Using your background knowledge, rank the following populations from least diversified to most diversified.

1. People
2. Cowboys
3. Democrats
4. Teachers
5. Cowboys who are teachers

Exercise 11-19 Think of as many variables as you can that are apt to be associated with each of the following attributes. For example, height and jumping ability are apt to be associated with being a professional basketball player: the more professional basketball players there are in a population, the more tall people who are good at jumping there are apt to be.

Your instructor may make this a timed competition, giving the person who wins an opportunity to go home after class.

▲ 1. Driving a Lexus
2. Owning a pet
3. Having no cavities
▲ 4. Being susceptible to poison oak or ivy
5. Owning a hand gun
6. Being afraid of the dark
▲ 7. Being nearsighted
8. Reading romance novels
9. Drinking Budweiser
▲ 10. Watching reality shows
11. Owning an iPad
12. Seeing a psychotherapist
13. Attending church once a week

Exercise 11-20 In each of the following pairs, identify the stronger argument. Some items may be ties.

▲ 1. a. The coffee in that pot is lousy. I just had a cup.
   b. The coffee at that restaurant is lousy; I just had a cup.

2. a. I've been to one ballet and I've never been so bored in my life. I'm sure they will all be the same.

   b. I love ballet! I've been to only one, but I fell in love instantly.

3. a. Cockers eat like pigs, judging from the cocker I had as a kid.

   b. Dogs eat like pigs, judging from the cocker I had as a kid.

4. a. Acura transmissions fail before 100,000 miles, judging from what happened to my car.

   b. Acura transmissions fail before 100,000 miles; at least that's what the *Consumer Reports* survey of Acura owners indicated.

5. a. Lupe's sister and father both have high blood pressure. It probably runs in the family.

   b. Lupe's sister, father, and brother have high blood pressure. It probably runs in the family.

6. a. Sherry doesn't write well, based on how poorly she did on this five-page paper.

   b. Sherry writes very well, based on how well she did on this five-page paper.

7. a. Blue Cross will cover that procedure. It covered it for me.

   b. Blue Cross will cover that procedure. It covered a similar one for me.

"Most Ohio State students I've met believe in God. Therefore, most Ohio State students believe in God."

Exercise 11-21

How should each of the following suppositions affect the speaker's confidence in his or her conclusion?

1. Suppose the students in the sample were interviewed as they left a local church after Sunday services. (Ohio State has no admission requirements pertaining to religious beliefs.)

2. Suppose the students in the sample were first-year students.

3. Suppose the students in the sample were on the university football team.

4. Suppose the students in the sample were selected by picking every tenth name on an alphabetical list of students' names.

5. Suppose the students in the sample were respondents to a questionnaire published in the campus newspaper titled "Survey of Student Religious Beliefs."

6. Suppose the students in the sample were randomly selected from a list of registered automobile owners.

Read the passage below, and answer the questions that follow.

Exercise 11-22

In the Georgia State University History Department, students are invited to submit written evaluations of their instructors to the department's personnel committee, which uses those evaluations to determine whether history instructors should be recommended for retention and promotions. In his three history classes, Professor Ludlum has a total of 100 students. Six students turned in written evaluations of Ludlum; two of these evaluations were favorable and four were negative. Professor Hitchcock, who sits on the History Department Personnel Committee, argued against recommending Ludlum for promotion. "If a majority of the students who bothered to evaluate Ludlum find him lacking," he stated, "then it's clear a majority of all his students find him lacking."

1. What is the sample in Hitchcock's reasoning?
2. What is the population?
3. What is the attribute of interest?
4. Are there differences between the sample and the population that should reduce our confidence in Hitchcock's conclusion?
5. Is the sample random?
6. Is the sample large enough?
7. Based on these considerations, how strong is Hitchcock's reasoning?

Exercise 11-23   Which of the following arguments would you regard as relatively strong? To a certain extent this will be a judgment call, but the class as a whole should reach approximate consensus on many items.

1. My cousin uses a Dodge truck on his ranch; it has over 300,000 miles on the original engine. Obviously, Dodge really does build tough trucks.
2. Drug abuse among pro athletes is unquestionably a serious and widespread problem. Why, last week three players from just one team said they used HGH!
3. Orange cats are easy to train. I had one once—Gross Kitty we called him—and you could teach that cat to ski if you wanted to.
4. You're gonna take a course from Toadstool? Two guys I know think he's terrible! He flunked both of them!
5. Most Americans favor a national lottery to reduce the federal debt, judging from a poll taken in Las Vegas where about 80 percent said they liked the idea.
6. Young people these days are too easily distracted by things. Just look at the kids in this class.
7. Most Ohio residents are worried about air quality. In a survey taken in Cleveland, more than half the respondents identified air pollution as the most significant environmental hazard.
8. It's time to take back our government. Most Americans agree with that.
9. I wouldn't buy anything from Ace. The lawn mower I got there didn't work worth beans.
10. Border collies are way smarter than Rottweilers. I know: I've owned both.
11. My Zenon plasma TV broke down three times in the first six month. It's a bad brand.
12. Did you know there's no Starbuck's in Pincus, Nebraska? I guess Starbuck's doesn't like the state.
13. Southwest doesn't assign seats. Leastwise they didn't on the flights I've taken.

CAUSAL STATEMENTS AND THEIR SUPPORT

As you've learned earlier in the book, an *argument* is intended to support or demonstrate a contention. A **causal statement** sets forth the cause of some event. Unfortunately arguments and causal statements use overlapping vocabulary.

This is an argument:

> The toilet is leaking because the floor is wet.

This, however, is a causal statement:

> The floor is wet because the toilet is leaking.

The first example gives evidence that the toilet is leaking. It is an *argument* that the toilet is leaking. The second example states the *cause* of the wet floor.

In this section, we are concerned with reasoning used to establish causal statements. Here is an example of such an argument:

> We dried the floor, turned off the toilet, and waited. The floor stayed dry. Then we turned the toilet back on and watched. Now there is a puddle on the floor. Therefore, the leaking toilet caused the puddle.

The conclusion of this argument is a causal statement; the rest of it offers reasons for thinking it is true.

Forming Causal Hypotheses

A statement that X causes or caused Y is often a hypothesis. A **causal hypothesis** is a tentative claim—a statement offered for further investigation or testing.

Normally, when we are concerned with the cause of something, our reasoning falls into two parts: (1) forming a hypothesis and (2) confirming the hypothesis. These are distinct activities (though they involve overlapping principles). If the car won't start, we first think of possible causes; those that seem most likely are the ones we offer as hypotheses. We then test them if we can.

Here are three principles often used to arrive at causal hypotheses:

Paired Unusual Events Principle*

The "paired unusual events principle" of arriving at a causal hypothesis is pretty straightforward: If something unusual happens, look for something else unusual that has happened and consider whether it might be the cause. If you wake up one morning with a splitting headache, and you remember doing something unusual the night before that might be a cause, such as reading in poor light or having a bit too much to drink, you hypothesize that it has something to do with the headache.

According to a report in the *Journal of the American Medical Association*, infants who are breastfed have higher IQs later in life.

Maybe parents with higher IQs are more aware of the health advantages of breastfeeding and as a result are more likely to breastfeed their children.

---

*This principle of hypothesis formation is sometimes called the Method of Difference, terminology invented by the English logician John Stuart Mill.

Here is another example of how a pairing of unusual events can suggest a causal hypothesis:

> As soon as my throat got scratchy I took Zicam. My sore throat went away and I never caught a cold.
> Therefore, maybe Zicam prevents colds.

Now, the fact that two unusual things happened around the same time is at best only grounds for *hypothesizing* causation. It does not *establish* causation. The previous argument does not establish that Zicam prevents colds or kept you from catching one. You don't know what would have happened if you hadn't taken Zicam. Take out the word "maybe" and you have the fallacy (discussed in Chapter 7) known as *post hoc, ergo propter hoc.*

To arrive at causal hypotheses one uses common sense and background knowledge of what causes what and how things work. Yes, if your scratchy throat goes away, you might recall that a raccoon had crossed your path before that happened. But it isn't plausible to think that a raccoon crossing your path could make a sore throat go away. Why isn't it plausible? Because given normal experience, one cannot see how a raccoon crossing one's path *could* make a sore throat go away. One cannot conceive of a mechanism by which this might happen.

The moment that declaration was made, oil prices jumped over $18 a barrel.

—*Post hoc, ergo propter hoc* from SENATOR JOSEPH BIDEN, criticizing a U.S. Senate resolution declaring the IRG (Iranian Revolutionary Guard) a terrorist organization.

Common Variable Principle*

The second principle for arriving at a causal hypothesis also straightforward: A variable common to multiple occurrences of something may be related to it causally. For example:

> When several people in Kearney complained to their physicians about acute intestinal distress, health officials investigated and found that all of them had eaten tacos at the county fair.
> Therefore, perhaps the tacos caused the distress.

This information logically justifies the hypothesis that tacos caused the intestinal problems suffered by Kearney residents. The conjecture might then be confirmed or disconfirmed by other means, such as testing the tacos for salmonella bacteria.

Here is another example of how identification of a common variable in multiple occurrences of something suggests a causal hypothesis:

> Some years the azaleas bloomed well; in other years they didn't bloom at all. In the years they didn't bloom, I fertilized heavily, but I didn't do that in the years they bloomed well.
> Therefore, perhaps heavy fertilizing caused them not to bloom.

Here, the variable common to the years the azaleas didn't bloom is also said to be absent in the years they did bloom. It is reasonable to hypothesize that heavy fertilizing prevented the azaleas from blooming.

---

*This principle of hypothesis formation was referred to by John Stuart Mill as the Method of Agreement.

Covariation Principle*

The third principle for arriving at a causal hypothesis works like this: When a variation in one phenomenon is accompanied by a variation in another phenomenon, we have a covariation or correlation, these being the same for our purposes. For example, if crime rates go up as gun sales increase, the two increases are correlated. You saw in Chapter 7 that "correlations don't prove causation." Nevertheless, when guided by common sense and background knowledge of what causes what, correlations can offer a reason for hypothesizing causation may exist, as in this example:

> Over the past few years online instruction has increased at San Diego State. During the same time the average GPA of San Diego State students has increased.
>
> Therefore, the increase in GPA may be due to the increase in online instruction.

The correlation does not "prove" causation, but it suggests a hypothesis.

Another example:

> When meat consumption in Holland went up after the Second World War, so did the rate of prostate cancer in that country. Therefore, perhaps eating meat causes prostate cancer.

The information doesn't establish that meat consumption in Holland after the Second World War caused the increase in prostate cancer there, but it warrants that hypothesis—that is, it *suggests* a cause-and-effect connection.

To repeat, correlation does not prove causation. The causal links suggested by correlation are only possible links. A girl's hair grows longer as she learns the multiplication table, but there is no causal link between the two things. Skiing accidents increase as Christmas sales pick up, but there is no causal connection. The principles we have discussed for developing causal hypotheses require common sense and some knowledge of what causes what and how things work. From our background knowledge, we can see how meat consumption *might* be related to prostate cancer, but we cannot see how hair length could have anything to do with learning arithmetic.

Weighing Evidence

Coming up with a causal hypothesis involves *weighing evidence*. The car isn't starting. Why? Well, we

It's well known that younger Americans are much more likely to favor gay marriage than older ones. But did you know that the most direct correlation so far, regardless of age, is between people who do not like sushi and people who do not favor gay marriage! Yes: no matter whether a person is a millennial, a gen X, a boomer, or a "greatest generation," the more likely they don't like sushi, the more likely they don't favor gay marriage.

—*MotherJones*, May/June 2013

■ Jeff Fulcher, a former student of ours, read this book and then flew airplanes in Alaska. These two "paired unusual events" do NOT suggest a causal hypothesis because it is difficult to think of a mechanism by which one of them might be the cause or effect of another. Background knowledge and common sense must guide us in the formation of hypotheses.

---

*Mill referred to this principle of hypothesis formation as the Method of Concomitant Variation.

Behavioral Causes

Consider these statements:

▪ Olivia isn't talking to Emma because Emma insulted her.

▪ The union approved the contract because their members wanted to end the strike.

▪ Christie was elected because he appealed to independent voters.

These statements explain the causes of behavior in terms of reasons and motives. Now, reasons and motives are not *physical* causes. Saying Christie was elected because he appealed to independent voters isn't like saying a puddle is on the floor because the toilet is leaking. Reasons and motives are said to be *behavioral* causes rather than physical causes.

heard funny clicking sounds when we tried to start it, the kind associated with having a battery that is almost dead. Unfortunately we also noticed gas fumes, like when an engine is flooded. We noticed other anomalies: we had just filled up with a new brand of gas; the steering wheel won't unlock; it is unusually cold out; and so forth. We had just installed a new radio, too. Could that have anything to do with the problem?

In real life, forming a hypothesis is not as simple as the preceding three principles suggest. We have to weigh things. For example, the association between clicking sounds and almost-dead batteries is more significant than the fact that the steering wheel won't unlock, or even that gasoline could be smelled. The smell of gasoline, which often accompanies engine flooding, might be explained by the fact we just filled up. We'd check battery connections and hope for the best.

Here is another example of weighing evidence:

> You go to a physician about numbness in a leg. The doctor asks a series of questions. Exactly where in the leg is the numbness? When did it begin? Did it begin suddenly? Did something unusual happen? Is it worse at some times of the day? Do you experience it in the other leg? Does it depend on your activities or the position of the leg? Do you smoke? Do you have high blood pressure? Are you experiencing other unusual symptoms? The investigation discloses various symptoms: Some of them might be associated with a neurological condition, another with an orthopedic condition, perhaps another is a psychiatric condition, and so forth.

The physician considers which symptoms are most important, and diagnoses your condition accordingly. The diagnosis is the physician's causal hypothesis. She doesn't arrive at it through any straightforward, formulistic application of the previous three principles. She is, however, looking for associations and correlations between symptoms and medical conditions, and she is looking for unusual events that might have accompanied the onset of numbness. "Did something unusual happen?" is a test to see if the Paired Unusual Events Principle applies. She, being a physician, is in the best position to gauge the comparative significance of our answers.

Three Principles for Forming Causal Hypotheses

- *Paired unusual events principle:* If something unusual happens look for something else unusual and consider whether it might be the cause.
- *Common variable principle:* A variable related to multiple occurrences of something may be related to it causally.
- *Co-variation principle:* If a variation in one phenomenon is accompanied by a variation in another, consider whether the two phenomena may be related causally.

These three principles only suggest a causal hypothesis. They do not "prove" cause and effect. It is a fallacy to think any of them establishes causation in and of itself.

One more example:

A murder has been committed, and investigators have narrowed the field to three suspects. Bullets from Adam's gun killed the victim, and Adam turns out to have lied about his whereabouts at the time of the murder. But Adam was a good friend of the victim, and investigators cannot discern a motive. Brady, on the other hand, owed the victim money, was known to have threatened him, and had access to Adam's gun. But Brady has an alibi. Cox was seen in the vicinity of the murder at the time it happened, knew the victim, and also might have had access to Adam's gun. But Cox has no apparent motive.

These factors suggest contradictory hypotheses. But some factors are more important than others. The fact that Adam lied about his whereabouts, while suspicious, may not be as suspicious as the fact that Brady owed the victim money and threatened him. We would guess the investigators will examine Brady's alibi carefully.

As you can see from these cases, formulating a causal hypothesis involves weighing various considerations, rather than applying one or more of the three principles according to a formula. Background knowledge is terrifically important when it comes to evaluating evidence. Physicians will be better than most at evaluating medical symptoms, police investigators better than most at solving crimes, and historians better than most when it comes to explaining the causes of historical events. Our own causal hypothesizing will be best in whatever areas we have the most knowledge.

Which are arguments and which are causal statements, depending on the most likely context? Exercise 11-24

1. The air is smoky because that house is on fire.
2. That house is on fire because the air is smoky.
3. She had a great workout because she is sweating.

2. The garage gets cluttered because we never throw anything away. So, if we want a neat garage, we'd better change our habits.

3. Mr. Snork is taking French so he can speak the language when he goes to Europe in the spring.

▲ 4. The reason the door keeps banging is that the windows are open on the south side of the house, and there is a strong breeze.

5. We eliminated the other possibilities. The puddle was caused by a leaking wax ring.

6. I am sure Professor York will end on time this evening. He always ends on time because he likes to watch the 11:00 news.

▲ 7. You think the mower won't start because it's old? That's not why. You let gas sit in the carburetor all winter, and it gums up the works. That's why it won't start. It has nothing to do with its being old.

8. The coffee I drink in the evening must explain why I can't sleep. The only other things it could be are sweet desserts and anxiety, and I don't eat dessert, and I'm not worried about anything.

▲ 9. Yes, I know Emily doesn't go out much, but you can hardly blame her. She doesn't go out because she wants to study.

▲ 10. The zucchini grows better than the eggplant because it gets more fertilizer.

11. Why didn't the tomatoes do better? I don't think we were fertilizing them enough. Right after I gave them Miracle-Gro, they did fine.

12. Just look at the cat hair on this keyboard! Where do you let your cat sleep? No wonder your computer doesn't work right.

▲ 13. Given your symptoms, Charles, I'd say your pain is due to a sprain, not a break. Plus, your X-rays don't show a broken bone.

14. Maria can tell what note you are playing because she has perfect pitch.

15. Give 'em a break. That kind of work makes noise, and they gotta start work early to get it done.

▲ 16. Why did Dr. York give a test on Friday? He wanted to surprise us.

17. TV watching leads to violent behavior. Studies show that adolescents who watch more television are more prone to act violently.

Exercise 11-29

Classify each of the following hypotheses according to the principle used to arrive at it. Use this key:

P = paired unusual events principle

C = common variable principle

COV = covariation principle

▲ 1. According to a report in the *American Journal of Cardiology,* people who reported the highest level of stress had the greatest likelihood of being hospitalized with heart disease. The higher the level of stress, the greater the likelihood. This suggests that stress is bad for the heart.

2. Pat never had trouble playing that passage before. I wonder what the problem is. It must have something to do with the piano she just bought.

3. Sometimes the fishing is pretty good here; sometimes it isn't. When I try to pin down why, it seems like the only variable is the wind. For some reason, wind keeps the fish from biting.

4. Texting doesn't impair academic performance? From what I've seen, the more the texting, the worse the grades.

5. Gas prices have gone up by 40 cents a gallon in the past three weeks. It all started when they had that refinery fire down there in Texas. Must have depleted the supplies.

6. Whenever we have great roses like this, it's always been after a long period of cloudy weather. Must be they don't like direct sun.

7. In a recent Chinese study reported in the journal *Alzheimer's & Dementia*, it was found that the people with the greatest exposure to secondhand smoke were twice as likely to develop Alzheimer's. Another study, appearing in *Occupational and Environmental Medicine*, linked passive smoking to severe dementia. The greater the cumulative exposure to secondhand smoke, the higher the risk of dementia, according to this study. A working hypothesis is that exposure to secondhand smoke can cause dementia.

8. All of a sudden, he's all "Let's go to Beano's for a change." Right. Am I supposed to think it's just coincidence his old girlfriend started working there?

9. You really want to know what gets me and makes me be so angry? It's you! You and your stupid habit of never closing your closet door.

10. I've noticed that the more stress I am under, the more colds I seem to get. I wonder if stress causes colds.

11. Why in heck am I so tired today? Must be all the studying I did last night. Thinking takes energy.

12. The computer isn't working again. Every time it happens, the dang kids have been playing with it. Why can't they just use the computers they have down at school?

13. Many studies seem to show that as meat consumption goes up, overall health declines, which suggests that the two are causally related.

14. What makes your dog run away from time to time? I bet it has to do with that garbage you feed him. You want him to stay home? Feed him better dog food.

15. I'll tell you what caused all these kids to take guns to school and shoot people. Every single one of them liked to play violent videogames; that's what caused it.

16. At our university we have observed that the more writing courses students take, the better they do on our university critical thinking exit exam. That's why we suspect that English courses may be among the better ways to teach critical thinking.

17. Gag! What did you do to this coffee, anyway—put Ajax in it?

18. Can you beat that? I set this battery on the garage floor last night, and this morning it was dead. I guess the old saying about cement draining a battery is still true.

19. Clinton was impeached. Then his standing went up in the opinion polls. Just goes to show: No publicity is bad publicity.

20. Young teenage men everywhere have observed that the more they shave, the heavier their beards seems to get. They believe that shaving may stimulate beard growth.

21. Why did the dog yelp? Are you serious? You'd yelp, too, if someone stomped on your foot.

22. Freddy certainly seems more at peace with himself these days. I guess psychotherapy worked for him.

23. Seems like now that kids spend more time playing these violent video games, there has been a lot more bullying. I wonder if video watching is connected to that.

24. Whenever we have people over, the next morning the bird is all squawky and grumpy. The only thing I can figure is it must not get enough sleep when we have company.

25. The mower worked fine last week, and now it won't even start. Could letting it stand out in the rain have something to do with that?

 26. Every time Greg plays soccer, his foot starts hurting. It also hurts when he jogs. But when he rides his bike, he doesn't have a problem. It must be the pounding that causes the problem.

27. You know, all of a sudden she started acting cold? She didn't like it when I told her I was going to play poker with you guys.

28. Your Suburban is hard to start. Mine starts right up. You always use Chevron; I use Texaco. You'd better switch to Texaco.

Exercise 11-30

Use your understanding of what causes what and how things work to answer the following questions. There is not necessarily a correct answer, but interesting controversies may be suitable for class discussion.

1. Do any of these explanations or any combination of them seem better or worse as an explanation of why more people come down with flu in the winter? Can you think of a better explanation?

   a. In winter, people wear warmer clothes.
   b. Flu viruses survive longer in cold air.
   c. More hot chocolate is consumed in winter.
   d. People stay indoors more and are in closer proximity to one another.

2. Reportedly, obesity among American children is increasing. Do any of these explanations seem better or worse?

   a. Children are eating more.
   b. Children are eating more fast food.
   c. Text messaging takes up so much time, kids have no time left for exercise.
   d. It's getting too hot to exercise, thanks to global warming.

3. In a recent study of more than 40,000 Japanese adults, it was found that those who drank lots of green tea were less likely to die from cardiovascular disease than were those who drank only a little. Do any of these explanations of that result seem better or worse?

   a. Green tea may be more popular than black tea.
   b. Green tea is better for your health than black tea is.
   c. Green tea is known to contain more antioxidants than black tea.
   d. Green-tea drinkers may be more likely to eat fruits and vegetables.

4. Japanese are less likely than Americans to die of stroke. Do any of these explanations seem better or worse?

   a. Japanese people drink more green tea.
   b. Japanese people eat more sushi.

   c. NASCAR racing is more popular in America than in Japan.

   d. Americans spend more time mowing lawns.

5. There is a strong association between lack of sleep and depression. Do any of these explanations seem better or worse?

   a. Sleeplessness causes depression.

   b. Depression causes sleeplessness.

   c. Sleeplessness and depression may both result from some underlying cause.

6. When Horace thinks of doing a dusty job like vacuuming his car or sweeping out the garage, he almost always sneezes. Do any of these explanations seem better or worse?

   a. Thinking of dust causes Horace to sneeze.

   b. A sneeze coming on makes Horace think of dust.

   c. It is probably just coincidence.

▲ 7. Every spring and summer, increased snow-cone consumption is correlated with each of the following. Which correlations seem most likely to be due to cause and effect, if any.

   a. Increased number of drownings

   b. Increased sales of swimsuits

   c. Increased sales of beer

   d. Increased number of lightning strikes

   e. Increased numbers of mosquitoes

8. The early 2000s saw a downturn in armed robbery, which coincided with increased cell phone ownership. Do any of these explanations seem better or worse?

   a. Robbers backed off because they knew more people could call for help.

   b. It's probably just coincidence.

   c. Criminals were becoming too busy talking on cell phones to rob anyone.

   d. Robbers know most cell phones can take photos; they worried about having their pictures taken.

9. In 2007, the homicide rate was higher than in 2006. To which of the following is that fact possibly related by cause or effect?

   a. In 2007, fewer hurricanes hit Florida.

   b. During the preceding two years, the war in Iraq went badly.

   c. Several years earlier, Bill Clinton had sex with an intern and lied about it.

   d. In 2007, the price of houses declined sharply.

▲ 10. The junior high basketball team played exceptionally well against a tough opponent. The coach rewarded the players with lavish praise and ice cream. In the next game, the team didn't play as well. Select the best responses:

   a. "Obviously, rewarding the team backfired."

   b. "The coach should have given them a better reward."

   c. "The coach should have rewarded only the best players."

   d. "The team probably still wouldn't have played as well, even if the coach hadn't rewarded the players."

11. Can mere reading of articles about dieting cause teenage girls to resort to extreme weight-loss measures? According to a study published in the journal *Pediatrics* (reported by Carla K. Johnson of the Associated Press in January

2007), the answer might well be yes. In the study, female middle school students were interviewed in 1999 and again in 2004 and their heights and weights were measured. Those in the first interview who said they frequently read magazine articles about dieting were more likely than those who said they never read such articles to report in the second survey that they indulged in extreme weight-loss measures like vomiting and taking laxatives. The effect was present whether or not the girls were overweight or considered their weight important when they started reading the articles, the researchers said.

Propose two explanations for the findings that seem likely or possible.

Exercise 11-31   In each of the following items cause and effect is asserted or implied. Using your background knowledge of how things work and what causes what, provide a believable alternative explanation for each assertion. Use the following key:

A = this may well just be coincidence

B = the stated "cause" might really be the effect, and the stated "effect" might really be the cause

C = the "cause" and "effect" might actually both be the effects of a third thing

D = legitimate cause and effect

 1. Whenever I mow the lawn, I end up sneezing a lot more than usual. Must be gas fumes from the mower.

2. Maybe the reason he's sick is all the aspirin he's taking.

3. The only thing that could possibly account for Clark and his two brothers all having winning lottery tickets is that all three had been blessed by the Reverend Jim Jome just the day before. I'm signing up for the Reverend's brotherhood.

 4. What else could cause the leaves to turn yellow in the fall? It's got to be the cold weather!

5. Perhaps Jason is nearsighted because he reads so many books.

6. First, Rodrigo gets a large inheritance. Then Charles meets the girl of his dreams. And Amanda gets the job she was hoping for. What did they all have in common? They all thought positively. It can work for you, too.

 7. It's common knowledge that osteoarthritis of the knee causes weakness in the quadriceps.

8. Ever since the country lost its moral direction, the crime rate has gone through the ceiling. What more proof do you need that the cause of skyrocketing crime is the breakdown in traditional family values?

9. Wow! Is Johnson hot or what? After that rocky start, he has struck out the last nine batters to face him. That's what happens when ol' Randy gets his confidence up.

 10. Research demonstrates that people who eat fish are smarter. I'm going to increase my intake.

11. What a night! All those dogs barking made the coyotes yap, and nobody could sleep.

12. Isn't it amazing how, when the leaves drop off in the winter, it makes the branches brittle?

▲ 13. What explains all the violence in society today? TV. Just look at all the violence they show these days.

14. On Monday, Mr. O'Toole came down with a cold. That afternoon, Mrs. O'Toole caught it. Later that evening, their daughter caught it, too.

15. Retail sales are down this year. That's because unemployment is so high.

▲ 16. Yes, they're saying electric blankets aren't really a health threat, but I know better. A friend had cancer, and know what? He slept with an electric blanket.

17. At finals time, the bearded man on the front campus offers prayers in return for food. Donald is thinking, "Sure. Why not?—can't hurt anything." He approaches the bearded man with a tidbit. Later: The bearded man prays. Donald passes his finals. To skeptical friends: "Hey, you never know. I'll take all the help I can get."

18. It is an unusually warm evening, and the birds are singing with exceptional vigor. "Hot weather does make a bird sing," Uncle Irv observes.

▲ 19. Why did Uncle Ted live such a long time? A good attitude, that's why.

20. Studies demonstrate that people who are insecure about their relationships with their partners have a notable lack of ability to empathize with others. That's why we recommend that partners receive empathy training before they get married.

21. Lack of self-confidence can be difficult to explain, but common sense suggests that stuttering is among the causes, judging from how often the two things go together.

▲ 22. When I went to Munich last summer, I went to this movie, and who was there? This guy I went to school with and hadn't seen in fifteen years! No way that could be coincidence!

23. It's odd. I've seen a huge number of snails this year, and the roses have mildew. Don't know which caused which, but one of them obviously caused the other.

24. Her boyfriend is in a bad mood, you say? I'll bet it's because she's trying too hard to please him. Probably gets on his nerves.

▲ 25. Many people note that top executives wear expensive clothes and drive nice cars. They do the same, thinking these things must be a key to success.

26. ". . . and let's not underestimate the importance of that home field advantage, guys."

   "Right, Dan. Six of the last seven teams that had the home field advantage went on to win the Super Bowl."

27. On your trip across the country, you note that the traffic is awful at the first intersection you come to in New Jersey. "They certainly didn't do anyone a favor by putting a traffic light at this place," you reflect. "Look at all the congestion it caused."

Go to Church and Live Longer

Exercise 11-32

According to Bill Scanlon, a reporter for the Scripps Howard News Service, researchers from the University of Colorado, the University of Texas, and Florida State University determined that twenty-year-olds who attend church at least once a week for a lifetime live on the average seven years longer than twenty-year-olds who never attend. The data came from a 1987 National Health Interview Survey that asked 28,000 people their income, age, church-attendance patterns, and other questions. The research focused on 2,000 of those surveyed who subsequently died between 1987 and 1995.

    a. Propose two different causal hypotheses to explain these findings.

    b. What data would you need to have greater confidence in these hypotheses?

Confirming Causal Hypotheses

Confirmation of many cause-and-effect hypotheses consists in trying to show that the hypothesized cause is the condition "but for which" the effect in question would not happen. For example:

> We dried the floor, turned off the toilet, and waited. The floor stayed dry.
> Then we turned the toilet back on and watched. Now there is a puddle on the floor.
> Therefore, the leaking toilet caused the puddle.

The hypothesized cause is the leaking toilet. The effect in question is the wet floor. The argument gives a reason for thinking that, but for the toilet, the floor would have stayed dry.

    A condition *but for which* the effect would not happen is expressed in the Latin legal phrase *conditio sine qua non* ("a condition without which nothing").

    Now, a critic might complain that the toilet would not have been leaking but for the fact that there is water in it. And he or she might also point out that there wouldn't be water in the toilet but for the fact that water exists on Earth. And that wouldn't happen, the critic might say, but for the fact that Earth is just the right distance from the sun to have water. What is the answer to this critic? The answer is that we were concerned only with whether the puddle was caused by the leaking toilet. Since that question has nothing to do with these other things, we logically can ignore them.

Randomized Controlled Experiments

Here is another example of reasoning that tries to show that something wouldn't have happened, but for the hypothesized cause. It's a long example, but you need to read it carefully.

> In an experiment, 50 willing volunteers were infected with a cold virus and then randomly divided into two groups. The subjects in one group were given a Zicam treatment, as per the instructions on the box. Two weeks later, the number of people with colds in both groups was compared. Eighteen of the subjects who had not been treated with Zicam had colds, and only 10 of the subjects who had been treated had colds, a difference that is statistically significant at the .05 level. Therefore, Zicam probably reduced the frequency of colds in the experimental group.

If you look at the new cases of death from AIDS, the fastest-growing category could be ladies over the age of 70. If last year one woman over 70 died from AIDS and this year two do, you get a 100 percent increase in AIDS deaths for that category.

—JOHN ALLEN PAULOS

Percentage increases from a small baseline can be misleading.

Is Hypothesis-Confirmation a Logic Fallacy?

- If the causal hypothesis in question is true, then such-and-such would have been observed.
- Such-and-such was observed.
- Therefore, the causal hypothesis is true.

This formula is an example of affirming the consequent (AC), a logical fallacy explained in Chapter 8. But when the results of a scientific experiment are presented this way as a step toward confirmation of a causal hypothesis, the reasoning would be better thought of as an inductive argument and represented by this formula:

- Such-and-such was observed.
- The best explanation of this fact is that the causal hypothesis in question is probably true.
- Therefore, the causal hypothesis is probably true.

Here's an example:

- The frequency of colds in the experimental group was observed to be significantly lower than in the control group.
- The best explanation of this fact is that Zicam reduced the frequency of colds in the experimental group.
- Therefore, probably Zicam reduced the frequency of colds in the experimental group.

The argument about Zicam on the preceding page is quite strong. It describes what is known as a **randomized controlled experiment**—one in which subjects are *randomly assigned* either to an "experimental group" (E) or a "control" (C), which differ from one another in only one respect: subjects in the E group are subjected to the suspected cause (in this case Zicam).

Could the low frequency of colds in the experimental group have been due to variables other than the Zicam? For example, could a disproportionate number of subjects in that group be resistant to colds? That's unlikely, because the subjects were randomly divided into the two groups. Randomization of subjects into the comparison groups helps ensure that both groups were identical (prior to administering Zicam to the subjects in one group).

Could the low frequency of colds in the experimental group be due to chance rather than to the Zicam? The odds against this happening can be calculated using the mathematics of statistics, and as it turns out, there is a 95 percent chance that the difference in frequency of colds between E and C did not occur by chance. To elaborate on this, notice this sentence in the previous argument:

Eighteen of the subjects who had not been treated with Zicam had colds, and only 10 of the subjects who had been treated had colds, a difference that is statistically significant at the .05 level.

Here is what this means. There were 25 subjects in both the experimental and control groups; 40 percent of the experimental group (10/25) caught colds, and

■ The Golden Compass. Just as it was supposed to, this picture makes us want to see this movie. We don't know why it has that effect, but we do not need an argument to know that it does have that effect.

72 percent of the control group (18/25) caught colds. According to the mathematics of statistics, a difference this large (32 percentage points) is "statistically significant at the .05 level," which just means there is a 95 percent chance it is not due to chance. Table 11-2 sets forth the approximate number of percentage points that the difference, d, in the experimental and control groups must exceed for it to be statistically significant at the .05 level. As you can see in the table, when there are 25 people in the experimental group, as in this experiment, a d of 27 percentage points or greater is statistically significant.

So, this randomized controlled experiment confirms an association (in this experiment) between (1) the members of a group taking Zicam and (2) having a reduced frequency of colds, and moreover, that association very probably did not

Table 11-2

Approximate Statistically Significant d's at .05 Level

Number in Experimental Group (with Similarly Sized Control Group)	Approximate Figure That d Must Exceed to Be Statistically Significant (in Percentage Points)
10	40
25	27
50	19
100	13
250	8
500	6
1,000	4
1,500	3

just occur by chance. Yes, it *could* just be chance: a 95 percent probability that it wasn't chance isn't the same as a 100 percent probability. But a 95 percent probability is still a very high probability.*

Prospective Observational Studies**

The randomized controlled experiment (RCE) is the standard for confirming and disconfirming hypotheses about causation in populations. Other confirmation techniques mimic it. Two of the most important of these are "prospective observational studies" and "retrospective observational studies." Observational studies are not experiments. The researcher does not control the assignment of people (or other things, if the study does not involve people) to the comparison groups, and does not experiment with either group. Instead the groups are "observed."

A prospective observational study is very similar to a randomized controlled experiment. Here is an example, which we will explain:

> Does partying on the weekends adversely affect academic performance? Students at San Diego State University were surveyed about their weekend study habits. The academic performance of 100 students who identified themselves as attending parties on most weekends was compared with that of 100 students who said they rarely or never attended weekend parties. It was found that 60 percent of the party-goers had GPAs below the mean for all San Diego State University students. Only 30 percent of the students who said they rarely or never attended weekend parties had GPAs below the mean. Therefore, attending weekend parties probably adversely affects a student's academic performance.

As you can see, in a **prospective observational study** two groups are compared as to the frequency of something (in this case low GPAs). All the members of one group say they have the suspected causal factor (in this case, attendance at parties on most weekends), and none of the members of the other group say they have it. A significant difference in the frequency of the "effect" (low GPAs) in the first group is unlikely due to chance.

But are the two groups really comparable? **Confounding variables** that may affect GPA may be present disproportionately in the comparison groups. For example, the partying group may contain a disproportionate number of first-year students who live in the dorms, and it may be the noise and distraction that is driving down their grades.

Confounding variables (sometimes called "lurking" variables) may be controlled to a certain extent in observational studies by *matching* them in the two comparison groups. For example, the researcher might attempt to make sure the comparison groups had the same number of first-year students. However, since researchers cannot know what all the confounding variables are, observational studies are inherently weaker than randomized controlled experiments. They can offer only a weaker form of hypothesis-confirmation.

---

*The fact that Zicam is associated with a diminished frequency of colds not attributable to chance does not entail that Zicam will diminish the frequency of colds for any specific individual.

**Prospective observational studies are also called cause-to-effect studies.

Retrospective Observational Studies*

In a **retrospective observational study** one reasons backward from a phenomenon of interest to a suspected cause or causal factor. In one comparison group the phenomenon is universally present. In the other it is universally absent. Both groups are then checked to see if there is a significant difference in the frequency of the suspected causal agent. Here is an example:

> Does partying on the weekends adversely affect academic performance? Students at San Diego State University were surveyed about their weekend study habits. It was found that of 100 students on academic probation, 60 percent identified themselves as attending parties on most weekends. By contrast, only 20 percent of 100 students not on academic probation identified themselves as attending parties on most weekends. Therefore, attending weekend parties probably adversely affects a student's academic performance.

In one comparison group, all students are on academic probation; in the other group none are. The only thing that could account for this difference—*if* the comparison groups otherwise are the same—is that most of the former group said they attended parties on most weekends. However, is it true that the two groups are otherwise the same? This type of reasoning suffers from the same problems as found in prospective observational studies: We cannot be sure the comparison groups do not disproportionately contain confounding variables. In this example, we cannot be sure that the students on academic probation are not disproportionately first-year students, for example.

Bottom line: Observational studies offer weaker confirmation of causal hypotheses because confounding variables may not be equally distributed in the comparison groups.

Methods Used to Help Confirm Causal Hypotheses

- *Randomized controlled experiment:* An experiment in which subjects are randomly assigned either to an "experimental group" (E) or a "control" (C), which theoretically differ from one another only in that subjects in E are subjected to a suspected cause. The groups are compared as to the frequency in each of a suspected "effect."

- *Prospective observational study:* A study of two groups, in one of which a suspected causal agent is universally present and in the other is universally absent. The groups are compared as to the frequency in each of a suspected "effect."

- *Retrospective observational study:* A study of two groups, in one of which a phenomenon of interest is universally present and in the other is universally absent. The groups are compared as to the frequency in each of a suspected causal agent for the phenomenon.

---

*Retrospective observational studies are also called effect-to-cause studies.

CALCULATING STATISTICAL PROBABILITIES

We constantly make decisions based on how probable we think an event is. If we think the likelihood of rain is small, we schedule the picnic; if we think the chances of our three kings winning the hand are good, we bet heavily; if we think the odds are that the prices of houses are about to go up, we're more inclined to buy one before they do. Sometimes, if it isn't a coin flip or a card game, it is very difficult to determine what the odds of a given event happening are. But our understanding of probabilities is further diminished by a failure to calculate probabilities correctly when more than one event is in question. Let us explain how to calculate some of these probabilities.

Joint Occurrence of Independent Events

The probability of an outcome can be calculated by simple division. Let's look at a simple case: What are the chances a flipped coin will come up "heads"? There are two possible outcomes when we flip a coin, one of which is the one we're interested in: heads. If we divide the number of outcomes we're interested in (1 in this example) by the number of possible outcomes, we get 1 divided by 2, or 1/2 (or .5 or 50 percent, all of which mean the same thing).

What is the probability of the coin coming up heads twice in a row? To find out, we must multiply the probability of each independent outcome. In this case, we multiply .5 times .5, getting .25 or 25 percent. So there is a 25 percent chance of getting two heads in a row.

Now, what is the probability of rolling dice and getting a 7? There are six ways you can produce a seven, that being the outcome we're interested in (6 + 1, 1 + 6, 5 + 2, 2 + 5, etc.), and there are 36 possible outcomes in all. (Each die has six faces, so 6 × 6 is the number of possible outcomes.) Divide 6 by 36 and you get 1/6 or a little under 17 percent. And that is the probability of a roll of fair dice coming up 7: one out of 6; almost 17 percent.

Notice, we spoke of two independent events. *Two events are independent when one happening does not affect the probability of the other happening.* Since one coin flip does not affect how the next will come up, these are independent. But what if we have a bag of ten marbles, nine of which are white and one of which is red. What are the chances that a random draw will produce the red marble? We know the odds are 1 in 10, or 1/10, or 10 percent. (If you like fancy terminology, this 1/10 figure is known as the "proportional frequency" of red to white marbles.) If the first marble drawn is white, what are the chances a second draw will produce the red marble? Notice that the answer is not 10 percent, because there are now only nine marbles left in the bag, so the answer is 1 in 9, or 1/9, or 11.1 percent. The two draws in this case are dependent events, because what happens in the first case does affect the odds in the second case. (Of course, if the red marble had been drawn in the first case, the odds of its being drawn in the second drop to zero!)

Many people don't realize that independent events really are independent. After flipping three heads in a row (the likelihood of which is .5 × .5 × .5, or 12.5 percent), one might think that it is more likely that tails will come up on the next flip. But this is a serious mistake known as the gambler's fallacy, as was explained in Chapter 8; the next flip has a 50 percent chance of being heads, just like every other flip.

Alternative Occurrences

Figuring the likelihood of two or more alternative occurrences is fairly straight forward, provided the events are mutually exclusive. Let's say you want to know the probability of drawing either a spade or a heart from a deck of fifty-two cards. (These are mutually exclusive events, since drawing a spade prevents drawing a heart and

Almost no one in Las Vegas believes the gambler's fallacy is in fact a fallacy.

—From an anonymous reviewer of this book

How does he or she know this?

vice versa.) Since one-fourth of the cards are spades and one-fourth are hearts, there is a 1-in-4 chance, or .25 chance, of a drawn card being a spade and similarly for it being a heart. To determine the likelihood of it being a spade or a heart, we simply add the probabilities of the two events: .25 + .25 = .5, or a 50 percent chance of it being a spade or a heart. This, of course, is exactly what we'd expect since spades and hearts comprise half the deck.

So, once again, to find the probability that either X or Y will happen, we simply add the probabilities of X and Y.

Expectation Value

How can you identify a good bet when you see one? Let's say you and a friend have lunch together. Your friend proposes that you flip a coin and the loser pays the entire lunch bill. Is this a good idea from your point of view? The answer is yes if your part of the bill is bigger than your friend's and no if his part is bigger than yours. Let's consider how we discover such answers, whether in simple cases like our example or in more complicated situations.

The relevant concept here is called **expectation value (EV)**, which is the result of how much you expect to gain combined with the likelihood of your gaining it. We return to our example: Let's say that your lunch was $20 and your friend's was $10, for a total of $30. (You didn't go to the Four Seasons, but you didn't go to Burger King either.) You stand to win $20 if you win the coin flip (since your friend would be buying your $20 lunch) and to lose $10 if you lose the flip (since you'd be buying his $10 lunch). The chances of your winning or losing the coin flip are the same: .5 or 50 percent. Now, your expectation value is found by multiplying the probability of your winning (.5) by the amount you might win ($20) and subtracting from this result the probability of your losing (also .5) times the amount you might lose ($10). So,

$$EV = (.5 \times 20) - (.5 \times 10)$$
$$EV = 10 - 5$$
$$EV = 5$$

Anytime the EV is greater than zero, it is a good bet, and this is a very good bet. Notice that, if both you and your friend had spent $15, your EV would be 7.5 minus 7.5, or zero. That means you and your friend have an equally good (or equally bad) bet. You have exactly the same chance of winning the same amount.

Let's look at another gambling situation. On a typical craps table, there is a bet called Big 6. If you put $5 on that part of the table, you are betting that a six will be rolled before a seven. If your six comes up first, the house pays you $5, and if the seven comes up first, the house takes your $5. What is the expectation value of this bet? First, you and the house both stand to win or lose $5. What are your odds of winning? There are six ways that a pair of dice can make a seven, and only five ways they can make a six. So the odds of the house's number coming up are 6 to 5; your probability of winning is about .45 and the house's probability of winning is about .55. (Over the long run, of every eleven times there is a winner, the house will win six and you will win five.) Your EV works out this way:

$$EV = (.45 \times 5) - (.55 \times 5)$$
$$EV = 2.25 - 2.75$$
$$EV = -.5$$

As mentioned, any bet with an EV below 0 is not a good bet. For this bet to be equally fair to both sides, the house would have to pay $6 when you win and you would pay $5 when you lose. This, in gamblers terminology, would make the money odds ($6 vs. $5) match the gambling odds (6-to-5 against), and the casino would soon be out of business.

One last example, since more people play poker than play craps. Let's say you are holding four hearts and are thinking about drawing one card to make a heart flush, which will make it almost certain you'll win the hand. What are the odds of drawing that fifth heart? There are 47 cards outside your hand, and 9 of them are hearts, so your chance of drawing a fifth heart is 9/47 or a little less than 5-to-1. So, to be worth your while, there needs to be at least $5 of other people's money in the pot for every $1 of yours. If that's the case, it's worth going for the fifth heart. But if there is less than $5 for every $1 of yours in the pot, it's time to fold 'em.

To speak generally, if the chances of winning and losing a bet are equal, then if what you gain from winning is greater than what you lose from losing, bet away!!!! If the chances of winning and losing are not equal, then you have to factor in not only how much you would gain or lose but what the odds are of your winning and losing. This is a good practice to follow whenever you are faced with a decision that has some sort of gain or loss attached to its outcome.

It is not always possible to calculate an expectation value because we may not know all the facts about our situation. But when we can, it is always a good idea; otherwise, you are operating from guesswork or, worse, ignorance.

Calculating Conditional Probabilities

Given the probability of B given A, what is the probability of A given B? Huh? Need an example?

> At your school of 1,000, the probability of being a male given you are a math major is .76. What is the probability of being a math major given you are a male?

Such questions can seem daunting, but the solution is to convert them to questions about proportions.

> At your school of 1,000, 76 percent of the math majors are males. What proportion of males are math majors?

You already know what proportion of math majors are males. If you know what proportion of the non-math majors are males, and you know how many math majors there are, you know what proportion of the males are math majors.

For example, let's say that at your school of 1,000 there are 50 math majors, 76 percent of whom are males; and let's say 50 percent of the non-math majors are males. Then you calculate as follows:

> 76 percent of the math majors are males = 38
> 50 percent of the non-math majors are males = 475
> Therefore, of the 513 males at the school, 38 are math majors = 7.4 percent

Knowing how to convert probabilities to proportions can be useful for calculating probabilities in medical tests, an ability that can be very important. For example:

> Ninety-nine percent of men who have prostate cancer have elevated levels of PSA. What is the probability that your uncle has prostate cancer given that he has an elevated PSA level?

You might think it is high. However, let's say that out of every 1,000 males, only 10 have prostate cancer, and let's say that 20 percent of men who don't have prostate cancer have elevated PSA levels. Then you reason as follows:

> Ninety-nine percent of the men who have prostate cancer have elevated PSA levels = 10
>
> Twenty percent of the men who don't have prostate cancer have elevated PSA levels = 198
>
> Therefore, of the 208 men (out of every thousand) who have elevated PSA levels, 10 have prostate cancer = 4.8 percent

The key to calculating the probability of B given A if you know the probability of A given B is to convert the problem to proportions, and obtain information about the proportion of not-As that are B, and the number of As there are in every 1,000 people.

CAUSATION IN THE LAW

In concluding this chapter, we direct your attention to an arena in which a great deal of money and sometimes even human life depend on establishing causation. In the law, causation is the connection between action and harm. Only if your action causes harm (or contributes to its cause) can you be said to be responsible for it. In civil law, it is a necessary condition of tort liability* that a person's action caused the harm in question. It is also a necessary condition for some, but not all, kinds of criminal liability. (Not all crimes involve harm—attempted crimes, for example.) It may seem simple to say that X caused Y, but as we will see, there are complications.

The broadest sense of the word "cause" is that of a *conditio sine qua non* ("a condition without which nothing"), mentioned earlier. Such causes are often called **but for causes,** a cause but for which the harm in question would not have happened. It would be wrong to punish a person for causing a harm by doing something when the harm would have happened even if the thing had not been done.

Of course a cause in this sense has antecedents *but for which* it would not have happened either. But for a physician having written a prescription in 1925, the father of Lee Harvey Oswald, the man who shot John Kennedy in Dallas, Texas, in 1963, would not have gone into the drugstore where he met Lee Harvey Oswald's mother, and Lee Harvey Oswald would not have been born.

Clearly we don't want to trace causes back this far in order to assign liability for a harm. In order to identify a *legal cause* (or a "proximate cause," as it is sometimes known), restrictions are placed on the notion of cause *sine qua non*. A legal cause is generally said to be a combination of fact and decision or fact and policy. That is because deciding what is "important" or "significant" requires a decision of some sort or a policy that indicates what is important. In a famous essay on the subject,** H. L. A. Hart and A. M. Honoré try to show that common sense can guide

---

*The legal obligation of one person to a victim as the result of a civil wrong or injury.

**H. L. A. Hart and A. M. Honoré, *Causation and the Law* (London: Oxford University Press, 1959), esp. 59–78.

the necessary decisions. They argue that in order to hold a person legally responsible for a harm, we must be able to trace the harm caused back to that person's action. If Smith throws a lighted cigarette into roadside brush, and the brush catches fire, and eventually much of San Diego County burns up, we do not excuse Smith when he claims that the breeze caused the fire to spread, because breezes are a "common recurrent feature," a part of the causal background, like oxygen in the air. Such features are not seen as intervening forces that mitigate Smith's responsibility.

But if Jones comes along and pours gasoline on the fire, which might have gone out otherwise, we say that Jones caused the destruction. That is because his intervention is voluntary and contravenes Smith's causal role.

Sometimes coincidence intervenes: Moore punches Merton, who falls to the ground. At that moment, a tree falls over in the wind and strikes Merton, killing him. Because the tree's falling is a pure coincidence, not foreseen by Moore, we cannot hold him responsible for Merton's death. We can say he caused Merton's bruises, but not his death. The idea here is that we do not hold a person responsible when coincidence intervenes in this way.

Obviously there is more to say about this subject, but a least you have seen some of the directions the discussion on causation in the law takes.

Recap

- An argument from an analogy is an argument that something has an attribute because a similar thing has that attribute.

- Thinking critically about arguments from analogy involves the principles stated on page 343.

- The time-honored strategy for rebutting an argument from analogy is to "attack the analogy" by calling attention to important dissimilarities between the premise-analogue and the conclusion-analogue.

- Arguments from analogy are especially important in ethics, history, and the law, and in rebutting other arguments.

- Generalizing from a sample happens when you reason that all, most, or some percentage of the members of a population have an attribute because all, most, or some percentage of a sample of the population have that attribute.

- Thinking critically about generalizations from samples involves the principles stated on page 349.

- Scientific generalizing from samples differs from the everyday variety in that everyday samples are not scientifically selected to eliminate bias, and probabilities in everyday generalizations cannot be calculated precisely.

- Statistical syllogisms have this form: Most Xs are Ys; this is an X; therefore, this is a Y.

- The strength of a statistical syllogism is distinct from the probability of its conclusion everything considered.

- Arguments and causal statements often use the same vocabulary.

- Causal statements can be conclusions or premises in arguments, but not entire arguments.

- A causal hypothesis is a tentative causal statement offered for further investigation or testing.

- Three principles are useful in arriving at causal hypotheses: the paired unusual events principle, the common variable principle, and the covariation principle.

Exercise 11-37

For each of the following passages:

a. Identify a causal hypothesis that might be raised by the passage.
b. Identify whether the passage reports on a randomized controlled experiment, a prospective observational study, or a retrospective observational study.
c. Identify the comparison groups.
d. State the difference in "effect" or "cause" between the comparison groups.
e. Identify any problems in the investigation or the report of it, including uncontrolled confounding variables.
f. State the conclusion you think is warranted by the report.

1. Michael Slepian of Tufts University and several colleagues conducted a study of professional poker players' actions during the play of their hands, looking for signs that indicated whether or not the players had strong hands. The researchers used college students (who were not poker experts) as judges of the players' confidence in their cards, randomly dividing 78 students into three groups: One group looked at 20 two-second clips of players' arms and hands as they placed their bets, a second group saw the same number of clips of just the players' upper bodies during that same action, and the third group saw only the players' faces. All clips were edited from the televised 2009 World Series of Poker.

   Each student participant judged each poker hand on a scale of 1 (very bad) to 7 (very good), based on what they could tell from the player's face, upper body, or arms/hands during the couple of seconds when the player moved his chips. Participants who saw only the arm/hand movements of the players scored best at estimating the actual strength of their poker hands, scoring significantly better than chance. Those who looked at players' upper bodies scored approximately the same as chance, and those who saw only players' faces scored a bit *worse* than chance. (This last result is probably due to the players' ability to send deceptive signals with their faces.) The students' ratings were compared to the statistical likelihood of each player's winning, a percentage calculated by the tournament and displayed to the television audience, although it was hidden from the study participants.

   A second study replicated the findings of the superior accuracy of estimating strength of poker hands from seeing only the arms and hands of poker players.

   —Adapted from Science News

2. Learning music can help children do better at math. Gordon Shaw of the University of California, Irvine, and Frances Rauscher at the University of Wisconsin compared three groups of second graders: 26 received piano instruction plus practice with a math videogame, 29 received extra English lessons plus the game, and 28 got no special lessons. After four months, the piano kids scored 15 to 41 percent higher on a test of ratios and fractions than the other participants.

   —Adapted from Sharon Begley, Newsweek

3. The Carolina Abecedarian Project [A-B-C-D, get it?] selected participants from families thought to be at risk for producing mildly retarded children. These families were all on welfare, and most were headed by a single mother who had scored well below average on a standardized IQ test (obtaining IQs of 70 to 85). The project began when the participating children were 6 to 12 weeks old and continued for the next 5 years. Half of the participants were randomly assigned to take part in a special day-care program designed to promote intellectual

development. The program ran from 7:15 to 5:15 for 5 days a week for 50 weeks each year until the child entered school. The other children received the same dietary supplements, social services, and pediatric care but did not attend day care. Over the next 21 years, the two groups were given IQ tests and tests of academic achievement. The day-care program participants began to outperform their counterparts on IQ tests starting at 18 months and maintained this IQ advantage through age 21. They also outperformed the others in all areas of academic achievement from the third year of school onward.

—Adapted from Developmental Psychology, *6th ed., David R. Schaffer*

4. Research at the University of Pennsylvania and the Children's Hospital of Philadelphia indicates that children who sleep in a dimly lighted room until age two may be up to five times more likely to develop myopia (nearsightedness) when they grow up.

The researchers asked the parents of children who had been patients at the researchers' eye clinic to recall the lighting conditions in the children's bedroom from birth to age two.

Of a total of 172 children who slept in darkness, 10 percent were nearsighted. Of a total of 232 who slept with a night light, 34 percent were nearsighted. Of a total of 75 who slept with a lamp on, 55 percent were nearsighted.

The lead ophthalmologist, Dr. Graham E. Quinn, said that "just as the body needs to rest, this suggests that the eyes need a period of darkness."

—Adapted from an AP report by Joseph B. Verrengia

5. You want to find out if the coffee grounds that remain suspended as sediment in French press, espresso, and Turkish and Greek coffee can cause headaches.

You randomly divide fifty volunteers into two groups and feed both groups a pudding at the same time every day. However, one group mixes eight grams of finely pulverized used coffee grounds into the pudding before eating it (that's equivalent to the sediment in about one and a half liters of Turkish coffee). Within three weeks, you find that 50 percent of the group that has eaten grounds have had headaches; only 27 percent of the other group have experienced a headache. You conclude that coffee grounds may indeed cause headaches and try to get a grant for further studies. (This is a fictitious experiment.)

6. Do you enjoy spicy Indian and Asian curries? That bright yellow-orange color is due to curcumin, an ingredient in the spice turmeric. An experiment conducted by Bandaru S. Reddy of the American Health Foundation in Valhalla, New York, and reported in *Cancer Research* suggests that curcumin might suppress the development of colon cancer.

Places where turmeric is widely used have a low incidence of colon cancer, so the research team decided to investigate. They administered a powerful colon carcinogen to sixty-six rats and then added curcumin at the rate of 2,000 parts per million to the diet of thirty of them. At the end of a year, 81 percent of the rats eating regular rat food had developed cancerous tumors, compared with only 47 percent of those that dined on the curcumin-enhanced diet. In addition, 38 percent of the tumors in rats eating regular food were invasive, and that was almost twice the rate in rodents eating curcumin-treated chow.

—Adapted from Science News

7. Does jogging keep you healthy? Two independent researchers interested in whether exercise prevents colds interviewed twenty volunteers about the

frequency with which they caught colds. The volunteers, none of whom exercised regularly, were then divided into two groups of ten, and one group participated in a six-month regimen of jogging three miles every other day. At the end of the six months, the frequency of colds among the joggers was compared both with that of the nonjoggers and with that of the joggers prior to the experiment. It was found that, compared with the nonjoggers, the joggers had 25 percent fewer colds. The record of colds among the joggers also declined in comparison with their own record prior to the exercise program.

8. In one fifty-seven-month study, whose participants were all male physicians, 104 of those who took aspirin had heart attacks, as compared with 189 heart attacks in those who took only a sugar pill. This means ordinary aspirin reduced the heart attack risk for healthy men by 47 percent. At least seven long-term studies of more than 11,000 heart attack victims have shown that one-half or one aspirin per day can reduce the risk of a second attack by up to 20 percent.

—*Adapted from the* Los Angeles Times

9. Although cigarette ads sometimes suggest that smoking is macho, new studies indicate that smoking can increase the risk of impotence. In a study of 116 men with impotence caused by vascular problems, done at the University of Pretoria, South Africa, 108 were smokers. Two independent studies, one done by the Centre d'Etudes et de Recherches di l'Impuissance in Paris, and reported in the British medical journal *Lancet,* and the other done by Queen's University and Kingston General Hospital in Ontario, found that almost two-thirds of impotent men smoked.

To test whether smoking has an immediate effect on sexual response, a group of researchers from Southern Illinois and Florida State universities fitted 42 male smokers with a device that measures the speed of arousal. The men were divided into three groups, one group given high-nicotine cigarettes, one group cigarettes low in nicotine, and one group mints. After smoking one cigarette or eating a mint, each man was placed in a private room and shown a two-minute erotic film while his sexual response was monitored. Then he waited ten minutes, smoked two more cigarettes or ate another mint, and watched a different erotic film, again being monitored.

The results: Men who smoked high-nicotine cigarettes had slower arousal than those who smoked low-nicotine cigarettes or ate mints.

—*Adapted from* Reader's Digest

▲ 10. "A study published in the July 27 *Journal of the American Medical Association* indicates that taking androgen (a male sex hormone) in high doses for four weeks can have important effects on the high density lipoproteins (HDLs) in the blood, which are believed to protect against the clogging of vessels that supply the heart. Ben F. Hurley, an exercise physiologist from the University of Maryland in College Park who conducted the study at Washington University, monitored the levels of HDL in the blood of sixteen healthy, well-conditioned men in their early thirties who were taking androgens as part of their training program with heavy weights. Prior to use of the hormone, all had normal levels of HDLs. After four weeks of self-prescribed and self-administered use of these steroids the levels dropped by about 60 percent.

"Hurley is cautious in interpreting the data. 'You can't say that low HDL levels mean that a specified person is going to have a heart attack at an earlier age. All you can say is that it increases their risk for heart disease.'"

—*D. Franklin,* Science News

11. "New studies reported in the *Journal of the American Medical Association* indicate that vasectomy is safe. A group headed by Frank Massey of UCLA paired 10,500 vasectomized men with a like number of men who had not had the operation. The average follow-up time was 7.9 years, and 2,300 pairs were followed for more than a decade. The researchers reported that, aside from inflammation in the testes, the incidence of diseases for vasectomized men was similar to that in their paired controls.

"A second study done under federal sponsorship at the Battelle Human Affairs Research Centers in Seattle compared heart disease in 1,400 vasecto-mized men and 3,600 men who had not had the operation. Over an average follow-up time of fifteen years, the incidence of heart diseases was the same among men in both groups."

—*Edward Edelson,* New York Daily News; *reprinted in* Reader's Digest

12. "A new study shows that the incidence of cancer tumors in rats exposed to high doses of X-rays dropped dramatically when the food intake of the rats was cut by more than half. Dr. Ludwik Gross of the Veterans Administration Medical Center noted that this study is the first to demonstrate that radiation-induced tumors can be prevented by restricting diet.

"The experimenters exposed a strain of laboratory rats to a dose of X-rays that produced tumors in 100 percent of the rats allowed to eat their fill—about five or six pellets of rat food a day.

"When the same dose of X-rays was given to rats limited to two pellets of food a day, only nine of 29 females and one of 15 males developed tumors, the researchers reported.

"The weight of the rats on the reduced diet fell by about one-half, but they remained healthy and outlived their counterparts who died of cancer, Gross said. He noted that the restricted diet also reduced the occurrence of benign tumors. There is no evidence that restriction of food intake will slow the growth of tumors that have already formed in animals, he said."

—*Paul Raeburn,* Sacramento Bee

▲ 13. Investigations conducted by researchers at the University of Washington in Seattle suggest that cheating may create more positive feelings than guilty ones. In one experiment, 179 participants were asked to unscramble as many of 15 words as possible in four minutes and told they would be given $1 for every correct word. Unknown to the subjects, their responses were recorded. When they were asked to check their own work in private before submitting it, 71 participants cheated by adding additional correct words to their answer sheets. Afterwards, cheaters reported on average a greater increase in excite-ment and positive feelings than non-cheaters did.

—*Adapted from* Science News

14. "A study released last week indicated that Type A individuals, who are char-acteristically impatient, competitive, insecure and short-tempered, can halve their chances of having a heart attack by changing their behavior with the help of psychological counseling.

"In 1978, scientists at Mt. Zion Hospital and Medical Center in San Francisco and Stanford University School of Education began their study of 862 predomi-nantly male heart attack victims. Of this number, 592 received group counseling to ease their Type A behavior and improve their self-esteem. After three years, only 7 percent had another heart attack, compared with 13 percent of a matched group of 270 subjects who received only cardiological advice. Among 328 men who continued with the counseling for the full three years, 79 percent reduced their Type A behavior. About half of the comparison group was similarly able to slow down and cope better with stress.

"This is the first evidence 'that a modification program aimed at Type A behavior actually helps to reduce coronary disease,' says Redford Williams of Duke University, an investigator of Type A behavior."

—Science News

Exercise 11-38

Researchers from Tenon Hospital in Paris reported to the American Urological Association that dogs can be trained to detect the odor of chemicals released into urine by prostate cancer. The researchers first trained a Belgian Malinois to identify urine samples from patients with prostate cancer and to differentiate them from urine samples from healthy subjects. They then determined whether the dog could select a urine sample from a prostate cancer victim when four urine samples from healthy people were present. The dog was correct in 63 out of 66 tests—more accurate than the PSA test now used to detect prostate cancer. The researchers currently are training other dogs.*

1. Do you think the dog's success rate was coincidental? Why or why not?
2. Do you see any weakness in the experiment?
3. If you were testing the ability of this dog to detect urine from victims of prostate cancer, would you do anything differently?

Exercise 11-39

Let's say you randomly divide 700 men in the early stages of prostate cancer into two groups. The men in one group have their prostates removed surgically; those in the other group are simply watched to let the disease take its course. Researchers did this to 700 Scandinavian men and reported the results in the *New England Journal of Medicine* in fall 2002. As it turns out, sixteen of those who underwent surgery died from prostate cancer, as compared with thirty-one of those who did not undergo surgery. On the face of it, these figures suggest your chances of not dying from prostate cancer are better if you have surgery. But put on your thinking caps and answer the following questions.

1. Suppose that, despite these findings, there was no statistically significant difference in how long the men in each group lived. What would that suggest?
2. The follow-up comparison lasted six years. Suppose that, after ten years, the death rates from prostate cancer were the same for the two groups. What would that suggest?
3. Suppose Scandinavian men are not screened for prostate cancer as aggressively as American men and tend to be older when they get the first diagnosis. What would that suggest?
4. Suppose Scandinavian men are screened more aggressively for prostate cancer than American men and tend to be younger when they get the first diagnosis. What would that suggest?

*http://phys.org/news194726672.html.

Here, as elsewhere, you need to know the whole picture to make a judgment. How old were the men to begin with? If they were relatively young men, how long did the study last? Was there a difference in how long the men in the two groups lived? (Note that prostate removal has risks and sometimes produces important negative side effects.)

Writing Exercises

1. Select one of the following general claims and explain how you might find out if it is true. Begin by making the generalization more precise by clearly specifying the population and attribute in question and how you might select a sample from the population. Alternatively, if you think you already have evidence the claim is true, produce an argument that supports it.

   a. Politicians can't be trusted.
   b. Government intrudes in our private lives/business affairs too much.
   c. Many welfare recipients take advantage of the system.
   d. Anyone who really wants a job can find one.
   e. University professors are liberals.
   f. The media are biased.

   When everyone is finished, the instructor will redistribute all papers to other members of the class. In groups of four or five, read the papers and select the best one to share with everyone in the class. Be prepared to explain why it is the best.

2. In a study reported by Gene Koretz in *BusinessWeek* (December 9, 2002). nine- and ten-year-old boys and girls ran a short race. There was no significant difference in the average speeds of the children when they ran solo, but when they ran the race again, paired with another child, the boys' speeds, but not the girls', increased. The boys' speeds increased most when they were paired on the second trial with a girl. In a brief essay offer a hypothesis to explain this result, and describe how your hypothesis might be (partially) confirmed or disconfirmed.

   When everyone is finished, the instructor will redistribute all papers to other members of the class. In groups of four or five, read the papers and select the best one to share with everyone in the class. Be prepared to explain why it is the best.

Moral, Legal, and Aesthetic Reasoning

Students will learn to . . .

1. Explain the role of value judgment in moral reasoning

2. Name and explain the major perspectives in moral reasoning in Western thought

3. Explain the elements of moral deliberation

4. Explain the principles that underlie legal reasoning and argument

5. Explain the principles involved in aesthetic reasoning and judgment

Let's imagine that you and an acquaintance have the same insurance agent, and you discover that the acquaintance, who lost his job during a recent recession, is involved in an insurance-fraud scam. He is trying to defraud the company out of tens of thousands of dollars. When you visit the agent to check up on your own policy, should you say anything about what your friend is doing?

From time to time, we all face tough moral decisions. A mother must decide whether her daughter's softball game has a higher priority than her professional responsibility. "Dear Abby" tries to answer a young woman with a serviceman fiancé serving abroad who has fallen in love with someone new. A governor must decide whether to send a convicted criminal to death row on circumstantial evidence. A president faces the decision of whether to take a nation to war.

When people think abstractly, sometimes they believe that moral issues are subjective. You hear them say such things as "When it comes to what you should do, the right thing is what seems right to you. End of story." However, we asked a class how many thought "Dear Abby" should have told her young correspondent, "Hey, do whatever you feel like"—not a single hand was raised. When people hear about a real moral dilemma, not to mention confront one for themselves, they usually *don't* think it's merely a matter of personal opinion. They discuss the issue with others, seek advice, consider options, and weigh consequences. When they do this, they find that some considerations and arguments carry more weight and are better than others. (You may remember our brief treatment of this topic in Chapter 1.)

In the first part of this chapter, we look at what actually is involved in moral reasoning and deliberation. Then we will do the same for aspects of legal reasoning and for aesthetic reasoning.

■ The "Dear Abby" column is now written by Jeanne Phillips, the original Abby's daughter. The column often employs moral reasoning, which is discussed in this chapter.

VALUE JUDGMENTS

Let's begin by fine-tuning what we mean when we talk about moral reasoning. Recently, our colleague Becky White debated what to do about a student who had copied parts of someone else's term paper and was silly enough to think Professor White wouldn't notice. Many things could be said about the student; what Professor White said was, "He deserves an F." And that's what she gave him—for the entire course.

Professor White's statement is what people call a "value judgment."* A **value judgment** assesses the merit, desirability, or praiseworthiness of someone or something. When our colleague said the student deserved an F, she wasn't describing him; she was *judging* him. She thought he had done something *wrong*.

Moral reasoning differs from other kinds of reasoning in that it consists mainly of trying to establish moral value judgments. Because moral reasoning is all about moral value judgments, you need to be able to identify one when you run into it.

A difficulty is that not every value judgment expresses a *moral* value judgment. When you say a movie is pretty good, you are judging the movie, but not its morality. When you say Pepsi is better than Coke, you are making a taste value judgment, not a moral value judgment.

See if you understand why, in the table below, the claims in the left column are all moral value judgments and those in the right are value judgments, but not of the moral variety. Exercises on moral reasoning are at the end of the section titled "Moral Deliberation" in this chapter.

Moral Value Judgments	Nonmoral Value Judgments
1. It was wrong for the senator to withhold information.	1. The senator dresses well.
2. The senator ought not to claim residence in one district when he actually lives in another.	2. *Why Him?* is one of the funnier movies of recent years.
3. Abortion is immoral.	3. Lorde is not quite good enough to have just one name.
4. Children should be taught to respect their elders.	4. Frank Zappa was a so-so guitarist.
5. I don't deserve to be flunked for an honest mistake.	5. Jessie J rocks.

*Value judgments are also known as "normative" or "prescriptive" statements. We'll stick with "value judgments" because the term is largely self-explanatory and we want to avoid terminological clutter.

Typically, moral value judgments employ such words as "good," "bad," "right," "wrong," "ought," "should," "proper," and "justified," "fair," and so forth, and their opposites. But you need to bear in mind that, although these words often signal a moral evaluation, they do not always do so. Telling someone she should keep her promise is making a moral value judgment; telling her she should keep her knees bent when skiing is assigning a positive value to keeping bent knees, but not a moral value.

It's also worth noticing that implicit value judgments can be made inside claims that are not themselves value judgments. For example, "David Axelrod, a good man, is a regular contributor to the *New York Times*" is not a value judgment, but the part about Axelrod being a good man is.

Moral versus Nonmoral

A source of confusion in discussions that involve moral reasoning is the word "moral." The word has two separate and distinct meanings. First, "moral" may be used as the opposite of "nonmoral." This is the sense in which we have been using the term. The claim "Chris Christie weighs more than 200 pounds" is a nonmoral claim, meaning it has nothing to do with morality. "Chris Christie is an evil man," by contrast, has a lot to do with morality: It is a moral value judgment, a claim that expresses a moral value. The same is true of the claim, "Chris Christie is a good man."

The second meaning of "moral" is the opposite not of "nonmoral" but of "immoral." Kicking a cat for the heck of it would be immoral; taking care of it would be moral. In this sense of the word, "moral" is used to mean "good," "right," "proper," and so forth.

To avoid confusion, when we use the word "moral" in this chapter, we always mean moral as opposed to nonmoral; that is, as having to do with morality. Thus, the statements "It was wrong to kick the cat" and "It wasn't wrong to kick the cat" are both moral judgments.

Two Principles of Moral Reasoning

Suppose Moore announces on the first day of class that the final exam will be optional. "Except," he says, pointing at some person at random, "for the young woman there in the third row. For you," he says, "the final is mandatory."

The problem here is that this student is no different from everyone else, yet Moore is treating her differently. And this brings us to the first principle of moral reasoning.

> **Moral Reasoning Principle 1**
>
> *If separate cases aren't different in any relevant way, then they should be treated the same way, and if separate cases are treated the same way, they should not be different in any relevant way.*

For convenience, let's call this the **consistency principle.** If Moore gives two students the same grade despite the fact that one student did much better than the other, Moore has violated the principle.

It is important to see that this is a principle of *moral reasoning,* not a moral principle. It's *not* like saying, "You should be kind to animals." It's like saying, "If all Xs are Ys, then if this thing is an X, then it is a Y"—"If all students are entitled to an optional final, then if the young woman in the third row is a student, then she is entitled to an optional final."

The second principle of moral reasoning is procedural rather than logical:

Moral Reasoning Principle 2

If someone appears to be violating the consistency principle, then the burden of proof is on that person to show that he or she is in fact not violating the principle.

For example, if Parker says, "Blue-eyed students can take tests with books open, but nobody else can," he needs to show that he is not violating the consistency principle. He must show that there is something about having blue eyes that should entitle such individuals to take their tests with their books open.

When do separate cases count as the same or different? Fortunately, principle 2 enables us to sidestep having to answer this question in the abstract. If Harlan approved of the war in Afghanistan but opposed the war in Vietnam, and the cases seem to us not to differ in any relevant way, then, if Harlan cannot point to a difference that seems satisfactory to us, we are justified in regarding him as inconsistent. If Carol treats black customers and white customers differently and cannot identify for us some relevant difference between the two, then we are justified in regarding her as inconsistent.

Suppose, however, that Carol thinks that skin color itself is a difference between blacks and whites relevant to how people should be treated, and she charges us with failing to make relevant discriminations. Here, it would be easy for us to point out to Carol that skin color is an immutable characteristic of birth like height or eye color; does Carol adjust her civility to people depending on those characteristics?

It isn't difficult to perceive the inconsistency on the part of a salesperson who is more polite to customers of one group; but other cases are far tougher, and many are such that reasonable people will disagree about their proper assessment. Is a person inconsistent who approves of abortion but not capital punishment? Is a person inconsistent who, on the one hand, believes that the states should be free to reduce spending on welfare but, on the other, does not think that the states should be able to eliminate ceilings on punitive damages in tort cases? No harm is done in asking, "What's the difference?" and because much headway can be made in a discussion by doing so, it seems wise to ask.

In Chapter 6, we talked about the *argumentum ad hominem,* a fallacy one version of which we commit when we think we rebut the content of what someone says by pointing out inconsistency on his or her part. Now, let's say Ramesh tells us it is wrong to hunt, and then we find out Ramesh likes to fish. And let's say that, when we press Ramesh, he cannot think of any relevant moral difference between the two activities. Then he is being inconsistent. But that does not mean that it is right to hunt, nor does it mean that it is wrong to fish. An *argumentum ad hominem* occurs if we say something like "Ramesh, you are mistaken when you say it is wrong to hunt, because you yourself fish." It is not an *argumentum ad hominem* to say, "Ramesh, you are being inconsistent. You must change your position on either hunting or fishing."

Similarly, let's suppose Professor Moore gives Howard an A and gives James a C but cannot think of any differences between their performance in his course. It would be committing an *argumentum ad hominem* if we said, "Moore, James does not deserve a C, because you gave Howard an A." Likewise, it would be committing an *argumentum ad hominem* if we said, "Moore, Howard does not deserve an A, because you gave James a C." But it is *not* illogical to say, "Moore, you are being inconsistent. You have misgraded one or the other of these students."

Moral Principles

Because separate moral cases, if similar, must be given similar treatment, a moral principle is a value judgment that is general in nature. That is, a moral principle refers to what should be done (or is right, proper, etc.) not just in a single case but in all similar cases. "Stealing is wrong" is a moral principle. "It is wrong to steal from Billy Bob" is just a true moral value judgment about a specific case. Likewise, "It is wrong for Billy Bob to steal" is a specific moral value judgment and not a moral principle. To qualify as a moral principle, a moral value judgment must be general in scope. Actually, this follows from the consistency principle. The largest part of everyday moral reasoning takes the form of deducing specific moral value judgments from general moral principles. We'll look next at how this works.

Deriving Specific Moral Value Judgments

From the standpoint of logic, there is something puzzling about deriving a specific moral value judgment from a premise that is not a value judgment. For example, consider this argument:

> Elliott's father depends on Elliott. Therefore, Elliott should take care of him.

We hear such arguments in everyday life and tend to think nothing of them; they certainly do not seem illogical. If facts and statistics are not grounds for making moral decisions, what is? Nevertheless, logically, arguments like this—the basic kind of argument of moral reasoning—are puzzling, because the premise ("Elliott's father depends on Elliott") is not a value judgment, whereas the conclusion ("Elliott should take care of him") is. How, logically, can we get from the "is" premise to the "should" conclusion? How does the "should" get in there?

The answer is that the conclusion of this argument follows logically from the stated premise, only if a *general* moral principle is assumed. In this case, a principle that would work is: Adult children should take care of parents who are dependent on them. Here is the argument with its conclusion:

> Premise: Elliott's father depends on Elliott.
> [Unstated general moral principle: Adult children should take care of their parents who are dependent on them.]
> Conclusion: Therefore, Elliott should take care of his father.

The result is a valid deductive argument. Likewise, any chain of moral reasoning that starts from a claim about facts and ends up with a moral value judgment assumes a general principle that ties the fact-stating "is" premise to the value-stating "should" conclusion.

So far, this is just a point about the logic of moral reasoning. But there is a practical point to be made here as well. It helps clarify matters to consider our general moral principles when we advance moral arguments. If we agree with the premise that Elliott's father depends on Elliott but disagree with the conclusion that Elliott should take care of his father, then our quarrel must be with the unstated general principle that adult children should take care of their parents who are dependent on them. For example, should an adult take care of parents even if it means sacrificing the welfare of his or her spouse? Considering the assumed general moral principle that ties the fact-stating premise with the value-judging conclusion can help clarify the issues involved in a moral decision.

For another example, you sometimes hear this said:

> Homosexuality is unnatural. Therefore, it ought not to be practiced.

A general moral principle assumed here might be: Whatever is unnatural ought not to be done. Bringing that principle to light sets the stage for fruitful discussion. What counts as unnatural? Is it unnatural to fly? To wear clothing? To live to 100? To have sex beyond one's reproductive years? And is it true that unnatural things never should be done? In the natural world, severely disabled offspring are left to fend for themselves; are we wrong to care for our own children who are severely disabled? Scratching oneself in public certainly qualifies as natural, but in our culture doing so is not considered proper.

Earlier, we mentioned our colleague Becky White, who failed a student for copying parts of another student's paper. As it so happens, Professor White also considered whether to penalize the student who allowed his paper to be *read* by the student who ended up copying parts of it. Was it wrong for Charles (whose name we have changed) to show his work to a classmate who then copied parts of it? Thinking that it was wrong would require a general principle, and one that would work would be: It is wrong to show your work to classmates before they have turned in their own work. This principle would yield a deductively valid argument, and there is something to be said for the principle. For example, showing your exam answers to the classmate sitting next to you is grounds for dismissal in many universities. At the same time, showing a term paper to a classmate to get constructive feedback is a good thing. Careful consideration of the earlier principle might lead to the conclusion that, in fact, Charles did nothing wrong.

After a few exercises, we'll have a look at the most general and fundamental moral principles assumed in most moral reasoning.

Deducing the Right Thing to Do

Nearly any kind of reasoning can appear in a discussion of moral matters. For example, we might need to reason inductively to support a claim about the effect of an action on the general happiness. On the other hand, the claim "You should do X" is ordinarily the conclusion of deductive reasoning. Something like this would be typical:

> Everybody who benefited from the program should contribute to its continuance.
> Denzil benefited from the program.
> Therefore, Denzil should contribute to its continuance.

That such arguments are frequently part of a discussion about what one should do is not surprising, for they reflect the consistency principle—that like cases be treated alike. This principle is embedded in the general claim in the premises regarding Denzil. It groups together everybody who benefited from the program as similar cases.

Exercise 12-1   Which of the following claims are value judgments?

▲ 1. Lizards make fine pets.
2. You can get a clothes rack at True Value for less than $15.
3. Melissa gives the best haircuts in this town.
▲ 4. It was a great year for regional politics.
5. Key officials of the Department of Defense are producing their own unverified intelligence reports about an arms buildup.
6. Texas leads the nation in accidental deaths caused by police chases.
▲ 7. Napoleon Bonaparte was the greatest military leader of modern times.
8. Racial segregation is immoral anytime, anywhere.
9. The president deployed a "missile defense" that wasn't adequately tested.
▲ 10. Air consists mainly of nitrogen and oxygen.

Exercise 12-2   Which of the following claims are value judgments?

▲ 1. T-shirts made by Fruit of the Loom are soft and luxurious.
2. Sanders was nearly as detailed as Clinton in reports to the press.
3. The Pentagon was not nearly as supportive of a war as it should have been.
▲ 4. Tens of billions of dollars have been wasted on worthless public transportation schemes.
5. Atlanta is sultry in the summer.
6. Religious school teachers are stricter than their nonreligious counterparts.
▲ 7. Six Flags has the scariest rides in the state.
8. The TV host with the most forceful delivery? That would have to be Al Sharpton.
9. Brandon is not nearly as happy as his wife, Hunter.
10. Hunter is more selfish than she should be.

Exercise 12-3   Which of the following are moral value judgments?

▲ 1. Marina's car puts out horrible smoke; for the sake of us all, she should get it tuned up.
2. After the surgery, Nicky's eyesight improved considerably.
3. Ms. Beeson ought not to have embezzled money from the bank.
▲ 4. Violence is always wrong.
5. Ryder ought to wear that sweater more often; it looks great on him.
6. Jen, you are one of the laziest people I know!
▲ 7. My computer software is really good; it even corrects my grammar.
8. Elizabeth has been very good tonight, according to the babysitter.
9. Judge Ramesh is quite well-informed.
▲ 10. Judge Ramesh's decision gave each party exactly what it deserved.

11. The editor couldn't use my illustrations; she said they were boring.

12. Wow. That was a tasty meal!

13. The last set of essays was better than the first.

14. Do unto others as you would have them do unto you.

15. People who live in glass houses shouldn't throw stones.

16. You really shouldn't make so much noise when the people upstairs are trying to sleep.

17. It is unfair the way Professor Smith asks questions no normal person can answer.

18. "Allegro" means fast, but not that fast!

19. Being in touch with God gives your life meaning and value.

20. Thou shalt not kill.

MAJOR PERSPECTIVES IN MORAL REASONING

Moral reasoning usually takes place within one or more frameworks or perspectives. Here, we consider perspectives that have been especially influential in Western thought.

Consequentialism

The perspective known as **consequentialism** is the view that the *consequences* of a decision, deed, or policy determine its moral value. If an action produces better consequences than the alternatives, then it is the better action, morally speaking. One of the most important versions of this view is **utilitarianism,** which says that, if an act will produce more happiness than will alternatives, it is the right thing to do, and if it will produce less happiness, it would be wrong to do it in place of an alternative that would produce more happiness. In short, act so as to produce the most happiness.

Many of us use a pro–con list of consequences as a guideline when considering what course of action to take. Your parents are divorced; should you spend Thanksgiving with your father's side of the family or with your mother's? Someone will be disappointed, but there may be more people disappointed on one side. Or the disappointment may be more deeply felt on one side. As a utilitarian, you calculate as best you can how your decision will affect the happiness of people on both sides of the equation. Plus, you must factor in how *certain* the outcomes of each alternative are with respect to happiness, assigning more weight to relatively more certain positive outcomes. Because you can generally be more certain of the effect of an act on your own happiness and on the happiness of others you know well, it is often morally proper to favor the act that best promotes your own or their happiness. Of course, you must not use this as an excuse to be entirely self-serving: Your own happiness isn't more important morally than another's. The best course of action morally is not always the one that best promotes your own happiness.

In sum, utilitarians weigh the consequences of the alternatives, pro and con, and then choose the alternative that maximizes happiness. One of the original and most profound intellects behind utilitarianism, Jeremy Bentham (1748–1832), even went so far as to devise a *hedonistic calculus*—a method of assigning actual numerical values to pleasures and pains based on their intensity, certainty, duration, and so forth. Other utilitarians think that some pleasures are of a higher quality (e.g., reading Shakespeare is of a higher quality than watching *The Quest!*). Although there are other important unresolved issues in utilitarianism, the basic idea involves weighing the consequences of possible actions in terms of happiness. Utilitarianism has considerable popular appeal, and real-life moral reasoning is often utilitarian.

Nevertheless, some aspects of the theory are problematic. Typically, when we deliberate whether or not to do something, we don't always take into consideration only the effect of the action on happiness. For example, other people have *rights* that we sometimes take into account. We would not make someone in our family a slave, even if the happiness produced for the family by doing so outweighed the unhappiness it created for the slave. We also consider our *duties* and *obligations.* We think it is our duty to return a loan to someone, even if we are still short of cash and the other person doesn't need the money and doesn't even remember having loaned it to us. If we make a date and then want to break it because we've met the love of our life, we think twice about standing up our original date, even if we believe that our overall happiness will far outweigh the temporary unhappiness of our date. To many, the moral obligation of a promise cannot be ignored for the sake of the overall happiness that might result from breaking it.

In estimating the moral worth of what people do, utilitarianism also seems to discount people's *intentions.* Suppose a mugger attacks somebody just as a huge flower pot falls from a balcony above. The mugger happens to push the individual the instant before the flower pot lands on the exact spot where the victim had been standing. The mugger has saved the victim's life, as it turns out. But would we say that the mugger did a morally good deed just because his action had a happy result? According to utilitarianism, we would—assuming the net result of the action was more happiness than would otherwise have been the case. So, utilitarianism doesn't seem to be the complete story in moral reasoning.

Another important consequentialist theory is **ethical egoism,** the idea that, if an act produces more happiness for *oneself* than will the alternatives, then it is the right thing to do, and if it produces less happiness for oneself than the alternatives, it is wrong to do it. In short, act so as to best promote your own happiness. But any well-thought-out theory of ethical egoism does not prescribe acting purely selfishly, for selfish behavior is not likely to produce the most happiness for oneself in the long run. Still, there is a difference between saying that the reason for doing something is to bring yourself happiness and saying that the reason for doing something is to bring others happiness. The latter doctrine is **ethical altruism,** which discounts one's own happiness as of lesser value than the happiness of others. From this perspective, utilitarianism is the middle ground, in which one's own happiness and others' happiness are treated as equally important.

Duty Theory/Deontologism

Immanuel Kant (1724–1804), who witnessed the beginning phases of the utilitarian philosophy, found utilitarianism deficient because of its neglect, among other things, of moral duty. Kant's theory is a version of what is called **duty theory,** or **deontologism.**

Kant acknowledged that our lives are full of imperatives based on our own situations and our objectives. If we want to advance at work, then it is imperative that we keep our promises; if we are concerned about our friends' happiness, then

Acts and Rules

Thinking of cheating on a test? Maybe the sum total of happiness in the world would be increased by this single *act* of cheating. But if the *principle* involved were adopted widely, the sum total of happiness would be decreased.

This raises the question: When calculating happiness outcomes, should we contemplate happiness outcomes of the particular *act* in question? Or should we contemplate happiness outcomes of adoption of the *principle* involved in the act?

Accordingly, some philosophers make a distinction between "act utilitarianism," which evaluates the moral worth of an act on the happiness it would produce, and "rule utilitarianism," which evaluates the moral worth of an act on the happiness that would be produced by adoption of the principle it exemplifies.

it is imperative that we not talk about them behind their backs. But this type of **hypothetical imperative,** which tells us we ought to do (or ought not to do) something in order to achieve such and such a result, is not a *moral* imperative, Kant argued. Keeping a promise so we'll get a solid reputation is neither morally praiseworthy nor morally blameworthy, he said. For our act to be *morally* praiseworthy, it must be done, not for the sake of some objective, but simply because *it is right.* Our action of keeping our promise is morally praiseworthy, he said, only if we do it simply because it is right to keep our promises. A moral imperative is unconditional or **categorical;*** it prescribes an action, not for the sake of some result, but simply because that action is our moral duty.

It follows from this philosophy that, when it comes to evaluating an action morally, what counts is not the result or consequences of the action, as utilitarianism maintains, but the intention from which it is done. And the morally best intention—indeed, in Kant's opinion the *only* truly morally praiseworthy intention—is that according to which you do something just because it is your moral duty.

But what makes something our moral duty? Some deontologists ground duty in human nature; others ground it in reason; in Western culture, of course, many believe moral duty is set by God. How can we tell what our duty is? Some believe our duty is to be found by consulting conscience; others believe that it is just self-evident or is clear to moral intuition. Those who maintain that human moral duties are established by God usually derive their specific understanding of these duties through interpretations of religious texts such as the Bible, though there is disagreement over what the correct interpretation is as well as who should do the interpreting.

Kant answered the question, How can we tell what our moral duty is? as follows: Suppose you are considering some course of action—say, whether to borrow some money you need very badly. But suppose you know you can't pay back the loan. Is it morally permissible for you to borrow money under such circumstances? Kant said to do this: First, find the *maxim* (principle of action) involved in what you want to do. In the case in question, the maxim is "When I'm in need of money, I'll

---

*Although it is related, this use of "categorical" should not be confused with its use in Chapter 9.

go to my friends and promise I'll pay it back, even if I know I can't." Next, ask yourself, "Could I want this maxim to be a *universal* law or rule, one that everyone should follow?" This process of *universalization* is the feature that lets you judge whether something would work as a moral law, according to Kant. Could you make it a universal law that it is okay for everybody to lie about paying back loans? Hardly: If everyone adopted this principle, then there would be no such thing as loan making. In short, the universalization of your principle undermines the very principle that is universalized. If everyone adopted the principle, then nobody could possibly follow it. The universalization of your principle is illogical, so it is your duty to pay back loans.

As you can see, the results of acting according to Kant's theory can be radically different from the results of acting according to utilitarianism. Utilitarianism would condone borrowing money with no intention of repaying it, assuming that doing so would produce more happiness than would be produced by not doing so. But Kant's theory would not condone it.

Kant also noted that, if you were to borrow a friend's money with no intention of repaying it, you would be treating your friend merely as a means to an end. If you examine cases like this, in which you use other people as mere tools for your own objectives, then, Kant said, you will find in each case a transgression of moral duty, a principle of action that cannot be universalized. Thus, he warned us, it is our moral duty never to treat someone else *merely* as a tool, as means to an end. Of course, Kant did not mean that Moore cannot ask Parker for help on some project; doing so would not be a case of Moore's using Parker *merely* as a tool.

Kant's theory of the moral necessity of never treating other people as mere tools can be modified to support the ideas that people have rights and that treatment of others must always involve fair play. Regardless of whether you subscribe to Kant's version of duty theory, the chances are that your own moral deliberations are more than just strictly utilitarian and may well involve considerations of what you take to be other moral requirements, including your duties and the rights of others.

Moral Relativism

One popular view of ethics, especially perhaps among undergraduates taking a first course in philosophy, is **moral relativism,** the idea that what is right and wrong depends on and is determined by one's group or culture.

A mistake sometimes made in moral reasoning is to confuse the following two claims:

1. What is *believed* to be right and wrong may differ from group to group, society to society, or culture to culture.

2. What *is* right and wrong may differ from group to group, society to society, or culture to culture.

The second claim, but not the first, is moral relativism. Please go back and read the two claims carefully. They are so similar that it takes a moment to see they are actually quite different. But they are different. The first claim is incontestable; the second claim is controversial and problematic. It may well have been the majority belief in ancient Greece that there was nothing wrong with slavery. But that does not mean that at that time there was nothing wrong with slavery.

It is worth noting that moral relativism suffers from three potential difficulties. First, exactly what counts as a group, society, or culture, and what are the criteria for membership in one? How many groups, societies, or cultures do you belong to? You probably find it hard to say. This makes it difficult to specify which set of general principles apply to a person.

The second difficulty is that conflicting views about moral principles are to be found within all but the very smallest groups. For example, even within small communities, people may disagree about gay marriage or abortion.

Mill's Fallacies

The founders of utilitarianism (discussed in the text) are the English philosophers Jeremy Bentham (1748–1832), John Stuart Mill (1806–1873), and Harriet Taylor Mill (1807–1858). After he died Bentham was paid the rare tribute of having his skeleton (dressed in his clothes) displayed at the University College in London. Apparently it still attends meetings of the College Council where Bentham is listed as "present but not voting."

Mill, Bentham godson, was a precocious young scholar who read Greek by the time he was 3. His book, *A System of Logic*, was a best seller in England, and not just among philosophers but among the general public. YouTube was not available. Harriet Taylor was a woman's rights advocate, and collaborated with John Stuart Mill on many books.

Every student of logic and philosophy should know that Mill gave the following infamous argument for utilitarianism, in the fourth chapter of his treatise that went by that name:

> The only proof capable of being given that an object is visible, is that people actually see it. The only proof that a sound is audible, is that people hear it . . . In like manner, I apprehend, the sole evidence it is possible to produce that anything is desirable, is that people do actually desire it . . . No reason can be given why the general happiness is desirable, except that each person, so far as he believes it to be attainable, desires his own happiness . . . we have not only all the proof which the case admits of, but all which it is possible to require, that happiness is a good: that each person's happiness is a good to that person, and the general happiness, therefore, a good to the aggregate of all persons.

Now Mill said that this was not a proof in the ordinary sense. That's just as well, because in the ordinary sense it contains three fallacies:

1. *Deriving an ought from an is*—deriving what people ought to do from what they actually do. We discussed this earlier, on pages 394–395, when we said that arguments that derive an ought-statement from an is-statement assume a general moral principle.

2. *Equivocation*—the argument moves from "desirable" in the sense of being sought after, to "desirable" in the sense of being something that should be sought after. (See Chapter 8 for a discussion of equivocation.)

3. *Composition*—the argument moves from the fact that individual happiness is a good thing, to the conclusion that the collective happiness is a good thing. (See Chapter 8 for a discussion of composition.)

Eminent philosophers have defended Mill by trying to show that he didn't really commit these mistakes. That he has defenders suggests they think he needs defending.

Our own view is that Mill knew what he was doing and that is why he said that this was not a proof in the ordinary sense. We agree that it is not a proof in the ordinary sense. Not knowing any other sense, we regard it as a piece of rhetoric (Chapter 4).

A third difficulty is perhaps less obvious. To understand the problem, if someone belongs to a society that believes it is permissible to kill Americans, then you, as a moral relativist, must concede it is permissible for that person to kill Americans. But if Americans in general agree on anything, it is that nobody should kill another person simply because of his or her national status. Therefore, if you are an American, you must also say it is *not* permissible for that person to kill Americans. Subscribing to moral relativism has placed you in a self-contradictory position.

Another popular moral perspective is **moral subjectivism,** the idea that what is right and wrong is merely a matter of subjective opinion, that thinking that something is right or wrong makes it right or wrong for that individual. We considered subjectivism in Chapter 1 and saw there the mistake in thinking that all value judgments are subjective.

Religious Relativism

As you might expect, **religious relativism** is the belief that what is right and wrong is whatever one's religious culture or society deems. The problems attending this view are the same as those for other versions of relativism. First, what counts as a religious culture or society and as membership within one? Are Baptists and Catholics part of the same culture? Are you a Christian even if you never attend church? Second, even within a single culture, conflicting moral views are likely to be found. When the Presbyterian Church voted in 2015 to recognize same-sex marriage, the vote was not unanimous.

Third, those who belong to one religion might well consider practices of other religions to be sinful. For example, members of the first religion may think it is sinful to worship a false god. Thus, according to religious relativism, if you belong to the first religion, then you must say that those who worship the other god are doing something sinful, because that is the view of your religion. But as a religious relativist, you must also say that those who worship the other god are *not* doing something sinful.

Religious Absolutism

One way out of this difficulty might be to subscribe to **religious absolutism,** which maintains that the correct moral principles are those accepted by the "correct" religion. A problem, of course, we cannot say which, if any, religion is the correct one.

I'm not guilty of murder. I'm guilty of obeying the laws of the Creator.

—Benjamin Matthew Williams, who committed suicide while awaiting sentencing for having murdered a gay couple

Virtue Ethics

Up to this point, the ethical perspectives discussed have focused on the question of what is the right or proper act, decision, practice, or policy. For that reason, these perspectives are referred to as "ethics of conduct." However, another approach, one predominant in classical Greek thinking, has regained popularity among some contemporary moral philosophers. This approach, known as **virtue ethics,** focuses not on what to do but on how to be.

To find an excellent example of virtue ethics, one need look no further than the Boy Scout pledge. A Boy Scout doesn't pledge to do or to refrain from doing this or that particular action; instead, he pledges to *be* a certain kind of person. He pledges to *be* trustworthy, loyal, helpful, friendly, courteous, kind, brave, and so forth. This is a list of "virtues," or traits of character. A person who has them is disposed by habit to act in certain ways and not to act in others.

The ancient Greeks believed it was supremely important for a person to achieve psychological and physical balance; and to do that, the person needed to develop a consistently good character. A person out of balance will not be able to assess a situation properly and will tend to overreact or to not react strongly enough; moreover, such a person will not know his or her proper limits. People who recognize their own qualifications and limitations and who are capable of reacting to the right degree, at the right time, toward the right person, and for the right reason are virtuous persons. They understand the value of the idea of moderation: not too much and not too little, but in each case a response that is just right.

Aristotle (384–322 B.C.E.) regarded virtue as a trait, like having wisdom, being just, or being courageous, that we acquire when we use our capacity to reason to moderate our impulses and appetites. The largest part of Aristotle's major ethical writing, the *Nicomachean Ethics,* is devoted to analysis of specific moral virtues as means between extremes (e.g., being courageous is the mean between fearing everything and fearing nothing). He also emphasized that virtue is a matter of habit; it is a trait, a way of living.

Virtue ethics is not an abstruse ethical theory. Many of us (fortunately) wish to be (or to become) persons of good character.

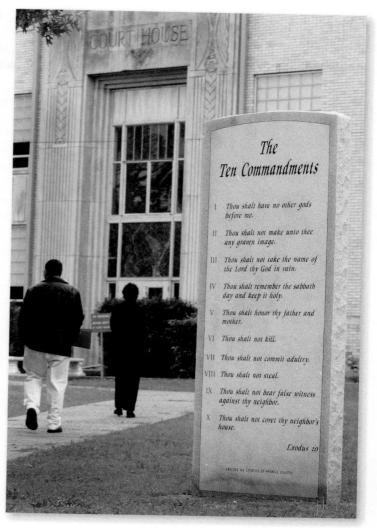

■ The Ten Commandments represent the perspective of religious absolutism.

And as a practical matter, when we are deliberating a course of action, our approach often is to consider what someone whose character we admire would do in the circumstances.

Still, it is possible that virtue theory alone cannot answer all moral questions. Each of us may face moral dilemmas of such a nature that it simply isn't clear what course of action is required by someone of good character.

Determine which ethical perspective is primarily reflected in each of the following statements. Choose from

Exercise 12-4

    A = consequentialism

    B = duty ethics/deontology

    C = virtue ethics

    D = moral relativism

    E = religious absolutism

1. Yes, innocent civilians have been killed in Syria. But in the long run, the world will be a safer place if Syria becomes a democracy.

2. Although many cultures have practiced human sacrifice, within the culture it was not thought to be wrong. So, human sacrifice within those cultures wasn't really immoral.

3. *(Note: "Preferential treatment" refers to the practice of some universities and professional schools of lowering entrance requirements for women and ethnic minorities.)* Preferential treatment is wrong, period. You shouldn't discriminate against anyone, no matter how much society benefits from it.

4. Sure, we might benefit from expanding Highway 99. But seizing a person's property against his or her wishes is just wrong, period.

5. Sure, we might benefit from expanding Highway 99. But it's wrong to seize someone's property, at least in this country. In our society, property rights are fundamental.

6. Sure, we might benefit from expanding Highway 99. But it's wrong to seize someone's property! You have a God-given right to own property.

7. If a company doesn't want to hire a woman, nobody should force it to. A company has a right to hire whomever it wants!

8. You have to balance a person's rights against the common good. Pornography isn't good for a society, and we should get rid of it.

9. Gay marriage? I think it is only fair! The right to happiness is a basic human right.

10. Gay marriage? I am against it. Once gays start marrying, the next thing you know, brothers and sisters will get married. Then moms and sons. Society will come apart at the seams.

Exercise 12-5

In each of the following passages, a general moral principle must be added as an extra premise to make the argument valid. Supply such a principle.

Example

Mrs. Montez's new refrigerator was delivered yesterday, and it stopped working altogether. She has followed the directions carefully but still can't make it work. The people she bought it from should either come out and make it work or replace it with another one.

Principle

People should make certain the things they sell work.

1. After borrowing Jacob's car, Mason had an accident and crumpled a fender. So, Mason ought to pay whatever expenses were involved in getting Jacob's car fixed.

2. When Sarah bought the lawn mower from Jean, she promised to pay another fifty dollars on the first of the month. Since it is now the first, Sarah should pay Jean the money.

3. Jayden worked on his sister's car all weekend. The least she could do is let him borrow the car for his job interview next Thursday.

4. Noah is obligated to supply ten cords of firewood to the lodge by the beginning of October, since he signed a contract guaranteeing delivery of the wood by that date.

5. Since it was revealed yesterday on the 11:00 news that Mayor Ahearn has been taking bribes, he should step down any day now.

6. As a political candidate, Havenhurst promised to put an end to crime in the inner city. Now that she is in office, we'd like to see results.

7. Since he has committed his third felony, he should automatically go to prison for twenty-five years.

8. Laura's priest has advised Laura and her husband not to sign up for the in vitro fertilization program at the hospital, because such treatments are unnatural.

9. Ali has been working overtime a lot lately, so he should receive a bonus.

10. It is true there are more voters in the northern part of the state. But that shouldn't allow the north to dictate to the south.

MORAL DELIBERATION

Before you began this chapter, you may have assumed that moral discussion is merely an exchange of personal opinion or feeling, one that reserves no place for reason or critical thinking. But moral discussion usually assumes some sort of perspective like those we have mentioned here. Actually, in real life, moral reasoning is often a mixture of perspectives, a blend of utilitarian considerations weighted somewhat toward one's own happiness, modified by ideas about duties, rights, and obligations, and mixed often with a thought, perhaps guilty, about what the ideally virtuous person (a parent, a teacher) would do in similar circumstances. It also sometimes involves mistakes—value judgments may be confused with other types of claims, inconsistencies may occur, inductive arguments may be weak or deductive arguments invalid, fallacious reasoning may be present, and so forth.

We can make headway in our own thinking about moral issues by trying to get clear on what perspective, if any, we are assuming. For example, suppose we are thinking about the death penalty. Our first thought might be that society is much better off if murderers are executed. Are we then assuming a utilitarian perspective? Asking ourselves this question might lead us to consider whether there are *limits* to what we would do for the common good—for example, would we be willing to risk sacrificing an innocent person? It might also lead us to consider how we might *establish* whether society is better off if murderers are executed—if we are utilitarians, then ultimately we will have to establish this if our reasoning is to be compelling.

Or suppose we have seen a friend cheating on an exam. Should we report it to the teacher? Whatever our inclination, it may be helpful to consider our perspective. Are we viewing things from a utilitarian perspective? That is, are we assuming that it would promote the most happiness overall to report our friend? Or do we simply believe that it is our duty to report him or her, come what may? Would a virtuous person report his or her friend? Each of these questions will tend to focus our attention on a particular set of considerations—those that are the most relevant to our way of thinking.

Why Moral Problems Seem Unresolvable

Ethical differences sometimes seem irreconcilable. Often the problem comes down to a difference in moral perspective. Proponents of affirmative action often speak of it as promising a greater good. Opponents regard it as treating people unequally. Those who favor gun control think public safety will be improved if more restrictions are placed on gun ownership. Those who oppose restrictions speak of gun control as violating Constitutional rights.

    This is not to say that ethical differences always come down to different moral perspectives. Pro-life and pro-choice adherents share a rights-based perspective; they disagree over which right is more basic, a woman's right to choose, or the rights of the unborn. Both parties presumably agree that in the absence of a compelling justification it is wrong to take a human life. They seem to disagree, however, as to when life as a human begins.

It may occur to you to wonder at this point if there is any reason for choosing among perspectives. The answer to this question is yes: Adherents of these positions, philosophers such as those we mentioned, offer grounding or support for their perspectives in theories about human nature, the natural universe, the nature of morality, and other things. In other words, they have *arguments* to support their views. If you are interested, we recommend a course in ethics.

Exercise 12-6

Identify each of the following questions as A, B, or C.

    A = moral value judgment

    B = nonmoral value judgment

    C = not a value judgment

▲   1. You should avoid making such a large down payment.

    2. You can't go wrong taking Professor Anderson's class.

    3. Misdemeanors are punished less severely than felonies.

▲   4. Anyone who would do a thing like that to another human being is beneath contempt.

    5. Anthony thought about homeschooling his kids.

    6. Anthony should have thought about homeschooling his kids.

▲   7. Anthony thought about whether he should homeschool his kids.

    8. Did Anthony think about homeschooling his kids? Apparently.

▲   9. It was a darn good thing Anthony thought about homeschooling his kids.

    10. You should have left a note when you dented that car.

Exercise 12-7

Identify each of the following statements as A, B, or C.

    A = moral value judgment

    B = nonmoral value judgment

    C = not a value judgment

▲   1. The employees deserve health care benefits.

2. Last year, the employees may have deserved health care benefits, but they don't now.

3. The employees' health care benefits consumed 40 percent of our operating costs.

▲   4. The health care benefits we gave the employees last year were excessive.

5. The health care benefits we gave the employees were generous, but not excessive.

6. Sophia is the best photographer in the department.

▲   7. Susan should not have used a filter when she made those photographs.

8. Olivia upset that man when she photographed him; she shouldn't have done that.

9. Madison's photographs are exquisite in their realism and detail.

▲ 10. Be more careful mowing the lawn! You could hurt yourself.

11. Be more tactful dealing with people! You could hurt them.

12. Use more fertilizer! You'll get better plants.

13. Use more deodorant! Your kids will thank you for it.

14. Avery works harder than anyone else in the office.

15. It was not right of Ava to dump Logan without giving him a chance to explain what happened.

Answer the question or respond to the statement that concludes each item.   Exercise 12-8

▲   1. Tory thinks women should have the same rights as men. However, he also thinks that, although a man should have the right to marry a woman, a woman should not have the right to marry a woman. Is Tory being consistent in his views?

▲   2. At Shelley's university, the minimum GPA requirement for admission is relaxed for 6 percent of incoming students. Half of those admitted under this program are women and minorities, and the other half are athletes, children of alumni, and talented art and music students. Shelley is opposed to special admissions programs for women and minority students; she is not opposed to special admission programs for art and music students, athletes, or children of alumni. Is she consistent?

▲   3. Marin does not approve of abortion because the Bible says explicitly, "Thou shalt not kill." "'Thou shalt not kill' means thou shalt not kill," he says. Marin does, however, approve of capital punishment. Is Marin consistent?

4. Koko believes that adults should have the unrestricted right to read whatever material they want to read, but she does not believe that her seventeen-year-old daughter Gina should have the unrestricted right to read whatever she wants to read. Is Koko consistent?

5. Jackson maintains that the purpose of marriage is procreation. On these grounds, he opposes same-sex marriages. "Gays can't create children," he explains. However, he does not oppose marriages between heterosexual partners who cannot have children due to age or medical reasons. "It's not the same," he says. Is Jackson being consistent?

6. Zoey thinks the idea of outlawing cigarettes is ridiculous. "Give me a break," she says. "If you want to screw up your health with cigarettes, that's your own business." However, Zoey does not approve of the legalization of marijuana. "Hel-loh-o," she says. "Marijuana is a *drug,* and the last thing we need is more druggies." Is Zoey being consistent?

7. California's Proposition 209 amends the California state constitution to prohibit "discrimination or preferential treatment" in state hiring based on race, gender, or ethnicity. Opponents say that Proposition 209 singles out women and members of racial and ethnic minorities for unequal treatment. Their argument is that Proposition 209 makes it impossible for members of these groups to obtain redress for past discrimination through preferential treatment, whereas members of other groups who may have suffered past discrimination (gays, for example, or members of religious groups) are not similarly restricted from seeking redress. Evaluate this argument.

8. Harold prides himself on being a liberal. He is delighted when a federal court issues a preliminary ruling that California's Proposition 209 (see previous item) is unconstitutional. "It makes no difference that a majority of California voters approved the measure," Harold argues. "If it is unconstitutional, then it is unconstitutional." However, California voters also recently passed an initiative that permits physicians to prescribe marijuana, and Harold is livid when the U.S. attorney general says that the federal government will ignore the California statute and will use federal law to prosecute any physician who prescribes marijuana. Is Harold consistent?

9. Dylan is of the opinion that we should not perform medical experiments on people against their will, but he has no problem with medical experiments being done on dogs. Chloe disagrees. She sees no relevant difference between the two cases.

   "What, no difference between people and dogs?" Dylan asks.

   "There are differences, but no differences that are relevant to the issue," Chloe responds. "Dogs feel pain and experience fear just as much as people."

   Is Chloe's position correct?

10. Mr. Bork is startled when a friend tells him he should contribute to the welfare of others' children as much as to his own.

    "Why on earth should I do that?" Mr. Bork asks his friend.

    "Because," his friend responds, "there is no relevant difference between the two cases. The fact that your children are yours does not mean that there is something different about them that gives them a greater entitlement to happiness than anyone else's children."

    How should Mr. Bork respond?

11. The university wants to raise the requirements for tenure. Professor Peterson, who doesn't have tenure, says that doing so is unfair to her. She argues that those who received tenure before she did weren't required to meet such exacting standards; therefore, neither should she. Is she correct?

12. Reverend Heinz has no objection to same-sex marriages but is opposed to polygamous marriages. Is there a relevant difference between the two cases, or is Reverend Heinz being inconsistent?

Exercise 12-9

1. Daniel needs to sell his car, but he doesn't have money to spend on repairs. He plans to sell the vehicle to a private party without mentioning that the rear

brakes are worn. Evaluate Daniel's plan of action from a deontological perspective—that is, can the maxim of Daniel's plan be universalized?

2. Defend affirmative action from a utilitarian perspective.

3. Criticize affirmative action from a deontological perspective. (*Hint:* Consider Kant's theory that people must never be treated as means only.)

4. Criticize or defend medical experimentation on animals from a utilitarian perspective.

5. Criticize or defend medical experimentation on animals from a religious absolutist perspective.

6. A company has the policy of not promoting women to be vice presidents. What might be said about this policy from the perspective of virtue ethics?

7. What might be said about the policy mentioned in item 6 from the perspective of utilitarianism?

8. Evaluate embryonic stem cell research from a utilitarian perspective.

9. In your opinion, would the virtuous person, the person of the best moral character, condemn, approve or be indifferent to bisexuality?

10. "We can't condemn the founding fathers for owning slaves; people didn't think there was anything wrong with it at the time." Comment on this remark from the standpoint of deontologism.

11. "Let's have some fun and see how your parrot looks without feathers." (The example is from philosopher Joseph Grcic.) Which of the following perspectives seems best equipped to condemn this suggestion?
    a. utilitarianism
    b. deontologism
    c. religious absolutism
    d. virtue ethics
    e. moral relativism

12. "Might makes right." Could a utilitarian accept this? Could a virtue ethicist? Could Kant? Could a moral relativist? Could someone who subscribes to divine command theory?

> This is Darwin's natural selection at its very best. The highest bidder gets youth and beauty.

Exercise 12-10

These are the words of fashion photographer Ron Harris, who auctioned the ova of fashion models via the Internet. The model got the full bid price, and the website took a commission of an additional 20 percent. The bid price included no medical costs, though it listed specialists who were willing to perform the procedure. Harris, who created the video "The 20 Minute Workout," said the egg auction gave people the chance to reproduce beautiful children who would have an advantage in society. Critics, however, were numerous. "It screams of unethical behavior," one said. "It is acceptable for an infertile couple to choose an egg donor and compensate her for her time, inconvenience, and discomfort," he said. "But this is something else entirely. Among other things, what happens to the child if he or she turns out to be unattractive?"

Discuss the (moral) pros and cons of this issue for five or ten minutes in groups. Then take a written stand on the question "Should human eggs be auctioned to the highest bidder?" When you are finished, discuss which moral perspective seems to be the one in which you are operating.

LEGAL REASONING

When we think about arguments and disputes, the first image to come to most minds is probably that of an attorney arguing a case in a court of law. Although it's true that lawyers require a solid understanding of factual matters related to their cases and of psychological considerations as well, especially where juries are involved, it is still safe to say that a lawyer's stock-in-trade is argument. Lawyers are successful—in large part—to the extent that they can produce evidence in support of the conclusion that most benefits their clients—in other words, their success depends on how well they can put premises and conclusions together into convincing arguments (This does not mean we discount the use of rhetorical devices and persuasive techniques of all sorts in courtrooms. Many cases have been decided on the basis of bad arguments accompanied by some powerful rhetoric.)

When one thinks of the many varieties of law—administrative law, commercial law, criminal law, international law, tax law, and so on—one is apt to think that there may be no distinctive common ground that one might call "uniquely legal reasoning." This conclusion is absolutely correct. Still, we can distinguish broadly between questions of *interpreting and applying the law in specific instances* and questions related to *what the law should be.* Typically, jurists and practicing attorneys are more interested in the former type of question and legal philosophers in the latter.

Reasoning used by jurists and attorneys in applying the law is both deductive and inductive; if deductive, the reasoning can be sound, valid, or invalid; and if inductive, it can range from strong to weak. Deductive reasoning, of course, includes categorical and hypothetical reasoning; and inductive reasoning includes generalizing, reasoning by analogy, and reasoning about cause and effect. Reasoning by analogy and reasoning about cause and effect deserve special mention in connection with applying the law.

One kind of argument occupies a special place in applying the law: the **appeal to precedent.** This is the practice of using a case that has already been decided as an authoritative guide in deciding a new case that is similar. The appeal to precedent is none other than an argument by analogy, in which the current case is argued to be sufficiently like the previous case to warrant deciding it in the same way. Appeal to precedent also assumes the consistency principle that is found in moral reasoning: Cases that aren't relevantly different must be treated the same way. To treat similar cases differently would be illogical; it would also be unjust.

The Latin name for the principle of appeal to precedent is *stare decisis* ("Don't change settled decisions," more or less). In the terminology of Chapter 11, the "analogues" are the earlier, settled cases on one hand and the current case on the other. The important question is whether the analogues are so similar that treating them differently would violate *stare decisis.* Apart from their significance to the parties involved, legal reasoning by analogy is not different in principle from reasoning by analogy in any other context.

The appeal to precedent is embodied in what is usually called the "common law." Originally

■ John Roberts, Chief Justice of the U.S. Supreme Court, which decides the constitutionality of legislation, actions of public officials, lower court decisions, and other public matters. This power, known as "judicial review," is not explicit in the U.S. Constitution but was established in *Marbury v. Madison* (1803), a landmark decision of the Supreme Court.

developed in England over a thousand years ago, common law is the reliance on precedent as the determining factor in present decisions. Its logical basis is the principle just described of treating similar cases similarly. Common law legal systems are distinguished from civil law systems, where the greater reliance is on statutory enactments. It is usual for modern legal systems to make use of a combination of these two influences, with English influence causing an emphasis on common law and Roman influence an emphasis on civil law. Anyhow, that similar cases must be decided according to consistently applied rules is, as Wikipedia puts it, at the heart of all common law systems. And that conforms to our principle of justice.

Also especially important when it comes to applying the law is reasoning about cause and effect. Causation is the foundation of legal liability. In some contexts, that a party is legally liable for something may mean more than simply that he or she caused it; but having caused it is normally a necessary condition for being legally liable for it. In Chapter 11, we discussed causation in the law.

Justifying Laws: Four Perspectives

The reasoning employed to justify or defend specific laws is similar to moral reasoning, discussed in the previous section. Both types of reasoning involve applying general principles to specific cases, and both refer ultimately to one or more of a handful of basic perspectives within which the reasoning takes place. Indeed, the moral perspectives already discussed can and are used to justify and defend specific laws. For example, the utilitarian idea that it is desirable to increase the sum total of happiness is used to defend eminent domain (by which a state seizes a person's property without his or her consent). And the deontological principle that others should not be used as the means to some end is used to argue against it. The harm principle, discussed below, which holds that only what harms others should be legally forbidden, is an extension of deontological ethics (although its most eloquent exponent was the utilitarian John Stuart Mill).

Of course, we are often most interested in the justification of laws that would forbid us to do something we might otherwise want to do or would require us to do something we would prefer not to do. Consider, then, whether a law that forbids doing X should be enacted by your state legislature.* Typically, there are four main grounds, or "perspectives," on which a supporter of a law can base his or her justification. The first is simply that doing X is immoral. The claim that the law should make illegal anything that is immoral is the basis of the position known as **legal moralism.** One might use such a basis to justify laws forbidding murder, assault, or unorthodox sexual practices. For a legal moralist, the kinds of arguments designed to show that an action is immoral are directly relevant to the question of whether the action should be illegal.

The next ground on which a law can be justified is probably the one that most people think of first. It is very closely associated with John Stuart Mill (1806–1873) and is known as the **harm principle:** The only legitimate basis for forbidding X is

---

*The example here is of a criminal law—part of a penal code designed to require and forbid certain behaviors and to punish offenders. The situation is a little different in civil law, a main goal of which is to shift the burden of a wrongful harm (a "tort") from the person on whom it fell to another, more suitable person—usually the one who caused the harm.

Stand Your Ground

More than half the states in the United States have adopted the "Castle doctrine"—the legal position that a person does not have an obligation to retreat from a threat in his or her own home, and further that the person may use deadly force in order to thwart an attacker in such circumstances. In Florida, as in several other states, a further law was passed in 2005 that extended the right to use deadly force in self-defense to any place the defender has a legal right to be. Such laws have come to be known as "stand your ground" (SYG) laws.*

Whether the SYG laws have reduced or increased violence is not clear. Proponents and opponents have both cited evidence, and there have been studies that interested parties can check before making up their minds.

These laws came into sharp focus in February 2012, when George Zimmerman, a 28-year-old "multiracial" Hispanic, shot and killed Trayvon Martin, a 17-year-old black youth during a much-disputed confrontation. Martin was walking home from a convenience store to the house where his father's fiancée lived and where he was staying. Zimmerman, the neighborhood watch coordinator, was in his vehicle when he spotted Martin, and he called police to report him as behaving suspiciously. Zimmerman left his car during the call, and soon after a violent encounter ensued, the only account of which is Zimmerman's, since Martin was shot dead in the fight. Zimmerman claimed Martin, who was unarmed, attacked him and that he fired in self-defense.

The Sanford, Florida, police were subjected to criticism for delaying bringing charges against the shooter. The cause of the delay, according to the police and local prosecutors, was the stand your ground law, which provides not only a defense in a criminal trial but also immunity from civil suits and from a criminal trial under the right circumstances.

Zimmerman went to trial in June 2013 on charges of second-degree murder and manslaughter. On July 13, 2013, a jury acquitted him of both charges. Although Florida's SYG law was clearly relevant to the case, Zimmerman's lawyers made scant reference to it during their defense. The extent to which it influenced the jury is not known.

*Some supporters of these laws, in a salute to Clint Eastwood's Dirty Harry character, refer to them as "make my day" laws; opponents of the laws, including the Brady Campaign to Prevent Gun Violence, refer to them as "shoot first" laws.

that doing X causes harm to others. Notice that the harm principle states not just that harm to others is a good ground for forbidding an activity but that it is the *only* ground. (In terms of the way we formulated such claims in Chapter 10, on propositional logic, the principle would be stated, "It is legitimate to forbid doing X *if and only if* doing X causes harm to others.") A person who defends this principle and who wants to enact a law forbidding X will present evidence that doing X does indeed cause harm to others. Her arguments could resemble any of the types covered in earlier chapters.

A third ground on which our hypothetical law might be based is legal paternalism. **Legal paternalism** is the view that laws can be justified if they prevent people from doing harm to themselves; that is, they forbid or make it impossible to do X, *for a person's own good.* Examples include laws that require that seat belts be worn while riding in automobiles and that helmets be worn while riding on motorcycles. Many laws prohibiting or limiting the use of drugs also fall into this category.

The last of the usual bases for justifying criminal laws is that some behavior is generally found offensive. The **offense principle** says that a law forbidding X can be justifiable if X causes great offense to others. Laws forbidding public urination and burning of the flag are often justified on this ground.

What is the law, and how should it be applied? These questions are perhaps somewhat easier than the question, What should the law be? But they are still complicated. An example will provide an indication. Back in Chapter 3, we discussed vague concepts, and we found that it is impossible to rid our talk entirely of vagueness. Here's an example from the law. Let's suppose that a city ordinance forbids vehicles on the paths in the city park. Clearly, a person violates the law if he or she drives a truck or a car down the paths. But what about a motorbike? A bicycle? A go-cart? A child's pedal car? Just what counts as a vehicle and what does not? This is the kind of issue that must often be decided in court because—not surprisingly—the governing body writing the law could not foresee all the possible items that might, in somebody's mind, count as a vehicle.

The process of narrowing down when a law applies and when it does not, then, is another kind of reasoning problem that occurs in connection with the law.

Exercise 12-11

For each of the following kinds of laws, pick at least one of the four grounds for justification discussed in the text—legal moralism, the harm principle, legal paternalism, and the offense principle—and construct an argument designed to justify the law. You may not agree either with the law or with the argument; the exercise is to see if you can connect the law to a justifying principle. For many laws, more than one kind of justification is possible, so there can be more than one good answer for many of these.

▲ 1. Laws against shoplifting

▲ 2. Laws against forgery

3. Laws against suicide

▲ 4. Laws against spitting on the sidewalk

5. Laws against driving under the influence of drugs or alcohol

▲ 6. Laws against adultery

7. Laws against marriage between two people of the same sex

8. Laws that require people to have licenses before they practice medicine

9. Laws that require drivers of cars to have driver's licenses

▲ 10. Laws against desecrating a corpse

11. Laws against trespassing

12. Laws against torturing your pet (even though it may be legal to kill your pet, if it is done humanely)

Exercise 12-12

This exercise is for class discussion or a short writing assignment. In the text, "Vehicles are prohibited on the paths in the park" was used as an example of a law that might require clarification. Decide whether the law should be interpreted to forbid motorcycles, bicycles, children's pedal cars, and battery-powered remote-control cars. On what grounds are you deciding each of these cases?

Exercise 12-13

The U.S. Supreme Court came to a decision some years ago about the proper application of the word "use." Briefly, the case in point was about a man named John Angus Smith, who traded a handgun for cocaine. The law under which Smith was charged provided for a much more severe penalty—known as an enhanced penalty—if a gun was used in a drug-related crime than if no gun was involved. (In this case, the enhanced penalty was a mandatory thirty-year sentence; the "unenhanced" penalty was five years.) Justice Antonin Scalia argued that Smith's penalty should not be enhanced because he did not use the gun in the way the writers of the law had in mind; he did not use it *as a gun*. Justice Sandra Day O'Connor argued that the law requires only the *use* of a gun, not any particular *kind* of use. If you were a judge, would you vote with Scalia or with O'Connor? Construct an argument in support of your position. (The decision of the Court is given in the answer section at the back of the book.)

AESTHETIC REASONING

Like moral and legal thinking, aesthetic thinking relies on a conceptual framework that integrates fact and value. Judgments about beauty and art—even judgments about whether something is a work of art or just an everyday object—appeal to principles that identify sources of aesthetic or artistic value. So, when you make such a judgment, you are invoking aesthetic concepts, even if you have not made them explicit to yourself or to others.

Eight Aesthetic Principles

Here are some of the aesthetic principles that most commonly support or influence artistic creation and critical judgment about art. The first three identify value in art with an object's ability to fulfill certain cultural or social functions.

1. *Objects are aesthetically valuable if they are meaningful or teach us truths.* For example, Aristotle says that tragic plays teach us general truths about the human condition in a dramatic way that cannot be matched by real-life experience. Many people believe art shows us truths that are usually hidden from us by the practical concerns of daily life.

2. *Objects are aesthetically valuable if they have the capacity to convey values or beliefs that are central to the cultures or traditions in which they originate or that are important to the artists who made them.* For example, John Milton's poem *Paradise Lost* expresses the seventeenth-century Puritan view of the relationship between human beings and God.

3. *Objects are aesthetically valuable if they have the capacity to help bring about social or political change.* For instance, Abraham Lincoln commented that Harriet Beecher Stowe's *Uncle Tom's Cabin* contributed to the antislavery movement.

Another group of principles identifies aesthetic value with objects' capacities to produce certain subjective—that is, psychological—states in persons who experience or appreciate them. Here are some of the most common or influential principles of the second group:

4. *Objects are aesthetically valuable if they have the capacity to produce pleasure in those who experience or appreciate them.* For instance, the nineteenth-century

■ Christo, The Gates. This particular art work occupied 23 miles of pathways in New York City's Central Park. Public reaction varied from lavish praise to outright ridicule. This section of the book considers principles on which artistic creation is commonly judged.

German philosopher Friedrich Nietzsche identifies one kind of aesthetic value with the capacity to create a feeling of ecstatic bonding in audiences.

5. *Objects are aesthetically valuable if they have the capacity to produce certain emotions we value, at least when the emotion is brought about by art rather than life.* In the *Poetics,* Aristotle observes that we welcome the feelings of fear created in us by frightening dramas, whereas in everyday life fear is an experience we would rather avoid. The psychoanalyst Sigmund Freud offers another version of this principle: While we enjoy art, we permit ourselves to have feelings so subversive that we have to repress them to function in everyday life.

6. *Objects are aesthetically valuable if they have the capacity to produce special nonemotional experiences, such as a feeling of autonomy or the willing suspension of disbelief.* This principle is the proposal of the nineteenth-century English poet Samuel Taylor Coleridge. One of art's values, he believes, is its ability to stimulate our power to exercise our imaginations and consequently to free ourselves from thinking that is too narrowly practical.

Notice that principles 4 through 6 resemble the first three in that they identify aesthetic value with the capacity to fulfill a function. According to these last three, the specified function is to create some kind of subjective or inner state in audiences; according to the first three, however, art's function is to achieve such objective outcomes as conveying information or knowledge or preserving or changing culture or

The watercolor by Alicia Alvarez on this page, and the pen and ink by Julia Ross on the next page: are lighthearted portrayals of the feminine, although they accomplish this in very different ways.

society. But there are yet other influential aesthetic principles that do not characterize art in terms of capacities for performing functions. According to one commonly held principle, art objects attain aesthetic value by virtue of their possessing a certain special aesthetic property or certain special formal configurations.

7. *Objects are aesthetically valuable if they possess a special aesthetic property or exhibit a special aesthetic form.* Sometimes this aesthetic property is called "beauty," and sometimes it is given another name. For instance, the early-twentieth-century art critic Clive Bell insists that good art is valuable for its own sake, not because it fulfills any function. To know whether a work is good aesthetically, he urges, one need only look at it or listen to it to see or hear whether it has "significant form." "Significant form" is valuable for itself, not for any function it performs.

Finally, one familiar principle insists that no reasons can be given to support judgments about art. Properly speaking, those who adhere to this principle think that to approve or disapprove of art is to express an unreasoned preference rather than to render judgment. This principle may be stated as follows:

8. *No reasoned argument can conclude that objects are aesthetically valuable or valueless.* This principle is expressed in the Latin saying *"De gustibus non est disputandum,"* or "Tastes can't be disputed."

The principles summarized here by no means exhaust the important views about aesthetic value, nor are they complete expositions of the views they represent. Historically, views about the nature of art have proven relatively fluid, for they must be responsive to the dynamics of technological and cultural change. Moreover, even though the number of familiar conceptions of aesthetic value is limited, there are many alternative ways of stating these that combine the thoughts behind them in somewhat different ways.

Consequently, to attempt to label each principle with a name invites confusion. For example, let's consider whether any of the principles might be designated

The story is told of the American tourist in Paris who told Pablo Picasso that he didn't like modern paintings because they weren't realistic. Picasso made no immediate reply. A few minutes later the tourist showed him a snapshot of his house.

"My goodness," said Picasso, "is it really *as small as that?*"

—JACOB BRAUDE

formalism, which is an important school or style of art. Although the seventh principle explicitly ascribes aesthetic value to a work's form as opposed to its function, the formal properties of artworks also figure as valuable, although only as means to more valuable ends, in certain formulations of the first six principles. For instance, some scholars, critics, and artists think certain formal patterns in works of art can evoke corresponding emotions, social patterns, or pleasures in audiences—for example, slow music full of minor chords is commonly said to make people feel sad. On the other hand, the art works on this and the preceding page would generally be seen as having a contrary effect.

You should understand that all of the principles presented here merely serve as a basic framework within which you can explore critical thinking about art. If you are interested in the arts, you will very likely want to develop a more complex and sophisticated conceptual framework to enrich your thinking about this subject.

Using Aesthetic Principles to Judge Aesthetic Value

The first thing to notice about the aesthetic principles we've just discussed is that some are compatible with each other. Thus, a reasonable thinker can appeal to more than one in reaching a verdict about the aesthetic value of an object. For instance, a consistent thinker can use both the first and the fifth principle in evaluating a tragic drama. Aristotle does just this in his *Poetics*. He tells us that tragedies are good art when they both convey general truths about the human condition and help their audiences purge themselves of the pity and fear they feel when they face the truth about human limitations. A play that presents a general truth without eliciting the proper catharsis (release of emotion) in the audience or a play that provokes tragic emotions unaccompanied by recognition of a general truth is not as valuable as a play that does both.

▲   4. Vincent van Gogh tells us that he uses clashing reds and greens in *The Night Café* to help us see his vision of "the terrible passions of humanity"; it is the intensity with which he conveys his views of the ugliness of human life that makes his work so illuminating.

5. The critics who ignored van Gogh's painting during his lifetime were seriously mistaken; by damaging his self-esteem, they drove him to suicide.

6. Moreover, these critics misjudged the aesthetic value of his art, as evidenced by the fact that his paintings now sell for as much as $80 million.

▲   7. By showing a naked woman picnicking with fully clothed men in *Déjeuner sur l'herbe*, Édouard Manet treats women as objects and impedes their efforts to throw off patriarchal domination.

Exercise 12-16 ▲   Asuka, a three-year-old chimpanzee in Japan, was sad and lonely, so the zoo director gave her paper, paints, and brushes to keep her busy. Look at the photograph of Asuka and her painting on the next page. Does the painting have aesthetic value? Use each of the eight aesthetic principles to formulate one reason for or against the aesthetic value of Asuka's work. You should end up with eight reasons, one appealing to each principle.

Asuka the chimpanzee.

Why Reason Aesthetically?

The various aesthetic principles we've introduced are among those most commonly found, either explicitly or implicitly, in discussions about art. Moreover, they have influenced both the creation of art and the selection of art for both private and public enjoyment. But where do these principles come from? There is much debate about this; to understand it, we can draw on notions about definition (introduced in Chapter 3) as well as the discussion of generalizations (Chapter 11).

Some people think that aesthetic principles are simply elaborate definitions of our concepts of art or aesthetic value. Let's explain this point. We use definitions to identify things; for example, by definition we look for three sides and three angles to identify a geometric figure as a triangle. Similarly, we can say that aesthetic principles are definitions; that is, these principles provide an aesthetic vocabulary to direct us in recognizing an object's aesthetic value.

If aesthetic principles are true by definition, then learning to judge art is learning the language of art. But because artists strive for originality, we are constantly faced with talking about innovative objects to which the critic's familiar vocabulary does not quite do justice. This aspect of art challenges even the most sophisticated critic to continually extend the aesthetic vocabulary.

Others think that aesthetic principles are generalizations that summarize what is true of objects treated as valuable art. Here, the argument is by analogy from a sample class to a target population. Thus, someone might hold that all or most of the tragic plays we know that are aesthetically valuable have had something important to say about the human condition; for this reason, we can expect this to be true of any member of the class of tragic plays we have not yet evaluated. Or, also by inductive analogy, musical compositions that are valued so highly that they continue to be performed throughout the centuries all make us feel some specific emotion, such as joy or sadness; so we can predict that a newly composed piece will be similarly highly valued if it also evokes a strong, clear emotion. Of course, such arguments are weakened to the extent that the target object differs from the objects in the sample class. Because there is a drive for originality in art, newly created works may diverge so sharply from previous samples that arguments by analogy sometimes prove too weak.

It is sometimes suggested that these two accounts of the source of aesthetic principles really reinforce each other: Our definitions reflect to some extent our past experience of the properties or capacities typical of valuable art, and our past experience is constrained to some extent by our definitions. But if art changes, of what use are principles, whether analytic or inductive, in guiding us to make aesthetic judgments and—even more difficult—in fostering agreement about these judgments?

At the very least, these principles have an emotive force that guides us in perceiving art. You will remember that emotive force (discussed briefly in Chapter 5) is a dimension of language that permits the words we use to do something more than convey information. In discussion about art, the words that constitute reasons can have an emotive force directing our attention to particular aspects of a work. If the critic can describe these aspects accurately and persuasively, it is thought, the audience will focus on these aspects and experience a favorable (or unfavorable) response similar to the critic's. If a critic's reasons are too vague or are not true of the work to which they are applied, they are unlikely to bring the audience into agreement with the critic.

The principles of art, then, serve as guides for identifying appropriate categories of favorable or unfavorable response, but the reasons falling into these categories are what bring about agreement. They are useful both in developing our own appreciation of a work of art and in persuading others. The reasons must be accurately and informatively descriptive of the objects to which they are applied. The reasons enable us (1) to select a particular way of viewing, listening, reading, or otherwise perceiving the object and (2) to recommend, guide, or prescribe that the object be viewed, heard, or read in this way.

So, aesthetic reasons contain descriptions that prompt ways of perceiving aspects of an object. These prescribed ways of seeing evoke favorable (or unfavorable) responses or experiences. For instance, suppose a critic states that van Gogh's brush strokes in *Starry Night* are dynamic and his colors intense. This positive critical reason prescribes that people focus on these features when they look at the painting. The expectation is that persons whose vision is swept into the movement of van Gogh's painted sky and pierced by the presence of his painted stars will, by virtue of focusing on these formal properties, enjoy a positive response to the painting.

To learn to give reasons and form assessments about art, practice applying these principles as you look, listen, or read. Consider what aspects of a painting, musical performance, poem, or other work each principle directs you to contemplate. It is also important to expand your aesthetic vocabulary so that you have words to describe what you see, hear, or otherwise sense in a work. As you do so, you will be developing your own aesthetic expertise. And, because your reasons will be structured by aesthetic principles others also accept, you will find that rational reflection on art tends to expand both the scope and volume of your agreement with others about aesthetic judgments.

Recap

The key points in this chapter are as follows:

- Value judgments are claims that express values.
- Moral value judgments express moral values.
- Certain words, especially "ought," "should," "right," "wrong," and their opposites, are used in moral value judgments, though they can also be used in a nonmoral sense.
- Reasoning about morality is distinguished from other types of reasoning in that the conclusions it tries to establish are moral value judgments.
- Conclusions containing a value judgment cannot be reached solely from premises that do not contain a value judgment ("you cannot get an 'ought' from an 'is'"). A general moral principle must be supplied to tie together the fact-stating premise and the value-judgment conclusion.
- In a case in which we disagree with a value-judgment conclusion but not with the fact-stating premise, we can point to this general moral principle as the source of disagreement.
- People are sometimes inconsistent in their moral views: They treat similar cases as if they were different, even when they cannot tell us what is importantly different about them.
- When two or more cases that are being treated differently seem similar, the burden of proof is on the person who is treating them differently to explain what is different about them.
- Moral reasoning is usually conducted within a perspective or framework. Influential Western perspectives include consequentialism, utilitarianism, ethical egoism, deontologism, moral relativism, religious absolutism, religious relativism, and virtue ethics.
- Often, different perspectives converge to produce similar solutions to a moral issue.
- Keeping in mind our own perspective can help focus our own moral deliberations on relevant considerations.
- Legal reasoning, like moral reasoning, is often prescriptive.
- Legal studies are devoted to such problems as justifying laws that prescribe conduct.
- Legal moralism, the harm principle, legal paternalism, and the offense principle are grounds for justifying laws that prescribe conduct.
- Determining just when and where a law applies often requires making vague claims specific.
- Precedent is a kind of analogical argument by means of which current cases are settled in accordance with guidelines set by cases decided previously.
- Whether a precedent governs in a given case is decided on grounds similar to those of any other analogical argument.
- To reason aesthetically is to make judgments within a conceptual framework that integrates facts and values.
- Aesthetic value is often identified as the capacity to fulfill a function, such as to create pleasure or promote social change.

■ Alternatively, aesthetic value is defined in terms of a special aesthetic property or form found in works of art.

■ Still another view treats aesthetic judgments as expressions of tastes.

■ Reasoned argument about aesthetic value helps us to see, hear, or otherwise perceive art in changed or expanded ways and to enhance our appreciation of art.

■ A critic who gives reasons in support of an aesthetic verdict forges agreement by getting others to share perceptions of the work. The greater the extent to which we share such aesthetic perceptions, the more we can reach agreement about aesthetic value.

Exercise 12-17

Additional Exercises

State whether the following reasons are (a) helpful in focusing perception to elicit a favorable response, (b) helpful in focusing perception to elicit an unfavorable response, (c) too vague to focus perception, (d) false or implausible and therefore unable to focus perception, or (e) irrelevant to focusing perception. The information you need is contained in the reasons, so try to visualize or imagine what the work is like from what is said. All of these are paraphrases of testimony given at a hearing in 1985 about a proposal to remove *Tilted Arc,* an immense abstract sculpture, from a plaza in front of a federal office building. You can find pictures of this sculpture online. Enter "Serra Tilted Arc" in your search engine.

▲ 1. Richard Serra's *Tilted Arc* is a curved slab of welded steel 12 feet high, 120 feet long, weighing over 73 tons, and covered completely with a natural oxide coating. The sculpture arcs through the plaza. By coming to terms with its harshly intrusive disruption of space, we can learn much about how the nature of the spaces we inhabit affects our social relations.

2. Richard Serra is one of our leading artists, and his work commands very high prices. The government has a responsibility to the financial community. It is bad business to destroy this work because you would be destroying property.

3. *Tilted Arc*'s very tilt and rust remind us that the gleaming and heartless steel and glass structures of the state apparatus can one day pass away. It therefore creates an unconscious sense of freedom and hope.

▲ 4. *Tilted Arc* looks like a discarded piece of crooked or bent metal; there's no more meaning in having it in the middle of the plaza than in putting an old bicycle that got run over by a car there.

5. *Tilted Arc* launches through space in a thrilling and powerful acutely arched curve.

6. *Tilted Arc* is big and rusty.

7. Because of its size, thrusting shape, and implacably uniform rusting surface, *Tilted Arc* makes us feel hopeless, trapped, and sad. This sculpture would be interesting if we could visit it when we had time to explore these feelings, but it is too depressing to face every day on our way to work.

■ Artemisia Gentileschi's *Judith*.

8. Serra's erotically realistic, precise rendering of the female figure in *Tilted Arc* exhibits how appealingly he can portray the soft circularity of a woman's breast.

9. *Tilted Arc* is sort of red; it probably isn't blue.

Exercise 12-18

The artist Artemisia Gentileschi (ca. 1597–after 1651) was very successful in her own time. Success came despite the trauma of her early life, when she figured as the victim in a notorious rape trial. But after she died, her work fell into obscurity; it was neither shown in major museums nor written about in art history books. Recently, feminist scholars have revived interest in her work by connecting the style and/or theme of such paintings as her *Judith* with her rape and with feelings or issues of importance to women. But other scholars have pointed out that both her subject matter and her treatment of it are conventionally found as well in the work of male painters of the Caravaggist school, with which she is identified. Based on this information, and using one or more of the aesthetic principles described in this chapter, write an essay arguing either that the painting *Judith* has aesthetic value worthy of our attention or that it should continue to be ignored.

Writing Exercises

1. In the movie *Priest*, the father of a young girl admits to the local priest—in the confessional—that he has molested his daughter. However, the man lacks remorse and gives every indication that he will continue to abuse the girl. For the priest to inform the girl's mother or the authorities would be to violate the sanctity of the confessional, but to not inform anyone would subject the girl to further abuse. What should the priest do? Take about fifteen minutes to do the following:

a. List the probable consequences of the courses of action available to the priest.
b. List any duties or rights or other considerations that bear on the issue.

   When fifteen minutes are up, share your ideas with the class.
   Now, take about twenty minutes to write an essay in which you do the following:

a. State the issue.
b. Take a stand on the issue.
c. Defend your stand.
d. Rebut counterarguments to your position.

   When you are finished, write down on a separate piece of paper a number between 1 and 10 that indicates how strong you think your argument is (1 = very weak; 10 = very strong). Write your name on the back of your paper.

When everyone is finished, the instructor will collect the papers and redistribute them to the class. In groups of four or five, read the papers and assign a number from 1 to 10 to each one (1 = very weak; 10 = very strong). When all groups are finished, return the papers to their authors. When you get your paper back, compare the number you assigned to your work with the number the group assigned it. The instructor may ask volunteers to defend their own judgment of their work against the judgment of the group. Do you think there is as much evidence for your position as you did at the beginning of the period?

2. Follow the same procedure as previously used to address one of the following issues:

   a. A friend cheats in the classes he has with you. You know he'd just laugh if you voiced any concern. Should you mention it to your instructor?

   b. You see a friend stealing something valuable. Even though you tell your friend that you don't approve, she keeps the item. What should you do?

   c. Your best friend's fiancé has just propositioned you for sex. Should you tell your friend?

   d. Your parents think you should major in marketing or some other practical field. You want to major in literature. Your parents pay the bills. What should you do?

3. Before a stand your ground (SYG) law such as that found in Florida (see the box on page 412), there was a presumed common-law requirement that a person attempt to retreat from a threat of bodily harm everywhere outside one's own home. Under this common-law requirement, only when retreat was impossible or unreasonable could one respond with deadly force. Under the Florida SYG law, one has the right to use deadly force in self-defense wherever he or she has a legal right to be. Under what circumstances do you think the Florida law should come into play? That is, what would one have to know about the confrontation between Zimmerman and Martin before applying the statute?

4. Generally speaking, do you think stand your ground laws are a good idea? Why, or why not?

5. Which of the four types of justification described in the chapter best apply to stand your ground laws? Is the justification successful?

Appendix

Note: Answers to all questions may be accessed through the Instructor Resources tab in the Connect® for Critical Thinking.

Exercise A-1

Identify (and explain, if your instructor requires) any fallacies you find in the following passages. There may be some that contain no fallacy.

1 The proponents of this spend-now–pay-later boondoggle would like you to believe that this measure will cost you only one billion dollars. That's NOT TRUE. In the last general election, some of these very same people argued against unneeded rail projects because they would cost taxpayers millions more in interest payments. Now they have changed their minds and are willing to encourage irresponsible borrowing. Connecticut is already awash in red ink. Vote NO.

2 Of course, Chinese green tea is good for your health. If it weren't, how could it be so beneficial to drink it?

3 Overheard: "No, I'm against this health plan business. None of the proposals are gonna fix everything, you can bet on that."

4 Rush Limbaugh argues that the establishment clause of the First Amendment should not be stretched beyond its intended dimensions by precluding voluntary prayer in public schools. This is a peculiar argument, when you consider that Limbaugh is quite willing to stretch the Second Amendment to include the right to own assault rifles and Saturday night specials.

5 You have a choice: Either you let 'em out to murder and rape again and again, or you put up with a little prison overcrowding. I know what I'd choose.

6 I think you can safely assume that Justice Thomas's opinions on the cases before the Supreme Court this term will be every bit as flaky as his past opinions.

7 The legalization of drugs will not promote their use. The notion of a widespread hysteria sweeping across the nation as every man, woman, and child instantaneously becomes addicted to drugs upon their legalization is, in short, ridiculous.

8 Way I figure is, giving up smoking isn't gonna make me live forever, so why bother?

9 Harvard now takes the position that its investment in urban redevelopment projects will be limited to projects that are environmentally friendly. Before you conclude that that is such a swell idea, stop and think. For a long time, Harvard was one of the biggest slumlords in the country.

10 Capital punishment was invented during barbaric times. No civilized society ought to tolerate it.

11 Dear Editor—I read with amusement the letter by Leslie Burr titled "It's time to get tough." Did anyone else notice a little problem in her views? It seems a little odd that somebody who claims that she "loathes violence" could also say that "criminals should pay with their life." I guess consistency isn't Ms. Burr's greatest concern.

12 I believe Tim is telling the truth about his brother, because he just would not lie about that sort of thing.

13 I think I was treated unfairly. I got a ticket out on McCrae Road. I was doing about sixty miles an hour, and the cop charged me with "traveling at an unsafe speed."

I asked him just exactly what would have been a safe speed on that particular occasion—fifty? forty-five?—and he couldn't tell me. Neither could the judge. I tell you, if you don't know what speeds are unsafe, you shouldn't give tickets for "unsafe speeds."

14 YOU: Look at this. It says here that white males still earn a lot more than minorities and women for doing the same job.

YOUR FRIEND: Yeah, right. Written by some woman, no doubt.

15 Suspicious: "I would forget about whatever Moore and Parker have to say about pay for college teachers. After all, they're both professors themselves; what would you expect them to say?"

16 "Steve Thompson of the California Medical Association said document-checking might even take place in emergency rooms. That's because, while undocumented immigrants would be given emergency care, not all cases that come into emergency rooms fall under the federal definition of an emergency.

"To all those arguments initiative proponents say hogwash. They say the education and health groups opposing the initiative are interested in protecting funding they receive for providing services to the undocumented."

—Sacramento Bee

17 "Creationism cannot possibly be true. People who believe in a literal interpretation of the Bible just never outgrew the need to believe in Santa Claus."

—*Melinda Zerkle*

18 It's obvious to me that abortion is wrong—after all, everybody deserves a chance to be born.

19 Overheard: Well, I think that's too much to tip her. It's more than 15 percent. Next time it will be 20 percent, then 25 percent—where will it stop?

20 CARLOS: Four A.M.? Do we really have to start that early? Couldn't we leave a little later and get more sleep?

JEANNE: C'mon, don't hand me that! I know you! If you want to stay in bed until noon and then drag in there in the middle of the night, then go by yourself! If we want to get there at a reasonable hour, then we have to get going early and not spend the whole day sleeping.

21 "Americans spend between $28 and $61 billion a year in medical costs for treatment of hypertension, heart disease, cancer, and other illnesses attributed to consumption of meat, says a report out today from a provegetarian doctor's group.

"Dr. Neal D. Barnard, lead author of the report in the *Journal of Preventive Medicine,* and colleagues looked at studies comparing the health of vegetarians and meat eaters, then figured the cost of treating illnesses suffered by meat eaters in excess of those suffered by vegetarians. Only studies that controlled for the health effects of smoking, exercise, and alcohol consumption were considered.

"The American Medical Association, in a statement from Dr. M. Roy Schwarz, charged that Barnard's group is an 'animal rights front organization' whose agenda 'definitely taints whatever unsubstantiated findings it may claim.'"

—USA Today

22 I know a lot of people don't find anything wrong with voluntary euthanasia, where a patient is allowed to make a decision to die and that wish is carried out by a doctor or someone else. What will happen, though, is that if we allow voluntary euthanasia, before you know it we'll have the patient's relatives or the doctors making the decision that the patient should be "put out of his misery."

23 You're wrong about Rudy Giuliani not knowing how to best to handle terror attacks. After all, when 9/11 happened, he was there.

24 Whenever legislators have the power to raise taxes, they will always find problems that seem to require for their solution doing exactly that. This is an axiom, the proof of which is that the power to tax always generates the perception on the part of those who have that power that there exist various ills the remedy for which can lie only in increased governmental spending and hence higher taxes.

25 Don't tell me I should wear my seat belt, for heaven's sake. I've seen you ride a motorcycle without a helmet! That's even *more* dangerous!

26 I'll tell you what Congress passed. They call it health care reform, but what it really is communism, pure and simple. It's designed to tax everybody who works so people who don't work can still have an easy life.

27 When it comes to the issue of race relations, either you're part of the solution, or you're part of the problem.

28 What! So now you're telling me we should get a new car? I don't buy that at all. Didn't you claim just last month that there was nothing wrong with the Plymouth?

29 Letter to the editor: "The Supreme Court decision outlawing a moment of silence for prayer in public schools is scandalous. Evidently the American Civil Liberties Union and the other radical groups will not be satisfied until every last man, woman and child in the country is an atheist. I'm fed up."

30 We should impeach the attorney general. Despite the fact that there have been many allegations of unethical conduct on his part, he has not done anything to demonstrate his innocence.

31 Amnesty International defends only criminals. This is obvious because the people it helps are already in jail, and that shows they're guilty of something.

32 Overheard: "Hunting immoral? Why should I believe that, coming from you? You fish, don't you?"

33 "Will we have an expanding government, or will we balance the budget, cut government waste and eliminate unneeded programs?"
   —*Newt Gingrich, in a Republican National Committee solicitation*

34 Despite all the studies and the public outcry, it's still true that nobody has ever actually seen cigarette smoking cause a cancer. All the antismoking people can do is talk about statistics; as long as there isn't real proof, I'm not believing it.

35 YOU: Clinton should have been thrown in jail for immoral behavior. Just look at all the women he has had affairs with since he left the presidency.
   YOUR FRIEND: Hey, wait a minute. How do you know he has had affairs since he was president?
   YOU: Because if he didn't, then why would he be trying to cover up the fact that he did?

36 On "The Colbert Report," Steven Colbert regularly asked his guests: "George W. Bush: a great president? or the greatest president?"

37 In 1996, a University of Chicago study gave evidence that letting people carry concealed guns appears to sharply reduce murders, rapes, and other violent crimes. Gun-control backer Josh Sugarman of the Violence Policy Center commented: "Anyone who argues that these laws reduce crime either doesn't understand the nature of crime or has a preset agenda."

38 Letter to the editor: "I strongly object to the proposed sale of alcoholic beverages at County Golf Course. The idea of allowing people to drink wherever and whenever they please is positively disgraceful and can only lead to more alcoholism and all the problems it produces—drunk driving, perverted parties, and who knows what else. I'm sure General Stuart, if he were alive today to see what has become of the land he deeded to the county, would disapprove strenuously."

39 Letter to the editor: "I'm not against immigrants or immigration, but something has to be done soon. We've got more people already than we can provide necessary services for, and, at the current rate, we'll have people standing on top of one another by the end of the century. Either we control these immigration policies or there won't be room for any of us to sit down."

40 Letter to the editor: "So now we find our local crusader-for-all-that-is-right, and I am referring to Councilman Benjamin Bostell, taking up arms against the local adult book-store. Is this the same Mr. Bostell who owns the biggest liquor store in Chilton County? Well, maybe booze isn't the same as pornography, but they're the same sort of thing. C'mon, Mr. Bostell, aren't you a little like the pot calling the kettle black?"

41 Letter to the editor: "Once again the *Courier* displays its taste for slanted journalism. Why do your editors present only one point of view?

"I am referring specifically to the editorial of May 27, regarding the death penalty. So capital punishment makes you squirm a little. What else is new? Would you prefer to have murderers and assassins wandering around scot-free? How about quoting someone who has a different point of view from your own, for a change?"

42 There is only one way to save this country from the domination by the illegal drug establishment to which Colombia has been subjected, and that's to increase tenfold the funds we spend on drug enforcement and interdiction.

43 It's practically a certainty that the government is violating the law in the arms deals with Saudi Arabians. When officials were asked to describe how they were comply-ing with the law, they said that details about the arms sales were classified.

44 Letter to the editor: "I would like to express my feelings on the recent conflict between county supervisor Blanche Wilder and Murdock County Sheriff Al Peters over the county budget.

"I have listened to sheriffs' radio broadcasts. Many times there have been danger-ous and life-threatening situations when the sheriff's deputies' quickest possible arrival time is 20 to 30 minutes. This is to me very frightening.

"Now supervisor Wilder wants to cut two officers from the Sheriff's Department. This proposal I find ridiculous. Does she really think that Sheriff Peters can run his department with no officers? How anyone can think that a county as large as Murdock can get by with no police is beyond me. I feel this proposal would be very detri-mental to the safety and protection of this county's residents."

45 Letter to the editor: "Andrea Keene's selective morality is once again showing through in her July 15 letter. This time she expresses her abhorrence of abortion. But how we see only what we choose to see! I wonder if any of the antiabortionists have consid-ered the widespread use of fertility drugs as the moral equivalent of abortion, and, if they have, why they haven't come out against them, too. The use of these drugs frequently results in multiple births, which leads to the death of one of the infants, often after an agonizing struggle for survival. According to the rules of the prolifers, isn't this murder?"

46 In one of her columns, Abigail Van Buren printed the letter of "I'd rather be a widow." The letter writer, a divorcée, complained about widows who said they had a hard time coping. Far better, she wrote, to be a widow than to be a divorcée, who are all "rejects" who have been "publicly dumped" and are avoided "like they have leprosy." Abby recognized the fallacy for what it was, though she did not call it by our name. What is our name for it?

47 Overheard: "Should school kids say the Pledge of Allegiance before class? Certainly. Why shouldn't they?"

48 Letter to the editor: "Once again the Park Commission is considering closing North Park Drive for the sake of a few joggers and bicyclists. These so-called fitness enthusiasts would evidently have us give up to them for their own private use every last square inch of Walnut Grove. Then anytime anyone wanted a picnic, he would have to park at the edge of the park and carry everything in—ice chests, chairs, maybe even Grandma. I certainly hope the commission keeps the entire park open for everyone to use."

49 "Some Christian—and other—groups are protesting against the placing, on federal property near the White House, of a set of plastic figurines representing a devout Jewish family in ancient Judaea. The protestors would of course deny that they are driven by any anti-Semitic motivation. Still, we wonder: Would they raise the same objections (of unconstitutionality, etc.) if the scene depicted a modern, secularized Gentile family?"

—National Review

50 "It's stupid to keep on talking about rich people not paying their fair share of taxes while the budget is so far out of balance. Why, if we raised the tax rates on the wealthy all the way back to where they were in 1980, it would not balance the federal budget."

—*Radio commentary by Howard Miller*

51 From a letter to the editor: "The counties of Michigan clearly need the ability to raise additional sources of revenue, not only to meet the demands of growth but also to maintain existing levels of service. For without these sources those demands will not be met, and it will be impossible to maintain services even at present levels."

52 A representative of the Catholic Church in Puerto Rico, in a radio interview (broadcast on National Public Radio), said that the Church was against the use of condoms. Even though the rate of AIDS infection in Puerto Rico is much higher than on the U.S. mainland, the spokesperson said that the Church could not support the use of condoms because they are not absolutely reliable in preventing the spread of the disease. "If you could prove that condoms were absolutely dependable in preventing a person from contracting AIDS, then the Church could support their use."

53 [Former California] Assemblyman Doug La Malfa said AB 45 [which bans handheld cell phone use while driving] is one more example of a "nanny government." "I'm sick and tired of being told what to do on these trivial things," he said. "Helmet laws, seat-belt laws—what's next?"

54 The U.S. Congress considered a resolution criticizing the treatment of ethnic minorities in a Near Middle Eastern country. When the minister of the interior was asked for his opinion of the resolution, he replied, "This is purely an internal affair in my country, and politicians in the U.S. should stay out of such affairs. If the truth be known, they should be more concerned with the plight of minority peoples in their own country. Thousands of black and Latino youngsters suffer from malnutrition in the United States. They can criticize us after they've got their own house in order."

55 It doesn't make any sense to speak of tracing an individual human life back past the moment of conception. After all, that's the beginning, and you can't go back past the beginning.

56 MOE: The death penalty is an excellent deterrent for murder.
JOE: What makes you think so?
MOE: Well, for one thing, there's no evidence that it's not a deterrent.
JOE: Well, states with capital punishment have murder rates just as high as states that don't have it.
MOE: Yes, but that's only because there are so many legal technicalities standing in the way of executions that convicted people hardly ever get executed. Remove those technicalities, and the rate would be lower in those states.

57 Overheard: "The new sculpture in front of the municipal building by John Murrah is atrocious and unseemly, which is clear to anyone who hasn't forgotten Murrah's mouth in Vietnam right there along with Hayden and Fonda calling for the defeat of America. I say: Drill holes in it so it'll sink and throw it in Walnut Pond."

58 Overheard: "Once we let these uptight guardians of morality have their way and start censoring *Playboy* and *Penthouse,* the next thing you know they'll be dictating every-thing we can read. We'll be in fine shape when they decide that *Webster's* should be pulled from the shelves."

59 It seems the biggest problem the nuclear industry has to deal with is not a poor safety record but a lack of education of the public on nuclear power. Thousands of people die each year from pollution generated by coal-fired plants. Yet, to date there has been no death directly caused by radiation at a commercial nuclear power plant in the United States. We have a clear choice: an old, death-dealing source of energy or a safe, clean one. Proven through the test of time, nuclear power is clearly the safest form of energy and the least detrimental to the environment. Yet it is perceived as unsafe and an environmental hazard.

60 A high school teacher once told my class that, if a police state ever arose in America, it would happen because we freely handed away our civil rights in exchange for what we perceived would be security from the government. We are looking at just that in connection with the current drug crisis.

"For almost thirty years, we've seen increasing tolerance, legally and socially, of drug use. Now we are faced with the very end of America as we know it, if not from the drug problem, then from the proposed solutions to it."

"First, it was urine tests. Officials said that the innocent have nothing to fear. Using that logic, why not allow unannounced police searches of our homes for stolen goods? After all, the innocent would have nothing to fear."

"Now we're looking at the seizure of boats and other property when even traces of drugs are found. You'd better hope some drug-using guest doesn't drop the wrong thing in your home, car, or boat."

"The only alternative to declaring real war on the real enemies—the Asian and South American drug families—is to wait for that knock on the door in the middle of the night."

61 The mayor's argument is that, because the developers' fee would reduce the number of building starts, ultimately the city would lose more money than it would gain through the fee. But I can't go along with that. Mayor Tower is a member of the Board of Realtors, and you know what they think of the fee.

62 Letter to the editor: "Next week the philosopher Tom Regan will be in town again, peddling his animal rights theory. In case you've forgotten, Regan was here about three years ago arguing against using animals in scientific experimentation. As far as I could see then and can see now, neither Regan nor anyone else has managed to come up with a good reason why animals should not be experimented on. Emotional appeals and horror stories no doubt influence many, but they shouldn't. I've always wondered what Regan would say if his children needed medical treatment that was based on animal experiments."

63 Not long before Ronald and Nancy Reagan moved out of the White House, former chief of staff Don Regan wrote a book in which he depicted a number of revealing inside stories about First Family goings-on. Among them was the disclosure that Nancy Reagan regularly sought the advice of a San Francisco astrologer. In response to the story, the White House spokesperson at the time, Marlin Fitzwater, said, "Vindictiveness and revenge are not admirable qualities and are not worthy of comment."

64 "People in Hegins, Pennsylvania, hold an annual pigeon shoot in order to control the pigeon population and to raise money for the town. This year, the pigeon shoot was disrupted by animal rights activists who tried to release the pigeons from their cages. I can't help but think these animal rights activists are the same people who believe in controlling the human population through the use of abortion. Yet, they recoil at a similar means of controlling pigeons. What rank hypocrisy."

—Rush Limbaugh

65 Dear Mr. Swanson: I realize I'm not up for a salary increase yet, but I thought it might make my review a bit more timely if I pointed out to you that I have a copy of all the recent e-mail messages between you and Ms. Flood in the purchasing department.

66 I don't care if Nike has signed up Michael Jordan, Tiger Woods, and even Santa Claus to endorse its shoes. It's a crummy company that makes a crummy product. The proof is the fact that it pays poor women a dollar sixty for a long day's work in its Vietnamese shoe factories. That's not even enough to buy a day's worth of decent meals!

67 I don't care if Nike has signed up Michael Jordan, Tiger Woods, and even Santa Claus to endorse its shoes. It's a crummy company, and I wouldn't buy its shoes no matter what the circumstance. You don't need any reason beyond the fact that it pays poor women a dollar sixty for a long day's work in its Vietnamese shoe factories. That's not even enough to buy a day's worth of decent meals!

68 Nike is a crummy company that makes crummy shoes. Look: it still sponsors Tiger Woods even after all the bad stuff that came to light about him.

69 POWELL FAN: Colin Powell said that diplomatic efforts to avoid war with Iraq were serious and genuine, and his word was good enough for me.
SKEPTIC: And what made you so sure he was telling it like it is?
POWELL FAN: Because he was the one guy in that administration you could trust.

70 If you give the cat your leftover asparagus, next thing you know you'll be feeding him your potatoes, maybe even your roast beef. Where will it all end? Pretty soon that wretched animal will be sitting up here on the table for dinner. He'll be eating us out of house and home.

71 Look, either we refrain from feeding the cat table scraps, or he'll be up here on the table with us. So don't go giving him your asparagus.

72 We have a simple choice. Saving Social Security is sure as hell a lot more important than giving people a tax cut. So write your representative now, and let him or her know how you feel.

73 Let gays join the military? Give me a break. God created Adam and Eve, not Adam and Steve.

74 So my professor told me if he gave me an A for getting an 89.9 on the test, next he'd have to give people an A for getting an 89.8 on the test, and pretty soon he'd have to give everyone in the class an A. How could I argue with that?

75 Those blasted Democrats! They want to increase government spending on education again. This is the same outfit that gave us $600 toilet seats and government regulations up the wazoo.

76 The way I see it, either the senator resigns, or he sends a message that no one should admit to his misdeeds.

77 Lauren did a better job than anyone else at the audition, so even though she has no experience, we've decided to give her the part in the play.

78 TERRY: I failed my test, but I gave my prof this nifty argument. I said, "Look, suppose somebody did 0.0001 percent better than I, would that be a big enough

difference to give him a higher grade?" And he had to say no, so then I said, "And if someone did 0.0001 percent better than that second person, would that be a big enough difference?" And he had to say no to that, too, so I just kept it up, and he never could point to the place where the difference was big enough to give the other person a higher grade. He finally saw he couldn't justify giving anyone a better grade.
HARRY: Well? What happened?
TERRY: He had to fail the whole class.

79 "Many, but not all, on the other side of the aisle lack the will to win," said Representative Charlie Norwood of Georgia. "The American people need to know precisely who they are." He said, "It is time to stand up and vote. Is it Al Qaeda, or is it America?"

—New York Times, *June 15, 2006*

80 Look, maybe you think it's okay to legalize tribal casinos, but I don't. Letting every last group of people in the country open a casino is a ridiculous idea, bound to cause trouble.

81 What, you of all people complaining about violence on TV? You, with all the pro football you watch?

82 You have three Fs and a D on your exams, and your quizzes are on the borderline between passing and failing. I'm afraid you don't deserve to pass the course.

83 I can safely say that no law, no matter how stiff the consequence is, will completely stop illegal drug use. Outlawing drugs is a waste of time.

84 If we expand the commuter bus program, where is it going to end? Will we want to have a trolley system? Then a light rail system? Then expand Metrolink to our area? A city this size hardly needs and certainly cannot afford all these amenities.

85 YAEKO: The character Dana Scully on *The X-Files* really provided a good role model for young women. She was a medical doctor and an FBI agent, and she was intelligent, professional, and devoted to her work.
MICHAEL: Those shows about paranormal activities are so unrealistic. Alien abductions, government conspiracies—it's all ridiculous.

86 Overheard: "The reason I don't accept evolution is that ever since Darwin, scientists have been trying to prove that we evolved from some apelike primate ancestor. Well, they still haven't succeeded. Case closed."

87 Ladies and gentlemen, as you know, I endorsed council member Morrissey's bid for reelection based on his outstanding record during his first term. Because you are the movers and shakers in this community, other people place the same high value on your opinions that I do. Jim and I would feel privileged to have your support.

88 It's totally ridiculous to suppose that creationism is true. If creationism were true, then half of what we know through science would be false, which is complete nonsense.

89 KIRSTI: I counted my CDs this weekend, and out of twenty-seven, ten of them were by U2. They were such a good band! I haven't heard anything by Bono for a long time. He had such a terrific voice!
BEN: Wasn't he bisexual?

90 Was Gerhard a good committee chair? Well, I for one think you have to say he was excellent, especially when you consider all the abuse he put up with. Right from the start, people went after him—they didn't even give him a chance to show what he could do. It was really vicious—people making fun of him right to his face. Yes, under the circumstances he has been quite effective.

91 Medical research that involves animals is completely unnecessary and a waste of money. Just think of the poor creatures! We burn and blind and torture them, and then

we kill them. They don't know what is going to happen to them, but they know something is going to happen. They are scared to death. It's really an outrage.

92 Dear Editor—If Christians do not participate in government, only sinners will.

93 The HMO people claim that the proposal will raise the cost of doing business in the state to such a degree that insurers will be forced to leave and do business elsewhere. What nonsense. Just look at what we get from these HMOs. I know people who were denied decent treatment for cancer because their HMO wouldn't approve it. There are doctors who won't recommend a procedure for their patients because they are afraid the HMO will cancel their contract. And when an HMO does cancel some doctor's contract, the patients have to find a new doctor themselves—if they can. Everybody has a horror story. Enough is enough.

94 From an interview by Gwen Ifill (PBS News Hour) with Senator Kit Bond, then ranking Republican on the Senate Intelligence Committee:
    IFILL: Do you think that waterboarding, as I have described it, constitutes torture?
    BOND: There are different ways of doing it; it's like swimming: freestyle, back-stroke. Waterboarding could be used, almost, to define some of the techniques that our trainees are put through. But that's beside the point. It's not being used. There are some who say that, in extreme circumstances, if there is a threat of an imminent major attack on the United States, it might be used.

95 The opposing party is going to give its reply to the president's speech in just a few minutes. Prepare yourself for the usual misstatements of fact, exaggerated criticism, and attempts to distract from the real issues. Their only reason for giving a reply is to score political points.

96 The proposal to reduce spending for the arts just doesn't make any sense. We spend a paltry $620 million for the NEA [National Endowment for the Arts], while the deficit is closing in on $200 billion. Cutting support for the arts isn't going to eliminate the deficit; that's obvious.

97 Year-round schools? I'm opposed. Once we let them do that, the next thing you know they'll be cutting into our vacation time and asking us to teach in the evenings and on the weekends, and who knows where it will end. We teachers have to stand up for our rights.

98 Romney was for abortion rights before he began running for president. Then he was antiabortion. I thought he should be ignored completely on the subject since you couldn't depend on what he says.

99 Even if we outlaw guns, we're still going to have crime and murder. So I really don't see much point in it.

Exercise A-2

Select the fallacy most clearly present (if one is present) from the lists following the passages.

1 The health editor for *USA Today* certainly seems to know what she is talking about when she recommends we take vitamins, but I happen to know she works for Tishcon, Inc., a large manufacturer of vitamin supplements.
   a. irrelevant conclusion
   b. apple polishing
   c. mistaken appeal to popularity
   d. *argumentum ad hominem*
   e. no fallacy

2 The president is right. People who are against fighting in Afghanistan are unwilling to face up to the threat of terrorism.
   a. mistaken to common practice
   b. peer pressure fallacy
   c. false dilemma
   d. straw man
   e. begging the question

3 Well, I, for one, think the position taken by our union is correct, and I'd like to remind you before you make up your mind on the matter that around here we employees have a big say in who gets rehired.
   a. wishful thinking
   b. *argumentum ad hominem*
   c. scare tactics
   d. apple polishing
   e. begging the question

4 On the whole, I think global warming is a farce. After all, most people think winters are getting colder, if anything. How could that many people be wrong?
   a. appeal to emotion (outrage)
   b. mistaken appeal to popularity
   c. straw man
   d. no fallacy

5 MARCO: I think global warming is a farce.
   CLAUDIA: Oh, gad. How can you say such a thing, when there is so much evidence behind the theory?
   MARCO: Because. Look. If it isn't a farce, then how come the world is colder now than it used to be?
   a. begging the question
   b. mistaken appeal to popularity
   c. irrelevant conclusion
   d. *argumentum ad hominem*
   e. no fallacy

6 Of course you should buy a life insurance policy! Why shouldn't you?
   a. irrelevant conclusion
   b. wishful thinking
   c. scare tactics
   d. peer pressure fallacy
   e. misplacing the burden of proof

7 My opponent, Mr. London, has charged me with having cheated on my income tax. My response is, When are we going to get this campaign out of the gutter? Isn't it time we stood up and made it clear that vilification has no place in politics?
   a. irrelevant conclusion
   b. wishful thinking
   c. mistaken appeal to common practice
   d. mistaken appeal to popularity
   e. *argumentum ad hominem*

8 Look, even if Bush did lie about the WMD threat, what's the surprise? Clinton lied about having sex with that intern, and Bush's own father lied about raising taxes.
   a. irrelevant conclusion
   b. straw man
   c. false dilemma

    d. *argumentum ad hominem*
    e. fallacious appeal to common practice

9 If cigarettes aren't bad for you, then how come it's so hard on your health to smoke?
    a. *argumentum ad hominem*
    b. misplacing the burden of proof
    c. slippery slope
    d. begging the question

10 GARRY: I think the people who lost their livelihood because of the Gulf oil spill ought to be paid their losses in full.
    HARRY: But there are disasters all over the place. You can't compensate everybody.
    a. perfectionist fallacy
    b. straw man
    c. mistaken appeal to tradition
    d. mistaken appeal to common practice

11 So what if the senator accepted a little kickback money—most politicians are corrupt, after all.
    a. argument from envy
    b. mistaken appeal to tradition
    c. mistaken to common practice
    d. *argumentum ad hominem*
    e. no fallacy

12 Me? I'm going to vote with the company on this one. After all, I've been with them for fifteen years.
    a. genetic fallacy
    b. appeal to emotion (call this an "appeal to loyalty")
    c. slippery slope
    d. misplacing the burden of proof
    e. no fallacy

13 Public opinion polls? They're rigged. Just ask anyone.
    a. slippery slope
    b. guilt tripping
    c. begging the question
    d. mistaken appeal to popularity
    e. no fallacy

14 Hey! It can't be time for the bars to close. I'm having too much fun.
    a. false dilemma
    b. misplacing the burden of proof
    c. wishful thinking
    d. mistaken appeal to tradition
    e. no fallacy

15 A mural for the municipal building? Excuse me, but why should public money, our tax dollars, be used for a totally unnecessary thing like art? There are potholes that need fixing. Traffic signals that need to be put up. There are a million things that are more important. It is an outrage, spending taxpayers' money on unnecessary frills like art. Give me a break!
    a. *argumentum ad hominem*
    b. argument from outrage
    c. slippery slope
    d. perfectionist fallacy
    e. no fallacy

16 Mathematics is more difficult than sociology, and I really need an easier term this fall. So I'm going to take a sociology class instead of a math class.
   a. *argumentum ad hominem*
   b. appeal to pity
   c. false dilemma
   d. begging the question
   e. no fallacy

17 Parker says Macs are better than PCs, but what would you expect him to say? He's owned Macs for years.
   a. mistaken to common practice
   b. *argumentum ad hominem*
   c. begging the question
   d. perfectionist fallacy
   e. no fallacy

18 The congressman thought the president's behavior was an impeachable offense. But that's nonsense, coming from the congressman. He had an adulterous affair himself, after all.
   a. *argumentum ad hominem*
   b. poisoning the well
   c. perfectionist fallacy
   d. genetic fallacy
   e. no fallacy

19 Your professor wants you to read Moore and Parker? Forget it. They are so right wing their book is falling off the shelf.
   a. poisoning the well
   b. *argumentum ad hominem*
   c. misplacing the burden of proof
   d. mistaken to tradition
   e. no fallacy

20 How do I know God exists? Hey, how do you know I'm wrong?
   a. perfectionist fallacy
   b. *argumentum ad hominem*
   c. misplacing the burden of proof
   d. slippery slope
   e. begging the question

21 Laws against teenagers drinking? They are a total waste of time, frankly. No matter how many laws we pass, there are always going to be some teens who drink.
   a. misplacing the burden of proof
   b. perfectionist fallacy
   c. line-drawing fallacy
   d. slippery slope
   e. no fallacy

22 Even though Sidney was old enough to buy a drink at the bar, she had no identification with her, and the bartender would not serve her.
   a. perfectionist fallacy
   b. *argumentum ad hominem*
   c. misplacing the burden of proof
   d. slippery slope
   e. no fallacy

23 Just how much sex has to be in a movie before you call it pornographic? Seems to me the whole concept makes no sense.
   a. perfectionist fallacy
   b. line-drawing fallacy
   c. straw man
   d. slippery slope
   e. no fallacy

24 Studies confirm what everyone already knows: Smaller classes make students better learners.
   a. perfectionist fallacy
   b. begging the question
   c. misplacing the burden of proof
   d. mistaken appeal to popularity
   e. no fallacy

25 The trouble with impeaching the president is this: Going after every person who occupies the presidency will take up everyone's time, and the government will never get anything else done.
   a. *argumentum ad hominem*
   b. straw man
   c. argument from outrage
   d. appeal to envy
   e. irrelevant conclusion

26 The trouble with impeaching the president is this. If we start going after him, next we'll be going after senators, representatives, governors. Pretty soon, no elected official will be safe from partisan attack.
   a. *argumentum ad hominem*
   b. slippery slope
   c. straw man
   d. false dilemma
   e. misplacing the burden of proof

27 MR. IMHOFF: That does it. I'm cutting down on your peanut butter cookies. Those things blimp me up.
   MRS. IMHOFF: Oh, Imhoff, get real. What about all the ice cream you eat?
   a. *argumentum ad hominem*
   b. misplacing the burden of proof
   c. straw man
   d. slippery slope
   e. argument from outrage

28 KEN: I think I'll vote for Andrews. She's the best candidate.
   ROBERT: Why do you say she's best?
   KEN: Because she's my sister-in-law. Didn't you know that?
   a. apple polishing
   b. appeal to pity
   c. scare tactics
   d. irrelevant conclusion
   e. no fallacy

29 Morgan, you're down-to-earth and I trust your judgment. That's why I know I can count on you to back me up at the meeting this afternoon.
   a. apple polishing
   b. appeal to pity
   c. scare tactics

d. guilt tripping

e. no fallacy

30 "Do you want to sign this petition to the governor?"

"What's it about?"

"We want him to veto that handgun registration bill that's come out of the legislature."

"Oh. No, I don't think I want to sign that."

"Oh, really? So are you telling me you want to get rid of the Second Amendment?"

a. false dilemma

b. *argumentum ad hominem*

c. genetic fallacy

d. misplacing the burden of proof

e. no fallacy

Exercise A-3

Answer the following questions and explain your answers. (Bases for class discussions.)

1 A brand of toothpaste is *advertised* as best-selling. How relevant is that to whether to buy the brand?

2 A brand of toothpaste *is* best-selling. How relevant is that to whether to buy that brand?

3 An automobile is a best seller in its class. How relevant is that to whether to buy that kind of automobile?

4 A movie is a smash hit. Would that influence your opinion of it? Should it?

5 Your friends are all Republicans. Would that influence your decision about which party to register with? Should it?

6 Your friends are all Democrats. Would that influence what you say about Democrats to them? Should it?

7 Your friend's father wrote a novel. How relevant is that to whether you should say nice things about the book to your friend?

8 Your friend's mother is running for office. How relevant is that to whether you should vote for her?

9 Your own mother is running for office. How relevant is that to whether she will do a good job? To whether you should vote for her?

10 The late movie critic Roger Ebert gave a 2012 movie a "thumbs-up" and calls it one of the best of the year. How relevant is this to whether you should rent and watch the movie?

Exercise A-4

Which of the following claims do you believe? Which of them do you *really* have evidence for? Which of them do you believe on an "everyone knows" basis? (Bases for class discussions.)

1 Small dogs tend to live longer than large dogs.

2 Coffee has a dehydrating effect.

3 Most people should drink at least eight glasses of water a day.

4 If you are thirsty, it means you are already dehydrated.

5 Rape is not about sex; it's about aggression.

6   Marijuana use leads to addiction to harder drugs.

7   The news media are biased.

8   You get just as much ultraviolet radiation on a cloudy day as on a sunny day.

9   If you don't let yourself get angry every now and then, your anger will build up to the exploding point.

10   Carrots make you see better.

11   Reading in poor light is bad for your eyes.

12   Sitting too close to the TV is bad for your eyes.

13   Warm milk makes you sleepy.

14   Covering your head is the most effective way of staying warm in cold weather.

15   Smoking a cigarette takes seven minutes off your life.

16   Government-run health care management is more (or less—choose one) expensive than private-run health care management.

Exercise A-5

Elegant Country Estate

- Stunning Federal-style brick home with exquisite appointments throughout
- 20 picturesque acres with lake, pasture, and woodland
- 5 bedrooms, 4.5 baths
- 5,800 sq. ft. living space, 2,400 sq. ft. basement
- Formal living room; banquet dining with butler's pantry; luxurious foyer, gourmet kitchen, morning room
- 3 fireplaces, 12 chandeliers

Maude and Clyde are discussing whether to buy this nice little cottage. Identify as many fallacies and rhetorical devices as you can in their conversation.

CLYDE: Maude, look at this place! This is the house for us! Let's make an offer right now. We can afford it!

MAUDE: Oh, Clyde, be serious. That house is way beyond our means.

CLYDE: Well, I think we can afford it.

MAUDE: Honey, if we can afford it, pigs can fly.

CLYDE: Look, do you want to live in a shack? Besides, I called the real estate agent. She says it's a real steal.

MAUDE: Well, what do you expect her to say? She's looking for a commission.

CLYDE: Sometimes I don't understand you. Last week you were pushing for a really upscale place.

MAUDE: Clyde, we can't make the payments on a place like that. We couldn't even afford to heat it! And what on earth are we going to do with a lake?

CLYDE: Honey, the payments would only be around $5,000 a month. How much do you think we could spend?

MAUDE: I'd say $1,800.

CLYDE: Okay, how about $2,050?

MAUDE: Oh, for heaven's sake! Yes, we could do $2,050!

CLYDE: Well, how about $3,100?

MAUDE: Oh, Clyde, what is your point?

CLYDE: So $3,100 is okay? How about $3,200? Stop me when I get to exactly where we can't afford it.

MAUDE: Clyde, I can't say exactly where it gets to be too expensive, but $5,000 a month is too much.

CLYDE: Well, I think we can afford it.

MAUDE: Why?

CLYDE: Because it's within our means!

MAUDE: Clyde, you're the one who's always saying we have to cut back on our spending!

CLYDE: Yes, but this'll be a great investment!

MAUDE: And what makes you say that?

CLYDE: Because we're bound to make money on it.

MAUDE: Clyde, honey, you are going around in circles.

CLYDE: Well, can you prove we can't afford it?

MAUDE: Once we start spending money like drunken sailors, where will it end? Next we'll have to get a riding mower, then a boat for that lake, a butler for the butler's pantry—we'll owe everybody in the state!

CLYDE: Well, we don't have to make up our minds right now. I'll call the agent and tell her we're sleeping on it.

MAUDE: Asleep and dreaming.

Exercise A-6

Where we (Moore and Parker) teach, the city council recently debated relaxing the local noise ordinance. One student (who favored relaxation) appeared before the council and stated: "If 250 people are having fun, one person shouldn't be able to stop them."

We asked our students to state whether they agreed or disagreed with that student and to support their position with an argument. Here are some of the responses. Go through them and identify any instances of rhetorical devices or bad reasoning.

1 I support what the person is saying. If 250 people are having fun, 1 person shouldn't be able to stop them. Having parties and having a good time are a way of life for Chico State students. The areas around campus have always been this way.

2 A lot of people attend Chico State because of the social aspects. If rules are too tight, the school could lose its appeal. Without the students, local businesses would go under. Students keep the town floating. It's not just bars and liquor stores, but

gas stations and grocery stores and apartment houses. This town would be like Orland.

3 If students aren't allowed to party, the college will go out of business.

4 We work hard all week long studying and going to classes. We deserve to let off steam after a hard week.

5 Noise is a fact of life around most college campuses. People should know what they are getting into before they move there. If they don't like it, they should just get earplugs or leave.

6 I agree with what the person is saying. If 250 people want to have fun, what gives 1 person the right to stop them?

7 I am sure many of the people who complain are the same people who used to be stumbling down Ivy Street twenty years ago doing the same thing that the current students are doing.

8 Two weeks ago, I was at a party, and it was only about 9:00 P.M. There were only a few people there, and it was quiet. And then the police came and told us we had to break it up because a neighbor complained. Well, that neighbor is an elderly lady who would complain if you flushed the toilet. I think it's totally unreasonable.

9 Sometimes the noise level gets a little out of control, but there are other ways to go about addressing this problem. For example, if you are a neighbor, and you are having a problem with the noise level, why don't you call the "party house" and let them know, instead of going way too far and calling the police?

10 I'm sure that these "narcs" have nothing else better to do than to harass the "party people."

11 You can't get rid of all the noise around a college campus no matter what you do.

12 The Chico noise ordinance was put there by the duly elected officials of the city and is the law. People do not have the right to break a law that was put in place under proper legal procedures.

13 The country runs according to majority rule. If the overwhelming majority want to party and make noise, under our form of government they should be given the freedom to do so.

14 Students make a contribution to the community, and in return they should be allowed to make noise if they want.

15 Your freedom ends at my property line.

Exercise A-7

For the past four years, Cliff has attempted the 100-mile bike ride on the Fourth of July. He has never had the stamina to finish. He decides to attempt the ride again, but is pessimistic about his chances of finishing. How should each of the following suppositions affect his confidence that once again he *won't* finish?

1 Suppose past attempts were done in a variety of weather conditions.

2 Suppose Cliff will ride the same bike this year as on all previous attempts.

3 Suppose past attempts were on the same bike, but that is not the bike Cliff will ride this year.

4 Suppose Cliff hasn't yet decided what kind of bike to ride this year.

5 Suppose past attempts were all on flat ground, and this year's ride will also be on flat ground.

6 Suppose past attempts were all on flat ground, and this year's ride will be in hilly terrain.

7 Suppose past attempts were all in hilly terrain, and this year's ride will be on flat ground.

8 In answering question 7, did you consider only the stated information, or did you consider other things you know about bike riding?

9 Suppose some of past attempts were on flat ground and others were in hilly terrain, but where this year's ride will be hasn't been announced yet.

Exercise A-8

Explain how each of the following public opinion poll questions is slanted, if it is.

1 Some say Republican plans to reduce environmental safeguards will lead to more ecological disasters. Do you favor or oppose these plans?

2 Was BP slow to respond to the Gulf Oil Spill because it didn't care or because it hadn't adequately prepared for drilling in deep water?

3 Do you agree or disagree that immigration laws should be more vigorously enforced?

4 Some say that the high cost of medicine is due to frivolous lawsuits. Do you favor or oppose ceilings on the amount doctors can be sued for?

5 Polls indicate that most Americans are satisfied with their health care. Do you agree or disagree that health care reform is needed?

6 To reduce the federal deficit, do you favor raising taxes on working families or reducing excessive government spending?

7 To reduce the federal deficit, do you favor raising taxes on the super wealthy or slashing services for the needy?

8 Should a doctor be able to withhold medical care from a baby who has survived an abortion?

9 When framing new laws, should legislators be guided by Judeo-Christian values or only by secular considerations?

10 Would you favor or oppose reasonable background checks on people who want to purchase deadly assault weapons.

11 Many portions of the Affordable Care Act (Obamacare) will begin later this year and the Congressional Budget Office's estimate of the program's cost has increased to $1.85 trillion. Do you:

a. Support the complete repeal of the law

b. Support adding the additional billions to trillions in spending needed to run the program

c. Support legislation to fix the main problem in the law without repealing it

d. Support eliminating funding for the implementation of the law if the Senate and president won't repeal the law

e. Support both A and D

f. Support both B and C

Exercise A-9

Find a confidence-level indicator (e.g., possibly, maybe, and probably) or an error-margin indicator (e.g., around, about, and approximately) in each of the following arguments. Then, create a new argument with a more appropriate indicator.

Example

Original argument:

It rained yesterday. Therefore, it absolutely, positively will rain again today.

New argument with a more appropriate confidence-level indicator:

It rained yesterday. Therefore, it could well rain again today.

1 Paulette, Georgette, Babette, and Brigitte are all Miami University students, and they all are members of Webkinz. Therefore, all Miami University students are members of Webkinz.

2 Paulette, Georgette, Babette, and Brigitte are all Miami University students and the first three are members of Webkinz. Therefore, exactly three out of every four Miami University students is a member of Webkinz.

3 Gustavo likes all the business courses he has taken at Foothill College. Therefore, he is bound to like the next business course he takes at Foothill.

4 Gustavo liked two of the four business profs he has had at Foothill College. Therefore, he will like 50 percent of all his business profs at Foothill.

5 Gustavo likes all the business courses he has had at Foothill. No doubt his brother Sergio will like all his Foothill business courses, too.

6 Twenty percent of York's 8:00 A.M. class watch PBS. Therefore, 20 percent of York's 9:00 A.M. class watch PBS.

7 Twenty percent of York's 8:00 A.M. class watch PBS. Therefore, it is certain that exactly 20 percent of all the students at York's community college watch PBS.

8 Bill Clinton lied about his relationship with Monica Lewinsky; therefore, he lied about Jennifer Flowers as well.

9 Seventy percent of Walmart shoppers own cars. Therefore, the same percentage of Target customers own cars.

10 Susan likes Thanksgiving. We can be very certain, therefore, that she likes Christmas too.

Exercise A-10

Arrange the alternative conclusions of the following arguments in order of decreasing confidence level. Some options are pretty close to tied; don't get into feuds with classmates over close calls.

1 Not once this century has this city gone Republican in a presidential election. Therefore,
   a. I wouldn't count on it happening this time.
   b. It won't happen this time.
   c. In all likelihood, it won't happen this time.
   d. There's no chance whatsoever that it will happen this time.
   e. It would be surprising if it happened this time.
   f. I'll be a donkey's uncle if it happens this time.

2 Byron doesn't know how to play poker, so
   a. He sure as heck doesn't know how to play blackjack.
   b. It's doubtful he knows how to play blackjack.
   c. There's a possibility he doesn't know how to play blackjack.
   d. Don't bet on him knowing how to play blackjack.
   e. You're nuts if you think he knows how to play blackjack.

3 Every time I've used the Beltway, the traffic has been heavy, so I figure that
   a. The traffic is almost always heavy on the Beltway.
   b. Frequently the traffic on the Beltway is heavy.
   c. As a rule, the traffic on the Beltway is heavy.

d. The traffic on the Beltway can be heavy at times.
e. The traffic on the Beltway is invariably heavy.
f. Typically, the traffic on the Beltway is heavy.
g. The traffic on the Beltway is likely to be heavy most of the time.

Exercise A-11

In which of the following arguments is the implied confidence level too high or low, given the premises? After you have decided, compare your results with those of three or four classmates.

1 We spent a day on the Farallon Islands last June, and was it ever foggy and cold! So, dress warmly when you go there this June. Based on our experience, it is certain to be foggy and cold.

2 We've visited the Farallon Islands on five different days, two during the summer and one each during fall, winter, and spring. It's been foggy and cold every time we've been there. So, dress warmly when you go there. Based on our experience, there is an excellent chance it will be foggy and cold whenever you go.

3 We've visited the Farallon Islands on five different days, all in June. It's been foggy and cold every time we've been there. So, dress warmly when you go there in June. Based on our experience, it could well be foggy and cold.

4 We've visited the Farallon Islands on five different days, all in June. It's been foggy and cold every time we've been there. So, dress warmly when you go there in June. Based on our experience, there is some chance it will be foggy and cold.

5 We've visited the Farallon Islands on five different days, all in January. It's been foggy and cold every time we've been there. So, dress warmly when you go there in June. Based on our experience, it almost certainly will be foggy and cold.

Exercise A-12

In each of the following, determine whether the sample, the population, or the attribute of interest is excessively vague.

1 The tests in the class are going to be hard, judging from the first midterm.

2 The transmissions in Chrysler minivans tend to fail prematurely, if my Voyager is an indication.

3 Judging from my experience, technical people are exceedingly difficult to communicate with sometimes.

4 Men cannot tolerate stress. My husband even freaks if the newspaper is a little late.

5 Movies are too graphic these days. Just go to one—you'll see.

6 Violence in movies carries a message that degrades women. The movies playing right now prove the point.

7 You need to get cooler clothing than that if you're going to Minneapolis in the summer. I've been there.

8 Entertainment is much too expensive these days. Just look at what they charge for movies.

9 Art majors sure are weird! I roomed with one once. Man.

10 The French just don't like Americans. I couldn't find anyone in Paris who would speak English to me.

11 All the research suggests introverts are likely to be well versed in computer skills.

12 Suspicious people tend to be quite unhappy, from what I've observed.

13 Everyone marries someone who looks like him or her. Just check out the married people you know.

Exercise A-13

If you can, specify a sampling frame for each of the following populations and attributes. In other words, define them so one could determine whether a person or thing is a member of the population and has the attribute.

1 The proportion of Denver residents who watch *The Bachelorette*.

2 The proportion of religious people in your city who are conservatives.

3 The proportion of blondes at your university.

4 The proportion of country songs about lost love.

5 The proportion of plumbers in Chicago who play the Illinois Lotto.

6 The proportion of people with long necks who make good listeners.

Exercise A-14

Some of the following items would normally be seen as arguments and others as explanations. Sort the items into the proper categories.

1 Collins will probably be absent again today. She seemed pretty sick when I saw her.

2 Yes, I know Collins is sick, and I know why: She ate raw seafood.

3 Did Bobbie have a good time last night? Are you kidding? She had a great time! She stayed up all night, she had such a great time.

4 You don't think the toilet leaks? Why, just look at the water on the floor. What else could have caused it?

5 You know, it occurs to me the reason the band sounded so bad is the new director. They haven't had time to get used to her.

6 What a winter! And to think it's all just because there's a bunch of warm water off the Oregon coast.

7 Hmmm. I'm pretty sure you have the flu. If you had a cold, you wouldn't have aches and a fever. Aches and fever are a sign you have the flu.

8 Hillary Clinton goes up and down in the opinion polls. That's cause sometimes she makes sense, and other times she sounds crazy.

9 VIKKI: Remember the California Raisins? What happened to them?
NIKKI: They faded. I guess people got tired of them or something.

10 Believe it or not, for a while there, a lot of young women were shaving their heads. It was probably the Britney Spears influence.

11 Couples who regard each other as equals are more likely to suffer from high blood pressure than are couples in which one perceives the other as dominant. This is an excellent reason for marrying someone you think is beneath you.

12 Couples who regard each other as equals are more likely to suffer from high blood pressure than are couples in which one perceives the other as dominant. This is apparently because couples who see their partners as equals argue more, and that raises their blood pressure.

Exercise A-15

For each of the following, identify the presumed cause and the presumed effect. Then identify which items contain or imply a causal claim, hypothesis, or explanation that isn't testable. If an item falls into that category, decide whether the problem is due to vagueness, circularity, or some other problem.

1 What causes your engine to miss? Perhaps a fouled spark plug?
2 Antonio had a run of hard luck, but that's to be expected if you throw away a chain letter.
3 Veronica is grouchy because she doesn't sleep well.
4 Divine intervention can cure cancer.
5 The CIA destroyed the files because it didn't want agents identified.
6 Having someone pray for you can cure cancer.
7 Having your mother pray for you brings good luck.
8 Oatmeal lowers cholesterol.
9 Why did Blake get the flu? Because he's susceptible to it, obviously.
10 Federer won the match mainly because Roddick couldn't return his serve.
11 Federer won the match because he wanted to win more than Roddick did.
12 The reason Tuck can play high notes so well is that he has command of the upper register.
13 Professor York's French is improving, thanks to his trips to Paris.
14 "Men are biologically weaker than women and that's why they don't live as long."
   —*Attributed to "a leading expert" by* Weekly World News
15 Smoking marijuana can cause lung cancer.

Exercise A-16

For each of the following, identify the presumed cause and the presumed effect. Then identify which items contain or imply a causal claim, hypothesis, or explanation that isn't testable. If an item falls into that category, decide whether the problem is due to vagueness, circularity, or some other problem. If you see some other problem, raise your hand and tell everybody what it is.

1 He has blue eyes because he had them in a previous incarnation.
2 The Pacers did much better in the second half. That's because they gained momentum.
3 Alcoholics can't give up drinking because they are addicted to liquor.
4 *Gone with the Wind* was a big hit because reviewers praised it.
5 Nicholas, you want to know why you have so much bad luck? It's because you want to have bad luck. You have a subconscious desire for bad luck.
6 Why do I like Budweiser? Maybe I was subjected to subliminal advertising.
7 This part of the coast is subject to mudslides because there's a lack of mature vegetation.
8 As Internet use grew, insurance costs fell. The Internet apparently drove down insurance prices.
9 Within eleven months of September 11, 2001, eleven men connected to bioterror and germ warfare died in strange and violent circumstances. Don't tell me that's coincidence!
10 When his dog died, Ryan was so upset he could hardly eat. In my opinion, he was transferring his grief from his mother's death to his dog's.
11 Why does she sleep so late? Obviously, she's just one of those people who have a hard time waking up in the morning.
12 When parapsychologist Susan Blackmore failed to find evidence of ESP in numerous experiments, *Fate* magazine's consulting editor D. Scott Rogo explained her

negative results as due to subconscious resistance to the idea that psychic phenomena exist.

—Reported in The Skeptical Inquirer

13 According to a report in *Weekly World News,* when tourists defied an ancient curse and took rocks home from Hawaii's Volcanoes National Park, they paid the consequences. According to the report, the curse caused a Michigan man to tumble to his death falling downstairs, a Massachusetts woman to lose her savings in the stock market, and a Canadian tourist to die in a head-on car accident.

14 Why is there so much violence these days? Rap music, that's why.

15 The reason I got into so much trouble as a kid was that my father was a heavy drinker.

16 According to Martin Gardner, in Shivpuri, a town in India, there is a large stone ball weighing about 140 pounds. It is possible for five men to stand around the ball and touch the lower half with a forefinger; if they recite a prayer while doing so, the ball rises. Some believe this is a miracle of the god Shiva.

Exercise A-17

Identify each of the following as (a) a claim about a specific case of cause and effect, (b) a general causal claim, or (c) neither of these.

1   The hibiscus died while we were away. There must have been a frost.
2   Carlos isn't as fast as he used to be; that's what old age will do.
3   Kent's college education helped him get a high-paying job.
4   The most frequently stolen vehicle of 2012 was a 1994 Honda Accord.
5   Vitamin C prevents colds.
6   The woman he returned to be with is Deborah.
7   The high reading on the thermometer resulted from two causes: This thermometer was located lower to the ground than at other stations, and its shelter was too small, so the ventilation was inadequate.
8   Oily smoke in the exhaust is caused by worn rings.
9   The initial tests indicate that caffeine has toxic effects in humans.
10 Neonatal sepsis is usually fatal among newborns.
11 WIN 51,711 halts development of paralysis in mice that have been infected with polio-2.
12 A stuck hatch cover on *Spacelab* blocked a French ultraviolet camera from conducting a sky survey of celestial objects.
13 An experimental drug has shown broad antiviral effects on a large number of the picornaviruses against which it has been tested.
14 Investigation revealed the problem was a short-circuited power supply.
15 Arteriovenous malformations—distortions of the capillaries connecting an arteriole and a small vein in the brain—can bleed, causing severe headaches, seizures, and even death.
16 Because of all the guns that its citizens own, the United States has never been invaded.
17 According to two reports in the *New England Journal of Medicine,* oil from fish can prevent heart disease.
18 The most important cause in the growing problem of illiteracy is television.
19 "Raymond the Wolf passed away in his sleep one night from natural causes; his heart stopped beating when the three men who slipped into his bedroom stuck knives in it."

—Jimmy Breslin, The Gang That Couldn't Shoot Straight

Exercise A-18

Match each item to a concept on this list:

A = overlooking prior probabilities or false positives
B = overlooking the possibility of regression
C = misplacing the burden of proof
D = argument from anecdote
E = *conditio sine qua non*
F = confusing explanations with excuses

1 The Amazing Vikings had an off night. Their shooting was poor, their defense uninspired. Everything was reflected in the lopsided score. "Laps," Coach Snort said after the loss. "Nobody showers before he does ten laps!" When the guys won their next game, the coach knew he had done the right thing. "You just gotta motivate them," he thought.

2 If your eyes are extremely sensitive to light, there is better than a 50–50 chance you have bacterial meningitis, since light sensitivity almost always accompanies the disease.

3 Wood smoke a health hazard? You kidding? We been using wood our entire lives to heat with. You gonna tell me we wouldn't know about it if it had hurt us?

4 Eat plenty of carbohydrates before an intense workout. Nobody has ever shown that carbo-loading doesn't enhance athletic performance.

5 The research team administered Deconolate to the men whose recent PSA readings were highly elevated, and then retested them. The average PSA reading for the group had declined markedly, suggesting that Deconolate may be useful in the fight against prostate cancer.

6 It is ridiculous for the FDA to ban ephedrine. I used the stuff for years to help with allergies, and I am as healthy as a horse.

7 Spokesperson for BP: Halliburton cemented the drill in place, not BP.
Congressperson: Don't try to put the blame on someone else.

8 "It's your fault!"
"What? I didn't run over the sprinkler! You did!!"
"Yeah, but if you had remembered the milk, I wouldn't even be going to the store."

9 After an evening when the mosquitoes were particularly bad, Tony rushed out to Ace and bought a Mosquito Magnet. That evening the mosquitoes didn't seem as bad. "It works," Tony told his wife.

10 If the HDL reading of a male over 50 is low, the odds are he has heart disease, since most men over 50 with heart disease have low HDL readings.

Glossary

Accident A fallacy that occurs when a speaker or writer assumes that a general statement automatically applies to a specific case that is (or could well be) exceptional.

Ad Hominem *See Argumentum Ad Hominem.*

Affirmative claim A claim that includes one class or part of one class within another: A- and I-claims.

Affirming the Antecedent *See Modus Ponens.*

Affirming the Consequent A fallacy, consisting of a conditional claim as one premise, a claim that affirms the consequent of the conditional as a second premise, and a claim that affirms the antecedent of the conditional as the conclusion.

Ambiguity Having more than one meaning. An ambiguous claim is one that can be interpreted in more than one way and whose meaning is not made clear by the context. *See also* Semantic ambiguity; Syntactic ambiguity.

Ambiguous pronoun reference A statement or phrase in which it is not clear to what or to whom a pronoun is supposed to refer.

Amphiboly A fallacy that occurs when a speaker or writer attempts to demonstrate or support a point by playing on the ambiguity of an expression, where the ambiguity derives from the expression's syntax.

Analogical argument *See* Argument from Analogy.

Analogues Things that have similar attributes.

Analogy A linguistic expression that treats two or more events or things as similar.

Analytic claim A claim whose truth or falsity is determined simply by the definitions of the words that make it up. Contrast with *Synthetic claim.*

Analytical definition Specification of the features a thing must possess in order for the term being defined to apply to it.

Anecdotal Evidence, Fallacy of *See* Argument by Anecdote.

Antecedent *See* Conditional claim.

Appeal to Common Practice See *Mistaken* Appeal to Common Practice.

Appeal to Emotion A fallacy that occurs when a speaker or writer "supports" a contention by playing on our emotions rather than by producing a real argument.

Appeal to Envy An appeal-to-emotion fallacy that occurs when a speaker or writer "supports" a contention by trying to make us envious rather than by producing a real argument.

Appeal to Ignorance A fallacy that occurs when a speaker or writer argues that we should believe a claim because nobody has proved it false.

Appeal to Jealousy An appeal-to-emotion fallacy that occurs when a speaker or writer "supports" a contention by trying to make us jealous rather than by producing a real argument.

Appeal to Pity An appeal-to-emotion fallacy that occurs when a speaker or writer "supports" a contention by playing on our sympathy rather than by producing a real argument.

Appeal to Popularity *See* Mistaken Appeal to Popularity.

Appeal to Precedent The claim (in law) that a current case is sufficiently similar to a previous case that it should be settled in the same way.

Appeal to Tradition *See* Mistaken Appeal to Common Practice.

Apple Polishing An appeal-to-emotion fallacy that occurs when a speaker or writer "supports" a contention by trying to flatter us rather than by producing a real argument.

Argument An attempt to support or prove a contention by providing a reason for accepting it. The contention itself is called the *conclusion;* the statement (or statements) offered as support or demonstration is referred to as the *premise* (or premises). Sometimes "argument" is used to refer only to the premise (or premises).

Argument by Anecdote A fallacy that occurs when a speaker or writer tries to support a general claim by offering a story.

Argument by Anecdote—causal variety A fallacy that occurs when a speaker or writer tries to support a causal statement by offering a story.

Argument from Analogy An argument that something has an attribute because a similar thing has that attribute.

Argument from Outrage An appeal-to-emotion fallacy that occurs when a speaker or writer "supports" a contention by trying to make us angry rather than by producing a real argument.

Argument pattern The structure of an argument. This structure is independent of the argument's content. Several arguments can have the same pattern (e.g., *Modus Ponens*) yet be about quite different subjects. Variables are used to stand for classes or claims in the display of an argument's pattern.

Argumentum Ad Hominem A fallacy that occurs when a speaker or writer attempts to dismiss someone's position by dismissing the person (rather than attacking his or her position).

Attacking the analogy An attempt to rebut an argument from analogy by calling attention to important dissimilarities between the analogues.

Attribute of interest The attribute ascribed to a thing or things in the conclusion of an inductive generalization, inductive Argument from Analogy, or statistical syllogism.

Atypical sample *See* Biased sample.

Availability heuristic Unconsciously assigning a probability to a type of event on the basis of how often one thinks of events of that type.

Background information The body of justified beliefs that consists of facts we learn from our own direct observations and facts we learn from others.

Balance of considerations reasoning Trying to determine which considerations, both for and against thinking or doing something, carry the most weight.

Bandwagon effect An unconscious tendency to modify one's views to make them consonant with those of other people.

Bandwagon Fallacy An appeal-to-emotion fallacy that occurs when a speaker or writer "supports" a contention not by producing a real argument for it but by playing on our desire to be in step with popular opinion.

Begging the Question A fallacy that occurs when a speaker or writer tries to "support" or "demonstrate" a contention by offering as "evidence" or "proof" what amounts to a repackaging of the very contention in question.

Belief bias The tendency to evaluate an argument by how believable its conclusion is.

Better-than-average illusion When a majority of a group estimates they are better at something than a majority of the group, the group is said to be subject to this illusion. When the majority of a group estimates they are worse at something than a majority of group, they are said to be subject to the "worse than average illusion."

Biased (skewed) sample A sample in which an important variable is disproportionately present or absent. *See also* Fallacy of Biased Sample.

But for cause A *conditio sine qua non,* a condition without which an effect could not have happened.

Category A group, collection, class, population, or division of things.

Categorical claim A claim that asserts or denies membership in second category by members of a first category. *See also* Standard-form categorical claim.

Categorical imperative Kant's term for an absolute moral rule that holds unconditionally or "categorically."

Categorical logic A system of logic based on the relations of inclusion and exclusion among categories. This branch of logic specifies the logical relationships among claims that can be expressed in the forms "All Xs are Ys," "No Xs are Ys," "Some Xs are Ys," and "Some Xs are not Ys." Developed by Aristotle in the fourth century B.C.E., categorical logic is also known as Aristotelian or traditional logic.

Categorical syllogism A two-premise deductive argument in which every claim is categorical and each of three terms appears in two of the claims—for example, all soldiers are martinets and no martinets are diplomats, so no soldiers are diplomats.

Causal hypothesis A tentative causal statement offered for further investigation or testing.

Causal factor A causal factor for an effect is a variable whose presence in a population raises the probability that the effect will be present as well.

Causal mechanism An interface between cause and effect that has the property of making the effect happen, given the cause.

Causal statement A statement that sets forth the cause of an event.

Cause-and-effect claim *See* Causal statement.

Chain argument An argument consisting of three conditional claims, in which the antecedents of one premise and the conclusion are the same, the consequents of the other premise and the conclusion are the same, and the consequent of the first premise and the antecedent of the second premise are the same.

Circularity The property of a cause-and-effect claim where the "cause" merely restates the effect.

Claim When a belief (judgment, opinion) is asserted in a declarative sentence, the result is a claim or statement.

Claim variable A letter that stands for a claim.

Cognitive bias A psychological factor that unconsciously affects belief formation.

Common variable principle A principle for forming a causal hypothesis that must be guided by common sense and background knowledge: a variable common to multiple occurrences of something may be related to it causally. *See* also Covariation principle and Paired unusual events principle.

Complementary term A term is complementary to another term if and only if it refers to everything that the first term does not refer to.

Composition A fallacy that happens when a speaker or writer assumes that what is true of a group of things taken individually must also be true of those same things taken collectively; or assumes that what is true of the parts of a thing must be true of the thing itself.

Conclusion In an argument, the claim thought to be supported or demonstrated by another claim (or claims) referred to as the premise (or premises).

Conclusion indicator A word or phrase (e.g., "therefore") that ordinarily indicates the presence of the conclusion of an argument.

Conclusion-analogue The analogue referred to in the conclusion of an argument from analogy. Sometimes called *target analogue.*

Conditio sine qua non A condition without which it could not be. Often referred to as a "but for cause."

Conditional claim A claim that state-of-affairs A cannot hold without state-of-affairs B holding as well—e.g., "If A, then B." The A-part of the claim is called the *antecedent;* the B-part is called the *consequent.*

Conditional probability The probability of an event if another has occurred.

Conditional proof (CP) A deduction for a conditional claim "If P, then Q" that proceeds by assuming that P is true and then proving that, on that assumption, Q must also be true.

Confidence level The probability that the random variation of a sample proportion from random sample to random sample will fall within the error margin. *See also* Sample proportion.

Confirmation bias A tendency to attach more weight to considerations that support our views.

Conflicting claims Two claims that cannot both be correct.

Confounding variable   A variable that, in an investigation of causation, may be causally linked with an effect of interest or cause of interest, but which is not the subject of the investigation.

Confusing Contraries and Contradictories   A fallacy in which two contrary claims are taken as contradictories or *vice versa*. *See also* Contrary claims and contradictories.

Confusing Explanations with Excuses   The fallacy of presuming that when someone explains how or why something happened, he or she is either excusing or justifying what happened.

Conjunction   A compound claim made from two simpler claims. A conjunction is true if and only if both of the simpler claims that compose it are true.

Consequent   *See* Conditional Claim.

Consequentialism   In moral reasoning, the view that the consequences of a decision, deed, or policy determine its moral value.

Consistency and inconsistency   A set of beliefs is consistent if it is possible for them all to be true at the same time, and inconsistent if it is not possible for them to all be true at the same time.

Consistency principle   The first principle of moral reasoning, which states that, if separate cases aren't different in any relevant way, they should be treated the same way, and if separate cases are treated in the same way, they should not be different in any relevant way.

Contradictories   Two statements that are exact opposites; they cannot both be true and cannot both be false.

Contradictory claims   *See* Contradictories.

Contrapositive   The claim that results from switching the places of the subject and predicate terms in a categorical claim and replacing both terms with complementary terms.

Contraries   Two statements that cannot both be true but can both be false.

Contrary analogue   *See* Contrary premise-analogue.

Contrary claims   *See* Contraries.

Contrary premise-analogue   A premise-analogue that weakens an argument from analogy; a disanalogy.

Converse   The converse of a categorical claim is the claim that results from switching the places of the subject and predicate terms.

Covariation principle   A principle for forming a causal hypothesis that must be guided by common sense and background knowledge: If a variation in one phenomenon is accompanied by a variation in another, consider whether the two phenomena may be related causally. *See* also Common variable principle and Paired unusual events principle.

Critical thinking   We think critically when we rationally evaluate our own or others' thinking.

Cum Hoc, Ergo Propter Hoc   "With this, therefore because of it." A fallacy that occurs when a speaker or writer assumes that the fact that two events happen at about the same time establishes that one caused the other.

Deduction (proof)   A numbered sequence of truth-functional symbolizations, each member of which

validly follows from earlier members by one of the truth-functional rules.

Deductive argument   An argument intended to prove or demonstrate, rather than merely support, a conclusion.

Definition by example   Pointing to, naming, or otherwise identifying one or more examples of the term being defined; also called *ostensive definition*.

Definition by synonym   Giving another word or phrase that means the same thing as the term being defined.

Demonizing   A rhetorical technique that tries to induce loathing of someone or something by portraying the person or thing as evil.

Denial   A fallacy that occurs when we forget that wanting something to be false is irrelevant to whether it is false.

Denying the Antecedent   A fallacy, consisting of a conditional claim as one premise, a claim that denies the antecedent of the conditional as a second premise, and a claim that denies the consequent of the conditional as the conclusion.

Denying the Consequent   *See* Modus Tollens.

Deontologism   *See* Duty theory.

Disanalogy   *See* Contrary premise-analogue.

Disinterested party   A person who has no stake in our belief or disbelief in a claim. *See also* Interested party.

Disjunction   A compound claim made up of two simpler claims. A disjunction is false only if both of the simpler claims that make it up are false.

Distribution   A term is distributed if and only if the category it names is referred to in its entirety.

Diversified sample   A sample whose members are heterogeneous.

Divine command theory   The view that our moral duty (what's right and wrong) is dictated by God.

Division   A fallacy that occurs when a speaker or writer assumes that what is true of a group of things taken collectively must also be true of those same things taken individually; or assumes that what is true of a whole is also true of its parts.

Downplayer   An expression used to play down or diminish the importance of something.

Duty theory   The view that a person should perform an action because it is his or her moral duty to perform it, not because of any consequences that might follow from it. Also called *Deontologism*.

Dysphemism   A word or phrase used to produce a negative effect on a reader's or listener's attitude about something or to minimize the positive associations the thing may have.

Emotive meaning   The positive or negative associations of an expression; an expression's *rhetorical force*.

Equivalent claims   Two claims are equivalent if and only if in exactly the same circumstances they would both have the same truth-value.

Equivocation   A fallacy that occurs when a speaker or writer attempts to demonstrate or support a point by playing on the ambiguity of an expression.

Error margin   The range of random variation of a sample proportion across multiple random samples of a given size.

Ethical altruism   The moral doctrine that discounts one's own happiness as being of lesser value than the happiness of others.

Ethical egoism   The moral doctrine that the rightness of an act is determined by the happiness it produces for oneself.

Euphemism   An agreeable or inoffensive expression that is substituted for an expression that may be found unpleasant or offensive by a listener or reader.

Expectation values (EV)   The likelihood of a result combined with the possible effects of that result (e.g., the likelihood of your winning a poker hand combined with the amount you would stand to gain).

Expert   A person who, through training, education, or experience, has special knowledge or ability in a subject.

Expertise   An unusual knowledge or ability in a given subject, most often due to specialized experience or education.

Explanation   A claim or set of claims intended to make another claim, object, event, or state of affairs intelligible. Also, an account of how an object, event, or state of affairs came to be.

Explanatory analogy   An analogy that is used to explain.

Explanatory definition   A definition used to explain, illustrate, or disclose important aspects of a difficult concept.

Extension   The set of things to which a term applies.

"Fact vs. opinion"   Sometimes people refer to true objective claims as "facts," and use the word "opinion" to designate any claim that is subjective.

Factual claim   An objective claim.

Fallacy   A common mistake in reasoning.

Fallacy of Biased Sample   A fallacy that occurs when a speaker or writer generalizes about a large or heterogeneous population on the basis of an atypical sample.

Fallacy of Induction   *See* Induction fallacy.

Fallacy of Small Sample   A fallacy that occurs when a speaker or writer generalizes about a large or heterogeneous population on the basis of too small a sample.

Fallacy of the Lonely Fact   *See* Hasty Generalization.

False Analogy   *See* Weak Analogy.

False consensus effect   Assuming that the views held by members of our group are held by society at large.

False Dilemma   A fallacy that occurs when a speaker or writer tries to establish a point by offering it as the only alternative to something we will find unacceptable, unattainable, or implausible.

Faulty inductive conversion   Mistakenly thinking that, from information about the percentage of As that are Bs, you can derive a conclusion about the percentage of Bs that are As.

Fear or hate mongering   A rhetorical technique that occurs when speakers or writers make inflammatory or scary statements intended to anger or frighten us, without

pretending that the statements support a specific conclusion.

Formal fallacy   A fallacy that occurs when a speaker or writer advances a deductive argument that has an invalid logical form.

Fostering xenophobia   *See* Xenophobia.

Fundamental attribution error   A tendency to attribute the mistakes of members of the in-group to extenuating circumstances, while attributing the same mistakes when made by members of out-groups to character defects.

Gambler's Fallacy   A failure to recognize that independent events do not affect one another's outcome—a belief that past performance of such events (as coin tosses) can affect later events.

General statement   A statement that refers to members of a population nonspecifically or in a nonspecific way.

Generality   Lack of detail or specificity. The more different kinds of Xs to which the word for Xs applies, the more general that word is.

Generalization   An argument used to support a general statement. The word also is used as a synonym for "general statement."

Generalizing   *See* Generalizing from a Sample.

Generalizing from a Sample   Reasoning that all, most, or some percentage of the members of a population have an attribute because all, most, or some percentage of a sample of the population have that attribute.

Generalizing from a Small Sample   *See* Fallacy of Small Sample.

Generalizing from Exceptional Cases   A fallacy that occurs when a speaker or writer arrives at a general statement by citing an atypical supporting case.

Generalizing from Too Few Cases   *See* Hasty Generalization.

Genetic Fallacy   A fallacy that occurs when a speaker or writer argues that the origin of a contention in and of itself automatically renders it false.

Good deductive argument   *See* Valid argument.

Good inductive argument   A relatively strong inductive argument. *See also* Stronger/weaker arguments.

Grouping ambiguity   A kind of semantic ambiguity in which it is unclear whether a claim refers to a group of things taken individually or collectively.

Guilt by Association   A fallacy that occurs when a speaker or writer tries to induce us to dismiss a belief by telling us that someone we don't like has that belief.

Guilt Tripping   An appeal-to-emotion fallacy that occurs when a speaker or writer "supports" a contention by trying to make us feel guilty rather than by producing a real argument.

Harm principle   The claim that the only way to justify a restriction on a person's freedom is to show that the restriction prevents harm to other people.

Hasty Generalization   A fallacy that occurs when a speaker or writer tries to support a general statement or rule by citing too few supporting cases. *See also* Fallacy of Small Sample.

Heterogeneous sample/population A sample/population whose members have a large variety of characteristics.

Heuristic A rule of thumb employed unconsciously by people when they estimate probabilities. In psychology, the field known as "heuristics and biases" was originated by Daniel Kahneman and Amos Tversky.

Homogeneous sample/population A sample/population whose members have the same characteristics.

Horse laugh *See* Ridicule.

Hyperbole Extravagant overstatement.

Hypothesis *See* Causal hypothesis.

Hypothetical imperative Kant's term for an imperative that tells us how we must act to reach a specific objective.

IBE *See* Inference to the Best Explanation.

In-group bias A predisposition to find fault with outsiders.

Inconsistency *See* Consistency.

Incorrectly Combining the Probabilities of Independent Events Adding rather than multiplying the probabilities of independent events.

Independent events Two events are independent when neither of them has an effect on the outcome of the other.

Indirect proof Proof of a claim by demonstrating that its negation is false, absurd, or self-contradictory.

Induction fallacy An argument that is supposed to raise the probability of its conclusion, but is so weak as to fail almost entirely to do so.

Inference to the Best Explanation (IBE) An argument that concludes that something exists or holds true or is a fact because that supposition best explains something we have observed or otherwise know.

Initial plausibility One's rough assessment of how credible a claim seems.

Innuendo An insinuation of something derogatory.

Intension The set of characteristics a thing must have for a term correctly to apply to it.

Interested party A person who stands to gain from our believing his or her claim. *See also* Disinterested party.

Invalid argument An argument that isn't valid.

Irrelevant Conclusion Any relevance fallacy that does not fit comfortably into the other categories discussed in this book.

Issue A point that is or might be disputed, debated, or wondered about. Essentially, a question.

Knowledge If you believe a claim, have an argument for it that is beyond reasonable doubt, and have no reason to think you are mistaken, you may be said to have knowledge that the claim is true.

Legal cause That combination of fact and policy that holds a person legally responsible for harm only if the harm caused can be traced back to that person's actions. Also referred to as *proximate cause*.

Legal moralism The theory that, if an activity is immoral, it should also be illegal.

Legal paternalism The theory that a restriction on a person's freedom can sometimes be justified by showing that it is for that person's own benefit.

Lexical definition The meaning of a word that is given in the dictionary.

Line-Drawing Fallacy A fallacy that occurs when a speaker or writer assumes that either a crystal-clear line can be drawn between two things, or they cannot really be differentiated.

Loaded question A question that rests on one or more unwarranted or unjustified assumptions.

Logic The branch of philosophy concerned with whether the reasons presented for a claim, if those reasons were true, would justify accepting the claim.

Logical analogy An analogy whose analogues are arguments.

Loss aversion Being more strongly motivated to avoid a loss than to accrue a gain.

Mean A type of average. The arithmetic mean of a group of numbers is the number that results when their sum is divided by the number of members in the group.

Median A type of average. In a group of numbers, as many numbers of the group are larger than the median as are smaller.

Method of Agreement *See* Common variable principle.

Method of Concomitant Variation *See* Covariation principle.

Method of Difference *See* Paired unusual events principle.

Misplacing the Burden of Proof A fallacy that occurs when a speaker or writer attempts to support or prove a point by trying to make us disprove it.

Mistaken Appeal to Authority A fallacy that occurs when a speaker or writer tries to support a contention by offering as evidence the opinion of a nonauthoritative source.

Mistaken Appeal to Common Belief *See* Mistaken Appeal to Popularity.

Mistaken Appeal to Popularity A fallacy that occurs when a speaker or writer treats an issue that cannot be settled by public opinion as if it can. Also known as Mistaken Appeal to Common Belief.

Mistaken Appeal to Common Practice A fallacy that occurs when a speaker or writer tries to justify a practice on the grounds that it is traditional or is commonly practiced.

Mistaken Appeal to Tradition *See* Mistaken Appeal to Common Practice

Mode A type of average. In a group of numbers, the mode is the number occurring most frequently.

Modus ponens An argument consisting of a conditional claim as one premise, a claim that affirms the antecedent of the conditional as a second premise, and a claim that affirms the consequent of the conditional as the conclusion.

Modus tollens An argument consisting of a conditional claim as one premise, a claim that denies the consequent of the conditional as a second premise, and a claim that denies the antecedent of the conditional as the conclusion.

Moral relativism   The view that what is morally right and wrong depends on and is determined by one's group or culture.

Moral subjectivism   The idea that what is right and wrong is merely a matter of subjective opinion, that thinking something is right or wrong makes it right or wrong for that individual.

Naturalistic fallacy   The assumption that one can conclude directly from a fact (what "is") what a rule or a policy should be (an "ought") without a value-premise.

Negation   The contradictory of a given claim; the negation of claim P is usually given as "not-P."

Negative claim   A claim that excludes one class or part of one class from another: E- and O-claims.

Negativity bias   An unconscious tendency to give more weight to negative evaluations than to positive evaluations.

Non sequitur   A statement that is unrelated to the statement that immediately preceded it.

Normative statement   *See* Value judgment.

Obedience to authority   The tendency to comply with instructions from an authority even when they conflict with our values.

Objective claim   *See* Objective statement.

Objective issue   *See* Objective question.

Objective question   A question whose answer is an objective statement.

Objective statement   A statement that is not made true or false by the speaker or writer's thinking it is true or false.

Obverse   The obverse of a categorical claim is that claim that is directly across from it in the square of opposition, with the predicate term changed to its complementary term.

Offense principle   The claim that an action or activity can justifiably be made illegal if it is sufficiently offensive.

Opinion   A claim that somebody believes to be true.

Ostensive definition   *See* Definition by example.

Otherizing   A rhetorical technique that divides people into two groups: Us and Them; and portrays Them as suspicious, dangerous, or repulsive. Them includes ideological opponents and other social groups who can be blamed for our problems. Minorities with their "unreasonable demands" are easy targets.

Overconfidence effect   A tendency to overestimate the percentage of correct answers we have given to questions on a subject we are not experts about.

Overestimating the strength of an argument Assigning an inappropriately high confidence-level indicator or an inappropriately narrow error-margin indicator to the conclusion of an inductive argument.

Overlooking a Possible Common Cause   A fallacy that occurs when a speaker or writer overlooks the possibility that two things may both be the effects of a third thing.

Overlooking Prior Probabilities   A fallacy that occurs when a speaker or writer estimates the probability of something only on the basis of new data, without taking into account its prior probability.

Overlooking the Possibility of Coincidence   A fallacy that occurs when a speaker or writer assumes that a coincidental temporal juxtaposition of two events is due to causation.

Overlooking the Possibility of Random Variation   A fallacy that occurs when a speaker or writer assumes that random fluctuation is due to causation.

Overlooking the Possibility of Regression   A fallacy that occurs when a speaker or writer assumes that a change in the value of a variable from more atypical to less on subsequent measurements is due to causation.

Overlooking the Possibility of Reversed Causation   A fallacy that occurs when a speaker or writer overlooks the possibility that the stated cause may actually be the effect, and the stated effect may actually be the cause.

Paired unusual events principle   A principle for forming a causal hypothesis that must be guided by common sense and background knowledge: If something unusual happens, look for something else unusual that has happened and consider whether it might be the cause. *See* also Common variable principle and Covariation principle.

Paralipsis   A passing over with brief mention so as to emphasize the suggestiveness of what is omitted. Also called *Significant mention.*

Peer Pressure Fallacy   A fallacy that occurs when a speaker or writer tries to persuade us to do or accept something by playing on our fear of becoming an outcast if we don't.

Perfectionist Fallacy   A fallacy that occurs when a speaker or writer ignores options between "perfection" and "nothing."

Poisoning the Well   A fallacy that occurs when a speaker or writer attempts to dismiss what someone is going to say, by talking about the person's character or circumstances or consistency.

Population   An identifiable group of things.

Post Hoc, Ergo Propter Hoc   "After this, therefore because of it." A fallacy that occurs when a speaker or writer assumes that the fact that one event came after another establishes that it was caused by it.

Precising definition   A definition whose purpose is to reduce vagueness or generality or to eliminate ambiguity.

Predicate term   The noun or noun phrase that refers to the second class mentioned in a standard-form categorical claim.

Predictable ratio   The ratio that the results of a series of events can be expected to have, given the antecedent conditions of the series. Examples: The predictable ratio of a fair coin flip is 50 percent heads and 50 percent tails; the predictable ratio of sevens coming up when a pair of fair dice is rolled is 1 in 6, or just under 17 percent.

Premise indicator   A word or phrase (e.g., "since it is the case that . . .") that ordinarily indicates the presence of the premise of an argument.

Premise   The claim or claims in an argument thought to support or demonstrate a conclusion.

Premise-analogue   An argument from analogy is an argument that something has an attribute because a similar thing has that attribute. The similar thing is the premise-analogue.

Principle of Total Evidence   The idea that in estimating probabilities of something, you must take into account all available relevant information.

Principle of utility   The basic principle of utilitarianism, to create as much overall happiness and/or to limit unhappiness for as many as possible.

Prior probability   *See* True proportion.

Probability of an event   The probability of an event is its likelihood of happening expressed as a proportion, percentage or decimal.

Proof surrogate   An expression used to suggest that there is evidence or authority for a claim without actually saying what it is.

Propositional logic   *See* Truth-functional logic.

Prospective observational study   A study of two groups, in one of which a suspected causal agent is universally present, and in the other of which it is universally absent. A significant difference in the frequency of a suspected "effect" in the comparison groups is evidence of causal linkage between it and the suspected causal agent. Also known as a nonexperimental cause-to-effect study.

Proximate cause   *See* Legal cause.

Random sample   A sample selected by a procedure that gives every member of a population an equal chance of being included.

Randomized controlled experiment   An experiment in which subjects are randomly assigned either to an "experimental group" (E) or a "control" (C), which theoretically differ from one another in only one respect: subjects in the E group are subjected to a suspected cause.

Red herring   *See* Relevance Fallacy.

Reductio Ad Absurdum   An attempt to show that a claim is false by demonstrating that it has false or absurd logical consequences; literally, "reducing to an absurdity."

Regression   *See* Statistical regression.

Relativism   The idea that truth is relative to the standards of a given culture. More precisely, relativism holds that if your culture and some other culture have different standards of truth or evidence, there is no independent "God's-eye view" by which one culture's standards can be seen to be more correct than the other's.

Relevance fallacy   Any fallacy that occurs when a speaker or writer attempts to support or prove a point by bringing up an irrelevant consideration. Includes several varieties, such as *Argumentum Ad Hominem,* Straw Man, and Appeal to Emotion.

Religious absolutism   The view that the correct moral principles are those accepted by the "correct" religion.

Religious relativism   The belief that what is right and wrong is whatever one's religious culture or society deems it to be.

Representative sample   A sample that isn't biased. *See also* Fallacy of Biased Sample.

Retrospective observational study   A study of two groups, in one of which a phenomenon of interest is universally present, and in the other of which it is universally absent. A significant difference in the frequency of a suspected causal agent in the comparison groups is evidence of causal linkage between it and the phenomenon. Also known as a nonexperimental effect-to-cause study.

Rhetoric   In our usage, "rhetoric" is language used primarily to persuade or influence beliefs or attitudes rather than to prove logically.

Rhetorical analogy   An analogy used to express or influence attitudes or affect behavior; such analogies often invoke images with positive or negative emotional associations.

Rhetorical definition   A pseudodefinition given to express our feelings or influence someone else's.

Rhetorical device   Rhetorical devices are used to influence beliefs or attitudes through the associations, connotations, and implications of words, sentences, and more extended passages. While rhetorical devices may be used to enhance the persuasive force of arguments, they do not add to their logical force.

Rhetorical explanation   An explanation intended to influence attitudes or affect behavior; such explanations often make use of images with positive or negative emotional associations.

Rhetorical force   *See* Emotive meaning.

Ridicule   A rhetorical technique whereby a speaker or writer seeks to discredit someone by mocking him or her, or to rebut his or her position by making fun of it.

Sample proportion   The proportion of a sample that has an attribute of interest.

Sample size   Sample size can affect the size of the error margin or the confidence level of inductive generalizations from a sample.

Sample   A subset of a population.

Sample-analogue   *See* premise-analogue.

Sampling frame   A precise definition of a sample or attribute that makes it unambiguous whether any given thing is a member of the sample and has the attribute.

Sarcasm   *See* Ridicule.

Scapegoating   Placing the blame for some bad effect on a person or group of people who are not really responsible for it but who provide an easy target for animosity.

Scare Tactics   A fallacy that occurs when a speaker or writer tries to scare us into accepting an irrelevant conclusion. Includes direct threats (which sometimes are called "arguments from force").

Self-contradictory claim   A claim that is analytically false.

Self-selected sample   A sample whose members are included by their own decision.

Self-Selection Fallacy   A fallacy that occurs when a speaker or writer generalizes incautiously from a self-selected sample.

Semantic ambiguity   *See* Semantically ambiguous claim.

Semantically ambiguous claim   An ambiguous claim whose ambiguity is due to the ambiguity of a word or phrase in the claim.

Significant mention   *See* Paralipsis.

Skewed sample   *See* Biased sample.

Slanter   A linguistic device used to affect opinions, attitudes, or behavior without argumentation. Slanters rely heavily on the suggestive power of words and phrases to convey and evoke favorable and unfavorable images.

Slippery Slope   A fallacy that occurs when a speaker or writer rests a conclusion on an unsupported warning that is controversial and tendentious, to the effect that something will progress by degrees to an undesirable outcome.

Social utility   A focus on what is good for society (usually in terms of overall happiness) when deciding on a course of action. *See also* Principle of utility.

Sound argument   A valid argument whose premises are true.

Spin   Statements using rhetorical devices and techniques to evoke positive or negative reactions to a politician or political party or perspective.

Square of opposition   A table of the logical relationships between two categorical claims that correspond to each other.

Standard-form categorical claim   Any claim that results from putting words or phrases that name categories in the blanks of one of the following structures: "All _____ are _____"; "No _____ are _____"; "Some _____ are _____"; and "Some _____ are not _____."

Stare decisis   "Letting the decision stand." Going by precedent.

Statistical regression   If the average value of a variable is atypical on one measurement, it is likely to be less atypical on a subsequent measurement.

Statistical syllogism   A syllogism having this form: Such-and-such proportion of Xs are Ys.

This is an X.
_____
Therefore this is a Y.

Statistically significant   From a statistical point of view, probably not due to chance.

Stereotype   A cultural belief or idea about a social group's attributes, usually simplified or exaggerated. It can be positive or negative.

Stipulative definition   A definition (of a word) that is specific to a particular context.

Straw Man   A fallacy that occurs when a speaker or writer attempts to dismiss a contention by distorting or misrepresenting it.

Stronger/weaker arguments   The more likely the premise of an inductive argument makes the conclusion, the stronger the argument, and the less likely it makes the conclusion, the weaker the argument.

Subcontrary claims   Two claims that can both be true at the same time but cannot both be false at the same time.

Subject term   The noun or noun phrase that refers to the first class mentioned in a standard-form categorical claim.

Subjective claim   *See* Subjective statement.

Subjective expression   *See* Subjective statement.

Subjective issue   *See* Subjective question.

Subjective question   A question whose answer is a subjective statement.

Subjective statement   A statement that is made true or false by the speaker or writer's thinking it is true or false.

Syllogism   A deductive argument with two premises.

Syntactic ambiguity   *See* Syntactically ambiguous claim.

Syntactically ambiguous claim   An ambiguous claim whose ambiguity is due to the structure of the claim.

Synthetic claim   A claim whose truth or falsity is not determined simply by the definitions of the words that make it up. Contrast with *Analytic claim.*

Target analogue   *See* Conclusion analogue.

Term   A noun or noun phrase.

Truth   In this book, we use the concept in a common-sense way: A claim is true if it is free from error.

Truth-function   A relationship between a complex sentence and its simpler parts. The truth of the larger sentence results entirely from (is a function of) the truth value of its simpler parts.

Truth-functional analysis   The result of producing a full truth-table for a truth-functional claim.

Truth-functional equivalence   Two claims are truth-functionally equivalent if and only if they have exactly the same truth table.

Truth-functional logic   A system of logic that specifies the logical relationships among truth-functional claims—claims whose truth values depend solely upon the truth values of their simplest component parts. In particular, propositional logic deals with the logical functions of the terms "not," "and," "or," "if ... then," and so on.

Truth-functional rule   A rule of deduction that allows the derivation of a line from one or more earlier lines.

Truth-functional symbolization   A representation of a sentence using only letters for its simplest parts—its independent clauses—and logical symbols for negation, conjunction, disjunction, and conditional claims

True proportion   The proportion of a population that actually has an attribute of interest.

Truth table   A table that lists all possible combinations of truth values for the claim variables in a symbolized claim or argument and then specifies the truth value of the claim or claims for each of those possible combinations.

Truth value   If a claim is true, its truth value is "true"; if it is false its truth value is "false."

Two Wrongs Make a Right   A fallacy that occurs when a speaker or writer thinks that the wrongfulness of a deed is erased by its being a response to another wrongful deed.

Undistributed Middle Fallacy   A fallacy that occurs when a speaker or writer assumes that two things related to a third thing are necessarily related to each other.

Untestable Explanation   A fallacy that occurs when a speaker or writer offers an explanation that could not be tested even in principle.

Utilitarianism   The moral position that if an act will produce more happiness than its alternatives, that act is the right thing to do, and if the act will produce less happiness than its alternatives, it would be wrong to do it in place of an alternative that would produce more happiness.

Vague claim   A claim that lacks sufficient precision to convey the information appropriate to its use.

Vagueness   A concept is vague if we cannot say with certainty what it includes and what it excludes.

Valid argument   An argument such that it would be self-contradictory to maintain that the conclusion is false and the premise (or premises) are true.

Value judgment   A claim that assesses the merit, desirability, or praiseworthiness of someone or something. Also called a *normative* or a *prescriptive statement*.

Variable   Something that varies. In deductive reasoning, the most important variables are terms, claims, and arguments. In inductive generalizing from samples, inductive arguments from analogy, and arguments for causal claims, the most important variables are attributes.

Venn diagram   A graphic means of representing a categorical claim or categorical syllogism by assigning classes to overlapping circles. Invented by English mathematician John Venn (1834–1923).

Virtue ethics   The moral position unified around the basic idea that each of us should try to perfect a virtuous character that we exhibit in all actions.

Weak Analogy   A weak argument based on debatable or unimportant similarities between two or more things.

Weak argument   *See* Stronger/weaker arguments.

Weaseler   An expression used to protect a claim from criticism by weakening or qualifying it.

Wishful Thinking   A fallacy that occurs when we forget that wanting something to be true is irrelevant to whether it is true.

Worse than average illusion   *See* Better than average illusion.

Xenophobia   Fear or dislike of what is foreign or strange.

Answers, Suggestions, and Tips for Triangle Exercises

Chapter 1: Don't Believe Everything You Think

Exercise 1-1

1. An argument consists of two parts, one of which, the premise, is intended to provide a reason for accepting the other part, the conclusion. Unfortunately, sometimes people use the word "argument" to refer just to the premise.
4. F
7. T
10. F. As an example of an opinion that isn't subjective, we (the authors) are of the opinion there is life somewhere else in the universe. If there is life, our opinion is true. If there isn't, then it is false. We don't know whether our opinion is true or false, but we do know that it is one or the other, and we know that whether it is true or false is independent of whether we think there is life somewhere else in the universe.
13. c. The first order of business is to determine what the issue is.
16. T
19. T

Exercise 1-2

1. This item belongs in one group.
4. This item belongs in the same group as item 1.
7. This belongs in a different group from 1 and 4.
10. This belongs in the same group as 1 and 4.

Exercise 1-3

1. Not objective
4. Not objective
7. Not objective
10. Objective

Exercise 1-4

1. Subjective
4. Subjective
7. Not subjective, assuming the speaker is expressing the opinion that the movie frightened his sister a lot.
10. Not subjective, unless the speaker intends to imply that Trump's hair is unattractive, in which case the assertion would be subjective.

Exercise 1-5

1. Argument
4. Not an argument
7. No arguments here
10. Argument. The last sentence is the conclusion.

Exercise 1-6

1. Does not contain an argument.
4. Argument, whose conclusion is that computers will never be able to converse intelligently through speech.
7. Argument, whose conclusion is that chemicals in teething rings and soft plastic toys may cause cancer.
10. Does not contain an argument.

Exercise 1-7

1. a
4. c
7. b
10. b

Exercise 1-8

1. We (the authors) think we probably tend to overestimate the probability of types of events that are fresh in our minds (availability heuristic).
4. Belief bias is the tendency to evaluate an argument on the basis of how believable its conclusion is to us. Confirmation bias is the tendency to attach more weight to evidence that supports our own point of view.

Exercise 1-11

1. Contains an argument whose conclusion is the stock market probably will go down.
4. Contains an argument whose conclusion is that probably more women than men are upset by pornography.
7. Does not contain an argument.
10. Subtle, but the speaker is giving a reason for thinking *AI* was the best talent show on TV. So the passage contains an argument whose conclusion is that contention.

Exercise 1-12

1. a
4. b
7. e. Reading the passage very closely, you can see that the premise (which follows "since") addresses the issue whether it is surprising that the winner of this year's spelling bee is a straight A student whose favorite subject is science.
10. c. But notice YOUR FRIEND hasn't given a reason for thinking the governor has been good.

Exercise 1-13

1. Whether police brutality happens often.

4. Whether we have a good reason to believe the world is independent of our minds.

7. Whether it is the case that you should sign up for lessons on how to use a synthesizer if you buy one.

10. Whether Native Americans, as true conservationists, have something to teach readers about their relationship to the earth. There are other points made in the passage, but they are subsidiary to this one.

Exercise 1-14

1. MRS. is addressing both issues raised by MR.

4. CAUTIOUS is addressing the issue raised by HEEDLESS, of whether people should complain about what we are doing in Afghanistan.

7. OLD GUY is addressing YOUNG GUY's issue of whether baseball players are better now than forty years ago.

10. SECOND NEIGHBOR is addressing the issue raised by FIRST NEIGHBOR, which is whether SECOND NEIGHBOR has a right to make so much noise at night. SECOND NEIGHBOR thinks he has the right.

13. DEVON is not addressing RAMON's issue, which is whether this English course is a complete waste of time.

16. PARKER isn't addressing MOORE's issue, which is whether Thomas Brothers or Vernon Construction does better work. Instead, he addresses whether Thomas Brothers charges too much.

19. On the surface, it may seem that both hands address the issue of whether a person such as ONE HAND can feel safe in her own home. But ONE HAND's real issue is whether the large number of handguns makes one unsafe in one's own home. OTHER HAND ignores this issue completely.

22. JENNIFER does not address the issue raised by KATIE, which is whether she (JENNIFER) would be better off riding a bike to school. JENNIFER in effect changes the subject. Instead of addressing whether she would be better off riding a bike to school, JENNIFER starts talking about KATIE, as if KATIE'S behavior somehow invalidates what KATIE has asserted. This is like item 5, in which MR. JR changes the subject in a similar way.

25. HERR UBERALLES thinks they spend more than they should on heating. FRAU UBERALLES reminds him that she gets cold easily, which she thinks justifies their heating expense. She addresses the issue raised by him.

Exercise 1-15

1. Pertains to moral right/wrong

4. Pertains to moral right/wrong

7. Doesn't pertain

10. Pertains to aesthetic good/bad

13. Doesn't pertain. It merely explains how to stop the decline in enrollments.

Exercise 1-16

1. b. Both are arguments.

4. b. Both are arguments.

7. b. Both are explanations.

10. a. Both contain two assertions, the second of which is implied to take priority.

Answer to question posed in box on page 9

Can animals think critically? Unquestionably animals think, but do they review and evaluate their thinking? We don't know, but we have our doubts.

Chapter 2: Two Kinds of Reasoning

Exercise 2-1

1. a. Premise;   b. premise;   c. conclusion

2. a. Premise;   b. premise;   c. conclusion

3. a. Conclusion;   b. premise

4. a. Premise;   b. premise;   c. conclusion

5. a. Premise;   b. conclusion;   c. premise;
   d. premise

Exercise 2-2

1. Premise: All Communists are Marxists.
   Conclusion: All Marxists are Communists.

4. Premise: That cat loves dogs.
   Conclusion: Probably she won't be upset if you bring home a new dog for a pet.

7. Premise: Presbyterians are not fundamentalists. Premise: All born-again Christians are fundamentalists.
   Conclusion: No born-again Christians are Presbyterians.

10. Premise: The clunk comes only when I pedal.
    Conclusion: The problem is in the chain, the crank, or the pedals.

Exercise 2-3

1. Conclusion: There is a difference in the octane ratings between the two grades of gasoline.

4. Conclusion: Scrub jays can be expected to be aggressive when they're breeding.

7. Conclusion: Dogs are smarter than cats.

10. Unstated conclusion: She is not still interested in me.

Exercise 2-4

1. Deductive demonstration

4. Inductive support

7. Inductive support

10. Deductive demonstration

Exercise 2-5

1. Inductive

4. Inductive

7. Deductive (with the unstated premise: If I didn't get enough sleep last night I should get to bed earlier tonight).

10. Inductive

Exercise 2-6

1. b

4. b

7. b

10. b

Exercise 2-7

1. a

4. a

7. b

10. c

Exercise 2-8

1. Inductive

4. True

7. Deductive

10. Inductive

13. T

17. F

Exercise 2-9

1. Deductive demonstration

2. Inductive support

4. Inductive support

7. Two arguments here. In the first argument, if the speaker is assuming that the universe's not having arisen by chance increases the probability that God exists, then his or her argument is inductive. Likewise, in the second argument, if the speaker is assuming that an increase in the number of believing physicists increases the probability that God exists, then his or her argument is inductive.

8. Inductive support

Exercise 2-10

1. ① North Korea is a great threat to its neighbors.

② It has a million-person army ready to be unleashed at a moment's notice.

③ It also has nuclear weapons.

6. ① You're overwatering your lawn.

② There are mushrooms growing around the base of that tree—a sure sign of overwatering.

③ There are worms on the ground.

④ They come up when the earth is oversaturated.

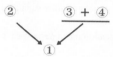

9. ① If you drive too fast, you're more likely to get a ticket.

② You're also more likely to get into an accident.

③ So, you shouldn't drive too fast.

10. ① You should consider installing a solarium.

② You can still get a tax credit.

③ You can reduce your heating bill.

④ If you build it right, you can actually cool your house with it in the summer.

13. ① We must paint the house now.

② If we don't then we'll have to paint it next summer.

③ If we have to paint it next summer, we'll have to cancel our trip.

④ It's too late to cancel the trip.

Exercise 2-11

1. "Because" is followed by a cause.

4. "Because" is followed by a cause.

7. "Because" is followed by a cause.

9. "Because" is followed by a premise.

Exercise 2-12

1. Could not possibly be false.

4. Could not possibly be false.

7. Could not possibly be false.

10. Could not possibly be false.

Exercise 2-13

1. Anyone who keeps his or her word is a person of good character.

4. One cannot murder someone without being in the same room.

7. Anyone who commits murder should be executed.

10. All squeaking fans need oil.

Exercise 2-14

1. Puddles everywhere usually indicate a recent rain.

4. The next day after a week of cold weather usually is cold.

7. Having leftovers is an indication that a party wasn't successful.

10. My cold probably would not have disappeared like magic if I had not taken Zicam.

Exercise 2-15

1.

4.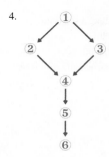

Exercise 2-16

1. a

4. a

Exercise 2-17

1. ① Your distributor is the problem.

   ② There's no current at the spark plugs.

   ③ If there's no current at the plugs, then either your alternator is shot or your distributor is defective.

   ④ [Unstated] Either your alternator is shot, or your distributor is defective.

   ⑤ If the problem were in the alternator, then your dash warning light would be on.

   ⑥ The light isn't on.

   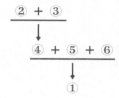

4. ① They really ought to build a new airport.

   ② It [a new airport] would attract more business to the area.

   ③ The old airport is overcrowded and dangerous.

Note: Claim ③ could be divided into two separate claims, one about overcrowding and one about danger. This would be important if the overcrowding were clearly offered as a reason for the danger.

Exercise 2-18

1. ① Cottage cheese will help you to be slender.

   ② Cottage cheese will help you to be youthful.

   ③ Cottage cheese will help you to be more beautiful.

   ④ Enjoy cottage cheese often.

4. ① The idea of a free press in America is a joke.

   ② The nation's advertisers control the media.

   ③ Advertisers, through fear of boycott, can dictate programming.

   ④ Politicians and editors shiver at the thought of a boycott.

   ⑤ The situation is intolerable.

   ⑥ I suggest we all listen to NPR and public television.

   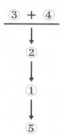

Note: The writer may see claim ① as the final conclusion and claim ⑤ as his comment upon it. Claim ⑥ is probably a comment on the results of the argument, although it, too, could be listed as a further conclusion.

7. ① Most schools should offer single-sex classes.

   ② Single-sex classes promote learning.

   ③ Girls do better in math and science courses when they are alone with other girls.

   ④ Gender offers distractions that interfere with learning.

   ⑤ Research also shows that in mixed classrooms most instructors will spend more time answering questions from boys.

   ⑥ Schools that offer single-sex classes always report learning gains for students of both sexes.

10. ① Well-located, sound real estate is the safest investment in the world.

② Real estate is not going to disappear as can dollars in savings accounts.

③ Real estate values are not lost because of inflation.

④ Property values tend to increase at a pace at least equal to the rate of inflation.

⑤ Most homes have appreciated at a rate greater than the inflation rate. . . .

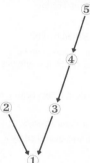

12. ① About 100 million Americans are producing data on the Internet. . . .

② Each user is tracked, so private information is available in electronic form.

③ One website . . . promises, for seven dollars, to scan . . . , etc.

④ The combination of capitalism and technology poses a threat to our privacy.

14. ① Measure A is consistent with the City's General Plan and City policies. . . .

② A yes vote will affirm the wisdom of well-planned, orderly growth. . . .

③ Measure A substantially reduces the amount of housing previously approved for Rancho Arroyo.

④ Measure A increases the number of parks and amount of open space.

⑤ Measure A significantly enlarges and enhances Bidwell Park.

⑥ Approval of Measure A will require dedication of 130.8 acres to Bidwell Park.

⑦ Approval of Measure A will require the developer to dedicate seven park sites.

⑧ Approval of Measure A will create 53 acres of landscaped corridors and greenways.

⑨ Approval of Measure A will preserve existing arroyos and protect sensitive plant habitats. . . .

⑩ Approval of Measure A will create junior high school and church sites.

⑪ Approval of Measure A will plan villages with 2,927 dwellings.

⑫ Approval of Measure A will provide onsite job opportunities and retail services.

⑬ [Unstated conclusion] You should vote for Measure A.

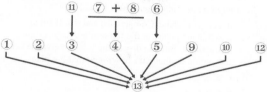

17. ① In regard to your editorial, "Crime bill wastes billions," let me set you straight. [Your position is mistaken.]

② Your paper opposes mandatory life sentences for criminals convicted of three violent crimes, and you whine about how criminals' rights might be violated.

③ Yet you also want to infringe on a citizen's rights to keep and bear arms.

④ You say you oppose life sentences for three-time losers because judges couldn't show any leniency toward the criminals no matter how trivial the crime.

⑤ What is your definition of trivial, busting an innocent child's skull with a hammer?

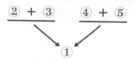

18. ① Freedom means choice.

② This is a truth antiporn activists always forget when they argue for censorship.

③ In their fervor to impose their morality, groups like Enough Is Enough cite extreme examples of pornography, such as child porn, suggesting that they are available in video stores.

④ This is not the way it is.

⑤ Most of this material portrays not actions such as this but consensual sex between adults.

⑥ The logic used by Enough Is Enough is that, if something can somehow hurt someone, it must be banned.

⑦ They don't apply this logic to more harmful substances such as alcohol or tobacco.

⑧ Women and children are more adversely affected by drunken driving and secondhand smoke than by pornography.

⑨ Few Americans would want to ban alcohol or tobacco even though these substances kill hundreds of thousands of people each year.

⑩ [Unstated conclusion] Enough Is Enough is inconsistent.

⑪ [Unstated conclusion] Enough Is Enough's anti-porn position is incorrect.

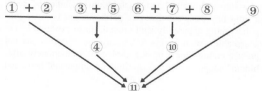

Chapter 3: Clear Thinking, Critical Thinking, and Clear Writing

Exercise 3-1

In order of decreasing vagueness:

1. d, e, b, c, f, and a. Compare (e) and (b). If Eli and Sarah made plans for the future, then they certainly discussed it. But just discussing it is more vague—they could do that with or without making plans.

4. c, d, e, a, b

7. a, c, e, b, d

Exercise 3-2

1. Somewhat too vague; same problem as in the example.

4. Ambiguous; who was in the car?

7. Ambiguous; he gave it to her or the cat?

11. Too vague; how much exercise is "modest exercise"?

Exercise 3-3

1. Answer b is more precise.

4. Answer a is more precise.

7. Answer b is more precise, but not by much.

10. a

15. b

Exercise 3-4

1. "Piano" is defined analytically.

4. "Red planet" is defined by synonym. (This one is tricky because it looks like a definition by example. But there is only one red planet, so the phrase refers to exactly the same object as the word "Mars.")

8. "Chiaroscuro" is defined by synonym.

11. "Significant other" is defined by example—several of them.

Exercise 3-5

1. Too imprecise. Sure, you can't say exactly how much longer you want it cooked, but you can provide guidelines; for example, "Cook it until it isn't pink."

4. Precise enough.

7. Precise enough.

10. For a first-timer or an inexperienced cook, this phrase is not sufficiently precise.

Exercise 3-7

"Feeding" simply means "fertilizing" and is precise enough. "Frequently" is too vague. "No more than half" is acceptable. "Label-recommended amounts" is okay, too. "New year's growth begins" and "each bloom period ends" seem a little imprecise for a novice gardener, but because pinpoint timing apparently isn't crucial, these expressions are acceptable—so it seems to us, anyhow. "Similar" is not precise enough for a novice gardener. "Immediately after bloom" suggests that precise timing is important here, and we find the phrase a bit too vague, at least for inexperienced gardeners. "When the nights begin cooling off" is too vague even if precision in timing isn't terribly important.

Exercise 3-8

1. The Raider tackle blocked the Giants linebacker.

4. How Therapy Can Help Victims of Torture

7. Chelsea's nose resembles Hillary's.

10. 6 Coyotes That Maul Girl Are Killed by Police

13. Second sentence: More than one disease can be carried and passed along to humans by a single tick.

16. We make good things happen.

19. Dunkelbrau—for those who crave the best-tasting real German beer

22. Jordan could write additional profound essays.

25. When she lay down to nap, she was disturbed by a noisy cow.

28. When Queen Elizabeth appeared before her troops, they all shouted "harrah."

31. AT&T, for as long as your business lasts.

32. This class might have had a member of the opposite sex for a teacher.

33. Married 10 times before, woman gets 9 years in prison for killing her husband.

Exercise 3-9

1. As a group

4. As a group

7. It's more likely that the claim refers to the Giants as a group, but it's possible that it refers to the play of individuals.

10. As individuals

12. Probably as individuals

15. Ambiguous. If the claim means that people are living longer than they used to, the reference is to people as individuals. If the claim means that the human race is getting older, then the reference is to people as a group. If the claim expresses the truism that to live is to age, then the reference is to people as individuals.

Exercise 3-13

7, 6, 4, 1, 3, 2, 5

Exercise 3-15

1. Students should choose their majors with considerable care.

4. If a nurse can find nothing wrong with you in a preliminary examination, a physician will be recommended to you. However, in this city physicians wish to protect themselves by having you sign a waiver.

7. Soldiers should be prepared to sacrifice their lives for their comrades.

10. Petitioners over sixty should have completed form E-7.

13. Language is nature's greatest gift to humanity.

16. The proof must be acceptable to the rational individual.

17. The country's founders believed in the equality of all.

20. Athletes who want to play for the National Football League should have a good work ethic.

24. Most U.S. senators are men. (Gender is important to the meaning of the sentence.)

27. Mr. Macleod doesn't know it, but Ms. Macleod is a feminist.

30. To be a good politician, you have to be a good salesperson.

Chapter 4: Credibility

Exercise 4-2

Something like number 9 is probably true, given the huge, almost unimaginable difference in wealth between the richest and the poorest people on the planet, but we have no idea what the actual numbers are. Regarding number 12, the warning went around on the web for a while, and even Click and Clack, the car guys on NPR's "Car Talk" allowed there might be something to this but they didn't want to conduct the appropriate experiments to find out. As it turns out, experience has shown there is a danger of explosion due to static electricity, and cars now have warnings against the practice. Number 15 is also true. We don't give any of the rest of them much of a chance.

Exercise 4-7

1. Of the first five, we'd say 1, 3, and 4 are probably interested parties. Of the last three, you must presume 8 is an interested party unless you can be assured he or she will not benefit more from the sale of one brand or the other. Numbers 6 and 7 depend entirely on the level of knowledge of the individuals and their lack of brand loyalty.

Exercise 4-10

10. One should be very cautious about expecting important results from such a plan. It should be noted that the plan includes hormone therapy that many believe is not healthy in the long run.

Exercise 4-11

1. In terms of expertise, we'd list (d), (c), and (b) first. Given what we've got to go on, we wouldn't assign expert status to either (a) or (e). We'd list all entries as likely to be fairly unbiased except for (a), which we would expect to be very biased.

3. Expertise: First (b), then (a), then (c) and (d) about equal, and (e) last. We'd figure that (b) is most likely to be unbiased, with (c), (d), and (e) close behind; Choker would be a distant last on this scale. Her bad showing on the bias scale more than makes up for her high showing on the expertise scale.

Exercise 4-12

1. The most credible choices are either the FDA or *Consumer Reports,* both of which investigate health claims of the sort in question with reasonable objectivity. The company that makes the product is the least credible source because it is the most likely to be biased. The owner of the health food store may be very knowledgeable regarding nutrition but is not a credible source regarding drugs. Your local pharmacist can reasonably be regarded as credible, but he or she may not have access to as much information as the FDA or *CR*. [We should add here that the FDA itself has come under considerable criticism in recent years, especially for making decisions on medical issues based on political considerations. The debate over approval of Plan B, the "morning after" pill, was a case in point. (See "Morning-After Pill," *The New York Times,* August 28, 2005.)]

2. It would probably be a mistake to consider any of the individuals on this list more expert than the others, although different kinds and different levels of bias are fairly predictable on the parts of the victim's father, the NRA representative, and possibly the police chief. The senator might be expected to have access to more data that are relevant to the issue, but that would not in itself make his or her credibility much greater than that of the others. The problem here is that we are dealing with a value judgment that depends very heavily upon an individual's point of view rather than his or her expertise. What is important to this question is less the credibility of the person who gives us an answer than the strength of the supporting argument, if any, that he or she provides.

3. Although problem 2 hinges on a value judgment, this one calls for an interpretation of the original intent of a constitutional amendment. Here, our choices would be either the Supreme Court Justice or the constitutional historian, with a slight preference for the latter because Supreme Court Justices are concerned more with constitutional issues as they have been interpreted by other courts than with original intent. (And Supreme Court Justices are not the most reliable historians of the Court.) The NRA representative is paid to speak for a certain point of view and would be the least credible, in our view. The senator and the U.S. president would fall somewhere in between: Both reasonably might be expected to be knowledgeable about constitutional issues but much less so than our first two choices.

Exercise 4-13

1. Professor St. Germain would possess the greatest degree of credibility and authority on (d), (f), and (h), and, compared with someone who had not lived in both places, on (i).

Exercise 4-15

1. We'd accept this as probably true—but probably only *approximately* true. It's difficult to be precise about such matters; Campbell will most likely lay off *about* 650 workers, including *about* 175 at its headquarters.

8. We'd accept this as likely.

12. No doubt cats that live indoors do tend to live longer than cats that are subject to the perils of outdoor life. If statistics on how much longer indoor cats live on the average were available, we'd expect the manufacturer to know them. But we suspect that such statistics would be difficult to establish (and probably not worth the effort), and we therefore have little confidence in the statistic cited here. Also, the source wants to sell cat litter, and this claim is surely designed to help do that.

20. This one is seriously nuts. But we're not sure whether most of the blame should go to the *Post* or to the *People's Daily*.

Solution to triangle puzzle on page 100

If you look carefully, you'll see that the hypotenuse (the topmost, longest line) of the two triangles are different. The upper one is slightly concave and the lower is slightly convex, thus allowing for extra space inside the lower triangle. That's where the "hole" comes from!

Chapter 5: Rhetoric, the Art of Persuasion

Exercise 5-1

1. Downplayer
4. Downplayer
7. Euphemism
10. Downplayer
13. Euphemism
16. Dysphemism
19. Euphemism

Exercise 5-3

1. Stereotype
4. Loaded question
7. Loaded question
10. Innuendo
13. Innuendo
16. Stereotype

Exercise 5-4

1. Rhetorical analogy
4. Rhetorical analogy
7. Rhetorical analogy
10. Rhetorical analogy

Exercise 5-6

1. Twenty percent more than what? Are there products with *fake* dairy butter?

4. This is not too bad, as long as we know what is meant by "the desert." Some deserts get more rain than others.

7. This one is straightforward, but remember that grading has changed a lot in the past twenty years, and grades nearly everywhere are higher (grade inflation); this doesn't necessarily mean today's students are better.

10. This doesn't make it a brilliant season all by itself. There may have been a big change in the economy, increasing attendance proportionately. Or attendance may have been miserable last year.

Exercise 5-8

1. Hyperbole
4. Proof surrogate
7. Ridicule/sarcasm
10. Hyperbole

Exercise 5-9

1. Ridicule/sarcasm
4. Proof surrogate
7. Proof surrogate
10. Ridicule/sarcasm

Exercise 5-10

1. Otherizing
4. Otherizing; fostering xenophobia
7. This contains elements of all the rhetorical categories listed in the directions to this exercise.
10. This passage does not fit any of the categories.
13. Primarily otherizing and fostering xenophobia

Exercise 5-11

1. c (probably the main theme here)
4. c, and a bit of d
7. a, c, and d
10. d
13. a
16. d
19. a

Exercise 5-12

1. Hyperbole
2. Dysphemism
3. Rhetorical analogy
4. Dysphemism
5. Downplayer
6. Dysphemism

Exercise 5-13

(1) Dysphemism, (2) dysphemism, (3) hyperbole, (4) weaseler, (5) proof surrogate, (6) mildly downplays the clause that immediately precedes it, (7) loaded question

Exercise 5-15

1. Whether the tax rate on carried interest is a good thing
2. That it is not a good thing
3. Yes, he does support his position with arguments. Here is a version of the most important one:

   Premise: No part of the tax code is acceptable if it is unfair.

   Premise: The "carried interest" portion of the tax code is unfair because it requires much less in taxes from wealthy money managers than it requires of other working people.

   Therefore the carried interest portion of the tax code is unacceptable.

4. We do find rhetorical devices and strategies going on in this passage. Dysphemisms include "tax giveaway" (for tax break), "stupendously wealthy" (a dysphemism in this context), "get away with" (for being exempt from the law), "crony capitalism" (is self-explanatory), and "cheating" (also self-explanatory). There is also "othering" going on, since the speaker clearly paints the beneficiaries of carried interest as very different from the rest of us. It would be too strong to call the passage hate mongering, but the speaker would probably not be disappointed if a listener were inclined to despise money managers and this tax break.

Exercise 5-20

1. b
4. a
7. c
10. d

Exercise 5-21

1. The quotation marks downplay the quality of the school.
4. Rhetorical definition
7. Euphemism
10. Rhetorical definition
13. Downplayer and proof surrogate

Exercise 5-22

1. "Shamelessly" is a downplayer and also is innuendo; "make sure Americans everywhere know" is hyperbole and ridicule; the rest of the passage is also hyperbole and ridicule.
4. Innuendo
7. Euphemism
10. Hyperbole
13. Innuendo
16. Downplayer; hyperbole; dysphemism
19. Dysphemism; innuendo ("still isn't right"); proof surrogate
22. "There is every reason to believe that this trend is going to continue," is a proof surrogate. There may be such reasons, but none is given or cited in the passage.
25. Lots of them here! To begin, "orgy" is a dysphemism; "self-appointed" is a downplayer. The references to yurts and teepees is ridicule, and "grant-maintained" is a downplayer. The rest of it employs a heavy dose of sarcasm.

Exercise 5-27

1. Superior? In what way? More realistic character portrayal? Better expression of emotion? Probably the claim means only "I like Paltrow more than I like Blanchett."
4. Fine, but don't infer that they both grade the same. Maybe Smith gives 10 percent A's and 10 percent F's, 20 percent B's and 20 percent D's, and 40 percent C's, whereas Jones gives everyone a C. Who do you think is the more discriminating grader, given this breakdown?
7. Well, first of all, what is "long-distance"? Second, and more important, how is endurance measured? People do debate such issues, but the best way to begin a debate on this point would be by spelling out what you mean by "requires more endurance."
10. This is like a comparison of apples and oranges. How can the popularity of a movie be compared with the popularity of a song?

Exercise 5-28

1. Smarter in what way? This is too vague.
4. "Attend church regularly" is a bit vague; a person who goes to church each and every Christmas and Easter is a regular, although infrequent, attender. We don't find "majority" too vague in this usage.
7. "Contained more insights" is much too vague. The student needs to know more specifically what was the matter with his or her paper, or at least what was better about the roommate's paper.
10. These two sorts of things are much too different to be compared in this way. If you're starving, the chicken looks better; if you need to get from here to there, it's the Volkswagen. (This is the kind of question Moore likes to ask people. Nobody can figure out why.)

Chapter 6: Relevance (Red Herring) Fallacies

Exercises

1. c. False dilemma (perfectionist fallacy)
5. c. False dilemma (you either support same-sex marriage or you are a homophobe who hates gays)
10. f. Appeal to emotion (scare tactics)
15. g. Irrelevant conclusion
20. b. Straw man
25. b. Straw man
30. e. Begging the question
35. d. Misplacing the burden of proof
40. e. Begging the question
45. g. Irrelevant conclusion

50. a. *Argumentum ad hominem* (genetic fallacy); poisoning the well also okay
55. b. Straw man
60. a. *Argumentum ad hominem* (guilt by association)
65. c. False dilemma
70. f. Appeal to emotion (flattery, apple polishing)
75. a. *Argumentum ad hominem* (genetic fallacy)
80. a. *Argumentum ad hominem* (genetic fallacy)
85. e. Begging the question
90. b. Straw man
95. g. Irrelevant conclusion
100. e. Begging the question

Chapter 7: Induction Fallacies

Exercises

1. h. Slippery Slope
5. d. Mistaken Appeal to Authority
10. a. Hasty Generalization
15. f. *Cum Hoc, Ergo Propter Hoc*
20. b. Accident
25. f. *Cum Hoc, Ergo Propter Hoc*
30. f. *Post Hoc, Ergo Propter Hoc;* Argument by Anecdote—causal variety
35. d. Mistaken Appeal to Authority
40. a. Hasty Generalization
45. d. Mistaken Appeal to Authority
50. b. Accident
55. e. Mistaken Appeal to Popularity
60. g. Overlooking the Possibility of Random Variation
65. e. Mistaken Appeal to Popularity

70. f. *Post Hoc, Ergo Propter Hoc;* Argument by Anecdote—causal variety
75. a. Generalizing from Exceptional Cases/Hasty Generalization
80. a. Generalizing from Exceptional Cases/Hasty Generalization
85. i, g. Untestable Explanation; Overlooking the Possibility of Regression
90. f. *Cum Hoc, Ergo Propter Hoc*
95. a. Generalizing from Exceptional Cases/Hasty Generalization
100. b. Accident
105. i. Untestable Explanation
110. h. Slippery Slope
115. d. Mistaken Appeal to Authority
120. d. Mistaken Appeal to Authority
125. h. Slippery Slope

Chapter 8: Formal Fallacies and Fallacies of Language

Exercise 8-1

1. Contradictories
4. Neither
7. Contraries
10. Contraries

Exercise 8-4

1. e. Equivocation
5. f. Composition
10. a. Affirming the Consequent
15. c. Undistributed Middle fallacy
20. e. Composition
25. c. Undistributed Middle fallacy
30. f. Division
35. b. Denying the Antecedent

40. g. Division
45. c. Undistributed middle fallacy
50. d. Excuse
55. b. Denying the Antecedent
60. g. Division
65. c. Undistributed middle fallacy
70. h. Miscalculating probabilities (faulty inductive conversion)
75. d. Sue might well be offering an excuse or justification, but we think there is a chance she might not be.
80. a. Affirming the Consequent
85. e. Equivocation
90. h. Miscalculating probabilities (Incorrectly combining the probabilities of independent events)
95. a. Affirming the Consequent
100. e. Equivocation
105. g. Division

Chapter 9: Deductive Arguments I: Categorical Logic

Exercise 9-1

1. All senators are politicians.
4. All senators are politicians.
7. Some politicians are not senators.
10. Some senators are not politicians.
13. Some scholars are not philosophers.

Exercise 9-2

1. All salamanders are lizards.
4. All members of the suborder Ophidia are snakes.
7. All alligators are reptiles.
10. All places there are snakes are places there are frogs.
13. All people who got raises are vice presidents.
16. All people identical with Socrates are Greeks.
19. All examples of salt are things that preserve meat.

Exercise 9-3

1. No students who wrote poor exams are students who were admitted to the program.
4. Some first basemen are right-handed people.
7. All passers are people who made at least 50 percent.
10. Some days I've had are days like this one.
13. Some holidays are holidays that fall on Saturday.
16. All people who pass the course are people who pass this test. Or: No people who fail this test are people who pass the course.
19. All times they will let you enroll are times you've paid the fee.

Exercise 9-4

1. Translation: Some anniversaries are not happy occasions. (True)
   Corresponding A-claim: All anniversaries are happy occasions. (False)
   Corresponding E-claim: No anniversaries are happy occasions. (Undetermined)
   Corresponding I-claim: Some anniversaries are happy occasions. (Undetermined)
4. Translation: Some allergies are things that can kill you. (True)
   Corresponding A-claim: All allergies are things that can kill you. (Undetermined)
   Corresponding E-claim: No allergies are things that can kill you. (False)
   Corresponding O-claim: Some allergies are not things that can kill you. (Undetermined)
7. Translation: Some herbs are medicinal substances. (False)
   Corresponding A-claim: All herbs are medicinal substances. (False)
   Corresponding E-claim: No herbs are medicinal substances. (True)
   Corresponding O-claim: Some herbs are not medicinal substances. (True)

10. Translation: Some colorful frogs are not poisonous frogs. (True)
    Corresponding A-claim: All colorful frogs are poisonous frogs. (False)
    Corresponding E-claim: No colorful frogs are poisonous frogs. (Undetermined)
    Corresponding I-claim: Some colorful frogs are poisonous frogs. (Undetermined)

Exercise 9-5

1. No non-Christians are non-Sunnis. (Not equivalent)
4. Some Christians are not Kurds. (Not equivalent)
7. All Muslims are Shiites. (Not equivalent)
10. All Muslims are non-Christians. (Equivalent)

Exercise 9-6

1. Some students who scored well on the exam are not students who didn't write poor essays. (Equivalent)
4. No students who were not admitted to the program are students who scored well on the exam. (Not equivalent)
7. All people whose automobile ownership is not restricted are people who don't live in the dorms. (Equivalent)
10. All first basemen are people who aren't right-handed. (Equivalent)

Exercise 9-7

2. All encyclopedias are nondefinitive works.
4. No sailboats are sloops.

Exercise 9-8

Translations of the lettered claims:

a. Some people who have been tested are not people who can give blood.
b. Some people who can give blood are not people who have been tested.
c. All people who can give blood are people who have been tested.
d. Logically equivalent to: "Some people who have been tested are people who cannot give blood" [converse]. Logically equivalent to: "Some people who have been tested are not people who can give blood" [obverse of the converse].
e. Logically equivalent to: "All people who have been tested are people who cannot give blood." Logically equivalent to: "No people who have been tested are people who can give blood" [obverse].

1. Equivalent to: "Some people who have not been tested are people who can give blood," which is equivalent to: "Some people who can give blood are people who have not been tested" by conversion. This in turn is equivalent to (b) by obversion.
4. Equivalent to "All people who can give blood are people who have been tested" (c).

Exercise 9-9

1. Equivalent to (b)

4. Equivalent to (d)

Exercise 9-10

1. Obvert (a) to get "some Slavs are not Europeans."

4. Obvert the conversion of (b) to get "Some members of the club are not people who took the exam."

7. Contrapose (a) to get "All people who will not be allowed to perform are people who did not arrive late." Translate (b) into "Some people who did not arrive late are people who will not be allowed to perform" and convert to "Some people who will not be allowed to perform are people who did not arrive late."

10. Begin with (b). First obvert, then convert the result to get "No drives that can be reformatted are devices capable of defragmentation."

Exercise 9-11

1. Invalid (this would require the conversion of an A-claim).

4. Valid (the converse of an I-claim is logically equivalent to the original claim).

7. Valid (the premise is the obverse of the conclusion).

10. Invalid. The premise translates "Some people in uniform are not people allowed to play," which is obverted and then converted to become "Some people not allowed to play are people in uniform." The conclusion becomes "Some people not allowed to play are not people in uniform." These are subcontraries, and one does not follow from the other.

Exercise 9-12

1. The converse of (a) is the contradictory of (b), so (b) is false.

4. Obvert (a) and convert (b). Since a false O-claim implies a false corresponding E-claim, (b) is false.

7. Translate (a) as "Some of GB's novels are novels in which the hero gets killed," and (b) as "Some novels in which the hero gets killed are GB's novels." Converting the latter, we have two subcontraries. If one subcontrary, (a), is false, the other, (b), must be true.

10. *This exercise is possibly the most difficult in the chapter for many students. Most cannot look at these claims and tell what follows about (b), and this inability justifies learning these techniques.* Correct translation is crucial: (a) becomes "All persimmons that have not been left to dry are astringent persimmons." Now find the contrapositive of that claim: "All persimmons that are not astringent are persimmons that have been left to dry."

    Next, obvert and then convert (b), arriving at: "Some persimmons that are not astringent are persimmons that have been left to ripen." (b) is now an I-claim that corresponds to the A-claim that resulted from (a). A true A-claim implies a true corresponding I-claim, so (b) is true.

Exercise 9-13

1. Valid:
   All P are G.
   No G are S.
   No S are P.

4. Invalid:
   All T are E.
   All T-T are E. (T = times Louis is tired, etc.)
   All T-T are T. (T-T = times identical with today)

7. Valid:
   All H are S.
   No P are S.
   No P are H.

10. Invalid:
    All C are R.
    All V are C.
    No R are V.

    (*Note:* There is more than one way to turn this into standard form. Instead of turning nonresidents into residents, you can do the opposite.)

Exercise 9-14

1. No blank drives are drives that contain data.
   Some blank drives are formatted drives.
   Some formatted drives are not drives that contain data.
   Valid:

4. All tobacco products are substances damaging to people's health.
   Some tobacco products are addictive substances.
   Some addictive substances are substances damaging to people's health.
   Valid:

7. All people who may vote are stockholders in the company.
   No people identical with Mr. Hansen are people who may vote.
   No people identical with Mr. Hansen are stockholders in the company.

Invalid:

People =
Mr. Hansen   Stockholders in
the company

People who may vote

Note: Remember that claims with individuals as subject terms are treated as A- or E-claims.

10. After converting, then obverting the conclusion:

No arguments with false premises are sound arguments.

Some arguments with false premises are valid arguments.

Some valid arguments are not sound arguments.

Valid:

Valid
arguments   Sound arguments

Arguments with
false premises

Exercise 9-15

1. A
4. B

Exercise 9-16

1. a
4. b

Exercise 9-17

1. 0
4. 1

Exercise 9-18

1. c
4. c
7. b
10. e

Exercise 9-19

1. All T are F.

Some F are Z.

Some Z are T.

Invalid; breaks rule 2

4. There are two versions of this item, depending on whether you take the premise to say *no* weightlifters use motor skills or only some don't. We'll do it both ways:

All A are M.

No W are M.

No W are A.

Valid

All A are M.

Some W are not M.

No W are A.

Invalid; breaks rule 3

7. Using I = people who lift papers from the Internet
   C = people who are cheating themselves
   L = people who lose in the long run

All I are C.

All C are L.

All I are L.

Valid

10. D = people who dance the whole night
    W = people who waste time
    G = people whose grades will suffer

All D are W.

All W are G.

All D are G.

Valid

Exercise 9-20

(Refer to Exercise 9-13 for these first four items.)

2. (Given in standard form in the text)
   Invalid: breaks rule 2

5. All voters are citizens.

   Some citizens are not residents.

   Some voters are not residents.

   Invalid: breaks rule 2

7. All halyards are lines that attach to sails.

   No painters are lines that attach to sails.

   No painters are halyards.

   Valid

8. No systems that can give instant access are systems with moving parts.

   All standard hard drives are systems with moving parts.

   No standard hard drives are systems that can give instant access.

   Valid; breaks no rule

(Refer to Exercise 9-14 for the next four items.)

2. After obverting both premises, we get:

   No ears with white tassels are ripe ears.

   Some ripe ears are not ears with full-sized kernels.

   Some ears with full-sized kernels are not ears with white tassels.

   Invalid: breaks rule 1

5. After obverting the second premise:

   Some digital players are machines with 3.0 transfer rates.

   All machines with 3.0 transfer rates are machines that cost at least twenty dollars.

   Some digital players are machines that cost at least twenty dollars.

   Valid

7. All people who may vote are people with stock.

   No [people identical with Mr. Hansen] are people who may vote.

   No [people identical with Mr. Hansen] are people with stock.

   Invalid: breaks rule 3 (major term)

8. No off-road vehicles are vehicles allowed in the unimproved portion of the park.

Some off-road vehicles are not four-wheel-
drive vehicles.

Some four-wheel-drive vehicles are allowed in the
unimproved portion of the park.

Invalid: breaks rule 1

Exercise 9-21

1. A = athletes; B = baseball players;
C = basketball players

Some A are not B.

Some B are not C.

Some A are not C.

Invalid: breaks rule 1

4. S = sportscasters; A = athletes; P = college
professors

All S are A

No A are P.

No S are P.

Valid

15. T = worlds identical to this one; B = the best of all
possible worlds; M = mosquito-containing worlds

No B are M.

All T are M.

No T are B.

Valid

18. P = plastic furniture; C = cheap-looking furniture;
L = their new lawn furniture

All L are P.

All P are C.

All L are C.

Valid

21. D = people on the district tax roll; C = citizens;
E = eligible voters

All D are C.

All E are C.

All D are E.

Invalid: breaks rule 2

24. C = people identical to Cobweb; L = liberals;
T = officials who like to raise taxes

All C are L.

All L are T.

All C are T.

Valid

29. P = poll results; U = unnewsworthy items;
I = items receiving considerable attention from the
networks

All P are I.

Some P are U.

Some I are U.

Valid

30. E = people who understand that the earth goes
around the sun; W = people who understand what
causes winter and summer; A = American adults

All W are E.

Some A are not E.

Some A are not W.

Valid

32. N = the pornographic novels of "Madame Toulouse";
W = works with sexual depictions patently offensive
to community standards and with no serious literary,
artistic, political, or scientific value; O = works that
can be banned as obscene since 1973

All O are W.

All N are W.

All N are O.

Invalid: breaks rule 2

Exercise 9-22

1. True. A syllogism with neither an A- nor an E-premise
would have (I) two I-premises, which would violate rule
2; or (II) two O-premises, which would violate rule 1; or
(III) an I-premise and an O-premise. Alternative (III)
would require a negative conclusion by rule 1, and a
negative conclusion would require premises that distribute at least two terms, the middle term and (by rule 3) at
least one other. Because an I-premise and an O-premise
collectively distribute only one term, alternative (III)
won't work either.

4. True. An AIE syllogism whose middle term is the
subject of the A-premise breaks exactly two rules. If
the middle term is the predicate of the A-premise, this
syllogism breaks three rules.

Exercise 9-23

1. All B are C.

4. Cannot be done.

7. Some B are not C.

10. Cannot be done.

Exercise 9-24

1. b

4. a

7. Some political radicals are patriots (or the converse of
this claim).

10. No conclusion validly follows.

Exercise 9-27

1. L = ladybugs; A = aphid-eaters; G = good things to
have in your garden

All L are A.

[All A are G.]

All L are G.

Valid

4. S = self-tapping screws; B = boons to the construction industry; P = things that make it possible to
screw things together without drilling pilot holes

All S are P.

[All P are B.]

All S are B.

Valid

Chapter 10: Deductive Arguments II: Truth-Functional Logic

Test Yourself Answer

Since you've gone to the trouble to seek answers to some exercises, we'll throw in an answer to the test in the box on page 290. Two cards must be turned over, the one with the "e" and the one with the "3."

Exercise 10-1

1. $Q \rightarrow P$
2. $Q \rightarrow P$
3. $P \rightarrow Q$
4. $Q \rightarrow P$
5. $(P \rightarrow Q) \& (Q \rightarrow P)$

Exercise 10-4

1. $(P \rightarrow Q) \& R$
2. $P \rightarrow (Q \& R)$

   Notice that the only difference between (1) and (2) is the location of the comma. But the symbolizations have two different truth tables, so moving the comma actually changes the meaning of the claim. And we'll bet you thought that commas were there only to tell you when to breathe when you read aloud.

5. $P \rightarrow (Q \rightarrow R)$. Compare (5) with (3).
11. $\sim C \rightarrow S$
12. $\sim (C \rightarrow S)$
16. $S \rightarrow \sim C$. Ordinarily, the word "but" indicates a conjunction, but in this case it is present only for emphasis—"only if" is the crucial truth-functional phrase.
20. $\sim (F \vee S)$ or $(\sim F \& \sim S)$. Notice that, when you "move the negation sign in," you have to change the wedge to an ampersand (or vice versa). Don't treat the negation sign as you would treat a minus sign in algebra class, or you'll wind up in trouble.

Exercise 10-5

1.

P	Q	R	$(P \rightarrow Q)$	$(P \rightarrow Q) \& R$
T	T	T	T	T
T	T	F	T	F
T	F	T	F	F
T	F	F	F	F
F	T	T	T	T
F	T	F	T	F
F	F	T	T	T
F	F	F	T	F

2.

P	Q	R	$(Q \& R)$	$P \rightarrow (Q \& R)$
T	T	T	T	T
T	T	F	F	F
T	F	T	F	F
T	F	F	F	F
F	T	T	T	T
F	T	F	F	T
F	F	T	F	T
F	F	F	F	T

5.

P	Q	R	$(Q \rightarrow R)$	$P \rightarrow (Q \rightarrow R)$
T	T	T	T	T
T	T	F	F	F
T	F	T	T	T
T	F	F	T	T
F	T	T	T	T
F	T	F	F	T
F	F	T	T	T
F	F	F	T	T

11.

C	S	$\sim C$	$\sim C \rightarrow S$
T	T	F	T
T	F	F	T
F	T	T	T
F	F	T	F

12.

C	S	$C \rightarrow S$	$\sim (C \rightarrow S)$
T	T	T	F
T	F	F	T
F	T	T	F
F	F	T	F

16.

C	S	$\sim C$	$S \rightarrow \sim C$
T	T	F	F
T	F	F	T
F	T	T	T
F	F	T	T

20.

F	S	$F \vee S$	$\sim (F \vee S)$
T	T	T	F
T	F	T	F
F	T	T	F
F	F	F	T

Since $\sim (F \vee S)$ is exactly equivalent to $\sim F \& \sim S$, the latter can be substituted for the former in the preceding table and it will still be correct. Columns for $\sim F$ and for $\sim S$ would need to be added to make it complete.

Exercise 10-8

1. Modus ponens; valid
4. Modus tollens; valid
7. Affirming the Consequent; invalid

Exercise 10-9

1. Invalid:

		(Premise)	(Premise)	(Conclusion)
P	Q	$\sim Q$	$P \vee \sim Q$	$\sim P$
T	T	F	T	F
T	F	T	T	F
F	T	F	F	T
F	F	T	T	T

(Row 2)

4. Invalid:

(Conclusion)			(Premise)			(Premise)
P	Q	R	(P → Q)	~ (P → Q)	(Q → R)	P → (Q → R)
T	T	T	T	F	T	T
T	T	F	T	F	F	F
T	F	T	F	T	T	T
T	F	F	F	T	T	T
F	T	T	T	F	T	T
F	T	F	T	F	F	T
F	F	T	T	F	T	T
F	F	F	T	F	T	T

(Row 4)

7. Invalid:

			(Premise)		(Premise)	(Conclusion)
P	Q	R	~ Q	P & R	(P & R) → Q	~ P
T	T	T	F	T	T	F
T	T	F	F	F	T	F
T	F	T	T	T	F	F
T	F	F	T	F	T	F
F	T	T	F	F	T	T
F	T	F	F	F	T	T
F	F	T	T	F	T	T
F	F	F	T	F	T	T

(Row 4)

10. The table is 16 rows long, and in no row are the premises true and the conclusion false. So the argument is valid.

Exercise 10-10

1. Invalid

S → T
~S
─────
~T

4. Valid

L
L → H
─────
H

7. Invalid

R → M
M
─────
R

10. Valid

F → A
F
─────
A

13. Invalid

P → S
~P
─────
~S

Exercise 10-11

We've used the short truth-table method to demonstrate invalidity.

1. Valid. There is no row in the argument's table that makes the premises all T and the conclusion F.

2. Invalid. There are two rows that make the premises T and the conclusion F. (Such rows are sometimes called "counterexamples" to the argument.) Here they are:

L	W	S	P
T	F	F	F
T	T	F	F

(Remember: You need to come up with only *one* of these rows to prove the argument invalid.)

3. Invalid. There are two rows that make the premises T and the conclusion F:

M	P	R	F	G
T	T	T	F	T
T	T	F	T	F

4. Invalid. There are three rows that make the premises true and the conclusion F:

D	G	H	P	M
F	T	T	T	T
F	T	F	T	T
F	T	F	F	T

5. Invalid. There are two rows that make the premises T and the conclusion F:

R	S	B	T	E
T	T	F	F	F
F	F	T	F	F

Exercise 10-12

1. Chain argument
2. Disjunctive argument
3. Constructive dilemma
4. Modus tollens
5. Destructive dilemma

Exercise 10-13

Modus ponens occurs in items 4, 10, and 15; modus tollens occurs in items 2, 5, and 14.

Exercise 10-14

1. 1. R → P   (Premise)
    2. Q → R   (Premise) /∴ Q → P
    3. Q → P   1, 2, CA

4. 1. P → Q   (Premise)
    2. ~ P → S   (Premise)
    3. ~ Q   (Premise) /∴ S
    4. ~ P   1, 3, MT
    5. S   2, 4, MP

7. 1. ~ S   (Premise)
    2. (P & Q) → R   (Premise)
    3. R → S   (Premise) /∴ ~ (P & Q)
    4. ~ R   1, 3, MT
    5. ~ (P & Q)   4, 2, MT

10. 1. (T ∨ M) → ~ Q   (Premise)
    2. (P → Q) & (R → S)   (Premise)
    3. T   (Premise) /∴ ~ P
    4. T ∨ M   3, ADD
    5. ~ Q   1, 4, MP

6. P → Q   2, SIM
7. ~ P   5, 6, MT

Exercise 10-15

1. 4. 1, 3, CA
   5. 2, CONTR
   6. 4, 5, CA
4. 4. 3, CONTR
   5. 2, 4, MP
   6. 2, 5, CONJ
   7. 1, 6, MP
7. 4. 1, SIM
   5. 2, CONTR
   6. 3, CONTR
   7. 4, 5, 6, CD
   8. 1, SIM
   9. 8, 7, CONJ
   10. 9, DIST

Exercise 10-16

There is usually more than one way to do these.

1. 1. P & Q   (Premise)
   2. P → R   (Premise) /∴ R
   3. P   1, SIM
   4. R   2, 3, MP
2. 1. R → S   (Premise)
   2. ~ P ∨ R   (Premise) /∴ P → S
   3. P → R   2, IMPL
   4. P → S   1, 3, CA
4. 1. ~ P ∨ (~ Q ∨ R)   (Premise)
   2. P   (Premise) /∴ Q → R
   3. P → (~ Q ∨ R)   1, IMPL
   4. ~ Q ∨ R   2, 3, MP
   5. Q → R   4, IMPL
8. 1. ~ Q & (~ S & ~ T)   (Premise)
   2. P → (Q ∨ S)   (Premise) /∴ ~ P
   3. (~ Q & ~ S) & ~ T   1, ASSOC
   4. ~ Q & ~ S   3, SIM
   5. ~ (Q ∨ S)   4, DEM
   6. ~ P   2, 5, MT

Exercise 10-17

1. 1. P → R   (Premise)
   2. R → Q   (Premise) /∴ ~ P ∨ Q
   3. P → Q   1, 2, CA
   4. ~ P ∨ Q   3, IMPL
4. 1. P ∨ (Q & R)   (Premise)
   2. (P ∨ Q) → S   (Premise) /∴ S
   3. (P ∨ Q) & (P ∨ R)   1, DIST
   4. P ∨ Q   3, SIM
   5. S   2, 4, MP

7. 1. (M ∨ R) & P   (Premise)
   2. ~ S → ~ P   (Premise)
   3. S → ~ M   (Premise) /∴ R
   4. P → S   2, CONTR
   5. P   1, SIM
   6. S   4, 5, MP
   7. ~ M   3, 6, MP
   8. M ∨ R   1, SIM
   9. R   7, 8, DA
10. 1. P ∨ (R & Q)   (Premise)
   2. R → ~ P   (Premise)
   3. Q → T   (Premise) /∴ R → T
   4. (P ∨ R) & (P ∨ Q)   1, DIST
   5. P ∨ Q   4, SIM
   6. ~ P → Q   5, DN/IMPL
   7. R → Q   2, 6, CA
   8. R → T   3, 7, CA

Exercise 10-18

1. D → ~ B
4. B → ~ D
7. C → (B & ~ D)

Exercise 10-19

1. Equivalent to (b)
4. Equivalent to (c)
7. Equivalent to (c)

Exercise 10-20

1. 1. P   (Premise)
   2. Q & R   (Premise)
   3. (Q & P) → S   (Premise) /∴ S
   4. Q   2, SIM
   5. Q & P   1, 4, CONJ
   6. S   3, 5, MP
4. 1. P ∨ Q   (Premise)
   2. (Q ∨ U) → (P → T)   (Premise)
   3. ~ P   (Premise)
   4. (~ P ∨ R) → (Q → S)   (Premise) /∴ T ∨ S
   5. Q   1, 3, DA
   6. Q ∨ U   5, ADD
   7. P → T   2, 6, MP
   8. ~ P ∨ R   3, ADD
   9. Q → S   4, 8, MP
   10. T ∨ S   1, 7, 9, CD
7. 1. P → Q   (Premise) /∴ P → (Q ∨ R)
   2. ~ P ∨ Q   1, IMPL
   3. (~ P ∨ Q) ∨ R   2, ADD
   4. ~ P ∨ (Q ∨ R)   3, ASSOC
   5. P → (Q ∨ R)   4, IMPL

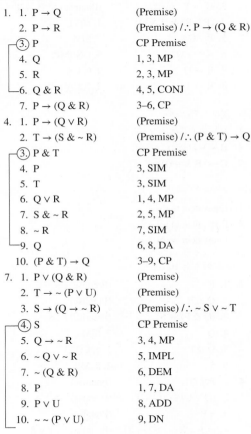

10. 1. (S → Q) → ~ R   (Premise)
     2. (P → Q) → R   (Premise) /∴ ~ Q
     3. ~ R → ~ (P → Q)   2, CONTR
     4. (S → Q) → ~ (P → Q)   1, 3, CA
     5. ~ (S → Q) ∨ ~ (P → Q)   4, IMPL
     6. ~ (~ S ∨ Q) ∨ ~ (~ P ∨ Q) 5, IMPL (twice)
     7. (S & ~ Q) ∨ (P & ~ Q)   6, DEM/DN (twice)
     8. (~ Q & S) ∨ (~ Q & P)   7, COM
     9. ~ Q & (S ∨ P)   8, DIST
    10. ~ Q   9, SIM

Exercise 10-21

1.   1. P → Q   (Premise)
     2. P → R   (Premise) /∴ P → (Q & R)
     3. P   CP Premise
     4. Q   1, 3, MP
     5. R   2, 3, MP
     6. Q & R   4, 5, CONJ
     7. P → (Q & R)   3–6, CP

4.   1. P → (Q ∨ R)   (Premise)
     2. T → (S & ~ R)   (Premise) /∴ (P & T) → Q
     3. P & T   CP Premise
     4. P   3, SIM
     5. T   3, SIM
     6. Q ∨ R   1, 4, MP
     7. S & ~ R   2, 5, MP
     8. ~ R   7, SIM
     9. Q   6, 8, DA
    10. (P & T) → Q   3–9, CP

7.   1. P ∨ (Q & R)   (Premise)
     2. T → ~ (P ∨ U)   (Premise)
     3. S → (Q → ~ R)   (Premise) /∴ ~ S ∨ ~ T
     4. S   CP Premise
     5. Q → ~ R   3, 4, MP
     6. ~ Q ∨ ~ R   5, IMPL
     7. ~ (Q & R)   6, DEM
     8. P   1, 7, DA
     9. P ∨ U   8, ADD
    10. ~ ~ (P ∨ U)   9, DN

    11. ~ T   2, 10, MT
    12. S → ~ T   4–11, CP
    13. ~ S ∨ ~ T   12, IMPL

10. 1. (P & Q) ∨ R   (Premise)
     2. ~ R ∨ Q   (Premise) /∴ P → Q
     3. P   CP Premise
     4. ~ Q   CP Premise
     5. ~ R   2, 4, DA
     6. P & Q   1, 5, DA
     7. Q   6, SIM
     8. ~ Q → Q   4–7, CP
     9. Q ∨ Q   8, IMPL
    10. Q   9, TAUT
    11. P → Q   3–10, CP

Exercise 10-22

1.   C → ~ S
     ~ L → S
     ――――――――
     C → L
     Valid

4.   ~ M ∨ C
     ~ M → ~ K
     C ∨ H
     T → ~ H
     ――――――――
     T → K
     Invalid

7.   C ∨ S
     S → E
     C → R
     ――――――――
     R ∨ E
     Valid

10. C → ~L
     (E → (~C → ~T)) & E
     ――――――――――――――――
     L → ~T
     Valid

13. S → ~ F
     ~S → ~ T
     T
     ――――――――
     ~F
     Valid

Chapter 11: Inductive Reasoning

Exercise 11-1

1. A
4. A
7. B
10. A

Exercise 11-2

1. Premise-analogue: rats. Conclusion-analogue: humans. Attribute of interest: saccharin as a cause of cancer.

4. Premise-analogue: Windex. Conclusion-analogue: this ant poison. Attribute of interest: being usable to clean windows.

7. Premise-analogue: December's heating bill. Conclusion-analogue: January's heating bill. Attribute of interest: being high.

10. Premise-analogue: abortion. Conclusion-analogue: capital punishment. Attribute of interest: being wrong.

ANSWERS, SUGGESTIONS, AND TIPS FOR TRIANGLE EXERCISES

Exercise 11-3

1. Premise-analogue: iPods. Conclusion-analogue: iPads. Attribute of interest: being easy to use.

4. Premise-analogue: Odwalla carrot juice. Conclusion-analogue: Odwalla orange juice. Attribute of interest: tasting moldy.

7. Premise-analogue: auto insurance. Conclusion-analogue: health insurance. Attribute of interest: being a good thing.

10. Premise-analogue: *Dancing with the Stars*. Conclusion-analogue: *So You Think You Can Dance*. Attribute of interest: being something you don't like.

Exercise 11-4

Football and rugby; football and basketball; football and tennis; football and bowling; football and golf; football and chess.

Exercise 11-6

1. This is stronger than a parallel argument that uses "Neptune" rather than "Mars" as an analogue.

4. This is stronger than a parallel argument that uses "Muammar Gadaffi" rather than "Saddam Hussein" as an analogue.

7. This is stronger than a parallel argument that uses "Ann's rubber plant" rather than "her dog" as an analogue.

10. This is stronger than a parallel argument that employs a non-Scandinavian country as an analogue.

Exercise 11-8

1. The new supposition introduces a difference between past crops and this crop, so it weakens the argument. Kirk should be less confident the new crop will be like the previous crops.

4. The supposition here is that this year will probably be different from previous years. This makes it less likely this year's crop will be like previous crops.

7. The new supposition introduces what is probably an irrelevant difference between this year's crop and the previous crops and has no bearing on the strength of the argument.

10. The new supposition introduces a potentially relevant difference between the analogues, so it weakens the argument and makes it less likely this year's crop will be like previous crops.

Exercise 11-9

1. Not a general statement
4. A general statement
7. A general statement
10. Not a general statement

Exercise 11-10

1. Generalization from a sample
4. Generalization from a sample
7. Generalization from a sample
10. Statistical syllogism

Exercise 11-11

1. A
4. B
7. A
10. A

Exercise 11-12

1. Most (all, nearly all, etc.) Otterhounds don't fetch.

4. Therefore most likely (probably, etc.) Dr. Walker is a liberal.

7. York is a member of the NRA.

10. Chabot Gap is a small town.

Exercise 11-13

1. Most professional dancers are pretty athletic.
4. Jim is a kid from around here.
7. It's hot now.
10. Christie probably won't be a very good president.

Exercise 11-14

1. Sample: the ten Disney movies I have seen. Population: Disney movies. Attribute of interest: being nonviolent.

4. Sample: my past experience at Columbus State. Population: all my experiences at Columbus State. Attribute of interest: being fun.

7. Sample: Costco store-brand coffee. Population: Costco store-brand products. Attribute of interest: being as good as name-brand products.

10. Sample: these McDonald's fries. Population: McDonald's fries. Attribute of interest: being too salty.

Exercise 11-15

1. Sample: this quart of milk. Population: things for sale at this joint. Attribute of interest: being overpriced.

4. Sample: life insurance salespeople I know. Population: life insurance salespeople. Attribute of interest: trying to sell you stuff you don't need.

7. Sample: my performance on the first test. Population: my performance on assessments in this class. Attribute of interest: being well done.

10. Sample: the English class I took. Population: English classes. Attribute of interest: being boring.

Exercise 11-16

Episodes of Survivor, movies staring Meryl Streep, television sitcoms, movies rated PG, movies.

Exercise 11-17

Olympic shot-putters, National Football League referees, major league baseball players, professional athletes, physically fit people.

Exercise 11-18

Cowboys who are teachers, cowboys, teachers, Democrats, people.

Exercise 11-19

1. We'd speculate that a disproportionate number of Lexus drivers (a) own swimming pools, (b) have a college degree, (c) are over 40 years old, and (d) think of themselves as knowledgeable about politics.

4. The population of people who are susceptible to poison ivy or oak might perhaps include a disproportionate number of people (a) who are fair-skinned, and (b) who are not elderly. Dog owners and hikers are more apt to have cases of poison oak or ivy, although they wouldn't necessarily be more susceptible to the plight.

7. We'd bet that a disproportionate number of nearsighted people (a) like to read, (b) own more than a single pair of vision glasses, (c) have family members who are nearsighted, and (d) suffer from glaucoma.

10. Those who watch reality shows, we conjecture, are more likely than the general population to (a) be under 50, (b) not have PhDs, (c) not be in the top 20% of income recipients, and (d) be impressed by expensive cars and clothes.

Exercise 11-20

1. a
4. b
7. a

Exercise 11-21

1. Given this supposition, the speaker should be less confident that most Ohio State students say they believe in God.

4. Given this supposition, the speaker should be more confident that most Ohio State students say they believe in God.

Exercise 11-22

1. The six students who turned in written evaluations.

4. Yes. The sample contains a disproportionate number of individuals who feel strongly enough about Ludlum to write something.

7. Poor reasoning. The sample is small and underrepresents those who do not have strong enough feelings about Ludlum to write.

Exercise 11-23

1. The speaker is implying that, in general, Dodge builds tough trucks, meaning, evidently, that in general Dodge trucks can be driven many miles on the original engine. This conclusion is derived from a sample of one. It must be allowed, however, that Dodge trucks as they emerge off the assembly line make up a relatively homogeneous population: Dodge no doubt spends a lot of money trying to ensure that all trucks within a given category come off the production line the same. It also must be allowed that this particular truck, having 300,000 miles on the original engine, qualifies as a very tough truck. But given the variations in the way trucks are driven, it still shouldn't be regarded as a strong argument.

4. Unless Toadstool teaches a single small class, this generalization is based on a relatively small sample and thus is not very strong.

7. This generalization is based on a potentially atypical sample and thus is not very strong.

10. This generalization is based on a small sample and is not very strong.

13. An airline's seating policy may be fairly uniform across its flights, so this is not a weak argument.

Exercise 11-24

1. Causal statement
4. Causal statement
7. Causal statement
10. Causal statement, but the lateness of the hour could have been offered as evidence that the bars are closed.

Exercise 11-25

1. Causal statement (behavioral variety)
4. Causal statement (behavioral variety)
7. Argument
10. Causal statement (behavioral variety)

Exercise 11-26

1. Implies cause and effect
4. Implies cause and effect (this is a behavioral causal statement)
7. Implies cause and effect, vaguely (this is a behavioral causal statement)
10. Implies cause and effect (this is a behavioral causal statement)
13. Implies cause and effect
16. Does not imply cause and effect

Exercise 11-27

1. Effect: cat is not eating; cause: cat has eaten mice
4. Effect: the little guy's not dehydrating; cause: giving him more water
7. Effect: that people cannot detect their own bad breath; cause: becoming used to the odor
10. Effect: a savings to the state in court expenses; cause: judges' not processing shoplifting, trespassing, and small-claims charges (this is a behavioral causal statement)

Exercise 11-28

1. A
4. C
7. A
9. A
10. C
13. B
16. C

Exercise 11-29

1. COV
5. P
9. C

13. COV

18. P

26. C

Exercise 11-30

1. Answer (d) is the generally accepted reason for more winter flu.

4. Answer (c) is the least plausible, because it is difficult to see how less NASCAR racing could reduce death by stroke. (d) is also fairly implausible.

7. None seem likely to be due to cause and effect.

10. Answer (d) is the best response. Statistical regression offers an attractive explanation of why the team didn't do as well.

Exercise 11-31

1. C. Long grass causes both the sneezing and the mowing (and thus the fumes).

4. C. Shorter days contribute to both.

7. B. Weak quadriceps might cause the knee problem.

10. B. Maybe smart people eat more fish.

13. B. If there is more violence, there is likely to be more on TV.

16. A. Coincidence seems likely.

19. C. Good health may have contributed both to Uncle Ted's attitude and to his longevity. For that matter, maybe being long-lived in itself gives him a good attitude. So B works, too.

22. A. Coincidence

25. B. Top executives can easily afford expensive clothes and nice cars.

Exercise 11-33

1. Outcomes

4. Adding the probability of each event

7. Treating independent events as if they were not independent events

Exercise 11-34

1. No. After the first draw, the remaining deck is smaller.

4. .11, or 11 percent

7. 40 percent

10. 4 in 52, or 1 in 13, or about 7½ percent

13. About 16 percent (.4 times .4 = .16)

16. You need to know two things: the proportion of males who aren't athletes and the proportion of all students are athletes.

Exercise 11-37

1. (a) Poker players' confidence in the strength of their cards causes differences in arm motions that can be interpreted by observers who are not poker experts. (b) This is a randomized controlled experiment. (c) One group saw clips of arm/hand motions; a second saw clips of upper bodies; a third saw clips of faces. All groups were measured against the likelihood of correct answers being due to chance. (d) In this report, only the first group performed significantly better than chance, the second group performed approximately as chance would have it, and the third performed rather worse than chance would have produced. (e) Further study, with larger numbers of participants, would seem to be in order. (f) Arm/hand motions are probably better indicators of the strength of an expert poker player's hand than other bodily indicators, particularly facial expressions.

4. (a) The lead ophthalmologist thinks that leaving a light on at night deprives infant eyes of the rest needed for nonmyopic development. In short, the causal hypothesis at issue is that leaving a light on at night when children are infants contributes to their becoming myopic. (b) This is a prospective observational study. True, the researchers are asking parents of children at the hospital to think back to when their children were infants. But the comparison groups are based on the presence or absence of the hypothesized causal factor (sleeping with light on at night). (c) There are three comparison groups: the 172 infants who (were said to have) slept in darkness, the 232 who slept with a night light, and the 75 who slept with a lamp on. (d) In the first group 10 percent were nearsighted; in the second group 34 percent were nearsighted; in the last group 55 percent were nearsighted. (e) The report does not rule out the possibility that nearsighted parents are more apt to leave lights on in their children's rooms. (f) Because of the possibility of the confounding variable mentioned in (e), the study offers very weak support for the hypothesis.

7. (a) The causal hypothesis at issue is that exercise prevents colds. (b) Presumably this is a randomized controlled experiment, although the report does not specifically state that the subjects were randomly divided into two groups; and one part of the experiment is a prospective observational study (as will be explained). (c) There are three comparison groups: the ten who participated in the six-month regimen of jogging three miles every other day; the same group prior to the regimen; and the ten who did not participate in the regimen. (d) The joggers had 25 percent fewer colds than the nonjoggers, and were said to have had fewer colds than they themselves had in some unspecified period prior to the experiment/study. (e) We don't know if the only difference between the joggers and the nonjoggers was the jogging. (f) The 25 percent fewer colds the joggers had could be due to chance or to confounding variables. For example, did the nonjoggers try to compensate for their lack of exercise by going to a gym during the six-month period?

10. (a) High doses of androgen lower HDL levels in the blood. (b) This is a prospective observational study. (c) There are two comparison groups: the sixteen men before taking androgen, and the same men after taking androgen. (d) The HDL levels of the men in the second group were 60 percent lower after four weeks of taking androgen. (e) We can't be sure there aren't confounding variables: We don't know that men in the second group didn't do something else while they were taking androgen that might have caused their HDL levels to drop. (f) This drop in HDL is

statistically significant, and occurred after a short period of time. However, we can't be sure there aren't confounding variables that account for it. Nevertheless, given the apparent health threat posed by low HDL, we would not take androgen if it were not prescribed by a physician.

13. (a) Cheating creates more positive feelings than guilty feelings (b) This is a controlled experiment. Its design does not require randomization except in the initial selection of subjects. (c) One group of 71 subjects cheated on a test; the other group of 108 did not.

(d) On average the cheaters, as compared to the noncheaters, reported a higher level of excitement and more positive feelings than guilty ones. (e) "Cheaters reported on average a greater increase in excitement and positive feelings than noncheaters did." This summary statement of the difference between the two groups is vague. (f) Maybe it isn't the cheating itself that thrilled the cheaters, but the money. Cheaters may also be more inclined to lie about their feelings. The most you could say is that these cheaters were more apt than the noncheaters to report excitement and positive feelings.

Chapter 12: Moral, Legal, and Aesthetic Reasoning

Exercise 12-1

1. Value judgment
4. Value judgment
7. Value judgment
10. Not a value judgment

Exercise 12-2

1. Not a value judgment, although it surely hints at one.
4. Value judgment
7. Not a value judgment in the ordinary sense, but since rides are often evaluated by degree of scariness, this may imply such a judgment.

Exercise 12-3

1. Moral value judgment
4. Moral value judgment
7. Not a moral value judgment
10. Moral value judgment

Exercise 12-4

1. A
4. B
7. B
10. A

Exercise 12-5

2. People ought to keep their promises.
5. A mayor who takes bribes should resign.
7. Anyone who commits a third felony should automatically go to prison for twenty-five years.
8. Whatever is unnatural is wrong and should be avoided.

Exercise 12-6

1. B
4. A
7. C, although the claim Anthony thought about is B, a nonmoral value judgment
9. B

Exercise 12-7

1. A
4. B (probably)
7. B
10. B

Exercise 12-8

1. Not really. To be consistent, Tory would have to say that if one gender has the right to marry whomever they want, so should the other gender have the same right. He does not say whether he denies men a right to same-sex marriage, but he does deny that right to women.

2. To avoid inconsistency, Shelley must be able to identify characteristics of art and music students, athletes, and children of alumni—for whom she believes the special admissions program is acceptable—and show that, aside from women and minority students who happen also to be in one of the listed categories, such students do not have these characteristics. Furthermore, the characteristics she identifies must be relevant to the issue of whether an individual should be admitted into the university. It may well be possible to identify the characteristics called for. (Remember that consistency is a necessary condition for a correct position, but not a sufficient one.)

3. Marin could be consistent only if he could show that the process of abortion involves killing and capital punishment does not. Because this is impossible—capital punishment clearly does involve killing—he is inconsistent. However, Marin's inconsistency is the result of his blanket claim that *all* killing is wrong. He could make a consistent case if he were to maintain only that the killing of *innocent* people is wrong, and that abortion involves killing innocent people but capital punishment does not. There is another approach: Marin could argue that only *state-mandated* killing (which would include capital punishment but not abortion) is permissible. (Each of these last claims would require strong arguments.)

8. To avoid inconsistency, Harold would have to identify a relevant difference between the discrimination law and the marijuana law. In fact, there is one fairly obvious one to which he can appeal: The former has been

declared contrary to the state constitution; the latter has not been alleged to be contrary to any constitution. So, Harold may object to the failure to implement the latter, even if it does conflict with federal drug laws—after all, if the law has not been found unconstitutional, shouldn't the will of the voters prevail? (It is a separate matter, of course, whether he can build a strong argument in the case of the marijuana law.)

Exercise 12-11

1. The harm principle: Shoplifting harms those from whom one steals.

2. The harm principle: Forgery tends to harm others.

4. We think the offense principle is the most relevant, because the practice in question is found highly offensive by most people (at least we believe—and hope—so). But one might also include the harm principle, because spitting in public can spread disease-causing organisms.

6. Legal moralism, because many people find adultery immoral; and, to a lesser extent, both the harm principle and legal paternalism, because adultery can harm the adulterer's partner emotionally and increase the spread of sexually transmitted diseases.

10. The offense principle

Exercise 12-13

Comment: In fact, a majority of the Supreme Court agreed with Justice O'Connor and sentenced John Angus Smith to thirty years in prison. Your authors take Justice Scalia's side and believe the Court's majority made a serious mistake.

Exercise 12-14

1. a. Principle 4
    b. Principle 2
    Compatible

4. a. Principle 5
    b. Principle 2
    Compatible

Exercise 12-15

1. Relevant on Principle 7

4. Relevant on Principle 1

7. Relevant on Principle 3

Exercise 12-16

Principle 1: Asuka's picture does not teach us anything, for no chimp can distinguish between truth and falsity; it is a curiosity rather than a work of art.

Principle 2: By looking at Asuka's very symbolic paintings, we are compelled to accept her vision of a world in which discourse is by sight rather than by sound.

Principle 3: Perhaps the most far-reaching impact of Asuka's art is its revelation of the horrors of encaging chimps; surely beings who can reach these heights of sublimely abstract expression should not see the world through iron bars.

Principle 4: Dear Zookeeper: Please encourage Asuka to keep painting, as the vibrant colors and intense brushstrokes of her canvases fill all of us with delight.

Principle 5: I never thought I would wish to feel like an ape, but Asuka's art made me appreciate how chimps enjoy perceiving us humans as chumps.

Principle 6: This is not art, for no ape's product can convey the highest, most valuable, human states of mind.

Principle 7: Whether by the hand of ape or man, that the canvases attributed to Asuka show lovely shapes and colors is indisputable.

Principle 8: What is art is simply what pleases a person's taste, and Asuka obviously finds painting tasty, as she tends to eat the paint.

Exercise 12-17

1. a

4. b

Photo Credits

Note: Page numbers followed by "n" indicate notes.